300 C.E. | 600 C.E. | 900 C.E. | 1200 C.E.

Early Christian Era

327 Macrina

354 Augustine of Hippo

355 Hypatia of Alexandria

Muslim Philosophers

ca. 873 Al-Farabi

1126 Averroes

Middle Ages

1033 Anselm of Canterbury

1098 Hildegard of Bingen

1225 Thomas Aquinas

1347 Catherine of Siena

a. 100 Pan Chao

DARK AGES | MIDDLE AGES | RENAISSANCE

. 29 eath Jesus

70 Romans destroy temple at Jerusalem

325 Council of Nicaea

ca. 476 Fall of Roman empire

529 St. Benedict founds monastery at Monte Cassino

632 Muhammad founds Islam

1150 Founding of University of Paris

ca. 100–300 Buddhism spreads to China

550 Buddhism enters Japan

ca. 730 Invention of printing in China

1100–1500 Islam spreads to eastern Europe, India, and southeast Asia

Roots of Wisdom

THIRD EDITION

Helen Buss Mitchell

Howard Community College

Australia • Canada • Mexico • Singapore • Spain • United Kingdom • United States

Philosophy Editor: Peter Adams
Assistant Editor: Kara Kindstrom
Editorial Assistant: Chalida Anusasananan
Marketing Manager: Dave Garrison
Print Buyer: April Vanderbilt
Permissions Editor: Bob Kauser
Production Service: Forbes Mill Press
Designer: Andrew Ogus
Copy Editor: Robin Gold
Cover Designer: Laurie Anderson
Cover Illustrator: Amy Kolman
Indexer: Rachel Rice
Compositor: Wolf Creek Press
Printer: Maple-Vail Book Manufacturing Group

Printed in the United States of America

1 2 3 4 5 6 7 05 04 03 02

For more information, contact
Wadsworth/Thomson Learning
10 Davis Drive
Belmont, CA 94002-3098
USA

For more information about our products, contact us:
Thomson Learning Academic Resource Center
1-800-423-0563
http://www.wadsworth.com

International Headquarters
Thomson Learning
International Division
290 Harbor Drive, 2nd Floor
Stamford, CT 06902-7477
USA

UK/Europe/Middle East/South Africa
Thomson Learning
Berkshire House
168-173 High Holborn
London WC1V 7AA
United Kingdom

Asia
Thomson Learning
60 Albert Complex, #15-01
Singapore 189969

Canada
Nelson Thomson Learning
1120 Birchmount Road
Toronto, Ontario M1K 5G4
Canada

Library of Congress Cataloging-in-Publication Data

Mitchell, Helen Buss.
Roots of wisdom / Helen Buss Mitchell. -- 3rd ed.
p.cm.
Includes bibliographical references and index.
ISBN 0-534-55299-4
1. Philosophy--Introductions. I. Title.

BD21 .M48 2001
100--dc21 00-054988

This book is printed on acid-free recycled paper.

In memory of Ruth and Joe, who believed in me from the beginning.

For Joe and Jason, who supported me to the end.

Brief Contents

Contents

The Making of a Philosopher Boxes

Preface

As we learn in our first course in philosophy, the concerns of this ancient discipline are those of people everywhere—who we are, how we know, how we should live. Drawing on what Huston Smith calls the world's wisdom traditions offers the teacher of philosophy rich resources for addressing the challenges and opportunities of the present age. It is in this spirit that I have written *Roots of Wisdom.*

To paraphrase Aristotle, all people desire to know. Yet, for nearly all students, philosophy is a foreign language, both in its specialized vocabulary and in its approach to knowledge. Students have to master the methods and tools of a subject they have not previously studied; this tends to be both frightening and exhilarating. Those of us who teach philosophy try to convey the power that made us fall in love with wisdom and to show our students how to use its methods to address all the questions of human life. Firmly grounded in the Western tradition, we are learning to incorporate the traditional wisdom of Asia, Africa, and the Americas as well as the voices of women into our search for meaning. This enlivens our teaching and provides an increasingly diverse student body with mirrors in which to see themselves as well as windows on a wider world.

These are the goals that animate *Roots of Wisdom.* Its ten chapters are framed with thought-provoking issues representing major topics in philosophy, beginning with metaphysics (reality, human nature, God), moving to epistemology (knowledge sources, truth tests, aesthetic experience), and concluding with axiology (political philosophy, social philosophy, ethics). Although they are topically organized, the chapters also move forward in time, following the canon of Western philosophy and including women, Asian and African thinkers/thought systems, and "The Peoples of the Americas" (Spanish language and indigenous thinkers of the past and present) as they speak to the questions raised by the Western discourse.

New to This Edition

This edition includes several new features. Each chapter now begins with a context-setting question for the student—Before you read, ask

yourself what it would take to make you truly happy, to enable you to live your life to the fullest, regardless of what circumstances you might eventually have to navigate (to use the example from the first chapter). At the conclusion of each chapter, following For Further Thought and For Further Exploration, is a new section called For Further Research, which contains 5 or 6 keywords that will yield research materials on the InfoTrac system. Each chapter also contains a new box labeled Philosophers Speak for Themselves, featuring more extensive primary material for student analysis. Some of these are short excerpts from the selections found in *Readings from the Roots of Wisdom,* the reader linked with this text, whereas others represent new material. Finally, an Appendix for the student on reading and writing philosophy has been added and difficult-to-pronounce glossary terms are followed by phonetic pronunciations.

The following reflect specific additions and changes to the chapters and historical interludes:

- Historical Interlude A discusses *The Alphabet versus The Goddess: The Conflict Between Word and Image* by Leonard Shlain, which links the rise in alphabet literacy with the decline in feminine values and Goddess worship.
- Chapter 2 has been reorganized and a summary of string theory ties together the section on quantum physics and relativity theory.
- In Chapter 3, there are new animal and electronic examples that challenge the claim of human uniqueness. Elizabeth V. Spelman points out Aristotle's circular reasoning, and we meet images from the *Tao Te Ching.* The section on Gender Identity has been rewritten and a response to determinism featuring James Hillman's *The Force of Character* has been added. Hinduism is introduced as a thought system in this chapter—From Hinduism and *Atman* to Buddhism and *Anatman.*
- Chapter 4 now includes Hinduism and Henotheism and the Is There Life After Death? section now includes a rejoinder by Bertrand Russell from his essay "What I Believe." Augustine shares his cosmic vision through an excerpt from *The City of God.*
- Chapter 5 now features an excerpt from Descartes' *Discourse on Method* and another from Alison M. Jaggar, challenging the Myth of the Objective Observer.
- Chapter 6 now includes an excerpt from Vision Eleven of Hadewjich of Antwerp.
- Chapter 7 introduces *Art and Physics: Parallel Visions in Space, Time, and Light* by Leonard Shlain, which demonstrates how artists show us in images what scientists will later tell us in words and formulas. Plato and Aristotle debate the value of art as imitation.
- Chapter 8 is now organized around the concept of "sovereignty." There is an excerpt from Locke's "Treatise on Civil Government" and another from Bart Kosko's Fuzzy Social Contract.
- In Chapter 9 the theme of justice as an organizing principle has been strengthened. We hear Audre Lorde on "Women Redefining

Difference" and read an excerpt from Mary Wollstonecraft's classic *A Vindication of the Rights of Women.*

- Chapter 10 includes a new section on Evolutionary Psychology and its implications for freedom/determinism, a section on Our Obligations to One Another, and another on Everyday Ethics, which includes issues related to friendship, work, and the information society. A new section on The Global Community contains the ideas of Peter Singer, Gloria Anzaldúa, and Benjamin Hoff. The section on Environmental Ethics has been expanded to include Ecocentrism and Ecofeminism. We also read an excerpt from Kant's *Foundations for the Metaphysics of Morals.*

The connections between this text and its accompanying reader *Readings from the Roots of Wisdom* have been strengthened. Selections from the reader, which are now discussed for the first time or expanded in the text, include the following: Plato's Cave Allegory, Augustine's *The City of God,* Descartes' *Discourse on Method.* Plato and Aristotle disagreeing on the question of the value of art as imitation, Locke's *Treatise of Civil Government,* Mary Wollstonecraft's *A Vindication of the Rights of Women,* Audre Lorde's *Age, Race, Class, and Sex: Women Redefining the Difference,* Gloria Anzaldúa's *Borderlands/La Frontera,* Benjamin Hoff's *The Te of Piglet,* and Kant's *Foundations for the Metaphysics of Morals.*

Some texts are written at such a difficult level that the instructor's task becomes explaining the text to the students. *Roots of Wisdom* takes a different approach. I have spared none of the rigor and retained all the essential vocabulary, yet the style is conversational, the examples plentiful, and the illustrations lavish. This is a book students can read on their own, freeing you to offer your own emphasis and add additional material if you choose. Your students will have the basics provided for them. This book makes difficult concepts simple without making them simplistic.

Special Content Features

Because formal philosophy is indeed a foreign language for beginning students, I have given special attention to offering many options for organizing and learning difficult new material. I have also taken care to provide the historical, cultural, and biographical context your students need to appreciate the roots of philosophical wisdom. The following special content features support these goals.

Philosophy in Context: Historical Interludes

There are five Historical Interludes that begin and end the text as well as link the major sections and topics. The first provides a worldwide context for the beginning of Western philosophy; the second describes the blending of Greek rationalist thought and Hebrew religious thought in the exportation of Christianity to the gentile world; the third and fourth provide transitions from the medieval to the modern world and from the modern to the post-modern world, respectively; the last considers the implications of discoveries in brain neuroscience for philosophy. Together these Historical Interludes provide transitions between the three major divisions of the text—metaphysics, epistemology, axiology—and include information on key historical and cultural events without interrupting the flow of a chapter.

Logic: "How Philosophy Works"

A mini-course in logic appears throughout the text with arguments drawn from the chapter content. Each chapter contains a "How Philosophy Works" box that you can use to teach reasoning while you cover content. Because the methods of reasoning are connected with the arguments of philosophers within the chapter, logic appears as the natural and indispensable tool of the philosopher, rather than something to be learned in isolation from content. Forms of argument range from Aristotle's formulation of the categorical syllogism to the new science of fuzzy logic that makes our air conditioners run efficiently by affirming the range of points at which something is neither A nor non-A.

Biography: "The Making of a Philosopher" Boxes

"The Making of a Philosopher" boxes provide biographical material and present thinkers as real people with human motivations and problems as well as great ideas. Because women as well as men inhabit these boxes and because some of the philosophers are Asian and African American, the multicultural focus of the text is maintained.

Applications: "Doing Philosophy"

From the early "sophistry" of one of O. J. Simpson's defense attorneys to the fuzzy social contract, each chapter brings the method and questions of philosophy into the everyday lives of ordinary people. An African woman's story about "knowing" how to cure malaria, Simone Weil's decision to starve herself to death in solidarity with her compatriots in France, and the limits we might want to place on both cultural relativism and deconstruction stand beside questions of individual liberty versus respect for tradition, and the possibility of life after death; a self-portrait in oil offers a visual method of exploring questions of identity. "Doing Philosophy" boxes explore the "real-life" dilemmas of being alive and make clear that philosophy is not merely a spectator sport.

Primary Material: Philosophers Speak for Themselves

In 250–400 word excerpts, philosophers across cultures and centuries speak in their own words about questions of vital importance to them. Plato, Aristotle, Augustine, Hobbes, Descartes, Locke, and Kant from the Western tradition are joined by the author of the Taoist classic *Tao Te Ching,* the medieval mystic Hadewjich of Antwerp, and Mary Wollstonecraft from the Western Enlightenment.

Visual Features

Many of your students will be strongly visual learners. Words alone may be inadequate to convey concepts. Even for those who respond best to words, illustrations provide valuable reinforcement.

Time Lines

The time lines on the inside cover embrace the entire scope of the book, highlighting the flow of ideas throughout human history and revealing the multicultural nature of the search for wisdom. They offer "the course at a glance" and give you and your students a ready reference for placing people and events in a historical context.

Maps

The roots of wisdom are deep in many cultures around the world, so some indication of where these cultures are geographically seems wise. You can use the maps that accompany each of the Historical Interludes to combat our national cultural illiteracy. By freezing a moment in history, each of these maps highlights a time period and illuminates it with significant dates, events, and historical figures. The last interlude contains a "map" of the brain to conclude our exploration of interesting (and somewhat uncharted) territory.

Cartoons, Photographs, and Illustrations

Cartoons are used strategically, captioned in each case with a statement or question, tying it to the text and raising a specific philosophical issue or query. Since they come from a wide variety of sources (Doonesbury, Mother Goose and Grimm, Bloom County, Bizarro, and the work of several talented, independent individuals) and represent a wide range of subjects, these cartoons offer some students memory devices for anchoring course content.

Photographs, like cartoons, appear in every chapter and are similarly captioned. Specific philosophical concepts are examined through the medium of world art. In each case the culture that produced the art is identified and the caption ties the photograph to the content of the chapter. Although some of the art may be quite familiar to you, some of it may appear exotic. One of the best ways to know a culture is by studying its art forms, and this book looks to art for important information about how philosophy is done around the world. This edition also features electronically-rendered "stills" from "For the Love of Wisdom," a multicultural telecourse based on *Roots of Wisdom,* that was produced by Howard Community College and is being distributed nationally by PBS. As the creator and host of this series, I thank both HCC and the Adult Learning Satellite Services division of PBS for allowing me to use these images.

Illustrations use graphic art or line drawings to visually represent difficult or challenging text material. As with the cartoons, each is captioned to tie the visual and verbal components together. Some of the African wisdom concepts are particularly well communicated through visual images.

In-Text Learning Aids

In addition to the special sections described earlier, each chapter includes the following elements to guide and reinforce students' learning.

"The Issue Defined"

"The Issue Defined" is an attention getting opening, designed to draw the student in and answer the unspoken "so what?" question. Artificial intelligence, national information databases, test tube babies, virtual reality—these are a few of the topics in the opening sections of chapters in this text.

Key Terms and Glossary

Key terms are bolded in the text, described etymologically, and defined in the running margin glossary as well as in the master glossary in the back of the book. The more difficult terms are followed by a phonetic pronunciation guide. By listing and learning these key terms, your students can create a philosophical skeleton on which to hang more complex ideas.

Follow-Up

Each chapter ends with For Further Thought and For Further Exploration. The former lead the student to apply and integrate chapter material with other text matter and with their own experiences; the latter are books (fiction and nonfiction) and films related to the chapter topic. For Further Thought offers thought-provoking questions designed to deepen student understanding, pull specifics together into concepts, and link philosophy with life. For Further Exploration suggests ways you and your students can go more deeply into the material covered in the chapter. Debates, informal writing and formal papers, group work, and individual presentations can all have their genesis in these books, short stories, and films. Keyword searches through InfoTrac constitute a new section: For Further Research.

Supplementary Materials

Two supplementary aids are available to complement the specific goals of the text outlined above. I have written them from the perspective of my own classroom experience over the last fifteen years, the experiences of my colleagues, and the honesty of my students.

Instructor's Manual

I have tried to make the Instructor's Manual for this book the aid I wished for (but couldn't find) the first time I taught Introduction to Philosophy with less than two weeks notice. Even if you are not facing this rigorous a challenge, the new material in this text may benefit from some teaching suggestions. In the Instructor's Manual (available only online at the

Wadsworth Web site), each chapter helps you guide your students through the language of philosophy. Vocabulary words are grouped into families, their etymologies and other interesting features explained, and ways to present them explored. The section on Method helps you relate the chapter's mini-lesson on logic to the overall chapter content. Next is a Discussion Starter for use during the class session when you begin each chapter; this is followed by Background to help you design a lecture or answer questions the text may raise for your students. Each chapter in the guide concludes with Questions—25 multiple choice, 15 true-false and 5 essay. The final section offers you one or two Resources unique to the chapter to get your students thinking or reinforce learning that has already occurred.

Study Guide

The study guide for students takes a similar approach to Vocabulary and Method. Treating philosophy as a foreign language, the guide lists new words (as foreign language texts typically do) at the beginning of each chapter and relates them to the overall "culture" of philosophy as well as to the specific instructional content of a given chapter. The Method section helps them think of logic as a useful tool for life as well as philosophy class and uses real-life illustrations as examples. Study Suggestions are intended to deepen students' understanding by nudging them beyond rote learning to a real application of the course content. Objective practice questions include: 25 multiple choice, 15 matching (statements/works to philosophers) and 10 true/false; there are also 5 essay Practice Questions. The questions are all unique. In some cases, student questions are reworkings of those in the instructor's manual, asking the same information in a different form.

Web Site

A dedicated Web site for *Roots of Wisdom,* third edition, is available through the Wadsworth Philosophy Web site, http://philosophy.wadsworth.com. Helpful student tips, practice quizzes, and links to other useful sites will be available.

Telecourse

Roots of Wisdom, third edition, and the accompanying reader, *Readings from the Roots of Wisdom,* third edition, also form a telecourse, produced by PBS adult learning. For information on the telecourse, call 800-257-2578. A telecourse study guide, also written by Helen Mitchell, can be obtained by contacting Howard Community College (410-772-4592, or fax 410-772-4592).

Acknowledgments

When Valerie Costantini sent two Wadsworth representatives to my office in December 1992, she probably had no idea she was launching me on a new adventure. I thank Philosophy and Religion Editor Peter Adams for believing in the project and Ruth Cottrell for overseeing the production phase so diligently and so kindly. Jason Mitchell and Jeannie Jeffrey read every chapter of the first edition, making helpful suggestions and reminding me of what matters to twenty-somethings. Jason took my words and turned them into computer graphics (in addition to supplying a stunning photograph); Jeannie took my ideas and turned them into visually striking concept sketches. Shannon Tenney provided a similar and equally valuable perspective for the second edition. In addition to reading and reflecting critically on every chapter, she went into the bowels of both the Library of Congress and the Catholic University Library and came back with the treasures I requested. Joe Mitchell took wonderful photographs on short notice and helped me remember the real world outside my office. Jean Moon, Mary Margaret Kamerman, Mary Young, Janis Cripe, Barbara Whorton, Marie Siracusa, Donna Canfield, JoAnn Hawkins, Diana Marinich, Judy Thomas, Peggy Armitage, Dawn Barnes, Virginia Kirk, Dee Weir, and Betty Caldwell helped me remember how important the voices of women are—in philosophy textbooks and in life. To all of you, and to my other friends and family who provided support and encouragement when I needed it most, I offer my deep and heartfelt thanks.

The Rouse Scholars: Jeff, Lindsey, Phil, Carrie, Chiara, Laura, Kelly, Dave, Posido, and Bruce in 1998 and Sarah, Laura, Meghan, Jen, Kelley, Kristina, Ila, Josh, Shaun, Jason, Jenny, Liana, Mike, Melissa, Justine, Jonathan, Amy, Jon, Matt, Adam, and Nina in 1999 tested the second edition in their seminars. I thank them for letting me know what worked and for gently pointing out what didn't as well as for their excellent proofreading and sleuthing out of typographical errors. Jonathan Ratican supplied a sidebar quote from his own powerful music for Chapter 4. All the students over the last twenty years who wondered aloud why we didn't read any women philosophers planted an idea that wouldn't go away. Without all of you, the idea of this book would never have germinated. And, Bob O'Brien, Matt Schulte, Matt McCabe, and Ruth Kastner locally, as well as many others with whom I am in contact through the worldwide web (especially Amy Hannon, Phil Ruge-Jones, and Michael Allen Fox), who have used *Roots of Wisdom* and *Roots of World Wisdom* as teaching texts, and have generously shared their classroom experience with me.

Doris Ligon opened the treasures of the African Art Museum of Maryland to me and Dianne Connolly, Julia Measures, Mary Ellen Zorbaugh, and Edna Brandt shared their knowledge of Chinese medicine and health. Rich' Walter taught me wonderfully simple ways to think and speak about Zen, the brain, and life. Phil Reitzel and Phillis Knill made special arrangements for me to photograph Civil War artifacts in the Howard County Historical Society. Yifei Gan painted "Early Spring" especially for this book and allowed me to use a photo of "Boy With Tree Apple." Hou Rong generously gave permission for two of his statues to be photographed and reprinted. Elaine Siegel provided the photo of the KanKouran West African Dancers. Jean Soto, Susan Myers, and Sharon Frey of the Howard Community College Library helped me borrow hard to locate books and find citations and references. Lt. Jay Zumbrun obtained a police warrant for Chapter

Whatever one does, one always rebuilds the monument in his own way. But it is already something gained to have used only the original stones.
MARGUERITE YOURCENAR
Memoirs of Hadrian

6. John Hernandez and Jose Lopez-Gonzalez made many valuable suggestions, pointing me toward Spanish-language philosophers, through whom some of our students might find a more familiar path to the world's wisdom. I appreciate the generosity with which all of you have shared your time and your resources to help me craft this book.

My special thanks to International Thomson Editores in Mexico City for translating the first edition of *Roots of Wisdom* into *Raices de la Sabiduria*. The Spanish edition is reaching an international audience and giving me greater insight into how the world's wisdom speaks to a multicultural world (as well as giving me another opportunity to learn Spanish). Victor Diaz and Miguel Angel Toledo (along with their technical reviewers Susana Leventhal and Gian Carla Brignole) have been especially easy to work with and have produced a beautiful product in record time.

When I took my first philosophy course at Hood College, it was love at first sight. Paul Mehl showed me how easy it is to fall in love with wisdom and what a thrilling ride it offers. Tom Scheye and Frank Cunningham from Loyola College opened my eyes to the possibilities that emerge when literature and philosophy meet, and Frank Haig, S.J. helped me see the philosophical implications of modern physics. Kimpei Munei introduced me to the thought systems of Africa while he was an AFS student in our home. From my colleagues at Howard Community College—especially Valerie Costantini, Yifei Gan, Ron Roberson, and Jane Winer—I have learned how art illuminates the philosophical quest.

Finally, I am as always indebted to the reviewers who provided uniformly constructive and sometimes brilliant suggestions. From the beginning, their thoughtful comments have shaped the manuscript. My thanks to Wayne Alt, Essex Community College; Roger Ebertz, University of Dubuque; John Hernandez, Palo Alto College; Doug Matthews, Toccoa Falls College; Isabel Luengo, MiraCosta College; Mathias Schulte, Montgomery College; Thomas Senor, University of Arkansas; Don Hanks, University of New Orleans; B. David Burke, Elgin Community College; Greg Weis, University of South Carolina; Sara Goering, University of Colorado; Truitt Hilliard, Odessa College; Thomas Korniak, Sam Houston; Samantha Brennan, University of Western Ontario; Shannon Tenney, Smith College; Erick Egertson, Midland Lutheran College; Eugene Sorenson, Rochester Community College; Arnold McMahon, Fullerton College; Marie Liberace, Rockland Community College; and Irene Byrnes, Broome Community College.

To my readers . . .

Please send your responses to *Roots of Wisdom* to me electronically: hmitchell@howardcc.edu. I am especially interested in what works for you and what doesn't, as well as your suggestions for augmenting and improving the text.

PART ONE

What Is Everything Really Like?

Questions of Metaphysics

HISTORICAL INTERLUDE A

A Worldwide Context for Western Philosophy

CHAPTER ONE

Why Philosophy?

Is This All There Is?

CHAPTER TWO

Reality and Being

Is What You See What You Get?

HISTORICAL INTERLUDE B

Philosophy and Early Christianity

CHAPTER THREE

Human Nature

Who or What Are We, and What Are We Doing Here?

CHAPTER FOUR

Philosophy and God

Who's in Charge?

HISTORICAL INTERLUDE A

A Worldwide Context for Western Philosophy

Philosophy—literally "the love of wisdom"—is a very ancient enterprise. People have probably been asking the "big questions"—Why am I here? How can I decide what's true and what isn't? What is everything made of? What's the right thing to do?—since the beginning of spoken language. We come into the world filled with questions. Children can't seem to stop asking them as they begin to wonder why things are the way they are. Why is the sky blue? Why does fire go up? Where is my dead goldfish now? How do you know it's time for me to go to bed? Why do I have to share my toys?

Philosophy assumes we never stop caring about the answers to those questions. What happens, for most of us, is that we get vague, unsatisfactory answers from grown-ups. At first we think they know better answers and are too busy to share the secrets with us. Later, we learn that they may not know either. Some people try to shut off the questions at this point, to concentrate on other things like making friends and money, seeking pleasure, popularity, and love. And, it works—for a while. But, the big questions have a way of coming back, especially during those moments when life gets our attention by stopping the ordinary flow of events with something startling and unexpected. A parent or friend dies young; a loved one betrays us; a cherished dream goes unfulfilled. At times like these, the questions come surging back. What is the purpose of life anyway? Does anything really matter? Are we on a short, unpleasant march toward death?

This book introduces some classical and some modern ways of thinking about those eternal questions. We begin with issues we all face at the beginning of a new millennium and link them with the roots of wisdom found in civilizations from ancient times to the present. There is wisdom in every culture, and no one culture has a monopoly on it. Although the principal thread running through this book is the story of Western philosophy, which began with the Greeks in the sixth century B.C.E. (before the common era), we will also be tracing lines of thought from other parts of the world, particularly China and Africa, but also India, Japan, and the Americas. Along the way we will be looking at often-neglected women philosophers as their arguments support or counter the classic conversation of Western philosophy and as they break new ground in engaging the big questions of life.

Before we begin looking at the Greeks, it is important to survey briefly what was going on in other parts of the world. The Greeks had an enormous influence on the Western philosophical tradition, but they were neither the first nor the only culture to "do" philosophy. In fact, the centuries during which Greek culture flowered were a time of extraordinary spiritual and philosophical awakening in many parts of the world. To put Greek thought in context, we will look first at several near contemporaries of Thales, the first Greek philosopher, whom we meet in Chapter 1. They include Siddhārtha Gautama, known as the Buddha, who lived in India; K'ung Fu-tzu, or Master K'ung, known to the West as Confucius; and Lao-tzu, the Old Master, who began the tradition of Taoism. Both Master K'ung and Master Lao were Chinese, and all three of these men (Buddha, Confucius, and Lao-tzu) lived around the sixth century B.C.E. We then expand our initial exploration of the quest for wisdom by touching on Zen Buddhism, Native American and African thought, and finally the Hebrews, whose story will appear in more detail in the next Historical Interlude.

As you may have done, people living in other times and places looked into the vastness of the night sky and wondered about the importance of human life. Like you, they asked themselves, "How should we live our lives?" "Why is happiness so difficult to find and keep?" "What can I be sure of?" "Where did everything come from?" When they posed these questions, they were doing philosophy. We could just as accurately say they were doing science or religion. The love of wisdom and the search for answers to the eternal questions led our distant ancestors to wonder, and wondering is the root of science and religion as well as of philosophy. Today, methods and focuses separate these three disciplines, but at the time when the Buddha (the Enlightened One) began asking himself about the meaning of life, there were only those persistent questions and the human need to find answers.

Buddhism

Siddhārtha of the Gautama clan was born around 560 B.C.E. in what is today Nepal, just below the foothills of the Himalayan Mountains. According to legend, the young Siddhārtha grew up in a palace, surrounded by pleasures and protected from the harsh realities of everyday life. He was married to a lovely woman and, in his late twenties, fathered a son, but he had grown restless and discontented. Escaping from the secure but artificial world created by his loving father, Siddhārtha saw for the first time people who were old and diseased—even dead. How, he wondered, could anyone live in peace and happiness if this was what life had in store.

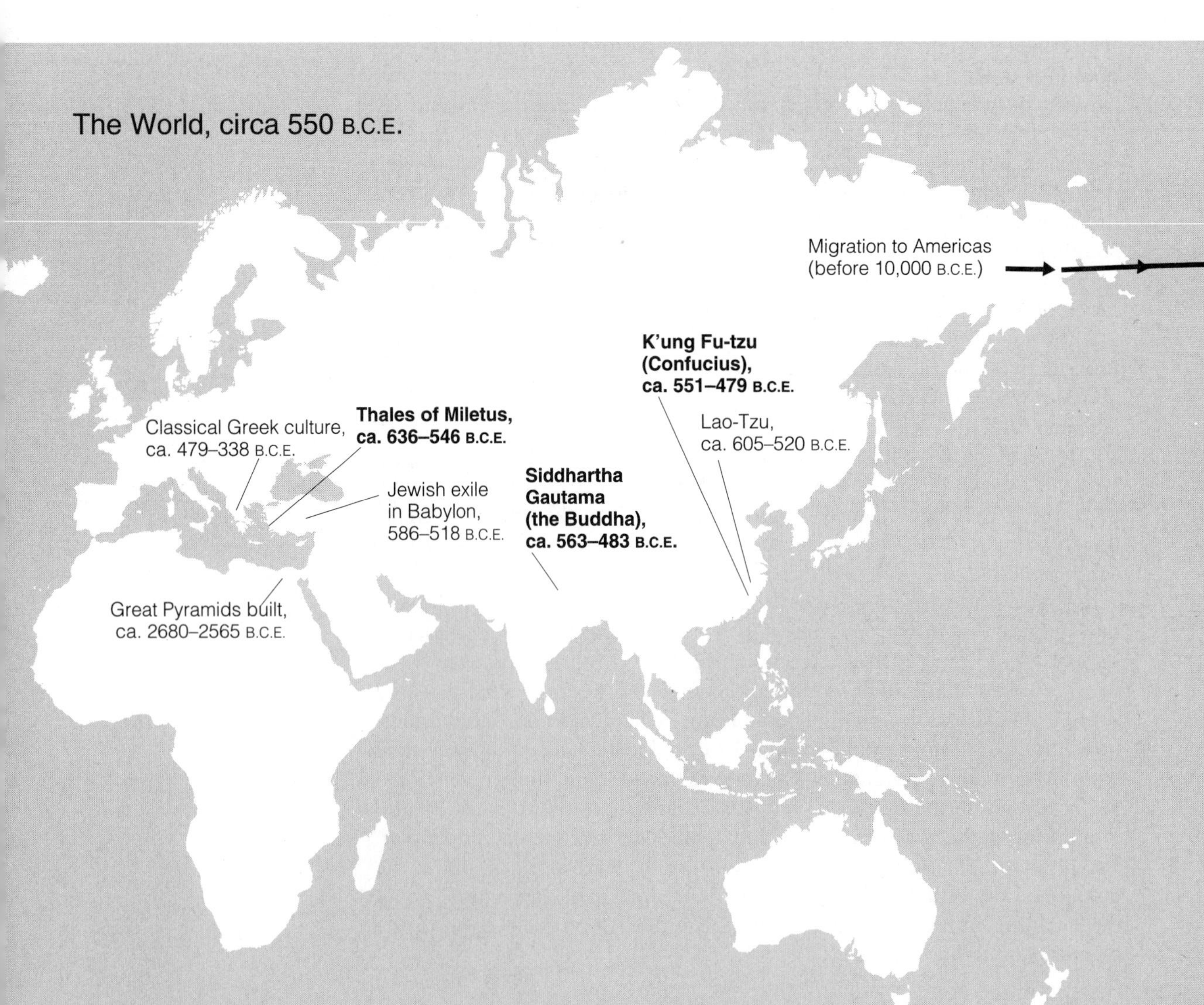

Renouncing his wife, child, father, and life of pleasure, he became a wandering beggar in search of answers. He spent some time with monks who lived in extreme **asceticism,** fasting and disciplining their bodies while they practiced yogic meditation. Although he fasted to the point that the texts claim he could feel his backbone when he sucked in his stomach and touched his navel, Siddhārtha did not find what he was looking for. According to tradition, enlightenment came when he sat beneath a bodhi (wisdom) tree on the night of the full Moon, resolving not to get up until he found the answer to life's riddles.

asceticism *the view that the body requires the discipline of mind or spirit, resulting in self-denial and even self-torture as a way of renouncing worldly longings in preparation for a happier existence after death*

During this experience he realized that life is characterized by change and that change is the clue to our suffering. We suffer because we desire and are attached to things that we want to fix in place and hold onto. We

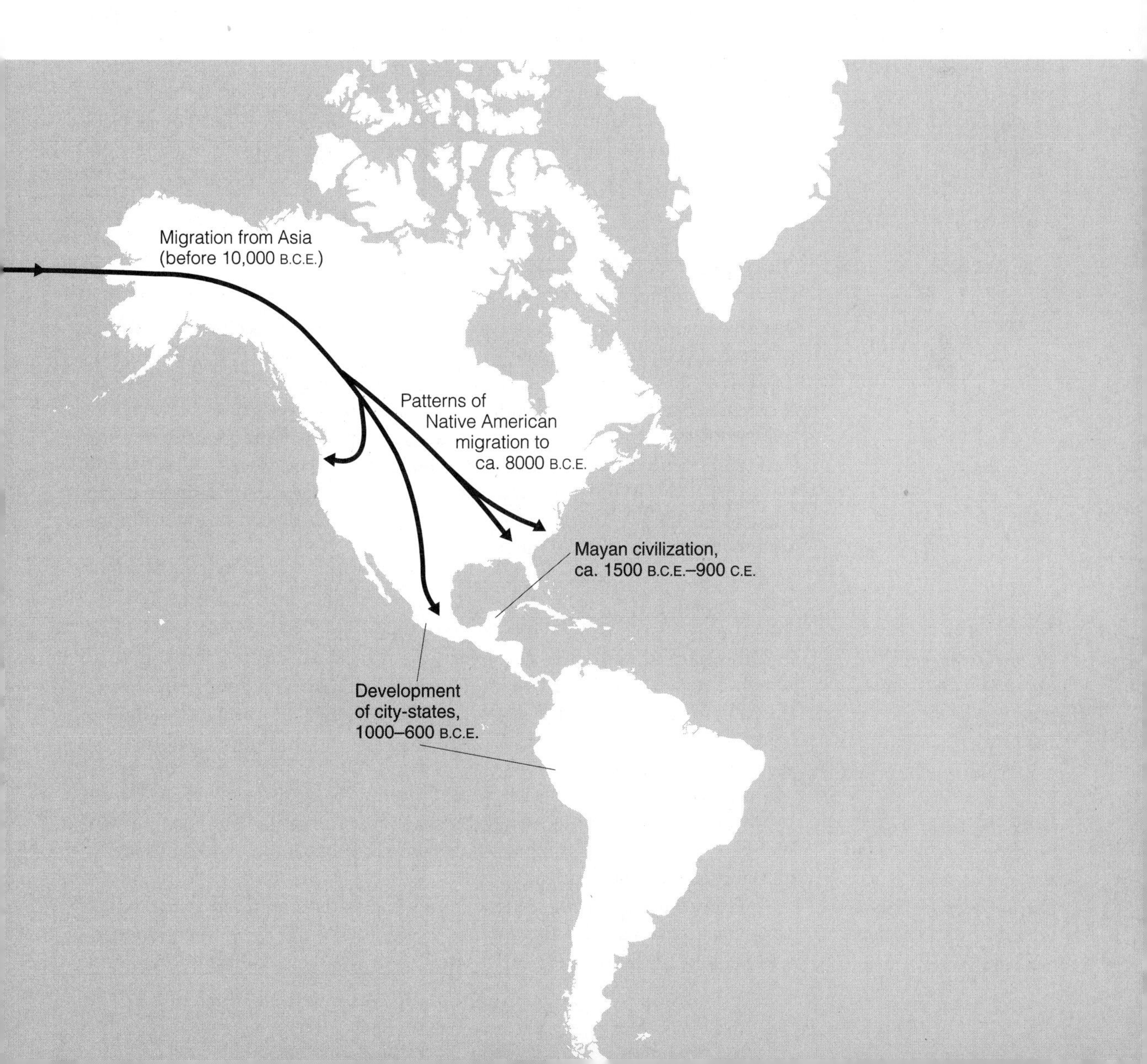

want to remain young and healthy; we want those we love never to die; we want to keep things just the way they are. Since all existence is characterized by constant change, this is impossible. By accepting the reality of impermanence and detaching ourselves from the desire to capture life and hold it fast, we, too, can become enlightened—we can see things as they are.

The only way to avoid the terror of aging, sickness and death is by withdrawing our anxieties about them, and this is accomplished by seeing that sensual pleasures, money, and power do not bring lasting joy. If we give up searching and yearning for youth, health, and wealth, we break the hold of the world and "blow out" the desire that binds us to it. This blowing out is ***nirvana,*** the state of enlightenment that, once attained, frees us from the cycle of birth, death, and rebirth. Once we become enlightened, there is no need to live additional lives—we will have learned all we need to know, all this world can teach us.

nirvana *a state in which individuality is extinguished or the state of enlightenment in which all pain, suffering, mental anguish, and the need for successive rebirths disappear*

Buddhism spread through India but had its real success in China, where it became established by the second century C.E. (common era) and incorporated many elements of Chinese culture. In China, Buddhism also blended with Taoism to form Ch'an, or, as it is known in Japan, Zen Buddhism.

Taoism

The dynasties of China stretch back before 2000 B.C.E. when the Sage Kings of the Hsia dynasty, including the semilegendary Yellow Emperor (Huang Ti), ruled China. Silk and ceramics, writing, painting and music, the use of a calendar, and the art of healing all date from this period. By 1000 B.C.E. leaders of the Chou dynasty were praised as model rulers, but the time of Lao-tzu is known as the Warring States period. The classic Taoist (pronounced "dowist") text, the *Tao Te Ching,* was supposedly written at the request of the gatekeeper as Lao-tzu left the strife-ridden city during the sixth century B.C.E. for the quiet life of a hermit.

Tao Te Ching means, roughly, the "book of the power, or virtue, of the Way." Reading from right to left, we arrive at the chief word in the title, ***Tao*** (pronounced "dow"). Lao-tzu and his disciple Chuang-tzu saw nature and the natural system as the heart of what is. To understand the *Tao,* which directs the natural system, is to understand everything. The *Tao* is the Way of nature that moves by perfect, effortless efficiency to fulfill its purposes. Summer turns to fall, which gives way to winter and then to spring. Night turns to day and day to night. We are born, grow up, grow old, and die. Only the foolish would attempt to oppose this system—to stand in the ocean and command a wave not to break. The wise person recognizes that—with a simple, egoless recognition of the way things are—all things can be accomplished.

Tao *the Way, the fundamental principle of the world, the cosmic order, nature in Taoism*

Wisdom lies in *letting* things happen rather than trying to *make* things happen. Just as nature is sometimes ***yang,*** full of the light, rising energy, and activity of the day, it is also ***yin,*** full of the dark, falling energy, and

yang *the active, male principle associated with action and doing*

yin *the receptive, female principle associated with quiet and being* receptivity of the evening. If one can let the *Tao* direct, things will always turn out right. As Lao-tzu puts it: "The *Tao* never does anything, yet through it all things are done."[1] Nature doesn't have to huff and puff to turn night into day; it just happens. Water, the softest and most yielding of elements, finds the lowliest places but can crack concrete with its power when it freezes. "Governing a large country," Lao-tzu says, "is like frying a small fish. You can ruin it with too much poking."[2] As the martial arts of T'ai Chi Ch'uan and Aikido recognize, the best way to oppose force is to yield to it: "When pushed, pull; when pulled, push."

Confucianism

Taoism urged withdrawal from the stress and conflict of city life in favor of quiet contemplation of nature. Confucianism, by contrast, was more worldly; it advocated embracing a common cultural heritage, with emphasis on observing the proper rituals. In the *Analects,* Confucius gave advice of a practical nature on how to live as a large-minded rather than as a small-minded person. The goal was living nobly and compassionately in the world, observing the appropriate dynamics of relationships. Subjects, for example, should obey their rulers who bear the Mandate of Heaven. Children should obey and respect their parents. Friends, however, have a more mutual relationship in which considerable give and take appropriately exists. As one of Confucius's students observed: "The Master is good at leading one on step by step. He broadens me with culture and brings me back to essentials by means of the rites."[3]

All three of these great teachers recognized that life is not always in harmony with the ideal; yet, each of them had a different response to the situation, according to Benjamin Hoff's analysis in his best-selling book *The Tao of Pooh*. These variations are captured in an ancient Chinese scroll painting called "The Vinegar Tasters." The three masters, who represent the three great teachings of China—Confucianism, Buddhism, and Taoism—have each dipped a finger in the vat of vinegar and tasted it. Confucius's expression is sour, Buddha's is bitter, but Lao-tzu's is sweet.[4]

For Confucius, the present was out of step with the past and government on Earth was out of harmony with the Way of Heaven; life for him was sour and in need of sweetening. The Buddha saw life as a generator of illusions and a setter of traps. Since life was filled with attachments and desires that lead to suffering, his reaction to it was bitter. Only Lao-tzu viewed the world as a teacher of valuable lessons and a reflection of the harmony between heaven and Earth. He taught that everything has its own nature and, if the laws of nature are followed, life, even with its vinegary moments, can be sweet. Winnie the Pooh who is neither smart nor obviously wise is the one for whom things always work out. He can always find his way home because he knows who he is, and that kind of wisdom is what makes a Taoist Master. When you finish reading this text, decide whether or not you agree with Hoff's analysis of "The Vinegar Tasters."

Native Americans

In the West, philosophers have tended to follow the Greeks in seeing themselves as objective observers of nature, but Native Americans, the people called "Indians" because Columbus thought he had landed in India, share with the Taoists of the Far East a profound respect for nature. In Native American thought, however, nature is more than a perfect teacher; nature is holy. Everything in nature possesses a life or spirit of its own—the earth, the sky, the trees, animals, and people. Before killing a deer or a rabbit, it was customary to ask the animal's spirit for permission to kill in order to eat. There is no sense of people as masters of creation, entitled to subdue the natural world, including other animals, as we find, for example, in the Western Judaic and Christian traditions.

According to a Cherokee creation story, in the beginning the white man was given a stone and the Cherokee a piece of silver; each threw away the gift, considering it worthless. Later the white man found and pocketed the silver as a source of material power, whereas the Cherokee found and revered the stone as a source of sacred power. Reflecting a similar attitude, Sioux author Luther Standing Bear has written that "the old people came literally to love the soil. They sat on the ground with the feeling of being close to a mothering power."[5] The worship of stones reflects this deep sense of the sacredness that pervades all nature.

Many legends recall a kind of Golden Age when humans and animals lived and talked together, each learning the other's wisdom. Native peoples revered the earth, the heavens, and the directions of North, South, East, and West as supernatural forces. The idea that all being is alive or animate is called ***animism***—from the Latin word for "spirit" ***anima.*** We will find a similar belief that everything is alive when we look at the first Greek philosophers.

animism *the philosophical theory that all being is animate, living, contains spirit*
anima *Latin word meaning "spirit"*

If the holy was everywhere around you, the first Americans assumed that was the place to look for divine power. In the Guardian Spirit Quest, common to several native traditions, a young brave would go off alone, then fast and wait. After many days and nights, he might be rewarded by meeting a strong animal spirit in human form, perhaps in a dream, who would teach him his family and tribal duties, as well as give him his own sacred song and a special gift to become a leader or even a healer.[6]

Many archaeologists believe the people we call Native Americans migrated to North America from Asia by walking over a land bridge from Siberia to Alaska, crossing what is now called the Bering Strait. During the last Ice Age, the water levels in the oceans were much lower, and the theory is that the land bridge is now submerged. This migration may have occurred from 10,000 to 50,000 years ago. There are some similarities between the physical appearance, myths, and rituals of Siberian tribes and those of Native Americans. Some myths from the Americas, however, speak of an island "where the star of day is born" from which all men came. The "star of day," or the Sun, rises in the east, and Sioux tradition speaks of an island toward the sunrise "where all the tribes were formerly one." These stories tell of people coming to their new home in canoes. Apparently, there are no myths about walking over a land bridge.[7]

We may never know for certain the origin of the many, varied peoples who came to populate the Americas before the arrival of European explorers. What we can be sure of are their enduring beliefs in the sacredness of nature and the infusion of supernatural power into the natural world. It may be useful to keep this in mind as you read of the beginnings of Western philosophy. The Greek notion of standing apart from nature to study it and understand its mysteries has split people from nature and made humans observers of rather than participants in the natural system. Some critics say the Greek emphasis on objectivity has meant the loss of wonder and reverence for the natural world; they urge Westerners to reenchant the world by recovering a sense of wonder and rediscovering the value of imagination.

The wealthy and high born pictured themselves in the afterlife surrounded by the pleasures of the world.

Egyptian musician, papyrus detail from tomb of Nakht, Sheikh Abd El Qurna/Photo by Quentin Kardos.

African Philosophy: Egypt

One of the world's most long-lived and fascinating civilizations developed in the land of Egypt on the continent of Africa. The Egyptian civilization was already ancient when the Greeks began their philosophical speculation. In fact, as we discuss shortly, the roots of Western thought may actually extend to this extraordinary culture. Like the Native Americans, early Egyptians believed the great powers of nature—including the sky, the sun, the earth, and the Nile River—to be gods. There was intense focus in Egyptian culture on the afterlife. The magnificent pyramids that awe tourists today were built as burial places for pharaohs, or kings, and bodies were mummified to prevent their decomposition. Although at first only the Pharaoh and the royal family were believed to be immortal, gradually even commoners had prayers recited over their bodies by the powerful priests of Egypt. The Pharaoh, however, was thought to be divine, a god-king ruling by divine right. Through him, the gods made known their wishes for the human family. There was no need for a code of laws because the word of the Pharaoh was the word of heaven.

The life of Egypt was controlled by the Nile River whose periodic overflowing and depositing of silt enriched the soil and made agriculture possible. Seeking to predict the annual flood, the Egyptians found a method in astronomy. Noting that the flood occurred after the star Sirius appeared in the sky, they developed a calendar based on this event. The Egyptian calendar divided the year into twelve thirty-day months and added five days at the end. Although this is not quite as accurate as present-day calendars, the Egyptian scheme was a major advance over the older calendar developed by the Babylonians of the Near East, which was based on phases of the Moon.

From ancient Egypt comes what may be the oldest surviving book in human history. Here are some "Instructions," or advice, for living in the world, written by Ptahhotep of Memphis between 3400 and 2150 B.C.E.

Don't be proud of your knowledge
Consult the ignorant and the wise;
The limits of art are not reached,
No artist's skills are perfect;
Good speech is more hidden than greenstone,
Yet may be found among the maids at the grindstones...
Follow your heart as long as you live . . .
Don't waste time on daily cares
Beyond providing for your household;
When wealth has come, follow your heart,
Wealth does no good if one is glum! . . .
Be generous as long as you live . . .
Kindness is a man's memorial . . .
If you listen to my sayings
All your affairs will go forward . . .[8]

This timeless advice, with its oddly modern sound, is as relevant now as it was in Old Kingdom Egypt. It also seems closely related to the attitudes expressed by Confucius and his disciples.

From a later period, about 600 B.C.E. (roughly the time of Buddha, Confucius, and Lao-tzu), comes this plea from the *Book of the Dead:*

The Address to the Gods

Behold me, I have come to you,
Without sin, without guilt, without evil,
Without a witness against me,
Without one whom I have wronged . . .
I have given bread to the hungry,
Water to the thirsty,
Clothes to the naked,
A ferryboat to the boatless.
I have given divine offerings to the gods,
Invocation-offerings to the dead.
Rescue me, protect me,
Do not accuse me before the great god![9]

These excerpts give us some insight into cultural ideals for behavior in Egypt. Ptahhotep's lengthy instruction attempts to cover all circumstances in which a person might find himself, while "The Address to the Gods" lists the good works the dead hope will be pleasing to the gods in the afterlife.

Egyptian civilization is a fascinating subject in its own right, but interest in it has been heightened by a major debate raging among scholars about the relationship between the cultures of Egypt and Greece. People in the West have been taught that Greece is the cradle of our civilization, but that tradition is being called "Eurocentric" by those who contend that much of Greek civilization was borrowed from Egypt. The "Afrocentric" thesis for the origins of Western civilization insists that much of what we call Greek or Western philosophy is copied from indigenous African philosophy of the "Mystery System."[10]

Supporters of the Afrocentric thesis argue that most of the early Greek philosophers, whom you will meet in Chapter 1, studied under Egyptian mystery priests or studied elsewhere under Egyptian-trained teachers. Pythagoras, some say, learned geometry in Egypt where it originated. Socrates, teacher of the great philosopher Plato, is credited with the maxim "Know Thyself," yet this saying was commonly written on Egyptian temple doors centuries before Socrates was born. As for Plato himself, it is said, his "alleged Theory of Ideas is borrowed from Egypt," while Aristotle, his foremost student, was educated in Africa before taking over an entire library of books on the Egyptian mystery system when Aristotle entered Egypt with Alexander the Great who had been *his* student.[11]

Although scholars continue to debate how much the Greeks may have learned from Egypt and other neighboring cultures, ancient evidence indicates that they did look to the Egyptians as a source of wisdom. Linked with ancient cultures by Phoenician sailing ships, the Greeks had the luxury of learning their wisdom from a distance. "There was Greece in her infancy on the one side, and the immemorial civilizations on the other . . . Thus it happened that the Greeks acquired the elements of culture from Babylon and Egypt without paying the forfeit of independence."[12]

Surviving fragments reporting the lives of such early Greek philosophers as Thales and Pythagoras suggest that they did in fact study in Egypt. Given the similarities between their ideas and those of Egypt and other surrounding cultures, there seems to be no reason to reject the hypothesis that Greek philosophy was influenced by the thought systems in Egypt and Babylon. The search for wisdom, even in ancient Greece, was international in scope.

A related question in the debate is, Were the Egyptians themselves black or white? If, as some contend, the Egyptians were black, then the unstated assumptions of many Westerners about white racial superiority would need to be reevaluated or at least questioned. Whatever their racial heritage may have been, the Egyptians remind us that the roots of wisdom are far older than Greek civilization.

Hebrews and Monotheism

Miles away from the Egyptians and the Greeks, a Hebrew religious tradition developed in what we now call the Middle East. King Solomon, who reigned about 950 B.C.E., collected wisdom sayings from around the known world, including Egypt. Solomon seems to have translated and paraphrased Egyptian wise sayings about nature and the living of one's life, adding his own contributions. The books of Proverbs and Ecclesiastes in the Hebrew Scriptures include Solomon's collection of Egyptian wisdom and elements of Greek philosophy. Like the Greeks, the Hebrews looked for wisdom wherever they could find it, and their quest had a similar international scope.

The concept of one God—known as **monotheism**—has been said to set the theology of the Jews apart from the polytheism of their neighbors. During the reign of Akhenaton, the Egyptians did adopt a kind of monotheism;

monotheism *belief in one God*

however, since the Pharaoh remained a god-king, the Egyptian system was not purely monotheistic. Although it is common in the West to credit the Hebrews with the development of monotheism, in recent years feminists have challenged this assumption.

Goddess Religions and Monotheism

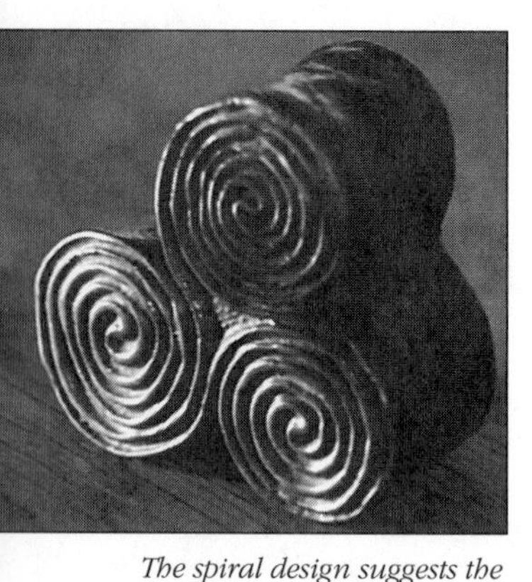

The spiral design suggests the eternal, life-giving power of the Goddess.

Goddess symbol from Ireland/Courtesy of Janis Cripe.

Using archaeological evidence, some scholars argue that from the dawn of history God was worshiped as a woman—the Great Goddess, the Mother of all life, and the source of all fertility. From France to Siberia, female figures—carved from ivory or bone, coupled with ancient hymns of worship and praise addressed to the Queen of Heaven under one of her many names—suggest that God was indeed One—the Great Mother. At first the Goddess reigned alone; later she was joined by a son or brother who was also her lover and consort. Only later, perhaps after the invasion of horse-riding Indo-Europeans who loved hard drinking and fighting, did God become a single "male" entity. The last of the Goddess temples was not destroyed until 500 C.E. This is monotheism, but of a very different sort from the worldview we have inherited from the Hebrews.

Leonard Shlain, a vascular surgeon, has suggested in *The Alphabet versus the Goddess* that the arrival of alphabet literacy (through the giving of the 10 commandments to Moses) set in motion a process that elevated what we have come to think of as left-brain ways of seeing the world over the more holistic right-brain-influenced ways of perception then in place. The result was dethroning of the Goddess and a corresponding decline in the status of women in society. According to Dr. Shlain:

> Goddess worship, feminine values, and women's power depend on the ubiquity of the image. God worship, masculine values, and men's dominance of women are bound to the written word. Word and image, like masculine and feminine, are complementary opposites. Whenever a culture elevates the written word at the expense of the image, patriarchy dominates. When the importance of the image supersedes the written word, feminine values and egalitarianism flourish.[13]

Much of this book will explore the patriarchal world of the last 5,000 years. Shlain believes that the increasing power of image—through photography, motion pictures, and television—has launched a new Golden Age, "one in which the right-hemispheric values of tolerance, caring, and respect for nature will begin to ameliorate the conditions that have prevailed for the too-long period during which left-hemispheric values were dominant."[14] Keep this thesis in mind as you read the later chapters and consider the rise of feminism and the emergence of environmental ethics. Is Shlain right in his assumptions?

Contemporary research into the origins of monotheism highlights a more general point. Just as traditional discussions of Western philosophy are being challenged as Eurocentric, so too have they been criticized for neglecting the contributions of women. Most philosophy textbooks include no women philosophers, although some now include a chapter on feminist thought. You will be reading women philosophers in every chapter of this book as their arguments speak to the chief line of thought we will be following. For now it is perhaps worth asking how the world might seem different if the God worshiped by most people in our culture were pictured as a woman. Suppose, too, that black Africans were the source of much of the philosophic wisdom of the West. Would you view the world or yourself differently?

How we image God reveals assumptions about what matters most in our culture. If God is the source of all that is, do women as well as men share in the divine nature? Like the Buddha, we are seeking enlightenment about the underlying nature of what is. If all existence is characterized by change, is there anything permanent beneath the flux? Can we look to nature as Native Americans and Taoists did and do or to Confucian rites and rituals for guidance in living our lives? Or, are the answers ultimately to be found within ourselves? What will be of lasting value and therefore make us happy? Keep these questions in mind as we turn to the Greeks and seek their guidance in answering the question: Is this all there is?

Notes

1. *Tao Te Ching,* trans. Stephen Mitchell (New York: HarperCollins, 1991), chap. 37.
2. *Tao Te Ching,* chap. 60.
3. Confucius, *Analects* IX:11, trans. D. C. Lau (New York: Penguin, 1979).
4. For this analysis I am indebted to Benjamin Hoff's *The Tao of Pooh* (New York: Penguin, 1983).
5. Peter Nabokov, ed., *Native American Testimony: A Chronicle of Indian-White Relations from Prophecy to the Present* (1492–1992) (New York: Viking Press, 1991), 32, 50.
6. Margot Edmonds and Ella E. Clark, eds., *Voices of the Winds* (New York: Facts on File, 1989), xv–xvi.
7. Vincent H. Gaddis, *American Indian Myths and Mysteries* (New York: Indian Head Books, 1977), 14.
8. Miriam Lichtheim, *Ancient Egyptian Literature,* vol. 1, *The Old and Middle Kingdom* (Berkeley: University of California Press, 1973), 63, 66, 72–73.
9. Miriam Lichtheim, *Ancient Egyptian Literature,* vol. 2, *The New Kingdom* (Berkeley: University of California Press, 1976), 128.
10. Innocent Onyewuenyi, "Is There an African Philosophy?" in *African Philosophy: The Essential Readings,* ed. Tsenay Serequeberhan (New York: Paragon House, 1991), 36.
11. Ibid.
12. *Selections from Early Greek Philosophy,* 3rd ed., ed. Milton C. Nahm (New York: Appleton-Century-Crofts, 1947), 5.
13. Leonard Shlain, *The Alphabet versus the Goddess: The Conflict Between Word and Image* (New York: Viking Penguin, 1998), p.7.
14. Ibid., p. 432.

CHAPTER 1

Why Philosophy?

Is This All There Is?

Before You Read ...

Ask yourself what it would take to make you truly happy, to enable you to live your life to the fullest, regardless of what circumstances you might eventually have to navigate.

We never cease to stand like curious children before the great mystery into which we are born.
ALBERT EINSTEIN

Children, as soon as they learn to speak, begin asking questions about what they see and experience. They seem to know, at least on an intuitive level, that what you see may not necessarily be what you get—that there may be more to objects and events than what is immediately apparent. Some things that look good taste awful; others that look awful taste good. TV puppies bark, but there is no soft fur to touch. Grandpa can take out some of his teeth. Bubbles look so solid but break when you try to grab them.

If mustard and the Sun are both yellow and hot, a child may draw the logical conclusion that the Sun must be made of mustard. Parents who explain the distinction between appearance and reality may not realize that they are introducing the subject matter of philosophy. As children we begin, as the first philosophers in any culture do, without the benefit of sophisticated scientific explanations. Struggling to make sense of the world, we quickly learn to question surface qualities and look for deeper or more essential levels of meaning.

The Issue Defined

In this chapter we take our first look at the early Greeks and their efforts to separate appearance from reality. As they examined the world around them in search of the basic "world stuff" from which every particular thing derived, another set of questions arose: How do we know what we think we know about what is apparent and what is real? Since I seem to have only my own private window on the world rather than an objective view of the world as it actually is, do I have a way to verify whether my perceptions are accurate?

If a child sees a monster under the bed or in the closet, but Mom and Dad do not, whose perceptions are correct, and who will decide between the two conflicting versions? Parental assurances that "there is nothing there" have little effect on a frightened child who "knows" the monster is only waiting for the light to go out before reappearing. Adults may "know" that eating spinach or practicing the piano are good for you, while you remain unconvinced. How we know seems to be intimately connected with what we know.

More critical still are questions about how to live and what (if anything) will make us happy. It may seem to us that some other state—being married or single, living alone or with a loved other, making your own money or not having to worry about earning money—holds the key to happiness. The grass always seems to be greener on the other side of the fence, but when we get there, the place we have just left takes on a romantic allure. And, we may find ourselves wondering if any place or any thing is really as wonderful up close as it appears to be from a distance.

As a human being, you have no choice about the fact that you need a philosophy. Your only choice is whether you define your philosophy by a conscious, rational, disciplined process of thought . . . or let your subconscious accumulate a junk heap of unwarranted conclusions, false generalizations, undefined contradictions . . . thrown together by chance.

AYN RAND

Even more confusing is the feeling we get when we achieve some goal we have been pursuing for years and find ourselves with an empty feeling and the taste of ashes in our mouths. Earning the degree, getting the perfect apartment, finding a soul mate, making a lot of money, becoming a name in the news—these do not necessarily bring with them happiness or peace of mind. The person who becomes a partner in a prestigious law firm and buys a dream house and a Ferrari may experience a midlife crisis—is this all there is?

Why philosophy? When questions like these arise, philosophy helps us sort the important from the trivial and determine what is of lasting value and may finally make us happy. Philosophy begins by asking about what is real, about what makes a person a person, about whether there is a God and, if so, what this God is like. Philosophy provides us a structure and a method for continuing to ask, "Is this all there is?"—about reality, knowing, the quest for human happiness, and the path we want to walk in life. To launch our exploration of this issue, we will start with the Greek philosophers who came before Socrates and look at how they first asked and answered the basic questions of philosophy 2500 years ago.

Philosophizing is the process of making sense out of experience.

SUSANNE K. LANGER

The Pre-Socratic Cosmologists

The earliest Greek philosophy we have on record consists of speculations about the nature of reality. It is called *pre-Socratic* in reference to Socrates, the first major figure in the Western tradition, and indicates that this early work came before Socrates and laid the groundwork on which his later, more sophisticated worldview could be constructed. We call these first Greek thinkers cosmologists because they saw the world as a **cosmos,** a comprehensible and ordered whole. **Cosmology** studies the basic principles of the cosmos with an eye to unlocking its secrets.

cosmos *the world as an ordered whole*

cosmology *the branch of metaphysics dealing with the study of the principles underlying the cosmos*

THE MAKING OF A PHILOSOPHER

Pre-Socratic Cosmologists
(6th to the 4th centuries B.C.E.)

Thales proved geometric theorems, measured the pyramids, and was an engineer and astronomer. He proposed a central federal government with common citizenship for the twelve Ionian cities. Anaximander drew a map of the known world and wrote a book—the first prose treatise in Europe. Heraclitus, born in 540 B.C.E., was a nobleman from Ephesus in what was then Asia Minor and is today Turkey. His ideas suggest he may have had contact with the East. Pythagoras developed a key geometric theorem and led a research institute—church in Croton, which was open to men and women. By 532 B.C.E. he had moved to southern Italy to live among the Dorian Greeks. He taught the transmigration of souls, a kind of reincarnation. Empedocles was a prince who was offered the kingship of his native city in Sicily but declined it. He wrote songs and practiced rhetoric. He saw himself as a prophet and claimed to have recalled the dead to life. His school of medicine was reputed to be the equal of the more famous one of Hippocrates. To prove his own immortality, or perhaps because he believed in reincarnation, he jumped into Mount Etna, the active volcano on the island of Sicily. A year later it spit out one of his sandals.

continues

Unlike children, these early Greek philosophers brought maturity and experience to their exploration of the basic questions of reality, knowledge, and values. Stories about the origins of things are as old as human speech, and Greek culture was alive with tales of the gods and goddesses who had brought humans into being and controlled the natural world while fighting among themselves for power and status. In asking and answering the basic question "Is this all there is?" what Thales and his fellow Milesians did was to take a new, more systematic approach, one that gave birth to what we now call philosophy.

The Milesians

If we wanted to assign a very arbitrary date, we could say that Western philosophy began May 28, 585 B.C.E. at 6:13 P.M. You might ask yourself what could have happened at that moment of sufficient significance to allow us to choose it as the beginning point for Western philosophy. It is not the birth or death of a philosopher, although those are logical guesses. In fact, what happened was that Thales, a Milesian mathematician, predicted an eclipse of the Sun would occur at that exact moment—and it did. Why was this event so striking?

The prevailing worldview attributed events like eclipses and other major cosmological events, as well as more minor occurrences like rainbows and thunderstorms, to the activities of the gods and goddesses. If lightning bolts flew across the sky, it meant the god Zeus was once again angry with his wife-sister Hera. Thales startled his fellow Milesians by figuring out that eclipses are caused by the movements of heavenly bodies and calculating mathematically when the next such alignment would occur. When his prediction was proved accurate, Thales had a ready audience for his theory that events have rational causes and that we, as rational beings, can understand and anticipate them.

Thales' feat was a world-changing event for the Greeks of Miletus. Instead of an unpredictable world, operating according to the whims of the all-too-human gods and goddesses who could at any moment turn things upside down, Thales postulated a rational cosmos in which things happen in an orderly and predictable manner. No less powerful was his assumption that humans are rational, or reasoning, creatures capable of unraveling the apparent mysteries of the cosmos. As we have seen, Thales' "givens" contain the seeds not only of Western philosophy but also of science. To those of us brought up in Western culture, they are so familiar that they seem obvious and hardly worth stating. Yet, these assumptions have far-reaching implications.

Thales' cosmology assumed that the "world" has an independent, objective existence separate from us knowers. Fortunately, as an orderly and rational place, the world can be known by us because there is a match between ourselves as rational creatures and the world as an intelligible place. If either condition is not met, no knowledge is possible. If the world is orderly and rational but we are not, we can never understand its order. On the other hand, if we are rational but the world is not, it will not yield itself to rational explanation.

Besides emphasizing rationality as the key to knowledge, Thales' account affirmed the characteristically Western distinction between the subject who knows and the object that is known. Understanding the world means standing back from it as if we, the knowers, were completely separate from it. To this day we in the West value "objective" knowledge that is obtained by rational means. Our philosophy and science generally presuppose Thales' distinction between an objective, rational world and the conscious subject who "knows" it. These assumptions are so fundamental to the way we approach the world that it is difficult for us to see the world, and knowledge, any other way. Yet, in some of the cultures we will be studying, the distinction between the knower and the known and the emphasis on reason as the key to knowledge are either denied or softened.

Worldviews that emphasize the interdependence and interrelatedness of all things, for instance, do not assume a separation between the knower and the known. If reality is characterized by interrelatedness rather than separateness, then knowing "reality" from the "outside" is impossible. We know only from the "inside" and by routes that are not exclusively "rational" in the sense affirmed by the Greeks. In fact, only in the West do we find such an absolute distinction between subject and object, knower and known. As we examine Eastern and African approaches to reality and knowing, you will see that different assumptions lead to quite different views of the world.

Thales was able to make the kind of intellectual detour he did largely because he lived in Miletus, a Greek colony across the Aegean Sea from Greece. It was part of what in the ancient world was called Asia Minor and on today's maps is labeled Turkey. As a trading colony, Miletus depended on foreigners to buy its products and to sell its citizens the goods they needed. There were always different-looking people in the marketplace, wearing a variety of clothes and speaking languages other than Greek. In a later period, Greeks would call all foreigners "barbarians" because their languages sounded to the Greeks like *bar, bar, bar,* but Milesians could not afford to alienate the foreigners who were so essential to their economy.

In fact, as a trading colony, Miletus fostered an openness to foreigners. If you want to sell something to someone else, you must try to understand not only their language but also the way they see the world. Every successful sales representative knows how to get inside the head of a client—to figure out what the client needs or to create a desire for what the salesperson has to sell. As good salespeople, the Milesians were probably more open to fresh ideas than other Greeks were.

Their flexibility and openness may have been the key ingredient in promoting acceptance of Thales' new ideas. There was also another factor. No one in Miletus worked full time or achieved social status based solely on religious activities. Unlike the powerful Egyptian priests, for example, those who presided over temple services in Miletus did so part time, and they had other roles in the community. If Thales proved that the gods and goddesses did not exist or were not nearly so powerful as previously supposed, no one's power or prestige was directly threatened.

THE MAKING OF A PHILOSOPHER

Pre-Socratic Cosmologists
continued

Anaxagoras was the first Athenian philosopher. Drafted into the army of the Persian General Xerxes, Anaxagoras defected when the Persians were defeated and then settled in Athens. Democritus (460–351 B.C.E.) devoted his life to science and travel. He wrote more than sixty books, but unfortunately none survives. He claimed he would rather "discover one causal explanation than gain the kingdom of the Persians." Together, these men took the first steps in establishing what we today call Western philosophy.

All things are full of gods.
THALES OF MILETUS

The arithmetic of life does not always have a logical answer.
INSHIRAH ABDUR-RAUF

After his startling eclipse prediction had gotten the attention of his fellow Milesians, Thales went on to apply his belief in rationality to the most basic question in philosophy—the difference between appearance and reality. How is it, for example, that cows eat grass and it turns into milk? Was the milk already present in some latent way in the grass or, if not, how did one substance turn into another? Questions like these soon led early philosophers to inquire into the fundamental nature of everything. If some things we observe are only appearances and not what is fundamentally real, then what permanent substance or substances exist behind those appearances? Is there some original, common substance from which all the variety in the world comes?

Assuming that such a substance exists, the Greeks called it the ***archē*** which means "first" or "beginning," and Thales reasoned that the *archē* might be water. After all, water is an excellent example of a substance that changes its appearance when it assumes different states—ice, liquid, and steam. Moreover, water is basic to all of life, another reason it seemed a good candidate for the original, fundamental substance.

archē *[AHR KAY] the first principle or basic stuff from which everything derives*

Milesians, no doubt, fished their dinner from the water. They had certainly noticed that humans can go weeks without food but only a few days without water. They probably had observed that just before the birth of a goat or human baby there is a bursting of the bag of waters (what we would name the amniotic sac) and a flow of water (amniotic fluid). Thales seems to have chosen an appropriate element on the level of symbol, too. Later Christians, wishing to symbolize new spiritual life in baptism, decided to sprinkle water or immerse a person in it to indicate a transformation from one form of life to another.

For Thales then, the permanent substance from which all the variety in the world derives was water. As the first of what later scholars would call the pre-Socratic cosmologists, he shared his ideas in Miletus and attracted students—the first people in the Western world to do what you are doing now, studying philosophy. One of them did what students often do; he listened to his teacher, learned what the teacher had to teach, and then went on to develop an original idea.

The student was Anaximander, and his theory was that water was much too particular to be the *archē*. After all, he mused, if water is the source of everything, where does dust come from? He theorized that the *archē* must be a far less specific substance, perhaps something with no characteristics of its own but the capability of becoming many things. By this process of reasoning, Anaximander arrived at the idea of a substance that in itself has no characteristics that we directly sense or observe. He called this substance the *infinite* or *boundless* (in Greek, *apeiron*).

Another student, Anaximenes, found Anaximander's boundless to be entirely too vague a concept. How could a material substance lack all specific characteristics? The idea seemed nonsensical to Anaximenes. He returned to something closer to Thales' original notion, but instead of water Anaximenes suggested *air* as the *archē*.

Just as air supports life in a person, so air in the form of wind supports life in the world. If a soldier fell in battle, the test for life was to check for breathing. Air meant life; the absence of it signified death. In a similar way, Anaximenes observed that air moves clouds and weather systems; in its full power, air can bend even strong trees. Anaximenes was the first in the Western world to reason by analogy from the *microcosm* to the *macrocosm*. What is true in the person (the microcosm) must also be true in the world (the macrocosm), and vice versa.

As the basic substance, air had to be the source of all the other apparently different substances in the world. Anaximenes used the principles of *rarefaction* and *condensation* to explain how this occurred. When rarefied (heated), air becomes fire; as it cools, air condenses more and more, becoming wind, water, earth, and stones. What appear to be *qualitative* differences between air and stone are explained as *quantitative* differences (stone is not qualitatively different from air, just more fully condensed).

Other Monists

monist *a pre-Socratic philosopher who believed the* archē *was a unified whole or any philosopher who believes reality is one*

All three Milesians were **monists**; they sought to explain all of reality in terms of a unified whole. Other monists, from different parts of the Greek Empire (southern Italy and Ephesus) during the fifth century B.C.E., were Pythagoras, Heraclitus, and Parmenides. Most of you have already met Pythagoras through his geometric theorem about the equal relationship between the square drawn on the hypotenuse of a right triangle and the sum of the squares drawn on the other two legs. Pythagoras ran a combination religious community and research institute to which hundreds of women and men belonged.

The qualities of numbers exist in a musical scale (harmonia) *in the heavens and in many other things.*
ARISTOTLE ON THE PYTHAGOREANS

Rejecting the material explanations of the *archē* favored by the Milesians, Pythagoras looked to mathematics to explain the rationality of the cosmos. In fact, he saw *numbers* imposing order on what would otherwise be a chaotic world. Since numbers enable us to count and bring clarity to objects and forces in the world, Pythagoras saw in them the basic explanation of reality. Numbers, for instance, help explain intervals between notes and chords in music. Noticing that stopping a lute string at fixed intervals produced sounds with mathematical relationships to each other, Pythagoras devised Greek music theory. He applied the same mathematical rigor to the movements of the heavenly bodies, which he calculated as operating in a similar kind of harmony, later called the "music of the spheres." To Pythagoras, understanding mathematical relationships was the key to unlocking the mysteries of the universe.

The most Eastern-sounding of our early Western philosophers, Heraclitus observed that all reality was characterized by change. He theorized that what was real might not be a substance at all but instead the very process of *change* itself. To symbolize this process of change, Heraclitus used the image of *fire*. He did not imagine fire to be the *archē* in the same way the Milesians had suggested water, the boundless, and air, but he did think fire would help us picture what reality is like.

If you have ever seen a beautiful fireplace fire and tried to capture it on film, you will have an idea of what Heraclitus was talking about. Your photo looks nothing like the fire you saw because the fire itself is constantly in motion while your photo artificially froze a split second of that action. Constantly exchanging elements with its surroundings, fire was for Heraclitus the clearest representation of the change he believed lay at the very heart of reality.

Making the same point, using a different analogy, Heraclitus wrote, "In the same rivers we step and we do not step."[1] What, after all, do we mean when we name a river? Surely not the water itself, since it flows ever onward toward the sea. The water we step in is not the same from one second to the next. It seems equally untrue to suppose the river is the bed where the water flows. What Heraclitus seems to be saying is that if you step into the river twice you will encounter two different rivers. In addition, you will have changed yourself in the intervening time. You will be a different person—warmer or colder, happier or sadder, certainly older if not wiser.

God is day and night, winter and summer, war and peace, satiety and hunger; but he assumes different forms, just as when incense is mingled with incense; everyone gives him the name he pleases.

HERACLITUS OF EPHESUS

Using still another metaphor, Heraclitus explained that the universe could be understood by observing the relationship between opposition and unity. "Men do not understand," he wrote, "how that which draws apart agrees with itself." Harmony, the reconciliation of opposites, "lies in the bending back, as for instance in the bow and lyre."[2] As the bow demonstrates when it bends then snaps to release an arrow, and as the lyre reveals when we pluck its harplike strings, opposite tensions can make effective unities. If we understand apparently opposing forces as parts of one whole, we can begin to grasp reality. As we will see later in this chapter, some Asian thought systems also see apparent opposites as complementary expressions of the way things are and regard process and change as key to understanding what is real.

Parmenides offered an analysis that was nearly the exact opposite of the one proposed by Heraclitus. Whereas Heraclitus thought change was the one ultimate reality, Parmenides argued that genuine change is impossible. What fundamentally exists—the *archē*—is *being* itself. For Parmenides, being was a material substance somewhat like Anaximander's *boundless,* which occupied all the space in the universe. By definition, what is *not*-being does not exist. But, if being is everywhere, then there is no place where being is not, and fundamental change is impossible. Change means motion, and motion supposes empty space, which, according to Parmenides, cannot exist. Just as the plastic number puzzles you may have played with as a child depend on the blank square for rearrangement, if there is no empty space, everything must remain exactly where it presently is.

It is necessary both to say and to think that being is; for it is possible that being is, and it is impossible that not-being is; this is what I bid thee ponder.

PARMENIDES

Notice that Parmenides developed his theory entirely on logical principles. If there is no empty space, there can be no motion. Those who think they see motion (everyone) must conclude that their senses deceive them. If motion (and therefore change) is logically impossible, then apparent motion and change must be illusion. So, Parmenides' theory takes the distinction between appearance and reality to perhaps its ultimate extreme.

Other philosophers covered in later chapters may reason themselves into theories that seem to deny common sense. Like Parmenides, they do not accept the evidence of the senses as certain. For this reason,

Parmenides is sometimes called the first logician, or the first philosopher to rely on logic rather than on sense experience or common sense.

Pluralists

Clearly, Heraclitus and Parmenides cannot both be correct. If reality is characterized by constant and unending change as Heraclitus supposed, then Parmenides must be wrong. If, on the other hand, Parmenides is right in his logical analysis that there can be no motion, then Heraclitus must be mistaken. The next group of philosophers reasoned themselves out of this impasse by broadening the base a little. Perhaps, they suggested, reality is too complex to be captured in a single element. It may be that reality is plural—that is, when things have been analyzed into their most fundamental elements, there are many of these elements instead of a single one. Philosophers who hold this view are called **pluralists.**

pluralist *a pre-Socratic philosopher who believed the* archē *was multiple or any philosopher who believes reality is plural*

Drawing on existing wisdom in fifth-century B.C.E. Sicily, Empedocles concluded that four elements could account for all the variety in the world: *earth, air, fire,* and *water.* Taken together, the four elements traditionally used in the ancient world to explain reality offered a wide enough range to accommodate everything in the natural environment. In Empedocles' way of thinking, alternating world cycles fully mixed and then fully separated the four elements. Thus, we observe the elements both as separate and as combined in complex objects. The mixing and separating were accounted for by the two opposing forces of love/attraction and strife/repulsion. These forces accounted for motion and change.

For before this I was born once a boy, and a maiden, and a plant, and a bird, and a darting fish in the sea.
EMPEDOCLES OF SICILY

Anaxagoras, a Greek contemporary, took Empedocles's theory to another level. If four elements helped explain variations, an even more complex explanation would arise from an *infinite number of seeds,* or *germs,* no two of which were alike. This, Anaxagoras believed, accounted for all the many qualitative differences we perceive in things. In all that exists, he wrote, there is a mixture of everything. The way a particular object appears is the result of the proportions occupied by the various seeds, or germs.

There is no smallest among the small and no largest among the large; but always something still smaller and something still larger.
ANAXAGORAS

To understand what Anaxagoras is saying, consider hair color. Observe any group of people and you will find a large variety of hair colors. Forced to categorize, you could place everyone into five main groups: black, blond, gray, red, and brown. Most people, however, have a unique hair color that is some combination of these categories—auburn, ash blond, salt and pepper. Anaxagoras would explain this phenomenon by asserting that all of us have some portion of every possible color; our own unique color reflects which colors predominate.

The last of the fifth-century B.C.E. pluralists, Democritus developed a theory that anticipates the understanding of the world expressed by classical physics. Reality, he wrote, is composed of *atoms and the void.* He conceived atoms as indivisible particles of matter that can neither be created nor destroyed. Unlike Parmenides, Democritus stipulated the void, the empty square into which the other squares in the puzzle can move.

One should cultivate much understanding, not much knowing.
DEMOCRITUS

Based on this theory, he concluded that the weight of composite bodies will depend on the density of their atoms. Small but very densely packed bodies could weigh more than larger, less densely packed ones. Colliding atoms, he stated, will behave according to mechanical principles, and since atoms are in motion, objects are not fixed and static but dynamic and changing. One intriguing aspect of his theory, already being discussed by a contemporary group of philosophers known as the Sophists (whom we discuss in the next section), was that if an object is composed of matter in motion it must appear differently to each observer.

For a summary of the different theories of the *archē* that we have just considered, see Table 1.1.

Cosmogony and Cosmology

cosmogony *[kos MAH go nee] theory about the origins of the cosmos*

The theories of many of these early Greek philosophers encompassed both *cosmology,* the basic principles of the universe, and **cosmogony,** an account of how the cosmos came to be. In describing the present state of the universe, these early thinkers offered rational, prescientific explanations for phenomena rather than attributing them to the actions of the gods and goddesses. Thales, for example, described Earth as a disk floating on water. This had the advantage of accounting for earthquakes; they were, he said, the result of water turbulence rather than the antics of the god Poseidon. When the boundless is in motion, Anaximander said, it spins off hot (fire) and cold (air, water, and earth). Air wraps fire in tubes with breathing holes; we call them the Sun and Moon. When the holes become blocked, we have eclipses and phases of the Moon. Earth is also a cylinder suspended in space.

Anaximenes adapted Thales' theory to say that Earth is a flat disk floating on air. The sky is a crystalline vault, with the Moon and stars stuck to it like leaves. Earth turns on a polar axis the way a cap turns on a person's head. When the Sun and Moon disappear, it is because they have gone behind high mountains. Rainbows are caused by the Sun's rays falling on dense air, not by the goddess Iris. Pythagoras was convinced that Earth is a spherical planet, one among many and not the center of the system; Parmenides accurately hypothesized that the Moon shines from the reflected light of the Sun.

Observing that human babies remain helpless for such a long time, Anaximander concluded that we must be descended from some other species, paving the way for the theory of evolution. Heraclitus reasoned that behind the change that was the very heart of reality there must be a rational principle responsible for its apparent order. He called it the *logos,* using a Greek word that literally means "word." As words impose order and meaning, so Heraclitus saw the *logos* ordering the cosmos. Anaxagoras said something similar in his theory of seeds, or germs. *Nous,* or mind, he argued, is the cause of all motion and contains the *telos* (end, or purpose) to which the motion is directed. *Nous,* or pure intelligence, was also the source of all creation.

TABLE 1.1 PRE-SOCRATIC PHILOSOPHERS *Each of these early Greek philosophers sought the basic stuff of which everything in the world was made. They fall into three general categories depending on how they conceived of the* archē.

PRE-SOCRATIC PHILOSOPHERS

	Philosopher	*Archē*
Milesian monists	Thales	Water
	Anaximander	The boundless
	Anaximenes	Air
Other monists	Pythagoras	Numbers
	Heraclitus	Change (fire)
	Parmenides	Being
Pluralists	Empedocles	Earth, air, fire, water
	Anaxagoras	Seeds, or germs
	Democritus	Atoms and the void

Perhaps more important than the specific answers offered by the early philosophers of the Western world is the process by which they went about speculating on fundamental questions. Instead of turning to the cultural wisdom found in religious myths and poetic explanations, each tried to reason his way to an accurate understanding of reality based on objective principles that would make the world intelligible on its own terms. This belief in the orderliness of the universe, and our human ability to understand it, is perhaps the most important legacy of the pre-Socratics. It is also what most clearly separates philosophical thought in the West from similar speculation in Asia and Africa.

Furthermore, the questions asked in sixth- and fifth-century B.C.E. Greece have not gone away. We are still struggling today with questions about what is real, how everything in the cosmos came into being, what accounts for change, and whether the universe is orderly and purposeful or merely chaotic. These are the basic questions of one of the three main branches of philosophy called **metaphysics.** Since Aristotle's writings about "being" followed his writings about physics, people began referring to them as *ta meta ta physica biblia* (literally, "the books that come after the Physics"). We will encounter the other two branches, **epistemology** (theories of knowledge and truth) and **axiology** (theories of values) later in this chapter.

metaphysics *the branch of philosophy investigating what is real*

epistemology *the branch of philosophy dealing with the study of knowledge, what it is, and how we acquire it*

axiology *the branch of philosophy dealing with the study of values*

Metaphysics is sometimes referred to as first philosophy because it deals with the first or most basic questions about what it means to call something or someone real. In this text we will be using the term *metaphysics* in its broadest sense to cover all questions related to reality and being. As we have seen, the early Greeks began doing philosophy by focusing on cosmology, the study of the principles underlying the cosmos. The next step in the development of Greek philosophy brings us to the

ontology *the branch of metaphysics dealing with the study of being*

other portion of metaphysics, which focuses on being. To keep our terms separate, we will call this branch **ontology.** You should keep in mind, however, that this division is somewhat arbitrary. For many people, metaphysics is synonymous with ontology.

The Sophists

philosophy *literally, the "love of wisdom"*

As you may remember from Historical Interlude A, the word **philosophy** literally means "love of wisdom." The prefix *phil-* occurs in words like *philharmonic,* an orchestra that loves harmony. Since *adelphi* means "brothers," we can see why Philadelphia is sometimes called the "city of brotherly love." The second part of the word *philosophy* comes from the Greek word *sophia,* meaning "wisdom." Those of you who are sophomores might have been told that the word *sophomore* literally means "wise fool." Freshmen, it seems, know nothing and know they know nothing; sophomores, on the other hand, still know very little but think they know a lot more than they do.

Sophist *a teacher of practical applications for philosophy in early Greece*

The **Sophists** are literally the "wise ones." Their name is derived from *sophia,* just like the last part of the word *philosophy.* To be called a Sophist, however, is not necessarily a compliment. Committed to individualism and relativism, the Sophists unsettled Greek society. Plato blamed them for the breakdown in values that he believed led to the death of his teacher and friend Socrates. He also treated them as a unified group when in fact there were at least three types: Sophists of culture, like Protagoras and Gorgias, who sought to stimulate the minds of the young; encyclopedists, like Hippias, who sought to systematize and classify knowledge and information; and, Sophists of eristic, who specialized in debate and disputation, preparing people for public life and the law.[3]

Unlike the pre-Socratic cosmologists, who pursued wisdom for the love of it, the third group of Sophists claimed to be wise enough to teach whatever you might want to know as long as you were willing to pay them the required fees. Although Plato felt these Sophists argued for the sake of argument—paying scant attention to truth or falsity—and had little or no true wisdom to offer, we must concede that their popularity indicates they were meeting a real need in Greek society.[4]

More men are good by training than by nature.
CRITIAS, A SOPHIST

Traveling from city to city from the mid-fifth to the mid-fourth centuries B.C.E., Sophists learned what people who stay at home never find out: People in other places may have a totally different way of doing something than you and all of your friends do, and they may be making assumptions about what is appropriate behavior that may be very different from your own. All of us tend to assume the way we and our families and friends see the world is the only way or at least the right way. Living with someone from another culture or even from a different region of your own country may be your first opportunity to learn what the Sophists learned: There may be no one, universally appropriate way of doing anything.

If this is the case, the Sophists concluded, then there can be no absolutes of any kind. We cannot say it is always right or wrong to do some-

HOW PHILOSOPHY WORKS
Sophistic Logic, or Sophistry

Sophists were accused of making the weaker argument appear the stronger and, generally, of distorting the truth. Here is a Sophist story. Read it and decide for yourself whether the charges are justified.

Protagoras took Euathlus as a student in rhetoric. Since Euathlus had no money, teacher and student agreed that when Euathlus won his first court case he would pay Protagoras for his education. Time went by, and Euathlus did not appear in court. Protagoras grew impatient and brought a suit against Euathlus for payment. Protagoras reasoned that whichever way the court decided he would win: If the court decided in his favor, Euathlus would have to pay, and if Euathlus won his first court case he would have fulfilled the original condition and be obliged to pay his teacher. Confident of the outcome, he arrived in court. Meanwhile, Euathlus had learned his lessons well. He reasoned this way: If the court decides I must pay Protagoras, I will still not have won my first case and not be obliged to pay, but if I win then the court will have decided I do not have to pay Protagoras.

Should Euathlus have to pay Protagoras?

thing; we cannot even speak about how something *is,* as if it had a fixed and absolute reality. The fact is, they concluded, everything is *relative.*

If you recall, Democritus and the atomists had reasoned that matter in motion implied that the same object might appear differently to different people who viewed it from unique angles or from various moments in time. The Sophists took this idea to its extreme and asserted that it makes no sense to ask "What is something like *really*?" The only "answer" is that it "really" is the way it appears to me, the way it appears to you, and the way it appears to everyone else when they observe it. If there are no absolutes and if everything is relative, then opposite conclusions can both be supported. The way something seems to me is the way it is. In a sense, the Sophists turned the distinction between appearance and reality on its head: Appearances *are* reality, at least the only reality any of us can know.

Protagoras, one of the best known Sophists of culture, claimed that "man is the measure of all things."[5] In other words, each of us—not some objective reality such as God or the world's inner nature—determines what is real. The world really is yellow to the person who has jaundice, if Protagoras is correct that "man is the measure of all things, of existing things that they exist, and of non-existing things that they exist not."[6]

In rejecting the idea of objective truth, the Sophists were making a claim (although a negative one) about the nature of being, the subject of ontology. From this metaphysical position it was a short step to a different and more practical focus—namely, what it means to be human and live well in this world. If there are no absolutes, the Sophists reasoned, and everything is relative, then we should not waste our time arguing about what is ultimately real. Instead, we ought to figure out how to be successful and happy. This is in fact what Sophists advertised they would teach their fellow Greeks.

DOING PHILOSOPHY

Shapiro for the Defense

Richard E. Vatz and Lee S. Weinberg

Awed by his aggressive defense tactics in the O. J. Simpson case, we researched Robert Shapiro's early career. It turns out that his first case was defending a man who had been ticketed for parking overtime. Here is his cross-examination of the officer who ticketed his client.

Mr. Shapiro: Officer, how long have you been ticketing cars?

Officer: For ten years, sir.

S: Now, the average meter cop has been ticketing for 15 years, is that right?

O: I don't know, sir.

S: You don't know? This has been your beat for 10 years, and you don't know the average time others have been on your own beat?

O: No, sir.

S: Now, officer, the meter in question was registered "expired," correct?

O: Correct, sir.

S: Now, officer, did anyone else witness the "expired" signal on the meter?

O: No, sir.

S: So, without verification, without eyewitnesses, you just took it on your own authority that the meter said "expired," right?

O: Yes, sir.

S: Officer, when is the last time you had an eye exam?

O: Five years ago.

S: Five years ago? Doesn't the department require meter cops to have regular eye exams?

O: No, sir.

S: So, in theory, officer, you could have terrible vision—be nearly blind—and no one in your department would know.

O: I guess not.

S: Now, officer, the meter which you THINK read "expired" was located in FRONT of the defendant's car, correct?

O: Correct, sir.

S: Now, many meters are located BEHIND parking spaces, is that not correct?

O: Correct, sir.

S: Now, if that's true, officer, how do you know that THIS meter was the meter for the defendant's car?

O: I could just see it, sir.

S: But you've had no training in differentiating between meters located in FRONT of parking spaces and meters located BEHIND parking spaces, have you?

O: Training in front and behind? No, sir.

S: And in 1984, when you started, you once read the wrong meter, erroneously giving an undeserved ticket, didn't you?

O: Well, yes, but . . .

S: And, finally, officer, another policeman in your precinct has testified that you have stated that people should buy American cars, right?

O: Well, yes, but . . .

S: And the defendant's car is a Toyota, isn't it?

O: Yes, but . . .

S: And you once said, and I quote, "I would ticket foreign cars for nothing," didn't you?

O: Well, I may have said that as a joke, but . . .

S: Of course, you wouldn't ticket all cars for nothing, would you?

O: No, but it was just a kind of joking . . .

S: So, you have no witnesses, your eyesight is untested and probably your vision is bad, you sought no corroborative testimony, you've erred on meter-readings in the past, and you are out to get foreign-car owners. How do you expect that 12 jurors would find it true beyond a reasonable doubt that the defendant's car was overparked?

O: I don't, sir.

"Shapiro for the Defense," *Baltimore Morning Sun,* 9/2/94. Courtesy of Richard Vatz and the *Baltimore Sun.*

Richard E. Vatz teaches rhetoric at Towson State University. Lee S. Weinberg teaches in the Graduate School of Public and International Affairs at the University of Pittsburgh.

Since the Greek culture was an oral-based culture, what made one person more successful than another was his ability to speak well. Success in the courts, in politics, and in the intellectual conversation that gave public and private gatherings their spice depended on the skillful use of words. Using the science of *rhetoric,* which literally means "public speaking," Sophists asserted they could teach the right argument for the right person at the right time. Anyone who had the required tuition and was willing to work hard could learn to be successful. In the hands of the Sophists, the logic of the early philosophers became a practical tool for advancing in the world.

Other philosophers were offended by what seemed to them crass commercialism. They thought the love of wisdom was a sacred calling, something worth devoting one's life to and not one cheap trick among many others for making what is wrong appear right and for getting ahead in the world. To call someone a Sophist today, or to accuse someone of "sophistry," is to charge that person with being all flash and no substance and possibly to accuse that person of being intentionally misleading. An example of sophistry is a speech that dazzles us with rhetorical flourishes and sways our emotions but, when examined critically, is found to have no real content or to be filled with errors and contradictions.

In their application of the basic principles of metaphysics to the problems and challenges of everyday life, the Sophists were also exploring the second of the three major branches of philosophy, epistemology. The Greek word *episteme* means "knowledge," so *epistemology* is literally the "study of knowledge," or of how we know what we know. By asserting that "man is the measure of all things," the Sophists were claiming that each of us determines what we know and what we do not. There are no outside standards to which knowledge claims can or should be submitted. In addition, their teachings led other philosophers, including Socrates, to explore the third branch of philosophy, *axiology,* or the study of values. These developments came to a head in what we now call the classical period of Greek philosophy.

THE MAKING OF A PHILOSOPHER

Socrates

(469–399 B.C.E.)

The son of a stonecutter and a midwife, Socrates made his living as a stonemason but also served as an infantryman in the Greek wars. Although he was not a wealthy man, he prided himself on not accepting payment for teaching philosophy. It was said that he wore the same cloak winter and summer, often went barefoot, ate simple foods, and preferred water to wine (although he could drink a lot without getting drunk when the occasion arose). When Aristophanes caricatured him in his play *The Clouds,* which premiered in 423 B.C.E., Socrates was in his forties and had already developed a reputation as a free-thinking intellectual who was not afraid to question established ideas and practices. According to those who knew him, he was short, stocky, muscular, pot-bellied, snub-nosed, and bald. Socrates was executed by the city of Athens as a capital criminal when he was seventy years old.

The Classical Period in Greek Philosophy

Three philosophers—Socrates, Plato, and Aristotle, who primarily lived and worked in the city of Athens as they were developing their ideas from the mid-fifth to the mid-fourth centuries B.C.E.—provided the classic formulations of Western philosophy. Their answers, more than any others, form the bedrock of Western philosophy. These three philosophers speculated about metaphysics, especially ontology. They pondered the issues raised by epistemology, and they explored axiology through earnest inquiries into what is moral or right. There is an interesting relationship among these three men. Socrates was the teacher of Plato, and Aristotle studied for many years in Plato's Academy. Because of this relationship, all three have much in common, but each developed his own distinctive philosophy as well.

Socrates

Socrates, as far as we know, never wrote a word of philosophy. Everything we know about him we know through Plato whose favorite form of writing was the *dialogue,* a literary creation that shows a discussion or exchange of ideas. Plato's dialogues usually featured Socrates and one or more other persons. Since Plato continued to write dialogues, featuring Socrates as the main character, long after his teacher had died, scholars know that some of these dialogues represent Plato's own ideas put into the mouth of Socrates. At least some of the early dialogues, however, seem to be the actual words and ideas of Socrates as remembered and recorded by Plato. We know that Socrates went around Athens questioning the apparently obvious and asking everyone he met to explain the most basic things. This, it seemed to him, was the best way of finding the truth. False ideas could be revealed as false and defeated by persistent questioning. Unlike the Sophists, Socrates, Plato, and Aristotle all believed that statements could be made about the way things *really* are.

Socrates' mother was a midwife, and he was fond of telling people that he was a kind of intellectual midwife. Whereas his mother assisted at the birth of babies, he assisted at the birth of ideas. Just as the baby already exists when the midwife helps the mother bring it into this world, Socrates contended that ideas already exist in our minds and a skillful questioner can bring to consciousness what we may not even realize we know. The Socratic **dialectic,** his method of asking questions, was designed to elicit the truth.

dialectic *a method of questioning used by Socrates in pursuit of the truth*

In the dialogue *Meno,* Plato uses Socrates to illustrate the value of the dialectic by leading a Greek slave boy with no formal education through a geometric proof as a way of proving to his friend Menon that "there is no such thing as teaching, only remembering."[7] Socrates scrupulously avoids giving any kind of instruction to the boy; instead, he only asks a series of questions. The problem: If a 2-foot by 2-foot space is 4 square feet, what must be the dimensions of an 8-square-foot space? Predictably, the boy's first thought is that doubling the length and width will double the square footage; but when this turns out to yield 16 square feet, the boy quickly grasps that doubling yields four times rather than double the area.

When Socrates persists with his questions, the boy next reasons that a dimension between 2 and 4—namely, 3—might yield the desired 8 square feet. Even this is progress, Socrates tells Menon, since the boy now realizes that he does not know the solution and is eager to figure it out.[8] This is a key ingredient in what is called the **Socratic method.** To find out where you are ignorant is the first step in pursuing knowledge or wisdom. As long as you are confident you know all there is to know, you will not seek the truth; and you may remain happily in error.

Socratic method *the method of the dialectic, reported in Plato's dialogues*

Continuing to question, Socrates leads the slave boy through a proof that begins with the 16-square-foot figure and inserts a square turned diagonally to appear as a diamond inside the space. By dividing each of the 4-foot square spaces (that make a 16-square-foot area) in half diagonally, it is possible to create an area of 8 square feet (see Figure 1.1). "Now then, Menon," Socrates concludes, "what do you think? Was there one single opinion which the boy did not give as his own?" When Menon agrees that Socrates is correct and asserts that no one has taught the boy geometry, Socrates reveals Plato's theory of knowledge. If no one has taught him and if Socrates was able to elicit this knowledge only by asking the right questions, then it must be the case that the knowledge (like the babies his mother helped deliver) was already there. Speaking of the ideas the slave boy has been revealed to have, Socrates asks Menon, "Then if he did not get them in this life, is it not clear now that he had them and had learnt at some other time?"[9]

If the boy was not taught geometry, he must be remembering what he knew at birth.

Socrates questioning a slave boy, from "For the Love of Wisdom"/Courtesy of Howard Community College.

The conclusion seems inescapable. If someone who has never even heard the word *geometry* can be led by skillful questioning to solve a geometric problem, it must be the case that knowledge even the boy did not realize he had was already there. And, if it was not learned in his earthly life (which Menon asserts it was not), then it must have been present all along. In fact, Plato's epistemology leads him to assert the immortality of the soul. In this somewhat later dialogue, we cannot be certain that Socrates is the source of this assertion.

For Plato, however, since we know things we could not possibly have learned in this earthly existence, it seems necessary to conclude that we brought this knowledge with us when we entered earthly life. The question of how we know what we appear to know leads directly to the issues of metaphysics or the nature of reality. What, for example, must we conclude about what it means to be a human being, if we have proved that human existence begins before birth and logically can continue after death? In the area of ontology, we cannot speak about what is real without, at the same time, dealing with epistemology—how we think we know the answer to this or any question.

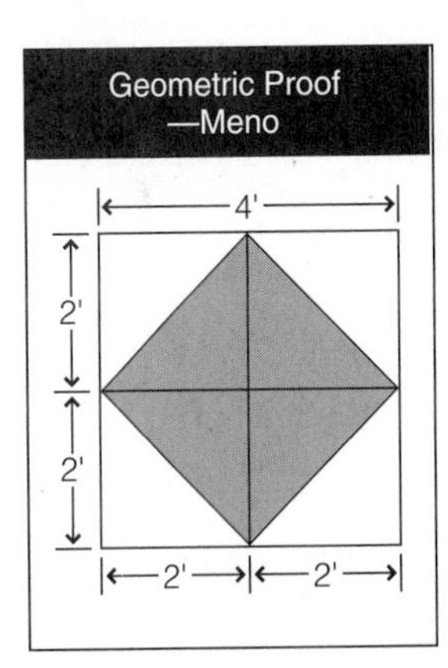

FIGURE 1.1 GEOMETRIC PROOF: MENO *The diagram of the proof that Socrates elicited from the slave boy illustrates that much of what we call knowledge is actually remembering. The area enclosed by the diamond equals 8 square feet.*

Questioning both revealed to Socrates essential truths and uncovered claims to knowledge that were unjustified. Under his relentless barrage of questions, most people were revealed to be quite ignorant about things they claimed to know and understand. Try explaining to someone the meaning of a concept like "truth" or "justice," and you will quickly learn how difficult a task it is to defend what you think you know, especially if the other person persists in probing everything you say.

As you might imagine, in his pursuit of truth, Socrates managed to embarrass most of the prominent citizens of Athens as he questioned them and they revealed their ignorance. Young men of the town started following him around to enjoy the sport of intellectual humiliation, and some of them began their own questioning of adults. It was not long before accusations were leveled against Socrates: He was corrupting the youth of the city and dishonoring the gods of the state.

At the age of seventy, Socrates was brought to trial before a group of 501 citizens (a subset of the larger group of 6000 citizens chosen by lot to

HOW PHILOSOPHY WORKS
The Dialectic

As developed and used by Socrates, the dialectic was a method of arriving at truth or of revealing falsity by persistent questioning. Socrates believed that by clarifying the use of terms and following each thought to its logical conclusion it would be possible to arrive at certainty. In many cases, Socrates' relentless interrogation quickly revealed the weakness or muddiness of an argument and, in the process, made the person answering look foolish. This earned him enemies in high places and no doubt contributed to the accusations made against him. As we have seen in this chapter, the dialectic could also be used as a tool for deriving knowledge already present. Using only skillfully constructed questions, Socrates assisted the slave boy in the *Meno* in recovering what he already knew about geometry. Much of what appears logical, Socrates thought, would, if dissected through questioning, be revealed as illogical. And, it is also true that we know more than we think we do. The method of dialectic draws out what is true and unmasks what is false. Conducted in the public eye, it is an essential tool for separating what can be relied upon from what cannot.

apology *a philosophical defense of an action, position, or viewpoint*

hear cases on a rotating basis). The charges against him were irreligion and corrupting the youth. In response to them, he gave a defense of his actions that has come down to us through Plato's dialogue *The Apology*. **Apology** in this context means a "philosophical defense." Socrates was not apologizing for his actions, since he regarded them as both moral and necessary.

In his defense, Socrates pointed out that, unlike the Sophists, he did not take money for his teaching. Indeed, his entire life was devoted to one thing—the search for wisdom. It is because he was successful in pursuing wisdom that he stands before the jury accused of crimes. Admitting that it sounded egotistical to claim to be wise, Socrates told the court a story about his friend Chaerephon and the oracle at Delphi.

You may know that the Delphic oracle was a priestess who, by entering a trancelike state, was believed to speak for the god Apollo. Many approached the oracle and asked her questions; often they received interesting and unexpected answers. Oedipus, for instance, was stunned to hear he would kill his father and marry his mother. Although he did everything he could to avoid this fate, circumstances led him unknowingly to do exactly these two things. When a general asked the oracle what would happen if he attacked an enemy army, he was told, "A great nation will be destroyed." He set off confidently, but the great nation he destroyed was his own.

The oracle's prophecies often had this enigmatic character. They were phrased in ways that turned out to be open to more than one interpretation. When Chaerephon went to see the oracle, he asked if anyone was wiser than Socrates, and the priestess answered that no one was wiser. Having learned not to take these pronouncements at face value, Socrates told the court, he had set out to prove the oracle wrong by finding someone wiser than himself.

When he approached those who had the reputation for being wise, Socrates explained, he had a strange experience:

> When I examined . . . one of our statesmen . . . I thought this man seemed to be wise both to many others and especially to himself, but that he was not; and then I tried to show him that he thought he was wise, but was not. Because of that he disliked me and so did many others who were there, but I went away thinking to myself that I was wiser than this man; the fact is that neither of us knows anything beautiful and good, but he thinks he does know when he doesn't, and I don't know and don't think I do; so I am wiser than he is by only this trifle, that what I do not know I don't think I do.[10]

The oracle's answers were usually true and often paradoxical.

Oedipus consulting the Delphic oracle/Photo by Quentin Kardos.

The difficulty was that poets thought their ability to compose verse made them wise in other matters as well. Similarly, craftsmen assumed their ability to manage their art qualified them to speak about greater things with wisdom. A genuine ability in a specific area made these Athenians arrogant about their claims to general knowledge and even wisdom. We see the same phenomenon today when athletes endorse products that have nothing to do with athletic accomplishment or when actors promote medical products, saying "I'm not a doctor, but I play one on TV."

By revealing that no one is as wise as he claims to be, Socrates acquired many enemies. Bystanders, he said, always assumed that Socrates himself was wise. When the rich and idle among the young imitated his example, they were able to find many people who thought they knew a lot but really knew little or nothing. These victims of Socratic questioning took their anger out on Socrates, he told the court, accusing him of harming Athenian society and corrupting the young.[11]

Although Socrates continued to insist he should be rewarded rather than punished for being a kind of god-appointed gadfly to Athenian society, he accepted the sentence they imposed on him, death by drinking a cup of hemlock (poison), with easy grace. In fact, he could easily have avoided it by proposing an alternate sentence. No one wished to see him dead, but many wished to shut him up. If he had agreed to stop questioning and live the remainder of his life in exile and silence, the court would almost certainly have accepted these conditions.

Unfortunately for Socrates, this was the one condition he could not meet. Speculating about his own reaction if the court should offer him this kind of bargain, Socrates vowed:

> If you should let me go free on these terms which I have mentioned, I should answer you, "Many thanks indeed for your kindness, gentlemen, but I will . . . never cease being a philosopher, and exhorting you, and showing what is in me to any of you I may meet, by speaking to him in my usual way . . ."[12]

In his search for what is true and what is real, Socrates could not agree to stop questioning. In his view, "Life without inquiry is not worth living for a man."[13] This saying is often translated as "The unexamined life is not worth living."

Relentless pursuit of what really matters in life is at the heart of philosophical speculation. Socrates was willing to drink the cup of hemlock rather than agree to stop doing philosophy. For him, a life lived on "automatic pilot"—a life in which your opinions and ideas are those of your parents, teachers, and friends rather than your own—is no life at all. It is a kind of existence, to be sure, but not a life. Living means searching for what you yourself believe and struggling with fundamental questions.

THE MAKING OF A PHILOSOPHER

Plato

(428–347 B.C.E.)

Plato spent ten years learning from Socrates and used Socrates as the main character in the dialogues he wrote to convey key ideas in philosophy. About eleven years after the death of Socrates, when Plato was forty years old, he founded his Academy. It was the first real university in the Western world, a place where people came together for higher education and research in mathematics, astronomy, and philosophy. It lasted for 915 years. He was invited on three different occasions to Siracusa in Sicily to put his theories on the training of a philosopher-king into practice, but on all three occasions, political changes canceled the experiment. Plato had studied mathematics with Pythagoras and was struck by the certainty of geometric proofs. Plato decided that since no one can argue that contradictory opinions about triangularity are both true, the Sophists must be wrong and certain knowledge about objects must be possible. Over the entrance to his Academy was written, "No one without geometry may enter." Plato died suddenly and peacefully at the age of eighty while attending a wedding.

Plato

Plato takes up this theme again in his long dialogue *Republic,* which explores what an ideal society would be like. This work contains many of his central ideas. Like Socrates, Plato believed most of us live in ignorance most of the time. The worst of this situation is that we do not even know we are ignorant.

To illustrate this point, Plato asks us to imagine a cave. The inhabitants are chained hand and foot, and their heads are in a fixed position so that they can only see the wall in front of them. On this wall shadows appear, and the prisoners assume these shadows are reality (Figure 1.2). What else could they think, since all of them have been in the cave since birth? This is the only reality they have known. As he explains this allegory, Plato lets us know that the shadows are produced by a fire burning at the cave's entrance, and they actually reflect objects carried above a wall by people walking by it. We know something the cave dwellers do not know. We recognize that they have mistaken shadow for substance. They think they know what is real, but we know they are in fact living in the dark, both literally and figuratively.

As the allegory progresses, Plato asks us to imagine that someone comes into the cave, unshackles one of the prisoners, and leads him or her out of the cave into the sunlight. What do you think this person's reaction would be? Blinded by the brightness of the Sun, the prisoner's first reaction would probably be to run back into the safety of the cave. It would require time and patience before the prisoner's eyes adjusted to the light and saw things as they really are. Once that happened, however, the former prisoner would clearly see that what had passed for knowledge was in reality only shadows.

Going back into the cave to explain "reality" to the other prisoners, this person would surely meet resistance. All of them would continue to believe the shadows were real. Hearing about a new and strange version of reality would most likely convince them that their fellow prisoner had gone crazy. "Wouldn't they say that he'd come back from his upward journey with his eyes ruined, and that it wasn't even worth trying to go up there?" Plato asks, "And wouldn't they—if they could—grab hold of anyone who tried to set them free and take them up there and kill him?"[14]

Ordinary life, Plato is telling us, is the life of the cave. This is the life from which Socrates had escaped and to which he was never willing to return. We are the prisoners, living in a world of untested assumptions, relying on our

FIGURE 1.2 PLATO'S CAVE ALLEGORY *The prisoners in the cave mistake shadows for reality as Plato suggests we do when we try to rely on the senses rather than reason.*

senses to tell us about reality, and assuming that only what we can see, hear, touch, taste, or smell is real. How much we are missing, Plato suggests:

> The region which is accessible to sight should be equated with the prison cell, and the firelight there with the light of the sun. And, if you think of the upward journey and the sight of things up on the surface of the earth as the mind's ascent to the intelligible realm, you won't be wrong.[15]

Plato may also be observing how strong the power of "group think" can be. If all our friends like or dislike something, if everyone in our country makes certain assumptions, if our family patterns have convinced us there is only one way to do something, we will be very comfortable with these preferences, assumptions, and patterns. If what is at issue is eating sauerkraut with the Thanksgiving turkey or assuming that toilet paper should feed over rather than under the roll, these patterns and assumptions may be harmless. The real danger is that we will trust our senses rather than our reason and accept what we see and what "everyone knows"

PHILOSOPHERS SPEAK FOR THEMSELVES

Plato

If you would like an allegory of the human condition, with special attention to the question of education and ignorance, then imagine people living in a cave. They have been there since birth, forced by the chains that bind them to sit in a fixed position and stare straight ahead. At the far end of the cave is an opening to the outside world but, of course, the prisoners are unaware of this. Above and behind the prisoners a fire blazes, and between the fire and the prisoners is a path running beside a low wall. People pass by this wall, carrying human statues and figures of animals and plants crafted from wood or stone and speaking to one another from time to time. The firelight casts shadows of these images on the wall the prisoners face and these shadows, accompanied by the intermittent sounds of voices, are the only reality the prisoners know. For as long as anyone can remember this has constituted the entire truth about the world . . .

This whole allegory depicts the human condition. The cave is the world revealed to us by our senses, dimly lit by firelight and filled with shadows we mistake for reality. The climb out of the cave and into the sunlight represents the ascent of the soul into the intellectual life—the life of the mind and the path of reason. By applying the tools of the intellect, one will come, finally, to the idea of The Good, which is the source of all that is beautiful and right. In truth, it is the only reliable ground for moral conduct as well.

Those who have seen things as they really are, using the full powers of the mind, will understandably be reluctant to return to the mundane world of human exchanges. Such a person might even seem a fool amid the shadows of the law courts and the hypocrisy of everyday life. We would do well to remember that those who seem disoriented are as likely to be moving from light to darkness as from darkness to light. And, we should be very careful whom we laugh at lest we find ourselves in the position of the happy prisoners who cling fiercely to their ignorance and mock what they do not understand.

The Cave Allegory, from *Republic,* Book VII. Translation:

as true and real rather than seek the truth for ourselves. If we mistake shadows for reality, Plato warns, our certainties will be based on incorrect or inadequate information.

Like the prisoners, Plato suggests, we may be mistaking the ordinary world of sense experience and snap judgments for reality and truth. Accepting things at face value often leads to error. Heroin and crack cocaine can make you feel wonderful for a minute and miserable for days; sexual pleasure carries the threat of AIDS; money and success do not necessarily lead to happiness. In other words, what you see may not be what you get.

Many people live in prisons of their own making, Plato seems to say. If you stay in the cave, you will have lots of company. There will be plenty of people to agree with you that the shadows you see are real. Leaving the cave will be difficult. Although someone may lead you, you will have to travel alone. Outside the cave, the Sun will hurt your eyes, and at first you may be disoriented. With patience and perseverance, however, your reward will be seeing things as they really are. When you return to the cave, though, be prepared for a hostile reaction.

Before you laugh at or pity a person who seems to be speaking nonsense, Plato cautions, find out whether that person has been outside the cave and seen what you have not. Going from bright sunlight back into the darkness of the cave causes disorientation; so does going from the cave into the sunlight. Cave dwellers are never confused. They understand the cave world very well, and it gives them security. Unfortunately, it is only a shadow of the real world. Plato suggests that if someone appears disoriented we would do well to find out the source of the confusion.

Plato's cave allegory is a literary picture of the classic Western version of what it is like to *do* philosophy. Plato is very clear that philosophy cannot be a subject you study from your armchair; it must be an activity you live. Like Socrates, you must question everything—even, or maybe especially, those things that seem so obvious, those things everyone agrees about. A life without philosophy is a life of shadows, a life lived inside the cave. You may feel content, but the price is much too high. What you give up is the world of reality that lies outside in the sunlight. Your knowledge of shadows may be excellent, but you will be ignorant of the objects that create those shadows.

There is only one way to know reality, Plato believes. You must rely on your reason rather than on your senses, your untested opinions, or your feelings. Reason will not deceive you. With it, you will be able to distinguish what is real from what is not. In the *Republic,* Plato has Socrates describe a situation in which a person might desire something on the level of the senses but refuse it, using the truer knowledge provided by reason. The question is, If there are conflicting impulses, one urging you to do something and another urging you not to, what does this tell us about human nature? Imagine that you have been playing volleyball on a hot summer day. At the break you find yourself very thirsty, and right beside the volleyball court is a small stream. You are tempted to cup your hands and drink some cool water from it. In fact, nothing sounds better at that moment. Then someone points out that the stream is badly polluted and drinking from it would surely make you sick.

Socrates explains the conflict this way:

> . . . Don't we have to say that their mind contains a part which is telling them to drink, and a part which is telling them not to drink . . . one of which we can describe as rational, and the other as irrational and desirous. The first is responsible for the mind's capacity to think rationally, and the second . . . for its capacity to feel lust, hunger, and thirst, and in general to be stirred by desire.[16]

We must conclude, Plato thinks, that the desiring part of our nature will pull us toward the world of the senses, urging us to satisfy our desires at any cost. Fortunately, he believes, we have another aspect, the reasoning part of our nature, that can and does override the desiring part. In our example, reason convinces us that the momentary pleasure of the cool water would not be worth severe intestinal distress later.

Let's take our example one step further by imagining that, having decided against drinking from the polluted stream, you go to the cooler and find all the bottles and cans empty. There is nothing safe to drink. Now, what you probably feel is anger or, in Plato's terms, spirit. This third part of your nature is separate from your desires or appetites and separate from your reason, although it tends to ally itself more with reason than desire. The spirited element is also what gives us the courage of our convictions.

tripartite soul *Plato's theory of a three-part human nature ideally ruled by reason*

What is unique about human beings, Plato asserts, is that we have these three aspects to our natures; he called it the **tripartite soul.** At times we seem lost in desire, slaves to our appetites for food, drink, sexual pleasure. Other circumstances can bring out the spirited aspect of our nature, and we may find ourselves becoming angry and self-assertive. Both these lower aspects—the desiring and spirited parts of us—must remain obedient to reason if we are to be fully human.

Being governed by reason is what it means to be a person, Plato believes, and the activity we call philosophy is the royal road of reason. It can lead us out of the cave and show us what is real. It can also guide us in living our lives. In this way, Plato's ontology blends with his view of a good life. Those who are lovers of wisdom, like Socrates, will follow a life of reason and keep both the desiring and spirited elements under proper control. As Socrates puts it, "Since the rational part is wise and looks out for the whole of the mind, isn't it right for it to rule, and for the passionate part to be subordinate and its ally?"[17]

As you can see, Plato's ontology (theory of being) and epistemology (theory of knowledge) join with his axiology (theory of values, especially morality). For Socrates and Plato, there is a direct link between what a person knows and what a person does. For this reason the questions raised by epistemology are linked with those raised by axiology.

Quite simply, Plato was convinced that the person who truly knows what is good or right will act accordingly. All people seek "the Good," or we might say perfect Goodness, by their very nature. No one who grasps the idea of the Good would voluntarily reject it. If people do wrong, then, it is because they have an incomplete or misguided view of what is good. Believing as he does in the power of reason, Plato concludes that intellect controls will. What we know will determine what we do. It follows that those who do wrong should be educated rather than punished. If they are brought to a deep understanding of what is right and good, they will act in accordance with it. People must be led from the cave of ignorance into the sunlight of true knowledge. When they are, the rational aspect will properly preside over the desiring and spirited elements.

In Plato we see for the first time in the Western tradition a philosopher concerned with uniting and integrating all three of the major branches of philosophy—metaphysics, epistemology, and axiology. What is real, what we know, and how we should live are not separate questions for Plato. Speculation in one area necessarily spills over into the other two. Conclusions must be consistent since the three areas are so closely related. As an enormously influential Western philosopher, Plato will appear in later chapters as we consider aesthetic experience, political philosophy, and social philosophy.

Do you see the Greek ideal of harmonia *in this temple?*
Greek temple at Segesta, Sicily/Photo by Joseph Mitchell.

Perictyone

Not all the philosophers in ancient Greece were men. Perictyone, who may have been the mother of Plato, was, like him, trained in the Pythagorean tradition. Pythagoras advocated the principle of ***harmonia,*** or harmony among diverse elements, which both Plato and Perictyone follow. Plato's three-part human nature—combining reason, spirit, and desire—reflects this tradition. In a similar way, Perictyone points out the value of philosophy for women within the home and in the wider world:

harmonia *[har moh NEE uh] the Pythagorean principle of desired harmony among elements*

> A woman should be a harmony of prudence and temperance. Her soul should be zealous to acquire virtue; so that she may be just, brave, prudent, frugal, and hating vainglory. Furnished with these virtues, she will, when she becomes a wife, act worthily towards herself, her husband, her children, and her family. Frequently, also, such a woman will act beautifully towards cities, if she happens to rule over cities and nations, as we see is sometimes the case in a kingdom. If she subdues desire and anger, there will be produced a divine symphony.[18]

As in Plato's cave allegory, Perictyone urges women to hate "vainglory" and, instead, to pursue "prudence and temperance." Like Plato, she sees the consciousness or awareness of goodness as the key to virtue. A woman who is able to subdue both desire and anger will be fit to rule her household and perhaps even a city.

My virginity,
oh my virginity,
Where will you go when
I lose you?
SAPPHO

Most Greek women, living at this time, led very restricted lives, confined by social custom to an existence centering on the home. Although a life of wisdom, governed by reason, might equip a woman to rule, there was very little likelihood that she would get such an opportunity. What all high-born or wealthy women did do, however, was rule over the home. This included authority over children and over household servants, some of whom were likely to be slaves.

Pythagorean thought compares both household management and city government to the care and tuning of a musical instrument. One must organize the elements and mingle them skillfully "according to virtue and the laws."[19] The little we know about Perictyone places her firmly within this Pythagorean tradition. The principle of *harmonia* and the image of the tuned string inspired both men and women as a model for personal and political balance.

Aristotle

Too loose and the string loses its tone; too tight and it snaps. What is needed is the right amount of tension to produce the proper note and to create harmony in the orchestra. This is the theme of Aristotle's master work on **ethics,** the philosophical discipline concerned with vice and virtue, the rightness or wrongness of actions. Dedicated to his son Nicomachus, the book has come to be known as the *Nicomachean Ethics.* In it, Aristotle describes the life of moderation that reason dictates for humans.

ethics *the branch of philosophy concerned with judgments about moral behavior and the meaning of ethical statements and terms*

He begins in Book 1 by examining what we mean by happiness. All human activities, he says, aim at some good. Happiness, however, is that good desired for its own sake (everything else being a means to this end), and it therefore assumes the status of chief good. Humans, Aristotle believes, are uniquely able to experience happiness. Since happiness is "one of our most divine possessions," it follows that "we do not speak of an ox or a horse or any other animal as happy, because none of them can take part in this sort of activity."[20]

Happiness or human flourishing (what the Greeks called *eudaimonia*) is tied to **virtue,** which for Aristotle means living in accordance with our highest human ability—the ability to reason. "Since happiness is an activity of the soul in accordance with perfect virtue," Aristotle reasons, "we must examine the nature of virtue; for perhaps in this way we shall be better able to form a view about happiness too." Moral virtue, in his view, is acquired by practice. As Aristotle puts it, "Moral goodness . . . is the result of habit . . . We become just by performing just acts, temperate by performing temperate ones, brave by performing brave ones."[21] We are not born good or bad; rather, we learn to be one or the other by the activities in which we engage.

virtue *for Aristotle, a life lived in accordance with the highest human capacity, reason*

The *Nicomachean Ethics,* like Pythagorean treatises on harmony, is a practical guide to moral decision making that stresses common sense and moderation. The good life, for Aristotle, involves intelligent decisions made in response to specific problems. Yet, he recognizes that people are not entirely rational—there is also a passionate nature that can neither be fully

FIGURE 1.3 ARISTOTLE'S GOLDEN MEAN *Aristotle conceived of virtue as a mean between two extremes.*

ignored nor totally eliminated. To surrender completely to desire is to descend to the level of a beast, but denying the passions is also a foolish and unreasonable rejection of human nature.

Our goal should be to avoid extremes of behavior and rationally choose the way of moderation. This middle way between extremes, sometimes called the **golden mean,** is the cornerstone of Aristotle's ethical thought (Figure 1.3). In Plato's system, the norms for ethical conduct are based on the idea of the Good, which in his system represents perfect goodness or goodness itself. Aristotle suggests that one does not necessarily have to know universal Good to choose the good in a practical situation. It may be enough to know that both too little and too much management will ruin the harmony. Greek scholar H. D. F. Kitto calls the idea of a mean a characteristically Greek concept. The model or the ideal is the tuned string—not "the absence of tension and lack of passion, but the correct amount of tension which gives out the true and clear note."[22]

When he speaks about ethics, Aristotle wants his listeners to understand that his focus is on practical wisdom and not on a purely intellectual wisdom that contemplates unchanging reality. In the realm of intellectual wisdom (such as that proposed by Plato), it may be possible to speak in absolutes, but day-to-day moral decision making must always take into account the variable aspects of a particular situation. Moral decisions, for Aristotle, must always be based on the circumstances surrounding the issue. It is not appropriate to speak about moral truth in an isolated and pure sense; rather, we must speak about it in harmony with right desire.

As in the Pythagorean writings, the goal is harmony. What Aristotle advocates is the right action, undertaken in the right way, toward the right person, to the right extent, at the right time, and with the right motive. Without knowing the details surrounding a particular situation, it is impossible to state in advance what someone ought to do. The only fixed and unchanging principle is, therefore, the *mean.* The goal must always be moderation, the appropriate response, the action that falls between two extremes.

Here is one of Aristotle's illustrations: The person who "exceeds in confidence is called Rash, and the one who shows an excess of fear and a deficiency of confidence is called Cowardly."[23] Both responses represent extremes. The life of virtue, which leads to happiness, contains neither cowardice nor rashness. Instead, the goal of a virtuous life is the mean between these two extremes: bravery.

THE MAKING OF A PHILOSOPHER

Aristotle
(384–322 B.C.E.)

Born in Thrace in northern Greece, Aristotle was the son of the official court physician to King Phillip of Macedon; however, Aristotle was orphaned early. At the age of eighteen he entered Plato's Academy and remained there twenty years, until Plato's death. King Phillip invited Aristotle to return to Macedon in 342 B.C.E. as tutor to his son Alexander. When Phillip died, Aristotle fled, fearing he might be put to death as Socrates was. Alexander later conquered the world and is known to us as Alexander the Great. In 335 B.C.E. Aristotle founded his own school, the Lyceum. It had a covered walkway, and students and teachers were fond of strolling along its shaded paths talking about philosophy. Graduates of Aristotle's Lyceum staffed the great library in Alexandria, Egypt. Aristotle died at the age of sixty-two of a chronic stomach ailment. According to those who knew him, he was thin-legged and bald, with small eyes set close together, and he lisped.

golden mean *the moderate action between undesirable extremes; used by Aristotle to describe an ethical ideal*

To consider another example, both boastfulness and false modesty are to be avoided. A person who is always bragging about what he or she has done is as far from virtue as is the person who cannot accept a compliment and insists on taking no credit for anything. The goal is truthfulness that accurately represents your own contribution. Extremes, in Aristotle's ethical system, are generally to be avoided:

> Thus there are three dispositions, two of them vicious (one by means of excess, the other of deficiency), and one good, the mean. They are all in some way opposed to one another: the extremes are contrary both to the mean and to each other, and the mean to the extremes . . . A brave man appears rash compared with a coward, and cowardly compared with a rash man . . .[24]

In any situation then, the virtuous action will usually be the one that falls between two possible extremes. Some ethical systems condemn all anger as wrong. Aristotle, however, would approve the right amount of anger, directed at the right person, in the right way, with the right motive. If the person in front of you in the grocery line has eleven items instead of ten, beating that person over the head with your frozen turkey would be excessive. At the other extreme, though, if you accept abuse without reaction, you would be deficient in anger.

Aristotle was very aware that the mean is difficult to attain. The life of virtue is not for everyone, and in some situations the most moral action possible may simply involve choosing the lesser of two evils. Clearly, there are also times when moderation does not apply. Aristotle speaks of adultery as one area in which it would be inappropriate to be moderate. Still, the mean remains the moral ideal, and the life of virtue continues to be the road to happiness.

Like Plato, Aristotle speculated about every area of philosophy. Although this chapter has explored only his views on axiology, you should be aware that Aristotle was interested in everything. He laid the foundations for Western formal logic, which we will begin examining in the "How Philosophy Works" boxes in Chapter 2. His theories about art and literature appear in Chapter 7. The early experiments he conducted in embryology anticipated the concerns of biology, and his desire to catalog and categorize classes of animals and plants established the disciplines of botany and zoology. In the next chapter we will investigate his theories of reality and knowledge and compare them with Plato's.

Metaphysics, Epistemology, and Axiology in Asian Thought

Both Asian and African philosophies differ from Greek philosophy in the assumptions they make about the three main branches of philosophy—metaphysics, epistemology, and axiology. Succeeding chapters will examine some of these differences in greater detail. We consider Asian variations in a preliminary way here, beginning with the ideas of the Buddha on some of the same questions that interested the early Greeks and concluding with a brief look at the Confucian tradition in China.

Buddhism

Let's begin by noting a similarity between Siddhārtha Gautama—known after his enlightenment as the Buddha, the one who woke up to the truth—and Aristotle. We have been considering Aristotle's practical bent, his insistence that virtue be considered not in the abstract but in the context of actual moral situations that are always particular and not subject to broad generalizations. The Buddha shared this practical outlook and went considerably further than Aristotle in his preference for it. Metaphysics, and in fact all abstract philosophical speculation, was of no interest to him.

His message focused entirely on the human situation and could be said to parallel Aristotle's search for happiness. The Buddha began by noting that life is characterized by suffering. Sooner or later, old age, sickness, and death will visit all of us. Youth, wealth, and health may temporarily blind us to these realities, but there is no escaping them. In fact, it is fear of these realities that makes us unhappy.

The root cause of our unhappiness (to use Aristotle's term) or our suffering (to use the Buddha's term) is our attachment to the things of this world—including objects and people—and our mistaken belief that they can bring us happiness. We suffer because we try to stop the change that *is* inevitable and hold onto things as they are at a particular moment in time. We want to maintain our youth and our health, or we want to keep our children young. Worse, we stake our happiness on having particular things or people in our lives.

"If only I had a BMW or a million-dollar house or a six-figure-a-year job, I would be happy," we may be tempted to think. Even more enticingly, we may convince ourselves that a certain person will bring us happiness. If only that person would love us, all our problems would be over. The difficulty is that no thing and no other person can ever bring us happiness. Either we are happy within ourselves or we are unhappy. No person and no thing, the Buddha suggests, can magically transform us from unhappy to happy. We may fool ourselves for awhile, but if the subject or object on which we have staked our happiness disappears, we are right back where we started—suffering and unhappy.

The Buddha would agree with Aristotle that happiness is to be found in living a life of virtue, but he had his own explanation of what the life of virtue meant. For the Buddha, the only way to end our suffering is to give up our attachment to people and things—to stop looking outside ourselves for happiness and to begin cultivating unattachment by following what he called the *Noble Eightfold Path*: Right Belief, Right Aspiration, Right Speech, Right Conduct, Right Means of Livelihood, Right Endeavor, Right Mindfulness, and Right

THE MAKING OF A PHILOSOPHER

Siddhārtha Gautama, the Buddha

(c. 563–483 B.C.E.)

Siddhārtha, sometimes known as Sakyamuni (sage of the Sakya tribe), was born into the Gautama family, a warrior caste in India. At the age of nineteen, he married his beautiful cousin Yasodhara and later fathered a son Rahula. Renouncing his fortune and family, he traveled through the Ganges River Valley as a begging monk. The disciples who began following him formed an order, which perpetuated the traditions after his death. The term *Buddha* means the Enlightened or Awakened One who awakens a sense of Truth in others. Siddhārtha had been protected by loving parents from the harsh realities of life. When he left the palace for the first time in his early twenties, he was shocked and saddened to find sickness, suffering, and death and set off to find the meaning of these things. He tried the life of an ascetic, punishing his body and eating only enough to stay alive, but found this did not bring him peace of mind. One night, he sat down beneath a tree vowing not to leave until he became enlightened. Spending the night in meditation, he relived past lives and eventually "saw" the Four Noble Truths that form the heart of Buddhism.

Let yourself be open and life will be easier.
A spoon of salt in a glass of water makes the water undrinkable.
A spoon of salt in a lake is almost unnoticed.
THE BUDDHA

Meditation; these and these alone will lead to an end to suffering. In a way, though, the Noble Eightfold Path is also a life of moderation not unlike Aristotle's golden mean.

In Buddhism, enlightenment can only be achieved by seeing the way things truly are and accepting our own full responsibility for either living a life in tune with this truth and being at peace or being in a state of denial and setting ourselves up for suffering. Although he might question the Buddha's unwillingness to speculate about metaphysics, Aristotle would certainly hold that happiness can only be achieved through an acceptance of things as they actually are.

The truth is that everything is One, and this of course is not a numerical one.
PHILIP KAPLEAU

Aristotle's philosophy, however, rests on the separatism that underlies all Western metaphysics: I am "me" and you are "you"; if you do something to anger me, I will respond with appropriate anger. Buddhism rejects this separatism and instead affirms that the world and all it contains are interdependent. All of what we might label "reality" is interrelated, without any separation or concept of individual entities. What appears to us as the multiplicity or the "manyness" of things and people is an illusion. Like Plato in the cave allegory, the Buddha urges us not to mistake appearance for reality.

If we could see things as they really are, we would know that there is no separate "me" and no separate "you." We only delude ourselves when we think that we, ourselves, and all parts of the universe are composed of separate and distinct bits (like atoms or molecules) that combine and recombine to produce the variety we see. Buddhism totally rejects this Western vision of reality. Rather, "reality" is a web of interconnectedness. Everything is mutually dependent on everything else and undergoing continuous change. What we think of as "ego" is an appearance, a temporary unity of body, emotions, perceptions, predispositions, and reasoning that will dissolve when we die and reform in a new combination as we are reborn. Reactions like anger only reinforce the illusion of separateness and keep us attached to things and people. It is here that the Buddha and Aristotle must part company.

The Enlightened One was "awake" even with his eyes closed in meditation.
Seated Buddha, Amitabha "Infinite Light," Hopei Province, ca. 610–630/The Walters Art Museum, Baltimore.

The Greek understanding of reality is based on rationality. The world, as Thales first suggested, is an orderly place and we, as reasoning creatures, have the right mental equipment to be able to figure it out. Socrates, Plato, and Aristotle share this assumption, identifying reason, or rationality, as the highest human ability. Furthermore, all their arguments take for granted that we humans have a self that stands apart from the world and from other selves. This self enables us to be subjects studying a world of objects and using our reason to make sense of them.

Buddhism rejects these notions. If the idea of an individual ego-self is an illusion, we must accept our basic interdependence and interrelatedness with what appear to be separate others. The Western idea that I as a knower stand apart from the object or person I wish to know makes no sense in the context of a Buddhist epistemology. Knowing must happen intuitively rather than rationally—imagine one drop of the ocean "knowing" another drop. And, knowing must be a process that works from the inside rather than from the outside. We might think of the way "I" know my emotions rather than the way "I" know geometry.

Similarly, Buddhist ethics begins with this concept of interrelatedness. Just as you cannot do harm to one part of yourself without the effects being felt throughout the system, so any injury you do to an apparent other is really an injury to yourself. A ripple at any point is felt throughout the entire pond, and the life of virtue, for a Buddhist, must take this understanding into account. In Chapter 10 we will explore the implications of the law of ***karma,*** which affirms this Asian understanding. In truth, I am free, but as long as I am ignorant of the way things are, I am bound. This seems paradoxical. If there is no separate "me," how can "I" continue to feel the effects of my actions through the law of *karma*?

The key is in the Buddhist epistemology. Once my knowing lines up with the way things are and I see that everything is interconnected, the illusion of a separate "I" disappears and, with it, all that bound that apparent "I" to ***samsara,*** the round of birth-death-rebirth. To be free of illusion is also to be free of *karma*. In Buddhism, the way things are, our understanding of the way things are, and how we act based on knowing how things are share an intimate connection. It is helpful to remember here that Siddhārtha Gautama was raised as a Hindu. There are many shared concepts as well as significant differences between the Hinduism in which the Buddha reached maturity and the Buddhism his new understandings created. Chapters 3 and 4 will explore some aspects of the Hindu view of human nature and ultimate reality.

karma *[KHAR muh] in Hinduism and Buddhism, the principle that all actions operate according to causal laws and what I do to another I do to myself; sometimes this law is referred to as the law of sowing and reaping*

samsara *[sahm SAHR uh] the continuous cycle of births, deaths, and rebirths resulting from* karma

Although Buddhism rejects Western rationality, it does affirm the power of the mind. With our thoughts, the Buddha points out, we create the reality in which we live. Whether we speak and act purely or impurely will determine the kind of life we experience:

> We are what we think.
> All that we are arises with our thoughts.
> With our thoughts we make the world.
> Speak or act with an impure mind
> And trouble will follow you
> As the wheel follows the ox that draws the cart . . .
> Speak or act with a pure mind
> And happiness will follow you
> As your shadow, unshakable.[25]

Millions of people—from Hong Kong to Tibet, from Burma to Tokyo, as well as throughout North America—call themselves Buddhists. There are several major doctrinal and practical divisions within Buddhism, but the influence of Siddhārtha Gautama has been considerable. Blending with existing ideas and practices as it moved into new geographical areas, Buddhism enriched what it found and was itself enriched. As the many statues of a meditating, slightly smiling Buddha suggest, the enlightened one, the one who woke up and saw things as they are, continues to inspire and intrigue people around the world today.

THE MAKING OF A PHILOSOPHER

Pan Chao
(ca. 48–117 C.E.)

Called the foremost woman scholar of China, Pan Chao lived and worked at the court of the Eastern Han Emperor Ho. Members of the Pan family had been court scholars since 32 B.C.E., and Pan Chao followed in the tradition of her father Pan Piao and one of her twin brothers, Ku. When Pan Ku died before completing the Hou Han Shou (a history of the Han family), Pan Chao was asked to complete it. Although she did not have the formal title of Historian to the Imperial Court, in effect this was the post she occupied. Working in the imperial library, she supervised the work of other scholars and furthered the work begun by her father and brother. And, at the emperor's request, she instructed the young empress and her ladies-in-waiting in the Confucian classics, history, astronomy, and mathematics. At the death of the emperor, his twenty-five-year-old widow Teng became regent first for an infant son, who died a year later, and then for the infant son's thirteen-year-old cousin. Teng relied on her teacher, "Mother Pan," for advice concerning affairs of state and at Pan Chao's death declared a period of mourning. Pan Chao is remembered for her narrative poetry and essays, as well as for her work as a scholar and teacher.

Pan Chao and the Confucian Tradition

When Buddhism made its way from India to China, it blended with existing systems of thought and behavior, especially Confucianism and Taoism. By the first century C.E., Confucianism had become well established in the Han Dynasty court where Pan Chao was acknowledged as the foremost woman scholar. Chosen to study, write, and teach in the library as well as instruct the empress in astronomy and mathematics, Pan Chao was also a significant contributor, along with her father and brother, to the *Han Shu,* an ambitious collection of literary and historical sources.[26]

From her surviving writings, it seems clear that Pan Chao revered the Confucian classics and modeled her life after their teachings. As we learned in Historical Interlude A, the Confucian ethical ideal was living nobly and compassionately in the world. In terms of cosmology, the emperor was seen as standing between heaven and Earth, receiving and interpreting the Mandate of Heaven. In terms of relationships, subjects and ministers would obey the emperor; children would honor parents; wives would submit to husbands; older siblings would lead younger ones; and friends would encourage one another in virtue.

When Pan Chao applied these instructions to her own life, however, she was forced to question the system of education then in effect that offered teaching only to boys. If only half the population has access to the classics, she observed, proper relationships might not be established:

> Now examine the gentlemen of the present age. They know only that wives must be controlled, and that the husband's rules of conduct manifesting his authority must be established. They therefore teach their boys to read books and (study) histories . . . Yet only to teach men and not to teach women,—is that not ignoring the essential relation between them? According to the "Rites," it is the rule to begin to teach children to read at the age of eight years, and by the age of fifteen years they ought then be ready for cultural training. Only why should it not be (that girls' education as well as boys' be) according to this principle?[27]

For Pan Chao, knowledge and wisdom hold the key for understanding both reality and virtue. In other words, epistemology leads to metaphysics and axiology. If a woman were to join what is sometimes called "the aristocracy of the wise," she would need a proper education. The wisdom of the past would lead her to understand both cosmology (humans as the link between heaven and Earth) and the ontology embodied in the five relationships. Most important, education would enable her to become a large-minded or superior person—in other words, a person of virtue.[28]

Pan Chao is the first of many women you will meet to claim for her own sex the benefits that flow from learning. Like Perictyone, she recognizes that a virtuous woman benefits the home in exactly the same way that a virtuous man enriches political and social life outside the home. Her argument for equal access to education comes from "Lessons for Women," a book of instructions she requested unmarried girls to copy. In Pan Chao's worldview, subjects would still obey emperors, and wives would continue to submit to husbands—she is clearly not advocating rebellion. Instead, she argues that education is indispensable for the life of virtue. This, incidentally, was also Plato's claim—that one who knew the good would do the good.

In later chapters, we will examine in detail the other major thought system of China—Taoism. Looking to nature rather than to the social order for the wisdom required for living a fully human life, Taoism sees no need for the kind of learning found in books. Books give us knowledge, but nature teaches us wisdom. As chapter 48 of the Taoist classic, the *Tao Te Ching,* points out:

> When we pursue knowledge,
> acquiring more is the goal.
> When we pursue wisdom,
> simplicity is the path . . . [29]

If one learns from others but does not think, one will be bewildered.
If, on the other hand, one thinks but does not learn from others, one will be in peril.
CONFUCIUS

Metaphysics, Epistemology, and Axiology in African Thought

In addition to Asian thought, each chapter of this book considers how the chief concerns of philosophy have been addressed in traditional African thought. Our focus will be on two cultural traditions: the East African, as articulated by the philosophy department of Makerere University in Uganda, and the West African, chiefly as expressed by the Akan and Ewe tribes, based principally in Ghana.

They must often change, who would be constant in happiness or wisdom.
CONFUCIUS

Western-educated, contemporary African philosophers are in the unique position of being able to reflect on traditional African cultures, using the categories of Western philosophy. They can help us examine how the indigenous peoples of Africa—before being influenced by the West—saw the cosmos, the human person, ways of knowing, and morality. Since these thinkers live in both worlds, they will be our cultural translators.

Sociological and intellectual differences exist between East and West Africa, as do differences within each of these traditions, but they all share some basic similarities. We will be exploring these common assumptions as we compare systems of African thought with those of Europe and Asia. In some significant ways, African philosophical thought represents a middle ground between Western and Asian traditions: It is neither as preoccupied with rationality and individualism as the West nor as convinced of essential interconnectedness as Buddhism.

In contrast with the West, the traditional African view is that all areas of life are part of an integrated whole, which includes nature. The Greek notion of standing apart from nature and studying it objectively would be incomprehensible to an African who does not feel separate from nature and whose goal is to "know" nature the way a child learns to know its mother. Mere intellectual knowing (the goal of the early Greeks) would be very limiting and would leave out the physical and emotional

Do you agree that the mother-child relationship is the most basic one in society?
Seated mother and child from Zaire/Courtesy of the African Art Museum of Maryland/Photo by Quentin Kardos.

knowing that, together with intellectual knowing, constitute a complete relationship.[30]

From the cycles of renewal at the heart of nature comes the idea that humans are also self-renewing. Like Buddhism, traditional African thought assumes the continuity of generations, believing "that ancestors do not die out but are reborn in the young."[31] The resemblance of children to dead relatives reinforces the idea of an ongoing cycle of birth-death-rebirth. If a baby is, at least in some sense, an honored elder reborn, that child has a sacred nature. Bearing children becomes a special blessing, miscarriage a curse, and abortion unthinkable.[32] As we have seen, metaphysics (what is real?) leads to axiology (which values are correct?).

Living apart from nature, Westerners may forget they have any connection with it. If food comes from the supermarket and water from a faucet, ecological implications may seem very distant. There is a temptation to try to exercise control over both nature and one's own body. African philosophy affirms that people and nature enjoy a reciprocal relationship. Hurricanes, earthquakes, floods, and droughts remind us we are connected with and dependent on nature. One cannot live a full life apart from nature any more than one can live an integrated life that ignores the body (another Western tendency) and focuses exclusively on the mind. It would be foolish to try.

In a traditional African society, a baby is seen as being born into a tribe or a clan and not just into an individual, nuclear family. The child's identity will, from the beginning, have social implications. All members of the tribe, as well as the ancestors, will have a stake in how that child behaves. As Professor Kwasi Wiredu puts it: "The primary responsibility for an action, positive or negative, rests with the doer, but a non-trivial secondary responsibility extends to the individual's family and, in some cases, to the environing community."[33]

This is a social concept of self that falls somewhere between the Western emphasis on individualism and the Asian insistence on interconnectedness. Traditional African epistemology also seems to blend some aspects of Asia and the West. It rejects exclusive reliance on either reason or intuition and insists on including the practical and the down to earth. To understand this version of epistemology, let's briefly review what we already know about Buddhism and Greek philosophy.

In the West we have favored rational and analytic thought, especially logic, as the best or only route to certain knowledge. Aristotle, as you know, developed and refined a system of logic that laid the bedrock for Western epistemology. Western technology rests upon this kind of thinking, and we have applied it to social and psychological challenges as well. At times we have discounted both intuition and the practical knowledge that comes from lived experience, insisting that if something cannot be proved logically it is not really true.

Asian cultures have tended to favor more intuitive ways of knowing over purely rational ones in pursuit of enlightenment. Although Buddhist and Hindu systems of rational argumentation share many interesting points of similarity with Aristotle's logic, the Buddhist truth that life is suffering can be felt or known intuitively. One can grasp it immediately and understand it "in a flash" without having to proceed through logical steps of analysis. Knowing intuitively that to harm another being is really to harm oneself is very different from knowing logically that individual actions have social consequences.

African cultures represent a third approach. They typically embody knowledge and wisdom in art motifs and in proverbs rather than in systems of logic. From the Akan culture of West Africa, we have this illustration: a crocodile with one stomach and two heads locked in combat. Human beings, this picture tells us, have many common interests (symbolized by the shared stomach), but they also have conflicting interests that can lead to struggle (symbolized by the fighting heads). The aim of morality, we might conclude, is to reconcile or harmonize these warring interests through adjustment and adaptation. In other words, axiology derives from lived experience.

Notice here that there is no absolute standard of right and wrong, as we found, for instance, in Plato's notion that the Idea of the Good should define human behavior. What is right is what will unlock the heads and get the food to the common stomach. In other words, individuals must learn to balance their own interests with the social good.[34] How this might work is not carved in stone or written in the sky but is determined by the lived experience of people in society. This particular African understanding has more in common with Aristotle than with Plato.

The proverbs that express African epistemology may be thought of as distilled human experience. Over many years, maybe many generations, people learn through trial and error what works and what does not. Through painful mistakes, a society learns what it can afford to tolerate and what it must condemn if the community is to prosper. These lessons are embodied in proverbs. Consider this one: "If you do not allow your neighbor to reach nine, you will never reach ten." Again, there is nothing here about absolute right and wrong, just the simple truth that holding your neighbor back harms not only your neighbor but yourself. "Sticking into your neighbor's flesh, it might just as well be sticking into wood" highlights the insensitivity to the pain of others that is the basis for all selfish behavior. It offers the moral basis for what is sometimes called the "silver rule." If the "golden rule" advises treating others as you would like to be treated, the silver rule suggests *not* treating others as you would *not* like to be treated.[35]

This is much closer to Aristotle than to Plato. There may be one basic principle—the silver rule or the golden mean—but it cannot be discussed in the abstract. Ethical principles, in both Aristotelian and Akan thought, must always be understood in the specific circumstances of a particular moral problem. Western thought has in general tended more toward absolutes. In the Judaic and Christian religious traditions, as well as in the philosophy of Plato, classic Western thought has favored moral ideals that are always true and mistrusted the notion that differing conditions might require differing actions.

The Peoples of the Americas

A final thread we will be following throughout this text involves the worldviews and value systems of both the indigenous peoples of the American continent and the Spaniards who conquered and intermingled with them as well as their varied descendants—those who live in or have emigrated from Centroamerica as well as those who sometimes call themselves the first Americans. You may notice similarities between the views of some of these diverse peoples and those of the Africans we have just met. We will hear their voices when we explore cosmology and ontology, when we take up questions of human nature and God, as well as in our investigations of knowledge, truth, and value.

What is life?
It is the flash of a firefly in the night
It is the breath of a buffalo in the wintertime
It is the little shadow on the grass, as it loses itself in the sunset.
CROWFOOT OF THE BLACKFEET

The first to speak is Rigoberta Menchú, 1992 winner of the Nobel Peace Prize for her work in organizing the peasants of Guatemala. Here she describes the welcoming of a new life into the community:

> Candles will be lit for him and his candle becomes part of the candle of the whole community . . . Candles are lit to represent all the things which belong to the universe—earth, water, sun, and man—and the child's candle is put with them, together with incense (what we call **pom**) and lime—our sacred lime. Then the parents tell the baby of the suffering of the family he will be joining. With great feeling, they express their sorrow at bringing a child into the world to suffer . . . It is also when the child is considered a child of God, our one father . . . To reach this one father, the child must love beans, maize, the earth. The one father is the heart of the sky, that is, the sun. The sun is the father and our mother is the moon. She is a gentle mother. And she lights our way.[36]

I am a medicine woman.
I live in the beyond and come back.
AGNES WHISTLING ELK

In this brief account we find a cosmology in which the Sun and the Moon are "pillars of the universe" and a child is born into a community as well as what we might call a nuclear family. What is known with certainty comes from a respected tradition and the life of virtue will honor both the ancestors and the earth.

A Look Ahead

As this first chapter indicates, we will be moving historically, seeing how philosophers both reflect and sometimes transcend their own cultures, and tracing the history of ideas. Since we are primarily following the Western tradition, European philosophers will predominate; however, every chapter will include both Asian and African philosophies as well as the thought systems of the peoples of the Americas.

Philosophers come in many varieties. They represent all races and both genders; women as well as men will speak to us about the love of wisdom. How each of them came to fall in love with wisdom is described in "The Making of a Philosopher" boxes. Many will have the title "philosopher," and some will merely share their wisdom with us. Most will speak with the utmost seriousness, whereas others will use humor and cartoon

The repeating right angles in this design, which also appear in Celtic and Greek cultures, suggest eternal recurrence.

Ecuadorian wall hanging/Courtesy of Jason Mitchell/Photo by Quentin Kardos.

drawings. Nearly all will write in prose, but the lyrics of a song can also help us ponder philosophical riddles.

The three parts of this book reflect the three main branches of philosophy—metaphysics, epistemology, and axiology. In Part 1 we will be asking "What Is Everything Really Like?" and addressing primarily questions of metaphysics. This first chapter has raised the basic philosophical questions in the context of "Is This All There Is?" Chapter 2 continues by looking at issues of reality and being while inquiring "Is What You See What You Get?" Philosophy, as you know by now, makes a distinction between the way something appears and the way it actually *is*. In Chapter 3, we analyze views of human nature by posing the question "Who or What Are We and What Are We Doing Here?," and Chapter 4 concludes Part 1 by asking "Who's in Charge?" and wondering about the existence and nature of God.

Part 2 focuses on issues relating to epistemology under the general heading "How Am I to Understand the World?" Chapter 5 examines sources of knowledge and wonders "Do You See What I See?" Chapter 6 considers "truth tests" by imagining how we might respond to the question "Do You Swear to Tell the Truth . . . ?" Chapter 7 explores the relationship between the beautiful and the true by looking at aesthetic experience and asking, in a paraphrase of the poet John Keats, "Is Truth Beauty and Beauty Truth?" Aesthetics is usually considered under axiology since it deals with values, but here it serves as a bridge between epistemology and axiology by considering beauty and truth as related concepts.

In Part 3 we examine questions of axiology or values as they relate to politics, justice, and private morality. Our overall question will be "By What Values Shall I Live in the World?" Political philosophy (Chapter 8) is introduced by the question "Is Big Brother Watching?" The question "Am I My Brother's or My Sister's Keeper?" introduces social philosophy (Chapter 9), which looks at our obligations to one another. In the final chapter, Chapter 10, we apply all we have learned to the issues raised by ethics. Our inquiry is "What Will It Be: Truth or Consequences?"

You have already read the first Historical Interlude, which set the stage for exploring the ancient world by looking at what was already going on when Western philosophy was born. The remaining four Historical Interludes will help you bridge the gap between events in one time period and those from a later era. In this way you will be able to appreciate and understand philosophical ideas in both their cultural and their historical contexts.

Let's end where we began. Why philosophy? If we do not ask the questions of philosophy, we may be more like sheep than people. And that, as the Pink Floyd song "Sheep" points out, can be dangerous because things are frequently "not what they seem." Harmlessly passing the time and following the leader were two actions Socrates felt to be unworthy of human beings. An "unexamined life" was, he thought, a mere existence and not a life at all. Philosophy asks us to wake up and critically examine what everyone else may be taking for granted. Is this all there is?

Is it true, as some claim, that in America philosophy has lost its "voice" in the public forum, that, despite greater efforts to apply philosophy to current issues, whatever philosophers are saying they are saying only to one another? Has the rest of the culture stopped paying attention? Does philosophy still have anything worthwhile to contribute as we struggle with personal and social issues? When then Vice-Admiral James Stockdale reported for duty on an aircraft carrier off the coast of Vietnam in 1965, he carried with him a copy of the *Discourses* of the Stoic philosopher Epictetus. Born as a slave in 55 C.E. on the eastern fringes of the Roman Empire, Epictetus had attracted followers with his message of rational control over the passions. Although we cannot control our external circumstances, we can choose how we respond to them. As he was shot down and parachuting into what would be a 7½ year ordeal in captivity, much of it spent in solitary confinement, Stockdale whispered to himself, "Five years down there at least. I'm leaving the world of technology and entering the world of Epictetus." Stockdale used the philosophy of **Stoicism** (see Historical Interlude B) not only to survive but also to rally his fellow prisoners, among whom he was the senior officer.[37]

Stoicism *[STOW us sism] the belief that virtue and happiness are achievable by mastering oneself and one's passions and emotions*

France, which has a long tradition of philosophical discussion in café society, is once again attracting thousands of ordinary citizens to the practice that Socrates felt made life worth living—asking and attempting to answer the fundamental questions of life. By 1998 Paris had 18 "cafés-philo," and there were about 100 throughout the country. Once a week people of all ages and walks of life gather for the "practice of philosophy." Topics are suggested by the group: "Is freedom anarchy?," "Is God dead?," "Can there be good and bad violence?," "Can one still speak of democracy without laughing?," "Are we what we do?" Since philosophy is a required subject in high school, most people have had some basic training and experience in acquiring the skills of thinking clearly and arguing coherently. There are no membership fees. Whoever shows up is eligible to participate.[38] Are these people better able to navigate the ups and downs of life as a result of engaging in philosophical inquiry? What does philosophy have to offer ordinary people? Why do they come back week after week?

Summary

In this chapter we have begun to explore the territory and the methods of philosophy. Beginning with the pre-Socratic cosmologists who launched the Western tradition of philosophy, we have marked off the traditional divisions of philosophical thought. Metaphysics considers what is real through cosmology (which studies the cosmos) and ontology (which studies being). Epistemology explores the sources of knowledge and considers how we know what we think we know. Axiology focuses on values, especially ethics and its emphasis on morality and rules for conduct.

If you enjoy what you do, you'll never work another day in your life.
CONFUCIUS

Western philosophy is said to begin with Thales because he and his fellow Milesians were the first in the West to ask and answer the eternal questions philosophically. In the process they postulated an understanding of the world as an orderly place and humans as rational knowers, which has provided the basis for Western science as well as philosophy.

Other monists, looking for a single explanatory principle, which the Greeks called the *archē,* brought Western philosophy to an impasse. Heraclitus's idea that reality is eternal change, suggested by the image of a burning fire, clashed with Parmenides' logical deduction that if only being is real, there can be no not-being and hence no empty space. What appears to be change must be an illusion since the possibility of change is excluded logically.

Pluralists resolved the impasse by postulating multiple explanations of reality. Empedocles' use of the traditional elements—earth, air, fire, and water—and Anaxagoras' imaginative speculation about an infinite number of seeds, or germs, stirred into being by *nous,* or mind, broadened the base of philosophical speculation and allowed for more commonsense explanations.

Some of the speculations about cosmogony or the origins of the universe that we find in these early pre-Socratic philosophers have an oddly modern sound. Pythagoras's idea that our world is one among several and not the center of the system, as well as Anaximander's evolutionary hypothesis, remind us that many "new" ideas have very ancient roots.

The relativism and individualism of the Sophists sparked interest in epistemology. If each of us can only know a private version of reality and if each person's version is equally valid, perhaps questions about metaphysics and ultimate reality are a waste of time. These controversial teachers of rhetoric were a great commercial success in ancient Athens, and they shifted the focus of philosophy from metaphysics to axiology, especially to questions about human happiness.

Socrates and his method of persistent questioning have created the model for the Western search for truth. Using the dialectic method, false ideas can be exposed and discredited. True ideas will be those that stand up to relentless probing. Although he wrote no philosophy, Socrates dignified philosophy as a lifework and the love of wisdom as something worth dying for.

Plato's cave allegory warns us against mistaking shadows for reality. Using our senses, we may become confused. Only reason can guide us unerringly to the truth. With it we have the tool for distinguishing what is real from what is merely appearance. The wise person will be certain that his or her desiring and spirited natures are subordinate to the rational element.

Similarly, Perictyone gives us insight into the Pythagorean goal of *harmonia* as it applied to the lives of Greek women. If harmony, or balance, was the highest human aspiration, men might practice it in the city while women practiced it in the home. Each would be living the life of reason and following the cultural ideal. The image of a well-tuned string captures the concept of a mean between extremes.

Aristotle's ethical theory develops this concept of the golden mean into a classic of Western philosophy. Both excess and deficiency are to be avoided in pursuit of an ideal of moderation. The right amount of reaction, at the right time, in the right manner—rather than adherence to an unvarying code of conduct—becomes the ideal.

The Buddha shares Aristotle's practical, down-to-earth focus but parts company with the West on the question of what is real. For the Buddha, the concept of a rational knowing subject and a separate known object, first articulated by the Milesians, misrepresents the way things actually are.

Buddhism makes every ethical decision a social one. The law of *karma* merely makes this obvious. And, Pan Chao's Confucianism acknowledges the importance of knowing the true nature of reality as an essential step in leading a life of virtue.

African metaphysics, as well as the worldviews of the peoples of the Americas, occupy a middle ground between a Western insistence on logical proofs and an Asian willingness to trust intuition, between the Western separation of knower from known and Buddhist interrelatedness. In the traditional thought of people in Africa and the Americas, all of life is an integrated whole, which includes nature. Humans have a communal destiny and cannot reasonably expect to be successful or happy apart from each other or apart from nature.

When in the sea of Buddha,
know that there is no sea, and no Buddha, and no in.
RICH' WALTER

Of course, questions about how to live, as well as about the nature of reality and knowledge, are addressed by many people besides philosophers. In particular, we have already seen that many of the same questions are asked in science and religion. Theology can be seen as a special field of philosophical inquiry dealing with questions about God, but, as we will see in Chapter 4, philosophers and theologians sometimes disagree about which knowledge sources are acceptable.

Psychology also asks many of the same questions philosophy does. Although these academic disciplines overlap in places, they are also distinct. Psychology has a narrower focus than philosophy does in that it concentrates on describing and explaining behavior and the mind and does not theorize about reality or values. Theology explores human and divine nature and addresses philosophical questions, but it may rely on the Bible or a religious tradition for assumptions, like the existence of God.

As individuals, many philosophers can and do rely on personal religious faith, including belief in divine revelation. In the practice of Western philosophy, however, Scripture and religious tradition are excluded as knowledge sources. In general, Western philosophers walk the path blazed by Thales, focusing on what can be thought and known purely through the exercise of human intelligence without the aid of divinely revealed truths or an ultimate religious faith. Following the path of philosophy, it is time to turn to Chapter 2 and begin our investigation of what is *really* real.

For Further Thought

1. Pretend you are the first to consider what the *archē* might be. Write your own definition of the basic "world stuff" from which everything comes.
2. Were the Sophists wrong to teach Greeks how to use speaking skills to achieve success? Should philosophy be used only for higher things, or are practical uses appropriate as well?
3. Plato hated the Sophists. How might the relativism they introduced have contributed to the decline in society that led to the execution of Socrates (Plato's theory)?

4. Philosophy is the love of wisdom, not the love of knowledge. What are some significant differences you might expect between one who loves wisdom and one who loves knowledge?
5. Which of the branches of metaphysics—cosmology or ontology—seems to you the shorter route to an understanding of what is real? Why do you choose it?
6. It has been said that we cannot answer the questions of metaphysics without, at the same time, addressing those of epistemology. Do you agree or disagree? Why?
7. Does a person's metaphysics influence that person's axiology and, if so, how?
8. Do you agree or disagree with Socrates that the dialectic method of persistent questioning is the best way to arrive at truth? Why?
9. In what ways does Socrates seem like an "intellectual midwife"—his own description of himself?
10. Should Socrates have done whatever he had to do so that he could go on pursuing truth, or was he wise to drink the hemlock? Explain your answer.
11. Socrates argued that the charges against him were not the real reason he was in court. What do you think really caused the prominent citizens of Athens to charge Socrates as a criminal? In what ways was it much "safer" to have him out of the way?
12. Apply the Pythagorean principle of *harmonia* to contemporary North American society. Is this an ideal we are striving to achieve? If yes, how is it working? If no, what are we pursuing instead?
13. What do you think of the golden mean as an ethical ideal? Are there situations in which you think doing the moderate thing would be clearly wrong, or does the mean seem to lead consistently to morality?
14. Do you tend more toward the metaphysics of Plato (two-world view) or Aristotle (one-world view)? On what basis did you decide?
15. Does the law of *karma*, which ensures that the good will be rewarded and the evil punished (if not in this lifetime then in another), seem fair to you? Why, or why not?
16. Would you live your life differently if you believed you would be reborn many more times? Does the thought of "coming back again" frighten or thrill you? Why?
17. Of the things you are pretty certain you know, how many do you know by reason and how many by intuition? Of the things you consider the most vital, did reason or intuition lead you to them?
18. African philosophers believe the West has lost something essential by severing the relationship with nature that is at the heart of traditional societies. Make a list of some things you think have been lost. Are there other ways to reclaim these lost things, or is a return to a relationship with nature the only way?
19. Does African philosophy represent a kind of golden mean between the extreme rationalism of the West and the interrelatedness of the East? Has the best of each been retained in the African approach, or have essential parts of either view been omitted?
20. If Socrates were to return to today's world, what do you think would please him the most and shock him the most profoundly? Why?

For Further Exploration

Achebe, Chinua. *Things Fall Apart*—London: Heinemann, 1983—and *No Longer at Ease*—London: Heinemann, 1962. Both these novels by a Nigerian writer deal with the clash between traditional tribal values and the influence of the technological West. In the first, the setting is the tribe; in the second, a young man goes to the big city and is corrupted.

American Beauty. In this 1999 Dream Works film, Lester undergoes a spiritual transformation—from a bored, robotic, and despairing man, facing a mid-life crisis, to an energetic person who is once again glad to be alive. He is inspired by his daughter's friend, a sexy cheerleader who is desperate in her own way, and the young man next door, who escapes the brutality of his own existence by making home videos of the wonders he finds all around him.

Aristophanes. "The Clouds." In *The Complete Plays of Aristophanes.* Edited and introduced by Moses Hadas. New York: Bantam, 1988. In this play by ancient Greece's most famous comic playwright, Socrates is lampooned as a Sophist who tries to persuade his students that "wrong things are right" and "make the weaker argument appear the stronger" (according to critics within the play). Socrates felt that these charges were what some people had in mind in bringing him to trial. Since the play was quite a success, it is worth speculating about how entertainment influences opinion. You might think about today's debate over violence shown on television and its possible effects on human behavior.

Bianco, Margery Williams. *The Velveteen Rabbit.* New York: Avon, 1960. This is a children's book that is really a philosophical musing on what it means to be "real" and how one goes about achieving it, as well as some of the costs involved.

Carroll, Lewis. *Alice in Wonderland.* New York: Norton, 1971. When a little English girl falls down a rabbit hole, she discovers a world in which nothing she has learned to do in the above-ground world works. Does the world ever seem that way to you? What is Carroll saying about metaphysics, epistemology, and axiology through the medium of this story?

H.H. The Dalai Lama and Howard C. Cutler, *The Art of Happiness.* New York: Riverhead, 1998. The fourteenth Dalai Lama shares practical wisdom from the Buddhist tradition for living a peaceful and happy life in the modern world.

Hesse, Hermann. *Siddhārtha.* Translated by Hilda Rosner. New York: Bantam, 1974. This book is a kind of retelling of the life of the Buddha (whose first name was Siddhārtha), a kind of explanation of Buddhism, and an entertaining story of one person's search for wisdom.

Little Buddha. In this film, director Bernardo Bertolucci gives an introduction to Buddhism by exploring the claim of some Tibetan monks that a young Caucasian boy from Seattle, Washington, may be the reincarnation of a Buddhist master.

Wolfe, Tom. *A Man in Full.* New York: Farrar, Straus, and Giroux, 1998. In this book, now also a movie, young prison inmate Conrad Hensley discovers Stoicism when he orders a spy novel called *The Stoics' Game* and receives, instead, the teachings of the Roman Stoic philosopher Epictetus. This book helps him survive the brutality of prison life.

For Further Research

Try these InfoTrac keywords:

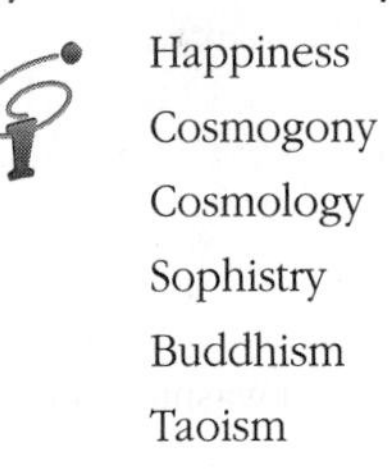

Happiness
Cosmogony
Cosmology
Sophistry
Buddhism
Taoism

Notes

1. Heraclitus, in *Selections from Early Greek Philosophy,* 3d ed., ed. Milton C. Nahm (New York: Appleton-Century-Crofts, 1947), 93.
2. Heraclitus, in *Selections,* 91.
3. Nahm, 221–222.
4. Nahm, 224.
5. Protagoras, in *Selections,* 237.
6. Protagoras, in *Selections,* 239.
7. Plato, "Meno," in *Great Dialogues of Plato,* trans. W. H. D. Rouse, ed. Eric H. Warmington and Philip G. Rouse (New York: New American Library, 1956), 42.
8. Plato, "Meno," 47.
9. Plato, "Meno," 49–50.
10. Plato, "Apology," in *Great Dialogues,* 427.
11. Plato, "Apology," 429.
12. Plato, "Apology," 435.
13. Plato, "Apology," 443.
14. Plato, *Republic,* bk. 7, trans. Robin Waterfield (New York: Oxford University Press, 1994), 243.
15. Plato, *Republic,* bk. 7, 243–244.
16. Plato, *Republic,* bk. 4, 150.
17. Plato, *Republic,* bk. 4, 153.
18. Perictyone, "On the Duties of a Woman," in *The Pythagorean Writings,* ed. Robert Navon (Kew Gardens, N.Y.: Selene, 1986), 72.
19. Eryphamus, in *Pythagorean Writings,* 25.
20. Aristotle, *The Ethics of Aristotle: The Nicomachean Ethics,* trans. J. A. K. Thomson, ed. Hugh Tredennick (New York: Penguin, 1976), 80–81.
21. Aristotle, *Ethics,* 87, 91–92.
22. H. D. F. Kitto, *The Greeks* (New York: Penguin, 1991), 252.
23. Kitto, 103.
24. Kitto, 107.

25. *The Dhammapada: The Sayings of the Buddha,* trans. Thomas Byrom (New York: Vintage, 1976), 3.
26. Nancy Lee Swann, *Pan Chao: Foremost Woman Scholar of China* (New York: Century, 1932), 61–69.
27. Swann, 84–85.
28. Swann, 142–144.
29. *Tao Te Ching,* chapter 48, author's translation.
30. P. Kaboha, "African Metaphysical Heritage," in *The Foundations of Social Life: Ugandan Philosophical Studies,* vol. 1, ed. A. T. Dalfovo et al. (Washington, D.C.: Council for Research in Values and Philosophy, 1992), 70.
31. Kaboha, 70.
32. Kaboha, 70.
33. Kwasi Wiredu, "Moral Foundations of an African Culture," in *Person and Community: Ghanaian Philosophical Studies,* vol. 1, ed. Kwasi Wiredu and Kwame Gyekye (Washington, D.C.: Council for Research in Values and Philosophy, 1992), 196.
34. Wiredu, 197.
35. Wiredu, 199.
36. *I, Rigoberta Menchú: An Indian Woman in Guatemala,* ed. Elisabeth Burgos-Debray, trans. Ann Wright (New York: Verso, 1984), 11–13.
37. James Rainey, "Revival of an ancient philosophy," *Baltimore Sun,* 3 May 1999, 2A.
38. Marlise Simons, "Thought for Food: Cafes Offer Philosophy in France," *New York Times,* 2 May 1998, A17.

CHAPTER 2

Reality and Being

Is What You See What You Get?

Before You Read . . .

Ask yourself how important it is to you to know what is real and what price you would pay for accepting as real what is only apparently real.

You are walking through the new kitchen you have designed, opening drawers, turning appliances on and off, testing the water faucet in the sink, even listening to birds chirping outside the window. Now, you are flying over the landscape of Mars, studying its rocky terrain. Next, you move a wand that leaves a trail of tiny, lighted triangles sparkling with color and a sea of musical notes that swirl around you. You can fly up and enjoy the perspective from behind a clock on the wall, swim the bottom of the ocean, or travel through your own bloodstream.

virtual reality *a computer-generated reality that is fully interactive for the participant*

This is called **virtual reality.** An observer would say that what you are "really" doing is sitting in a chair wearing goggles and a glove, experiencing an artificial, or "virtual," reality in an environment created by a computer. Unlike other computer simulations, however, in virtual reality you do not experience a picture on a screen. Instead, you are in another environment, experiencing it in three dimensions and with your senses of touch, sight, and hearing. To you the experience is "real."

The Issue Defined

Virtual reality seems like a dramatic technology, yet something like the telephone, which all of us take for granted, long ago began to alter our sense of reality. What Alexander Graham Bell had in mind was piping music to people; instead, we listen to electromechanical representations of people's voices and believe we are encountering the people themselves. Soon we will see faces, too. Will this be as real as a face-to-face encounter? Maybe it will seem more real.

Virtual reality is already commonplace in television shows and movies. In *Star Trek: The Next Generation,* for example, crew members on a future starship visit the "holodeck" to indulge their fantasies, play a game of racquetball, or make "human" contact. Captain Jean-Luc Picard likes to live as a private detective in San Francisco during the 1940s. Data, the android, takes on the identity of Sherlock Holmes. Men dance with and kiss beautiful women. All of it seems real until the command "Computer, end program" reveals an empty room.

Quark, the Ferengi bartender and general hustler on *Star Trek: Deep Space Nine,* entices customers with offers of a visit to the "holosuites." In the twenty-fifth century, there is no need for human prostitution, no fear of sexually transmitted diseases, no risk of unpleasant entanglements; all of it is done in a computer-generated environment. The virtual experience is so close to the "real thing" as to be indistinguishable from it.

Technology is the knack of so arranging the world that we do not experience it.
MAX FRISCH

Even today it's possible to "feel" the designs in a clay vase that only exists in the hard drive of a computer, thanks to the Phantom, invented by Thomas Massie, a twenty-five-year-old MIT graduate. What the Phantom gives you is the "unshakable impression that there's something there, even though it has no physical reality."[1] A man in New Jersey sues for divorce, charging his wife with having a "virtual affair"; a French bishop, disciplined by Pope John Paul II and given a diocese that no longer exists, retaliates by setting up a "virtual diocese" and becoming the first bishop in cyberspace; Japanese children experience emotional trauma when their Tamagotchis, virtual reality pets, grow ill or "die" because the children are too busy studying to give them the love and attention they need to "survive." The line between ordinary and virtual reality has begun to blur.

The advent of virtual reality challenges our absolute faith in the version of "reality" we encounter daily. To what extent do we define what is real? If we cannot distinguish between the reality "out there" and the reality we experience through our minds and senses, does that mean we *construct* even everyday reality?

The universe was a vast machine yesterday. It is a hologram today. Who knows what intellectual rattle we'll be shaking tomorrow.
R. D. LAING

When we question the independent existence of what seems to be "out there," we have begun to alter the way we think about ourselves. Emerging technologies accelerate the process. Already, many of us are members of virtual communities as we electronically talk via a computer with like-minded people. We may not know our neighbors in the dorm or apartment complex, we may be alienated from our families, but in the world of the Internet we can find the friends and colleagues the "real world" has failed to provide.

Unlike face-to-face encounters, exchanges on the Internet allow us to keep certain things invisible if we choose. We need not reveal our gender, race, age, whether we are able-bodied, what our gifts and challenges are. Those with whom we "speak" can converse with us independent of the boxes society creates around some of these terms. We may find ourselves attracted to someone whose external features might put us off in ordinary reality. Meeting the "real person" on the Net opens up possibilities excluded by "chemistry" or the lack of it.

All of this raises some interesting questions. Who *am* I if no one knows my race, gender, or sexual orientation; what my face looks like; or how much I weigh? Can I be a different person under these conditions? And if so, which is the more "real" me? The questions raised by these new technologies invite us to rethink our ideas of "self" and "reality." As columnist Howard Rheingold points out, virtual reality is already having a profound effect on the "big questions" of philosophy:

> Our most intimate and heretofore most stable personal characteristics—our sense of where we are in space, who we are personally, and how we define "human" attributes—are now open to redefinition. The technology that can replicate the human mind's fanciest trick—weaving sense-mediated signal streams into the fine-grained, three-dimensional, full-color, more-or-less consistent model we call "reality"—is in its infancy today. But . . . what will we think of each other, and ourselves, when we begin to live in computer-generated worlds for large portions of our waking hours?[2]

In fact, virtual worlds are creating what Michael Heim, known as "the philosopher of cyberspace," calls an ontological change in the world itself—a change "in the whole context in which our knowledge and awareness are rooted."[3] It is not just our perceptions that are changing; it is the world beneath our feet. Changes of this type often take place before we even realize what is happening. Before we are aware of it, the world becomes a different place.

The implications of virtual reality provide a good context in which to consider the questions of metaphysics we began addressing in Chapter 1. What is "real," and how will I know when I encounter the "real thing"? Is there something "real" that underlies the world of appearances? Were Thales and company on the right track in searching for an *archē,* and, if so, how do I tell the apparently real from the really real?

These and other questions have occupied philosophers and other thinkers for centuries. As they consider the structure and basic laws of the cosmos, scientists ask what philosophers would call metaphysical questions. Do things happen at random in the cosmos, or is there order and purpose—what Aristotle called *telos*? More clearly ontological questions—questions about the nature of being and ultimate reality—intersect with the cosmological questions first asked by Thales. Both scientists and philosophers want to know, for example, whether it is possible to speak about external reality in a definitive way.

Why does the universe go to all the bother of existing?
STEPHEN W. HAWKING

Reality and the Brain: The Visual World and Constructed Reality

Imagine a person who has been blind since birth and who, thanks to advances in medical technology, receives the gift of sight. What do you suppose that person's experience of the world will be? Common sense tells us that the world of visual stimuli—the one we see every day—will present itself to the newly sighted person just as it does to already sighted people. We imagine the gift of sight to be all benefit with no strings attached.

In fact, in several well-documented cases, this is not at all what happens. Virgil, a man blind almost from birth, recently had surgery to remove cataracts and replace lenses. When the bandages were removed, he stared blankly at what he later described as a meaningless blur of light, movement, and color—all mixed up. Only when the familiar voice of the surgeon said, "Well?" did Virgil realize that "this chaos of light and shadow was a face and, indeed, the face of his surgeon."[4]

Virgil behaved not like a sighted person, not like a blind person, but like a person whose eyes can "see" but who is "mentally blind." He "saw" what sighted people see—light, movement, color—but what he saw had no coherence. Virgil found his dog and cat very confusing visually. He would see "a paw, the nose, the tail, an ear, but could not see all of them together, see the cat as a whole." Motion offered special challenges, since objects in motion appeared to change constantly. Virgil reported that his dog "looked so different at different times that he wondered if it was the same dog."[5]

Before his surgery Virgil had lived exclusively in a tactile world, a world revealed through the sense of touch. It is a world made up of sequences of impressions—first, one touch, sound, or smell and then another and another—constructed through time. Indeed, for the blind, the simultaneous perception of objects placed in space that is commonplace for the sighted does not happen automatically. It has to be learned and, for some like Virgil, the task can never be fully mastered.

According to neurologist Oliver Sacks, whereas the blind construct a world based on time, the sighted depend on visual space to make an "instantaneous visual scene." The integration of perceptions into a visual map of the world is mastered early. For those who fail to master it or later lose their sight, the very "*idea* of space becomes incomprehensible—and this even for highly intelligent people blinded relatively late in life."[6]

What happens automatically—thousands of times a day for most of us—does not happen without learning. Constructing a visual world requires work, and ordinarily, half the cerebral cortex in the brain is devoted to this enormously complex task, which even the most sophisticated computers have yet to accomplish. Seeing, as we now understand, is at least as much a mental process as a physiological one.

If the world that seems to present itself to us composed of objects in space is largely a mental construction, there are ontological implications. As Plato and Aristotle describe the process, we make a world out of Form and matter. When we look at an object, both Form and matter are present. Lacking either, the object does not exist. With his eyes Virgil could perceive the matter but not the Form. We are back with the fundamental question these two Greek philosophers debated: Is the Form, or Idea, of something more real than the matter of that something? Virgil's experience seems to confirm that the Form is at least as vital as the matter and in fact may be the more critical of the two.

HOW PHILOSOPHY WORKS

Reductio Ad Absurdum

This form of argument takes a premise and follows it to an insupportable conclusion as a way of denying it. It reduces to the absurd, as the name implies. Here is the form:

Suppose A.
If A, then B.
If B, then C.
If C, then not-A.
Since not-A is true, A must be false.

Now let's consider an example from this chapter:

The world as it is matches my perceptions of it: A.
If so, my perceptions must be the same as those of all sighted people: If A, then B.
If this describes all sighted people, we must include a blind person whose sight is restored: If B, then C.
Virgil's perceptions (after restored sight) of the world did not match mine: If C, then not-A.
The world may not be as I perceive it: Truth of not-A challenges A.

Is the world of Forms, or Ideas, more real than the world of matter? Plato's answer—that Forms, or Ideas, exist perfectly in their own realm as well as imperfectly in this one—receives a new twist with the advent of virtual reality. In visiting an ideal world, are we seeing what is more or less real than the ordinary world we see every day? Are we prisoners to our ordinary sight, able to escape its confines through access to computer-generated worlds? Or is virtual reality simply a dangerous "drug," amusing us but taking us farther from actual reality?

If the world as it presents itself to us every day is, as Virgil's experience and quantum mechanics suggest, largely constructed by our minds, what exactly is the difference between everyday reality and virtual reality? Isn't everything in a sense constructed? How would we go about testing what is real and distinguishing it from what we might label mere appearance? These are the fundamental questions of ontology, and they are as "alive" for us today as they were for Thales, the first philosopher and the first scientist in the Western world. What is real, and how can we be sure we have the real thing and not some imitation?

Ontology: What Is Real?

Searching for the "world stuff" from which everything else is derived, the pre-Socratic philosophers were struggling to understand ultimate reality. In this section we consider a variety of answers to the most basic ontological question: What is real? Both Plato and Aristotle speculated about what is "really real" and ultimately disagreed about where it can be found. In Asia, Buddhists and Taoists, asking the same question, arrived at answers that would have shocked both Plato and Aristotle. Finally, explanations of reality can be found in the relatively new subsets of contemporary physics called quantum mechanics and relativity theory. Using their own methods, which are different from those of philosophy, physicists and other scientists are also asking ontological questions.

Ontology in Plato and Aristotle

We had our first look at Plato and Aristotle in Chapter 1. As you remember, they were both curious about a number of basic questions and wrote on the subjects we now call metaphysics, epistemology, and axiology. In this chapter we narrow our focus to their ideas on metaphysics, looking especially at how each understood being or the nature of reality.

Plato: Forms, or Ideas, as the "Really Real"

Plato began his formal education at Pythagoras's research institute. There, among many interesting pursuits, students and teachers unlocked the mysteries of the three-dimensional world through the study of geometry. They marked off space into segments, defined by points and lines; created shapes; and discovered the rules that govern mathematical existence.

Mathematics is the only good metaphysics.
LORD KELVIN

Yet this work involved a paradox. Plato noticed that they spent a lot of time talking about *the* square, *the* circle, and *the* triangle, and they did not mean the particular square, circle, or triangle in front of them. Geometric definitions imply an "ideal" square, circle, or triangle, having all the relevant properties of that shape. Even though geometry can help us understand the world of experience, its perfect shapes do not seem to exist in this world at all.

Every particular line, for instance, took up space as it was drawn in sand or on papyrus. But lines as defined in geometry do not actually take up space. Similarly, circles in geometry are perfectly round, but the circles drawn for illustration are always a little lopsided and their radii are never exactly equal. Plato began to realize that what can be said about the "real" figures in geometry cannot be accurately or fully represented in this world. Instead, the perfect prototypes, or **Forms,** he concluded, must exist somewhere else.

Forms *in Plato's ontology, intelligible Ideas, the ultimate realities from which the world of objects has been patterned*

The best we can do in this world is to imitate or mimic the perfect Forms. Doing this will allow us to talk about circles and triangles as they actually exist in a perfection we can never replicate. This world, he came to believe, is a world of appearances, and we make a big mistake if we confuse it with the real thing.

Gradually, Plato expanded his theory of ideal Forms to include everything we see imperfectly represented in the ordinary course of events. There are many tables in the world, in all kinds of shapes and sizes. What makes them all *tables* is that they each participate to a greater or lesser extent in the Form of a table—what we might call "tableness" (Figure 2.1). It is this ideal that an artisan must have in mind in order to make a particular table out of wood. The raw material, the matter, is shaped and given form by the Idea of "tableness" that the artisan brings to it.

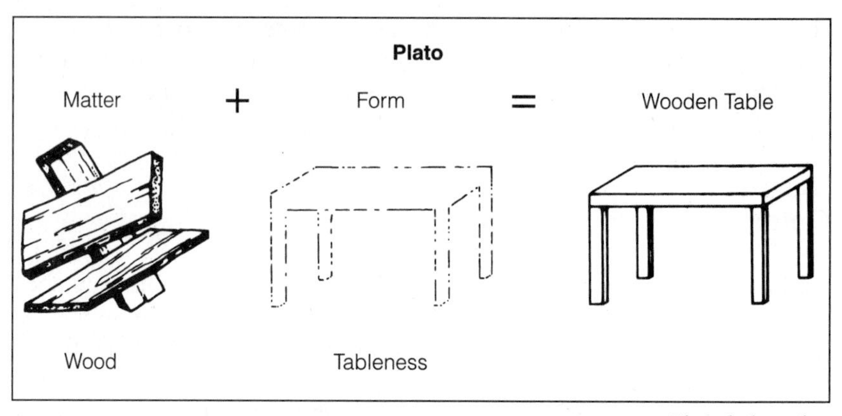

FIGURE 2.1 FORM AND MATTER AS CONCEIVED BY PLATO *Plato believed that the Form of a table existed in a world of perfect Forms.*

Plato applies the same line of thinking to other ideas, including those that concern social life and morality. For instance, how do we judge whether a particular act is just or fair? When we see a just act, and maybe especially when we do not, we compare it with an ideal standard, the perfect Form of Justice that no single act captures in its entirety. Even three-year-olds understand this. Take away a toy and the child will protest, "That's not fair—it's mine; give it back!" But if Forms don't exist in the everyday world, how can we know about them? How does a child know what fairness is?

Plato came to believe we can recognize the imperfect imitations of the perfect Forms that exist in this world because we had a glimpse of the other world—the world of Forms—before our birth. Plato put this idea into Socrates' mouth in *Meno,* the dialogue between Socrates and the slave boy (see Chapter 1). For Plato, much of what we think we are learning might more accurately be called *remembering.*

It is important to note here that when we speak of Forms, or Ideas, we mean a great deal more than the ideas that exist only in our minds and nowhere else. For Plato, the Forms have a real existence outside our minds. When we compare them with mere matter, Plato thinks we will agree that Forms, or Ideas, are the most real things that exist.

idealism *in metaphysics, the belief that the most real entities are ideas and other immaterial entities*

Plato's philosophy has been called **idealism** because of his belief that the most real things are these otherworldly Forms, or Ideas. Through the centuries other thinkers have agreed that the "really real" is what we grasp through our minds rather than through physical experience. You might think of religious worldviews in which the "really real" is something spiritual, such as God, heaven, or the soul—things we cannot know through our senses. In fact, as we will see later on, some religious thinkers, both Christian and non-Christian, have adapted Plato's philosophy to enhance their explanation of reality.

You can also see that Plato's ontology is directly tied to his epistemology (theory of knowledge) and axiology (theory of values). Consider, for example, the Idea of Beauty. There is the danger of mistaking beautiful objects for the beautiful itself and settling for something of inferior value. Plato thinks that loving a beautiful object gives us only a glimmer of what it would be like to love Beauty itself. Our senses show us beautiful objects, but only our reason can reveal the Form, or Idea, of Beauty. In the *Republic* Plato has Socrates make this point by asking us to imagine two classes of people:

> Theatre-goers and sightseers are devoted to beautiful sounds and colours and shapes, and to works of art which consist of these elements, but their minds are constitutionally incapable of seeing and devoting themselves to beauty itself . . . And what about someone who does . . . think that there is such a thing as beauty itself, and has the ability to see it as well as the things which partake in it, and never gets them muddled up? Do you think he's living in the real world or in a dream-world?[7]

The prisoners from the cave allegory, which we discussed in Chapter 1, are mistaken in their assessment of reality because they are relying on the evidence of their senses. Using this standard, shadows can indeed be confused with reality. When we look at a pencil partially standing in a glass of water, our senses tell us the pencil is bent; but when we pull it out, the pencil is as straight as ever. We call this an "optical illusion" and use our reason to override the misinformation our senses give us. Plato thinks that relying on reason is the only method that can lead us to real knowledge.

Since he equated the sense world with the cave of ignorance and illusion, Plato was not willing to trust what the senses offered as information about reality. He had some negative things to say about artists (see Chapter 7) since their work essentially involved the creation of illusion. As far as Plato was concerned, illusion was an ever-present threat. Its dangers and confusions were everywhere, and the last thing we ought to do is willingly create more of it. The task of the philosopher, he believed, was to turn away from the sense world and rely upon rationality.

This is Plato's "promo" for philosophy. It is fourth-century B.C.E. advertising copy for the benefits of doing philosophy and the dangers of not doing it. If you prefer to remain in the cave, Plato suggests, you have that choice; but now you know that something far superior awaits you outside the cave. Try philosophy—it can change your life!

The Real is the rational and the rational is the Real.
G. W. F. HEGEL

Plato, however, is no mere huckster. He passionately believed in what he was selling. We might think of the poster that proclaims, "If you think education is expensive, try the cost of ignorance." Plato's life had been changed by the geometry he did with Pythagoras and by the inspirational life of his teacher Socrates. He saw the benefits for individuals and for society of using the mind to apprehend reality in the perfect Forms and the dangers of remaining in the cave.

Our Western culture has been forever changed because of the distinction Plato made between a world of perfect Forms and a world of imperfect objects of sense perception. When we say "It's just a question of mind over matter," we are echoing his assumption that reason controls reality. Deeply imbedded in our culture is the notion that our bodies are inferior to our minds and not really to be trusted, that our emotions can get us into trouble, that only reason and logic can lead us to truth. It tends to make us feel superior to those of lesser intellect in the human family, to other animals, and to the natural world. It helps us live almost exclusively in our heads and forget we have bodies until they break down and get our attention.

And reason is the source of some of our greatest ideals. Only a culture that accepts Plato's ontology, or something close to it, believes there are absolutes—Ideas and ideals worth dying for. Socrates chose death over a life without philosophy. To live without being able to question and pursue the truth would be to exist as a robot, in his judgment, but not really to live.

Logic is the beginning of wisdom, not the end.
SPOCK, *STAR TREK*

One implication of this view is that our proper home is not in this imperfect world but in another realm where things exist in a perfect state, the world of Forms revealed by our reason. In the dialogue called *Phaedo,* Plato has Socrates say shortly before his death,

> But those who are thought to have lived in especial holiness, they are those who are set free and released from these places here on earth as from a prison house and come up into the pure dwelling place . . . those who have purified themselves enough by philosophy live without bodies altogether forever after . . .[8]

Aristotle: Form and Matter as the "Really Real"

Like many students, Aristotle began by accepting the theories of his teacher Plato. Later, however, he made a significant departure. He continued to accept Plato's basic division of the world into Form and matter and to agree with Plato that Form is superior to matter, shaping and defining it, making it what it is. Where he came to disagree with Plato was on the question of a *separate* world of perfect Forms. In *Metaphysics,* he writes:

> Above all one might discuss the question what on earth the Forms contribute to sensible things, either to those that are eternal or to those that come into being and cease to be. For they cause neither movement nor any change in them. But again they help in no wise either towards the knowledge of the other things . . . or towards their being, if they are not in the particulars which share in them . . .[9]

In other words, although the Forms may appear to serve no purpose in sense objects, Aristotle agrees with Plato that they give the object its form or identity. If they existed somewhere other than in association with matter, however, Aristotle believes they would have no effect on the being, or reality, of the object. At this point Aristotle, the student, rejects his teacher Plato's theory that Forms exist in a separate, otherworldly state (Figure 2.2).

Apart from particular tables, Aristotle argues, "tableness" is a slippery and not very meaningful concept. If asked the question "How can I learn what makes a table a table?" Plato would probably advise the use of reason to contemplate the Form of a table—its "tableness." Asked the same question, Aristotle would be likely to reply, "Go and look at fifty tables; then you will understand what makes a table a table!"

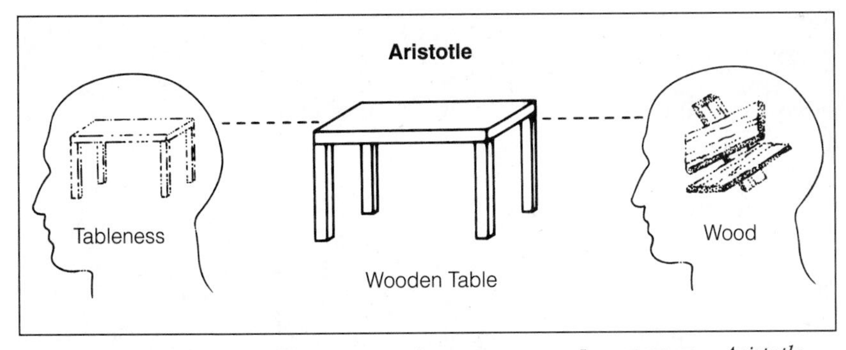

FIGURE 2.2 FORM AND MATTER AS CONCEIVED BY ARISTOTLE *Aristotle rejected Plato's theory, believing Form and matter could only be sprarated in a mental exercise, not in reality.*

Aristotle is willing to grant that in our minds we could make the distinction between "tableness" and wood and then combine both into the one concept of a wood table, but he insists this could only be done as a mental exercise. In fact, no one ever encounters "tableness" except in actual tables. "Again," he writes, "it would seem impossible that the substance and that of which it is the substance should exist apart; how, therefore, could the Ideas, being the substances of things exist apart?"[10] A separate world of Forms, or Ideas—disconnected from material reality—seems nonsensical.

Logic is the anatomy of thought.
JOHN LOCKE

In Aristotle's view, to exist is to exist as a specific something, composed of Form and matter. Each of these two ingredients, which make up all the specific somethings in the world, has a reciprocal relationship with the other. Form gives matter its particularity, whereas matter gives concreteness to Form. Each needs the other for completion, for existence. Wood is only wood until "tableness" gives it Form, and "tableness" requires wood (or some other matter) in order to express itself.

Matter has within it what Aristotle calls ***entelechy,*** meaning "inner purpose" or "end." This gives matter the potential for becoming formed. To describe this process a little more poetically, we might say that matter yearns for Form and with it matter becomes Formed. When its potential becomes actual, matter becomes real. Since all matter possesses *entelechy,* all of it is formed. There is no matter without Form and no Form without matter. For Aristotle, a kingdom of matterless Forms was self-contradictory.

entelechy *[EN tuh leck ee] in Aristotle's ontology, the inner purpose, or end, in something that brings it to actuality*

Aristotle's insistence on a "this world" orientation has distinguished his philosophy from that of his teacher and mentor Plato. Whereas Plato wrote a book (*Republic*) outlining what an ideal society would be like and how it should be governed, Aristotle approached the same challenge by studying 158 actual constitutions and then examining the societies they produced to see which were the most successful.

As with Plato, Aristotle's metaphysics was related to his epistemology and axiology. Aristotle was convinced we could learn the Forms of things only by studying and examining the things themselves. Actual constitutions

HOW PHILOSOPHY WORKS
The Categorical Syllogism

With the categorical syllogism, we begin our study of formal logic. Using deductive reasoning, the patterns of argument we will explore help us determine whether or not the correct *form* of reasoning has been followed. We set aside the *content* of the propositions and concentrate instead on their logical form. If we are not reasoning correctly, there is no possibility of arriving at the truth or of learning what we want to know about reality. A logically sound argument follows the rules of deductive reasoning. In the West, logic has been a primary and sometimes exclusive criterion for knowledge. Much of the rest of the world, however, looks beyond logic for other methods of validating knowledge claims.

Aristotle pioneered the use of the *categorical syllogism* as a way of testing the *validity* of an argument. This form of argument contains two *premises* and a *conclusion* and includes three *terms* that are related to one another. Here is a typical example:

All men are mortal.
Socrates is a man.
Therefore, Socrates is mortal.

Notice that the two terms, *Socrates* and *mortal*, appear in both the conclusion and the premises. The argument also contains a third term that appears in the premises but not the conclusion. The *middle term* links the other two terms together. In this particular syllogism, the middle term is *man* or *men*. When the first premise uses the adjective *all*, that tells us that all men are being described by the second term, *mortal*. The term *Socrates* in the second premise also describes all members of the class—in this case, the class has one member, named Socrates.

When we examine a syllogism, we need to ask whether or not it is valid. This means, Do the premises support the conclusion? Philosophers have developed validity tests for syllogisms. Passing all four of these tests guarantees the validity of the argument:

1. The middle term (the one appearing in both premises but not the conclusion) must refer to all members of the class at least once.
2. A term in the conclusion referring to all members of a class must also refer to all members of the class in the premises.
3. The premises must not both be negative.
4. If one of the premises is negative, the conclusion must also be negative.

(continued)

and the societies they produce tell us what we need to know about government. Observing and noting the similarities shared by all horses will allow us to figure out what makes a horse a horse and also what separates it from a donkey or a zebra. Aristotle believed the sense world was a great laboratory and a source of endless learning.

Unlike Plato, Aristotle was eager to use his senses as a legitimate route to knowledge. If the perfect Forms can only exist in the material world, then studying that world is the best way to study reality itself. Indeed, it is the only way. Whereas Plato scorned poets and artists as weavers of illusion, Aristotle greatly admired the work of the Athenian playwrights whose tragic verses had much to teach humankind about what is real and how to recognize it (see Chapter 7).

The Western world's debate about what is real took shape through the tension created by the contrasting theories of Plato and Aristotle. It has even been said that all subsequent metaphysics in the West is a footnote to Plato and Aristotle. For centuries there were two camps—those who defined

HOW PHILOSOPHY WORKS

The Categorical Syllogism (continued)

Let's apply the tests to our syllogism. The middle term *man* or *men* applies to all members of the class in the first premise, so the first condition is satisfied. The term *Socrates* refers to all members of that class of one in both the conclusion and the second premise; this meets the second condition. The third and fourth conditions do not apply since none of the premises is negative. We can conclude that this syllogism is valid.

However, validity does not *guarantee* truth. Consider this example:

All philosophy students are extraterrestrials.
John is a philosophy student.
Therefore, John is an extraterrestrial.

The form of the argument is the same as the preceding one. The difference is that in this second argument at least one of the premises is simply not true. It is *not* the case that all philosophy students are extraterrestrials. Even though the *form* of the argument is valid, the conclusion is not true because it rests on a false premise. However, *if* it were true that all philosophy students are extraterrestrials and that John is a philosophy student, then it would also be true that John is an extraterrestrial. Valid arguments are true *if* their premises are true. Even with false premises, however, they are still valid. That is, the correct form of reasoning has been followed.

When you apply the tests listed to a syllogism, be especially careful when one or more of the premises is negative—rules 3 and 4 must be taken into account—or when the premises refer to "some men" or "some philosophy students," for all members of a class are not being described.

Try the tests on these syllogisms:

All men are mortal.
No women are men.
No women are mortal (all women are immortal).

(Notice that the word *men* is used with two different meanings, rendering this argument automatically invalid.)

Some children like toys.
Some chimps like toys.
Some children are chimps.

All television programs are a waste of time.
Some college courses are a waste of time.
Some college courses are televison programs.

No baseball players are artists.
Jackie is a baseball player.
Jackie is not an artist.

reality in terms of perfect Forms, or Ideas, and those who insisted Forms have reality only when they are given tangible or touchable expression. What effect will virtual reality have on this debate?

If I can sit in a chair but, at the same time, inhabit a completely different world, which is the real one? Is reality defined and encountered by my body as it occupies space and meets standard definitions of matter, or is reality what my mind experiences as revealed through the wonders of technology? Can matter and Form be separated? Are we being seduced by the ultimate in shadow play or seeing more deeply into what is real? With virtual reality, the world itself seems to change.

If I can no longer be absolutely certain whether what I see and touch "really" exists, the whole question of what is real shifts. What seemed so clear to Plato and Aristotle is suddenly much less so for us. Although they disagreed over a basic question, they shared a common understanding of the difference between Form and matter. We may no longer share their confidence in the distinction.

DOING PHILOSOPHY

The Riddle of the Nature of Reality

Philosophy isn't only something you study—it's something you can learn to *do*. Doing philosophy means using your critical thinking skills to analyze a question and think through possible responses to it. By studying the philosophers of the past and present, we can learn how to do philosophy ourselves. Let's begin by considering our own responses to the riddle of the nature of reality. It seems we have two extreme positions—the interrelatedness and interconnectedness of Buddhism at one pole and the "discrete bits of something" traditional Western view at the other pole. As you begin to think this question through, you will learn something about which approach to knowledge you favor. Is your instinct to reason your way to an answer, to look for evidence and then analyze that evidence, to trust your intuitive sense about what's real? Now, here are some other questions: If everything is interrelated, what happens to individuality? If individuality is important, is there any kind of underlying unity? Can I trust my senses and my common sense to tell me about the nature of reality? If I can't, what do I trust? To what extent do we create our own reality by the interpretation we attach to what we perceive? Who are the experts—scientists, philosophers, theologians, artists, economists, psychologists? Once you have decided your own view of reality and who you trust to guide your judgment, what implications does this view have for you? How will you live your life based on what you think is real? In many ways these are the most basic questions any human being faces. From your analysis of reality will flow your view of human nature, your interpretation of the cosmos, and your value system.

Asian Views of Reality

Outside the Western world, the reality debate between Plato and Aristotle had little to contribute to the ontological search. In Asia, philosophers and other thinkers were just as eager to learn what is "really real," but their metaphysical speculation led them along different paths and to quite different conclusions. Here we look more deeply into Buddhism's insistence on the interdependence of all that is and encounter the mysterious *Tao* that moves nature and all of life effortlessly.

Buddhism: Reality as Interdependence

How admirable!
to see lightning and not think
life is fleeting
BASHO

Buddhism describes our experience of life in words that suggest virtual reality and also share some assumptions with Plato's ontology. If you remember the introductory discussion of Buddhism in Chapter 1, life is characterized by suffering, and suffering is caused by desire. But desire is trapped in an illusion. In the world of appearances, we may think it is possible to hold on to things as they are at a particular moment—to enjoy forever the things we desire, like wealth, health, particular relationships. Our desire could be fulfilled, however, only if these things had permanence, and an accurate view reveals that they do not. It is their very impermanence that causes us suffering. As Heraclitus from the Greek tradition reminds us, we can never step twice into the same river.

In Buddhism, the position of the unenlightened person—the person who does not see things as they actually are—resembles the position of the cave dweller in Plato's cave allegory. Like the cave prisoners who cling to their false version of reality, Buddhism suggests the unenlightened remain caught in the world of ***samsara,*** a continually repeating cycle of birth-death-rebirth. We seem to be isolated, separated individuals, and reality seems capable of being fixed and held on to. We cling and we suffer all through our lives, and when we die the process begins all over again.

samsara *the continuous cycle of births, deaths, and rebirths resulting from* karma

The possibility of seeing in another way seems frightening and makes us insecure. As the cave dwellers in Plato's allegory resisted being dragged out of the cave and closed their minds against those who had seen the "real world," so do the unenlightened embrace their chains and deny the true state of affairs. Things are as they are, Buddhism reminds us, and refusing to acknowledge that only leads to more suffering.

In virtual reality, too, we experience what appears to be something real. Afterward, however, from our ordinary perspective, we may dismiss virtual reality as merely a computer simulation. From this perspective, the fact that something seems real does not make it real. Just as a very vivid dream is shattered when we awaken, virtual reality ends when the computer is unplugged or the goggles and glove are removed. Yet there are cultures that believe we dream our reality and then work to give that reality form in our everyday lives.

Is a female figure an appropriate choice to represent the Buddhist ideal of bodhisattva *who postpones* nirvana *to help others reach enlightenment?*

Guanyin, *bodhisattva* or goddess of mercy/The Baltimore Museum of Art: The Julius Levy Memorial Fund, BMA 1944.80.

From a Buddhist perspective, much of what seems to have form is really empty, in the sense of being devoid of a self-nature. This is a dramatic reversal of Plato's ontology. For Plato, the Forms are the essence of reality; for the Buddhist, form is a kind of illusion.

From the point of view of the unenlightened, feeling, perception, impulse, consciousness, and form all seem to have the fullness of existence. In other words, they all seem real. Seen from the vantage point of enlightenment or transcendent wisdom, however, all these terms are revealed to be empty. To recognize them as empty is to gain detachment from them and be on the road to enlightenment. To use the virtual reality analogy, we might worry about someone who believed what he or she experienced in virtual reality was identical with ordinary reality. Buddhism points out that ordinary perception is a kind of virtual reality trap, and the way things appear should not be confused with the way things are. Emptiness rather than form marks the true state of affairs.

To see this we must radically shift our perspective, and the invitation to do so provokes all the natural, human resistance we saw in Plato's cave allegory. Those who have seen things as they are may be available to help us. In the Mahayana branch of Buddhism, the ideal person is a ***bodhisattva***—one who has achieved enlightenment but stays around to help others do the same.

bodhisattva *[bohd hee SAHT vuh] in Buddhism, a wise and enlightened person who postpones* nirvana *in order to help others gain enlightenment*

We can see the tension between perspectives expressed in a popular Buddhist Scripture known as the Heart Sutra. Its full title is *The Heart of*

skandhas *[SKAHN duhs] in Buddhism, the five elements (feeling, perception, impulse, consciousness, and form) that make the world and the person of appearances*

Transcendent Wisdom, and it is one of the best known in Buddhism. The theme of the Heart Sutra is emptiness. In it, ***skandhas*** are the heaps of what appear to be reality—feeling, perception, impulse, consciousness, and form. From the ordinary, commonsense point of view, they seem full of essence. "Here," by contrast, from an enlightened perspective, things are revealed as they truly are—empty of essence:

> Here, Sariputra, form is emptiness, emptiness is form . . . Therefore, Sariputra, emptiness is not form, nor feeling, perception, impulse, nor consciousness. It is not the eye, ear, nose, tongue, body, or mind. It is not shape, sound, odor, flavor, nor object of touch or thought . . . The *bodhisattva,* bound to Transcendent Wisdom, lives with nothing clouding his mind. Lacking confusion, he is intrepid, and having passed beyond error, reaches *nirvana* . . .[11]

To speak of form being emptiness and emptiness as full of form is to use language in a way that makes rational thought very difficult. Words may lead us away from truth rather than bring us closer to it. Our attempts to explain may take us farther from what is. It may be time to use images rather than words. Buddhism also uses a web or net of interconnectedness to picture reality.

Imagine a spider web or a fishing net. At every cross point there is a jewel—perhaps it is a luminous pearl, perhaps it is a crystal. Every jewel reflects all the others; look at any one and you see the entire system. In the same way, each particle or object in the world is not merely its own existence; it also includes or involves every other particle or object. In fact, it is everything else. Known as the **Net of Indra,** this web of jewels, which is said to hang over the god Indra's palace, gives us a way to describe the interpenetration of all things.

Net of Indra *in Buddhism, an image of the world as interrelatedness and interconnectedness—pictured as a net of jewels, each of which reflects all others and itself*

Buddhism also describes the great wheel of life that turns to reveal birth-death-rebirth; life is constantly changing and the dance never ends. According to the Buddha, enlightenment means seeing things as they are, knowing that all is interconnected and that all time is the present moment:

> For consider the world—
> A bubble, a mirage.
> See the world as it is,
> And death shall overlook you.
> Come, consider the world,
> A painted chariot for kings,
> A trap for fools.
> But he who sees goes free.[12]

I am not a teacher, I am an awakener.
ROBERT FROST

Taoism: Reality as the *Tao*

Although some important differences occur between Buddhism and Taoism, they share a perspective in which reality is interconnected rather than singular, dual, or multiple. The name Taoism derives from ***Tao*** (pronounced "dow"), which is the Way, the path, the central mystery of life. The Chinese classic *Tao Te Ching* proclaims the *Tao* as beyond form and sound:

Tao *the Way, the fundamental principle of the world, the cosmic order, nature in Taoism*

> Look, it cannot be seen—it is beyond form.
> Listen, it cannot be heard—it is beyond sound.
> Grasp, it cannot be held—it is intangible . . .
> Stand before it and there is no beginning.
> Follow it and there is no end.
> Stay with the ancient *Tao*,
> Move with the present.
> Knowing the ancient beginning is the essence of *Tao*.[13]

Like the Heart Sutra, this passage emphasizes that form and sound are not the core of reality. To a greater extent than Buddhism, however, Taoism studies nature as a key source of wisdom. It is in the natural world that the workings of the mysterious *Tao* can be most easily observed. If we study nature, we can learn what is at its heart. In somewhat the same way that Aristotle brought Plato's Forms into ordinary reality, Taoism brings the heart of transcendent wisdom directly into nature.

Taoism sees everything as flowing from the *Tao,* which has two aspects or manifestations, two ways we can perceive it. The Chinese call these aspects ***yin*** and ***yang.*** *Yin* matches our holistic, intuitive, creative nature, whereas *yang* describes our linear, logical, rational nature. *Yin* and *yang* are always represented in a complementary relationship (Figure 2.3). A more accurate way of expressing these two concepts would be *yin-yang* and *yang-yin. Yin* and *yang* are two aspects of the *Tao*. It is impossible and unthinkable to have one without the other.

yin and ***yang*** *the complementary principles through which the* Tao *is expressed;* yin *reflects receptivity and being, whereas* yang *reflects activity and doing*

If you want to know the way things are, say Taoists, observe nature. The *Tao* moves the natural system with perfect efficiency. There is no forcing, no ego, no "me" versus "you." Day fades into twilight and then into night; dawn leads to day. It was ever so and ever it will be. If you want to understand what is, do not try to analyze it—dance with it!

Taoists observe that nature is wise enough to know that the Sun shines by day and the Moon by night; winter and summer each have their place, and each is birthed out of the other when the time is right. If we attune ourselves with the *Tao,* our lives can also approach this inner harmony. We will reflect the *Tao* and, at the same time, be happy. Resisting this natural rhythm is wasteful of energy and leads to unhappiness.

The miracle is not to walk on water. The miracle is to walk on the green earth in the present moment, to appreciate the peace and beauty that are available now.

THICH NHAT HANH

Appropriate, realistic behavior, according to Taoism, calls for each of us to be *yin* when *yin* is called for and *yang* when *yang* is demanded. As we awake in the morning, we will gradually leave the *yin* energy of the night and move into the *yang* energy of the day. By afternoon, however, we should begin to move around toward *yin* so that we are ready for the restful sleep that prepares us for another day of more active energy.

A person or a culture that is all *yin* or all *yang* expresses a distortion. All logic and no creativity is just as one-sided as all creativity and no logic. Life contains both aspects, and each slides effortlessly into the other when the time is appropriate—unless we intervene. Of course, we can stay in our *yang* energy way past the time of natural return to *yin*—at an all-night party or even through days of frantic activity; it is also possible to retreat into a withdrawn and inward life, with all *yin* and no *yang*.

In ancient Chinese metaphysics, the *Tao,* or the oneness, is expressed in the twoness of *yin-yang/yang-yin* and is observable as a dance of energy. The energy of the cosmos—what the Chinese call the sacred ***ch'i***—gives life to the world and to all of us who live as creatures in the world. In Chinese cosmology the relationship between heaven and Earth is envisioned as a dance of *ch'i* continually moving between them. Heaven sends forth its *yang* energy, which *yin* Earth receives and makes manifest in the 10,000 things of this world. We will amplify this idea in Chapter 8.

ch'i *[CHEE] in Taoism, the energy of the life force that flows between heaven and Earth and within nature*

Using nature imagery, the *I Ching (Book of Changes)* chronicles the ever-changing, ever the same, dance of *ch'i.* We might think of *ch'i* as a kind of breath flowing between heaven and earth. One image is that of a lake whose water evaporates into the heavens and falls as rain upon the earth. The dance of *ch'i* is like this—the heavens breathe in (draw up water), then breathe out (the water falls as rain). In the world of living things, we humans are seen as standing midway between Earth and heaven. If we are wise, we will learn to take in the life-giving, energy-producing *ch'i.*

FIGURE 2.3 T'AI CHI SYMBOL (YIN AND YANG) *The* Tao *can be thought of as the complementarity and interplay between* yin *and* yang.
By permission of Julia Measures, The Traditional Acupuncture Institute.

T'ai chi ch'uan—with its slow, graceful, yet athletically powerful martial arts movements—is one way to gather in the *ch'i.* The postures alternate between *yin* and *yang* movements, helping to balance and center by drawing in the heavenly *ch'i.* Another way is through quiet meditation, perhaps including rhythmic breathing. If you can remember how it feels to be filled with creativity and the life force, seemingly able to accomplish anything, and also how it feels to be physically, emotionally, and spiritually exhausted, with no energy to live your life, you may better appreciate why gathering *ch'i* is desirable.

If the cosmos is a great energy system and we humans occupy the middle ground between heaven and earth, then everything becomes a question of the expression and balance of energy. The Sun climbs higher and higher in the sky until at noon it stands overhead; then, inevitably and appropriately, it begins its decline. In a day, a week, a month, a year, a lifetime, there will be many of these cycles.

By honoring these cycles, rather than fighting them, Taoists say, we can use the *yin* cycle, the time of *being,* to gather *ch'i* so that when it is time for *doing* we have the *yang* energy we need. Sometimes reality is *yin,* and at these times observing nature would suggest that your best course of action is simply to *be,* to let what happens happen; at other moments reality is yang, and you are invited to *do,* to take the lead. Always remember, though, that today you may lead and tomorrow you may follow. Why waste your vital energy commanding the Sun not to rise? It is far wiser to bathe in its golden rays and wait for evening when other activities will be more appropriate.

The wisdom of the Taoist classic *Tao Te Ching* (the book of the virtue or the power of the Way) suggests conquering by yielding. If something or someone refuses to move, do not exert yourself. Be like water that seeks the lowest places and fills the shape of whatever container it is placed in but that has the power to wear away rock (by dripping relentlessly) or move a house (at flood tide):

> Yield and overcome;
> Bend and be straight;
> Empty and be full;
> Wear out and be new;
> Have little and gain;
> Have much and be confused . . .
> Be really whole,
> And all things will come to you.[14]

Like nature, much of life can seem paradoxical. A frontal assault is frequently unsuccessful, perhaps costly in lives, and always wasteful of energy. Far better to do as the trees do—bend with the wind and then stand straight for another day. The paradoxes above are known as feminine, or *yin,* paradoxes because they emphasize the strength of yielding. Notice that one of the paradoxes—"Empty and be full"—seems somewhat similar to the Heart Sutra's "Form is emptiness and emptiness is full of form."

THE MAKING OF A PHILOSOPHER

Lao-tzu
(6th century B.C.E.)

The name literally means "old master," and the truth is we are not at all sure who Lao-tzu was. There are stories of course. According to the *Historical Records,* Lao-tzu was an historian in the secret archives of Chou. He learned to work quietly and anonymously, drawing no attention to himself. Confucianism, the dominant philosophy, put great emphasis on ritual as a symbol for the orderly relations between people and god, as well as between one person and another. By the time of Lao-tzu, there was an elaborate code of conduct, containing more than 3000 rules, all of which had to be mastered by anyone hoping to succeed in politics or government. Lao-tzu represents a more mystical tradition, concerned with the oneness of the cosmos rather than rules of conduct. Legend says that Lao-tzu grew weary with society and prepared to leave Chou to live as a hermit. At the frontier, so the story goes, the official Lin Hsi urged him to write down his wisdom before departing. The result is the *Tao Te Ching*.

Materialism: Reality as Purely Material

We began this chapter by discussing the two major theories of reality as articulated by Plato and Aristotle. Even earlier, Democritus, a pre-Socratic philosopher like Thales, articulated the theory that all of reality could be described as matter in motion. Known as **materialism,** this ontology rejects the concept of Form, or Idea, altogether and insists that matter alone provides a sufficient explanation for reality. There is no need to attribute intelligence, purpose, or final causes to the universe; understanding its physical processes is sufficient. As you can see, materialism reached its fullest expression in the scientific method.

The world as understood and described by Isaac Newton and as explained philosophically by René Descartes (whom we meet in Chapter 5) appeared to be a giant machine. Moving with great precision, the world machine resembled a watch. Everything was governed by the laws of classical physics: Hit a tennis ball against a wall, and it rebounds with equal force; from tennis balls to planets, objects in motion tend to remain in motion (modified by external forces like friction and air resistance), while objects at rest tend to remain at rest (inertia).

materialism *in ontology, the belief that reality is essentially matter*

In what came to be called the "clockwork universe," every event had a cause, and all motion seemed to be clearly determined. Nothing was free and nothing was random. Moving bodies exerted force on other moving bodies, if not direct force then indirect force such as gravity. Like an intricate, well-oiled machine, the world was thus completely predictable. If we could understand all the forces, scientists and philosophers agreed, we would be able to know in advance what every object would do. There could be no surprises in the materialism of the clockwork universe.

We are the dust of long dead stars.
Or, if you want to be less romantic,
we are nuclear waste.
SIR MARTIN REES, ASTRONOMER ROYAL OF ENGLAND

Perhaps there was a divine "clockmaker" long ago who created the clockwork universe and set it in motion—perhaps not (we return to this point in Chapter 4). In any case, once in motion the universe was self-regulating. There would be no need, some said, for any divine interference. The machine would wind down slowly, according to its own rules or laws, which science was steadily uncovering and explaining. Asked by Napoleon why his system of physics, or mechanics, omitted God, Pierre LaPlace responded that God was an "unnecessary hypothesis."

For centuries materialism was the philosophical view that best corresponded with the scientific understanding of reality. As physicists brought large chunks of reality out of the realm of mystery and into the realm of science, it appeared to be only a matter of time before everything previously left to religion and philosophy could be explained by human means in materialistic terms. Materialist philosophers, like Thomas Hobbes, whose political theories we will consider in Chapter 8, could take comfort in the compatibility that appeared to exist between their philosophical explanation of reality and the theories of science.

Imagine the shock to this kind of scientific and philosophical materialism produced by quantum mechanics and relativity theory. The first jolt was the discovery that at its heart matter does not seem to be material at all. As we have seen, matter and energy now seem to be two ways of saying the same thing. Most of the atom contains nothing we could call material. It appears to be empty space but energy-charged empty space. In fact, quantum field theory tells us that only the field is real (you might think here of one already familiar type of field, the gravitational field that surrounds Earth)—and the field is energy, not matter.

What we call matter is simply a momentary manifestation of interacting fields. These interactions seem to produce particle-like matter only because the field interactions happen abruptly and in very small regions of space. What appears to us as the continual creation and destruction of particles at the subatomic level is instead the result of the continual interaction of fields. Quantum mechanics describes subatomic particles as "tendencies to exist" or "tendencies to happen." Probability expresses how likely the "tendency" is to be expressed.[15]

You don't need to leave your room
Remain sitting at your table and listen
Don't even listen, simply wait
Don't even wait
Be quite still and solitary
The world will freely offer itself to you
To be unmasked it has no choice
It will roll in ecstasy at your feet.
FRANZ KAFKA

Scientific materialism had described a world in which the order of physical law underlay the apparent chaos of ordinary experience. Newton had told the world that the same law of gravity that causes apples to fall from trees also explains the motion of planets. These laws in fact continue to hold for objects with many atoms and at relatively low speeds.

What we now know about the subatomic level, however, reveals a quite different picture—chaos underlying apparent order. The laws in operation here do not tell us what must happen (as Newton's laws do); they only say what cannot happen. There are twelve conservation laws, and according to quantum theory, everything not forbidden by those laws actually happens (has the potential for happening). Quantum theory tells us how *probable* it is that any of the many possibilities may occur.[16]

Does this mean that there is no longer any justification for being a materialist philosopher? Not necessarily. What it does mean is that the former easy correspondence between philosophical and scientific materialism has been ruptured. Instead of assuming certain "facts" about the physical universe (as Democritus and Thomas Hobbes did) and using them to construct an ontology, materialist philosophers will need to rethink what they mean by "matter."

Pragmatism: Reality as What We Can Know

We turn now to **pragmatism,** another way of looking at reality—one that had its origins in nineteenth-century America and has more radical implications for ontology than either idealism or materialism does. Unlike Plato and Aristotle, who were concerned with how things actually are, pragmatists believe this may be an unanswerable question. Like the Sophists, who took a similar position in fifth- and fourth-century B.C.E. Greece, pragmatists do not care what something is *really* like; what they do care about is how something works.

pragmatism *in ontology, the belief that what is real is what works and predicts what is likely to happen next*

Let's turn to an illustration of scientific pragmatism. Quantum field theory tells us that electromagnetic force (like the repulsion of one electron for another) is the mutual exchange of virtual photons.[17] The same thing happens with two protons (both positively charged), causing repulsion; however, when a proton (positive) and an electron (negative) exchange virtual photons, they attract one another.[18]

This nicely explains something you may have learned in a science class—that like charges repel, whereas opposite, or unlike, charges attract—but it is important to remember we are talking here about *virtual photons,* photons that are inferred mathematically (but cannot be observed because of their extremely short lives) and may or may not actually exist. Physicists readily admit that this theory, which explains attraction and repulsion in terms of the exchange of virtual particles, is only a theory. It does not necessarily tell us anything about what nature is really like, but it does help us correctly predict what nature is likely to do.

In other words, the theory may or may not be true, but it definitely works. This also captures the essence of the philosophical view of reality known as pragmatism. Right now, the scientific theory that electromagnetic force is the exchange of virtual particles matches our experience. If a better theory comes along, we will immediately adopt it. For philosophical pragmatists, it makes little or no difference what is "really real." What matters much more is what will enable us to manage the world we find ourselves in and predict, with some accuracy, what is likely to happen in it.

As far as the laws of mathematics refer to reality, they are not certain; as far as they are certain, they do not refer to reality.
ALBERT EINSTEIN

When quantum mechanics was a new field, a group of scientists working with it met in Brussels, Belgium, in 1927 to figure out what reality quantum mechanics describes. Their conclusion was shocking: It does not matter what reality it describes. The important thing is that it accurately describes what we will observe under certain conditions—in other words, it works. This is pure pragmatism, and for philosophers who apply it to their own ontological questions, it offers a clear alternative to the Greek rationalist

What would be your test?

We don't know yet about life;
How can we know about death?
CONFUCIUS

explanation of reality that began with Thales of Miletus and reached its high point with nineteenth-century science.

Most of us live our lives pragmatically. We are much more interested in what's likely to happen next than we are in a more philosophical analysis of reality. This is especially true for those who lack power and money and don't expect justice. In the epic saga of his own family history, *Rain of Gold,* Mexican-American novelist and screenwriter Victor Villaseñor tells the story of Juan Salvador, who at the age of twelve lands in jail, convicted of stealing copper from the Copper Queen Mining Company. When a "rich Mexican from Sonora" offers to give Juan's mother 200 American dollars if Juan will confess to the murder of a Texas Ranger committed by the rich man's "high-spirited son," Juan finds himself forced to think pragmatically. It may be true that in reality he is innocent of the crime and that under the law a person is innocent until proven guilty; it is also true that the money will make a huge difference for his struggling family in turn-of-the-century California:

> Juan calmed down and looked into the eyes of the old man who, it was said, owned more cattle in the State of Sonora than the rails had ties. "Your mother, look at her," he continued, "see how desperate she is. This is a terrible time for us mejicanos." He went on and on, and Juan didn't curse him and send him packing—as the gringos said—but, instead, he listened and looked at his mother and sisters and nephew

> and nieces over there by the far wall. Finally, Juan . . . spoke. "Make it five hundred in gold!"[19]

For Juan, the only reality is his desperate family and the life that $500 can buy for them. Like the virtual protons, justice may or may not exist, especially for a twelve-year-old Mexican American in the penitentiary. What is real is the situation Juan faces in his prison cell. And, for the rich man, reality looks quite different. His money can buy freedom for his "high-spirited" son. Is reality "out there" and the same for everyone? Or, must we acknowledge that the version we accept or are forced to accept as real is the only reality?

Contemporary Physics and the Nature of Reality

As we consider how Plato and Aristotle, Buddhists and Taoists, Materialists and Pragmatists view reality, some of what they say may seem very strange. Think for a moment how you would describe reality. Perhaps your own view incorporates some of the understandings about reality developed in particle physics. In the context of these explanations, Plato and Aristotle as well as Buddhists and Taoists may seem a little less strange. Even without virtual reality, science currently describes reality in dramatically different concepts from those it used 100 years ago.

Classical physics, as explained by Isaac Newton and others, described a physical universe of solid, indestructible particles moving in a void and a three-dimensional world of absolute space (length, width, and depth) that existed independent of the material objects it contained. Time was also believed to be absolute, moving at an even rate, independent of the material world. During the last 100 years, all these assumptions have been questioned and radically redefined. The laws of classical physics appear to hold only for objects containing large numbers of atoms and at velocities that are slow compared with the speed of light. In the world of the very small and the very fast, a whole new set of laws takes over that, interestingly enough, does not replace Newtonian physics but includes it.

One distinction physicists used to feel comfortable making was that between a particle and a wave. A particle is a small chunk of matter, and a wave is an expression of energy. One of the most disturbing revelations has been that light has a dual nature: Sometimes it acts like a particle, and other times it behaves like a wave. The same can be said of electrons.

In a famous experiment, called by physicist Richard Feynman "the business of the holes," electrons behaved one way if they were observed, another way if they were not. Imagine a barrier with two holes and a plate behind it to record "hits." Watched electrons, those measured by instruments, followed the expected path—they passed through one hole or the other and were stopped by the plate. If experimenters simply examined the plate, however, it seemed as if each electron had passed through both holes.

> *Nature uses only the longest threads to weave her patterns, so each small piece of her fabric reveals the organization of the entire tapestry.*
>
> **RICHARD FEYNMAN**

The conclusion: Unobserved electrons behave like waves, and part of the wave passes through each hole; observed electrons behave like particles.[20]

So, which are they *really*—particles or waves? The answer appears to be both—at different times or in different contexts. Like the Sophists, physicists appear to be affirming a radical relativism.

Quantum Mechanics

Early in this century a new subdiscipline opened up in physics that studied the behavior of particles and energy within the atom, until then thought to be the smallest possible unit of matter. This field has become known as *quantum mechanics*. Its remarkable discoveries led to a radical change in the way physicists "picture" the physical world.

It is often stated that, of all the theories proposed in this century, the silliest is quantum theory. In fact, some say that the only thing that it has going for it is that it is unquestionably correct.
MICHIU KAKU

Fundamental to classical physics are measurements of both position (where something is) and momentum (how fast it is moving, but also how big it is and in which direction it is moving). If we know your car is moving at 60 miles an hour, we can mark your position and project 60 miles ahead along the road. If you maintain your present momentum, in an hour's time you will have moved 60 miles farther. Your new position will be at the 60-mile mark we made earlier.

In the world of the very small, however, it turns out we can take one of these two measurements but not both. The more accurately we know the position of an electron, for example, the less accurately we can speak about its momentum. Measure its momentum accurately, and we sacrifice certainty about its position. Developed by Werner Heisenberg, this *uncertainty principle* affirms that we can know something about both measurements, but in doing so we have to give up any hope of precision in both cases. In the world of quantum mechanics, we must speak in probabilities rather than certainties. To paraphrase one of Albert Einstein's most quoted remarks, it is as if God were playing dice with the universe.

Relativity Theory

Along with the very small, studying the world of the very large—the realm of planets, stars, and galaxies—has also brought about a revolution in physics. Whereas quantum mechanics challenged the idea that the universe obeys rigid and precisely knowable laws, Albert Einstein's famous *theory of relativity* challenged the absolute reality of time and space described by Newton. In Einstein's theory, time and space are not two separate things but two aspects of the same thing. In fact, physicists now speak about a four-dimensional continuum—the three dimensions of space plus time. As Gary Zukav explains it, in a continuum there are no breaks—one unity flows continuously:

> The Newtonian view of space and time is a *dynamic* picture. Events *develop* with the passage of time. Time is one-dimensional and . . .

1997 World Series: First pitch exceeds the speed of light

If time and space are relative rather than absolute, interesting things are possible.

> past, present, and future happen in that order. The special theory of relativity, however, says that it is preferable, and more useful, to think in terms of a *static,* non-moving picture of space and time. This is the space-time continuum. In this static picture, the space-time continuum, events do not develop, they just are. If we could view our reality in a four-dimensional way . . . we would see all, the past, the present, and the future with one glance.[21]

Like the prisoners in Plato's cave, using our senses, we can experience only the "shadows" of a three-dimensional world, but we "know" the world is really four dimensional. We might remember that Buddhism holds a similar view of time. In a sense, all time is the present moment, and realizing this is a step toward enlightenment.

According to relativity theory, there is nothing absolute about either space or time. Universal time, for instance, does not exist. The only meaningful way to speak about time is to limit your remarks to time as it appears to unfold for a particular observer. Different observers may have conflicting experiences, since at sufficiently great relative speeds, time seems to slow down (relative to the point of view of an observer at rest) as you (the observed) speed up.

Einstein illustrated his theory with paradoxes like the following. One of your parents could board a spaceship and travel at a high rate of speed for what, to him or her, is a year. When the space ship returns, fifty years might have passed for you—and you could find yourself older than your parent! Time will have moved at one rate of speed for your parent and at another rate for you. Absolute time, as we used to think about it before relativity, does not exist.

In the new world depicted by relativity theory, the only constant is the speed of light. Light always travels about 186,000 miles a second, and this figure is an absolute "speed limit" for the entire universe. When astronomers talk about a light-year, they mean the distance light can travel in a year, at 186,000 miles a second. Given this understanding, what does it mean to talk about "now"?

Suppose you say "The Sun is shining now." In actuality, because light takes time to travel, you are not seeing the Sun as it is "now," but as it was about eight minutes ago. Even more dramatically, your view of the night sky is a snapshot of the past rather than a glimpse of the present. Some of the light you see left its star centuries ago. If you have ever seen the Andromeda Galaxy, the light that fell on your eyes started its journey long before human life appeared on Earth. And Andromeda is the nearest galaxy to our own.

Time and space, once thought to be separate, appear to be related aspects of reality that occupy one continuum. Similarly, energy and matter were once believed to be distinct. Albert Einstein's most famous equation, $E = mc^2$, gives us the startling information that E (the energy contained in matter) equals m (its mass) times c (the speed of light) squared. In other words, under certain conditions, energy converts to matter and vice versa. This change of state happens routinely at the subatomic level, and we now understand that stars shine by converting matter into energy, following the relationship described in Einstein's equation.

String Theory

What physicists are looking for and all of us would be happy to hear about is a grand explanatory principle, often referred to the Theory of Everything (T.O.E.) that would tie everything we know about the cosmos together. The difficulty is that, although both quantum mechanics and general relativity—the two foundations of modern physics—are both highly predictive, they are also mutually incompatible. As they are currently formulated, Brian Greene, in his wonderfully lucid book *The Elegant Universe* claims, "general relativity and quantum mechanics cannot both be right."[22] Fortunately, a relative newcomer—superstring theory—resolves the tension between them. In fact, within the new framework of superstring theory, "general relativity and quantum mechanics require one another for the theory to make sense."[23] Although it will require a radical reformulation of the way in which we understand space, time, and matter, string theory has vast explanatory potential. In fact, Greene claims that string theory may be able to show us ". . . that all of the wondrous happenings in the universe—from the frantic dance of subatomic quarks to the stately waltz of orbiting binary stars, from the primordial fireball of the big bang to the majestic swirl of heavenly galaxies—are reflections of one grand physical principle, one master equation."[24]

The current conflict between general relativity and quantum mechanics is actually the third major conflict that, over the last two centuries, has brought us to our current understanding of the world. Einstein's theory of special relativity resolved the conflict between Isaac Newton's laws of motion, which indicate that at a fast enough speed one could catch up with a departing beam of light, and James Clerk Maxwell's laws of electromagnetism, according to which this is impossible because light waves (a particular kind of electromagnetic wave) never slow down. Light waves always travel at light speed—about 186,000 miles per second. By realizing that space and time are not universal concepts, experienced in the same way by everyone, but rather constructs that show up differently depending on one's state of motion, Einstein, through his theory of special relativity, was able to resolve this first conflict into a higher unity.[25] The second conflict arose because one of the findings of special relativity is that nothing can travel faster than the speed of light, whereas Newton's universal theory of gravitation postulates the instantaneous transmission of gravity over millions of miles of space. Einstein's 1915 general theory of relativity resolved this conflict by theorizing that, if space and time can warp and curve in response to the presence of matter or energy, then these distortions can account for the transmission of gravity from one location to another.[26]

However, as in the previous case, resolving one conflict has led to another. How can we mesh the "gently curving geometrical form of space emerging from general relativity" with the "frantic, roiling, microscopic behavior of the universe implied by quantum mechanics"?[27] Superstring theory, or string theory for short, emerged in the mid-1980s as a resolution for this conflict. According to string theory, if we could examine so-called elementary particles, with much greater precision than is now possible, we would discover that, instead of being pointlike, each of these consists of a tiny one-dimensional loop—"a vibrating, oscillating, dancing filament that physicists . . . have named a string."[28] Different patterns of vibration produce what appear to us as various kinds of particles [such as quarks] as well as what appear to us as the various forces of nature—in other words, everything is unified under the theoretical framework of a spectrum of "notes" (to speak metaphorically) that strings can play. Strings themselves appear to be fundamental—that is, they don't resolve into any constituent ingredients. Whether they interact smoothly, as general relativity seems to suggest, or chaotically, as quantum mechanics indicates, depends on the frequency with which they oscillate. String theory itself may actually be part of an even grander synthesis of everything, currently called M-theory.[29]

Science and Physical Reality

If, as physicists theorize, space and time are unified, matter equals energy, and electrons, like light, can be both particles and waves, what then is physical reality? Subatomic particles, the so-called building blocks of matter, seem to be more like bundles of energy (remember this when we study Leibniz in Chapter 5), and everything in the universe appears to be connected with everything else. Perhaps only strings can be described as basic or fundamental, and there are no "building blocks" in the Newtonian sense of that term.

Like early Greek metaphysics, classical physics tells us that we get to know something by standing outside it and observing it. Quantum mechan-

When we open our eyes each morning, it is upon a world we have spent a lifetime learning *to see. We are not given the world: we make our world through incessant experience, categorization, memory, reconnection.*
OLIVER SACKS

To observe the very small is to change it.

"Dilbert," reprinted by permission of UFS, Inc.

ics challenges this commonsense view of things, insisting that the "something" we observe is not really there until we observe it. Although this is true at the subatomic level, one question that arises is, When does it stop being true? In other words, when is a system large enough to be described by the rules of classical rather than quantum mechanics? In a famous thought experiment, a cat is put into a box with a vial of poison gas that will either be released or not released depending on a random occurrence (the radioactive decay of an atom). The question is, What has happened to the cat?[30]

Classical Newtonian physics (or mechanics) responds that either the cat is alive or the cat is dead; all we have to do is open the box to find out which. Quantum mechanics disagrees, insisting that the fate of the cat is not determined *until* we look into the box. The cat is neither alive nor dead until we observe it. According to one theory, at the moment we open the box, one possibility is reinforced and becomes an actuality (the cat is alive or the cat is dead), and the other possibility disappears. According to another theory, when we open the box, the world splits in two. In one world, the cat is alive; in the other, the cat is dead.

Star Trek: The Next Generation based an entire episode around the theory of parallel universes—a theory that is being seriously proposed by some physicists. Returning from a tournament, the Klingon officer Worf records a personal diary, documenting his victory. Back home on the starship *Enterprise,* however, strange things begin to happen. In another version of reality, he placed ninth. Scenes repeat with varying results and varying casts of characters as the universe continues to split into parallel worlds.

Although the cat paradox is intended to show that the theories of quantum mechanics cannot be applied to large objects—say, the size of a cat—things are apparently quite puzzling and paradoxical in the world of the very small (smaller than the size of an atom). At this subatomic level, the ancient distinction between observer and observed, between knower and known breaks down. As Gary Zukav explains,

> The new physics tells us that an observer cannot observe without altering what he sees. Observer and observed are interrelated in a real and fundamental sense . . . and there is a growing body of evidence that the distinction between the "in here" and the "out there" is illusion . . . In short, what we experience is not external reality, but our interaction with it.[31]

What we call reality is an agreement that people have arrived at to make life more livable.
LOUISE NEVELSON

To many thoughtful people, the implications of the new physics are extraordinary. Our minds cannot think about reality; they can think only about *our ideas about reality.* Have we then reached the limits of rational thought? For Western philosophers, the insights of contemporary physics raise ontological questions. If there is no observation without alteration, one metaphysical question is, How do we talk about what is real? Thales' assumption that there is a rational self capable of observing and understanding an intelligible cosmos seems less clear, and perhaps less self-evident, than it once did.

Cosmology: Is There Order and Purpose in the Universe?

Besides ontology, or the nature of reality, metaphysics is also concerned with cosmology, investigation of the principles underlying the cosmos. Like the questions of ontology, those of cosmology touch on what is real and what is not. Did the universe come into being at some point in time, or has it always existed? Will it one day end? Is there a set of unalterable laws governing the universe? Is everything working toward some purpose or end, or are events random and meaningless?

Greek Cosmology

The idea that order and purpose exist falls under the heading **teleology** (from the Greek word *telos,* meaning "end" or "purpose"). Before the Milesian philosophers, the gods and goddesses had represented the *telos.* Events might be unpredictable, but they were not random. Earthquakes could be traced to the god Poseidon and rainbows to the goddess Iris. Violent weather only indicated that the all-too-human Olympians were once again quarreling among themselves. Many of the pre-Socratic philosophers explicitly addressed themselves to how things came into being, changed form, and passed away—and they specifically excluded heavenly explanations.

teleology *the theory that there is order and purpose in reality*

To speak, as Thales did, of the earth floating on water was to offer water turbulence in place of an angry Poseidon to account for earthquakes. When Anaximenes explained the rainbow as the result of the Sun's rays falling on dense air, he also dethroned the goddess Iris. Protagoras, whom you may

PHILOSOPHERS SPEAK FOR THEMSELVES
Aristotle: The Four Causes

"Cause" means [1] the material from which something is made—for instance the bronze that made possible the statue or the silver from which the plate was crafted. (We might say that metals are the material causes of these beautiful objects). [2] the form or pattern according to which something is made. (We might say that the ratio 2:1 and number in general are the formal causes of the musical octave). [3] that from which a change begins or ceases. For instance, the adviser is a cause of the action, the father is a cause of the child and, in general, the maker is a cause of the thing made. (We might say that the one who makes a change is the efficient cause of the change). [4] the end or that for which a thing exists. For example, health is the cause of walking. Why does one walk? We say one walks in order to be healthy and, in saying this, we believe we have stated the cause. We speak in a similar way about all the various means that might be employed along the way to reach the general end of health—for example, dieting or purging or instruments might intervene before health is reached. All these are for the sake of the end, though they differ from one another in that some are instruments and others actions. (We might speak of all of them as final causes . . .).

Metaphysics, Book V, Chapter 2

recall from Chapter 1, was also not prepared to attribute what happened in the universe to the actions of the gods and goddesses. "As to the gods," Protagoras said, "I have no means of knowing . . ." whether or not they exist.[32]

relativism *the view that truth has no objective standard and may vary from individual to individual, from group to group, and from time to time*

The **relativism** introduced by the Sophists challenged the idea that there was an objective, absolute reality and an implied moral order. Plato had certainly believed in such an order. In his Kingdom of Ideas, the perfect prototypes existed in all their splendor. Perfect Justice might not exist here on Earth, but it was available for contemplation by those who learned to cultivate their reason. The highest and purest of his Forms—the Idea of the Good—established moral standards against which particular acts might be measured. To know the Good, he and Socrates maintained, would be to do the good: "And no one can deny that all beings who have apprehension of the good hunt after it, and are eager to catch it and wear it about them, and care not for the attainment of anything which is not accompanied by good."[33]

Aristotle was even more explicit on the subject of the *telos.* Scientific inquiry, he insisted, must concern itself with the four varieties of causes that together account for observed order. If we imagine a statue of Aristotle, we can identify and describe the causes that ultimately bring it into being. First, there is the *material cause,* the material from which the statue will be made. Let's suppose it will be made of wood. Second, there must be an *efficient cause* by which the statue comes into being—in this case, the wood-carver who makes it. The *formal cause* of the statue conveys its essence. It is in fact a statue of Aristotle. Last, there is a *final cause*—its end, or reason for being. Let us imagine this particular statue is one of a pair designed as bookends (the other is Plato).

Knowing what we know about Plato's belief in a separate world of perfect Forms, it is not surprising that Plato found in the world of Forms a moral order with implications for everything and everyone. The Form of the Good defines goodness and issues a call to goodness, which those who use their reason will naturally seek to answer. Aristotle, the more down to earth of the two, was concerned with describing what he saw in the ordinary life of Athens. His four causes accounted for scientific order and demonstrated that events and processes are not random. Observing what occurs will reveal an underlying order.

As we will see in the next Historical Interlude, Christianity began with a Hebrew worldview but defined its theology in the Greek world, using Greek words and Greek concepts. The Greek idea of the *logos,* or rational principle of the universe, described by Heraclitus and other early thinkers, came to be associated with Jesus as early missionaries tried to explain his uniqueness. The concept of the *telos* has deep resonance in Western culture, not only for religious thinkers who see in God the end and purpose of the universe and human life but also for many who simply affirm the inherent intelligibility of the cosmos.

Quantum Theory and Astronomy

It can be difficult to make judgments from within the system.

"Dim Wits" by David Rogers from the *Harvard Crimson.* Reprinted by permission of David Rogers.

For those accustomed to thinking the world a comprehensible place, the theories of quantum mechanics can be unsettling. Assuming what we now know about the world of the very small and very fast, teleology may seem less obvious and self-evident than it did to the ancient Greeks. Let's look now at the world of the large and slow. On the scale of solar systems and galaxies, what does modern science have to say about cosmology?

Speculating about the origin of the universe, most astronomers support a theory that has come to be called the *big bang.* According to this theory, all the matter in the universe was once compressed by gravity into a molten ball. Under constantly increasing pressure, the ball of matter collapsed on itself as temperatures reached unbelievable levels, and then exploded in a big bang. This will continue until there is no more heat or light left in the system, and the universe will die or reverse itself at some point, producing what some have called the "big crunch."

According to current theory, as the energy produced by the big bang expanded and cooled, it condensed into equal amounts of matter and antimatter. Antimatter atoms are like regular atoms except that their particles have electrical charges opposite those in regular matter. Regular protons are positive, whereas antiprotons are negative. When matter meets antimatter, the result is mutual annihilation. So, why is there any matter at all—why didn't everything annihilate everything else immediately following the big bang? According to a complicated theory, for every billion particle-antiparticle pairs, there was one extra particle. Matter as we know it owes its existence to that. To make things a bit more interesting, in May 1997 astronomers from Northwestern University identified a "fountain" of antimatter 3000 light-years long, spewing into space from the center of our Milky Way Galaxy. They aren't sure how this antimatter is being created.[34]

Even stranger is the theory that as much as 90 percent of the universe is composed of dark matter, matter that can't be seen but must exist to account for what we observe if our current explanations are correct. For instance, galaxies should be rapidly flying apart unless the gravity produced by vast quantities of unseen mass, or dark matter, is holding them together. What this theory would predict is the scattering and random clumping of galaxies throughout space. According to actual observations made by Harvard's Margaret Geller and John Huchra, however, galaxies sometimes line up in ribbons or (strangest of all) align themselves into what appears to be a giant stick figure. Surrounding these structures are voids—regions with no galaxies at all.[35]

Each galaxy represents a collection of stars, like our Sun (perhaps with planets and moons), and appears as a pearly luminous light in the darkness of space. Gravitation is widely believed to be the only force acting on these galaxies, but gravitation tends to draw objects into roughly spherical clusters. The sheets of galaxies astronomers are finding look more like soapsuds or a sponge. Are there natural laws we do not yet understand, or are our current theories simply wrong? Will dark matter ultimately account for an increasingly perplexing set of observations, or is there something else we don't know about at work?

At the scale of the very large, we meet the same dilemma as in the world of the very small. There is very little we can say with certainty. In describing our corner of the vast universe, it is difficult to know whether we are describing only a local condition or saying something valuable about the universe as a whole. To the person who lives in the desert, the world appears one way; another person who lives on a lush green mountain sees it otherwise; the houseboat dweller disagrees with both.

When astronomers thought the distribution of galaxies was more or less uniform, hope of understanding the universe as a whole grew. If the universe were homogeneous throughout, examining one section could tell us much of what we want to know about the whole. We might avoid the problem of the three blindfolded people examining the elephant, each of whom described a very different animal. Now that we think the universe, which may be infinite in nature, is quite ununiform, what can we say about cosmology?[36]

Does the apparent order (represented by galaxies lining up in ribbons or as stick figures) in our corner of the galaxy signify a cosmic order? If galaxies appear not to be obeying the law of gravity, what are we missing? Will the universe expand until all its energy dissipates (as the big bang theory suggests), or will it at some point reverse itself and begin to contract, leading the whole process to begin again with another big bang? As in all good science and philosophy, there are many more questions than there are answers.

The Possibility of Eternal Dimensions

As we discussed earlier, the idea of *telos* is an enduring one in the Western philosophical tradition. For people with a religious worldview, order and purpose flow from a divine creator-lawgiver. In this final section we explore four views of reality as tinged with eternal dimensions. Neoplatonism combines Plato's cosmology with a mystical spirituality; Seneca, African, and African-American religious worldviews describe a sacred cosmos.

Hypatia of Alexandria and Neoplatonism

Astronomy was one of the passions of Hypatia who lived in Alexandria, Egypt, during the fifth century C.E. For her, as for her philosophical and scientific contemporaries, astronomy, mathematics, and physics seemed the most direct route to understanding the cosmos and the place of humans within it.

Best known for her commentaries on the great mathematical works of her time, Hypatia also taught philosophy. Although none of her philosophical works survives, we are able to reconstruct the *Neoplatonism* she taught from letters written by her students. One of these students, Synesius, discovered in the Neoplatonism he learned from Hypatia a way to reconcile pagan Greek philosophy with Christianity. Other historical figures, including the more famous Christian convert Augustine of Hippo (discussed in Historical Interlude C), also found Neoplatonism to be an essential link.

Articulated in the Christian era by Plotinus, an Egyptian who had studied in Alexandria in the third century, Neoplatonism combined Plato's idealism with a mystical spirituality compatible with Christianity. According to its philosophy, the Supreme Deity is One and unknowable by humans in any direct way. Everything else derives from the One by way of emanations that flow from the One but are not the One.

The first of these is ***nous*** (the Greek word for "mind"), which unites the multiplicity of ideas. *Nous* emanates a world soul, which brings both the universe and sentient beings into existence. Whereas *nous* is holy, matter is evil, and humans—having parts of each—are a mixture of evil and holiness. Choosing to identify with the evil, sensual side of one's nature was always a possibility. But, by subduing it, a person could aspire to mystical union with the universal *nous*. This ethical path would lead to divine truth and an ultimate return to the One.[37]

nous *[NOOS] Greek for "mind," expressing the rationality of the cosmos*

Although this is clearly a pagan philosophy, lacking all the specifics of Christian revelation, it is also compatible with Christianity because it stipulates an eternal, spiritual dimension to the world and to the human person. Neoplatonism affirmed the compatibility of Greek rationalist thought and Hebrew religious thought (the original basis for Christianity), which we will examine in Historical Interlude B. Plato's idealism had assumed a cosmos with moral order and an immortal human soul. What Neoplatonism offered later seekers after truth was a solid intellectual transition from the power of Greek philosophy to the intellectual power of Christianity. For Neoplatonists, as for Christians, the cosmos has a divine dimension.

Synesius, whose study of Neoplatonism under the exclusive direction of Hypatia prepared him to accept Christianity, had traveled from Cyrene to Alexandria about the year 393 for the privilege of learning from her.[38] Synesius remained devoted to Hypatia for the rest of his life, writing letters

THE MAKING OF A PHILOSOPHER

Hypatia of Alexandria
(c. 355–415)

Hypatia was born in Alexandria, Egypt, when it was the intellectual center of the Western world and spent all her life there. Its museum and library were centers for scientific, mathematical, and philosophical study, presided over by her father Theon. From him she probably learned mathematics and astronomy, and she seems to have collaborated with her father in scholarly work in these two fields. Best known for her commentaries on mathematical works, Hypatia was also respected and loved as a teacher of philosophy and a model of the philosophical life. By the early 390s, she was teaching Neoplatonism to a circle of students who came from Alexandria and other parts of Egypt, as well as from more distant cities. At least one of them, Synesius of Cyrene, later became a Christian and a bishop. She remained a virgin throughout her life and wore the simple tribon, or coarse robe, used by ascetics. Both she and her school of philosophy seemed to coexist peacefully with Christian church leaders until 415 when a mob murdered her and burned her body, believing they were carrying out the wishes of Cyril, Bishop of Alexandria. Eventually, a tide of antipaganism led to the burning of the great library.

to his revered teacher and seeking her opinion—even though Hypatia remained a pagan and Synesius became first a Christian and then a bishop. In a letter to a friend, Synesius writes: "Salute for me the most holy and revered philosopher [Hypatia], and give my homage also to the company of the blessed who delight in her oracular utterance."[39]

In a letter to Hypatia, Synesius describes a book he has felt compelled to write and asserts his unwillingness to accept the criticism of fanatics:

> There are certain men among my critics whose effrontery is only surpassed by their ignorance, and these are the readiest of all to spin out discussions concerning God. Whenever you meet them, you have to listen to their babble about inconclusive syllogisms . . . The rest, who have more taste, are, as sophists, much more unfortunate than these . . . Their philosophy consists in a very simple formula, that of calling God to witness, as Plato did, whenever they deny anything or whenever they assert anything . . .[40]

For Synesius, the only kind of Christianity he could ultimately accept would have to be compatible both with Greco-Roman culture and with his own philosophical analysis of reality and truth. One of the most exemplary aspects of Hypatia's school was its tolerance for religious diversity. Jews, Christians, and pagans all studied philosophy under her direction. Each of these traditions was acknowledged to contain some aspect of the truth, but it was understood that complete truth could be reached only through the study of philosophy, which must retain "its primacy as both the key to the riddles of the universe and the path of the soul's salvation."[41]

The true philosopher would have to reserve the right to evaluate even Christian doctrine in the light of philosophical truth. Although Synesius was able to find in the emanations of Neoplatonism an image for the Christian Trinity of Father, Son, and Holy Spirit, he remained absolutely committed to philosophy and only provisionally committed to Christianity. That is, he embraced Christian doctrine only to the extent that he could reconcile it with Neoplatonism. Augustine of Hippo, by contrast, used Neoplatonism as a bridge and, once across it, asserted Christianity as his touchstone for judging all other systems of belief. For Augustine, philosophy's proper role was as the "handmaid of theology."

Synesius, by contrast, remained fiercely loyal to Hypatia, whom he regarded as the personification of philosophy—a person who lived her life devoted to the pursuit of perfection and a search for the divine motivated by the love of wisdom. Under her influence he became convinced that "philosophy is the highest way to the divine." Throughout his life and especially in times of emotional or spiritual crisis, it was Hypatia to whom Synesius turned for guidance and insight.[42] Regarding the book he had written, Synesius left the final decision to Hypatia:

> Concerning all this I shall await your decision. If you decree that I ought to publish my book, I will dedicate it to orators and philosophers together. The first it will please, and to the others it will be useful, provided of course that it is not rejected by you, who are really able to pass

If stones like these could speak, what might we learn from them?
Stonehenge/Photo by Fred Espenak, Photo Researchers, Inc.

> judgment. If it does not seem to you worthy of Greek ears, if, like Aristotle, you prize truth more than friendship, a close and profound darkness will overshadow it, and mankind will never hear it mentioned.[43]

The Peoples of the Americas: A Sacred Cosmos

The identification of matter with evil and of spirit with good that we have just seen in Neoplatonism is typical of the Greek rationalist view of the cosmos. Matter is identified as separate from mind or spirit and as occupying an inferior role. In contrast, Native American cosmology tends to see everything—matter and spirit—as holy.

One of the six members of the Iroquois Confederation of Nations, the Seneca tribe believed the cosmos to be sacred and captured the oneness and the holiness of all things in a creation myth. "Other Council Fires Were Here Before Ours" is a reminder to us "Two-leggeds" (human creatures) that we are not the first. Before us were our Ancestors, before them were the Creature-beings and Plant People, and before them the Stone Tribe. Even the stones are holy and have much to teach us. By letting go of the spiritual arrogance that insists only the Two-leggeds have access to wisdom, we can learn from other life-forms.

The creation myth is narrated by a member of the Stone Tribe:

> Our Earth-forged bodies have been fashioned from the erupting heat of volcanic creation and the ice-blue cold that tempers our ancient spirits . . . From other Stone People who have fallen from the Great Star Nation [meteorites, for example], we have learned much of other galaxies . . . We have many stories to tell the Children of Earth about the worlds that came before the written histories of the Two-legged humans.[44]

Even the stones are a source of wisdom. Notice how the language in parts of this story mirrors the energy dance described by both Taoism and particle physics and the interconnectedness described by the Buddhist Net of Indra while it affirms the beauty and holiness in every aspect of creation.

Before creation, the Stone Tribe speaker recalls existing in the vastness and total darkness of the Void, fearless and aware of ecstasy in merging with the Original Source: "Great Mystery, you live in me as in all other thoughts here in the emerging Void."[45] Creation was an eruption of brightness in the inky blackness:

> A cloudlike substance began to arise and encircle Eternal Land as Great Mystery [Swenio] created the Field of Plenty. All that would ever be needed in Creation began as patterns of light and thought . . . I felt the goodness and beauty of every new part of Creation as each emerged. Patterns of color traveled through the mists uniting and dancing with one another in endless space.[46]

All creation occurs out of the Field of Plenty as Swenio, Great Mystery, rolls some of its matter into spheres and breathes upon them to give them physicality. Like Yahweh, the Creator God of Genesis, Swenio begins with Grandfather Sun, whose golden light was to be a reminder to all that each "carried a part of the Eternal Flame of Great Mystery's love," and Grandmother Moon, whose mission was to weave emotions into dreams as we slept.[47]

A "swirling blue-green orb of light" became Mother Earth, and from inside her body the Stone Tribe narrator watched the rest of Creation as "Swenio continued to arrange patterns of eternal beauty and set them in motion, dancing and playing throughout the Void . . . Eternal Land was an indivisible Uni-world created in wholeness as a unified expression of Swenio's love."[48]

Notice here the themes of oneness and goodness, as well as the playful dance of energy. Each part of Creation is endowed with equality and wholeness, wisdom, love, and beauty, along with life. Like Buddhism and Taoism, this creation story emphasizes interdependence and interconnectedness. There is the familiar pulse of energy we now associate with quantum mechanics, as well as Taoism, and a joyous interplay of light and color.

Like the Genesis creation story—accepted by Judaism, Christianity, and Islam—everything is created good and endowed with love. Unlike Genesis, there is no Fall, no loss of goodness. And there is a noticeable lack of hierarchy such as we find in Genesis—inert objects (like stones), plants, animals and, at the top, humans. Instead, each aspect of Creation is affirmed as holy and valuable with its own wisdom to teach.

Sinik *(sleeps) is not a distance, not a number of days or hours. It is both a spatial and a temporal phenomenon, a concept of space-time that describes the union of space and motion and time that is taken for granted by Inuits but that cannot be captured by ordinary speech in any European language.*

PETER HØEG, *SMILLA'S SENSE OF SNOW*

There is also a remarkable similarity with the worldview of current physics. The quantum field, which is the only reality, produces what appear to be particles. Like the Field of Plenty in the Seneca myth, the quantum field is the source of all creation. It is a dance of light and energy, capable of appearing as matter under the right conditions. One significant difference, however, is that quantum physics attributes the movement of subatomic particles to pure chance.

This is how Chris-in-the-Morning, the philosopher-deejay of K-BEAR in Cicely, Alaska (on the TV series *Northern Exposure*), describes the new "magic" science has discovered:

> When we think of a magician, the image that comes to mind is Merlin—long white beard, cone-shaped hat—you know. Well, in one version of the Arthurian legend, this archetypal sorcerer retires, checks out of the conjuring business. His reason? The rationalists are taking over. The time for magic is coming to an end.
>
> Well, ol' Merlin should've stuck around, 'cause those same rationalists, trying to put a rope around reality, found themselves in the psychedelic land of physics . . . a place that refuses to play by Newtonian rules, that refuses to play by any rules at all—a place much better suited to the Merlins of the world.[49]

The Seneca myth attributes the appearance of matter out of the Field of Plenty not to chance or to magic but to the loving creative act of Swenio, the Great Mystery. All of creation is consciously and caringly done by an intelligent creator who has a plan, who first makes the pattern (somewhat like a Platonic ideal) and then the matter to express it. The Seneca cosmos is sacred and everything in it, both matter and spirit, is holy.

An African View of a Sacred Cosmos

We can find something similar in African thought. Although there are of course many differences among the indigenous people of Africa with respect to metaphysics, a number of similarities in concept and belief underlie the differences. One of these is that, in traditional African society, all of life is seen as an integrated whole. Nature, living things, humans, the ancestors, and a supreme being or beings all share in one world, a world to which all of them equally belong.

Even the Niger River must flow around an island.
HAUSA PROVERB

There is a hierarchy of being, beginning with inanimate objects, continuing through plants, lower animals, and humans to the ancestors and arriving at a supreme being or beings at the top. Not all beings are conceived as equal—as described in the Seneca creation myth, for instance—but they occupy different parts of one comprehensive universe. This is in contrast with the traditional Judaic and Christian concept of a natural order and a supernatural deity. In that system, God—who exists outside the natural order—makes a decision and creates a world out of nothing.

If the Creator and the created share the cosmos, everything in it is sacred.
KanKouran West African Dance Company/Courtesy of Siegel Artist Management and KanKouran West African Dance Company.

Among the Akan people of Ghana, traditional thought tells us that God created the world because it was in the nature of God to create. Creation was not a willful act undertaken after careful thought and decision making. Looking for why creation occurred is in fact a waste of time. As a famous drum text asks:

> Who gave word,
> Who gave word,
> Who gave word,
> Who gave word to Hearing,
> For Hearing to have told the Spider,
> For the Spider to have told the Creator,
> For the Creator to have created things?[50]

Who told the Creator to create? This is an unanswerable question. Reasons always demand other reasons and then the reason behind those reasons. Creation occurred because of the nature of the Creator. "The creator created the world by the very law of his own being"[51] and, like all of creation, is subject to its laws. The Akan deity can accomplish any well-defined task but cannot violate the laws of the cosmos in which all beings (including the Creator) live. (For more about the nature of the Akan deity, see Chapter 4.)

In the Akan system, creation itself is not creation out of nothing, as in the Judaic and Christian system. Instead, creation is seen more as a process of transformation. Out of some unstructured stuff, already present, the Creator fashions order. If the stuff of creation is already present, we have a system a little like Plato's view of the creation of human souls, as found in the *Timaeus*:

> Having said this, he turned once more to the same mixing bowl wherein he had mixed and blended the soul of the universe, and poured into it what was left of the former ingredients, blending them this time in somewhat the same way, only no longer so pure as before . . .[52]

If the Creator and the unstructured stuff inhabit the same world, creation, seen as transformation, does nothing to separate them. There is no distinction in the Akan system between the natural order—the world and its inhabitants, both animate and inanimate—and a supernatural one. There is only *one* order. Another way of saying this is that the Creator and the created share this world.

This is the sense in which the traditional Akan cosmos might be thought of as sacred. In it, both the Creator and the created exist. There is a sense of continuity among all the parts, and if causes appropriate to one part do not explain what is happening, then it makes sense to turn to causes pertaining to another part. If, despite the best medicines and psychological interventions, an illness persists, a traditional Akan might turn to the world of ancestors and assume that one of them is punishing the patient.

There is no sense of going outside a natural explanation in search of a supernatural one. If, as the Akan believe, there is a good explanation for everything, then an explanation must be found. The patient who remains ill clearly remains ill for a reason. If the interventions of one area do not work, the next logical step would be to turn to another area in search of a cause and perhaps a cure. "By the Akan definition of the universe, everything is a regular part of the system of reality."[53]

African-American Christianity and the Sacred Cosmos

African-American Christianity, forged under slavery, fuses the concept of a sacred cosmos that underlies traditional African thought with the orthodox beliefs of Christianity. Taught by their white owners of the Judaic and Christian God who creates and saves, African-American slaves, to varying degrees, integrated that teaching into the traditional African worldview they had brought with them. Often it was a question of where to place the emphasis.

Independent black churches, which existed during slavery, as well as the informal and secret gatherings of African-American Christians, often stressed the personal involvement of God in history and the role of God as liberator of the oppressed. To slaves the story of the Jews as captives in Egypt had a very different resonance than it did for those who held them in bondage. Similarly, the central Christian concept that the God of the universe took human form in Jesus—suffering, dying, but ultimately triumphing over suffering and death—had special meaning for those who felt oppression in their bodies and souls.

At the heart of the African-American sacred cosmos was the notion of freedom. Dr. Martin Luther King's "jubilant cry of 'Free at last, free at last, thank God Almighty, we are free at last,' echoed the understanding black folk always had with the Almighty God whose impatience with unfreedom matched their own."[54] Denied citizenship by the Constitution, African-American slaves who were also Christians understood that their religion opposed discrimination, even if white Christian churches did not.

Between the seventeenth and nineteenth centuries in the United States, evangelical revivals swept the country, in what were called Great Awakenings. Through the deeply life-changing experience of conversion, people were led through acknowledgment of personal sinfulness to an emotional experience of salvation. Being "born again" meant changing one's orientation to life and, for many African Americans, that involved the recognition of a sacred cosmos.

Religion always expresses itself in cultural forms. The music and song, modes of worship, and the style and content of preaching have a unique form in most black churches regardless of their denomination. W. E. B. Du Bois, describing his visits to black churches in the South, emphasized the intensity of feeling and the open display of emotions he observed. Some shouted; others rolled on the floor, possessed by the Spirit; people stood in their pews, clapping in time with the music and calling approval or encouragement to the preacher.

As in Athenian tragedies and African rituals, the participants sought both catharsis (emotional cleansing) and transcendence (the ability to step outside the ordinary world of space and time)—in the American case, a period of intense intimacy with God. Ecstatic religious experience came to be one of the marks of a black sacred cosmos that cut across denominational lines. First Baptists and Methodists, but eventually even Roman Catholics, incorporated a unique religious experience into their worship. Most black churches, regardless of denomination, have a "qualitatively different cultural form of expressing Christianity."[55]

Seeing the cosmos as holy provides a strong sense of *telos*. If God is in charge, whatever happens will ultimately weave itself (or be woven) into a divine plan. This can provide a very comforting cosmology. Regarding all things as sacred also sets up a sense of unity, an ontology of shared being. In a sacred cosmos there is no hierarchy, such as we find in the writings of Plato and Aristotle, with reason on top and the body on the bottom. All is holy. All is blessed.

Summary

Across cultures and nations, the big questions of metaphysics remain the same: What is real, and how can I tell what is real from what is not? What is the cosmos like, and is it characterized by order and purpose or by randomness and chaos? Is God watching over everything, or does God play dice with the universe? Is there a divine being at all?

In the West we have been very influenced by the division of the world into Form and matter first given its classical expression by Plato and Aristotle more than 2000 years ago. Its elevation of Form over matter has led us to view ourselves and the world in terms of subject and object, observer and observed, rather than as intimately interrelated and interdependent.

One consequence of this has been the elevation of the mind and the devaluation of matter. Since patriarchal political regimes have identified men with rationality and women with nature and emotion, the problem is compounded. Women can claim rationality only by accepting the devaluation of emotion and the natural world that goes with it.

Some people today are questioning whether our culture has placed too much emphasis on the rational and denied the world of nature and emotion to our own peril. This rethinking of the Greek rationalist worldview could be easily cast in Taoist terms. Has *yang* energy been overly emphasized and *yin* energy destructively ignored? Can we arrive at a balanced worldview that includes and balances both reason and emotion, that integrates technology with nature?

Consistent with the Greek devotion to rationalism, the metaphysics of Plato and Aristotle assumes the world to be "out there," separate from me and capable of being understood by a separate "I." Another unstated assumption is that things have an independent existence if they are properly constituted of Form and matter. In other words, tables are tables and chairs are chairs, regardless of whether or not I am perceiving them. These solid objects make up the everyday world I can take for granted.

The discoveries and theories of quantum mechanics and relativity have cast doubt on all these assumptions. If reality is an energy field, the solid world of matter seems to evaporate. If time is relative to the speed of the observer, rather than moving at a fixed and absolute rate, getting a handle on what we mean by past, present, and future, as well as age, is difficult. The theoretical concept of a space-time continuum throws many of our most stable notions right out the window.

Virtual reality, with its computer-generated images, causes us to wonder which version of reality is the more reliable one—the view from inside the goggles or the one I see when I wake up in the morning. Experiences like Virgil's of receiving sight but not being able to make sense of visual stimuli, not being able to construct a world out of them, further complicate the picture. With what we now know, it seems harder rather than easier to be sure about what is real and what is not.

Other traditions, from Africa and Asia as well as from Native American people, suggest a world of "oneness" rather than "twoness" in which everything exists as a web of interconnectedness. Using strikingly different imagery, some of these alternative versions of reality seem closer to the world that Western science now describes. And the Neoplatonism taught by Hypatia assumes both eternal dimensions and the possibility of union with the One—the end, or purpose, of human life.

Is it, as the Beatles song "Tomorrow Never Knows" suggests, just a matter of turning off your mind and surrendering to the void? Must we give up the strictly rationalist way of approaching the world that is our inheritance from the Greeks to truly apprehend what is real? If we "play the game 'Existence' to the end," will we find ourselves back at the beginning? Does the Buddhist version of the wheel of birth-death-rebirth more accurately represent the way things are?

When we get to the heart of being—if we ever do—will we find love? Is love the kind of knowing that comes when you "listen to the color of your dreams" and "relax and float downstream"? Does the cosmos have an eternal dimension, as religion has traditionally insisted? Is everything interdependent and interconnected as Buddhism and Taoism suggest or sacred as the Seneca creation myth and traditional African cosmology believe?

Are we getting closer to understanding what is real and how to judge whether we have the real thing or an imitation? Or, as pragmatism suggests, is the only important question: What works? If we can predict what will happen with some success and make technology serve our needs, does it matter what the world is really like?

Philosophers, in general, are less willing to settle for a working model and continue to search for the real nature of the cosmos and the human person. In the next chapter we will look at the expression these questions of metaphysics take when directed not out at the world but in to ourselves. What are we like, as human beings?

Now, let's turn to the world of the first century and observe the interaction of Hebrew religious thought, formed in Palestine, with the Greek rationalist thought we have been discussing. In trying to describe the reality of Christianity they had originally experienced in a Jewish environment, early Christian missionaries learned that what you can say about reality depends on the words and the concepts available to say what you want to say. Using the Greek language and the social and intellectual concepts available in the Greek culture, missionaries learned how hard it could be to express what could be said so easily in Hebrew or Aramaic. Not only the words, but sometimes the very concepts, were simply not available in Greek. At times reality itself seemed to shift in the process of cultural translation.

For Further Thought

1. If you were participating in a virtual reality experience, what standard or test could you employ to determine which was more "real"—the experience of your mind or the experience of your body?
2. If you were observing someone else participating in a virtual reality experience, what standard or test could you use to describe what is "real" for that person?
3. Are you more or less the "real you" in a virtual community like the Internet than you are in your ordinary experience? Why?
4. Suppose the memories you have stored from virtual reality experiences are indistinguishable from the memories you have stored from ordinary reality. Is there any difference between them? If so, what is the difference? If not, why not?

5. Suppose you could go on vacation via virtual reality and experience all the sensations that would be available to you if you took the trip in ordinary reality. Would there be any reason for your body to take the trip? If so, what would you be seeking?
6. Knowing that you live in a four-dimensional world (length, width, depth, and time) but experience only the first three of those dimensions, are you more inclined to subject your ordinary commonsense view of the world to skeptical analysis? What else might you be missing?
7. If different rules apply in the world of ordinary size and speed than apply in the world of the very small and the very fast, which is the "real" set of rules? Is it possible to hold that there are two realms of reality, each operating according to its own set of instructions?
8. In what ways have the discoveries of quantum mechanics and relativity theory brought Western metaphysics closer to Buddhist and Taoist worldviews? If these new scientific understandings are more fully integrated into Western culture, what effect might they have on the way we see ourselves, our world, and our culture?
9. If all red objects were to disappear, would the color red still exist as a concept? If so, what would be the nature of its reality? If not, did the concept ever exist?
10. How has the debate between Plato and Aristotle about whether or not ideas can exist apart from material reality been affected by relativity theory? In other words, if we are only able to know how the world works—essentially, pragmatism—how can we consider whether materialism or idealism more accurately describes the world as it "really" is?
11. If Virgil, who had his physical sight restored, was never able to see the world as sighted people do, what questions does his "mental blindness" raise for the rest of us?
12. What concerns might we have if God "plays dice with the universe"—that is, if events are random and without order or purpose? If, in the world of the very small, we can only speak in probabilities and never in certainties, what implications does this have for the world of ordinary-sized objects?
13. What effect, if any, do questions about the origin and age of the universe have on our ordinary experience of reality? If we could determine how the universe was "born" and how it will "die," would we live our lives differently or perceive the world differently?
14. Gaze up into the night sky on a clear evening and remember that what you are seeing is a portrait of the past. Some of the light you see began its journey to you thousands and even millions of years ago. Is your concept of time altered by what you "know" to be true, even though it violates your commonsense understanding of reality?
15. If the space-time continuum makes all events present events that only our limitations prevent us from seeing as parts of one whole, what implications are there for the way you consider the future and the past?
16. Was Protagoras right to claim that "man is the measure of all things"? If so, what are the implications for "reality"? If not, who or what might be the measure? What are the implications of holding another view?
17. Suppose the Seneca creation myth accurately portrays reality. What might it be possible to learn from the Stone Tribe and other creatures here before us "Two-leggeds"? How might we go about learning from other species?

18. Does the world appear differently to you if everything in it is sacred? What implications are there in this worldview?
19. If God shares this world with human beings and creates out of what is already here, does the world seem more or less predictable, more or less safe than it does if God exists outside the world and creates it out of nothing?
20. List five things you are sure are "real" and describe how you know they are "real."

For Further Exploration

Albee, Edward. *Tiny Alice.* New York: Pocket Books, 1966. In this play, an old crone turns out to be a young, sensual woman, and a fire in the castle's tiny model chapel mirrors a fire in the actual chapel. What's real and what isn't?

Card, Orson Scott. *Ender's Game.* New York: Doherty, 1986. A young man is recruited and harshly trained to play simulated war games resembling virtual reality; the final game is revealed as "real" while he is playing it.

Esquivel, Laura. *The Law of Love.* New York: Crown, 1996. Azucena, an "astroanalyst" in twenty-third-century Mexico City, tries to help people deal with their past lives. Since she has not worked through the *karma* of her own 14,000 past lives, they intrude on events in the present.

Gibson, William. *Neuromancer.* New York: Gibson, 1985. A novel about "cyberspace" or virtual reality in which an artificial intelligence (AI) computer criminal tries to become "unlimited."

The Lawnmower Man. In this film, a scientist uses virtual reality to reprogram a slow but decent young man and ends up creating a monster. Interesting virtual reality sequences.

The Matrix. This film, from Andy and Larry Wachowski flips our perceptions of ordinary reality by presenting our everyday world as a "matrix," designed to entrap us. Reality is much more brutal and, ultimately, much more worth living, according to the film's thematic premise.

MindWalk. This film, a critique of the Descartes/Newton mechanical model of the universe, is based on the insights of particle physics. Based on *The Turning Point* by Fritjof Capra, whose first book—*The Tao of Physics*—explores similarities between quantum mechanics/relativity theory and Buddhist mysticism.

The Philadelphia Experiment. Reportedly based on a true World War II incident, this film involves an antiradar experiment that lands a sailor in 1984 via a time warp.

Purple Rose of Cairo. Woody Allen's film has a dashing, romantic movie character leave the screen and sweep a housewife off her feet.

Star Wars. This film explores the nature of the Force, an energy source that can be used for good or evil.

Time After Time. This film features H. G. Wells (inventor of the time machine), who pursues Jack the Ripper into present-day San Francisco, using his invention.

Total Recall. Are the memories of a Martian vacation the character has had implanted reality, or is his ordinary life the implant? How is the character to tell the difference? This film poses some interesting questions.

The Truman Show. This 1998 film by director Peter Weir raises disturbing questions about the nature of what we take to be independent reality. It suggests that we all accept the reality of the world with which we are presented. Even when Truman begins to suspect his world is being created, Christoff challenges, "There's no more truth out there than in the world I created for you." How would we be able to tell whether or not we are part of someone else's ongoing drama?

Vonnegut, Kurt. *Slaughterhouse Five.* New York: Delacorte, 1969. Billy Pilgrim disconnects from time, jumping back and forth among different periods of his life. Also a movie.

Wargames. In this film, a young hacker accidentally starts World War III when he breaks into a video-game manufacturer's computer and selects a "game" called "Global Thermonuclear War."

Zukov, Gary. *The Dancing Wu Li Masters: An Overview of the New Physics.* New York: Morrow, 1979. A readable nonfiction introduction to a complex field.

For Further Research

Try these InfoTrac keywords:

Virtual Reality
String Theory
Ontology
Pragmatism
Materialism

Notes

1. "To Touch What's Not Really There," *Baltimore Sun,* 30 January 1997, 2A.
2. Howard Rheingold, *Virtual Reality* (New York: Summit, 1991), 46.
3. Michael Heim, *The Metaphysics of Virtual Reality* (New York: Oxford University Press, 1993), xiii.
4. Oliver Sacks, "To See and Not See," *New Yorker,* 10 May 1993, 61.
5. Sacks, 64, 66.
6. Sacks, 64–65.
7. Plato, *Republic,* bk. 5, trans. by Robin Waterfield (New York: Oxford University Press, 1994), 196–197.
8. Plato, "Phaedo," in *Great Dialogues of Plato,* trans. W. H. D. Rouse, ed. Eric H. Warmington and Philip G. Rouse (New York: New American Library, 1956), 518.
9. Aristotle, *The Pocket Aristotle,* ed. Justin D. Kaplan, trans. W. D. Ross (New York: Washington Square, 1958), 131.
10. Aristotle, 132.
11. "The Heart of Transcendent Wisdom," in *Anthology of World Scriptures,* ed. Robert E. Van Voorst (Belmont, Calif.: Wadsworth, 1994), 85–86.
12. *The Dhammapada: The Sayings of the Buddha,* trans. Thomas Byrom (New York: Vintage, 1976), 65.

13. Lao Tsu, *Tao Te Ching,* chap. 14, trans. Gia-Fu Feng and Jane English (New York: Vintage, 1972), 14.
14. Lao Tsu, chap. 22.
15. Gary Zukav, *The Dancing Wu Li Masters: An Overview of the New Physics* (New York: Morrow, 1979), 219.
16. Zukav, 213.
17. Zukav, 243.
18. Zukav, 243.
19. Victor Villaseñor, "Rain of Gold," in *Hispanic American Literature,* ed. Nicholas Kanellos (New York: HarperCollins, 1995) 29.
20. "The Business of the Holes," *Baltimore Sun,* 25 April 1995, 13A.
21. Zukav, 171–172.
22. Brian Greene, *The Elegant Universe,* (New York: Vintage, 2000), 3.
23. Greene, 4.
24. Greene, 5.
25. Greene, 24
26. Greene, 6.
27. Greene, 6.
28. Greene, 14.
29. Greene, 20.
30. This is the famous thought experiment known as the paradox of Schrödinger's cat, named after its originator Erwin Schrödinger. Introduced in 1935, it has continued to intrigue physicists interested in quantum mechanics.
31. Zukav, 115–116.
32. *Selections from Early Greek Philosophy,* 3d ed., ed. Milton C. Nahm (New York: Appleton-Century-Crofts, 1947), 237.
33. Plato, "Philebus (20d)," in *The Dialogues of Plato,* vol. 3, trans. Benjamin Jowett (New York: Oxford University Press, 1953), 571.
34. "The Real World of Antimatter," *Baltimore Sun,* 22 June 1997, 2A.
35. "Astronomy Crisis Deepens as the Hubble Telescope Sees No Missing Mass," *New York Times,* 29 November 1994, C1.
36. George Greenstein, "Our Address in the Universe," *Harvard Magazine,* January–February 1994, 47.
37. *Dictionary of Philosophy,* ed. Dagobert D. Runes (Savage, Md.: Rowman & Littlefield, 1983), 256.
38. Jay Bregman, *Synesius of Cyrene: Philosopher-Bishop* (Berkeley: University of California Press, 1982), 20.
39. *The Letters of Synesius of Cyrene,* trans. Augustine Fitzgerald (London: Oxford University Press, 1926), 90.
40. *Letters of Synesius,* epistle 154, 251–252.
41. Bregman, 38.
42. Bregman, 24–25, 38.
43. *Letters of Synesius,* epistle 154, 253.

44. Jamie Sams and Twylah Nitsch, *Other Council Fires Were Here Before Ours: A Classic Native American Creation Story as Retold by a Seneca Elder and Her Granddaughter* (New York: HarperCollins, 1991), 6.
45. Sams and Nitsch, 9.
46. Sams and Nitsch, 10.
47. Sams and Nitsch, 11–12.
48. Sams and Nitsch, 15, 11.
49. Louis Chunovic, ed., *Chris-in-the-Morning: Love, Life, and the Whole Karmic Enchilada, based on the Universal Television Series* Northern Exposure *created by Joshua Brand and John Falsey* (Chicago: Contemporary Books, 1993), 52–53.
50. Kwasi Wiredu, "African Philosophical Tradition: A Case Study of the Akan," *Philosophical Forum,* 24, no. 1–3 (1992–1993), 42.
51. Wiredu.
52. Plato, *Timaeus* (41d), trans. Francis M. Cornford (New York: Macmillan, 1987), 37.
53. Wiredu, 46.
54. C. Eric Lincoln and Lawrence H. Mamiya, *The Black Church in the African American Experience* (Durham, N.C.: Duke University Press, 1990), 5.
55. Lincoln and Mamiya, 6–7.

HISTORICAL INTERLUDE B

Philosophy and Early Christianity

Separating either Hebrew religious thought or Greek rationalist thought from our cultural heritage is difficult. They are both interwoven permanently, whether or not you are religious, whether or not you read Greek philosophy. To be a Christian in the twenty-first century is to think in an essentially Greek way about God, about the special status of Jesus, and about the meaning of human life. To read the literature of the West is to confront the images and language of both Jewish and Christian theology.

Even the most secular among us stands between the two pillars of Hebrew religious thought and Greek rationalist thought that together support the Western worldview. With Christianity's acceptance as the state religion of Rome and its subsequent spread throughout the Roman Empire, Western culture came to call itself Christendom. Medieval philosophers in the West were also theologians, and by the time of the Renaissance, both Plato and Aristotle had been "Christianized," their pagan ideas modified by theologians and made compatible with Christianity. Much earlier, however, Greek rationalist thought had its first tentative encounter with the worldview of Palestinian Jews.

Ideas take shape within a culture in a reciprocal relationship: Ideas shape the culture and the culture shapes the ideas. Over time, ideas and their cultural context become virtually inseparable. As a consequence, interesting things happen when an idea conceived in one culture is transmitted to another. A new idea will influence any culture into which it is introduced, but it will also be transformed in significant ways by the cultural forms available to express it. In this Historical Interlude, we look at the blending of Greek rationalist thought and Hebrew religious thought that occurred when Christianity (at its heart, a Jewish religion) was exported during its infancy to the Greek world.

If you speak more than one language, you already know that some things that can be said easily in one language cannot be accurately translated into another. The same can be said for "translating" concepts. Imagine going to a culture that believes Earth to be flat, striking up a conversation with someone (assume some common language), and complaining about the long journey you have just taken halfway around this spherical world, forced to live on airplane food. You would be met not with disagreement but with incomprehension—the same incomprehension you might exhibit if your acquaintance expressed worry over the favor of fertility gods/goddesses and the danger inherent in planting the crops during an unfavorable phase of the Moon.

A similar culture jolt occurred when Christianity, a new religion born in Palestine, spread into the Greek world. The existing worldview of Palestinian Jews provided the cultural, intellectual, and religious context in which the original ideas of Christianity were formed. Greeks had a significantly different worldview, however, and the early Christian missionaries to the Greek world struggled to translate concepts from one culture to another. Over a period of 300 years, Christianity, which began as a Jewish sect, came to understand itself and express its theology in Greek terms, since Greek converts to Christianity rapidly outnumbered those in Palestine.

Judaism

Let's begin by looking at the worldview of the Hebrews, as the Jews were called when Abraham unified a number of nomadic tribes into a people under the worship of one God during the second millennium B.C.E. This belief in one God, rather than many gods—called *monotheism*—distinguished the Hebrews from their neighbors. After a period of exile in Egypt, lasting from about 1650 to 1280 B.C.E. (scholars vary in assigning an end date), the Hebrews were led by Moses, to whom God was to reveal the law in the form of the Ten Commandments. Through Moses, God established a covenant with the Hebrew people, agreeing to care for them in exchange for their faithfulness.

For Jews and Christians, the Ten Commandments summarize God's law for humanity.

The Ten Commandments/Courtesy of Sara Baum/Photo by Quentin Kardos.

Moses led the Hebrew Exodus from Egypt. On the way, according to the Hebrew Scriptures, sometimes called the Old Testament, God allowed the Hebrews to pass through the sea by parting the waters; when the pharaoh's army tried to follow, however, the wall of water collapsed and drowned them. During a period of wandering in the desert, the Hebrews believed God spoke to them through Moses, and they came to see themselves as a people chosen by God and under his protection.

The Hebrew Scriptures began as oral tradition, passed on from generation to generation through the telling of stories. They were collected and

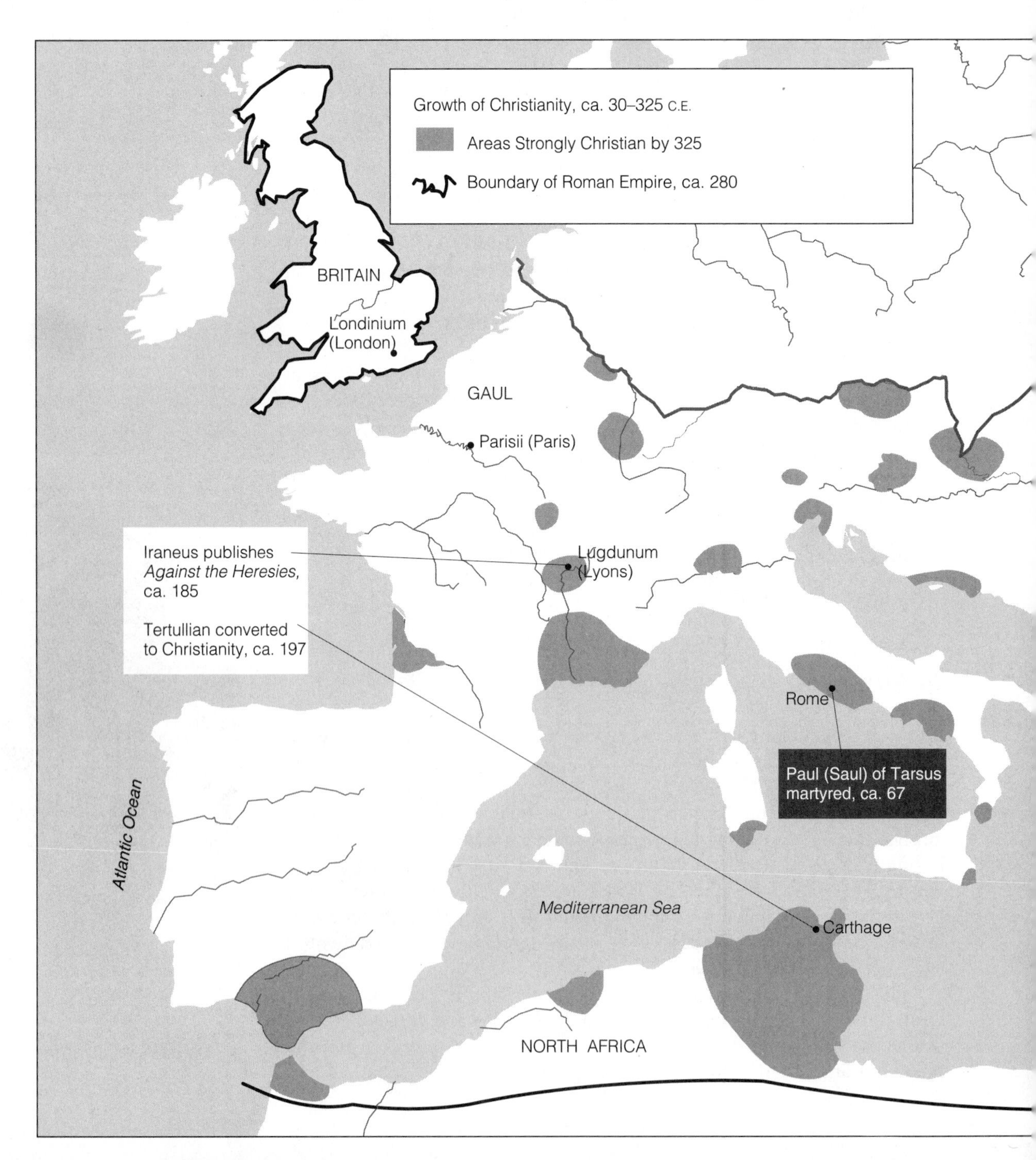

compiled from various sources probably around 400 B.C.E. and now consist of the Torah, the first five books that describe events from the Creation of the world through the formulation of the law; historical books that describe kings, wars, and the faithfulness/unfaithfulness of the people; words of the prophets who arose from time to time, calling the people to repentance and

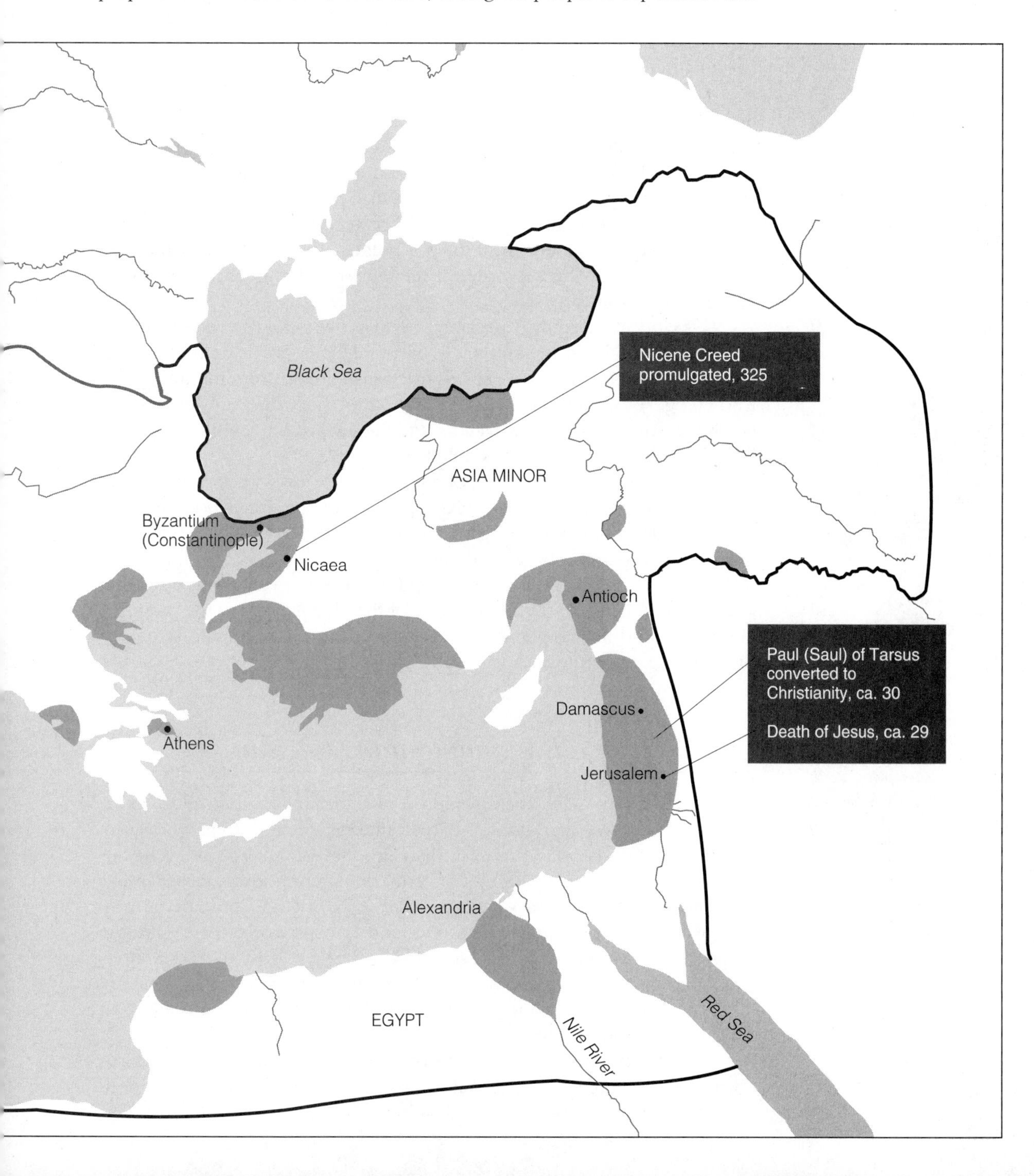

threatening the wrath of God if they did not; and the wisdom literature, proverbs and other advice on living a holy and happy life.

For the Jews, as they are called after the fall of Jerusalem to the Babylonians and their allies in 586 B.C.E., the one God (whom they frequently called Yahweh) was *transcendent,* meaning independent of the space-time world we live in. God was not to be identified with nature but was perceived as revealed yet concealed in a burning bush, flaming without being consumed, or through a voice speaking to Moses on Mount Sinai and delivering the law. Yet, this mighty God was also personal—not an unmoved mover or uncaused cause as Aristotle would later argue or even the Idea of the Good in Plato's *Republic*.

The God of Judaism was considered both as awesome and powerful and as taking a personal interest in the Jewish people, even to the point of intervening in human history to save and protect them (as in the parting of the sea during the Exodus from Egypt). In fact, some of the great religious festivals of Judaism are set aside for remembering the mighty acts of God in the events of history.

This God was also the Creator of the world who made everything from nothing and declared it all to be "good." Only later, after the first people, Adam and Eve, disobeyed God's instructions and ate from the tree of the Knowledge of Good and Evil, did evil enter the world. Observance of God's law was the route to salvation, and the Jews saw themselves as God's holy people living under God's holy law.

Lighting eight candles in this menorah at Hanukkah celebrates a miracle that accompanied the rededication of the Temple.

Menorah/Courtesy of Sara Baum/Photo by Quentin Kardos.

At the time of the birth of Christianity, the Jews were living under Roman occupation. As a politically oppressed people, their hope focused on the coming of the Messiah who had been promised by God. Descended from King David, the long-awaited Messiah would, it was said, come in power and glory to establish the Kingdom of God on Earth and begin a golden age of peace and freedom. Jews of that time looked to the promised Messiah to end the Roman occupation and restore a freed and righteous Judaism to earthly rule.

Greek Rationalism and Roman Stoicism

To provide a context for the emergence of Christianity, we need to take a brief survey of two worldviews—Greek rationalism and Roman Stoicism. As we follow Christianity from its origins in a Jewish cultural and religious context, we will find it gaining converts, first among lower-class Greeks and later among upper-class Romans. A key task of early Christian missionaries was comprehending both Greek and Roman worldviews. Like the Milesian philosophers we discussed in Chapter 1, Christian missionaries needed to understand the mind-set of those they hoped to convert. Openness to existing philosophies proved to be essential in the "translation" of concepts from one culture to another.

As you may remember, the Greeks at this time placed great emphasis on reason. Beginning with Heraclitus, many Greek philosophers had used the word *logos* to speak of the rational principle that governs the cosmos. They viewed reason as the distinguishing characteristic of humans and the tool by which people could understand the world and their place in it. One of the focuses in the Greek world was on the origin of things, on finding the *archē*. Alexander the Great, who had been tutored by Aristotle during the fourth century B.C.E., had conquered the eastern world and introduced Greek culture as far as North Africa where the city of Alexandria was a major cosmopolitan and intellectual center.

In the Roman Empire of the first and second centuries C.E., Stoicism—a form of pagan, ethical thought—had attracted Seneca, Epictetus, and Emperor Marcus Aurelius. Stoicism stresses the relationship between an intelligent and self-conscious world soul and human reason, which shares the rationality of the *logos* that orders the cosmos. Since there is one reason or wisdom for all, there is also one code of conduct for all. Stoicism advocates the moral freedom of all persons and insists that one's station in life is an accident. Both the emperor and the slave are brothers. To obey reason, or *logos,* is the goal of human life; the passions, enemies of the obedience to reason that leads to happiness, are to be avoided.

The Emergence of Christianity

This was the world into which Jesus was born. According to the uniquely Christian Scriptures, called by Christians the New Testament, he was a pious Jew who went up to Jerusalem for the great religious festivals and a teacher who took a middle-of-the-road position with regard to the Romans, advocating neither armed rebellion against them (as the Zealots did) nor fraternization with them (as the Sadducees did). Politically, he was closest to the Pharisees who urged keeping the law and waiting for vindication from God.

Jesus angered the Pharisees, the most strongly monotheistic and legalistic of the Jewish sects, by breaking the law—healing people on the Sabbath, for instance. At the same time, he intensified the ethical demands of the law, insisting that not only were murder and adultery sinful but the hatred and lust that led to them were also sinful. Jesus urged love of God and love of neighbor, linking unlimited forgiveness of others with God's forgiveness.

The first five books of the uniquely Christian Scriptures tell the story of Jesus' life, death, and resurrection, as well as events in the lives of his followers in the period after his death. After three years of teaching and healing, Jesus entered the city of Jerusalem during Passover week to the acclaim of a noisy crowd, gathered for the festival. To the Romans he must have seemed like a potential threat to an uneasy peace. Since his priorities were uniquely his, he disappointed all three of the major Jewish sects—Pharisees, Sadducees, and Zealots. The result was his arrest, trial, and execution by the Roman authorities, with support from the Jews.

In the confusing days after the death of Jesus, most of his followers were in hiding. They had not expected their leader to be put to death and feared that a similar fate might await them. Since all the followers of Jesus had been Jews, they built their new religion on the bedrock of Judaism. In fact, they saw themselves as members of the "true Judaism" since they came to believe that Jesus was the Messiah.

Neither the Jewish leadership nor the Romans accepted this analysis, of course, but many early Christians, called Nazarenes because Jesus had come from Nazareth, continued to think of themselves as Jews. Just as they had always done, these early Christians affirmed all the central truths of Judaism and observed the long-familiar religious rituals, now filled with additional meaning. To reflect their experience as followers of Jesus, they added new rituals, primarily a sacrificial meal of bread and wine that represented the body and blood of Jesus and drew them closer to him in its observance.

They believed in one God, but they also believed Jesus to be an extraordinary being, more than merely human, more like Yahweh. They struggled to express what came to be called the divinity of Jesus in a way that did not threaten the monotheism that was so central to Judaism. They believed Jesus to be the Messiah and, viewing him as the risen Savior, they began also to call him the Son of God. This presented problems in a religion that had long prided itself on monotheism. As Christianity matured, it eventually proclaimed a Trinitarian monotheism—that God is one but expressed in three persons—Father, Son, and Holy Spirit.

One of the early points of contention between Christians and Jews was this insistence that Jesus, too, was God. Stephen, the first Christian martyr, was stoned to death in Jerusalem, at least in part for espousing the blasphemy that there was another God besides Yahweh. Among those at the stoning was Saul of Tarsus, who had been raised as a Pharisee, devoted to the Jewish law and strongly monotheistic. After watching the death of Stephen, he left for Damascus in search of other blasphemers. On the way he had a vision that he believed to be of the risen Jesus, and instead of persecuting Christians, he became one. After this dramatic, life-changing experience, Saul, who spoke Greek and had been exposed to Greek philosophy, changed his name to Paul and became the chief missionary to the Greek-speaking world.

Blending of Greek Rationalist and Hebrew Religious Thought

Early Christians believed that soon, certainly within their lifetimes, Jesus would return to Earth. This Second Coming would signal the end of time and the beginning of a new era, the Kingdom of God on Earth. As Paul began to explain Christianity in the Greek world, he quickly realized that this emphasis on the end of time was a liability, because Greeks were much more interested in the origins of things. The origins of Christianity, he soon grasped, would have to be explained in terms Greeks could understand.

Knowing both Hebrew theology and Greek ideas, Paul blended the two, associating a figure from Hebrew theology, the Wisdom, with the philosophical concept of the *logos* as the rational principle of the universe. The book of Proverbs, in the Hebrew Scriptures, describes the Wisdom as being with God at the time of the Creation. By linking Jesus with the

Wisdom, Paul allowed his explanation to resonate against the Greek idea of a preexisting, rational principle.

Philo of Alexandria, a contemporary of Jesus, had already begun the blending of Greek rationalist and Hebrew religious thought by declaring that the idea of the Good, described by Plato, was identical with the transcendent God of the Bible. Thus, because Paul was not the first to bring Hebrew ideas into a culture familiar with Greek philosophy, his attempts to integrate the two may have met with greater initial acceptance.

In their efforts to explain the uniqueness of Jesus, early Christians had written accounts of his life, ministry, death, and resurrection. The first four books of the uniquely Christian portion of the Bible tell this story. Called the Gospels, they are attributed to Matthew, Mark, Luke, and John. In the earliest gospel, the one called Mark, Jesus is identified as the Son of God when he enters the Jordan River at about the age of thirty to be baptized by John the Baptist. The gospels called Matthew and Luke assume Jesus to be divine from birth, and the first describes the star of Bethlehem, as well as angels announcing a heavenly nativity.

The gospel attributed to John, the last to be written, was probably conceived in the Greek world, perhaps even under the influence of Paul. In it, the divine nature of Jesus is apparent at the beginning of time. According to this gospel: "In the beginning was the Word (*Logos*) and the Word (*Logos*) was with God and the Word (*Logos*) was God. . . ." Like the Wisdom, then, the *Logos* was present "in the beginning." In this fourth gospel, Jesus seems to remember the glory he has left and to be conscious that he has a divine mission.

Perhaps the chief problem facing missionaries like Paul was the fact that the key Jewish concept of a Messiah had no meaning in the Greek world. The writers of the Gospels had used the term *Lord* to refer to Jesus. The Greek term Paul used, *Christos,* which is translated into English as "Christ," had kingly associations but came to be almost a last name since it lacked the meaning and power the word *Messiah* had in the Hebrew language and in the Jewish religion and culture.

Only the gospel narratives and letters to newly established churches sent by missionaries like Paul were included in what became the uniquely Christian portion of the Bible, sometimes called the New Testament. Around 150 C.E., however, a group of apologists, including Justin Martyr, attempted to further translate Christian concepts into a Greek cultural context. Like Paul, Justin knew Greek ideas and had in fact studied Greek philosophy extensively at Ephesus before being converted to Christianity.

In his writings, Justin united Christian concepts with the ideas of Plato, Aristotle, and the Stoics. Socrates, he said, was the model for Christian martyrs, since he died for what he believed in, and both Abraham and Socrates were "Christians before Christ." Neither Judaism nor Greek philosophy accepted this status as precursors of Christianity, but those who became Christians tended to see every system of thought as leading up to perfect truth as expressed in Christianity.

Justin also contributed a very useful image to the emerging concept of the Trinity. The Son-*Logos*, he said, mediates between the Father and the material world. The *Logos* is derived from the Father in a process that in no way diminishes or divides the being of the Father—as one torch is lighted from another. Jesus is "light of light" or "light from light."

Doctrinal Controversies in Early Christianity

Not all attempts at cultural blending worked as smoothly as Justin's had. As the Gospels and the letters to churches were written down and as apologists like Justin continued blending Christian concepts with the existing Greek culture, points of conflict sometimes arose. In the process of working out its theology and its practice, Christianity's Jewish roots were the source of some problems, and the thought systems Christianity encountered in the Greek world created others.

Judaism as a Precondition for Christianity

Since all the first Christians had been Jews and thus saw Christianity as the fulfillment of Judaism, they naturally assumed that anyone who became a Christian would first have to become a Jew. This was not an issue in Palestine where likely converts were already Jews, but in the Greek world it led to a potentially serious problem. For one thing, Judaism insists that Jewish males be circumcised, an event that occurs when they are eight-day-old babies. Most men in the Greek world, however, were unwilling to undergo the pain of circumcision as a precondition for becoming Christians.

The issue of requirements for conversion was resolved when Paul brought Titus, an uncircumcised Greek convert, to Jerusalem for a meeting with the original leaders. They recognized the value and genuineness of the work Paul was doing in the Greek world and agreed on a compromise. The mission to convert Jews would continue to maintain the Jewish law, but Paul and his partner Barnabas would take their message to Gentiles (non-Jews) who could become Christians without first converting to Judaism.

The Compatibility of Gnosticism and Christianity

Some of the best minds of the second century C.E. were drawn to Gnosticism, a pre-Christian system that attempted to encompass all wisdom and that had appeared in varying forms in both Greek and Roman culture and as far away as Egypt. In general, Gnostics believed that the Fall of humanity (which Jews and Christians maintain happened when Adam and Eve disobeyed God after the world was created good) occurred before Creation. The world, they said, was an evil place, and humans struggle to return to the good world of spiritual ideas. Since the world is evil, it could not have been created by a good God; perhaps an inferior demiurge, or second-level deity, was responsible.

The most serious problem for the Christian Church was the Gnostic insistence that the good God could not possibly take human form and come to this evil world to suffer and die. This taking of human form, called the *Incarnation,* is at the very heart of Christianity. Without it, according to Christian theology, the world cannot be reconciled to God. Gnostics argued that Jesus only *seemed* to suffer and die; it was only an appearance because God is good and exists only apart from this evil world.

Gnostics accepted Christian ideas, along with many other wisdom sources, and believed Jesus was a messenger from the good, heavenly realm. Christians, however, insisted that the *Logos* was incarnate, or made flesh in Jesus, and that they had exclusive claim to the truth. Gnostics had their own gospels as well as those that came to be included when Christian leaders formally decided which writings should be included in the Scriptures, in about the fourth century. They claimed authority for their gospels, and this threatened the Christian Church's insistence that it had a unique truth claim.

Irenaeus of Lyon (in what was then Gaul and is now France) stated that, since all Christian churches shared the same set of beliefs, any ideas that conflicted with these were wrong. Arguing that the followers of Jesus had perfect knowledge of his teachings, which they transmitted to churches they established, Irenaeus asserted that anything not in agreement with beliefs held by those churches was unacceptable. The secret knowledge, claimed by Gnostics, failed the test set up by Irenaeus in his influential book *Against the Heresies,* published around 185; Gnosticism was the first belief system to be condemned as heresy. One could not be a Gnostic and a Christian. It was necessary to choose.

The Compatibility of the Trinity and Monotheism

So sensitive was the issue of calling Jesus God that some began to openly resist the idea. The *Logos* was sounding suspiciously like a rival God; since there could only be one God, some suggested that Jesus might be thought of as God's son by adoption. If the Roman emperors had done this, maybe God did, too. Others declared that Father, Son, and Holy Spirit are modes of the same being. According to this way of thinking, Jesus was a temporary manifestation of the one God in human form.

In the third century, Tertullian of Carthage in North Africa developed what has come to be the official, orthodox Christian understanding of the Trinity. God, Tertullian said, is three persons in one being. He used the Greek word *homoousios,* which means "one in being," and translated it into Latin as *consubstantial.* Both words mean that God is a unity, one in being or of one substance, even if expressed in three persons. By the third century, members of the upper classes were becoming Christians and their language, Latin, began to replace the Greek spoken by the first Gentile converts, who were mostly slaves and members of the lower classes.

Struggles with the concept of the Trinity continued into the beginning of the fourth century. In Alexandria, a priest named Arius began preaching that Jesus, the Christ, was a created being, not of the same substance as God but created out of nothing like every other person. Furthermore, Arius said, in the Incarnation the *Logos* entered a human body and took the place of a human, reasoning spirit. The result was neither divine nor human but a third thing.

Although he was forbidden to say these things by Alexander, his bishop, Arius persisted since he was concerned that the unity of God was being threatened by talk of the Trinity. The bishops of the Christian Church soon began to take sides; some sided with Arius and others with Alexander. Emperor Constantine, who had recently conquered the eastern empire, was no theologian but he did recognize a threat to unity within the empire.

He called the first Ecumenical Council, inviting all the bishops to the city of Nicea in Asia Minor at government expense, to resolve the controversy and restore unity. Constantine, like others at this time, was waiting to be baptized on his deathbed, thinking this would guarantee a sinless entry into heaven. So he was technically not even a Christian, but he *was* the emperor. At the council meeting, he used all the power of his office to press for a *creed,* or belief statement, that would guarantee unity.

In the end his will prevailed: The council adopted what has come to be called the Nicene Creed (or the Creed of Nicea) in 325. Using language designed to reject Arius's position, the creed declared the Son "begotten, not made" and "one in being" (*homoousios,* as Tertullian had put it) "with the Father." Reflecting other controversies, this creed declared (against the Gnostics) that God is "maker of heaven and earth" and insisted that Jesus "suffered, died and was buried." It also used a phrase that might have been lifted from Justin Martyr by calling the relationship between Son and Father "God from God, Light from Light."

The Legacy of the Early Christian Period

The Nicene Creed reflects the coming of age of the Christian Church far from its Jewish roots. By this time, the ethical precepts of Judaism had been overlaid with a lot of Greek philosophical concepts and language. The central idea of the Trinity—three persons who are one God—came to have a very Greek formulation in the word *homoousios.* Had Christianity developed its key concepts in the Jewish world, they would have been quite different.

As we will see in the next chapter, the Western concept of an essential self has its roots in both Hebrew and Greek ways of thinking. The experiences of Paul and others in transplanting religious concepts from one culture to another produced an amalgam that is neither purely Hebrew nor purely Greek but is heavily indebted to both. The blending of these two traditions has played a significant role in shaping how we Westerners understand our human nature and our place in the world, the topics we examine next.

CHAPTER 3

Human Nature

Who or What Are We, and What Are We Doing Here?

Before You Read . . .

Ask yourself whether there is a "real you," fixed at birth, or whether you see yourself more as a work in progress.

Imagine that you have been having an Internet relationship with John for the past six months. During that time you have discussed many issues, and you have gradually come to respect John's intelligence and perceptive questions. The two of you have connected on so many levels that you have begun to look forward to your evening meetings on the Net. Although many of the people with whom you live and work seem preoccupied with trivial and superficial things, John always focuses on the "big picture" and appears to understand what really matters.

When you suggest a face-to-face meeting, John puts you off. As you become more insistent, John finally admits that this will be impossible because "he" is a computer program. But this revelation should not harm your relationship, John contends. You can go on just as you have done for the past six months. Still, you feel confused and a little betrayed by this new information. How, you wonder, could you have been fooled for so long? Realizing that you have had a relationship with a computer, you are embarrassed, and even angry. Continuing these conversations now seems out of the question.

The Tom Hanks character in the movie *Splash* faced a similar problem when the beautiful woman who seemed to return his affection and readily agreed to move in with him turned out to be a mermaid, Hanks responded with indignation, "I can't love you. You're a fish." The mermaid took the same approach as John, the computer, insisting that this new revelation need not have any effect on the relationship: "Whatever you connected with, fell in love with, I'm still that. The fact that I'm a mermaid has nothing to do with anything."

The Issue Defined

Would you be able to accept a skillfully constructed android, made to appear and act human in every way, as a love partner? What about a mermaid, if this were possible? Or is there something in you that recoils from the less than human and insists that only a member of your own species can be an acceptable mate? Paying close attention to your feelings as you consider this question might give you some insight into your own view of human nature.

As a variation on this thought experiment, imagine yourself in a room with two computer terminals. You know that one is connected with a computer program and the other with a human being, but you don't know which is which. Your task is to sit at both keyboards and carry on conversations with whoever or whatever is on the other end. At the conclusion you must render a judgment about which is the human and which the computer. Known as the Turing test—after its inventor, British mathematician Alan Turing—this experiment assumes that if a computer can convince you it is human, perhaps it could reasonably be said to think.

A few years ago, a program called "PC Therapist III" convinced half the people who interacted with it that it was indeed a therapist and not a series of computer bytes. Part of the program's success was due to its stock phrases, each useful in many contexts, such as "Does that interest you?" "How does that make you feel?" and "Tell me more." Its whimsical creator, Joseph Weintraub, did not stop there, however; he added some original questions ("Were you always so sick, sick, sick?") and some literary lines (such as "What is moral is what you feel good after, and what is immoral is what you feel bad after"—from Ernest Hemingway's *The Sun Also Rises*) to convince PC Therapist III's "clients" of its rationality.[1]

David Cope, a composer at the University of California at Santa Cruz, created a program called EMI (Experiments in Musical Intelligence) as a way to generate ideas for his own compositions. When he taught it to scan pieces by the musical genius J. S. Bach and to pick out the musical "signatures" unique to Bach, it created new compositions using the same ingredients. E.M.I does its job so effectively that audiences are convinced they are listening to the real thing. Music theorists are now wondering how a machine can create engaging music with no experience of what we call "life" or the world. What makes Bach's music so special if a computer program can imitate it? And, what can E.M.I. possibly "mean" when it composes the music it does?[2]

If a computer can pass for a human being, does this mean there are no essential differences between humans and computers? More to the point, are we unique among animals? Is there something that sets us apart and makes us human? Over the centuries we have claimed that toolmaking, culture, language, reason, and morality make humans distinct from and superior to other animals. The difficulty is that, one by one, these supposedly human characteristics have been observed or cultivated in other animals.

Chimps, for instance, make tools and plan ahead for their use. After breaking off a long reed, stick, or stalk of grass, a chimp strips off any excess leaves or twigs, shortens it to the appropriate length, carries it to another, often distant location, inserts it into a termite tunnel, shakes it to attract the tasty insects, and then carefully removes it without dislodging too many. Because the technique takes years to perfect, adults teach it to their eager young as they mature. One anthropologist spent months trying to learn it and found that, despite intense instruction from a chimp named Leakey, he was unable to find the entrances to the termite mounds and remained hopelessly inept at selecting, preparing, and using the stalks.[3]

Macaques can be inventive, too. On the small Japanese island of Koshima, scientists began leaving sweet potatoes and wheat on the beach to feed a colony of macaques, once their natural food supply dried up. One young female named Imo discovered that dipping the sand-covered potatoes in a brook washed off the inedible grit. Later, she transferred the technique to the more difficult task of separating sand from wheat. When she dropped them both into the water, the sand sank while the wheat floated. Other macaques noticed Imo's cleverness and soon her playmates and young relatives began imitating her. Gradually, adult females learned the tricks and taught them to their offspring.[4]

Mankind differs from the animals only by a little, and most people throw that away.
CONFUCIUS

Andrew Whiten, of the Scottish Primate Research Group at the University of St. Andrews in Scotland, synthesized the field studies of nine of the world's top primatologists, including Jane Goodall. Whiten's report covers 151 years' worth of chimpanzee observations. Citing 39 behaviors found in seven chimpanzee communities, the primatologists conclude that humanity's "closest cousins" display what has long been thought to be a uniquely-human ability: cultural variation. Subtle and not-so-subtle variations in behavior from site to site offer convincing evidence that chimps can observe and imitate behaviors and then pass those learned skills on to neighbors and kin. Many of these skills involve styles of insect retrieval or methods of grooming, but some of the cultural behaviors have an almost religious sense to them. In six of the seven communities, for example, the chimpanzees perform a rain dance. "You're in awe when you see this," one human observer said. "The chimpanzees go into a quasi-trance, dancing even when they're alone, with no [observed] spectators, as if they were ritually celebrating the rainstorm."[5]

Although apes lack organs of speech and can never make the sounds humans use, some of them have learned to use language quite proficiently. Researchers tried unsuccessfully to teach an adult pygmy chimp named Matata to communicate using symbols on a computer keyboard and then were astounded to find that her six-month-old son Kanzi, who had come along for the lessons, had mastered the skill. Described as functioning at the level of a two-year-old child in 1991, Kanzi also understands hundreds of words of spoken English and can execute such complex commands as,

"Put the backpack in the car," "Take the mushrooms outdoors," "Go get the lettuce in the microwave," and "Do you see the rock? Can you put it in the hat?"—even when the commands come through a microphone from another room and no visual cues are possible.[6]

Some chimps have gone beyond computer keyboards to learn American Sign Language, the manual language used by deaf and hearing-impaired humans. Using this language, they display the ability to lie and deceive, make jokes, uncover trickery in others, and even relate cause and effect. Chimps who have mastered the significance of word order use their knowledge of signs to demand that it be respected. Kanzi, for example, has learned to request activities in the order in which he desires them. If he has asked to be chased and then tickled, Kanzi will not allow the tickling unless a little chasing occurs first.[7]

Quite astounding is the ability of Kanzi and other chimps to use word order to convey meaning. On his own, Kanzi figured out the difference between "Matata bite" and "bite Matata." Using what appears to be a form of abstract reasoning, he deduced the difference in meaning that results when the words in these simple sentences are transposed. All of us understand that "man bites dog" differs from "dog bites man." What is significant is a chimp's discovery of the principle.

Rio, a sea lion, seems to understand the basics of logic. Trained to match pictures of objects, Rio quickly mastered the logical principles of symmetry and transitivity. After learning that object A matched object B and object B matched object C, Rio was able to match object A with object C. This is transitivity. If A equals B and B equals C, then A equals C. The principle of symmetry asserts that if A equals C, then C also equals A. On Rio's first trial, after learning the principle of symmetry, she correctly made A–C connections eleven out of twelve times and correctly made C–A connections seventeen out of eighteen times. She is the only nonhuman animal known to display this ability.[8]

Each species may look at others with curiosity and interest.

Killer whales form groups, called pods, that have distinct cultural patterns and language dialects. Some pods hunt in large groups, apparently using sounds to exchange information during the hunt, whereas others hunt in small groups, maintaining total silence. Moreover, each pod has its own language dialect, distinct from others and apparently determined by family connections rather than by geography. One theory is that unique dialects may be used during mating to prevent inbreeding.[9]

In May 1999, Damini, an elephant at the Prince of Wales Zoo in Lucknow, India, died—apparently losing the will to live after the death of her companion. When the younger elephant Champakali died after giving birth to a stillborn calf, Damini lost interest in food and could not be tempted, even by her favorites—sugar cane, bananas, and sweet grass. She stood for days in her enclosure. When her legs swelled and eventually gave way, she lay listlessly on her side. Tears rolled down her face and she rapidly lost weight. Finally, Damini stopped drinking, despite the 116 degree heat. Veterinarians pumped more than 25 gallons of glucose, saline, and vitamins through a vein in her ear, but, despite their efforts, Damini died.[10]

This empathy for a fellow creature might help explain the ethical behavior displayed by a group of macaques presented with two very undesirable alternatives. If they were willing to pull a chain and administer an electric shock to an unrelated macaque, they were fed; if not, they went hungry. In one experiment, only 13 percent pulled the chain; 87 percent preferred to go hungry rather than hurt another macaque. One went without food for nearly two weeks rather than harm another.[11]

This experiment is particularly impressive when we recall a similar model using humans. Participants, who received a small amount of money for being part of the study, were told that its purpose was to investigate the effects of punishment on memory. Each time a human subject in another room (actually, researchers only feigning participation) failed to remember correctly, participants were instructed to move levers to administer electric shocks of increasing severity. Despite hearing moans and screams from the other room, 87 percent moved the lever to a zone marked "Danger! Severe Shock" when instructed to do so. The conclusion of this study by Stanley Milgram was that 87 percent of humans (receiving money and instructions from authority figures) will hurt others. What caused the macaques (facing the deprivation of food) to resist?

If we are indeed unique, the task of proving it seems to be getting more difficult. The central questions of this chapter are, Who or what are we (a little lower than the angels? a little higher than the aardvarks?), and what are we doing here? We will delay the exploration of what we are doing here until a little later in the chapter; first we will ponder who or what we are. Another way to pose this question is to ask, Is there is a distinct human nature?

Who or What Are We?

To aid in our inquiry, we can use the structures of the avocado and the artichoke as metaphors for human nature (Figure 3.1). An avocado is a pear-shaped tropical fruit with yellowish flesh and a single large seed at the center. If the avocado seed is planted, an entire new avocado plant may grow, which, if it reaches full maturity, is capable of producing another generation of avocado fruit. The seed at the center contains all the essential information about what makes an avocado an avocado.

For contrast, consider the artichoke. Sometimes cooked as a vegetable, an artichoke is the flower head of a thistle plant. It consists of spiny layers that can be peeled off one after the other. When the last layer has been removed, there is nothing left. The "heart" of the artichoke is actually the base of the flower. Although it is tasty to eat, the heart does not contain the essence of the artichoke. The artichoke is nothing but its layers. Since it is a flower, no part of the artichoke—not even its heart—can be induced to produce another generation.

So, we might want to ask, Are we more like avocados or like artichokes? If we could peel away our layers, would we find a central core or

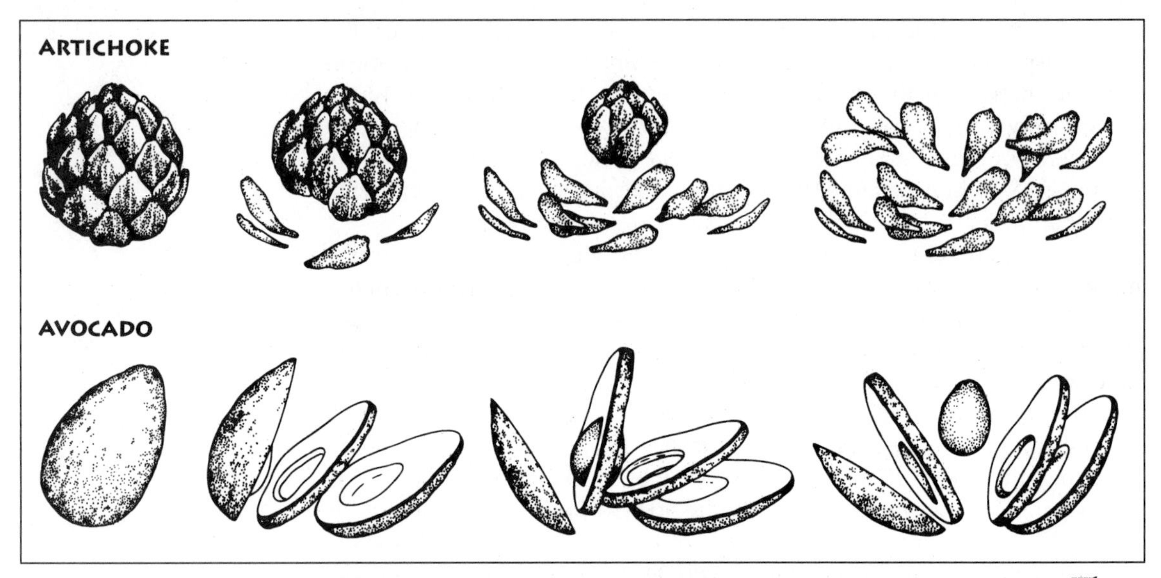

FIGURE 3.1 AVOCADO AND ARTICHOKE VIEWS OF HUMAN NATURE *When we peel away an avocado's outer layers, we find the seed that contains its essence, but when we remove an artichoke's outer layers, we find no central core.*

merely emptiness as the last layer is removed? Do we consist entirely of our layers—genetic instructions and environmental effects—or is there something central that contains and represents the essence of who and what we are?

Is There an Essential Human Nature?—The Avocado View

We will begin our study with the avocado view, because it has had a profound impact on Western culture. As we saw in Historical Interlude B, Greek rationalist thought and Hebrew religious thought became intertwined as Christianity came to theological maturity and planted its Hebrew roots in Greek soil. These two thought systems represent the avocado view of human nature in the West. After discussing each of them, we will look at their impact on ideas about women and consider the influence of technology on the assumption that organic human nature is unique.

The Judaic and Christian Traditions

The Hebrew Scriptures assert that we humans are made in the image and likeness of God. Into the mud of our material stuff, the book of Genesis tells us, the Creator breathed the breath of life. Humans, in a special way, are believed to share in the divine nature. Other animals, according to this tradition, may have excellent instincts and perhaps even intelligence, but they are not made in the image and likeness of God.

Like the Creator, we know who we are—we are self-conscious—and we have the capacity for love. Indeed, we are moral selves obliged to love and serve our Creator. Like the avocado, we have a fleshy outward appearance, which makes us appear similar to other animals, but at our core we share the divine nature and that makes us unique.

The essence of the avocado is not in its flesh but in its seed. The proof of this can be found by planting the seed, which so contains the essence of "avocadoness" that it can produce another whole avocado plant. Whatever it is that makes an avocado an avocado—and not, for instance, a peach or an apple—is condensed into that seed. In a similar way, the Judaic and Christian traditions affirm that what makes you a person, rather than a chimp or a computer, is your special creation in the image of God.

The Greek Rationalist Tradition

We have already met the other avocado view of human nature in Chapters 1 and 2. For Plato and Aristotle, it is our reasoning ability that sets us apart from other creatures. Recalling the prisoners in Plato's cave allegory may make it easier to understand the essential role of reason in the philosophy of the Greek rationalists. While relying only on their senses, the prisoners seem subhuman. Trapped in a world of shadows, they are missing what is real. To be fully human and to understand reality as it is, Plato tells us, they must leave the cave and use their reason to become enlightened.

It costs so much to be a full human being that there are very few who have the enlightenment or the courage to pay the price. One has to abandon altogether the search for security and reach out to the risk of living with both arms. One has to embrace the world like a lover and yet demand no easy return of love. One has to accept pain as a condition of existence.

MORRIS L. WEST, *LAZARUS*

In imagining what an ideal society would be like, Plato makes a connection between the classes of people in society and the parts of a human being. Most people, Plato suggests in his utopia, *Republic,* are driven by their appetites. A good meal, some sensual pleasures, and the gadgets that money can buy are the things this class of people values most. And, we all have in ourselves this element. We crave food, sex, and material comfort to satisfy these appetites.

A second class of people is driven by their emotions. In *Republic* they are the soldiers who guard the city. Their spirited nature makes them capable of strong words and even stronger deeds when conditions demand. We, too, Plato believes, share this element. It gives us the energy to commit ourselves to causes and the enthusiasm to carry a project to completion.

At the highest level in *Republic* are the rulers. They have the same appetites and emotions as the other two classes do, but through training and education, they have cultivated the highest human faculty and live their lives chiefly in accordance with reason. We will discuss Plato's political system in depth in Chapter 8; for now, it is enough to observe that in society and in the human person Plato believes rationality to be the highest element. To be fully human we must exercise our reason; to do otherwise would be to risk slipping to the level of animals or being ruled by our passionate impulses.

Using our avocado image, it is reason that lies at the core of the human person for both Plato and Aristotle. As discussed in Chapter 1, the *Nicomachean Ethics* emphasizes the role of reason in determining the golden mean of proper ethical conduct. Aristotle explains that our passions may drive us to rashness and our animal survival instincts may make us cowards; only reason reveals the path of courage.

Recall that Plato, speaking through the character of his mentor Socrates, thought much of what we call learning is more accurately remembering. Like the slave boy who used reason to understand geometry without being taught it, we have memories of the world of Forms, which we glimpsed before our birth and to which we return at our death. For Plato, the soul is the immortal part of us. Its true home is not in this world of matter and the senses but in the higher world of pure Forms—a world that only our reason can reveal.

Aristotle agrees that at our core we are rational beings. He begins *Metaphysics* by asserting that "all men by nature desire to know" and continues by distinguishing humans from other creatures. "The animals other than man live by appearances and memories, and have but little of connected experience; but the human race lives also by art and reasonings."[12] Where he and Plato part company is on the question of the soul's origin and final home. For Aristotle, the Forms exist and can exist only in matter. In most of his writings, this ontology implies that souls can exist only in bodies and that when the body dies the soul dies with it. Only Plato's theory of a separate world of Forms makes possible the pre- and postexistence of the soul in another world.

It is in the darkness of men's eyes that they get lost.
BLACK ELK

For Plato and Aristotle, the soul represents the highest faculty of human nature. By proclaiming the uniqueness and superiority of human reason, Plato and Aristotle mean to capture our essence (in the avocado sense we have been using) and to distinguish us from other animals. Although we clearly have the capacity to behave like beasts and are just as likely to be swept away by our emotions or passions, only humans are capable of living in accordance with reason. To do this, Plato and Aristotle agree, is to be fully human—to express most truly what we are (in avocado terms, the seed at our core).

The Influence of Western Essentialism on Women

According to the avocado view, there is an essential human nature, analogous to the seed at the core of the avocado. In the Western intellectual tradition, both Judaic and Christian religious thought and Greek rationalist thought have been filtered through the social system of **patriarchy.** Literally meaning "father rule," patriarchy has come to stand for government in society and in the family as well as image making controlled by men. In more recent times, **feminism**—the theory that women should have political, legal, economic, and social rights equal to those of men—has challenged some aspects of both of these traditional thought systems, as well as the assumptions of patriarchy.

patriarchy *a form of social organization in which the father is recognized as head of the family or tribe and men control most of the formal and informal power, as well as define the role of women*

feminism *the theory that women should have political, legal, economic, and social rights equal to those of men and should define their own roles*

In considering the influences of essentialism on women, let's begin with the Greeks. As a result of the strength of the Greek rationalist tradition and especially Plato's tripartite soul, a life dominated by reason has been a cultural ideal in the West for more than 2000 years. Elevating reason to the highest place and commanding it to rule over emotions and appetites seems harmless enough. The difficulty is that Western culture has identified rationality with men and emotionality with women. From that connection, it was an easy step to declare that, just as reason must rule over emotion and the desires of the body, so men must rule over women in human society.

Aristotle reaches a similar conclusion, although his model is based on two rather than three elements of the human soul—the rational and the irrational elements. Like Plato, Aristotle asserts that the political condition of women being ruled by men is understandable because, although both sexes share a rational principle, in women the rational element is easily overruled by the irrational element. One of the difficulties with this argument, according to Elizabeth V. Spelman of Smith College, is that Aristotle argues circularly. Our understanding of why the rational element in the souls of women is often overruled by the irrational element depends on our understanding of relationships in the political arena, and the reverse is also true: we can understand the political realities of Athenian life, in which men rule over women, by reference to the relationship between the rational and irrational elements within women's souls. In other words, men rule over women because women are by nature more likely to be influenced by the irrational elements in their souls, and this is clear because women are ruled by naturally-more-rational men.[13] While each of these premises justifies the other, there is no independent or outside justification for either of them. René Descartes, in Chapter 5, will be accused of a similarly circular type of reasoning in his proof for the existence of God.

Although the reasoning is flawed, the argument has prevailed. There is, in Western culture, a presumption that men are more rational and women more emotional. Given this equation, women who want to be taken seriously as rational decision makers appear to have two options. One is to deny their emotions and desires and strive to fit into the rational, male model as fully as possible. Women entering the workforce during the 1970s did something like this. They bought plainly cut dark suits (with skirts) and wore them with plain blouses and ties. Looking as much like men as possible, many women also went out of their way to prove that they could work as hard, act as tough, and be as distant from their emotions as the male cultural ideal demanded.

The other extreme option for women is to affirm the value of a rich emotional life and identify themselves with it. To do so, they must risk accepting second-class status. As long as emotionality is devalued, there are few socially acceptable ways for women or men to express and cultivate healthy emotional lives. Yet, by insisting that only logic can lead to knowledge, suppressing our feelings, and denying whenever possible and for as long as possible that we have bodies at all, we risk both physical and mental/emotional illness.

As some social critics have observed, the physical ideal for women in Western culture is an emaciated body. Models must deny themselves food, dieting continually to achieve the kind of no-fat body image that allows clothes to simply hang. At the extreme are the illnesses of anorexia and bulimia. Continuing to see a fat image, some ninety-five-pound women starve their bodies, and most middle or junior high school girls have been or are now on diets. Others are out of control, bingeing on rich foods and then vomiting or taking laxatives to prevent the food from turning to fat. And this is not just a modern-day problem. Mary Wollstonecraft, whose ideas we will examine in Chapter 8, wrote in 1792: "Genteel women are, literally speaking, slaves to their bodies."

If we maintain this patriarchal view in which the virtues of the mind are projected onto men and the vices of the body attributed to women, men as well as women must pay the price. Many of us ignore the messages of our bodies—that we are sleep- and rest-deprived, that eating while engaging in stressful telephone conversations interferes with digestion—until severe illness forces us to stop or at least slow down. Heart attacks and strokes, as well as cancer, may be our bodies' last, desperate attempts to get our attention. By pretending we are only rational minds, it is possible to suppress emotions and ignore physical symptoms—at least for a while.

A better solution might be questioning the Greek ideal and asking whether a life lived in accordance with reason has to mean a life lived without emotion and without attention to the body. Acknowledging that we have limits and stopping at regular intervals to enjoy our food, to play, and to rest takes nothing away from our commitment to reason as an ideal. The Greeks themselves led much more balanced lives than we, holding as an ideal "A sound mind in a sound body" and honoring the place of leisure and sports in a life devoted to rational thinking.

Women in the workforce in the early years of the twenty-first century are wearing softer clothing. Rejecting the model of the driving and driven emotionless "boss," some women and some men have discovered that being a leader means empowering everyone to act rather than giving orders from the top. Collaborative leadership ignores hierarchies—one manager at the top, a layer of submanagers next, and a large bottom layer of workers—in favor of a more organic model in which everyone has a task and all share in leading.

The Chinese classic *Tao Te Ching* has been given a new twist under the title *The Tao of Leadership*. In this translation, the message remains the same, but the language reflects the modern world:

> The leader can act as a warrior or as a healer. As a warrior, the leader acts with power and decision. That is the *Yang* or masculine aspect of leadership. Most of the time, however, the leader acts as a healer and is in an open, receptive, and nourishing state. That is the feminine or *Yin* aspect of leadership. This mixture of doing and being, of warrior and healer, is both productive and potent.[14]

If I am not for myself, who will be for me? If I am not for others, what am I? If not now, when?
THE TALMUD

The Western division into reason and emotion, into doing and being, is overcome in this more holistic version of reality. It avoids the either/or choice between reason and emotion that has its roots in Western interpretations of the ideas of Plato and Aristotle and suggests the way to a fuller life for both women and men.

Let's now consider the patriarchal influence on Hebrew religious thought. It is not necessary to be a religious person in Western society to be influenced by Judaic and Christian views of human nature. John Milton's

1667 epic poem *Paradise Lost* gives us the story. Adam, the first man, is created in God's image. Lonely for a companion, he petitions God for other creatures. As God obligingly provides a variety of animals, Adam names them. They are fine, but only when God removes one of Adam's own ribs and creates woman (literally, "out of man") is he fully satisfied. As Milton has God say in the poem:

> Return, fair Eve,
> Whom fliest thou? Whom thou fliest, of him thou art
> His flesh, his bone; to give thee being I lent.[15]

Indeed, this story does appear in the second chapter of Genesis, the first book of the Bible. The first chapter of Genesis, however, tells the story another way. It begins with the familiar "In the beginning God created the heavens and the earth." After dividing the seas from the dry land and placing the Sun and Moon in their proper positions, God begins creating living things—plants, animals, and, finally, humans. Here is the last part of Chapter 1:

> Then God said, "Let us make humankind in our image, according to our likeness; and let them have dominion over the fish of the sea, and over the birds of the air, and over the cattle, and over all the wild animals of the earth, and over every creeping thing that creeps upon the earth." So God created humankind in his image, in the image of God he created them; male and female he created them. God blessed them, and God said to them, "Be fruitful and multiply, and fill the earth and subdue it." And it was so. God saw everything he had made and indeed, it was very good.[16]

There is nothing in this version about Adam's rib. Instead, woman and man are created together at the high point of Creation and together given dominion over Earth. Chapters 1 and 2 of Genesis each contain a separate and complete creation account. They derive from two different oral traditions and both were included, yet our patriarchal culture has popularized only the second chapter. Some people are totally unaware that the first even exists.

When the Western religious tradition speaks of man being created in God's image, it has sometimes seemed to mean human males only. Woman has appeared to be created in Adam's image, not God's. As Milton puts it in *Paradise Lost,* "He [Adam] for God only, she [Eve] for God in him." Today's philosophers wonder what the implications are for women if we define human nature this way. Does our human uniqueness apply to men only? When the culture emphasizes the Adam's rib story to the exclusion of the other more egalitarian account, how can women identify with this tradition and see themselves as created in the image of God and sharing equally in the divine essence?

Macrina on Emotions and the Soul

Macrina of Cappadocia had an extended conversation with her brother Gregory on this very question during the fourth century. Her response spoke to an urgent theological question of her day because, as she lay

THE MAKING OF A PHILOSOPHER

Macrina
(ca. 327–380)

Born into a wealthy Christian family in Cappadocia (present-day Turkey), Macrina grew up on stories of the persecutions her great-grandparents and grandparents had suffered because of their faith. Her mother's father had lost his life and all his possessions, yet the family's faith remained strong. Macrina was the eldest child of ten, and after her father died when she was only twelve, she took over the education of her baby brother Peter. She also persuaded her mother to convert the family home into a monastery in which former slaves and servants were treated as sisters and equals. Although she had been engaged at the age of twelve to a lawyer, when the young man died, Macrina decided to remain unmarried and devote her life to asceticism. As an architect of the monastic ideal, she can perhaps be seen as a cocreator with her more famous brother Basil the Great, of the Eastern form of monasticism. Her brother Gregory, like Basil also a bishop, recorded the dying words of his sister in *On the Soul and the Resurrection,* and he also wrote a tribute to her called *The Life of Macrina.* We are told that when Basil came home from the university smug with learning, it was Macrina who converted him to the humility of a seeker after wisdom. She remained at the center of a remarkable family and regarded both philosophy and religion as paths to truth.

dying, the church fathers of Western Christianity were arguing about whether or not women were made in the image of God. Because in the secular world women typically played subordinate roles, some Fathers linked this with the story of Eve's creation from Adam's rib and contended that woman was made in the image of man rather than the image of God.

We must consider Macrina's views on the soul and women's place in the divine order of Creation against this theological background. Raised in a highly intellectual and spiritual family (two of her brothers were bishops), Macrina appears as a virgin-philosopher and even as the "Christian Socrates" in *On the Soul and the Resurrection,* her deathbed dialogue with her brother Gregory, which he later recorded.[17] Grieving the recent death of their brother Basil, Gregory presses Macrina for a clear explanation of the nature of the soul. The conversation quickly turns to the relationship between the passions and the soul. Macrina states the question and offers a thesis:

> . . .What must we think of the desiring and spirited faculties; are they part of the essence of the soul and present in it from the beginning or something additional which come to us later . . . For the one who says that the soul is "the image of God" affirms that what is alien to God is outside the definition of the soul. So, if some quality is not recognized as part of the divine nature, we cannot reasonably think that it is part of the nature of the soul.[18]

When Gregory questions how what is clearly in us (the passions of anger and desire) can be seen as alien to us, Macrina replies that reason struggles to subdue these passions and that some people such as Moses have succeeded in conquering them:

> This would not have been so if these qualities had been natural to him and logically in keeping with his essence . . . These qualities are alien to us so that the eradication of them is not only not harmful, but even beneficial to our nature. Therefore, it is clear that these qualities belong to what is considered external, the affections of our nature and not its essence . . .[19]

This dialogue reminds us of the *Phaedo,* Plato's description of Socrates' last day of life. As he prepares to drink the hemlock, Socrates discusses with his friends the possible fate of the soul after death. Significantly, there are no women present; even Xanthippe, Socrates' wife, has been banished. In this dialogue we hear two possibilities for the soul's fate after death. If the soul has consistently practiced disassociating itself from the body during life, Socrates explains, it will be free at death to join the unseen. On the other hand, the impure soul will remain under the influence of the body:

> Why, because each pleasure and pain is a sort of nail which nails and rivets the soul to the body, until she becomes like the body, and believes that to be true which the body affirms to be true; and from agreeing with the body and having the same delights she is obliged to have the same habits and haunts, and is not likely ever to be pure at her departure . . .[20]

This basket, woven in a traditional design, also expresses the uniqueness of the woman who made it.

Apache basket/Courtesy of Carol Galbraith/Photo by Quentin Kardos.

In this image, the ***pathe,*** what we might call the passions, can make the soul impure. As we have just seen, Macrina offers another image: The *pathe* are not part of the soul's essence. In the *Phaedo,* Socrates believes his body will be appropriately discarded at the time of death, but Macrina defends the Christian belief that the body will be reunited with the soul on the day of resurrection at the end of time. Using an analogy, she likens the soul to the art of painting and the elements of the earth to colors. Just as the painter knows the colors he has used, both individually and in combination, so the soul does not forget:

pathe *[PAH thay] the plural of* pathos, *a Greek word that, when used in connection with the soul, means "emotion" and "passion"*

> Thus the soul knows the individual elements which formed the body in which it dwelt, even after the dissolution of those elements. Even if nature drags them far apart from each other and, because of their basic differences prevents each of them from mixing with its opposite, the soul will, nevertheless, exist along with each element, fastening upon what is its own by its power of knowing it and it will remain there until the union of the separated parts occurs again in the reforming of the dissolved being which is properly called "the resurrection."[21]

In all of this, Macrina is clear that the soul, which is "the image of God," is without gender. Women as well as men are created in the image and likeness of God. As we turn from the fourth to the twenty-first century, we consider a similar controversy: the possible "humanness" of artificial intelligence. Just as the issues raised by feminism have caused us to take a second look at Western essentialism, so the possibilities opened up by technology have further complicated the question of what it means to be a human being.

Sing a black girl's song. Sing the song of her possibilities. Sing a righteous gospel, the making of a melody. Let her be born. Let her be born and handle warmly.

NTOZAKE SHANGE

Technology and Western Essentialism

The line between human and machine is beginning to blur. When IBM's Deep Blue defeated reigning chess grandmaster Garry Kasparov in May 1997, some called the victory a "turning point in history." Others likened it to a Greek tragedy. If we define our humanity in terms of our rationality, the superior computational skills of a computer program may threaten us. Equally unsettling to us is the idea of a computer made out of DNA. Although its applications are restricted, it "solves" problems through parallel processing: addressing all possible solutions simultaneously, rather than working serially the way an adding machine tallies a sum. A DNA computer does each step slowly but can work on billions of sites at once. This style is just what is needed for breaking a code or searching the Library of Congress for a particular piece of information.[22]

With the continuing progress of work in artificial intelligence, it is easy to imagine an android that appears human but is actually a very sophisticated machine. The original *Star Trek* TV series gave us Spock, half Vulcan and half human, who at times struggled to deny his human side and imitate the totally logical, totally unemotional Vulcan ideal.

Star Trek: The Next Generation took the idea one step further by introducing Data, an android with a positronic net for a brain and a very human-looking body. He is extremely strong, able to calculate and absorb information at an extraordinary rate, but unable to experience human emotions. In one episode, "The Measure of a Man," a scientist's request to disassemble Data in the name of science leads to a debate on whether or not Data is a sentient being with the right to control his own fate.

Insisting that Data is in essence a sophisticated toaster, the scientist is perplexed when Captain Jean-Luc Picard refuses permission. At a hearing convened to decide the matter, both sides agree on three characteristics of a sentient being, creating, in effect, a definition and test of human nature. Everyone agrees that Data has intelligence, and he clearly has self-awareness—he is aware of himself and of his options. Data passes the key third test—possession of consciousness—when he demonstrates "human" attachment to a book of poetry and the hologram of a deceased lover. "Does Data have a soul? I don't know if *I* have," the adjutant replies in denying permission to disassemble, "but he must have the ability to choose."

In another episode, Data refuses to send a group of repair modules called Exocomps to their death/destruction, even though the lives of his best friend Geordi La Forge and Captain Picard are at risk, because he believes the Exocomps may be like himself, a life-form. With a twist worthy of the ethical macaques we discussed earlier, the Exocomps put their own lives at risk, and one of them voluntarily sacrifices itself so that the humans can escape. The message is that self-aware beings, whether human or mechanical, may choose martyrdom but it may not be forced upon them. As sentient beings, their own wishes must be considered.

A man is born into the world with only a tiny spark of goodness in him. The spark is God, it is the soul; the rest is ugliness and evil, a shell. The spark must be guarded like a treasure, it must be fanned into flame.
CHAIM POTOK, *THE CHOSEN*

If, as in the Western religious definition, a human being must possess a soul or be made in the image of God, it seems clear that Data and the Exocomps fail the test. Clearly, they have been created by humans and not by God. If, however, we apply the Greek rationalist definition of a human being as one whose life is ruled by reason, then androids would seem to be candidates. But, would we be prepared to grant human status in any legal or social sense to an artificial life-form like Data or the Exocomps?

Much of what probably seems most obvious and familiar to you derives from the combination of Greek rationalism and Judaic and Christian theology that supports the Western worldview. Yet, as we have seen, those views have been overlaid with patriarchy to the detriment of women and men and caused some to describe the West as out of balance or excessively rationalist. Both feminism and technology have introduced new questions. Still, the avocado view of human nature remains the commonsense explanation for anyone raised in the West. Since it currently seems to present almost as many problems as solutions, let's consider the other possibility—the artichoke view of human nature.

Is There an Essential Human Nature?—The Artichoke View

Tom Wolfe's *The Bonfire of the Vanities* introduces us to Sherman McCoy, a Wall Street bond trader who, at the beginning of the novel, sees himself as a "master of the universe." Arrested for vehicular manslaughter and financially ruined, he is taken from his elegant Park Avenue apartment to a downtown New York police station for booking. Somewhere during this dehumanizing experience, the "self" he thought was so durable begins to deteriorate. Stepping in to editorialize, novelist Wolfe tells us that we need the "whole village" of our social relationships to keep our "self" in place. Citing scientific data, Wolfe tells the reader that healthy college students, if subjected to total sensory deprivation, begin to hallucinate in a few hours. When deprived of constant feedback to fuel its image, the self, it would seem, simply disintegrates. If this is so, then was the self ever real to begin with?

What you have become is the price you paid to get what you used to want.
MIGNON MCLAUGHLIN

The Protean Self

One artichoke view of human nature assumes that disintegration and reformation of the self is not necessarily a bad thing. Based on Proteus—the shape-shifter of Greek mythology who was able to appear as a green tree, an old man, a blinding fire—this view agrees that we are nothing but our layers and finds this reasonable and healthy. Lacking a central core, as posited by the avocado view, we are able to respond to the lack of continuity we find in the world by adapting to it. If reality were stable and filled with meaning, it might make sense to strive for a core self; because it is not, the psychologically healthy approach might be to imitate Proteus and change with a changing world.

Psychiatrist Robert Lifton suggests that people could be hippies when young and, years later, conservative businesspeople, with no loss of identity or fragmentation. In this view, a "self," like an artichoke, is composed of many layers, each of which is real and functional only at particular times or in particular circumstances. Viewing the self as a collage rather than as a single, unchanging picture might better enable us to move successfully among incomplete, changing realities. Since the world is unpredictable, we need a whole collection of selves with which to meet it. Some would say that Bill Clinton's success as president of the United States was due in part

Nothing, nothing am I but a small, loving watercourse.
ROSARIO CASTELLANOS

to his ability to negotiate among a repertoire of "selves." We might think here of a pomegranate that contains many seeds, each representing a version of the self.[23]

Looking for certainty in a single truth to explain the world has been called **modernism.** Western essentialism developed in a modernist world. The protean self, by contrast, is a product of **postmodernism,** which denies moral absolutes and certain truth. Instead of despairing over the loss of unitive meaning, the protean self celebrates pluralism. If the realities of life are always changing, the sensible thing to do is move easily among them, altering your "self" to suit the conditions you find. Embracing postmodernism, a group of twentieth-century philosophers celebrated the chaos and hailed the freedom it would provide.

modernism *the quest for certainty and unitive truth, a single and coherent explanation of reality that gives it meaning*

postmodernism *the recognition that certainty and unitive truth are not possible because existence and reality are partial, inconsistent, plural, and multiple*

Existentialism: The Self-Created Self

According to existentialism, whose ethical theory we will consider in Chapter 10, the key fact about human nature is that we come into being and exist without a fixed essence. Spanish philosopher José Ortega y Gasset put it this way in his 1941 book *History as a System:*

> The stone is given its existence; it need not fight for being what it is—a stone in the field. Man has to be himself in spite of unfavorable circumstances; that means he has to make his own existence at every single moment. He is given the abstract possibility of existing, but not the reality. This he has to conquer hour after hour. Man must earn his life, not only economically but metaphysically . . . We are dealing—and let the disquieting strangeness of the case be well noted—with an entity whose being consists not in what it is already, but in what it is not yet, a being that consists in not-yet-being.[24]

We grow neither better nor worse as we get old, but more like ourselves.
MAY LAMBERTON BECKER

Indeed it is of the essence of man that he can lose himself in the jungle of his existence, within himself, and thanks to his sensation of being lost can react by setting energetically to work to find himself again.
JOSÉ ORTEGA Y GASSET

French existentialist Jean-Paul Sartre takes for granted the twentieth-century despair over loss of meaning and flatly rejects belief in God. Without God, the cosmos lacks purpose and there is no moral law that must be obeyed. The positive aspect of all this negativism is that humans are not squeezed into society's preconceptions and are therefore free to become whatever they choose—to create themselves. Sartre had this to say at a 1946 lecture:

> Atheistic existentialism, of which I am a representative, declares with greater consistency that if God does not exist there is at least one being whose existence comes before its essence, a being which exists before it can be defined by any conception of it. That being is man . . .What do we mean by saying that existence precedes essence? We mean that man first of all exists, encounters himself, surges up in the world—and defines himself afterwards . . . Thus there is no human nature, because there is no God to have a conception of it.[25]

With no fixed essence—with no "avocado seed"—people take their bare existence as a starting point and begin choosing a life path for themselves. Since there are no rules, choosing can be difficult. The key requirement, according to existentialist philosophers, is that we must choose and,

Which qualities, described by atheistic existentialism, do you find in this image?
The Subway by George Tooker/Whitney Museum of American Art, New York.

having chosen, we must stand accountable for our choices. Each time you do this, you add a brushstroke to the painting that will be yourself or shape a bit more distinctly the clay of the sculpture that is you.

In the most powerful of creative actions, you create a self for yourself. In a world lacking purpose and meaning, in the absence of guidelines, you make a decision and accept responsibility for it. Since you have this radical freedom from all restraint, you behave less than humanly if you try to claim a lack of freedom. It is tempting to blame your childhood, your ethnicity, or your previous experiences for what you say and do. The result might be to justify your actions or let yourself off the hook by claiming "It's not my fault." To do so, however, is to sacrifice the opportunity to be fully human.

Power is knowing your past.
SPIKE LEE

At every moment, existentialism affirms, you have the possibility of being different than you have been in the past. Nothing is fixed; there are no boxes in which you are imprisoned; nothing can defeat you without your cooperation. As the nineteenth-century poem "Invictus" puts it, "I am the master of my fate; I am the captain of my soul."[26] Its author, William Ernest Henley, lived with chronic, crippling pain and died young; yet he remained "unconquered" (the Latin meaning of the title) by life's challenges. It is frightening to think that even facing what Henley had to face we might be expected to be brave and self-reliant, unconquered to the end, yet existentialism insists that all our responses to life, all our states of mind, are totally within our control.

I change myself, I change the world.
GLORIA ANZALDÚA

If you are sad, Sartre insists, it is because you have chosen to be sad. Your sadness is like a coat you put on, and you could just as easily wear another—the coat of happiness. While you are alone or with a loved one, you may decide to indulge your sadness, walking around with stooping shoulders and sighing frequently. The proof of your ability to alter your mental state occurs when the telephone or doorbell rings. If a stranger appears, Sartre writes, "I will assume a lively cheerfulness. What will remain of my sadness except that I obligingly promise it an appointment for later after the departure of the visitor."[27]

Existentialism asserts that by facing the lack of meaning all around us, making our choices, and standing accountable for them, we have the possibility of putting together the layers that will make a self for ourselves. It will not be an easy task. The world in which we find ourselves is absurd. Sartre's existentialist colleague Albert Camus put it this way:

> In a universe suddenly divested of illusions and lights, man feels an alien, a stranger. His exile is without remedy since he is deprived of the memory of a lost home or the hope of a promised land. This divorce between man and his life, the actor and his setting, is properly the feeling of absurdity.[28]

Life has no inherent meaning. Existentialism celebrates the absence of a solid center in the avocado sense. Lacking an essence, the human person is not fixed, not predetermined to be anything. Instead, each person is free to create those layers that will make a functional self. As circumstances change, the layers may change with them. At every moment, however, humans are the masters of their fate. The good news is you can be anything you want to be; the bad news is there is no one to blame but yourself.

Non-Western Views of the Self

Besides Western views of the protean self and existentialism, there are three non-Western examples of the artichoke view of human nature to consider. Buddhism, beginning at the time of the Milesian, or pre-Socratic, philosophers, proclaimed that there is no need to think of a solid, separate self. To proclaim a permanent self is to live in a world of illusion. From ancient Chinese medicine, we find a conception of self with five elements—found in both the self and nature. Like nature, the self is in flux, and in a healthy person or ecosystem, the elements take their places at appropriate times. One African view of a fully realized human person describes the creative, complementary relationship between men and women as a model for healthy living, as well as an indication of what divinity might be like.

From Hinduism and *Atman* to Buddhism and *Anatman*

As we begin to look at non-Western views of the self, we are fortunate that in India we can see the transition from what we have been calling an avocado view of the self (in Hinduism) to what we are calling an artichoke view of the self (in Buddhism). Keep in mind that Siddhārtha Gautama was raised a Hindu, and, through a long struggle to understand how happiness is possible in the face of suffering, he reached a new understanding of the self. From the most philosophical of the Hindu scriptures, the Upanishads (also known as the Vedanta because they are the end or conclusion of the

Veda) we have a very avocado-like image of the core self at the heart of every human person, which travels from life to life through the process of reincarnation, taking on new bodies but remaining intact.

In a dialogue between father and son, popularly known as "The Education of Svetaketu," a young man has returned home after twelve years of studying all the Vedas. He considers himself quite well educated and is even a bit conceited. Realizing this, the father begins questioning his son and, in the process, giving him additional instruction. "In the beginning," the father explains, "there was that only which is, one thing only, without a second. It thought, May I be many, may I grow forth." The inner essence of all that is, the father goes on to tell Svetaketu, is the cosmic Self—present in an unlimited way in the cosmos and in a more limited way in each of us. In truth, what is in each of us—and what is known in Vedanta as ***atman***—is identical with ultimate reality—what is known as *Brahman*. "This body indeed withers and dies when the living Self has left it; the living Self dies not," the father concludes. And, in a stunning affirmation, the father tells his now humbled son, "That subtle essence is the self of all that exists. It is the True. It is the Self, and that, Svetaketu, you are."[29]

atman *[AHT muhn] in Hinduism, the Self or soul, which endures through successive reincarnations as an expession of the divine and as a carrier of* karma

This is quite similar to the Western religious view of the self as marked by its resemblance to the divine. The thought system that came to be known as Buddhism departs from this view of a core self and offers instead a very artichoke-like view. Concluding that impermanence characterizes all of existence and—giving rise to sickness, old age, and death—is the cause of most of our suffering, Siddhārtha Gautama set out to resolve this conflict. What he concluded was that acceptance of the fleeting nature of all that is offers the only possiblity for happiness. If we accept that change is the nature of our existence, that might be a good starting place. The man who came to be known as the Buddha offered humankind an analysis of and a prescription for what he referred to as "the disease of living." The prescription is the Four Noble Truths (Table 3.1). The First Noble Truth of Buddhism is that, for all of us, life is marked by suffering. The Second Noble Truth is that we suffer because we desire—to remain always young; to keep our children with us always; to find a special person who can make all our loneliness disappear.

You are all the Buddha.
THE BUDDHA—LAST WORDS

In the first flush of love, all we feel is completion, lost in a love that makes us feel ten feet tall. Nothing else seems to matter or even to be real. A very special and wonderful person treasures us, and that seems to be all we need. Unfortunately, there will inevitably be the first conflict in which the beloved, rather than meeting all our needs, seems intent on making us

TABLE 3.1

FOUR NOBLE TRUTHS OF BUDDHISM

1. Life is suffering.
2. Desire causes suffering.
3. Ending desire ends suffering.
4. Following the Noble Eightfold Path ends desire.

Letting go of the idea of "self" can be enlightening.
Ioanna Salajan, *Zen Comics*. Used with permission.

miserable. The very desire we have for that person becomes the cause of our suffering. It is the same with parents and children. In their innocent perfection, babies and young children represent all the unrealized and perhaps unrealizable dreams of their parents, but if they are psychologically sound, they will one day need to separate from the dreams of their parents to create dreams of their own. Parents may feel betrayed or rejected by their growing children.

Buddhism offers the same reply to both the disappointed lover and the clinging parent: Your desire or, to put it another way, your attachment to particular people and outcomes is the cause of your suffering. Nothing in this world can bring you permanent pleasure since nothing is permanent. If you look to this world for happiness, you can only be disappointed:

> From attachment springs continued existence, which is sensual, possessing form or formless. From existence arises birth through a returning to various wombs. On birth is dependent the series of old age, death, sorrow and the like. By putting a stop to ignorance and what follows from it, all these cease successively.[30]

It may seem painful to accept the transitory nature of everything, but reality is what it is, and kidding yourself for a while only postpones the suffering. No one escapes. In the end, everyone you love will die and you yourself will meet the same fate. All the beauty of nature will one day perish, as will all the creations of humankind. The self that seems so stable is only another manifestation of the world of flux. Accept this and you will save yourself the pain and suffering attachment is sure to bring.

Ending this desire means ending the suffering. This is the Third Noble Truth, and with it we come to the Buddhist view of ***anatman.*** Our desires or attachments originate from a fiction we have created: the fiction of a stable, permanent, and real self. The truth is we are only a collection of ***skandhas,*** or yarnlike strands, temporarily united but in no sense permanent or real. Once we grasp this essential truth, we can begin to escape the desires that cause us so much suffering. All of life is characterized by change, and we are no exception to this rule. There is no separateness, as we discussed in Chapter 2; everything is interconnected and everything is in flux. There are temporary combinations of the five *skandhas*—form, feeling, perception, impulse, and consciousness—in what we think of as our separate selves and in what appears to be external reality. The temptation is to delude ourselves that these loose, ever-shifting associations of *skandhas* represent something permanent.

anatman *[ahn AHT muhn] the Buddhist doctrine that there is no permanent, separate, individual, ego-self*

skandhas *in Buddhism, the five elements (feeling, perception, impulse, consciousness, and form) that make the world and the person of appearances*

Delusion is the cause of our pain, and letting go of this delusion is the only route to peace of mind. Since we are at every moment different selves, there is really nothing to hold on to. One Buddhist text puts it this way:

> The body is composed of the five *skandhas,* and produced from the five elements. It is all empty and without soul, and arises from the action of the chain of causation. This chain of causation is the cause of coming into existence and the cessation of this chain is the cause of the state of cessation.[31]

DOING PHILOSOPHY
Oneness with Other Beings

For French philosopher and mystic Simone Weil, the sacred part of the human person was his or her "ineradicable expectation of goodness." In a universe ruled by impersonal necessity, divinely created humans give up their particularity (their individual selves) and become annihilated in divine love. For Weil, this mystical sense of connection with other human beings led to an extreme renunciation of self during World War II. Born into a well-to-do Jewish family in Paris, she experienced a mystical union with Christ while in her twenties. Living in exile in England during the Nazi occupation of France, she deliberately starved herself to death (at the age of thirty-four) to place herself in the position of her compatriots starving involuntarily in France.

Weil's act represents both the Judaic and Christian ideal of loving one's neighbor as oneself and the Buddhist ethical ideal of compassion for one's fellow beings. Weil herself was deeply influenced by all these traditions. In a poem commemorating Weil's sacrifice of herself, Gjertrud Schnackenberg put this prayer in Weil's mouth:

> Father, I cannot stand
> To think of them and eat.
> Send it to them, it is theirs.
> Send this food for them,
> For my people still in France.*

* Gjertrud Schnackenberg, "The Heavenly Feast," in *The Lamplit Answer* (New York: Farrar, Strauss and Giroux, 1983).

In another lifetime, a different combination of *skandhas* will present itself as apparently permanent, and there will be the continuing temptation to accept this one, too, as real. What is correct is *anatman,* the absence of an enduring self. Whereas attachment to a false self leads to the pain caused by desire, letting go of this illusion can lead to **enlightenment.** Accepting things as they are not only ends suffering but also lets us off the wheel of birth-death-rebirth that binds us to this world.

enlightenment *the Buddhist term for the realization that comes from seeing the world as it actually is*

To face reality about the self and the world is to gain a kind of freedom. No one but you can make you happy. If you put your happiness in the hands of another, that person always has the power to make you unhappy—not only by rejecting you but by moving away, growing older, or dying. Enlightenment is the recognition that you hold your fate in your own hand. True seeing earns you escape from the round of births and deaths that characterizes this plane of existence:

> This is to be meditated upon by you who enjoy dwelling tranquilly in lonely woods. He who knows it thoroughly reaches at last to absolute thinness. Then he becomes blissfully extinct . . . Then, set free from the bonds of the prison-house of existence, you . . . shall attain *Nirvana.*[32]

nirvana *a state in which individuality is extinguished or the state of enlightenment in which all pain, suffering, mental anguish, and the need for successive rebirths disappear*

This is the Buddha's description of ***nirvana,*** a literal "blowing out" of the candle flame of the false self. To many Westerners, the concept may sound very negative. Accustomed as we are to taking a solid self for granted, we may find it difficult, if not impossible, to imagine why anyone would want to annihilate that sense of self. But we have some experience that can help us appreciate what the Buddha was describing. At the moment of orgasm, the sense of self may blur or disappear as the world falls away, and even your partner may fade from your experience. There is a kind of joy in the abandonment of self in orgasm that comes close to what mystics from many cultures experience in meditation.

As one gives up the illusion of a separate self, there is a feeling of interdependence with everything that in Buddhist terms is the accurate view. What you lose is your sense of a separate identity, with boundaries and limits; what you gain is the sense of interconnectedness with all things that the false sense of separateness can block. *Nirvana,* the "blowing out" of the false sense of a separate self, has been described by Alan Watts as, "joy and creative power . . . to lose one's life is to find it—to find freedom of action unimpeded by self-frustration and the anxiety inherent in trying to save and control the Self."[33] To hold on to a puny separate self seems foolish and petty in the presence of something vast and wonderful.

I came to understand that I am not the light or the source of the light. But light—truth, understanding, knowledge—is there, and it will only shine in many dark places if I reflect it. I am a fragment of a mirror whose whole design and shape I do not know.

ALEXANDER PAPADEROS

Chinese Five-Element View of the Self

Taoism shares with Buddhism the view that life is a state of interconnectedness rather than separateness. *Tao* is the inside of the circle, that which cannot be named, for to name it is to give it particularity and destroy its wholeness. The *Tao* manifests itself in a dance of energy that in Chapter 2 we called *yin-yang* or *yang-yin*—sometimes actively doing and sometimes quietly receptive. In the *t'ai chi* symbol we saw that *yin* spills into *yang* and *yang* is already moving to *yin*. These are two aspects of the same thing, like the two sides of a coin or the front and back of a hand. They flow into each other in a circular movement.

In Taoism, nature is our guide for healthy living. Each season (five in the Chinese system) is a particular manifestation of the whole process, and each has its appropriate time and role to play. Spring melts the snows of winter and pushes green shoots out of what seemed to be dead earth. In summer the Sun rises early and sets late, calling us to be active and energetic and to bloom like the flowers and the trees. Late summer brings the harvest when the fruits of the growing season are gathered and stored. Autumn turns the leaves red and gold, signaling the transition from activity to rest. In winter the earth rests; days are short and nights are long and cold. Humans and other animals seek shelter, and much activity is curtailed.

Like the cosmos, we are composed of five elements: earth, air or metal, water, wood, and fire (Figure 3.2). Each element corresponds to a season, and together all five express the oneness of nature. When we are in harmony, the elements are balanced within us, and we move smoothly around the circle of the seasons—throughout the year and, indeed, throughout each day. Taoism views health as balance, or harmony, among the elements and disease as imbalance among them.

In our Western view, life-giving blood pulses through us in the circulatory system, the network of arteries, veins, and capillaries that connects everything with everything else. Taoism uses the image of a parallel energy

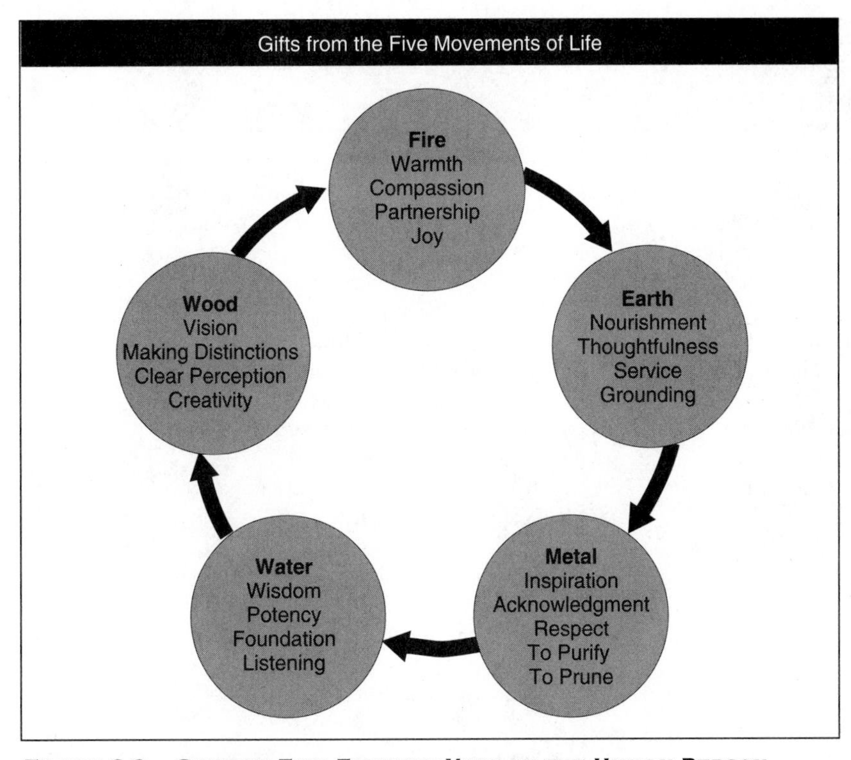

FIGURE 3.2 CHINESE FIVE-ELEMENT VIEW OF THE HUMAN PERSON
As in nature, the human person is composed of five elements.
By permission of Julia Measures, The Traditional Acupuncture Institute.

system. Instead of blood, this system carries ***ch'i,*** the energy of the life force that expresses the dance between heaven and Earth. In a healthy person, *ch'i* flows unobstructed throughout the body. Pain and disease result from blockages in the system; the art and science of acupuncture is concerned with restoring the flow.

ch'i *in Taoism, the energy of the life force that flows between heaven and Earth and within nature*

In her book *Traditional Acupuncture: The Law of the Five Elements,* Dianne Connelly describes acupuncture's role in Chinese medicine:

> Traditional Acupuncture is a healing art and science which teaches how to see the entire human being in bodymindspirit, how to recognize the process of health and illness, and how to go about the restoration of lost health in an individual. The main difference between Western medicine and Oriental medicine is the basic theory of the Chinese that there is a Life Force called *Ch'i* Energy, and that this Life Force flows within us in a harmonious, balanced way. This harmony and balance is health. If the Life Force is not flowing properly, then there is disharmony and imbalance. This is illness.[34]

Ch'i makes the Sun shine, the rain fall, the seasons change; it is the source of life and breath in the human person. Taoism suggests: If you want to understand yourself, study nature.

PHILOSOPHERS SPEAK FOR THEMSELVES
Tao Te Ching

Chapter 23

Speak and then be still and listen
Observe the wisdom of Heaven and Earth
Hurricanes blow—then the winds grow calm
Showers soak—then the sun returns
Nothing lasts forever
Natural forces follow their own rhythms
We would do well to imitate them

Follow the Tao and share its simplicity
Practicing virtue unites you with Virtue
Experiencing loss immerses you in loss
and brings acceptance

Trust the wisdom of Nature
It is your guide to wholeness

Chapter 55

The person in harmony with the Tao
has the vitality of a baby
Impervious to scorpions and wild bears,
Soft-boned and weak-muscled,
but with a strong grip
Unaware of sexual union,
he maintains an erection
She screams all day
without becoming hoarse
Such vitality!
It is the expression of perfect harmony
and the goal of life

Courting excitement wastes our vital energy
Rushing from project to project wears us out
These are the marks of disharmony

Separated from the natural vitality of the Tao,
we exhaust our strength

O to be self-balanced for contingencies, to confront night storms, hunger, ridicule, accidents, rebuffs, as the trees and animals do.

WALT WHITMAN

Think of a young, healthy tree in springtime, as its wood pushes up toward the heavens and its branches sprout green leaves. The young tree is well rooted in the earth, so it has stability, yet it is supple and able to bend when the wind blows. An unhealthy or dying tree can be hard and dry; branches may snap off in the wind, or the whole tree may become uprooted. In nature and in the human person, the wood element is associated with growth and vitality, with new possibilities.

Healthy trees spontaneously do what is appropriate; humans, unfortunately, can get out of harmony by trying to resist what cannot be resisted or by yielding too easily what should be held on to. Consider this passage from the *Tao Te Ching:*

> When a man is living, he is soft and supple.
> When he is dead, he becomes hard and rigid.
> When a plant is living, it is soft and tender.
> When it is dead, it becomes withered and dry . . .
> What is well planted cannot be uprooted.
> What is well embraced cannot slip away.[35]

Fire is another element, or energy pattern, in the natural world and in us. In its balanced state, the Sun lights and warms the earth, helping plants grow as they convert its energy into food by the process of photosynthesis. Its fire is so vital to life itself that without it we cannot survive. Imagine Earth in a nuclear winter, when the Sun's life-giving rays are blocked and ice spreads over the planet, to understand the absence of fire. Equally frightening, however, is the prospect of being lost in the desert without water, subject to an excess of the Sun's brutal, dehydrating glare. Too much Sun can cause heatstroke and even death.

Like plants we need the warmth and energy of the Sun to get us going and accomplish our daily tasks. The warmth of fire creates intimacy and companionship; when the fire goes out, we can become cold and distant from each other. People who are physically and emotionally cold are deficient in the fire element. The heat of passion and the warmth of friendship are wonderful parts of a full and harmonious life, but we cannot be on fire all the time. Too much fire and we burn out. High-energy work—like healing, teaching, and governing—can turn eager idealists into weary cynics. The key is pacing—balancing work with time for rest. No one can be in the fire element all the time without being consumed by it. Even the Sun gives way each evening as it slips below the horizon and allows the evening to come.

Chinese philosophy and medicine affirm that we are also the element earth. The source of all life, the earth is a great nourisher. It provides the food all living beings need to survive, and it holds the roots of trees to give them stability. In human persons the earth element can give us a sense of balance and centeredness. It represents our connection with life, its cycles and harmonies, and reflects our ability to be at home in the world and within ourselves. When out of balance, the earth element may be manifested in a lack of nourishment—whether physical, emotional, or spiritual. If we neglect to rest our "soil," we may become depleted and even infertile. Constant summer would exhaust even the earth.

Chinese philosophy reminds us that we must nourish ourselves before we can expect to nurture anyone else. Carrying eighteen credits and working twenty-five hours a week may sound possible at the beginning of a semester, but there is very little time in a schedule like this for a quiet walk in the woods, sleeping in on Saturday morning, or listening to music while lying on the beach. Even human companionship may begin to seem like something we simply do not have time for any longer. When we feel depleted and exhausted, it's time to become grounded again.

Autumn is the season of letting go, and the element of metal or air represents the breathing out that marks the end of the year and the onset of the time for rest. From the remains of each growing season, the earth makes its treasures. Diamonds and other gems are the hard-packed debris of the earth. Minerals and ores are other manifestations of the metal element. Just as the earth receives the remains of the harvest and honors its value, it is important for us to acknowledge our accomplishments before rushing on to do more.

Autumn evening
it is no light thing
being born a man

ISSA

In a life filled with doing, doing, doing, one project very often runs into the next, or many projects are underway simultaneously. There is no opportunity to savor a small success at work or celebrate a good grade on an exam because there remains a long list of things still waiting to be done. In Taoist terms, there is no emptiness and therefore no room to receive treasure.

The water element may be the easiest to recognize because the human body is 78 percent water. Saliva, perspiration, and tears all remind us that we are made of water. In its natural state, water flows freely, like a mountain stream rippling over its rocky bed. Because it is fluid, moving water bends easily around obstacles, occupying whatever space is available to it. And it always seeks the lowest level, pooling at rest in the depths.

Water can be as calm as a pond in the sunlight or as violent as a tidal wave. It can come as life-giving fluid to quench our thirst and irrigate our crops, or it can flood our houses and leave us afloat. Too little of it and we die; too little of it and the earth dies. Surprisingly, we find ourselves where we began—with Thales who theorized that water was the *archē,* or first substance from which everything else derived.

Water seems so—elemental—and we are so clearly dependent on it for survival. Although water yields to force and takes the shape of any container in which it is placed, when water freezes it can crack rocks and rupture concrete and macadam. Much of its power is hidden. In ourselves, Taoism says, water represents the not-yet formed, the pool from which ideas emerge. It has the power of unknowing and is filled with possibilities. Deciding too quickly on one solution may preclude you from seeing other, perhaps better ones. Water never confronts; it always yields, and yet it has the power to conquer.

The integrated person, the one who lives in harmony with the *Tao,* will be the one whose life shows a balance among the five elements. Each will be expressed as it is in nature—spontaneously, cyclicly, naturally—and none will be blocked or ignored.

African Synthesis Model

A similar ideal is revealed in the African model of a fully realized human person. As in the Chinese model, reality in the larger world shows us the reality of human nature. The ideal model is life itself. As proverbs observe, "Life sows seeds" and "Life hatches things." So, to become a person one must, in a similar way, be creative. Achieving a creative personality and learning to maintain productive relationships are the marks of a person in the Akan culture of West Africa.[36]

Mawu *[MAH woo] the female principle in West African thought*
Lisa *[LEE sah] the male principle in West African thought*

A Tanzanian proverb puts it this way: "In the world all things are two and two" (Figure 3.3). In other words, everything is a fusion of opposites that form a unity while remaining separate. They are two; they become one; they remain two. In the West African country Benin, "***Mawu,*** the female principle, is fertility, motherhood, life, creativity, gentleness, forgiveness, night, freshness, rest and joy, while ***Lisa,*** the male principle, is power,

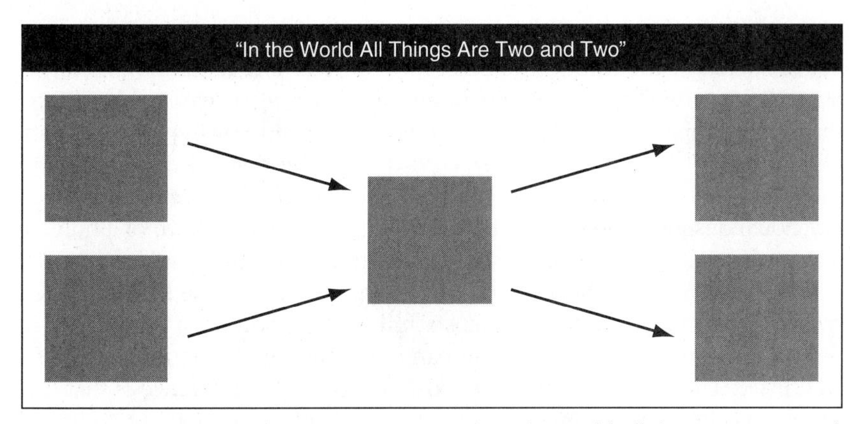

FIGURE 3.3 EAST AFRICAN VIEW OF REALITY *"In the world all things are two and two"—Tanzanian proverb.*

warlikeness, death, strength, toughness, destructivity, day, heat, labor, and all hard things."[37]

The descriptions of *Mawu* and *Lisa* bear a striking resemblance to the Chinese principles of *yin* and *yang*. The idea of a unity expressed as a duality occurs frequently in the non-Western world. The fundamental model of unity in duality and duality in unity found in African thought is the female-male polarity. Women in relation to men and men in relation to women express complementarity, tension, and balance; each represents otherness and together they model creativity.[38]

Sometimes the High God embodies the principle of female-male polarity. In Benin the supreme deity bears the name *Mawu-Lisa,* the embodiment of the two sexes. The Ga of Ghana call their High God a name that translates as Father Mother Sky God. The Akan of Ghana express this unity-in-duality by giving two-part personal names; one-half is female, the other half male. An Akan child might be named *Dua-Agyeman,* which translates as "tree" (female principle) "warrior" (male principle).

African philosophers see in this synthesis model a striking contrast to modern Western theories that are rooted in conflict. Consider Charles Darwin's theory of evolution and Sigmund Freud's insights into psychology, both of which have significantly shaped Western views of human nature. Darwin's principle of the survival of the fittest assumes competition among species that results in the elimination of the weak and defines progress. Freud stressed the driving force of the libido, or sexual energy, and, later, the continual struggle between the life instinct and the death instinct. Thus, in Western models the basic image of the human person is that of an aggressive or predatory individual. African cultures, in contrast, depict humans as social beings. A person is seen as being born into a culture, into a social structure that is the source of his or her very being. We might say the community exists for the good of the individual and the individual exists for the good of the community. An individual outside a community is nothing.[39]

This androgynous figure carves a woman from the block of wood on its head and then "morphs" into a male. Does this seem to tell the "truth" about our human origins?

Makonde "origins" figure/Courtesy of the African Art Museum of Maryland/Photo by Quentin Kardos.

Among the Akan people of West Africa, becoming a responsible member of society is the true test of personhood—learning to harmonize one's own interests with those of the community, earning a reasonable living, showing a human sensitivity to the needs of others. Endowing every human person before birth with an *okra,* a particle of the divine being, God ensures that each will have dignity and intrinsic worth. Each *okra* receives an individual destiny to be fulfilled before going to Earth to be born of a human man and woman, and the *okra* survives death to become an ancestor.

Generally, by the time you are Real, most of your hair has been loved off, and your eyes drop out and you get loose in the joints and very shabby. But these things don't matter at all, because once you are Real, you can't be ugly, except to people who don't understand.

MARGERY WILLIAMS, *THE VELVETEEN RABBIT*

At the same time, there are degrees of personhood, based on social responsibility. In an existentialist sense, full personhood must be earned. A person becomes a fully realized human being through the journey of a life well lived. This resembles Western existentialism. The difference is that the African model does not imagine a solitary, individual journey but, rather, a communal and social one. One learns to be a person under the guidance and with the support of a nurturing community.[40]

Female and male elements are equally essential in divinity and in humanity. An androgynous name that calls the child who bears it to the best in female and male nature offers an ideal of synthesis—of unity within duality. One illustration of a contrasting Western ideal is the custom of lighting two candles at a wedding ceremony—one to represent the bride, the other to represent the groom—using both candles to light a third—that represents their unity—then blowing out the original candles. Using this symbolism, the African synthesis model would insist that all three candles remain lighted.

Assumptions about the self often tell us something about how a given culture views the world and the place of human life within it. Western glorification of the individual has produced a legal system that lays great stress on protecting individual rights and a theological system that emphasizes the value of each individual, made in the image of God. Postmodernist preoccupation with a loss of meaning has shifted emphasis in the Western world from a solid, essential self to a more flexible and human-controlled protean or existential self.

Non-Western cultures have usually not taken the individual as the starting place for metaphysics. Reality is assumed to be interconnected and much too large to be understood or expressed in terms of the individual. Indeed, in Buddhism, the very idea of separateness and individuality is a mark of illusion. Taoist and African philosophies both paint a much more social picture of human life and emphasize balance and complementarity over competition and conflict.

What Are We Doing Here?

Non-Western Views

It is time to take up the second half of this chapter's inquiry by asking now how non-Western cultures view the purpose or meaning of human life. In

African thought, because unity in duality as expressed in the female-male polarity is basic, the purpose of human life is creativity. The creative principle in humans often has a name linguistically related to the name for the high god, showing its importance. Expressing this creative power, by bringing forth children and by developing and maintaining creative relationships, is the purpose of human life. Someone who has achieved a creative individual life within productive, social relationships with others is said to have become a person.

In Taoist thought, the meaning of life is to be found in aligning oneself with the wisdom at the heart of nature. If nature is interdependent and if the cycle of *yin-yang/yang-yin* is basic to reality, humans would do well to recognize this. Because the same five elements are in the cosmos and in us, we may profitably look to nature to see their right use and free expression. The *Tao* directs the natural system and accomplishes every task with perfect, effortless efficiency; we cannot hope to do better than this. If the elements of wood, fire, earth, metal or air, and water are out of balance in us, we need only look to the model of nature for our healing.

Buddhism understands the meaning of life as reaching enlightenment, that is, seeing what actually is. It is as if each of us is a sleeping or drunken person who needs only to awaken or sober up in order to see things as they really are. The delusion that most of us accept includes the fiction of a permanent, unchanging self. If we can see past apparent separateness to the interconnectedness that underlies everything, perhaps we can let go of our tiny egos and embrace the interdependence of all life.

Seeing accurately—that is, achieving enlightenment—means we need not be reborn. There is nothing left to learn; this is *nirvana*. While still in this world of illusion, the master or the enlightened one remains detached from it. Using an image of a charioteer taming unruly horses (which Plato also liked), the Buddha describes the master this way:

> He is the charioteer.
> He has tamed his horses,
> Pride and the senses.
> Even the gods admire him.
>
> Yielding like the earth,
> Joyous and clear like the lake,
> Still as the stone at the door,
> He is free from life and death.[41]

Western Views

Because the question of existence is asked differently in the West, there have been different answers given for the purpose of human life. Most Western thinkers would not be entirely comfortable with the Buddha's description of the master as free from life as well as from death. "Yielding like the earth, joyous and clear like the lake" is similarly too Taoist to appeal to believers in a uniquely human individual self.

Rationalist and Religious Essentialism

Western essentialism—what we have called the avocado view—assumes the uniqueness of human nature. The Judaic and Christian traditions affirm a human sharing in the divine nature, and the Greek rationalist tradition exalts the power of human reason: the ability to step back, observe, and make sense of the world and of ourselves. Both traditions share a belief that humans have a separate and essential self that defines us and makes us who and what we are.

An "I" without a body is a possibility. But a body without an "I" is utterly impossible.

EDITH STEIN

In contrast with non-Western views, Western essentialism takes for granted the existence of a permanent self that is unique to each individual. Some parts of the tradition assert that this self is immortal and will not die when the body dies. Plato, you recall, believed the soul exists both before and after its earthly life in another realm he called the Kingdom of Ideas, or the World of Forms. Christianity, too, is founded on a strong belief in life after death and the continuation of the individual soul.

The purpose of human life derives from assumptions about the self, and in the West the human person has been seen as the peak of creation, the highest expression of life. Plato and Aristotle agreed that humans, although lower than the gods, were certainly superior to other animals; even a slave boy could use reason to master the principles of geometry. In Genesis the story of the Creation ended with God's final, crowning accomplishment: the fashioning of beings in God's image.

But questions arise. If we are distinguished by our ability to reason, what are we to say about the severely retarded or those in comas? Are they somehow less than human because they lack the full capacity to reason? Even though that conclusion seems logically to follow, we shrink from this judgment.

If we have a soul, when does it enter the body? Following Aristotle's theories about *ensoulment,* the Western world declared, until the nineteenth century, that the male embryo received a soul about the fortieth day after conception, whereas the female embryo had to wait until about the eightieth day. The conclusion seemed to be that the soul—what makes us human—animates males sooner than it animates females. During the Middle Ages, theologians like Thomas Aquinas argued that the soul entered the body at the time of *quickening,* when the mother began to feel the baby moving. Abortion was less sinful if it occurred before the time of quickening, since what was destroyed lacked a soul and was not therefore human.

If the purpose of life for the Greeks at the time of Plato and Aristotle was to become as rational as possible, the purpose of life in the Judaic, Christian, and Islamic traditions is to become as loving as possible. The commandments to love God and love neighbor are at the heart of the religious view of what it means to be a person in the West.

Postmodernism and the Loss of Meaning

Until the end of the Middle Ages, the Western view of what it means to be human remained pretty firmly in place. (Historical Interlude C, which precedes Chapter 5, considers the breakdown of what is called the medieval synthesis.) The Greeks had looked around them, at other animals, and at

HOW PHILOSOPHY WORKS
Inductive Reasoning

In Chapter 2 we began examining deductive logic by looking at the categorical syllogism developed by Aristotle. Deductive reasoning is the chief analytic tool of philosophy, and it is capable of leading to certain knowledge. Inductive reasoning, used in philosophy, is primarily the province of science and, because it deals with a changing world, yields only probable knowledge.

Scientists reason from particular sense observations to general laws. The basic laws of genetics, for instance, were developed by Gregor Mendel, a nineteenth-century monk, who repeatedly crossbred peas and noted which characteristics appeared in the next generation. If additional crossbreeding were to reveal different outcomes, the laws of heredity would be altered to reflect the new knowledge. Since we never know anything completely or fully and there is always the possibility that something new will show up, inductive reasoning is said to lead to probable knowledge.

Broad and comprehensive theories, like Charles Darwin's theory of evolution and Sigmund Freud's theory of psychology, use inductive reasoning but also depend on intuition to arrive at a hypothesis. Darwin's theory of natural selection, for example, hypothesizes that the fittest in each generation survive and reproduce characteristics adapted for survival. Freud hypothesized about the role of the unconscious mind in directing human behavior. From their original observations, Darwin and Freud used a little creative imagination to develop a hypothesis, or theory, to explain what happens.

Once a hypothesis has been formulated, it must be one that is capable of being proved false. A valid scientific theory must survive repeated attempts to prove it wrong. When a theory remains valid after many attempts at proving it false, it is said to be reliable. No matter how reliable a theory is, however, and no matter how many times it is verified by experimental methods and observation, the possibility always exists that it may at some future date be proved false and made invalid.

For centuries, the Earth-centered theory appeared to synchronize with observations. Since the movement of the Sun seemed so obvious and since everyone took for granted the privileged place of Earth in Creation, other possibilities were rejected. Copernicus's theory of a Sun-centered solar system replaced the Earth-centered theory because his mathematical calculations were simpler and his theory better synchronized with observational data.

As we will see in Chapter 6, the scientific community tends to hold on to paradigms, like the Earth-centered theory, even in the face of some conflicting evidence, because a theory is whatever the scientific community agrees is true and everyone likes and needs a coherent explanation of reality. Revolutions in science, like the Sun-centered theory, occur when enough surprising results and/or data that do not match the theory are recorded.

what they called their barbarian neighbors and had found themselves clearly superior. Christians believed that God so loved them he would send his only Son to die for their reconciliation and salvation. Human uniqueness was at the heart of basic assumptions made by both groups. The first major blow to the conviction that human life had special meaning came with the mathematics of Copernicus who proved that the Sun, not Earth, was at the center of our solar system. When Copernicus convinced scientists (and eventually theologians) that Earth is one of several planets, rather than the center of a cosmic religious drama, the crisis of meaning began. Were there other cultures on other planets? Had God made similar arrangements with them? It was a bit like the feelings of the first child when a new sibling arrives.

During the nineteenth century, Darwin and Freud challenged humans' pride in themselves as rational beings. If we were evolutionarily descended from apes, as Darwin insisted, the case for human uniqueness became a little more difficult to make. Freud further eroded our confidence in our rationality by demonstrating the primitive urges he said actually determined our decisions. Seething with libido, drawn as strongly to the death principle as to the life principle, humans seemed suddenly rather more irrational than rational.

behaviorism *a psychological theory that focuses on objective or observed behavior, as opposed to introspection or reflections about inner states*

As the discipline of psychology matured, further theories were developed. In the twentieth century, B. F. Skinner introduced **behaviorism,** the theory that we are solely the product of our conditioning. We begin life, Skinner said, as organic machines, set up and ready to run. What we are is almost entirely the product of the rewards and punishments we receive. A baby, making random sounds, will one day accidentally say "Mama." At that point the most important person in the world, the meeter of all needs, will hug the baby, cover it with kisses, and speak reassuring words. The baby, behaviorism contends, will strive mightily to make this experience recur.

However, when the child grows older and tries out another four-letter word on the same mother, the result is likely to be quite different. Now, she may become angry or at least coldly distant. Although the child may learn not to use the word in mother's hearing, its use on the schoolbus may make the child a hero. Behaviorism thus asserts that positive and negative conditioning makes us who we are; we are nothing but the product of our experiences.

Perhaps as an antidote to this reduction of the human person to a kind of biological machine, writers such as psychologist James Hillman offer a humanist response to the question of human existence. In *The Soul's Code* Hillman argued that each of us is born with an innate character—the "daimon" that calls us to what we are meant to be. Notice that this is closer to Socrates's notion of his own purpose for living than to a Jewish/Christian/Islamic sense of divine purpose. In his latest book, *The Force of Character,* Hillman provides a rethinking of old age. As we grow older, he insists, we become more ourselves—our true natures tend to emerge. Thus, our final years have an important purpose: the fulfillment and confirmation of our own character. Reclaiming "oldness" as an archetypal state of being, Hillman resurrects the valuable notion of the old person as ancestor—model for the young and bearer of societal memory and traditions. Maybe our human purpose is to grow into a conscious old age and share the wisdom we have acquired for the good of society.

Whether or not there is a clear purpose to human life seems to be an important question. Few of us are comfortable with the notion of total randomness, but the purpose of human life might be conceived in a wide spectrum of ways. If human life comes from God, for example, there may be reciprocal responsibilities: things that humans owe to God. If, at the other extreme, humans are more animal-like, driven by unconscious urges and conditioning, it is hard to see much purpose at work. Since the avocado view, which began this discussion of human nature, has suffered some serious challenges, it is time to consider the issue of who we are in the light of those challenges. To speak about human nature today is to touch on questions of identity and freedom. As we begin the twenty-first century, we have many more questions than we have answers.

Issues of Human Identity and Freedom

To what extent do racial and ethnic labels, as well as gender, shape how we think of ourselves? Is it even possible to ignore our physical characteristics, and, if it is, what difference would it make to be color- or gender-blind? Are these labels the source of prejudice and the basis of discrimination or the foundation for racial pride and ethnic solidarity, to say nothing of gender identity?

Race and Ethnicity: One Aspect of Identity

Golf phenom Tiger Woods identifies himself as Cablinasian, a childhood attempt to acknowledge all the parts of his identity. Uncomfortable with being labeled the first black to win the Masters Tournament, Woods explained that he is one-half Asian—one-fourth Thai, one-fourth Chinese—one-fourth black, one-eighth white, and one-eighth Native American. Which category should he check on the census form? Would a "multiracial" category be more appropriate for the many like Woods who identify with more than one racial category?

Race, what is that? Race is a competition, somebody winning and somebody losing . . . Blood doesn't run in races! Come on!
BEAH RICHARDS

Twin sisters arrive at Harvard having checked the same boxes on their college applications—Native American, African American, Irish, and Scottish. One immediately begins receiving correspondence from the Black Students Association, and the other is invited to meetings of the Native American Students Association. How can identical twins have different racial identities? How should we classify mixed-race children? Forcing a person, like Tiger Woods or the Harvard twins, into only one category forces them to deny others. A "multiracial" category might more accurately represent reality, but it also has the potential to decrease federal funding for programs and realign voting districts.[42]

Sociologist Orlando Patterson suggests that dropping racial classification altogether would be a step in the right direction, since race is a social construction with no basis in fact. If we must categorize, Patterson sees ethnic choices as being both more accurate and more meaningful than racial ones:

> "Asian" . . . is at best a pan-ethnic term meant to include everyone from Filipino-Americans to Korean-Americans to Pacific Islanders. Having learned from the census form that a person is Japanese-American, Chinese-American or Pakistani-American, what useful information is gained by the additional data that he or she belongs to the "Asian" race? None whatsoever. The Asian category only reinforces and legitimizes the notion of race as a separate, meaningful entity.[43]

If a "white" person is no different biologically from a "black" person, Patterson observes, ethnic categorization has the advantage of not reinforcing racial tensions or prejudices.

Among those who identify themselves as "Hispanic," 6.7 percent also identify themselves as multiracial. Is "Hispanic" a meaningful category? What exactly does it represent? Nearly 10 percent of all Americans are foreign-born, double the ratio of twenty-five years ago. Of black and Asian men, 12 percent are in interracial marriages, as are 25 percent of Asian women and 60 percent of Native Americans of both genders. Of white men, 4 percent have a spouse of a different race.[44] Does it make sense to continue using either racial or ethnic categorization? Whom does it help and whom does it harm? And how much of our human freedom is compromised by forcing us into racially- or ethnically-labeled boxes?

Light came to me when I realized that I did not have to consider any racial group as a whole. God made them duck by duck and that was the only way I could see them.
ZORA NEALE HURSTON

Questions of identity become even more complex when one is transplanted from one culture to another. Writing about the experience of emigrant Latinos, Denis Lynn Daly Heyck describes the challenge of trying to transplant some elements of one's native culture into new soil while developing some new reference points by which to define relationships with other people and the world. A clash in values is the likely result:

> The questions that all Latinos must ask as they seek signposts for identity often involve pitting traditional against modern values. The process of adaptation often involves juxtaposing a personalistic, religious, spiritual, integrated, hierarchical, communitarian, static view of the world and one's place in it to a worldview that is impersonal, secular, materialistic, fragmented, egalitarian, individualistic, and in constant flux.[45]

Is it in everyone's best interest to emphasize our common humanity and downplay racial and ethnic differences, or are there discussions and debates we can have only from within existing camps? We will explore questions of assimilation versus separatism much more fully in Chapter 9. Meanwhile, consider how large a role racial or ethnic identity plays in your own life.

Biological Sex and Gender: Another Aspect of Identity

In Plato's dialogue *Symposium,* the participants debate the meaning of love. Aristophanes, the comic playwright, tells of a time when humans were all four-legged, four-armed, two-headed creatures who threatened the gods with our arrogance. To cut us down to size, Zeus, the head of the gods, sliced each creature in half so that now, the story goes, each of us is wandering the world in search of our missing other half. This, says Aristophanes, is the origin of and explanation for love.

In this myth some of the originally united creatures were what we might call opposite-sex unions and some were same-sex unions. Among upper-class Greek men of the time, sexual relationships might unite them with their cloistered wives in the home, for the purpose of having children, or with courtesans of either sex—an intellectual and cultured female hetaera or a beautiful and docile young boy—for the purpose of erotic pleasure. Clearly, their sense of gender identity existed in a different context than our own. Today, some of us believe erotic attractions are a matter of preference, whereas others of us insist such attractions are a matter of orientation and not something that can be controlled by will power.

Who decides whether one or both of these expressions of our sexuality is an acceptable part of our human nature? And, what about other variations? If we begin with our genetic blueprints, we learn that, in addition to XX and XY, other known chromosomal types include XXX, YYY, XXY, XYY, and XO. Most of these combinations produce bodies that eventually develop one or the other set of secondary sex characteristics—beards or breasts—but not always. Some babies are born with ambiguous sexual organs and others with one incompletely formed set. As we now know, for the first six weeks of prenatal life, all fetuses appear "female." Regardless of genetic typing, if a fetus is to develop into what the hospital staff will identify as a "male" infant, it is essential that the mother's body produce a bath of androgens, the male sex hormones that make a penis out of a clitoris and move ovaries down to become testicles. If this does not occur, the result will be a person who is biologically male—XY in the chromosome department—but female in appearance. Such a person might have a different experience of gender identity than will someone, also genetically XY, who did receive the androgen bath.

Are we talking about life style or orientation?

How much about us is "fixed," and how much is "plastic"?

In addition to the labels "homosexual" and "bisexual," there are now individuals who identify as "transgenders"—their identities literally cross the gender lines drawn so emphatically in Western culture. Some transgenders feel they are trapped in the wrong kind of body and undergo hormone therapy and even surgery to acquire a body that more closely resembles the image they have of themselves. Others keep the bodies they were born with but live a gender role that does not match their biological type. Alice Myers was playing lacrosse at Phillips Exeter Academy when she decided to apply to Harvard, her father's alma mater. On the way to Harvard, Alice realized some important things about her own identity. Living as a lesbian (because "it was the only community that let women be masculine"), she met people who had "transitioned" from one gender to another and realized that she was transgendered herself. Changing her name to Alex at 18, Myers was interviewed with his girlfriend at Harvard in 1997, where he had successfully lobbied to expand legal protections then available to gays, lesbians, and bisexuals to transgenders as well. "It's 100 percent wrong for me to be referred to as a woman," he says, "and it feels 60 percent wrong to be called a man. I wish there was a pronoun that easily described me."[46]

One question we might ask ourselves is: Who benefits from insisting that there are two and only two boxes available for gender identity and that everyone must fit into one of the two? Penalties for failing to conform to societal expectations regarding gender identity can be severe, as a spate of recent hate crimes has amply demonstrated. Some cultures have valued **androgyny,** blending the characteristics of both genders, as the route to artistic creativity and even a richer spirituality. Just as racial pigeonholing

androgyny *[an DRAH jin ee] the state of having all or some of the characteristics of both sexes/genders* can type us and invite harmful stereotyping, insisting that gender identity be limited to two and only two possibilities may harm both individuals and the societies in which they live. Ethnic identity is fixed by our genes, but, as Tiger Woods has eloquently showed us, how we name ourselves to others and how we internalize our identity is up to us. A key question in the arena of gender identity is, of course, How much is fixed and how much is changeable?

Innate or Plastic: One Question in the Free Will Versus Determinism Debate

plastic *capable of continuous changes in shape or form*

How much of our gender identity can be thought of as **plastic**—capable of being shaped into many forms, just as plastic can be when it is molten? Plastic surgery, which remolds human faces and bodies, can help us understand this meaning of the word plastic. Or are we the prisoners of our genes and our hormones—destined to appear and act in certain ways and to find one and only one group of people erotically attractive? To pose the question in the traditional way: How much of the way we are is the result of nature and how much the product of nurture? And, to complicate this dyad, how much about ourselves can be altered through the exercise of our human freedom?

If we did not make such strong distinctions on the basis of gender, gender identity might not be as crucial an issue. But, because we do, it matters quite a bit whether I am perceived by myself and others to be a woman or a man. At various times in our history as a human species, we have insisted that women must do certain things and may not do others, while men are responsible for a different set of obligations and prohibitions. And, biological body type at birth has traditionally determined who gets the dolls and who gets the trucks. If my physical appearance does not match the way I feel about myself and my place in the world, who decides who and what I am? How much choice do I really have when it comes to my own gender identity?

Greek rationalist and Judaic and Christian religious traditions have all insisted that humans, as distinct from other animals and machines, have free will. In the Greek tradition, our freedom to choose is a product of our ability to think: The more aware we are, the freer we become. In the Judaic and Christian traditions, free will is both a gift from God and the source of moral responsibility. If we are made in the image of God, then God has expectations for us, and we are free to either obey or disobey God's commands—with eternal consequences, of course. In Chapter 10 we will examine the issue of free will versus determinism much more thoroughly as we consider questions of personal moral responsibility. For now, consider this question: Is gender identity fixed by God or by an evolutionary mandate and do we defy our assigned gender roles only at our own peril?

If you find yourself attracted to a member of your own gender in a society that forbids this attraction and calls it unnatural, are you free to conform to society's expectations for you, or is your sexual orientation fixed and beyond your control? If you find your gender identity does not match the body you were born with, can you exert your will and force a match? How much of who and what I think myself to be is determined, and to what extent am I free to remold myself? Can I be held responsible for the choices I make and fail to make, and, if so, by whom?

Summary

Whether or not we can accept a skillfully constructed android as human and how strongly we feel the need to emphasize differences between ourselves and other animals can tell us something about our own view of human nature. The West has traditionally affirmed the uniqueness of humans in contrast with both machines and other animals. Its view of human nature as being closer to an avocado than to an artichoke has shaped our culture and our ideas.

Although in Western culture, reason is designated a human trait, the identification of men with rationality and women with emotionality has implied that women might not be as fully human as men. And, by weaving one creation story into our culture while ignoring another, the Western world has underlined women's derivative status as Adam's rib. During the fourth century, women like Macrina felt it necessary to philosophically defend the notion that women, too, are made in the image of God. Denying that the *pathe,* or passions, are part of the essential nature of the soul, Macrina was able to disassociate women both from exclusive identification with emotionality and from second-class theological status. Because the soul, in Macrina's view, is genderless, it is the same for women and men, both of whom are made in the image of God.

Sophisticated androids, like the fictional Data on *Star Trek: The Next Generation,* pass many existing tests of human personhood. Even computer programs created in the late twentieth century have been considered indistinguishable from people by their human users. As our technology grows evermore sophisticated, will we be able to create in a laboratory a creature that is indistinguishable from ourselves? If so, we will have two options: (1) Deny the creature human nature because it lacks a soul, which only God can create, or (2) appreciate its rational qualities and welcome it to the human family.

Not everyone accepts this traditional Western view. Some suggest that human nature is like what we have called the artichoke view, layers surrounding an empty center. Forced to question any and all certainties—including that of an essential human nature—the postmodernist West has struggled to redefine human nature. If our identities are not fixed at birth, we have limitless possibilities to explore. We can put a positive "spin" on the artichoke view by affirming the flexibility of the protean self or the self-actualizing aspects of existentialism.

Buddhism includes the sense of a separate self—what we have called the avocado view of human nature—in the illusions one must give up on the way to enlightenment. Holding on to our illusions not only causes us suffering, it also keeps us tied to this world and forces us to endlessly repeat the cycle of birth-death-rebirth. By waking up and seeing things as they actually are, Buddhism tells us, we will realize that a temporary combination of *skandhas* does not make a self and cannot be expected to endure. This may loosen our unhealthy attachments to the objects of our desires who are, like us, *anatman*—lacking a core self. Losing our false sense of security in an ego self, we can realize our vastness and experience *nirvana*.

Chinese philosophy and medicine tell us that we are a microcosm of the cosmos. The elements we see in the world around us are also the elements that comprise our own human nature. We have met this microcosm-macrocosm view among the pre-Socratic cosmologists such as Anaximenes, who observed that air as breath keeps a person alive and air as wind keeps the world alive. In the Chinese view, we are, like nature, composed of earth, metal or air, water, wood, and fire. When they are in balance, we are healthy; when they are in disharmony, we become ill.

We come spinning out of nothingness—trailing dreams like dust.

RUMI

Unity within duality is the theme of the African synthesis model of human nature. Taking the female-male polarity as the fundamental one, we can see all of life as expressing this model of creativity, arising from resolvable tensions between complementary opposites. Naming the High God and human children with female-male combination names is a way of affirming that all things are two and can unite as one while still remaining two. Thus, women and men retain their individuality even while becoming one in creating new life. All people learn and experience their identity within a social context, so the idea of an individual choosing to live apart from society is unthinkable.

In the postmodern world we are left to wonder how much (if anything) of who we are is the product of our racial and/or ethnic identity? As we seek our place within the world and the human family, should we emphasize what makes each of us unique or what we all have in common? Are we all the same, despite superficial differences, or is what distinguishes some of us from others part of our core identity? What must we hold on to and what is expendable as we seek our identity in a culture other than the one into which we or our parents were born?

The goal or purpose of human life may be creativity, as in African thought; harmony and balance, as in Chinese thought; or enlightenment, as in Buddhist thought. In these views, all that is seems part of a continuum of life. Because the Western world has insisted on an essential human nature, the meaning of life in the West is tied to an understanding of what it means to be human, as opposed to, say, a machine or a chimp. Blows to our collective psyche—from the Copernican revolution in science, which removed Earth from center stage in the cosmos; from evolution, which blurred our claims to unique status; and from psychology, which further questioned our rationality and our freedom—have led to a loss of meaning and something of a human identity crisis. We are still asking a basic question: Is there something unique about human nature?

As we have seen, here and in Chapter 2, whether or not the cosmos has meaning seems to matter a lot to us. If God determines human destiny and the destiny of the cosmos, we can relax, knowing that everything will turn out all right in the end. Without a divine-meaning maker, however, we have only ourselves to rely on, and the more we learn about human nature, the less confident we may be about the future.

Who we are and what we may be doing here is directly connected with whether or not there is a God. Indeed, how we approach many other far-reaching issues also hinges on this question. Issues concerning how we know and how we test for truth (Part 2 of this text) will be influenced by whether or not we can count on a good God who will not deceive us. In Part 3, questions about how we should constitute a human society, who should rule, and how we should behave toward one another will be answered differently if we assume or deny the existence of God. Thus, it is time now to turn our attention to the fundamental philosophical questions concerning the nature and existence of God.

For Further Thought

1. Suppose you meet someone who might or might not be an android. What questions or tests would you use to decide if you were in the presence of a person or a machine?
2. Some have called our insistence on human uniqueness "species arrogance," and others suggest that animals besides ourselves might even have souls. Assuming there is a God, on what basis does God endow humans with souls? Could this basis be extended to other animals? Why, or why not?
3. If you were fooled by the Turing test, would you be willing to grant the status of "thinker" to the computer program that fooled you? Why, or why not?
4. Suppose you are despondent and depressed. You dial up a "hotline" on your computer and have an extended conversation with a counselor, after which you feel much better. Does it matter if you later learn you were conversing with the program PC Therapist III?
5. Imagine that biblical scholars find an ancient scroll revealing that woman was created first and gave birth to man and that previous versions had reflected translation errors. What effect might this revelation have on women and men?
6. If we agree with Plato and Aristotle that the more rational we are the more human we become, how can we avoid the conclusion that the less rational we are the less human we are? Are very young children, those with severe mental retardation, and Alzheimer's patients human? If so, on what do you base your defense?
7. As a society, have we sacrificed anything worthwhile by elevating reason, mistrusting emotion, and ignoring the body? If we have, what is it? What have we gained by doing this, and was the sacrifice worth the cost?
8. Does it matter, even to nonreligious people, if theologians decide woman is not made in the image of God? Why, or why not?
9. If we succeed in building a very sophisticated android who seems human in most ways, should that android have the same legal and social rights as we do? Why, or why not?

10. If a few hours of sensory deprivation cause us to lose our sense of having a permanent, indestructible "self," should we conclude that the "self" was an illusion? Does the fact that the sense of "self" returns after feedback begins again increase the credibility of the "self" or make it seem more fictional than ever? Explain.
11. Does the notion of having many selves to meet the varying conditions one encounters during a lifetime frighten and disorient you or fill you with the thrill of adventure? Explain.
12. Try this thought experiment: For one day, in your own mind at least, take complete responsibility for everything you do and every choice you make, including your emotional states. At the end of the day, record your feelings. Are you exhilarated or depressed? Explain.
13. Does the fact that many people have experienced a loss of the sense of self and a feeling of merging with something larger during meditation add credibility to the Buddhist theory of *anatman*? How would you decide which is the truer version of reality: the one experienced on the day-to-day level or the one available during meditation?
14. Some pre-Socratic cosmologists and practitioners of Chinese medicine agree that the human person is a microcosm, or smaller version of the macrocosm that is the world. What lessons about living do you think it might be possible to learn from nature?
15. Democritus saw the value of empty space. If atoms exist and there is a void, motion is possible. What value could the empty space advocated by Eastern philosophies have in a person's life? What might be possible if there were empty space? What is impossible if there is none?
16. Most Western names are clearly masculine or feminine, and a popular song of some years ago explored the fate of "A Boy Named Sue." Try to imagine what your self-concept might be like if you and everyone you know were given a name that reflects both the female and male principles, as many African children are. Could this cause you to see yourself differently? If so, how?
17. Does it make a difference in your life here and now if you believe you have a soul that is immortal and so do other people? What difference does it make if you accept this belief and if you reject it?
18. Imagine that you conduct a radical philosophical experiment. When you move to a new town, you adopt the opposite gender: If you have been a boy, you become a girl; if you have been a girl, you become a boy. Try to imagine what that experience might be like and what you might learn from it.
19. What if your mother became your father or your father became your mother through transsexual surgery. Could you continue to accept loving parenting even if the external appearance of your parent changed? Assume that the personality and approach of your parent will not change, only his or her appearance and social role.
20. Try to decide to what extent you are the product of your conditioning and the prisoner of your subconscious urges and to what extent you are the master of your fate and the captain of your soul. On what basis will you make this decision?

For Further Exploration

Anderson, Kevin J. "Therefore I Am, The Tale of IG-88." In *Star Wars Darksaber,* edited by Kevin J. Anderson. New York: Bantam, 1995. This story explores the question, Can a machine ever achieve human status?

Anna to the Infinite Power. This movie portrays a brilliant but troubled child who undergoes a scientific experiment, which is conducted without her knowledge or consent, to determine her identity.

Beauty and the Beast. The 1946 classic movie by Jean Cocteau and the 1990s remake both explore the dimensions of beauty and beast in all of us.

Being John Malkovich. This film raises intriguing questions about the nature of the self and the freedom of the will.

Blade Runner. This movie traces the exploits of rebel androids in 2817 Los Angeles. Cyborgs, who are given a lifespan of only four years, yearn for more time, and develop a reverence for life that includes their oppressors.

Boys Don't Cry. This movie presents the challenges and ultimate costs of living a transgendered existence.

Charlie. Would it be worth the disappointment to have your mental powers raised, briefly, to extraordinary heights before being dropped slowly back to their below normal condition?

The Cider House Rules. An orphan learns that his search for a sense of self and a vocation to match his talents can be realized by responding to these imperatives: Go where you are wanted; go where you are needed; go where you belong.

The Crying Game. In this movie, an Irish Republican Army soldier looks up the girlfriend of a dead hostage, falls in love with her, and then finds she is socially female but anatomically male.

Ellison, Harlan. "A Boy and His Dog." In *As Tomorrow Becomes Today.* Edited by Charles William Sullivan. New York: Prentice-Hall, 1974. After a nuclear holocaust, a boy and his telepathic dog roam Earth. Also a movie.

E.T. This movie makes us ask, Can an extraterrestrial become human?

Gattaca. When a DNA test is the job interview, who would take their chances with genetics by having a "faith" child who might turn out to be fatally flawed?

Golding, William. *Lord of the Flies.* New York: Coward-McCann, 1962. This novel asks, Is civilization a mask, and are we beasts masquerading as humans? Also a movie.

James, Henry. "The Real Thing." In *The Real Thing and Other Tales.* New York: Macmillan, 1922. This short story explores why actors can portray us more accurately than we can protray ourselves.

Kingsolver, Barbara. *Pigs in Heaven.* New York: HarperCollins, 1993. This novel explores the question of racial-ethnic identity: Should a Cherokee girl be taken from her adoptive Anglo mother and returned to her people because only they can provide her with an identity?

Mariama Bâ. *So Long a Letter.* Portsmouth, N.H.: Heinemann, 1989. Can a Senegalese schoolteacher create a new self when her husband abruptly takes a second wife as sanctioned by Islamic law?

Morrison, Toni. *Beloved.* New York: New American Library, 1988. This novel asks, Can a child, murdered by her mother to avoid her capture by slave catchers, return in the body of another?

Powder and Phenomenon. These two movies explore extraordinary power and its ability to alter reality for a human being.

Rain Man. This movie tells the story of an autistic savant, gifted in some areas and dysfunctional in others. It asks, What does his life tell us about human nature?

Saint, Harry F. *Memoirs of an Invisible Man.* New York: Macmillan, 1987. Rendered invisible by a physics accident, a man confronts questions about his identity. Also a movie.

The Shawshank Redemption. This movie asks, Can a man unjustly imprisoned use the experience to create a new self for himself?

Short Circuit. In this movie, a sophisticated robot comes alive after being struck by lightning and learns the value of life from an animal lover.

Splash. This movie asks whether it is possible to love a mermaid who has the capacity to appear and act human most of the time.

The Talented Mr. Ripley. Is human identity so plastic that a clever con man can assume the identity of another without being exposed? Are we nothing more than the layers we acquire, the roles we play?

Terminator 2. This movie asks, Can a machine be a father figure to a lonely boy?

2001: A Space Odyssey. What happens when an IBM computer drops each letter back one space, becomes HAL, and takes over?

Woolf, Virginia. *Orlando.* New York: Penguin, 1946. Beginning in sixteenth-century England, a young man moves through four centuries, changing gender along the way in a fascinating exploration of continuity within change. Also a fine movie.

For Further Research

Try these InfoTrac keywords:

Human Nature
Human Uniqueness
Artificial Intelligence
Atman
Determinism
Gender Identity

Notes

1. Michael Specter, "A Computer Mistaken for a Human," *New York Times,* 16 November 1991.
2. Glenn McNatt, "Pondering the meaning of computer compositions," *Baltimore Sun,* 16 November 1997, 1E.

3. Summary from *Shadows of Forgotten Ancestors* by Carl Sagan and Ann Druyan, quoted in Parade Magazine, 20 September 1992, 4.
4. Sagan and Druyan, 5.
5. Natalie Angier, "Chimps Exhibit, er, Humanness, Study Finds," *New York Times,* 17 June 1999, A1.
6. Sagan and Druyan; Frederic Golden, "Clever Kanzi," *Discover* (March 1991): 20.
7. Sagan and Druyan; Golden.
8. Charlene Crabb, "Rio, the Logical Sea Lion," *Discover* (February 1993): 20.
9. Glen Martin, "Killer Culture," *Discover* (December 1993): 111–113.
10. "Grieving elephant starves self after companion's death," *Baltimore Sun,* 6 May 1999, 23A.
11. Martin.
12. Aristotle, "Metaphysics," in *The Pocket Aristotle,* ed. Justin D. Kaplan, trans. W. D. Ross (New York: Washington Square, 1958), 108.
13. Elizabeth V. Spelman, "Aristotle and the Politicization of the Soul," in *Discovering Reality,* Sandra Harding and Merrill B. Hintikka, eds., (Boston: Kluwer Academic, 1983), pp. 17–30.
14. John Heider, *The Tao of Leadership: Lao Tzu's Tao Te Ching Adapted for a New Age* (New York: Bantam, 1986), 55.
15. John Milton, *Paradise Lost,* book 4, ll. 480–490.
16. Genesis 1:26–28, 31, *Bible,* NRSV (Nashville, Tenn.: Nelson, 1989).
17. Gregory, Bishop of Nyssa, *The Life of Saint Macrina,* trans. Kevin Corrigan (Toronto: Peregrina, 1989), 21.
18. Macrina, "On the Soul and the Resurrection," in Saint Gregory of Nyssa, *Ascetical Works,* trans. Virginia Woods Callahan (Washington, D.C.: Catholic University of America Press, 1966), 216–217.
19. Macrina, 218–219.
20. Plato, "Phaedo," in *Plato: Five Great Dialogues,* ed. Louise Ropes Loomis (New York: Gramercy, 1969), 118.
21. Macrina, 229.
22. "The Gene in the Machine," *New York Times,* 15 May 1995, A17.
23. This image was suggested by one of my students, Faisal Ali.
24. José Ortega y Gasset, "History as a System," in *Existentialism from Dostoevsky to Sartre,* ed. Walter Kaufmann (New York: New American Library, 1975), 153–154.
25. Jean-Paul Sartre, "Existentialism as a Humanism," in *Existentialism from Dostoevsky to Sartre,* ed. Walter Kaufmann (New York: New American Library, 1975), 349.
26. William Ernest Henley, "Invictus," in *The Norton Anthology of English Literature,* 5th ed. M. H. Abrams (New York: Norton, 1986), 1657.
27. Jean-Paul Sartre, *Being and Nothingness* (New York: Washington Square, 1966), 316.
28. Albert Camus, "An Absurd Reasoning: Absurdity and Suicide," in *The Myth of Sisyphus and Other Essays* (New York: Vintage, 1955), 5.

29. *Chandogya Upanishad* 6.1–2, 9–11, in *Anthology of Sacred Scripture,* 2nd ed., Robert E. Van Voorst, ed. (Belmont: Wadsworth, 1997), 36–37.
30. Camus, 85.
31. "The Skandhas and the Chain of Causation," in *Anthology of World Scriptures,* ed. Robert E. Van Voorst (Belmont, Calif.: Wadsworth, 1994), 84.
32. "The Skandas."
33. Alan W. Watts, *The Way of Zen* (New York: Vintage, 1957), 50.
34. Dianne M. Connelly, *Traditional Acupuncture: The Law of the Five Elements* (Columbia, Md.: Centre for Traditional Acupuncture, 1979), 3. The succeeding analysis of the five-element view of human nature is adapted from this book.
35. Lao Tzu, *Tao Teh Ching,* chaps. 76 and 54, Asian Institute Translations, no. 1, trans. John C. H. Wu, ed. Paul K. T. Sih (New York: St. John's University Press, 1961), 77, 109.
36. N. K. Dzobo, "The Image of Man in Africa," in *Person and Community: Ghanaian Philosophical Studies I,* ed. Kwasi Wiredu and Kwame Gyekye (Washington, D.C.: Council for Research in Values and Philosophy, 1992), 131.
37. Dzobo, 128.
38. Dzobo.
39. Dzobo, 132.
40. Kwasi Wiredu, "African Philosophical Tradition: A Case Study of the Akan," *Philosophical Forum* 24, no. 1–3 (1992–1993): 49–51.
41. *The Dhammapada: The Sayings of the Buddha,* trans. Thomas Byrom (New York: Oxford University Press, 1976), 38.
42. *Harvard Magazine* (May–June 1997): 19–20.
43. Orlando Patterson, "The Race Trap," *New York Times,* 11 July 1997, A25.
44. "How About Just Being an American?" *Baltimore Sun,* 29 April 1997, 11A.
45. Denis Lynn Daly Heyck, "My Roots Are Not Mine Alone: La Identidad Cultural," in *Barrios and Borderlands: Cultures of Latinos and Latinas in the United States,* ed. Denis Lynn Daly Heyck (New York: Routledge, 1994), 372.
46. "Is Biology Destiny?," *Baltimore Sun,* 24 September 1997, 5E, 1E.

CHAPTER 4

Philosophy and God

Who's in Charge?

Before You Read . . .

Ask yourself how important (or unimportant) belief in a personal God is to your concept of human nature and your understanding of the cosmos.

I want to know how god created the world. I am not interested in this or that phenomenon, in the spectrum of this or that element; I want to know his thoughts; the rest are details.
Albert Einstein

Philosophers take the question of the existence or nonexistence of God seriously because it is so intimately connected with the other questions of metaphysics. If there is a God who is in charge of the universe, then we must see reality itself, as well as human nature, in a divine context. On the other hand, if we are the most powerful beings in the cosmos, we are responsible for what happens to us and to our world. "If only God would send me a sign!" Woody Allen once observed, "like making a large deposit in my name in a Swiss bank." How can we determine whether or not there is a God? Can you imagine, as Woody Allen did, what kind of evidence it would take to convince you?

In the song "Terrible Lie," Trent Reznor of Nine Inch Nails blames God for his anger and loneliness as well as for the sad state of the world. Is the idea of God a "terrible lie" that teases us but ultimately provides no answers? If things go wrong in our lives, are we being punished by a higher power or just having bad luck? Which is easier to bear? If we believe the "promises and lies," are we deluded fools? Or is God trying to help us figure out how to live our lives—trying as all parents do with both love and discipline? Do we, like Reznor, "need someone to hold on to," and, more to the point, is there anyone out there to fill the bill?

What could move these fleas to theism or atheism?
"Mother Goose and Grimm." Reprinted by permission. Tribune Media Services.

The Issue Defined

theism *the conception of God as a unitary being*
atheism *the denial of theism, usually on the basis that everything can be explained without God*
agnosticism *the philosophical position that whether God exists or not cannot be known*

Philosophers have offered three answers to the "who's in charge?" question: (1) there is a God, (2) there is no God, and (3) we can't know whether there is or is not a God. The assertion that there is a God is called **theism,** from the Greek word *theos,* meaning "God." The contrary argument, that there is no God, is called **atheism** (the prefix *a-* means "not" or "without"). Finally, the position that we do not and cannot know the answer to this question is called **agnosticism,** from the Greek word *gnosis* meaning "knowledge." Both theism and atheism are positions that require philosophical defense—arguments stating why there is or is not a God—but agnosticism asserts that on this question no position can be taken. Its philosophical justification is that human knowing is not capable of answering this question. Language analysts, whom we will consider in Chapter 5, assert that the propositions "God exists" and "God does not exist" are equally meaningless, since there is no possible way they could be verified.

The nineteenth-century American philosopher William James, who is best known as a pragmatist, believed passionately that agnosticism was just not a useful position to take. For James, the decision to believe or not to believe in God is too important for fence straddling. He calls the choice a "live, forced, momentous option." The choice is "live" because both the decision to believe and the decision not to believe are *real* choices for you. Deciding whether or not to believe in Santa Claus may no longer be a "live" choice for you, but it may remain a "live" option for your younger siblings or children.

The decision about belief in God is also a "forced" choice in the same way that the decision about getting a haircut this week is *not* a "forced" choice. Choosing to have faith or not to have faith in a higher power is for James a decision you must make because your decision will probably affect the way you live your life. Finally, this is a "momentous" option; the stakes are potentially very high. If there is a God in whom you choose not to believe, there may be consequences. Of course, if there is no God, it really does not matter whether you believe in God or not.

The seventeenth-century mathematician Blaise Pascal proposed that we consider whether or not to believe in God as we would consider any

TABLE 4.1. PASCAL'S WAGER *Believing in God seems to be the safer wager.*

PASCAL'S WAGER

	I Choose to Believe	I Choose Not to Believe
There Is a God	Infinite gain (eternal life)	Infinite loss (eternal suffering)
There Is No God	Finite loss (give up a few pleasures)	Finite gain (being right—after death)

wager. The problem highlighted by **Pascal's wager** is a simple one: Either there is a God or there is not. Your choices are also simple: Believe or do not believe. There are four possible outcomes (Table 4.1). If there is a God and you choose belief, the reward may be eternal life. If God exists and you choose not to believe, you risk unpleasant eternal consequences. If there is no God and you live as if there were, you may give up a few selfish pleasures. If there is no God and you correctly withhold your belief, you will have the satisfaction of being right—after you are dead, of course. For Pascal, the wager is obvious; in three of the four possibilities, you are better served by acting as if there were a God—just in case. There is little to lose and much to gain:

Pascal's wager *the advice to wager and live your life as if God exists, in case God does*

> Let us then examine this point, and let us say: "Either God is or he is not." But to which view shall we be inclined? Reason cannot decide this question. Infinite chaos separates us. At the far end of this infinite distance a coin is being spun which will come down heads or tails. How will you wager? Reason cannot make you choose either, reason cannot prove either wrong . . . Let us weigh up the gain and loss involved in calling heads that God exists. Let us assess the two cases: if you win you win everything, if you lose you lose nothing. Do not hesitate then; wager he does exist.[1]

Wagering that God exists might raise other issues for you. God may expect things of you and hold you accountable for living your life in a certain way. If there is a God, life has an eternal dimension, lasting longer than your own life and longer even than the life of the cosmos. If there is no God, we will find the answers to the significant metaphysical questions here in the natural world. We, not God, are the ones in charge.

Not everyone agrees with Pascal, of course. Atheists, for instance, assert that everything can be accounted for without bringing God into the explanation. Although deists and pantheists believe in God, the God they acknowledge makes no demands upon believers apart from intellectual assent. Only panentheism and especially traditional monotheism—belief in one, personal God—raise serious philosophical questions for believers. For James, the decision to believe or not to believe in a theistic God was a live, forced, momentous option. Consequently, most of this chapter explores possible routes to knowledge of God and various qualities that have been attributed to God.

Atheism

What we need is not the will to believe but the wish to find out.
BERTRAND RUSSELL

Arguments in support of atheism generally have their basis in scientific materialism. Our current scientific explanation of the origin of the universe, the big bang theory, postulates a huge explosion many billions of years ago that set the galaxies in motion and created the conditions out of which life could arise. Charles Darwin's theory of the origin of the species postulates a gradual evolution of life from lower to higher forms. Although it is possible to see the hand of God in both the big bang and evolution, it is also quite possible to argue, as atheists do, that God is an unnecessary and unverifiable hypothesis. Insisting on the application of the empirical method of observation and verification through experiment, atheists find no "proof" for any supernatural entities and reject them as they would reject any unsupported hypothesis. Commitment to empiricism focuses their attention on the natural world.

Deism

deism *the belief that an impersonal, mechanical genius began the world and has since left it alone*

It is actually possible to believe in God in a way that has no more effect on your life than being a Republican or a Democrat might, if you think of belief in God as merely a matter of intellectual assent. Many French and American thinkers during the late eighteenth century were attracted to **deism**—from *deus,* the Latin word for "God." Determined to make religion compatible with a scientific understanding of nature, they rejected most of Christianity, including the idea of revelation (divinely inspired words such as those found in the Bible), miracles, original sin, clerical authority, and the divine nature of Jesus. What seemed reasonable to retain was belief in God as Creator of what science was discovering to be an incredibly efficient, mechanical universe. Once God had set the machine in motion, however, there was no further need for intervention. Deists regarded Jesus as an effective moral teacher and believed the best way to serve God was to treat one's fellow humans justly.

Some of the founders of the American republic were deists, and the God evoked in phrases such as "In God We Trust" is the distant First Cause of the mechanical universe, which had recently been described by Isaac Newton. It is certainly true that these men believed in God, but the God they believed in was no longer actively involved with the world or with human beings. Believing or not believing in the God of deism is probably not a live, forced, momentous option for most people in the Western world in the twenty-first century.

Pantheism and Panentheism

pantheism *the belief that God is fully expressed in nature or the material world*

Another fairly neutral position to take is called **pantheism** (literally, "all God"). Pantheism received its classic formulation in the *Ethics* of the seventeenth-century philosopher Baruch (Benedictus) Spinoza who argued that "besides God no substance can be, nor can be conceived."[2] Spinoza's conclusion is that "whatever is, is in God, and nothing can either be or be conceived without God."[3] If the universe is a unity, it would be correct to name it either God or Nature. Pantheism literally claims that God is everything and everything is God. Some philosophers assert that God and the universe are identical. If God is one with nature and its processes, then God is in the storm, in the gentle breeze, in the ice and snow and not apart from those things. Another way of saying this is to call God **immanent,** or totally expressed in nature.

I said to the almond tree, "Speak to me of God" and the almond tree blossomed.
NIKOS KAZANTZAKIS

Like deism, pantheism describes a God who is not intimately connected with human life. If you are a pantheist, nothing much is expected of you apart from a kind of intellectual assent. On the other hand, a pantheistic God does not offer any answers to the significant questions of human life. In addition to immanent, God can also be described as **transcendent** (literally, to "climb over"). The transcendent aspect of God is revealed in the voice giving the Ten Commandments to Moses on Mount Sinai or in the burning bush that continues to flame without being consumed. To be transcendent is to be wholly other, awesome and powerful.

immanent *indwelling within a process, as God is described as indwelling in creation*

transcendent *existing beyond and thus independent of the space-time world*

We have called Spinoza a pantheist, but he also insists that God has an infinite number of attributes, of which only two (thought and extension) are known directly in the natural world. What Spinoza's pantheism points toward is a modern variation called **panentheism,** meaning "all in God," that tries to strike a balance between extreme immanence and extreme transcendence. According to panentheism, God has both a timeless, unchanging nature (is transcendent) and a historical, changing nature (is immanent in this world). God is expressed temporally in nature, but all nature and everything that is exists within a transcendent God. So, God is large enough to reconcile an apparent contradiction. God is both expressed in the world and existing beyond the world, both immanent and transcendent.

panentheism *the belief that God is expressed in the world and that the world and all that is exists in God*

According to twentieth-century philosopher Alfred North Whitehead, reality is a dynamic process in which God both affects and is conditioned by events in the temporal world. Referred to as *process philosophy* or *theology,* this view suggests that events in this world, transformed by the love and wisdom of God, exert a reciprocal influence on God. In the ongoing interchange, God is part of the process but not contained or limited by it. As Whitehead puts it:

To go to Rome—great the effort, little the gain;
You will not find there the King you seek, unless you bring Him with you.
NINTH-CENTURY IRISH POEM

> I have envisioned a union of Plato's God with the God of the universe . . . God is *in* the world or nowhere, creating continually in us and around us. This creative principle is everywhere, in animate and so-called inanimate matter . . . But this creation is a continuing process, and "the process is itself the actuality" since no sooner do you arrive than you start on a fresh journey. Insofar as man participates in this creative process does he partake of the divine, of God . . .[4]

God ever geometrizes.
PLATO

As we saw in Spinoza's philosophy, pantheism asserts that God is expressed in the world. What Whitehead adds is a constant cycle of interaction—a feedback loop—between the world and God in which everything is seen as in the divine nature. Panentheism is a twentieth-century attempt to merge pantheism with more traditional theism.

Theism

Theism refers to belief in a personal God who created the world and who continues to be connected with its processes and with us. The choice that James described involves, as we have said, belief in this kind of God rather than in the absentee landlord of deism or the impersonal force of pantheism. Theism describes the God of the Judaic and Christian traditions who is the source and creator of the natural world as well as its loving protector. The God of theism, like the God described in Whitehead's process theology, loves us and expects love in return. To believe in a theistic God requires much more than mere intellectual assent—it requires the commitment of one's life.

A theistic God makes demands on people and offers rewards, including the possibility of eternal life. There is an implied relationship between this God and human beings. If a theistic God is in charge, then we are in "good hands," as the insurance commercial suggests. We also have significant obligations to respond in a loving manner to this God and to our fellow human beings. When we address philosophical questions related to the nature of God, we mean this kind of God.

theology *the rational organization of religious beliefs into a logical system*

We need to distinguish between philosophy and theology. Literally, "the study of God," **theology** usually refers to religious beliefs. Although philosophy and theology cover similar topics and issues, a fundamental epistemological difference exists between them. Theology accepts certain things, like the existence of God, on the basis of *faith*. Usually, faith derives from revelation (divinely inspired words) or the authority of a church or religious leader. Philosophy insists that the proposition "God exists" is just like the proposition "the world exists" and that both must be examined and defended using ordinary methods of analysis. When we speak of theism, we will be examining it from a philosophical, rather than a theological, point of view.

monotheism *belief in one God*

polytheism *the belief in many gods*

To be a theist in Western culture is to practice **monotheism,** or belief in one God. There have, of course, been many cultures in the past and there are some in the present that practice **polytheism,** or belief in many gods. Indeed, as we have seen, the Greek culture into which Thales introduced his philosophical ideas was a polytheistic one.

Trinity *the Christian doctrine asserting that God is three persons in one nature*

Historically, what distinguished the Jews from their sometimes polytheistic neighbors was their strong belief in one God. Retaining the monotheism of their Jewish roots, Christians nonetheless insist that the God they worship is three-in-one. The concept of the **Trinity** asserts that God is three persons—Father, Son, and Holy Spirit—in one nature. All three persons of the Trinity—God the Creator; Jesus the Savior; and the Holy Spirit, or Sanctifier—share the same nature and so retain their unity. Historical Interlude B reviews some of the difficulties involved with defining a Trinitarian monotheism in a way that preserves the oneness or unity of God.

Arguments for the Existence of God

A church or religious leader may tell you that God exists and a sacred text may claim to do the same. Faith can answer all your questions, but as we

TABLE 4.2 NATURAL THEOLOGY *These three arguments demonstrate the existence of God using only human reason—not faith or revelation.*

GOD MUST EXIST BECAUSE . . .

Ontological Argument	Cosmological Argument	Teleological Argument
A perfect being, whom I can imagine, must possess *all* perfections, including the perfection of existence.	There must be • An unmoved mover. • An uncaused cause. • A necessary being. • A standard of perfection. • A source of order and purpose.	The universe is so skillfully and intricately made that there must be a universe maker—just as the existence of a watch argues for a watchmaker.

have said, the method of philosophy usually demands more. Let's now examine two ways to "know" that God exists—one based on reason, the other based on intuition.

Knowledge Based on Reason

Some theists have tried to demonstrate the independent existence of God philosophically, using reason, the power of the human mind. Theologians have sometimes joined philosophers in attempting to establish that God exists without relying on faith. Called **natural theology,** this process focuses on a natural way of understanding God using human reason instead of a supernatural way using revelation or the revealed word of God as found in the Bible or the Qur'an.

natural theology *the pursuit of knowledge of God, using natural intelligence rather than supernatural revelation*

In this section we look at three of the natural theology proofs (Table 4.2) for the existence of God and some objections that have been raised to them. The arguments will use ontology, cosmology, and teleology—three concepts we have already begun to explore.

Reasoning Ontologically

The **ontological argument,** developed by a priest named Anselm in the eleventh century, depends on an understanding of *ontology,* the study of being or the essence of things. Anselm reasoned that if he could imagine a perfect God (which he called "that than which nothing greater can be conceived"), then that perfect God must exist; for to lack existence would be to cease being perfect. If the perfect God Anselm conceived in his mind did not exist in reality, then it would be possible for something or someone else to be greater, something or someone that did exist:

ontological argument *a logical argument for the existence of God, based on the nature of thought, developed by Anselm and used by Descartes*

> Therefore, if that, than which nothing greater can be conceived, exists in the understanding alone, the very being, than which nothing greater can be conceived, is one, than which a greater can be conceived. But obviously this is impossible. Hence, there is no doubt that there exists a being, than which nothing greater can be conceived, and it exists both in the understanding and in reality.[5]

THE MAKING OF A PHILOSOPHER

Anselm of Canterbury
(1033–1109)

Born in Aosta (northwestern Italy), Anselm spent time as a Benedictine monk in Bec (Norman France) and finished his career as Archbishop of Canterbury in England. These were the years before the division of Europe into nation-states, and the Western world was unified under the name Christendom. All Christians, especially those who spoke and read Latin, were in a sense citizens of one state. Anselm is often called the father of scholastic philosophy, which is so named because those who later practiced it were scholars, professors at universities. Scholastic philosophy is characterized by its rational approach to Christianity, and Anselm was the first of many who would contend that with faith all the truths of religion could be rationally proved. He wrote his ontological proof for the existence of God on his knees—in gratitude to God for showing him a way to rationally prove God's existence.

Anselm thus argues that it is in the nature or being of God to exist. To be God, according to Anselm, is to be what philosophers call a necessary being—one who must exist and always will exist. Humans are contingent beings, and there is no logical contradiction in thinking of ourselves as not existing, but God is different. Anselm's conclusion is that a perfect being cannot be conceived not to exist.

Anselm believed he had found a proof, based on reason alone, that would convince the doubter that God, an absolutely necessary being, must exist. Critics have pointed out, however, that Anselm seems to be defining God into existence. If existence were a property like other properties we might attribute to God, such as goodness or power, then Anselm's argument would prove that a perfect being must indeed have all those properties, including existence. But is existence such a property? Or does existence instead describe something about the relationship this perfect being has with the world?

Another way of phrasing Anselm's argument is to say: If there is a perfect being, then that perfect being must exhibit all perfections, including existence. Immanuel Kant, whose ideas on knowledge we will consider in the next chapter, points out that to say "If there is a perfect being, then that perfect being exists" is not the same thing as saying "A perfect being exists." We might agree that if birds exist they will have wings, but this says nothing about whether there *are* any birds.

Properties like wingedness belong to birds, and properties like transcendence and immanence may belong to God; however, just as there may not be any birds, there may not be a perfect being. It does not contradict the laws of logic to say that there is no perfect being. Kant argues that we do not really add anything to a concept of God by positing existence. What we do is to assert a relationship of existence between God and the world. Existence is not a quality—as goodness is, for example—and thus it constitutes a separate question.

This argument retains its liveliness even in the twenty-first century. Modern proponents of the ontological argument object that critics like Kant attack and refute their own, weaker versions of the argument rather than the argument itself. For example, the contemporary philosopher Charles Hartshorne asserts that if we examine the proposition "A perfect being exists," we will discover that it is both logically possible for contingent beings like ourselves to know the truth of this proposition and logically impossible for contingent beings like ourselves to know its falsity.

A perfect mind can know its own existence, and an imperfect mind can know the existence of a perfect mind; it is a logical contradiction, however, to assert that an imperfect mind could know the nonexistence of a perfect mind. Hartshorne's conclusion is that the "logical possibility of knowing the truth of a proposition, coupled with the logical impossibility of knowing its falsity, is one of the clearest implications of 'necessary truth.'"[6] In his view a perfect being cannot be conceived not to exist, and we must therefore take Anselm's argument seriously.

Reasoning Cosmologically

The **cosmological arguments** for the existence of God (from the Greek *cosmos,* or "world") had their first important formulation in the Western world at the hand of the medieval theologian Thomas Aquinas, who used rationalist arguments developed by Aristotle and derived from the world. Aquinas offers five cosmological proofs, each based on some observed phenomenon, in his thirteenth-century *Summa Theologica.* The first three follow a similar line of reasoning—from motion to first mover, from effects to first efficient cause, from contingent beings (for whom nonexistence is always a possibility) to a necessary being. By looking at one, we can consider the pattern common to all three before considering the fourth and fifth.

cosmological argument *an argument for the existence of God, based on the contingent nature of the physical world, developed by Aristotle and popularized in the Middle Ages by Aquinas*

In the first proof, Aquinas observes motion and reasons that whatever is moved must be moved by another. A chain of motion exists between objects we observe moving now and the beginning of the chain of motion in the distant past. The chain is not infinite, since if it were there would be no beginning to motion and thus no motion at all. "Therefore," Aquinas concluded, "it is necessary to arrive at a first mover which is moved by no other."

Although Aristotle had ended the argument at this point, Aquinas concluded his argument by adding, "And this everyone understands to be God."[7] Critics have questioned this connection. Why not stop with a first mover, as Aristotle did? Why is a first mover necessarily identical with God? A more serious objection is that if the basis of the argument is correct and "whatever is moved must be moved by another," why exempt God from this requirement?

The second and third proofs follow this pattern. Nothing, Aquinas argues, can be the efficient cause of itself (otherwise, it would have to exist prior to itself and that is impossible) and there must be a necessary being (otherwise, there would have been a time when nothing existed and nothing would now be in existence). Like the first mover, the first efficient cause and the necessary being are for Aquinas the one "all men speak of as God."[8]

The fourth proof is based on degrees of perfection:

> . . . A thing is said to be hotter according as it more nearly resembles that which is hottest. There is then something which is truest, something best, something noblest . . . Now the maximum in any genus is the cause of all in that genus; as fire, which is the maximum of heat, is the cause of all hot things . . . Therefore there must also be something which is to all beings the cause of their being, goodness, and every other perfection. And this we call God.[9]

In the final proof, Aquinas argues from design or purpose. Observing that natural bodies that lack knowledge nevertheless nearly always act to obtain the best result for themselves, he concludes that they achieve this end "because they are directed by some being endowed with knowledge and intelligence, as the arrow is directed by the archer." The intelligent being who directs natural bodies with order and purpose is again, Aquinas asserts, "this being we call God."[10]

THE MAKING OF A PHILOSOPHER

Thomas Aquinas
(1225–1274)

As the son of a noble Italian family, young Thomas had to overcome strong family resistance to become a priest. When he was finally allowed to go to the University of Paris, he studied with the famous Dominican theology professor Albertus Magnus. As an overweight student who remained very quiet in class, Thomas was called the "dumb ox" by his classmates. His professor knew better and told the class, "The bellows of this dumb ox will awaken all of Christendom." Thomas taught theology for twenty-five years, most of them at the University of Paris. He also wrote massive works of theology of which the *Summa Theologica* may be the best known. In all, he wrote sixty books, dictating them to secretaries (sometimes to four secretaries at once since he could think faster than they could write) before he had a mystical experience. After that, he never wrote another word and died at the age of forty-nine.

teleological argument
an argument for the existence of God, based on the design, order, and apparent purpose of the universe; developed by Aquinas and attacked by Hume

Reasoning Teleologically

This **teleological argument** (from the Greek *telos,* meaning "end" or "purpose"), which was originated by Thomas Aquinas, was further developed in 1802 by theologian William Paley. The order and purpose apparent everywhere, according to Paley, require an orderer, a designer who fashioned the whole mechanism and set it working. As the teleological or design argument is sometimes rendered, if you came upon a watch lying on the ground and wondered about its origins, you would look around for the existence of a watchmaker rather than assume that the watch just came into being by itself.

Since the universe is so skillfully wrought, this argument goes, we can see the hand of the designer in its perfection. Even something so basic as the cycle by which water is purified through evaporation and returns to Earth as life-giving rain illustrates the forethought of an efficient planner.

The eighteenth-century empiricist philosopher David Hume took on arguments of this type in his three-part *Dialogues Concerning Natural Religion*. If we are to argue from the evidence of the world, Hume says, we must be sure we argue no further than the evidence can reasonably take us. A character in the dialogues, Philo, who speaks for Hume, questions attributing infinity to the Deity since "the cause ought only to be proportioned to the effect" and the world is clearly finite. Even more doubtful is the attribute of perfection, if we use the world as evidence:

> If we survey a ship, what an exalted idea must we form of the ingenuity of the carpenter who framed so complicated, useful, and beautiful a machine? And what surprise must we feel when we find him a stupid mechanic who imitated others . . . Many worlds might have been botched and bungled, throughout an eternity, ere this system was struck out . . . In a word, Cleanthes, a man who follows your hypothesis is able, perhaps, to assert or conjecture that the universe sometime arose from something like design; but beyond that position he cannot ascertain one single circumstance . . . The world, for aught he knows . . . is the work only of some dependent, inferior deity, and is the object of derision to his superiors . . .[11]

Rationalist arguments, for all their apparent persuasiveness, have had their share of critics, and to many they seem flawed. As we have seen, the developers of these rationalist proofs for the existence of God were all clergymen and at least two were theologians. They already believed in God and were using these arguments to convince others. Probably they would have gladly agreed with Anselm's declaration: "I believe in order that I might understand." Although believers find rationalist proofs for the existence of God comforting, skeptics rarely find their way to belief in God through logic. If one is to believe in a theistic God, then, must it be through "blind faith" or Pascal's wager?

mystical experience
intuitive knowledge of a larger reality, based on personal experience that convinces the recipient of its accuracy

Knowledge Based on Intuition

There have always been those whose belief in a higher power was based not on reason but on what has come to be called **mystical experience.**

Having had an intense, often very personal experience of a more inclusive reality, these people are convinced that a higher power exists. Although they willingly grant that they are unable to "prove" the content of their experience, they contend that we are also unable to "prove" the love of a spouse or child but do not and cannot doubt its existence.

Any God I ever felt in church I brought in with me. And I think all the other folks did too. They come to church to share *God, not find God.*

SHUG AVERY, FROM ALICE WALKER, *THE COLOR PURPLE*

As we consider the writings of some mystics, recall the prisoner who was taken out of the cave in Plato's allegory. At first blinded by the greater light, the prisoner was eventually able to see things as they "really" are. On returning to the cave, however, the prisoner had no words to describe his experience. Anyone whose experience had always been limited to the cave would find it very difficult to accept the enlightenment brought by someone who claimed to know a deeper, fuller, more complete reality.

Encountering the Holy

By definition, the experience of the holy—what the early twentieth-century theologian Rudolf Otto has called the "numinous"—cannot be put into words. It is not a logical, rational, linear experience, like that of taking a trip to Disneyworld (which can be described). But the numinous experience does have certain characteristics. The first of these is the feeling of dependence; Otto calls it a "creature feeling," a recognition of the insignificance of everything in the world of ordinary experience. Thomas Aquinas, who spent his life using reason to build theological systems and explain theological concepts, had a mystical experience near the end of his life and, after it, never wrote another word, referring to all his previous work as utterly insignificant compared with what he had experienced. Two other aspects of the numinous experience are mystery and terror that occur as the ordinary world falls away, taking with it everything that previously helped explain reality. Then, too, there is an element of fascination, of being drawn to something awesome, of lacking defenses but having intense interest. Finally, there is in these experiences a feeling of bliss, of the kind of ecstasy we glimpse when lovemaking is perfect. Let's look at a few examples of knowledge of God through intuition.

The bliss of body and soul captured in this statue reminds us of the earthly and heavenly pleasures oneness brings.

Ecstasy of St. Theresa sculpture by Giovanni Lorenzo Bernini (1598–1680) Santa Maria della Vittoria, Rome, Italy/Bridgeman Art Library, London/New York

God as Lover

Mechthilde of Magdeburg (near today's city of Berlin), a thirteenth-century German mystic, found poetic language more conducive than prose to expressing her experience. Calling herself God's "Fiancée," Mechthilde describes her relationship with God this way:

> This I ask Him earnestly, when we go
> Among the flowers of holy knowledge;
> And I beg Him, brimming over with desire,
> To reveal to me, in His pleasure, the flux
> Which flows in the Holy Trinity,
> And on which the soul alone lives.
> If I must be consoled according to my nobleness,
> The breath of God must draw me to Him
> And there must be no weight detaining me . . .

Nothing attracts me except God alone;
And so, in a most wonderful way, I am dead . . .
But I cannot bear that one single consolation should touch
me, unless it comes from my Most Beloved.[12]

Keep in mind that the image Mechthilde evokes here of lover and Beloved depicts her soul in ecstatic union with God. The analogy is to the sexual union in which earthly lovers are made one. Filled with desire, she is dead to all but God, her "Most Beloved."

THE MAKING OF A PHILOSOPHER

Hildegard of Bingen
(1098–1179)

More of a visionary than a philosopher, Hildegard von Bermersheim, as the tenth child born to her parents, was offered as a "tithe" to God and taken at the age of eight to a nearby Benedictine Abbey. She seems never to have questioned this decision or regretted it. She took her vows as a nun at the age of eighteen and twenty years later was chosen to lead her community. In her forty-third year, she had a life-changing, spiritual awakening; as a result, she felt called to write about the visions she had been having most of her life. Over the next ten years, she wrote about her insights and supervised the creation of artistic illuminations to depict what she saw, compiling all of it in a book she called *Scivias*. She also found time to preach at cathedrals throughout the region; to compose more than seventy poems and an equal number of songs and chants (available on Hyperion and Vision), including an opera; and to write commentaries on the Gospels, instructions in the use of plants for healing, two biographies of saints, and a treatise on ethics. Abbess Hildegard considered herself a "prophet" and called on bishops and even the pope to purify the corruption in the Church.

Divinity as Viriditas, or "Greening Power"

Hildegard of Bingen (near Bonn in modern Germany), a near contemporary of Thomas Aquinas, described the voice of God appointing her to write of what she has learned through her visionary experiences:

> It was in my forty-third year, when I was trembling in fearful anticipation of a celestial vision, that I beheld a great brightness through which a voice from heaven addressed me: O fragile child of earth, ash of ashes, dust of dust, express and write that which thou seest and hearest. Thou art timid, timid in speech, artless in explaining, unlearned in writing, but express and write not . . . under the guidance of human composition, but under the guidance of that which thou seest and hearest in God's heaven above . . .[13]

One of her most striking images is that of *viriditas,* or "greening power"—a Latin word she invented to express the creative, nourishing, life-giving power of divinity. *Viriditas* is the spring flowering that animates creation and stirs the life force in humans as well.[14] As she explained at a sermon in the Cologne cathedral, without it, all is parched and wilted:

> He Who Is made all creation and showed the testimony of testimonies in all His works, so that each created thing appeared . . . For the sun is like the light of His eyes, the wind like the hearing of His ears, the air like His fragrance, the dew like His taste, exuding viridity like His mouth . . . If the clouds did not have fire and water, there would be no firm bond, and if earth did not have moisture and viridity, it would crumble like ashes . . .[15]

In a poem to honor St. Disibod, Abbess Hildegard praises the saint for being the "greening finger of God," the instrument of God's "greening power:"

O Viriditas Digiti Dei

O invigorating power of the finger of God,
in which God planted a garden
which shimmers on the heights
like a steadfast column:

You are glorious in the eternal garden of God[16]

Mary, the mother of Jesus, receives even higher praise as *viridissima virga,* the "greenest branch" that brings the life-giving power of God to Earth. In Mary, the "greening power" overcomes the sin of Eve:

Less traditional images, such as this Ethiopian triptych icon, offer a fresh way to consider this mother and child.

Mary with her Son/The Walters Art Museum, Baltimore.

Hail, O greenest branch . . .
So the time has come
that your sprays have flourished . . .
For the beautiful flower sprung from you
which gave all parched perfumes
their aroma
And they have radiated anew
in their full freshness . . .
O sweet Virgin,
no joy is lacking in you.
Eve rejected all these things . . .[17]

I am the breeze that nurtures all things green . . .
I am the rain coming from the dew
that causes the grasses to laugh with joy of life.
HILDEGARD OF BINGEN

These startling images of God as lover and divinity as "greening power" both have a **noetic** quality—a conviction of certainty. Both Mechthilde of Magdeburg and Hildegard of Bingen are convinced that they know something about God because of intense, personal, intuitive experience. Although we may be a little shocked to think of God as a lover or hadn't really thought of God as being a greening power, there is a certain level of familiarity in these images that makes them understandable to us.

noetic *having the quality of knowledge, seeming to be knowledge*

Interconnectedness Without the Divine

From the Buddhist tradition, we see an intuitive understanding of what is that contains no divine figure. In this vision of the simultaneous existence of all that is, has been, or will be, from Hermann Hesse's *Siddhārtha,* only "time" stands between the images Govinda sees when he bends to kiss the forehead of his boyhood friend Siddhārtha near the end of both their earthly lives:

> He [Govinda] saw the face of a newly born child, red and full of wrinkles, ready to cry. He saw the face of a murderer, saw him plunge a knife into the body of a man; at the same moment he saw this criminal kneeling down, bound, and his head cut off by an executioner. He saw the naked bodies of men and women in the postures and transports of passionate love. He saw corpses stretched out, still, cold, empty . . . Yet none of them died, they only changed, were always reborn, continually had a new face: only time stood between one face and another . . . and over them all there was continually something thin, unreal and yet existing, stretched across like thin glass or ice, like a transparent skin, shell, form or mask of water—and this mask was Siddhārtha's smiling face which Govinda touched with his lips at that moment.[18]

Govinda's mystical vision of life existing in a kind of eternal present requires no divine figure. In this image of existence, there is no past and no future; to be born is to die and to die is to be reborn. The murderer and the murdered are the same. All of existence is interrelated, and only ignorance keeps us from understanding this truth. When he kissed Siddhārtha's forehead, Govinda recognized the "thousand-fold smile of Gotama, the Buddha," and it reminded him of everything he had ever loved, everything that had ever been holy for him. Like Mechthilde and Hildegard, Govinda was granted a moment of pure bliss.

Govinda's vision is of many births and deaths that are all one birth-death or death-birth. It is only our perception of "time" that separates the moment of our birth and the moment of our death, so in a sense both exist simultaneously. As Fritjof Capra, a contemporary theoretical physicist, has observed, this Eastern conception of the universe bears a striking resemblance to the Western scientific understanding of reality as described by quantum theory and relativity:

> The Eastern mystics see the universe as an inseparable web, whose interconnections are dynamic and not static. The cosmic web is alive; it moves, grows and changes continually. Modern physics, too, has come to conceive of the universe as such a web of relations and, like Eastern mysticism, has recognized that this web is intrinsically dynamic. The dynamic aspect of matter arises in quantum theory as a consequence of the wave-nature of subatomic particles, and is even more essential in relativity theory . . . where the unification of space and time implies that the being of matter cannot be separated from its activity. The properties of subatomic particles can therefore only be understood in a dynamic context; in terms of movement, interaction and transformation.[19]

It seems that scientists and mystics sometimes use a common language to describe what both agree is in many ways indescribable: the inner essence of reality. Like Anselm, Thomas Aquinas, and William Paley, Christian mystics claim knowledge of God. Their certainty arises not out of the linear logic of reason but intuitively, based on their experience. What they "know" cannot be proved, but then again, much of what we "know" about the world cannot be proved either, at least not using the traditional methods of science.

If we are to know anything, we must interact with it; and yet, we know that by interacting we are altering what we set out to observe. Perhaps the Taoist image of the cosmic dance found in the Chinese classic *Tao Te Ching* will be helpful:

> Every being in the universe
> is an expression of the Tao.
> It springs into existence, unconscious, perfect, free,
> takes on a physical body, lets circumstances complete it.
> That is why every being
> spontaneously honors the Tao.
> The Tao gives birth to all beings,
> nourishes them, maintains them,
> cares for them, comforts them, protects them,
> takes them back to itself, creating without possessing,
> acting without expecting, guiding without interfering.
> That is why the love of the Tao
> is in the very nature of things.[20]

Like the visions of the mystics in the preceding discussion, the *Tao* cannot be described. The moment you try, you separate the *Tao* out of its inner integrity and into the particularity of the Ten Thousand Things. *Tao* can be experienced but not talked about: "The *Tao* that can be told is not the eternal *Tao*. The name that can be named is not the eternal Name. The unnameable is the eternally real. Naming is the origin of all particular things."[21]

Hinduism and Henotheism

As archaeologist Michael Wood reminds us, Hinduism is a convenient Western label for a vast array of beliefs and practices, sometimes widely divergent from one another. Anything we say about Hinduism can easily be countered by reference to an apparently contradictory belief or practice. Having said that, let's begin with one generalization: many Hindus practice ***puja***—personal devotions that invite a god or goddess into the home. Since there are thousands of deities from which to choose, we might immediately categorize Hinduism as an example of polytheism. Instead, it might more accurately be described as an example of **henotheism.** Many gods are worshiped individually, but each is believed to be a window on the One or the All. Let's see how this happens.

A statue of a particular god or goddess might be the focal point of a home altar and a devotee would rub the statue with sandalwood paste and perfume it with scented oils, draping it with silk and jewels, offering the

puja *[POOH jah] in Hinduism, personal ritual worship, either at home or in a temple*

henotheism *[HEN oh THEE ism] attributing supreme power to a number of deities, one-at-a-time, so that each becomes a window on the One or the All* deity flowers, fruit, milk, or incense before presenting a prayer. In that moment of prayer, focused on a particular deity, the worshiper would hope for an experience known as ***darshan***—a moment of fusion with the divine. As you see the sacred image, you, too, are being seen and being blessed. The particular deity in your home shrine is your window on the One, the All. In the later Hindu sacred texts known as the Upanishads, the divine or supreme reality is known as ***Brahman***—the vital principle of the cosmos whose attributes are infinite being, awareness, and bliss. For those who find these attributes admirable but excessively abstract, *puja* offers the possibility of an encounter with ***Saguna Brahman,*** God-with-attributes. This vision of deity is very close to the Jewish and Christian image of God as loving Father, which we will be discussing in the next section.

darshan *[DHAR shan] in Hinduism, uplift in the presence of greatness and, in* puja, *a moment of fusion with the divine*

Brahman *[BRAH muhn] in Hinduism, the ultimate, absolute reality of the cosmos, the world-soul with which* atman *is identified and seeks union*

Saguna Brahman *[SA goon uh BRAH muhn] in Hinduism, the absolute conceived with attributes*

Nirguna Brahman *[NIR goon uh BRAH muhn] in Hinduism, the absolute conceived without attributes*

For those more comfortable with the impersonal, philosophical contemplation of an entity that is pure being with nothing excluded, Hinduism offers the other face of *Brahman*—***Nirguna Brahman*** or God-without-attributes. "He cannot be seen, for when breathing he is called breath. When speaking he is called speech; when seeing, eye; when hearing, ear; when thinking, mind. All these are only the names of his acts. He who worships him as the one or the other does not know him."[22] There are no mental pictures to bring this image into focus, no words with which to make a more specific connection. For the sages, this is all that can be said and it is enough. This concept is much closer to the impersonal *Tao* than to the God of theism. Huston Smith, who has been studying and writing about the world's religions for more than 50 years, uses this analogy: *Nirguna Brahman* is the ocean, smooth as glass, totally without waves or swells; *Saguna Brahman* is the ocean with waves and swells, with variations that produce particularity.[23]

Which is more accurate? Each interpretation has had its eloquent champions—Ramanuja of the personal *Saguna Brahman* and Shankara of the impersonal *Nirguna Brahman*—as well as those like Ramakrishna who claim that both are correct. The logical West finds this a contradiction, but Hinduism is more tolerant of apparent contradictions. We are at such a distance from *Brahman* and our minds are so finite that whatever we say can be at best an approximation. Perhaps logic itself collapses within the divine light or, with much less mental stretching, perhaps both descriptions are true from different points of view.[24]

If there is a theistic God, whether known rationally or intuitively, then perhaps the most important questions remain to be asked. They focus on what this God is like, for the images we have of God also have implications for human life.

Traditional Images of God

imago dei *[ih MAH go DAY ee] literally, "image of God"; how humans picture an infinite deity, using finite terms*

The God of Western religion and philosophy has been described traditionally as eternal, omnipotent, omniscient, good, the source of truth as well as moral law, and a loving father. In this section we consider the implications of these traditional images of God and examine the ***imago dei,*** or image of God.

God as Eternal

To speak about God in the Western tradition of religion and philosophy is to speak about a being who is *eternal*—who always has been and who always will be. God must have existed prior to Creation, since there must first be a creator before there can be a creation and even if we succeed in destroying ourselves and our planet, presumably God will go on existing. This aspect of eternal existence is closely bound with the definition of God in Western culture.

For this reason, the bold assertion of Friedrich Nietzsche's madman in *Thus Spake Zarathustra*—that "God is Dead!"—shocked nineteenth-century intellectuals to the core. What Nietzsche's madman meant, of course, was that the idea or concept of God was no longer useful, no longer had explanatory power, and no longer made a difference in the way most people lived their lives. Not only is God dead, according to the madman, but we have killed him with our science and our so-called progress. We can explain so much of our universe that the power the idea of God once had to transform human lives has simply evaporated. When the madman realizes he has come too soon with this announcement, he throws down his lantern and departs, but the implication he leaves behind is that sooner or later the rest of us will wake up and acknowledge that God is indeed quite dead.

The fact that even today this phrase can be jarring indicates just how essential to the nature of God is the attribute of eternity. Even deists, who allow God on stage only long enough to create a self-regulating machine before being politely but firmly ushered into the wings, seem to assume that God is eternal. If not very involved in creation at the moment, God is presumably at least taking pride in a job well done. In the 1960s, Death-of-God theologians proclaimed that God—like sexual morality, swing music, and the military-industrial complex—had outlived all usefulness and should be discarded. During the exhilarating chaos of that period, God seemed to some the prime example of a whole group of ideas and institutions that had not kept pace with the times and no longer met the deepest human needs. If God were dead, human beings could re-create themselves and their culture and do a better, fairer job than God had done the first time around.

Judging by the lively debates that still occur in philosophy classes concerning the subject of God, it seems that a funeral would be a bit premature. Theists believe an eternal God will always have the last laugh, witness this well-known piece of graffiti:

> GOD IS DEAD!
> —Nietzsche
>
> NIETZSCHE IS DEAD!
> —God

God as Omnipotent and Omniscient

Omnipotent means "all powerful," and omniscient, "all knowing"; in both cases, the prefix *omni-* means "all." These two attributes of a theistic

omnipotence *the state of unlimited power, usually attributed to God*

omniscience *the state of unlimited knowledge, usually attributed to God*

God—**omnipotence** and **omniscience**—are related, but we will consider them separately.

Philosophy students sometimes have fun with the following puzzle that gets at the notion of the omnipotence of God: Can God make a rock so big that God cannot lift it? Think about the puzzle for a minute. If you answer yes, you preserve the idea that God can do anything and is therefore omnipotent; but if by being omnipotent God places a limit on omnipotence (and as a result cannot lift the rock), does this not negate the whole idea of omnipotence? On the other hand, if you answer no, meaning that God's omnipotence is so great it cannot be limited (and God can lift any rock), then you are left with a situation in which God cannot do something that seems much more significant—create an unliftable rock. Either way, it seems, God's omnipotence is in doubt.

This is a frivolous question (although lots of fun to ponder at parties), but it raises serious questions about the important issue of omnipotence. Could God, for instance, decide not to exist? Could God make a person into a cockroach? If to be all powerful is to be able to do anything, then how can we argue that there are some limits—some things God cannot do and still insist that God is omnipotent?

Let's consider existence. In Western religion and philosophy, as we have just observed, God is thought of as an eternal being. For an eternal being to cease to be would be a self-contradiction. To imagine yourself as not existing would not involve a contradiction, because at some point all humans will cease to be. God, by contrast, is considered a necessary being, one who by definition will always and in fact must exist.

To speak of a necessary being as not existing, then, is to speak nonsense. Just as you cannot speak about a triangle without assuming three sides and three angles, so you cannot speak about God without assuming existence. Presumably, God could not make a triangle that did not have three sides and three angles. And, presumably, a necessary being does not have the option of nonexistence. This is in the nature of the way things are. The limitation here is not on omnipotence but on the rational structure of the universe.

The theological answer Thomas Aquinas provided for the puzzle concerning omnipotence is that if things that lead to contradiction cannot be done, that is a limitation on logic and not a limitation on the power of God. In other words, God is capable of all rationally possible actions. Contradictory things are essentially not real, and so they cannot be brought into being. God creating the unliftable rock is like God turning a person who has reason (and was made in the image of God) into a cockroach that does not (and was not)—it is a contradiction. God, it is said, can do all that is possible—all that does *not* involve contradiction.

God is also described as omniscient, which literally means "all knowing" or sometimes "all wise." Understood positively, the omniscience of God puts every aspect of reality in divine hands: Not a sparrow can fall without God's knowledge. Understood negatively, if God knows everything, in what sense are we free to act as we choose? Theology asserts that God made people free to choose good or evil. To hold humans accountable for moral choices, we must assume we are in fact free to make those choices. But how can our choices be described as free if God already knows what we will choose to do?

This question cuts to the heart of both divine and human nature. How are we to hold on to the seemingly essential human freedom to choose while still affirming that God knows everything? Suppose that humans had no option but to love God. Although all of us have wished we could command someone to love us, it takes only a moment's reflection to realize that forced love is not love at all; only when someone freely chooses to love us do we feel loved. God is in more or less the same position: For our love to be freely given to God, we must have the option not to love God. Yet God knows what our choices will be since God knows everything.

The explanation most often given for this apparent paradox is a deceptively simple one. Being who you are, you will act in a certain way in any given situation. That does not mean you are not free to do otherwise; it simply means that your actions are predictable. If I know you very well, I may be able to predict what you will do, but my ability to predict in no way limits your freedom. God, who has an omniscient vantage point, can predict everything with absolute certainty. The final act of the play is already written, and I will play my part in what is to God a very predictable way. Still, in every scene, indeed with every line, I am free to act as I choose to act. Could God have done this differently—elected not to know how I will choose and leave me free to fool even God? Not without contradicting God's omniscience.

God as Good

The really thorny question involves the goodness, or benevolence (which means "willing good"), of God. Theists insist that God is good—it seems impossible to do otherwise—and yet, if God is good, why is the world so full of evil and suffering? There seem to be two possible explanations, both of them unsatisfactory. Either God is responsible for the evil and suffering (and is therefore not good), or evil and suffering exist in spite of God, who either cannot (and is therefore not omnipotent after all) or will not (and is therefore not good) eliminate them. The dilemma is sometimes posed in the form of this puzzle:

> If God is God, God is not good.
> If God is good, God is not God.

It seems to me that in our time faith in God is the same thing as faith in good and the ultimate triumph of good over evil.
SVETLANA ALLILUYEVA, DAUGHTER OF JOSEF STALIN

In other words, if we grant the reality of evil and suffering in the world, we must question either God's power (to stop them) or God's goodness (in allowing them to exist). If God is God (meaning all powerful), then God is responsible for everything (including evil and suffering) and thus is not good. On the other hand, if God is good (and thus not responsible for evil and suffering), then apparently God is not powerful enough to stop them—or worse, chooses not to stop them.

Where is God while evil seems to triumph? One way of looking at the problem is to consider evil as simply the absence of good, in which case

PHILOSOPHERS SPEAK FOR THEMSELVES
Augustine

As we can see, therefore, two cities arise from two types of love. The earthly city has its roots in a selfish love that will go so far as to defy God. The heavenly city rests in a love of God that does not shrink from conquering the self. One celebrates its own accomplishments; the other gives glory to God through a life well lived. The earthly city lifts up its head to boast of its greatness; the other acclaims God as "my glory, and the one who lifts up my head."[1]

Domination and the love of domination rule in the earthly city; whereas, in the heavenly city rulers and subjects serve one another in love. The former city delights in its own strength; the latter says, "I love you, O Lord, my strength."[2] Even the so-called wise people in the earthly city seek only the pleasures of mind and body. If they stumble upon knowledge of God, they are not wise enough to be humble and grateful; instead, they congratulate themselves on their intelligence. "Claiming to be wise, they became fools; and they exchanged the glory of the immortal God for images resembling a mortal human being or birds or four-footed animals or reptiles."[3] They either lead or follow the people in worshiping these images, mistaking creature for Creator. In the City of God, by contrast, there is no merely human wisdom but only the worship and love of God and the pursuit of holiness in the company of saints and angels, "so that God may be all in all."[4]

The Earthly City and the Heavenly City, from *The City of God* Book XIV (26-28). Translation: Copyright 2000 by Helen Buss Mitchell

Notes

1. Psalm 3:3 *The New Revised Standard Version* (Nashville: Thomas Nelson Publishers, 1989)
2. Psalm 18:1 *The New Revised Standard Version* (Nashville: Thomas Nelson Publishers, 1989)
3. Romans 1:22-23 *The New Revised Standard Version* (Nashville: Thomas Nelson Publishers, 1989)
4. I Corinthians 15:28 *The New Revised Standard Version* (Nashville: Thomas Nelson Publishers, 1989)

we are left with good and the absence of good. Because evil is then the absence of something, it is not a "something" that can be laid to God's account. Notice that this argument does not deny the existence of evil; it simply denies the *reality* of evil.

Augustine, a fourth-century Christian Platonist, took this position, arguing in his *Enchiridion on Faith, Hope and Love* that "all beings were made good, but not being made perfectly good, are liable to corruption."[25] According to this argument, if you get a cold, your health is "corrupted." When you get better, nothing actually goes away except the temporary corruption and your health is restored. Augustine saw evil this way, as a temporary corruption of an essential state of goodness. If we take this position, the goodness of God is retained. Sometimes the goodness that God created is not fully present in limited beings, which are liable to corruption, but this absence cannot be blamed on God.

I would rather believe that God did not exist than believe that he was indifferent.
GEORGE SAND

A stronger explanation for the apparent strength of evil locates evil in human free will. As we have already seen, if humans are free to do good, they must also have equal freedom not to do good. Even though God did not will evil, the possibility of evil is a necessary consequence of human freedom. Much of what we would call evil in the world can be traced directly or indirectly to our own choices and the choices of our fellow human beings. Wars, famines, and neighborhood violence are all to a greater or lesser degree under the control of humans like ourselves. If we want to find someone to blame, we need look no further than into our own hearts.

What this solution does not take into account, however, are natural disasters like earthquakes and hurricanes, as well as the deaths of apparently innocent children from disease. Blaming these evils on human freedom is difficult. In these cases, it is sometimes suggested that evil is apparent, rather than real. From our limited perspective, something may seem catastrophic, but from a God's-eye view it may be part of some greater good.

The matter of perspective is important; things might look very different from the divine point of view. Suppose, by way of analogy, that while we were having a picnic one of us discovered an anthill and totally destroyed it without a second thought. We would have achieved a good from our perspective, but for the ants our good would be paid for with an unimaginable catastrophe. From the ants' perspective, this would be unmitigated evil, but from our perspective it would be good. Theists say that all apparent evil is working toward an ultimate good, a good that may be visible only from a God's-eye view.

Hardest to accept may be the suffering of the innocent and the good. What does it mean when bad things happen to good people and why would a good God permit this? Sometimes a tragedy brings out the best in people, but, if people are already good, then what purpose can there be to their suffering? Perhaps the nearest we can get is to say, as some theologians do, that it is a "mystery." In *The Prophet,* the Lebanese poet Kahlil Gibran puts it this way:

> Your joy is your sorrow unmasked.
> And the selfsame well from which your laughter rises
> was oftentimes filled with your tears.
> And how else can it be?
> The deeper that sorrow carves into your being,
> the more joy you can contain.
> Is not the cup that holds your wine the very cup
> that was burned in the potter's oven?
> And is not the lute that soothes your spirit,
> the very wood that was hollowed with knives?[26]

In his novel *All The King's Men,* Robert Penn Warren suggests that only by separating humans from the divine (good) nature could God set up a condition under which humans could reject sin and create good. This is perhaps the ultimate in **theodicy,** the explanation and justification of evil as an integral part of this best of all possible worlds:

> The creation of man whom God in His foreknowledge knew doomed to sin was the awful index of God's omnipotence, for it would have been a thing of trifling and contemptible ease for Perfection to create

THE MAKING OF A PHILOSOPHER

Augustine of Hippo
(354–430)

As the son of a pagan father and Christian mother, Augustine grew up in Tunisia (North Africa). He was intellectually attracted first to Manichaeism, a dualistic system with a god of good and a god of evil perpetually at war, and then to Neoplatonism, which stressed mystical union with God and declared evil merely the absence of good. In Milan, Italy, Augustine met Bishop Ambrose, a Christian intellectual, and after opening the Bible and reading a verse that seemed aimed at him, Augustine gave up drunken parties and a series of mistresses, to become a Christian. He wrote *The City of God* in response to pagan critics who said Rome had been sacked by Alaric in 410 because the Romans had abandoned the gods who had protected them when they turned to Christianity. Augustine declared that in the end the City of God, the true "eternal city," will triumph although the devil may win temporary victories in the City of Man. Charlemagne used this book as his model for the Holy Roman Empire.

theodicy *[thee AH dih see] the justification of the goodness of God in the face of the fact of evil*

HOW PHILOSOPHY WORKS
The Hypothetical Syllogism

One form of deductive reasoning takes the form "If P, then Q" and is called a *hypothetical syllogism.* In the proposition "If P, then Q," the term "P" is called the *antecedent* and the term "Q" is called the *consequent.* Both affirming the antecedent P and denying the consequent Q lead to valid conclusions. The first form, affirming the antecedent, is called *modus ponens;* the second form, denying the consequent, is called *modus tollens.*

Modus Ponens	*Modus Tollens*
If P, then Q.	If P, then Q.
P.	Not-Q.
Therefore, Q.	Therefore, not-P.

Let's look at a simple example of these two forms:

If the pond is frozen (P), the temperature must be below 32 degrees F (Q).

The pond is frozen (P).

Therefore, the temperature is below 32 degrees F (Q).

If the pond is frozen (P), the temperature must be below 32 degrees F (Q).

The temperature is 50 degrees F (not-Q).

Therefore, the pond is not frozen (not-P).

Now, let's examine the argument

If God is God, God is not good.

If God is good, God is not God.

We must first acknowledge some unexpressed definitions. The first is that the word *God* as used here means "all powerful," and the second is that the word *good* as used here means "not the source of evil."

If God is God (all powerful) (P), God is not good (the source of evil) (Q).

God is God (all powerful) (P).

Therefore, God is not good (the source of evil) (Q).

If God is good (P), God is not God (Q).

God is good (not the source of evil) (P).

Therefore, God is not God (not powerful enough to destroy evil) (Q).

These two examples illustrate *modus ponens.* Let's try *modus tollens,* keeping in mind that the "nots" may get in our way:

If God is God (P), God is not good (Q).

God is good (not-Q).

Therefore, God is not God (not powerful enough to destroy evil) (not-P).

If God is good (P), God is not God (Q).

God is God (not-Q).

Therefore, God is not good (the source of evil) (not-P).

> mere perfection. To do so would, to speak truth, be not creation but extension. Separateness is identity and the only way to create, truly create, man was to make him separate from God Himself, and to be separate from God is to be sinful. The creation of evil is therefore the index of God's glory and his power. That had to be so that the creation of good might be the index of man's glory and power. But by God's help. By His help and in His wisdom.[27]

For some people, all these attempts to put a good face on evil remain unconvincing. What is your own response? If human freedom—even that described so glowingly by Warren—does not account adequately in your mind for what you can only describe as very real suffering and evil, then what would a world with no suffering, no evil, be like?

In *The Brothers Karamazov,* Dostoyevsky poses this ethical dilemma: Would you eliminate all the evil and suffering in the world by transferring it to one innocent but relatively insignificant creature—one small baby, for instance? It may be interesting to ask yourself this question, which has a greater bearing on ethics than on the attributes of God. Or imagine this: What if all evil and suffering simply disappeared? Would this be a satisfactory world?

To begin with, we would rapidly become overpopulated, since no one would die to make room for the next generation. There would be no crime and no accidents; no jealousy, hate, or anger. Each day would be just like the last—perfect. This may sound like paradise to you or it may sound very bland. With no challenges would you grow and develop as a person? If never faced with a problem to overcome, might you become complacent, even bored?

There are those who feel a little adversity is absolutely necessary to achieve even very limited human goals. Suppose you could play the piano flawlessly without ever having had to practice. Would you take the same pleasure in your accomplishment? If athletic prowess came naturally and were available to everyone, would this diminish your sense of having done something profoundly worth doing? It is worth pondering whether you would wish to live in a world completely devoid of evil and suffering.

God as Source of Truth and Moral Law

As you may recall from Chapter 1, the Greeks considered the cosmos an intelligible system and believed humans qualified by their reason to unlock its mysteries. Several of the early Greek cosmologists used the word ***logos*** (in the sense of "reason") to describe the rational principle they believed lay behind all the workings of the cosmos. John, the writer of the fourth gospel in the Bible, also used the word *Logos* (in the sense of "word") to describe Jesus as the *Logos* made flesh. Remember that every usage of "the Word" represents the Greek word *logos:*

logos *the rational, ordering principle of the cosmos, for the Greeks*

> In the beginning was the Word and the Word was with God, and the Word was God. He was in the beginning with God; all things were made through him, and without him was not anything made that was made . . . And the Word became flesh and dwelt among us . . .[28]

In the second century after the death of Jesus, Justin Martyr, who had studied philosophy in Ephesus before being converted to Christianity, asserted that the *Logos* of God became incarnate in the person of Jesus and, as a result, the *logos,* or rational principle, of the universe is universally active and present in the highest goodness and intelligence, wherever they may be found.

Paul Tillich, a twentieth-century Protestant theologian, says that the intelligible structure of the universe is expressed in the world through the *Logos.*[29] In one sense, the divine *Logos* is in every aspect of creation, since all creation is the self-manifestation of God. But, the divine *Logos* is present in a unique way in the life of Jesus as the Christ.[30] It is this understanding that has led Christianity to claim a unique and therefore exclusive claim to religious truth. If God, the ultimate source of all truth, chooses to take on human form, bringing into the world a unique expression of the *Logos,* and if that embodiment of the *Logos* founds a church, then truth is ever-after present in an enhanced way in that church.

If God is truth, then we must look to God as the arbiter, or decision maker, on all questions, including how we should behave. For those who accept the Bible as the word of God, it is only a small step to believing that divine law must govern human society. When a civil government is based on divine law, we call it a **theocracy,** which literally means "rule by God."

theocracy *literally, "rule by God"; the fusion of church and state*

The Puritans who left England to establish the Massachusetts Bay Colony set out very self-consciously to establish a "Holy Commonwealth" that would operate on God's law. The colony they established was a theocracy because God (*theos*) was literally the ruler. Those who live in a democracy in which the people (*demos*) rule often make an explicit distinction between religious and secular law. The separation of church and state guarantees that citizens must obey only civil laws—those developed by its citizens—and not the laws of a particular religion. In a theocracy, church and state are one; to break the laws of one is to break the laws of the other.

Anthropomorphism

anthropomorphism *representing something nonhuman (such as animals or God) in human likeness*

To think of God as the ruler of a state is to engage in **anthropomorphism**—ascribing human characteristics to nonhuman beings, including God and animals. We know that God is by definition larger than our finite, human categories of race and gender and even age, and most of us would be quick to say that we know that God (if there is a God) is not an old, white man. Still, what lives in our imagination is probably William Blake's white-bearded *The Ancient of Days* or Michelangelo's painting on the Sistine Chapel ceiling of God giving life to Adam by touching his finger.

New gods arise when they are needed.
JOSEPHINE W. JOHNSON

This tendency has been a human practice for a long time. Writing in the fifth century B.C.E., Xenophanes, one of the pre-Socratic philosophers, notes that "mortals suppose that the gods are born (as they themselves are), and that they wear man's clothing and have human voice and body." Observing that Ethiopian gods are dark and snub-nosed whereas the Thracian gods have blue eyes and red hair, Xenophanes concludes that the tendency to depict gods as like ourselves is a universal one: "But if cattle or lions had hands, so as to paint with their hands works of art as men do, they would paint their gods and give them bodies in form like their own—horses like horses, cattle like cattle."[31]

The modern tendency to anthropomorphize is examined in Ludwig Feuerbach's *The Essence of Christianity.* Published in 1841, this short treatise led Karl Marx to a materialist understanding of the world. Feuerbach's thesis is that religion arises out of human needs and wants. People create ideals for themselves—that is, for human nature—and then project them onto the world and worship them as God. God is nothing more (and nothing less) than an idealized human being:

> Reason can only believe in a God who is in accordance with its own nature, in a God who is not beneath its own dignity, who, on the contrary, is a realization of its own nature; i.e., reason believes only in itself, in the absolute affirmation of its essence. What, therefore, do you affirm, what do you objectify in God? Your own reason! God is your highest idea, the highest conception of your intellect, the highest conception you can possibly have. What I recognize as belonging to the essence of reason I posit in God as existing.[32]

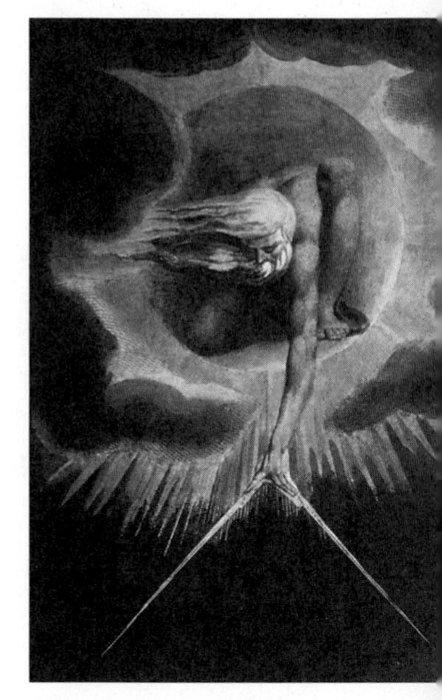

What do we gain and what do we lose by imaging God as an old, white male?

The Ancient of Days by William Blake (1757–1827) British Museum, UK/Bridgeman Art Library, London/New York

In the movie *Oh God!,* a supermarket clerk, played by John Denver, receives a visit from God, played by George Burns. The clerk is surprised that God is so ordinary looking, really indistinguishable from hundreds of other rather old men one might meet on the street, and no better dressed. "God" explains that he has taken on this appearance so as not to frighten a human. "I picked a look you could understand," God explains, "I could even be a woman."

Suppose God appeared to you. Is there a form, other than the human one, that you could accept? Theism tells us that God is a spirit and has no need for a body. What options does a disembodied spirit have for communicating with us humans? Would a burning bush be more convincing? It is easy to see why the tendency toward anthropomorphism is so strong. If there is a God who wishes to communicate with humans, a human form might be essential; any other form could be too easy for us to miss or too frightening.

Although God, being infinite, cannot be described as a person, we associate personal qualities with the God of the Hebrew Scriptures, sometimes called the Old Testament. God is repeatedly shown intervening in human history to save the children he has so lovingly created. Even when the children are unfaithful and break the Covenant (the sacred relationship of trust and mutual responsibilities God has entered into with them), the God of the Bible remains a loving father.

There are many positive aspects to this image. A personal God, unlike the God of deism, for instance, seems to care what happens to people and to exist as a source of love and support in times of trouble. If one holds the view that there is a divine plan and everything is working toward a greater good, the idea of a loving father makes adversity easier to bear. Christianity has taken the notion of love to the extreme by insisting that the infinite, eternal, all-powerful, all-knowing God voluntarily took human form and died in order to reconcile humankind to God.

Although the image of God as loving father may be psychologically satisfying, it is not without its problems. Clearly, we are only speaking by analogy: God is *like* a loving father is in the human world. But once we use such terms it becomes very difficult, if not impossible, not to form a mental image of God as an old, white male. Visual art in the Western world has created this image, and it has seemed to validate male leadership in the world and in the family. As lines have blurred between "men's work" and "women's work," some have begun to reexamine the image of God as implicitly male. Seeing God as Father, no matter how loving, is limiting and

Why indeed must "God" be a noun? Why not a verb . . . the most active and dynamic verb of all?
MARY DALY

"You don't look anything like your pictures"

God has never sat for a portrait, but we have images of God.

can restrict women from fully identifying with God. As we saw in Chapter 3, fourth-century women like Macrina felt compelled to justify women's inclusion in the image of God.

i found god in myself
& i loved her
i loved her fiercely
NTOZAKE SHANGE

Nontraditional Images of God

If traditional images of God are too restrictive or too culture bound to capture the fullness of divinity, let's consider some less traditional images from feminist and racial/ethnic points of view, a traditional Western culture, and a West African image of God that assumes a different worldview. Each of these images challenges some aspect of the traditional Western concept of God.

God as Mother, Jesus as Mestizo

If God is both male and powerful, what of those who are not male and/or not powerful? The image of God as constructed by theologians and artists has served to exclude as well as to include. What if God were imaged as female and Jesus thought of as a marginal person of mixed blood?

The image of God as loving father and the maleness of Jesus have both been cited as reasons for excluding women from the Christian priesthood. If to mediate between the divine and the human one must be male, where does this leave women? What do these restrictions say about God, and what do they say about women? Mary Baker Eddy, the founder of Christian Science, called God "our Father our Mother," and there are no doubt rich possibilities in the idea of God as mother, which might be interesting to explore.

One of them appears in the feminist fantasy *Herland,* written in 1915 by Charlotte Perkins Gilman, whose ideas about women and economics we'll explore in Chapter 9. Male explorers discover an all-female society—a world of mothers and children in which divinity is conceived as a Loving Power with maternal concern for humankind. There was no formal worship, the male narrator Van explains, but temple mothers offered love and wisdom to help people through life's challenges:

> Their cleanliness, their health, their exquisite order, the rich peaceful beauty of the whole land, the happiness of the children, and above all the constant progress they made—all this was their religion . . . As for those little temples everywhere—some of the women were more skilled, more temperamentally inclined, in this direction, than others. These, whatever their work might be, gave certain hours to the Temple Service, which meant being there with all their love and wisdom and trained thought, to smooth out rough places for anyone who needed it.[33]

If there has to be a god, can she be a committee of women dedicated to wiping out earthly oppression?
HATTIE GOSSETT

Here are women imaging divinity and mediating between the human and the divine. Do you find this comforting or unsettling? What about thinking of Jesus as mestizo? Virgil Elizondo claims that "being a Jew in Galilee was very much like being a Mexican-American in Texas."[34] Galilee, Elizondo says, was a borderland between Judean Jews and Greeks, and its residents were too Jewish to be accepted by the Greeks, and too pagan to be accepted by the Jews:

> By growing up in Galilee, Jesus was a cultural mestizo assuming unto himself the great traditions that flourished in his home territory . . . Culturally and linguistically speaking, Jesus was a mestizo . . . He appeared to be a half-breed. . . . No wonder they kept saying, "What good can come out of Galilee? . . . This man is possessed by the chief of demons."[35]

If Jesus is depicted as a blond, blue-eyed figure who resembles the rich and powerful in the world, those who share his maleness but not his power may feel excluded in the same way women do. Those who feel themselves to be marginal, however, can find much to identify with in a Jesus who lived between two cultures, never quite fitting into either, and whose accent always gave him away. Elizondo, who is a priest, sees this point of connection as essential for Mexican Americans such as himself and his parishioners:

> The *mestizo* affirms both the identities received while offering something new to both. Being an inside-outsider and an outside-insider to two worlds at the same time, we have the unique privilege of seeing and appreciating both worlds . . . Jesus did not give in to the fashion of many of the educated Jews of his time by assuming the ways of Greek culture, but neither did he simply affirm and purify his Jewish ways. He offered a new alternative to both and through them to everyone else. It is in this alternative that all the previous traditions are assumed and transcended. Thus it is in the very way of Jesus that mestizos find their mission: to create.[36]

existentialism *emphasizes the uniqueness and freedom of the human person as an individual (what makes each life a unique, personal experience) as opposed to the essence of a human being (what makes all of us alike)*

God as Ground of Being

Religious existentialism asks us to step outside the traditional images of God and rethink the idea of Being itself from the inside out. **Existentialism** began in the mid-nineteenth century with Søren Kierkegaard, who shifted the focus of philosophy from essence (in this case, what human nature is like) to existence. He used words like *dread, anxiety,* and *despair* to characterize the human condition.

One of his books, *Fear and Trembling,* was built around the biblical story of Abraham and Isaac. Kierkegaard finds Abraham's willingness to sacrifice his son Isaac at God's request admirable, if impossible to understand. No process of logic or rationality would lead a person to murder his own child, and Kierkegaard understands that Abraham did not arrive at his decision through analysis. Although in the end God did not demand the sacrifice of Isaac, the point for Kierkegaard is that Abraham was prepared to make it. What Abraham did is what everyone must do in the face of absurdity and despair: Make a "leap of faith."

For Kierkegaard, existence is what really matters, and the key question is, How shall I act? We will not, he believes, find any worthwhile answers to the "big questions" about God and human existence through objective analysis and reasoning. In the face of objective uncertainty, a person must passionately and trustingly jump into the unknowable and choose faith:

> Without risk there is no faith. Faith is precisely the contradiction between the infinite passion of the individual's inwardness and objective uncertainty. If I am capable of grasping God objectively, I do not believe, but precisely because I cannot do this I must believe . . . For this reason Socrates was in the truth by virtue of his ignorance, in the highest sense in which this was possible within paganism.[37]

If God is not knowable in an objective sense, then the questions produced by overly specific images of God disappear. Whether God is omnipotent, omniscient, or even eternal is really beyond the reach of human knowing and perhaps even a little beside the point. With the advent of existentialism, the focus always remains on the solitary existence of the human subject. Faced with the reality of suffering and the certainty of death, the individual is concerned primarily with questions of meaning.

For religious existentialists, the question really is what sort of relationship we may have with God, because it is this relationship that overcomes the loneliness and despair of the human condition. God's specific attributes may be unknowable, but we can be sure that God is a "Thou" rather than an "It," according to twentieth-century Jewish existentialist Martin Buber. It is possible to become an "I" only through experience of a "Thou," and this same kind of personal relationship is the basis for the divine-human encounter that occurs in faith. Consider the story of an encounter between the young Buber and a dapple-gray horse:

> If I am to explain it now, beginning from the still very fresh memory of my hand, I must say that what I experienced in touch with the animal was the Other, the immense otherness of the Other, which, however, did not remain strange like the otherness of the ox and the ram, but rather let me draw near and touch it. When I stroked the mighty mane . . . it was as though the element of vitality itself bordered on my skin, something that was not I was certainly not akin to me, palpably the other, not just another, really the Other itself; and yet it let me approach, confided itself to me, placed itself elementally in the relation of *Thou* and *Thou* with me.[38]

Every Thou, even a dapple-gray horse, points to the Eternal Thou with whom the authentic "I" is in dialogue. What matters is the experience, the relationship, not the particular qualities of the Thou. Here, as with Kierkegaard, I become an authentic person and have an authentic encounter with God not through objective knowing but through subjective experiencing.

For Buber, this means that if I wish to know something about Being, then I must come to the knowing as an "I"; that is, I must understand myself before I can hope to understand Being. To know God, I must stand alone like Abraham: "Not before a man can say I in perfect reality—that is, finding himself—can he in perfect reality say *Thou*—that is, to God. And even if he does it in a community he can only do it 'alone.'"[39]

Existentialists like Kierkegaard and Buber do not focus on the images associated with a theistic God we discussed earlier, and some existentialist thinkers think these images reduce God to an object. Objects can be known "objectively," dispassionately, but God cannot.

Paul Tillich defines faith as "ultimate concern" and "the most centered act of the human mind." Since faith always implies faith in something, if that something is the "ultimate," then faith has the possibility of overcoming the traditional subject-object split:

> In true faith the ultimate concern is a concern about the truly ultimate; while in idolatrous faith preliminary, finite realities are elevated to the rank of ultimacy. The inescapable consequence of idolatrous faith is "existential disappointment," a disappointment which penetrates into the very existence of a man![40]

It is not enough to have faith. People may, for instance, have faith in a nation in the form of intense patriotism, but this kind of faith will ultimately disappoint, and the distance that may have been temporarily overcome

THE MAKING OF A PHILOSOPHER

Søren Kierkegaard
(1813–1855)

Born in Denmark and raised in the Pietist tradition of Protestantism, Kierkegaard felt guilty most of the time. He first reacted against his upbringing by eating, drinking, and carousing, but these only plunged him deeper into "melancholy," or depression. He became engaged to seventeen-year-old Regine Olson but broke the engagement after an anguished struggle in which he decided God must have first place in his life. Having decided to become a Lutheran pastor, Kierkegaard studied the Bible and became overwhelmed by the huge gap between an infinite God and finite human beings. He realized that the central issue was faith—belief that God would keep his promise of eternal life, despite the fact that this can in no way be proved rationally. Since there can be no question of proof, we must make an absolute and unconditional "leap of faith," Kierkegaard concluded. As a result of his emphasis on the loneliness and despair of the human condition and the irrationality of human life, Kierkegaard is called the first existentialist philosopher.

between subject and object may then seem greater than before. For a while I may see myself exclusively as a member of a team, a club, or a peer group, and this identification may be deeply satisfying; I may lose for a time my sense of loneliness and isolation by rooting my identity in something larger than myself—my friends, my team, my country. But all finite things are unworthy as objects of faith, and belief in them will ultimately lead to cynicism. Only the "ultimate," Tillich believes, will not disappoint.

I don't want a God that
blesses America
I don't want a God that
fills me with terror
Love springs from the
Goddess
Energy is above and
beyond us
Sacred Universe, Cosmic
Christ
A new Solar Birth is
within sight
Spiritual revolution to set
us free
Let it start with me.
JONATHAN RATICAN

Tillich is not even comfortable with the term *God*. Traditional images have, in his view, objectified God. Tillich prefers terms like the "God above God" or the "Depth" or the "Ground of Being." By using these terms, Tillich hopes to escape the traps of objectification and anthropomorphism we discussed earlier. If God is the "Ground of Being," for instance, God is both a person and not a person:

> Religiously speaking, this means that our encounter with the God who is a person includes the encounter with the God who is the ground of everything personal and as such not a person. Religious experience, particularly as expressed in the great religions, exhibits a deep feeling for the tension between the personal and the nonpersonal element in the encounter between God and man . . . The God of Abraham, Isaac, and Jacob and the God of the philosophers is the same God. He is a person and the negation of himself as a person.[41]

God as Cosmic Architect and Bagworm

It may be useful at this point to step outside the Western tradition and look at how the Akan people of West Africa view God. We will benefit by keeping in mind the discussion of Western views of the omnipotence of God. If you recall, God can do anything that does not involve a contradiction, such as creating a rock so big it could not be lifted even by God. In this conception of omnipotence, God is bound by the laws of logic and capable only of things that are possible.

A similar but even more stringent limitation on the omnipotence of God exists among the Akan people. According to philosopher Kwasi Wiredu, the state drummer at a "funeral," while offering condolences to an Akan ruler on the loss of a person, would be likely to "say" in drum language: "The creator created death and death killed him." This emphasizes the inevitability of death as well as limitations on the omnipotence of the creator. If people are created to die, then they must die; and when the time comes for a person to die, both the physician and the creator are equally powerless to stop the process.[42]

Notice the difference between this view and the traditional Western one. Thomas Aquinas bound the Western God to the laws of logic, but once the Akan God has created the cosmic order, that God is also bound by them. The Akan God can accomplish any well-defined task but cannot change the cosmic order, which includes the inevitability of death. Even creation itself is less an act of will and more a necessary result of the Creator's nature. If the Western God has "reasons" for creating the world, then, according to Akan philosophy, it only makes sense to ask where God got those reasons. But this question will lead us in circles and will never come to a reasonable conclusion. Rather, creation proceeds from the built-in law of the Creator's being.

Unlike the Western God, the Akan Creator does not create out of nothing, because to create in the Akan language is to fashion a product—to mold, shape, design the form of something—rather than bring something into being out of nothing. The Akan Supreme Being is more like a cosmic architect than like a creator. But if the Akan Creator did not create something out of nothing, how did things come about? This problem can be posed in terms of a paradox involving the bagworm, the larva of a moth, that lives in its own silk case: How did the bagworm get into its case?

In the beginning was God
Today is God
Tomorrow will be God
Who can make an image of God?
He has no body
He is as a word which comes out of your mouth
That word! It is no more
It is past, and still it lives!
So is God
PYGMY HYMN

There are two possibilities. Either the bagworm wove the case before getting into it, or the bagworm got into the case before weaving it. The second alternative seems clearly impossible; how can you get into a case that has not yet been woven? In the first alternative, however, whatever wove the "bag" was not yet a bagworm; only when within the bag does the bagworm deserve its name. The real paradox is this: "Either the Creator was somewhere before creating everywhere, or he was nowhere while creating everywhere." Just as with the bagworm, in either case there is a contradiction. Therefore, it must be the case that creation really is a process of transformation.

The Akan view is that both creature and Creator are part of this world. "To exist" in the Akan language is to be somewhere. The concept of purely mental existence apart from any physical space (which we will discuss in the next chapter) is linguistically impossible in Akan and, in Wiredu's view, in any language. So, a creator must exist in space somewhere. Thus, there must be a somewhere, and that somewhere has something in it—an indeterminate something that has the possibility of being transformed into something else.[43]

In Akan culture then, creature and Creator are somewhat closer together than in the Western tradition. Both share the same world, and both are bound by the laws of that world and the laws of their own being. Rather than reducing the religious dimension, this view may enhance it. If the Supreme Being is in the same world as we are, everything is made holy.

As we have seen, the question of the existence or nonexistence of God (if answered affirmatively) leads to an equally important question about what kind of God exists. Images associated with God are culture specific and can make it relatively easier or more difficult for a person in any given culture to believe in God. But how a person answers the most basic question—whether or not there is a God—will probably affect how that person views related questions of metaphysics.

Imagine yourself in a ritual mask with a beak—part bird and part human—soaring over the earth like a god.

Dan ritual mask, courtesy of the African Art Museum of Maryland/Photo by Quentin Kardos.

Theological Implications for Human Nature and Cosmology

Whether or not you believe in a personal God will probably influence your views of both human nature and the nature of the cosmos. As we have seen in this chapter, Buddhism, Taoism, and some followers of Hinduism speak about ultimate reality using impersonal terms. So, it might be a good idea to remind ourselves at this point that our discussion of terms such as theism, atheism, and agnosticism reflects a Western worldview. There are alternatives outside the Western worldview that don't fit tidily into the terms we have been using. Within the Western context, however, if there is a personal God, we might say that humans are made in the image of God and the cosmos is ruled by divine law. If a personal God does not exist, we might describe ourselves and the world using only finite terms. Let's look at some of the implications of the "who's in charge?" question we posed at the beginning of the chapter.

Atheistic Worldview

In this view, if the God of theism does not exist, then all meaning might be said to derive from human values. According to Protagoras, without God, "man is the measure of all things." Without a personal God, we might conclude that all creative and technological accomplishments are monuments to human potential and should be celebrated as the legacies one generation leaves to the next so that continuous progress is possible. We are responsible to ourselves and to our fellow travelers to behave reasonably and to be true to our human nature. The purpose of life is what we bring to it: our dreams and hopes for a better present and a brighter future. The purpose of my life is whatever I decide it should be, and the measure of a life well or poorly lived can be taken only by the person who has lived it. When I die, my consciousness will die with me; my contributions to human knowledge and the creative spirit, as well as the people whose lives I have touched, will be my immortality. While they live and while my accomplishments endure, I will not be forgotten. My children and grandchildren are my legacies to the future.

Cats are atheists; but dogs almost certainly believe in God!
VLADIMIR MARINICH

Deistic, Pantheistic, and Panentheistic Worldviews

I can catch a glimpse of a power more splendid than I through the natural and mechanical processes of nature, and it may inspire me to more fully realize my own potential. Everything that intrigues my intellect or touches my emotions has a bit of the divine in it, nudging me to fulfill my potential. To know nature is to know God, and so my attention is focused on the world and my place within it. Because this world is an awesome place of wonder and complexity, I may never understand or grasp it fully, but I can enjoy an exhilarating attempt to do so. What better definition of life?

Theistic Worldview

God is eternal, all powerful, all knowing, and the source of every good and every truth. By bringing the world into being out of nothing, God made a wonderful realm where created beings can exercise their free will. The purpose of life is to love God in an eternal relationship, but we also have the freedom to reject God. There will be consequences for our choices: for sin, terrible punishments; for virtue, great rewards. My life here on Earth has an eternal dimension, and I must live it in its full, eternal context: I may make sacrifices now in order to obtain much greater pleasures hereafter.

Death is a passage from this dimension to another. Far from being the end, it is a return to my source, to God who created me. When I die, I will see God face-to-face and will give an accounting of the way I have chosen to live my life. Death holds no fear for me because it will deliver me from the evil and suffering of this world and bring me to the loving arms of God.

If you bring forth what is within you, what you bring forth will save you. If you do not bring forth what is within you, what you do not bring forth will destroy you.

The Gnostic Gospel of Thomas

Is There Life After Death?

Does human life end with death? According to a recent Gallup Poll, 70 percent of Americans believe in life after death. A great deal of interest has been generated by accounts of people who have been close to death, even clinically dead, and then returned to life. Everyone naturally wants to know what the experience of death is like and what, if anything, lies beyond it.

Several physicians and psychologists have popularized the accounts of people who have returned from a near death experience (NDE). Most accounts include the experience of leaving the body and looking at it as a spectator might, often from some height; encountering a bright light; meeting others, who may include deceased family members or a being of light; and an almost instantaneous review of one's life. Survivors often describe being sucked at great speed through a dark corridor or tunnel toward a bright, white light, and many recall a voice explaining "You aren't ready to come here yet" or "It's not your time." Some describe seeing or talking with divine figures from their own religious traditions.

Almost to a person, those who have had an NDE describe death as "easy," even "joyous," and insist they no longer fear it. The experience, however, does not make them wish to die; rather, it seems to intensify their commitment to live life to its fullest. Most describe the experience as profoundly spiritual and say it has brought about changes in their lives.

For many years scientists have known that by stimulating the right temporal lobe of the brain, in the area just over the right ear, they can cause people to have out-of-body sensations and experience their lives passing before them, but they have been unable to replicate the experience of light often described as "brilliant," "warm," "loving," and "totally accepting of your being."

Compelling as the accounts of life after death may be, we currently have no way of verifying their truth by means of a controlled experiment. In the instances in which NDEs occur in hospital settings, the focus is on saving the person's life rather than on verifying the claim of an NDE. Even if there were time to set up such an experiment, what should it be? How can one measure the existence of conscious life beyond the threshold of clinical death?

Twentieth-century philosopher Bertrand Russell suggests that if a drop of water were to insist that it had a quality of aqueousness that would survive its dissolution into hydrogen and oxygen, we would be skeptical. In the same way, Russell recommends skepticism as the appropriate response to claims that human consciousnes can survive the body's dissolution at death. "All the evidence," Russell argues, "goes to show that what we regard as our mental life is bound up with brain structure and organized bodily energy. Therefore it is rational to suppose that mental life ceases when bodily life ceases. The argument is only one of probability, but it is as strong as those upon which most scientific conclusions are based."[44]

Since we lack an experimental base, NDE accounts do not establish life after death empirically—that is, through the scientific method of objective data gathering and hypothesis testing. The evidence is simply not there. And yet, listening to accounts of NDEs, it is also clear that these people feel they "know" what they have experienced. Children make particularly compelling witnesses because they tell of their experiences so matter of factly.

The Sacred and the Secular

In this world
we walk on the roof of hell
gazing at flowers
ISSA

Often, belief in life after death is rooted in the assumption that the ordinary life of this world is not sacred. Only another dimension, a realm in which God dwells in perfect goodness, can properly be called sacred. This reminds us of Plato's philosophical claim that the perfect Forms are somewhere else. If this world of "shadows" is our secular life, and we leave it for an hour on Saturday or Sunday to touch the sacred, then boundaries between the sacred and the secular are secure. Not all cultures make this distinction. Father Jerome Martínez, a native of New Mexico explains:

> Our spirituality is definitely not influenced by secular humanism. There is no division between religion and your daily life. My grandfather would go out in the morning before he went out to work, and he would sing the alba to the rising sun. He would go out and work in the field, and before he came home at night, he would kneel down on the ground that took his energy that day and give thanks. It was a whole web, a way of seeing the divine interpenetrate into everyday life and interpreting it as such: seeing the saints as daily, constant companions, the voice of God as constantly present . . .[45]

Rigoberta Menchú, whose description of welcoming a new baby into the community we read in Chapter 1, describes beliefs and practices that predate the Spanish, Christian conquest of Guatemala and remain meaningful today:

> We Indians have more contact with nature. That's why they call us polytheistic . . . We worship—or rather not worship but respect—a lot of things to do with the natural world, the most important things for us. For instance, to us water is sacred . . . Without water we cannot survive . . . and we never stop thinking of it as something pure. The same goes for the earth . . . The sun as the channel to the one God, receives the pleas from his children that they should never violate the rights of all the other beings which surround them . . . cows, horses,

DOING PHILOSOPHY
Speculating on Life After Death

Suppose you had a near death experience (NDE) and experienced either a loving light infused with divinity or a horror show that filled you with fear and anxiety. Would you live the rest of your life differently? Would "knowing" something about what awaits us after death change everything about this existence? Do you think everyone, either consciously or subconsciously, makes a decision about whether or not life has a divine dimension and lives life with those (perhaps unspoken) assumptions? Why are NDEs so fascinating? Isn't it possible to just live our lives as they unfold without regard to whether or not there is another dimension? If you had the chance to opt for an NDE, would you take it or run from it? Does it matter to you whether this life is the main event, a series of illusions, or a rehearsal for the real thing that awaits us after death? How can these questions be answered? Should we try experiments like the medical students in *Flatliners*? Can we figure them out ourselves, based on logical analysis of what we have observed—about what we call "life"? Do theologians and mystics have the inside track, or are they deluded and untrustworthy sources of information? Are these the most significant questions of human existence or merely a way to entertain ourselves?

> dogs, cats. All these. We mention them all. We must respect the life of every single one of them . . . We must not do evil while the sun shines upon his children.[46]

Both of these examples reveal a worldview in which what we might call the secular-and-sacred intermingle, in which the divine interpentrates the ordinary, everyday world.

Summary

The traditional Western assumption—that the secular and sacred are distinct—places enormous importance on whether there is or is not a God. If a "being of light" waits to welcome us on the other side of death, then life has an eternal dimension, and our own existence in this world is dramatically transformed. If God is a certainty rather than a "terrible lie," then both humans and the universe are in good hands, and much of the anxiety in the modern world may be laid to rest. If there is no God, we and the cosmos are on our own.

The cherry blossoms
fallen—
through the branches
a temple
BUSON

In Asia, life and death are seen not as opposites but as complements, as two sides of the same coin, of which both are necessary to describe what is. For Buddhists, death is merely the transition from one lifetime to the next, and the way to escape the wheel of birth-death-birth is to see this world as it actually is. From a Buddhist point of view, the West has objectified what is and called it God. There is no someone or something outside us and apart from the world, but instead a dynamic flux much more like the dance of electrons in the heart of the atom. We are one with this flux, and lifetimes are provided for us to eventually wake up to this realization.

For a Hindu or a Buddhist, the nature of what is can be revealed and validated not through rational proofs but through meditation or meditative experiences that place one in direct contact with what is.

If you have been shaped by the Western world, you might ask yourself what kind of evidence would be capable of convincing you that there is a God. Would it be necessary for you to have either a personal encounter like the one the John Denver character had in the movie *Oh God!* or a near death experience? How would God have to appear to you, to be convincing? Would you insist on having scientific proof of some kind? If so, what would that proof look like?

If there is a God, is it helpful for us to see ourselves as made in his or her image? Is the line we draw between the secular and the sacred a useful one, or does God interpenetrate what we like to call ordinary reality? What would happen if we thought of everything as sacred?

Is it possible that belief in God is so basic that it can be accepted as rationally sound, even in the absence of supporting evidence? Alvin Plantinga, a contemporary analytic philosopher, calls belief in God a "basic belief" and compares it with our belief that there is an external world. As we will see in the next chapter, philosophers are not at all in agreement about how the existence of an external world might be proved, and yet we all act as if there is one.[47]

In Chapter 5 we consider which kind of "knowing" might be regarded as reliable. John Updike's novel *Roger's Version* features a debate between a theology professor and a student who believes he is on the verge of proving the existence of God with the aid of his computer. The professor objects to the whole idea:

> For myself, I must confess I find your whole idea aesthetically and ethically repulsive. Aesthetically because it describes a God Who lets Himself be intellectually trapped, and ethically because it eliminates faith from religion, it takes away our freedom to believe or doubt. A God you could prove makes the whole thing immensely, oh, uninteresting. Pat. Whatever else God may be, He shouldn't be pat.[48]

Does true knowledge rest on logical deduction? Must we test everything and prove it to our senses before we believe it? Was natural theology a step in the right direction? And, if we were finally able to prove something such as the existence of God, would you, like Updike's professor, find the idea unsatisfying? This puzzle is worth keeping in mind as we turn first to an Historical Interlude concerning the Middle Ages and explore questions of epistemology, or knowledge theory, that focus on faith and reason.

For Further Thought

1. For many centuries, God was worshiped as a woman—the great Goddess from whom all life flowed. If you believe in God and currently image God as male, try thinking of God as female and notice any changes that may develop

in your self-concept and in the way you relate to God. Ask a friend, preferably of the opposite gender, to try this experiment and listen carefully to his or her answers.

2. Try picturing God as belonging to the same race or ethnic group that you do (maybe you already do this) and then to a different race or ethnic group. What effect does picturing God as racially different have on your self-concept and ability to relate to God? Ask a friend, preferably one of a different racial or ethnic group, to try this and listen carefully to his or her answers.
3. If you are a theist, write a defense of atheism. If you are an atheist, do the opposite. If you are an agnostic, reread the section on William James at the beginning of the chapter and take a position if only for the extent of this exercise. Try to really understand how a person can sincerely hold a view different from your own.
4. What are the consequences if God is a "terrible lie"? Is Pascal right—that there is very little to lose and everything to gain by believing in God anyway, to hedge our bets? Explain.
5. If you were a dictator, would you prefer your people to believe in God or not? Why? Karl Marx called religion the "opiate of the people," and yet religion has led some to bloody wars and revolutions.
6. Would you live your life differently if you had positive proof that there is no God? Or positive proof that a divine being exists? What changes would you make, and why?
7. If death is not the end of human consciousness, what qualities of your present life would you like to take with you into the next?
8. In a republic, citizens have civil and legal rights. If there is a theistic God, what rights (if any) do human beings have in the divine world order?
9. Try coming up with your own view of life and death (humorous or otherwise). What assumptions are you making? Are you arguing from the nature of God, the nature of the world, or the nature of human beings?
10. What ways does a theistic God have of communicating with people? What forms might these communications take? What could they tell us about the nature of God?
11. What do you think Eastern thinkers mean by saying the West has objectified God? How can God be thought of other than as an object?
12. Suppose, instead of a machine, we were to think of the universe as a huge, complex, living organism. What kind of God could be proved? How would such a proof be constructed?
13. Can God really create out of nothing—be a bagworm without a bag? According to process theology, there was no beginning, and creation is the gradual bringing of order out of chaos. Also, God does not have unilateral power and must rely on evoking responses in creatures who are partners in creativity. If this is true, can God be held solely responsible for either evil or good?
14. How might an agnostic flea prove the existence or nonexistence of a dog? Pretend you are one and give it a try.
15. How does existentialism differ from traditional theism? What historical conditions in the 1940s might have made it popular, and why? How does starting from the existentialist view of human nature lead to a different understanding of God than that of traditional theism? Is this evidence of anthropomorphism—that

we remake God in every age to meet our current needs—or simply evidence that God is too large to be contained in any one concept or way of thinking?

16. Suppose a person long dead returned to life. Make a list of questions you would ask him or her.
17. Why do you think the United States has chosen to separate church and state? What are the advantages and disadvantages of uniting them? Of separating them? Have we lost anything in the separation? What would we sacrifice by uniting them?
18. Suppose aliens landed in your backyard (able to speak English, of course) and asked you how you and your world came to be. What would you answer?
19. Does the prospect of immortality thrill or frighten you? If you could live forever in your present state, what conditions would you place on your own immortality? Would you want to stay the same age, for instance? How would you feel about living on as everyone you know died? What would be your goals for yourself for eternity?
20. Do you have a conscience? If so, where did it come from, and how does it function?

For Further Exploration

Fiction and Film

After Life. This Japanese film explores the value of personal memories. A group of recently deceased men and women arrive at a halfway house where they are given a week to select one moment from their lives to carry with them into eternity. A production crew has been provided to recreate and film the chosen memory for each person.

Bradley, Marian Zimmer. *The Mists of Avalon.* New York: Ballantine, 1984. A retelling of the Arthurian myth from the viewpoint of the women; it features a sensitive portrayal of Goddess worship and its eventual defeat by Christianity. Bradley has also written two prequels, *The Forest House* and *Lady of Avalon.*

Camus, Albert. *The Plague.* New York: Knopf, 1962. Why would God send a plague? (In this case, the bubonic plague during the Middle Ages, but you might want to think of AIDS.) Why do some survive and others die? What answers, if any, do science, religion and our sense of our own humanity provide in the face of a plague?

Corman, Avery. *Oh God!* New York: Simon & Schuster, 1971. God appears to a supermarket clerk and asks him to "spread the word that I exist . . . I set the world up so it can work." All the questions raised in this chapter are covered in this book. The movie version features John Denver as the clerk and George Burns as God.

Dillard, Annie. *Holy the Firm.* New York: HarperCollins, 1988. Dillard creates an interesting theodicy in which the suffering of a seven-year-old girl appears as a link to the order of things.

Dogma. This film poses a theological riddle: What if the price for two angels getting back into heaven is an acknowledgement that God made a mistake (in casting them out), a realization that would immediately and inevitably bring about the end of everything? When God finally makes an appearance, it is as an athletic young woman—and it is clear that this image by no means exhausts the possibilities.

Eco, Umberto. *The Name of the Rose.* New York: Warner, 1986. Theological controversies, political intrigue, and human squabbling in a medieval monastery are the subjects of this novel. A real slice of medieval life. The movie is also pretty good.

Kazantzakis, Nikos. *The Last Temptation of Christ.* New York: Bantam, 1965. The author speculates on the temptation God must feel to live an ordinary human life with struggles, a family, and all the simple pleasures we take for granted. Also an excellent movie.

Sartre, Jean Paul. *No Exit.* New York: French, 1972. In this play, three characters discover that they are in hell; each will torture the others more effectively than devils with pitchforks might, just by being the people they are. Sartre suggests that hell is other people.

The Sixth Sense. This film suggests that the dead are always with us, in ways we cannot understand. The transition from life to death may depend on accepting certain realities that are difficult to accept and we may be caught between realities until we do accept them.

Updike, John. *Roger's Version.* New York: Knopf, 1986. A theology professor and a young computer student debate the possibility and the advisability of trying to prove the existence of God, using a computer. This novel also covers the key questions raised in this chapter in fictional form.

Walker, Alice. *The Color Purple.* New York: Pocket, 1982. This Pulitzer-Prize–winning novel features letters written by a poor, abused black woman in the South to God and to her missing sister. Walker has a character say that if you walk by a field of radiant purple flowers God has gone to a lot of trouble to create without noticing it, this pisses God off. You've probably seen the movie.

What Dreams May Come. This film is a stunning example of the Buddhist maxim that with our thoughts we make the world—in this case the afterlife. What if each of us creates our own reality and the only limitation is on what we are ready to see? The suggestion is that good people end up in hell because they cannot forgive themselves.

Nonfiction

Augustine of Hippo. *Confessions.* New York: New American Library, 1963. This spiritual autobiography reveals a very human person who struggled all his life to be what he thought he ought to be.

Buber, Martin. *I and Thou.* New York: Scribner's, 1970. This book has become a classic of Jewish personalism. It is clear and understandable.

Camus, Albert. *The Myth of Sisyphus and Other Essays.* New York: Knopf, 1969. An introduction to the existential view of the absurdity of life, this book uses the myth of Sisyphus who was condemned by the gods to push a large stone up a hill, only to have it roll down and to begin the process all over again—a metaphor for life.

Feuerbach, Ludwig. *The Essence of Christianity.* New York: Harper & Row, 1957. This is the attack on anthropomorphism that inspired Karl Marx's interest in dialectical materialism. It is short and readable.

Hildegard of Bingen. *Illuminations of Hildegard of Bingen,* commentary by Matthew Fox. Santa Fe, N.M.: Bear, 1985. This book is about the images from Hildegard's visions, with commentaries linking them to her worldview.

Hume, David. *Dialogues Concerning Natural Religion.* New York: Routledge, 1992. These dialogues are Hume's answer to Natural Theology. Once you know the argument being made, they are readable and interesting.

John of the Cross. *Dark Night of the Soul.* New York: Doubleday, 1990. This is a medieval account of numinous experiences written by a Spanish mystic.

Kierkegaard, Søren. *Fear and Trembling.* New York: Penguin, 1995. In this story of the readiness of Abraham to sacrifice his son Isaac to God, we may read Kierkegaard's struggle to sacrifice the dearest person in his life, Regine. A glimpse at a man in love, as well as an anguished philosopher.

Merton, Thomas, trans. *The Wisdom of the Desert.* Boston: Shambhala, 1994. These very articulate musings of a modern Western man who gave up the world to become a Trappist monk and live in silence provide an introduction to a mystical, intuitive approach to religion.

Teresa d'Avila. *The Life of St. Teresa of Avila.* New York: Penguin, 1957. Written by Teresa—a sixteenth-century Catholic nun—at the request of her superiors, this book is filled with energy, humor, and extraordinary experiences.

Tillich, Paul. *Dynamics of Faith.* New York: Harper, 1958. This brief statement of Christian existentialism by a Protestant theologian will introduce you to what is sometimes referred to as radical theology.

For Further Research

Try these InfoTrac keywords:

Anthropomorphism

Atheism

Theism

Existentialism

Mysticism

Natural Theology

Notes

1. Blaise Pascal, *Pensees* (London: Penguin Group, 1966), 150–151.
2. Baruch (Benedictus de) Spinoza, "Ethic Demonstrated in Geometrical Order and Divided into Five Parts, Part 1," in *Philosophers Speak for Themselves: From Descartes to Locke,* ed. T. V. Smith and Marjorie Grene (Chicago: University of Chicago Press, 1957), 265.
3. Spinoza.
4. Alfred North Whitehead, *Dialogues of Alfred North Whitehead* as recorded by Lucien Price (Boston: Little, Brown, 1954), 218, 370–371.
5. Anselm of Canterbury, *Treasury of Philosophy,* ed. Dagobert D. Runes (New York: Philosophical Library, 1955), 57.

6. Charles Hartshorne, *The Logic of Perfection and Other Essays in Neoclassical Metaphysics* (LaSalle, Ill.: Open Court, 1962), 70–73.
7. Thomas Aquinas, "Summa Theologica," in *Great Books of the Western World: Thomas Aquinas: I,* ed. Robert Maynard Hutchins (Chicago: Benton, 1952), 12–13.
8. Aquinas, 13.
9. Aquinas.
10. Aquinas.
11. David Hume, *Dialogues Concerning Natural Religion,* ed. Henry D. Aiken (New York: Hafner, 1960), 38–41.
12. Mechthilde of Magdeburg, "How the Fiancée Who Is United to God Refuses the Consolation of All Creatures, Desiring Only That of God, and How She Sinks into Suffering" (IV, 12), in *Women Mystics in Medieval Europe,* ed. Emilie Zum Brunn and Georgette Epiney-Burgard, trans. Sheila Hughes (New York: Paragon House, 1989), 62–63.
13. Hildegard of Bingen, "Scivias," in *Medieval Women's Visionary Literature,* ed. Elizabeth Alvilda Petroff (New York: Oxford University Press, 1986), 139.
14. *Illuminations of Hildegard of Bingen,* Text by Hildegard of Bingen with commentary by Matthew Fox (Santa Fe, N.M.: Bear, 1985), 30–33.
15. Hildegard of Bingen, *The Letters of Hildegard of Bingen,* Vol. 1, letter 15r, trans. Joseph L. Baird and Radd K. Ehrman (New York: Oxford University Press, 1994), 55.
16. *The Letters of Hildegard of Bingen,* p. 160.
17. "O Viridissima Virga," in *A Feather on the Breath of God: Sequences and Hymns by Abbess Hildegard of Bingen,* Hyperion, lyrics from Wiesbaden, Hessische Landesbibliothek M 52, ed. Christopher Page.
18. Hermann Hesse, *Siddhartha* (Cutchogue, N.Y.: Buccaneer, 1976), 150–151.
19. Fritjof Capra, *The Tao of Physics* (New York: Bantam, 1984), 178.
20. Lao-tzu, *Tao Te Ching,* trans. Steven Mitchell (New York: HarperCollins, 1988), 51.
21. Lao-tzu, 1.
22. *Brihad-Aranyaka Upanishad* 1.4.5-7 in *Anthology of Sacred Scriptures,* second edition, Robert E. Van Voorst, ed. (Belmont, Calif.: Wadsworth, 1997), 34.
23. Huston Smith, *The Religions of Man* (New York: Harper & Row, 1958, 1986), 73.
24. Smith, 74.
25. Augustine of Hippo, *The Enchiridion on Faith, Hope and Love,* ed. Henry Paolucci (Chicago: Regnery, 1961), 11–13.
26. Kahlil Gibran, *The Prophet* (New York: Knopf, 1963), 29.
27. Robert Penn Warren, *All The King's Men* (New York: Random House, 1953), 462–463.
28. Gospel according to John 1:1–15, *Holy Bible,* RSV (New York: Nelson, 1952), 103.
29. Paul Tillich, *Systematic Theology,* vol. 2 (Chicago: University of Chicago Press, 1962), 111.
30. Paul Tillich, "Biblical Religion and the Search for Ultimate Reality," in *Four Existentialist Theologians,* ed. Will Herberg (Garden City, N.Y.: Doubleday, 1958), 293.

31. Xenophanes, in *Selections from Early Greek Philosophy,* ed. Milton C. Nahm (New York: Appleton-Century-Crofts, 1947), 109.
32. Ludwig Feuerbach, *The Essence of Christianity,* eds. E. Graham Waring and F. W. Strothmann (New York: Ungar, 1957), 20–21.
33. Charlotte Perkins Gilman, *Herland,* introduction by Ann J. Lane (New York: Pantheon, 1979), 115.
34. Virgil Elizondo, *The Future Is Mestizo: Life Where Cultures Meet* (New York: Crossroad, 1988), 77.
35. Elizondo, 79.
36. Elizondo, 85.
37. Søren Kierkegaard, "Concluding Unscientific Postscript," in *The Search for Being: Essays from Kierkegaard to Sartre on the Problem of Existence,* trans. and ed. Jean T. Wilde and William Kimmel (New York: Farrar, Straus and Cudahy, 1962), 77.
38. Martin Buber, "Dialogue," in *Four Existentialist Theologians,* 176.
39. Martin Buber, "Between Man and Man," in *Four Existentialist Theologians,* 207.
40. Paul Tillich, *Dynamics of Faith* (New York: Harper & Brothers, 1957), 4, 12.
41. Paul Tillich, "Biblical Religion and the Search for Ultimate Reality," in *Four Existentialist Theologians,* 298–299.
42. Kwasi Wiredu, "African Philosophical Tradition: A Case Study of the Akan," *Philosophical Forum* 24, nos. 1–3 (1992–1993): 41.
43. Wiredu, 42–45.
44. Bertrand Russell, "What I Believe," in *The Basic Writings of Bertrand Russell: 1903–1959,* Robert E. Egner and Lester E. Denonn, eds. (New York: Simon & Schuster, 1961), 379.
45. Jerome Martínez, interview, in *Barrios and Borderlands: Cultures of Latinos and Latinas in the United States,* ed. Denis Lynn Daly Heych (New York: Routledge, 1994), 417–418.
46. *I, Rigoberta Menchú: An Indian Woman in Guatemala,* ed. Elisabeth Burgos-Debray, trans. Ann Wright (New York: Verso, 1984), 56–58.
47. Alvin Plantinga, "Advice to Christian Philosophers," *Journal of Faith and Philosophy* 1, no. 3 (July 1984): 253–271.
48. John Updike, *Roger's Version* (New York: Knopf, 1986), 24.

PART TWO

How Am I to Understand the World?

Questions of Epistemology

HISTORICAL INTERLUDE C

From the Medieval to the Modern World

CHAPTER FIVE

Knowledge Sources

Do You See What I See?

CHAPTER SIX

Truth Tests

Do You Swear to Tell the Truth . . . ?

CHAPTER SEVEN

Aesthetic Experience

Is Truth Beauty and Beauty Truth?

HISTORICAL INTERLUDE C

From the Medieval to the Modern World

We closed the last Historical Interlude with the Council of Nicea in 325 and the writing of an official creed, or belief statement, for the Christian Church. This Interlude will review the events between this council and the 1596 birth of René Descartes, generally regarded as the first philosopher of the modern world.

Legacies of Monasticsim and the Dark Ages

During the fourth century, the practice of some Christians to withdraw from the world in search of spiritual renewal was institutionalized in the monastic movement. Beginning in Egypt, monasteries sprang up in the Eastern world and attracted growing numbers of men and women who elected to live in sex-segregated communities and observe standard rules of behavior. Saint Basil, inspired by the example of his sister Macrina, established the standards in the East, requiring monks to refrain from bodily indulgences, to engage in physical labor to keep the monastery self-sufficient, and to spend much of their time in silence.

This movement spread from the East to the West where the principal architect was Saint Benedict, who founded a monastery at Monte Cassino, Italy, in 529 and established a rule that became standard in the West. Monks were required to surrender their private property and live in poverty; pray with the community at regular intervals and privately; study, work hard, and observe silence. You may remember from Chapter 4 that Hildegard of Bingen spent most of her life under the Benedictine rule and that Augustine established a monastery.

Augustine had found philosophy useful in substantiating the truths of faith, but he had insisted, "I believe in order that I may understand." Without faith, Augustine believed, human reason was too corrupted by original sin to arrive at truth; only with faith could reason be useful and reliable. Augustine

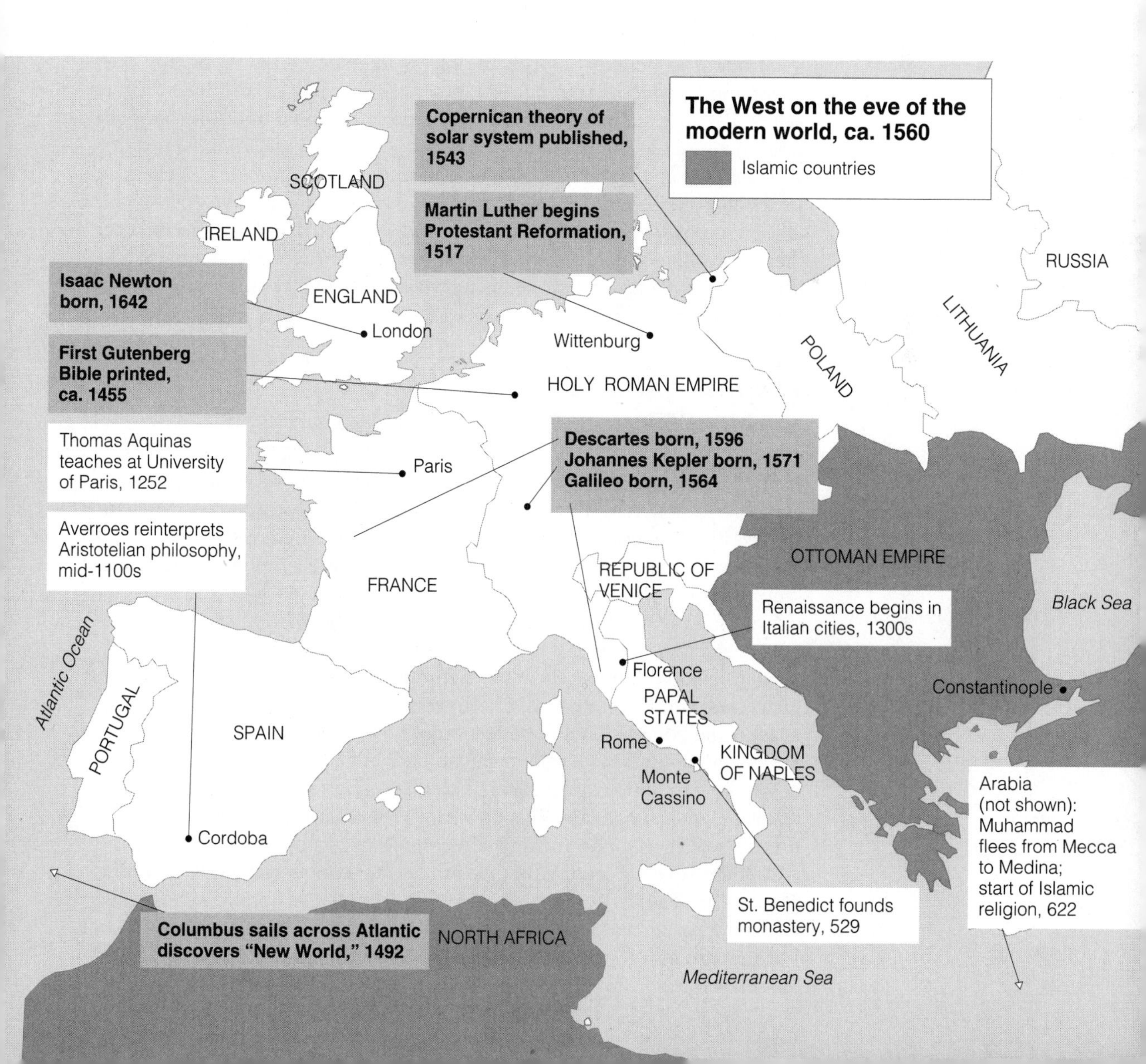

was in fact quite explicit about the secondary role that philosophy must play, calling it the "handmaid of theology." All the important questions about the origins of the cosmos, about human life and about ethical standards could be answered only by faith, Augustine insisted. If philosophy began with faith, it had a role to play; alone it could contribute nothing.

This mistrust of independent rationality fostered a climate of anti-intellectualism, which reached its peak in the so-called Dark Ages of the sixth, seventh, and eighth centuries. Greek culture was condemned as pagan and stamped out by those in power, and the Greek reliance on reason as the gateway to all understanding and wisdom was replaced by an aggressive reliance on faith alone. Monasteries usually receive the credit for keeping the "light of learning" alive during the otherwise intellectually dreary Dark Ages, but many classic Greek texts were, essentially, preserved accidentally.

Under the Benedictine rule, monks were expected to work, and one occupation was copying manuscripts of prayer books and lives of the saints. Because trade with Egypt had been interrupted and thus papyrus was unattainable, the alternative was parchment, made from sheepskin, which was both expensive and time-consuming to prepare. It was cheaper to acquire old books, scrape off the ink, and reuse the parchment. Monks tended to collect more books than they needed for de-inking and to keep them in relatively safe places. When these "pagan" works came back into acceptance in Christian Europe, many were found in monastery storerooms.

The Rise of Islam and Its Effects on Western Civilization

At the beginning of the seventh century, the Arab world came alive with fervor for a new religion called Islam. Muhammad, a prosperous merchant in the city of Mecca (in what is now Saudi Arabia) believed he had been visited by the angel Gabriel and chosen to serve as a prophet. *Islam* means "surrender to Allah," the monotheistic Deity; standards of morality are set out in the Qur'an (a holy book comparable to the Bible), which Muslims believe contains the words of Allah as revealed to his prophet Muhammad. Muslims value the prophets of the Hebrew Scriptures and regard Jesus as a great prophet, but they do not believe that he was divine. For Muslims, Islam is the completion and perfection of both Judaism and Christianity.

Within a few decades, Muhammad had unified the often-feuding tribes of Arabia into an Islamic theocracy in which Allah was seen as the source of divine and human law. This powerful idea of a society governed by the precepts of the Qur'an remains alive today in Islamic revivalism. By the end of the seventh century, Islamic armies had conquered the Persian Empire and moved across North Africa to the Straits of Gibraltar where they crossed into Europe early in the eighth century. Spain fell to the Moors, but the spread of Islam was stopped on the other side of the Pyrenees Mountains near Tours, France, in 732.

The Islamic archbitecutre of this mosque was radically altered when later Christians built a cathedral inside it.

La Mezquita mosque in Cordoba, Spain/Photo © Robert Frerck/Odyssey Productions/Chicago.

The Founding of the Papacy

During this time, there were four major centers of Christianity: Alexandria, Antioch, Constantinople, and Rome. The first two fell quickly to the armies of Islam, and Constantinople was under siege most of the time. Only Rome enjoyed the luxury of peace. The Eternal City had been the center for Western Christianity since the second century. Toward the end of the sixth century, the bishop of Rome—Gregory the Great—took advantage of events in the Eastern world to assume a position of greater leadership in the Church. His strength of personality led him to fill a power void, and the harassment of Alexandria, Antioch, and Constantinople by Islamic forces ensured that he would have no rivals. This period in history thus established the Church at Rome as the center of Western Christianity and its bishop as pope.

The Preservation and Recovery of Aristotle's Works

During the early Middle Ages, when philosophy had low status in Western Europe, learning and culture flourished in the Arab world. Arab scholars took great interest in Greek philosophical texts, preserving them during a time when they were lost to the Western world. Aristotle's treatises, which had been translated from Greek to Arabic around 800, received wide attention from Arabic scholars—until they were perceived to be in conflict with the truth of Islam.

In early tenth-century Aleppo, Al-Farabi saw philosophy, and particularly Aristotelian logic, as useful in developing intelligence, Allah's greatest gift to humankind. Avicenna (980–1037), a Persian genius, memorized Aristotle's *Metaphysics* by reading it forty times but understood it only after reading Al-Farabi's commentaries on it. When Al-Farabi's texts were translated into Latin in the twelfth century, they began the revival of Aristotle in the West.

The Doctrine of the Double Truth and Its Role in Legitimizing Philosophy

One sticking point for both Muslims and Christians involved Aristotle's insistence that Form and matter must always exist together. If this doctrine were true, the world must always have existed in its present form, and Allah or God could not have created it out of nothing. In Moorish Cordoba, Spain, Averroes (1126–1198) resolved this problem temporarily by asserting that a proposition could be theologically true and philosophically false, or vice versa. So, there was a "double truth," and Averroes maintained that religion expresses the higher truth through the use of religious imagery.

Averroes had also sidestepped another consequence of Aristotle's thought (that the soul, as the form of the body, would perish with the body at death) by declaring immortality possible. What survived death, however, was what Averroes called the "active intellect"—what we do geometry with, not what we use to remember our experiences. Aristotle's insistence on the necessary union of Form and matter made survival of the individual soul after death impossible. Although Averroes was a physician and astronomer, as well as a philosopher, his status could not save him. When Islam became intensely focused on doctrinal purity, his books were burned and he died in exile in Morocco.

The notion of the "double truth" enjoyed a revival in the West when the works of Aristotle, along with Arabic commentaries, made their way back as a result of the Crusades and the opening of trade routes with the Arab world. Universities—an Arab creation—were springing up everywhere and students were flocking to them, eager to discuss new ideas. In the thirteenth century, the University of Paris—where Thomas Aquinas (ca. 1224–1274) was professor of theology—was said to have had an enrollment of more than 3,000 students. Even though the works of Aristotle made an intriguing subject, universities were still controlled by the Christian Church, and Aristotle was a pagan whose theory that Form and matter were eternal and inseparable contradicted Christian assumptions about the creation of the world and the immortality of the soul.

Latin Averroists (students living in the Latin Quarter of the University of Paris) claimed a "double truth." The philosophical truth that the world has always existed (proved by Aristotle's *Physics*) and the religious truth that it was created out of nothing (revealed in the Bible) were each, they said, truths within a closed system; both were true.

Unable to suppress Aristotle, the Church found a diplomatic solution in the distinctions drawn by Thomas Aquinas. Some questions must always remain mysteries as far as reason is concerned because they can be grasped only by faith; creation of the world and the doctrine of the Trinity were two examples for Aquinas. In certain matters, however—most notably the existence of God—Aquinas asserted that natural, human reason could arrive at theological truths.

Moving away from Augustine's insistence that only with faith could reason arrive at the truth, Aquinas—the great theological system builder—insisted that philosophy and religion were separate systems. He argued that each was capable of arriving at truth within its own domain and neither could overrule the other. Although the "double truth" did not endure, an independent role for philosophy did.

The link between faith and reason, forged by Aquinas, did not survive the later Middle Ages, when scholars insisted on drawing a sharp distinction between reason and faith. The content of faith, it was argued, has nothing to do with reason. Religious doctrines were to be believed, of course, but they certainly could not be proved. Reason would be much more useful in exploring the processes of the natural world.

The medieval view that God had created the world for human beings to subdue and even exploit led to the development of laborsaving devices that used animal (and later, mechanical) power. As technology in the Western world proliferated, it produced ever more complex explanations of the forces of nature—elements that had recently been mysteries.

Awakening and Change: The Renaissance and Reformation

The Renaissance—a rebirth of independent, humanistic learning and exploration during the fourteenth, fifteenth, and sixteenth centuries—led to a rediscovery of classic Greek and Roman ideas and ways of doing things. Art became humanized as painters used their neighbors as models and painted human as well as religious themes. Individual artists began to sign their names to their creations, a radical departure from the Middle Ages, when creating art was seen as an act in the service of God. During the late Renaissance, sculptors such as Michelangelo Buonarroti secretly dissected corpses to learn human anatomy. His creations, especially the fourteen-foot-high statue of a young David about to hurl a stone at the giant Goliath, have an amazingly lifelike quality.

Renaissance humanism also included a rejection of religious restrictions on human knowledge. The revival of classical learning provided an alternative to the theological scholasticism of Thomas Aquinas, and a new prototype emerged—a secular human being, able to seek and find wisdom apart from the authority of the Church. Renaissance philosophers stressed enjoyment of earthly life and followed knowledge and wisdom wherever they led.

With the Protestant Reformation, beginning in the sixteenth century, the temporal power of the Church as well as the unity of all Christians was broken. First Martin Luther in Germany in 1517, then King Henry VIII of England in 1534, and, eventually, other reformers, too, split from the Roman Catholic Church to form new Protestant branches of Western Christianity. Even Latin, which had been the language of scholarly discourse, began to give way to the spoken languages of various regions.

Ultimately, the unity that had been Christendom broke up into what we know today as separate nation-states, and the Western Church fragmented into many denominations. With the Reformation, emphasis came to be placed on the individual believer's relationship with God. Martin Luther translated the Bible into German so that ordinary, educated people might discover the word of God for themselves without having to depend on the clergy to interpret it.

When Dante Alighieri (1265–1321) wrote the *Divine Comedy* in Italian, literature, too, came within the reach of literate people outside the clergy. Johannes Gutenberg's invention of movable type around 1445 made possible mass production of books; as technology became more sophisticated, inexpensive forerunners of today's paperbacks became available. Knowledge had broken free of the Church and begun to have a life of its own in secular society.

Plato's writings enjoyed a revival in the fifteenth century and came to be seen as an alternative to medieval scholasticism. His belief that reality lies beyond appearances inspired theologians and scientists alike to look deeper into nature's mysteries. As the medieval concept of God lost much of its explanatory power, Plato's search for the truth underlying appearances was reinterpreted during the Renaissance as being compatible with a religious quest for knowledge about God.

For their part, Renaissance scientists were inspired by the universality of truth in Plato's system and its similarity to the intellectual purity of mathematics. If God is truth, then the methods of science could be seen as leading one directly to God. Why not use human reason, a gift from God, to understand the mysteries of the cosmos and perhaps even the mind of its Creator? For many, science and religion came to share a common impulse during the Renaissance.

Nowhere was this clearer than in the Hermetic tradition of magic, drawn from the ideas of an ancient Egyptian priest, Hermes Trismegistus, who was believed to have had secret knowledge of the forces at work in the universe. *Hermeticism* emphasized the inner mathematical harmony within nature and urged contemplation of the One, the highest spiritual reality that some writings identified with the Sun. Pythagorean and Neoplatonic influences in this tradition made it compatible with both mathematics and magic.

The sharp distinctions we make today between science and magic simply did not exist during the Renaissance. Astrologers, astronomers, alchemists, and mathematicians all sought nature's wisdom and the explanation of her

Before the divisions of the Reformation, these columns represented the arms of the Church reaching out to embrace all of Christendom.

Bernini columns of St. Peter's Church in Rome/Photo by Jason Mitchell.

mysteries. Working to reform the calendar to more accurately date Roman Catholic festivals, the Polish astronomer and priest Nicolaus Copernicus (1473–1543) reached into the distant past—before Ptolemy and Aristotle—for evidence to support his mathematically simpler concept of a Sun-centered, or heliocentric, system. Although the Catholic Church condemned his thesis, its gradual acceptance over the course of centuries did more to undermine the medieval synthesis than perhaps any other single act.

In the medieval worldview, Earth was the center and focus of a human drama in which the stakes are the ultimate ones of eternal bliss or eternal punishment. Having created the world and found it good, God left human beings, his highest creation, free to choose either good or evil. Each human life has meaning in an eternal scheme of which this earthly life is but a part, and the entire human race is the hero of the cosmic battle between God and the devil. So unique and valuable were humans, medieval theology affirmed, that God sent his only Son to Earth to die and be reborn so that humanity might be reconciled with divinity.

If Earth is not the focus of divine intervention, not a one-of-a-kind creation but rather one speck among many in a vast and impersonal cosmos, then the whole theological synthesis that sustained the medieval world begins to crumble. Even (or maybe especially) common sense received a body punch. Surely the clearest and most indisputable truth is that the Sun rises in the east, moves all day across the heavens, reaching its highest point at midday, and finally sets in the west. If this can no longer be believed because mathematical formulas say otherwise, what else must be doubted?

The Scientific Revolution

The scientific revolution took human vision to the stars with the invention of the telescope and toward the infinitesimally small with the creation of the microscope. Whole worlds, previously invisible but obviously there all the time, emerged. Bacteria, identified as causes of disease, could be observed swimming in a newly accessible microscopic world. On a much larger scale, European explorers redrew the map of the world by finding unexplored continents, virtually entire worlds, like the Americas, that had lain hidden from Europeans for centuries.

Johannes Kepler (1571–1630), a German astronomer, discovered the three fundamental laws of planetary motion and provided a mathematical basis for Copernicus's theory. Searching for a Platonic harmony lying beneath appearances, Kepler also sought a direct, mystical understanding of reality through contact with the Hermetic tradition. He believed in and used mathematics; he also believed in and used astrology.

Galileo Galilei's (1564–1642) studies of motion went beyond the logic used by Aristotle to incorporate mathematics and empirical observation into studies of the Moon, other planets, and physical objects on Earth. Discovering that bodies of unequal weight fall at the same rate, Galileo realized that motion could be treated mathematically, and his use of the telescope brought the moons of Jupiter into view, supporting Copernicus's theory by revealing heavenly bodies that do not orbit Earth. Physical laws governing matter in motion, so crucial to the work of Isaac Newton (see Chapter 5), rested on the assumption that nature is orderly and predictable.

Imagine yourself a person living in these times. All the physical and spiritual certainties of your life, all the things you have always taken for granted, have one by one been disproved, discredited, or displaced by something new and different. If you are the adventurous type, there is a certain exhilaration that comes when barriers drop and new possibilities emerge, but always there is a great deal of uncertainty. After all, what's next? To get a slight sense of what it must have been like to be alive in Europe during the fifteenth and sixteenth centuries, we might consider Neil Armstrong bouncing on the surface of the Moon, surrogate mothers and test-tube babies, cloning, and even the breakup of the Soviet Union.

Nothing would ever be so absolute again. Expectations that had stood for centuries had fallen. Human nature was a much slipperier concept, and the world slipperier still. Even God seemed relegated to first cause, a mechanical engineer and nothing more. Most of the mysteries, it seemed, had been explained by science, and life would never be the same.

This medieval world, rocked to its core by science and technology, was the environment into which Descartes was born. Educated by the Jesuits, he received a solid grounding in certainties that were already beginning to crumble. As the world fell apart around him, Descartes would search for the undoubtable truth—the certainty no new discovery could touch. On this, he would build his system of knowledge.

CHAPTER 5

Knowledge Sources

Do You See What I See?

BEFORE YOU READ . . .

Ask yourself how you know whatever you care most about knowing reliably.

When we begin to examine the large issue of Part 2—how am I to understand the world?—the first questions we must consider have to do with the process of knowing. All of us began asking questions early in life—about the world (what is above the sky?), about events (what does it mean to die?), about ourselves (where was I before I was born?). These very philosophical questions assume that we can know things, that there is a world outside us to be known, and that we have the mental and physical equipment to be able to know.

Lack of knowledge is darker than the night.
HAUSA PROVERB

You may be surprised to learn that philosophers have questioned all of these assumptions. Some philosophers, called skeptics, wonder whether knowledge is even possible, and others have doubted the independent existence of a world outside of and independent of our minds. Is knowledge a meeting between us and reality, or is what we call knowledge restricted to mental processes within us that may or may not match the world as it actually is?

The Issue Defined

All of us have been fooled by optical illusions into seeing things that are not actually there, or not there in the way we think they are (Figure 5.1). We are more seriously deluded by our ego-bound point of view—the perception that events in the world occur as a drama, with each of us the center of the drama as it unfolds for us. We are, in a manner of speaking, trapped inside our own perspective.

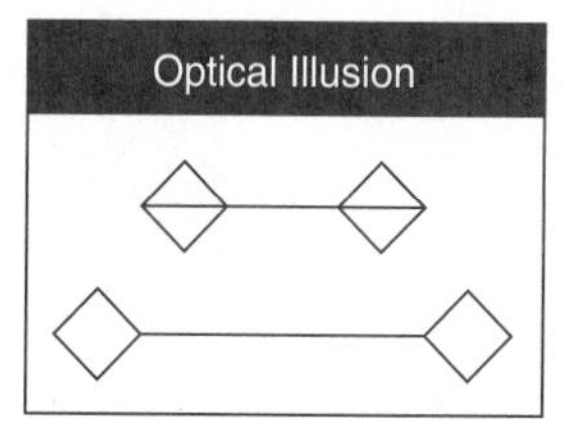

FIGURE 5.1 WHICH LINE IS LONGER?
When we trust our senses, we can easily be deceived.

egocentric predicament *the human condition of being unable to leave the boundaries of our individual selves to determine what anything is really like, as opposed to how it seems to us*

epistemology *the branch of philosophy dealing with the study of knowledge, what it is and how we acquire it*

None of us is able to get inside the head of another person in order to "know" what that person knows. Even worse, none of us can step outside our own perceptions to determine what something is "really" like. Philosophers call this dilemma the **egocentric predicament.** Trapped inside our own heads, we can only guess or make assumptions (and hope they are valid) about what others think and about reality itself. The questions about reality—the questions of metaphysics—that we considered in Part 1 really depend on knowledge theory, or **epistemology.** Unless we can agree about "how" we know, we will never be able to agree on "what" we know.

Because the egocentric predicament limits all human knowing, some philosophers have taken what may seem to you an extreme position: Reality is not "out there" waiting to be discovered but instead is created by us in the act of perceiving. Perhaps even the most basic things, like space and time, exist only in our heads, and we filter all our perceptions through them. What all philosophers seem to agree on, however, is that knowing is crucial if we wish to understand reality.

In the first book of the *Metaphysics,* Aristotle writes, "All men naturally desire to know." Do you agree? Living in a time when knowledge seems to be exploding, we may be tempted to wish for a little less knowledge rather than a little more; however, for many of the thinkers we consider in this chapter, the freedom to know and the ability to follow knowledge wherever it might lead were privileges that had to be fought for and defended.

He who knows not and knows not he knows not
He is a fool, shun him
He who knows not and knows he knows not
He is ignorant, teach him
He who knows and knows not he knows
He is asleep, wake him
He who knows and knows he knows
He is wise, follow him

ARABIAN PROVERB ATTRIBUTED TO KING DARIUS, THE PERSIAN

The Peoples of the Americas: Sor Juana Inés de la Cruz

In seventeenth-century New Spain (present-day Mexico), a girl was born with an insatiable desire to know. At the age of three she followed her older sister to school and "tricked the mistress—or so I thought—by telling her that my mother had directed her to give me lessons . . . I learned to read in so short a time that I already knew how when my mother found out . . ."[1] When her mother refused her pleas to dress as a boy and study in Mexico City, Juana took some consolation from the books in her grandfather's library.

Later, she did go to Mexico City to live at the court of the Spanish viceroy, where she astonished people with her learning (including "forty learned men" who were summoned to examine her) and wrote poetry, plays, and *villancicos* to be used at religious services.[2] As an illegitimate child with no money, her only hope for an intellectual life lay in the convent. So, she professed her vows as a nun in 1669 at the age of eighteen in the Convent of Saint Jerome in Mexico City.[3]

> I became a nun because, although I knew that that way of life involved much that was repellent to my nature—I refer to its incidental, not its central aspects—nevertheless, given my total disinclination to marriage, it was the least unreasonable and most becoming choice I could make to assure my ardently desired salvation.[4]

Sor Juana was fortunate that her "cell" was a private, two-story living space with its own kitchen, bath, bedroom, and a parlor, which she quickly converted into her study and filled with thousands of books. The viceroy and vicereine were frequent visitors, as Juana presided over a *tertulia,* or conversational gathering, that featured music, improvisational poetry, and philosophical discussion.[5]

When she was in her forties, Sor Juana received a letter from her bishop, instructing her to give up secular study and concentrate on matters of the spirit. Her elaborate defense of the intellectual life—for herself and all women—begins with the assertion that it is God who has made her want to know:

> What is true . . . is that from my first glimmers of reason, my inclination to letters was of such power and vehemence, that neither the reprimands of others—and I have received many—nor my own considerations—and there have been not a few of these—have succeeded in making me abandon this natural impulse which God has implanted in me.[6]

Being a woman and a nun in patriarchal New Spain created special problems for Sor Juana, and she shared with René Descartes in France the threat of the Spanish Inquisition. The Holy Office considered some things—such as the contention that Earth was not the center of the cosmos—inappropriate for discussion or study and conclusions that would not be permitted. Those who challenged the Church's authority were silenced. Those who persisted could end up tortured or even dead. In the end, Sor Juana gave away her books and abandoned the love of learning that had sustained her all her life.

THE MAKING OF A PHILOSOPHER

Juana Inés de Asbaje y Ramirez (Sor Juana Inés de la Cruz)
(ca. 1650–1695)

As an illegitimate child with no dowry in patriarchal New Spain, Juana had few propects for fulfilling her intellectual gifts. When she arrived at the Spanish viceroy's court in Mexico City as a beautiful prodigy, her only long-term option—if she wanted time to study, think, and write—was the convent. After joining the Convent of San Jeronimo, she turned her "cell" into a meeting place for intellectuals and artists. Asked by her bishop to write down her sophisticated criticism of a sermon, Juana was stunned when he published it and urged her formally to turn her attention from secular to sacred subjects. In her response (*Respuesta*), she cites many women from the Bible and the classical past, including Hypatia, to justify women's right to the life of the mind. She cleverly explains that to study theology, the queen of sciences, she had to prepare herself by mastering the lesser disciplines of logic, rhetoric, physics, music, geometry, and architecture. She died nursing other nuns during a plague.

The Rationalist Approach of René Descartes

The medieval world into which René Descartes was born in 1596 was beginning to come apart. The great synthesis that had held knowledge together under the control of the Church and the authority of Aristotle was unraveling, and many things that had seemed settled or obvious were being questioned. The stable if somewhat stifling world of his childhood—in which the Church was the keeper of all knowledge and books were written in Latin, thereby limiting access to knowledge to scholars and churchmen—had been jolted by the scientific revolution.

When he was in his twenties, Descartes had a kind of intellectual crisis. Taking seriously the questions we have been considering, he began to wonder whether there was anything in his mind that he could know with certainty.

The Use of Methodic Doubt to Examine Knowledge

When Descartes began his search for certain knowledge, he decided to doubt everything systematically and see whether anything remained after this process. Any knowledge that was left would have, by surviving such a test, achieved the status of certainty. Much of what he found in his mind seemed to have arrived there on the authority of someone else; he had been told many things and read others, without questioning the authority of the source. In other words, like most of us, he accepted as facts both things his teachers told him and things he read in books. He had no independent verification for this apparent knowledge; he had only the word or the authority of the source as assurance that what he thought was true was indeed true.

What about the senses? Could they be relied upon to provide knowledge? To test the reliability of his senses, Descartes took a piece of beeswax and heated it in a candle flame, watching every property of the wax change before his eyes:

> Let us take, for example, this bit of wax which has just been taken from the hive. It has not yet completely lost the sweetness of the honey it contained; it still retains something of the odor of the hive from which it was collected; its color, shape, and size are apparent; it is hard and cold; it can easily be touched; and, if you knock on it, it will give out some sound . . . But now while I am talking I bring it close to the fire. What remains of the taste evaporates; the odor vanishes; its color changes; its shape is lost; its size increases; it becomes liquid; it grows hot; one can hardly touch it; and although it is knocked upon it will give out no sound.[7]

If he were to use the evidence supplied by his senses, Descartes concluded, he would have to declare that the wax after being heated was completely different from the wax before being heated. To conclude that the wax re-

THE MAKING OF A PHILOSOPHER

René Descartes
(1596–1650)

Born in Tours, France, into a prominent family, Descartes received a classical education from the Jesuits and at age twenty took a law degree from the University of Poitier. He joined the Dutch army and later the army of Bavaria. Since armies didn't fight during the winter months, he had time to think and write. First, he used mathematics to solve problems of military engineering and eventually invented analytic geometry. At the age of twenty-three, he "discovered the foundations of a wonderful science," which was published as the *Discourse on Method* in 1637. Descartes was a loyal Catholic who wanted to be the Thomas Aquinas of his day, reconciling the teachings of the Church with the new science as Thomas had done with Aristotle. Invited to Sweden to instruct Queen Christina in philosophy (she sent an ambassador and a warship to fetch him), he caught pneumonia trudging through the snow at 5 A.M. and was dead within two weeks.

"Am I a Chinese philosopher dreaming I'm a butterfly or a butterfly dreaming I'm a Chinese philosopher," and how can I decide?

Butterfly/Photo by Ernest Braun/Bonnie Kamin Collection.

PHILOSOPHERS SPEAK FOR THEMSELVES
René Descartes

It is true that we never tear down all the houses in a city just to rebuild them in a different way and to make the streets more beautiful; but we do see that individual owners often have theirs torn down and rebuilt, and even that they may be forced to do so when the building is crumbling with age, or when the foundation is not firm and it is in danger of collapsing. By this example I was convinced that a private individual should not seek to reform a nation by changing all its customs and destroying it to construct it anew, nor to reform the body of knowledge or the system of education. Nevertheless, as far as the opinions which I had been receiving since my birth were concerned, I could not do better than to reject them completely for once in my lifetime, and to resume them afterwards, or perhaps accept better ones in their place, when I had determined how they had fitted into a rational scheme. And, I firmly believed that by this means I would succeed in conducting my life much better than if I built only upon the old foundations and gave credence to the principles which I had acquired in my childhood without ever having examined them to see whether they were true or not. For though I noticed several difficulties in the way, they were neither insurmountable nor comparable to those involved in the slightest reform of public affairs . . .

From *Discourse on Method*

tained its identity during this transformation, Descartes realized that he had relied on his understanding, not on his senses.

As the next step in his systematic process, Descartes applied methodic doubt to his ordinary perceptions of reality, comparing them with dreams and finding no clear way to distinguish between the two. In a very vivid dream, you are sure the events are really happening to you—until you wake up; only then can you look back and label as a dream the experience you had. While it is going on, a very realistic dream is virtually indistinguishable from waking reality. Although he was convinced that he was sitting at his writing table before the fire, Descartes realized that he had dreamed himself in this exact situation. While the dream was going on, it had seemed just as verifiable as ordinary reality.

To test this, think about how you would go about proving to yourself or to someone else that you are not dreaming right now. Chuang-tzu, the Taoist philosopher, once had an incredibly realistic dream in which he was a butterfly, flying luxuriously from flower to flower and enjoying the warmth of the Sun. When he "awoke" to find himself sitting solidly on the earth and in his usual identity as a philosopher, he asked himself this question: Am I a Chinese philosopher who has dreamed himself a butterfly, or am I a butterfly who now dreams himself to be a Chinese philosopher?

Another area of knowledge Descartes examined for possible certainty was mathematics, a field in which he, as the inventor of analytic geometry, was intellectually very comfortable. Surely, 2 and 2 must always equal 4, right? Descartes felt just as certain as you do that 2 and 2 do indeed add up to 4. He assumed, as we do, that what seems logically certain is very reliable as knowledge. What he questioned was the ultimate foundation for

HOW PHILOSOPHY WORKS
Methodic Doubt (Zero-Based Epistemology)

You may be familiar with a budget-building method called zero-based budgeting. Instead of carrying everything in your present budget forward into the next year and writing justifications only for the new things you wish to add, zero-based budgeting starts from zero. Every item must be justified. All the things you spent money on in the current year must be rejustified, along with any new expenditures you'd like to make next year. Descartes does something like this with his method of doubt. He is unwilling to assume anything in his mind to be true, so he casts it all out by doubting in a systematic or methodic manner. This is a kind of zero-based epistemology because he will allow nothing into his mind as certain knowledge unless and until he justifies it by deducing or reasoning its certainty. Once he deduces the *Cogito* and admits his existence as a certainty, he insists that every other item be similarly justified—God, the material world, even his own body.

Descartes went to his favorite restaurant for dinner. After recommending several good dishes, the Maitre d' said, "The duck is really excellent, Monsieur Descartes, may I bring you the duck this evening?"

After thinking for a moment, Descartes replied, "I think not"—and disappeared.

AUTHOR UNKNOWN

our certainty. Suppose a very powerful but very evil deity has amused himself or herself by making all of us believe that 2 and 2 add up to 4 when they really add up to 5, or to the square root of 10 or to anything other than 4. The fact that we are all secure in our agreement that 2 plus 2 equals 4 does not make it so if such a malevolent superior being has decided to confuse us. We really have no way of *knowing* that this is not the case, so even the so-called truths of mathematics must be doubted.

In applying this process of systematic or methodic doubting, Descartes realized he was rapidly eliminating almost everything he had previously thought of as "knowledge." Finally, however, he came to something he felt was impossible to doubt—something, at last, of which he could be certain. In the following famous passage, Descartes concludes that, without doubt, he is doubting. If he is doubting, he is thinking and must therefore exist as a thinking thing:

> Even though there may be a deceiver of some sort, very powerful and very tricky, who bends all his efforts to keep me perpetually deceived, there can be no slightest doubt that I exist, since he deceives me; and let him deceive me as much as he will, he can never make me be nothing as long as I think that I am something. Thus, after having thought well on this matter, and after examining all things with care, I must finally conclude and maintain that this proposition: *I am, I exist,* is necessarily true every time I pronounce it or conceive it in my mind.[8]

Cogito *[KO ghi toe] the proof by which Descartes established his mental existence*

solipsism *belief that only my mind exists and everything else is a perception of that mind*

When the essence of this now famous proof was rendered in Latin, the translation of "I think, therefore I am" became "Cogito ergo sum." As a result, this proof is known as the ***Cogito.***

With the *Cogito,* Descartes has finally arrived at certain knowledge, but it is unfortunately very limited knowledge. What Descartes can be sure of is only the contents of his own mind. In philosophy this is called **solipsism,** the belief that only minds and their contents exist. Even if

SOURCE: *Doonesbury*.

Descartes can be sure he exists as a thinking thing, he still cannot trust his perceptions that he has a body and that there is a world outside his mind; nor can he be sure that the mathematical certainties he has are correct. In other words, he has reasoned himself into a very small box.

Beyond Solipsism to Belief in a Material World

To get out of this box, Descartes must prove to himself that a very powerful and very good God exists to serve as the guarantor that the certainties of mathematics are true and that Descartes's perceptions are not hallucinations. Only a powerful yet good deity—a nondeceiving God—would assure Descartes that his perceptions of his own body and of the material world were accurate and matched reality. You may recall that Thomas Aquinas used the world to prove God in his cosmological proofs (the Prime Mover, the First Cause, the Necessary Being). Paradoxically, Descartes must use God to prove the world, and to do so he must first define God into existence without being able to use any of Aquinas's proofs. Whether or not he does this successfully is for you to judge.

In his *Meditations,* Descartes used several proofs for the existence of God. The first is an ontological proof, similar to the one devised by Anselm in the eleventh century (see Chapter 4). Like Anselm, Descartes reasoned that, if I can conceive of a perfect God, then that perfect God must exist; otherwise, lacking existence, God would not have all the properties of perfection and would cease to be "perfect."

Ideas that are both clear and distinct are, for Descartes, the only ones on which a thinking person may rely. Because Descartes does indeed have in his mind a "clear and distinct" idea of a perfect God, he reasons that the subject of this idea must have a real existence:

> I find it manifest that we can no more separate the existence of God from his essence than we can separate from the essence of a triangle the fact that the size of its three angles equals two right angles, or from the idea of a mountain the idea of a valley. Thus it is no less self-contradictory to conceive of a God, a supremely perfect Being, who lacks existence—that is, who lacks some perfection—than it is to conceive of a mountain for which there is no valley.[9]

Another proof concludes that only God could be the source of Descartes's idea of God, because any other source (like Descartes himself, for instance) would present the paradox of the lesser being the source of the greater. To Descartes, it seemed clearly illogical to believe that an inferior being such as himself was the cause of the idea of a superior being like the one he had in his mind as a "clear and distinct" idea. Only God was great enough to be the cause of this concept:

> And consequently we must necessarily conclude from all that I have previously said that God exists. For even though the idea of substance exists in me from the very fact that I am a substance, I would nevertheless have no idea of an infinite substance, I who am a finite being, unless the idea had been placed in me by some substance which was in fact infinite.[10]

Notice here that Descartes assumed certain ideas to be part of every rational being's mind from birth. Because he had observed the presence of

HOW PHILOSOPHY WORKS

Circular Reasoning (Begging the Question)

This is actually a logical fallacy, or an invalid form of reasoning. To beg the question is to begin with something you have already concluded, as in this example: "Of course that joke is funny; every joke he tells is funny!" The argument is a circle: The joke is funny because he is a funny joke teller. The conclusion "The joke is funny" is already assumed in the evidence (he's a funny joke teller). Descartes makes a similar mistake in the judgment of some critics by arguing that his "clear and distinct idea of God" proves God exists, while assuming that God guarantees the accuracy of his "clear and distinct" ideas. It may be perfectly true that each component justifies the other, but there is no outside justification for either of them. If every joke someone tells is funny, then the current one must be funny, too; but we have no evidence that every joke the person tells is funny. This critical piece is simply assumed as true. When you examine an argument, look for circular reasoning, or begging the question. That kind of reasoning does not lead to valid conclusions.

certain ideas in his mind for as long as he could remember, Descartes concluded that these ideas had been present since birth. They were therefore **innate,** or inborn. Some rationalist philosophers, including Plato and Descartes, accept the possibility that certain ideas can be fully or partially present at birth, whereas others deny even the possibility of innate ideas. Empiricist philosophers, whom we consider later in this chapter, believe the mind to be totally without ideas until experience provides it with content.

innate *literally "inborn," present from the moment of birth, not learned or acquired*

Once Descartes had demonstrated that God must exist, he was then able to trust his perceptions of his own body and of the world revealed to him by his senses, because a good God would, also by definition, not be a "deceiver." Critics have argued that Descartes argues circularly, using the "clear and distinct" idea of God as the basis for his proofs of God and, at the same time, using God, the nondeceiver, as the guarantor of the accuracy and trustworthiness of his "clear and distinct" ideas. Each of these terms—*God* and *clear and distinct ideas*—does in fact "prove" the other, but it is a closed system and there is no outside justification for either of them. Critics refer to this as the **Cartesian circle** (a shorthand version of the Descartesian circle, or the circle created by Descartes).

Cartesian circle *the argument by which Descartes uses his clear and distinct idea of God to prove God's existence and uses God's existence as the justification for the accuracy of his clear and distinct ideas; each proves the other, but there is no outside justification for either*

In the course of deciding what was really knowable, Descartes made what was for him a very useful distinction between the substance called mind and the substance called *matter.* A **substance** is something primary, something about which things can be said. This split between mind and matter was not invented by Descartes: You may recognize it from our study of Plato and Aristotle who used the terms *Form* and *matter* to make a similar distinction. What Descartes did, however, was to apply this distinction to the most significant knowledge problem of his day—how to find an independent role for the new science that would not threaten the Catholic Church. Let's look at how he accomplished this.

substance *the underlying reality of something, containing its primary qualities; the essence of something that remains constant despite changes in its perceptible qualities*

Catholic Free Will in the "Clockwork Universe" of Science

According to Descartes, reality is composed of two substances that possess opposite and complementary qualities: Mind is thinking and unextended, meaning it does not take up space, whereas matter is unthinking and extended (Figure 5.2). Because matter is both unthinking and extended in space, it is subject to the laws of physics. In the "clockwork universe" then being uncovered by the invention of telescopes and microscopes and by the discoveries of electricity, magnetism, and optics, it seemed as if it were only a matter of time before human reason could unlock all of nature's mysteries and demystify her deepest secrets.

The realm of mind, by contrast with the realm of matter, was both thinking and unextended. (Recall that Descartes reasoned himself into being as a "thinking thing.") Being unextended, mind was not determined by the laws of physics; its actions were not part of the "clockwork universe," and so the very significant Catholic doctrine of the "freedom of the will" was not threatened. Unlike matter, mind was free to act independently on its own behalf. As free entities, human minds could make their own decisions and be held accountable as moral agents.

My mind is a handgrenade—catch!
ICE-T

Descartes began by systematically doubting everything and ended with the *Cogito*. Only by proving the existence of a nondeceiving God was he able to move from solipsism to belief in the material world, including his own body. The reality of his rational mind was much clearer and more distinct to Descartes than that of his material body, and as we have seen, the two substances had separate and contrasting characteristics. His method had led him to affirm a basic distinction between mind and matter that had the additional advantage of being what today we might call "politically correct." By affirming two substances, Descartes was able to assign the "clockwork universe" to science while reserving the mind (and the soul) as the province of the Catholic Church. However, there was an unanticipated consequence: the **mind-body problem.**

mind-body problem
a problem of metaphysics created when Descartes divided reality into mind and matter, making each a separate substance; how can two completely distinct substances interact in one person?

The Mind-Body Problem

By solving a problem in epistemology, Descartes had unknowingly created another in metaphysics. If mind and body are opposite in every respect (as Descartes had successfully argued), the next reasonable question is, How can they possibly interact? What connection can there be between a thinking and an unthinking substance, between an extended and an unextended substance? What possible point of contact could coordinate the smooth interaction of polar opposites? And yet, it seems clear to most people that mind-body interaction takes place all the time. Instruct your hand to move and it moves; tell your body to lie down and it obeys. Thinking, unextended substance (mind) tells unthinking, extended substance (body) to act and it acts.

Forced to deal with this truth of common sense, Descartes theorized that the pineal gland in the brain was the center of interchange between mind and body; at that location mental instructions were translated into

Descartes's Division of Substances				
Mind =	Thinking	Unextended	Substance	(province of the Church)
Matter =	Unthinking	Extended	Substance	(province of the new science)

FIGURE 5.2 DESCARTES'S MIND-MATTER DISTINCTION *Separating mind and matter into two distinct substances created a domain in which the new science could operate without threatening the Church.*

physical responses. This explanation is the obvious weak point in Descartes's elaborate theory because pinpointing a location tells us nothing about how such an interchange might take place. Having convinced us too thoroughly that body and mind inhabit different realms, Descartes cannot successfully convince us that these realms can and do interact.

Descartes did something all of us have done at one time or another: He concentrated so intently on solving one problem that he failed to see that he was creating another. In his eagerness to make clear the distinction between thinking, unextended mind and unthinking, extended body, Descartes seems to have painted himself into a metaphysical corner. Having declared mind and body as separate and distinct, he had no credible way to unite them in the mind-body interactions that are part of every person's lived experience. Even though Descartes more than any other philosopher defined the terms of the modern world's philosophical discourse, his unresolved mind-body problem remained for others to address.

Responses to the Mind-Body Problem

Although Descartes died before working out a satisfactory resolution of the mind-body problem, it remains an issue in the Western world. Because Descartes's system had been so successful in resolving a potential conflict between religion and science, his successors tried to modify the absolute separation between mind and body without losing the distinction between them. Baruch Spinoza, Gottfried Leibniz, and Anne Finch Conway are all Descartes's heirs in the rationalist tradition. As the epistemology of the Akan of West Africa demonstrates, the mind-body problem arises out of a Western worldview and does not exist if one does not make Descartes's assumptions.

Baruch (Benedictus) Spinoza

Baruch Spinoza, Descartes's contemporary, was one of the first philosophers to take seriously the dilemma posed by the mind-body problem. His

THE MAKING OF A PHILOSOPHER

Baruch (Benedictus) Spinoza
(1632–1677)

Spinoza's Jewish family had left Spain to escape the Inquisition and settled in the Netherlands. He studied Hebrew literature and Jewish philosophy in Amsterdam in his youth but eventually learned Latin, the "priests' language," which gave him access to the writings of Descartes and descriptions of the new science. Spinoza's writings were judged to be heretical, and he was excommunicated in 1656. After this he spent his life in quiet philosophic study, supporting himself by the trade of lens grinding. He corresponded with prominent thinkers and writers of his day, wrote an impassioned defense of free speech, but declined a professorship of philosophy at Heidelberg University, fearing restrictions on his own freedom to speak. Glass dust from his trade eventually weakened his lungs and made him vulnerable to tuberculosis. He had always maintained that being obsessed with the fear of death was a kind of slavery and, true to that intellectual conviction, he died calmly and peacefully.

solution, like Descartes's, solved one problem while creating another. For Spinoza, the mind-body problem could be solved very simply by considering both thinking and extension to be attributes, or characteristics, of God. If God is a single substance with two attributes—thinking and extension—then the characteristics associated with being a thinking substance and those of being an extended substance are not separate and distinct, as they were for Descartes. Instead, both are united in the one substance we call God.

Even Descartes had admitted that though we use the word substance to refer both to finite thinking and extended substances (like ourselves) and to God (who is an infinite, thinking substance), the word substance is used in two different ways. Taking what he believed was already implicit in Descartes, Spinoza argued that the one substance, God, has an infinite number of attributes, of which we know two: thought and extension. Human minds are finite modifications of God considered under the attribute of thought, whereas human bodies are finite modifications of God considered under the attribute of extension.

For Spinoza, mind and body are the same thing viewed in two different ways. The mind is the idea of the body, and the body is the extended aspect of the mind. If God is the ultimate substance, then his two attributes will have a necessary relationship with each other, much as our own minds and bodies are interrelated. Spinoza had neatly solved the mind-body problem, but his argument suggests that God actually has a body, and that body is the world. If the price of solving the mind-body problem was assigning God a body, some found the cure worse than the original disease. Spinoza was condemned as a heretic. As we saw in Chapter 4, describing precisely what kind of God you believe in is much more difficult, and sometimes much more perilous, than simply proving the existence of an abstract deity.

THE MAKING OF A PHILOSOPHER

Gottfried Wilhelm Leibniz
(1646-1716)

Leibniz worked as a librarian, historian, mathematician, political theorist, jurist, and philosopher, often with prominent political families, including the Prussian royal family. He spent a good portion of his life trying to demonstrate the power of logic to solve problems—like the royal succession in Poland and the reconciliation of Protestant and Catholic theologies. As the inventor of the integral calculus, Leibniz hoped to create a logical calculus, a universal language by which two philosophers who disagreed could take out their pencils and "calculate" a solution to their differences. His conclusion that this must be the "best of all possible worlds" was easily satirized, most famously in Voltaire's *Candide* in which Dr. Pangloss represents Leibniz.

Gottfried Wilhelm Leibniz and Monads

monad *Leibniz's word for the simple, unextended, teleological substances that make up the universe*

Like Spinoza, Gottfried Wilhelm Leibniz solved the mind-body problem by reducing the world to a single substance. For Spinoza, that substance was God and everything else was an attribute; for Leibniz, however, the primary substance, which he called the **monad,** was the basic constituent of everything. A monad is a simple, nonmaterial substance that can neither be created nor destroyed. It is both active and teleological—meaning it acts purposefully. What you think of as your mind is a monad. What you think of as your body is a collection of monads. Leibniz, another Western rationalist of this period, argues that bodies and minds are both spiritual substances or souls created by God—the ultimate spiritual substance, a kind of *Monad of Monads*. The only difference between what we call bodies and what we call minds is that some monads perceive more clearly than others and are called rational.

The most startling thing about Leibniz's theory of monads is his declaration that, although all substances are intrinsically related to one another, no direct interaction occurs between them; they only appear to interact because of a **preestablished harmony** set up by God at the time of Creation. God knows the thoughts and perceptions that will pass through each monad's consciousness from the time of its creation and, acting as a divine orchestrator, harmonizes the thoughts and perceptions of all. So well regulated is the system that soul and body, each acting independently and following its own divinely implanted laws, agree "just as if there were mutual influence, or as if God in addition to his general cooperation constantly put his hand thereto."[11] In a bizarre way this solves the mind-body problem. What we are left with, however, is a situation that appears to contradict common sense—that substances do not interact.

preestablished harmony *the harmony between body and soul or between the world of efficient causes and the world of final causes established by God, according to Leibniz*

What is most interesting about Leibniz is the character of his monads. They are not like the atoms that Democritus and others described as the building blocks of matter; they more closely resemble energy and might be thought of as zones of force. Our current understanding of the universe, discussed in some detail in Chapter 2, depicts matter and energy as two aspects of the same thing ($E = mc^2$). You may recall that in the heart of the atom, as well as in the macrocosm of the universe, what seems to be fundamental is the *energy field*. Especially within the atom, matter seems not to be very material. In the context of current particle physics, Leibniz's monads have an oddly modern character.

Anne Finch, Viscountess Conway

Anne Conway, a contemporary of the seventeenth-century rationalist philosophers we have been discussing, is credited with influencing Leibniz, who read her work twenty years after her death. Since he began using the term monad at this time, he may have borrowed it from Conway as well. Leibniz's monads were purely spiritual, but Conway's monads have both physical and spiritual qualities.

In *The Principles of the Most Ancient and Modern Philosophy,* written in the mid-1670s and published in 1690, Conway insists that matter and spirit both exist on the same continuum, but spirit exists at a higher level than matter. God is pure spirit, and human creatures, which are a mixture of body and spirit, tend either toward higher things as a reflection of spirit or toward sin as a reflection of matter.

Speaking directly to the mind-body problem, Conway wrote:

> To prove that Spirit and Body differ not essentially, but gradually, I shall deduce my Fourth Argument from the intimate Band or Union, which intercedes between Bodies and Spirits, by means whereof the Spirits have Dominion over the bodies with which they are united, that they move them from one place to another, and use them as Instruments in their various Operations.[12]

For Conway, asserting a complete separation between Spirit and Body creates absurd scenarios. Why, for instance, does Spirit not simply "leave the Body behind it when it is moved from place to place . . ." if there is no relationship between the two? More to the point, "Why is it [Spirit] grieved or

THE MAKING OF A PHILOSOPHER

Anne Finch, Viscountess Conway
(1631–1678)

Anne Finch was born in London and, like many other women of her time, educated at home. After learning Latin and Greek, she could discuss philosophy with her brother John and others of his classmates at Cambridge University, one of whom she married (Edward, Viscount Conway). Through John she also met his tutor, Henry More, the Cambridge Platonist. Encouraged to think for herself, Anne Conway eventually undertook a formal criticism of both the rationalist philosophers Descartes and Spinoza and the materialist Thomas Hobbes. She suffered from what were probably migraine headaches and, influenced by Francis Mercury van Helmont, who tried to ease her suffering, she became a Quaker. Leibniz may have been influenced by her work—at the very least their ideas were remarkably similar. She died at the age of forty-seven, and her only published philosophical work is *The Principles of the Most Ancient and Modern Philosophy.*

wounded when the Body is wounded which is quite of a different Nature?" Recognizing that they are related though different allows reason and common sense to prevail:

> But if it be granted, that the Soul is of one Nature and Substance with the Body, although it is many degrees more excellent . . . then all the aforesaid difficulties will vanish, and it will be easily conceived, how the body and Soul are united together, and how the Soul moves the Body, and suffers by it or with it.[13]

The Akan of West Africa

The extent to which the mind-body problem is a distinctively Western problem can be seen by examining the conception of a person among the Akan people of West Africa. In the making of a human person, God fashions an ***okra,*** which is a life force or spirit, out of a portion of himself, then sends it to Earth with the blueprint for its life. This is similar to Leibniz's view of the monad into which God has built every thought and perception that will pass through its consciousness.

okra *[OAK rah] the life force in the Akan system*

Mogya (bloodline and clan identity), which derives from the mother, is material; ***sunsum*** (the distinctive aspects of personality), which derives from the father, is only partly material. The *sunsum* perishes with the body at death, whereas the *okra* (which is also quasi-material) goes on to become an ancestor in a world that seems strikingly like the present one in many ways.

mogya *[MAHG yah] bloodline and clan identity in the Akan system*

sunsum *[SUHN suhm] the distinctive aspects of personality in the Akan system*

The important difference from Descartes occurs with the concept of mind, or ***adwene.*** In the Akan language, *adwene* "is primarily the capacity to think thoughts, feel emotions, construct arguments, imagine things, perceive objects and situations, dream dreams of both night and day and so on."[14] *Adwene* does not signify anything like the thinking, unextended substance Descartes described when he used the word "mind."

adwene *[ahd WAY nay] the mind, meaning the capacity to think and feel in the Akan system*

In fact, although Descartes used the words *mind* and *spirit* more or less interchangeably, "to identify either the *okra* or the *sunsum* with *adwene* would be the sheerest gibberish" in the Akan language.[15] Because there is no "mind" in the Cartesian sense—meaning an immaterial entity, separate and distinct from a material aspect of the person—the mind-body problem cannot arise.

For the Akan, as for Conway, the parts that make up a human person are arranged on a continuum. Conway's continuum moves from more or less spiritual to more or less material, whereas the Akan continuum moves from purely material to quasi material. In both cases, the result is the same: an integrated person rather than a body and a mind essentially different one from another and unable to interact.[16] (For a summary of some solutions to the metaphysical mind-body problem, see Figure 5.3.)

The New Science Leads to Empiricism: Isaac Newton

Descartes's theory of the clockwork universe led others to deepen the investigation into nature's mysteries, and in 1687 Isaac Newton stunned the

The Mind-Body Problem and Some Solutions			
Descartes:	Mind is thinking and unextended Body is unthinking and extended Point of contact is the pineal gland		
Spinoza	**Leibnitz**	**Conway**	**Akan**
Mind and body are both attributes of God.	Mind and body are both monads.	Mind and body occupy the same continuum, which ranges from material (matter) to spiritual (God).	*Okra, sunsum,* and *mogya* occupy the same continuum, which ranges from material (*mogya*) to quasimaterial (*okra*); no unextended mind.

FIGURE 5.3 SOLUTIONS TO THE MIND-BODY PROBLEM *If mind and body are completely separate, the question becomes, How do they interact?*

scientific community with his *Principia Mathematica (Mathematical Principles of Natural Philosophy).* Working from mathematical laws, Newton was able to use a few relatively simple principles to describe a vast array of phenomena in the physical universe. Things that had only recently been labeled "mysteries" and thus credited to a divine power were explained clearly and precisely by human reason. With no exaggeration, the poet Alexander Pope expressed the awe of his age:

> "Nature and Nature's Laws lay hid in Night
> God said, Let Newton be! and all was light"[17]

Whereas Descartes had worked from one basic premise, the *Cogito*, and from it deduced a world in the same way that Euclid had deduced geometry, Newton had begun with nature. His laws of motion arose out of observation. Only after the data of sense experience were analyzed and developed into basic axioms did Newton use those axioms to generate a deductive system. His method was a major departure from Descartes's insistence that only reason—not the world of the senses and not even mathematics—could be the basis for knowledge about the world. After Newton, philosophers, too, began to turn their attention to observable phenomena, studying them with the expectation that they would provide a new route to knowledge.

British Empiricism

Once Newtonian science had become firmly enthroned as the explanatory principle of the physical universe, philosophers looked to the methods of science to provide a new understanding of how we know. The approach they took, beginning in the late seventeenth century, has come to be called **empiricism.** In the face of the big epistemological question

empiricism *the belief that meaningful knowledge can be acquired only through sense experience* of the relationship (if any) between my ideas of things and things themselves, Descartes had taken refuge in the guarantee of a nondeceiving God. Once he had reasoned a perfect God into existence, Descartes could assert with confidence that the contents of his mind bore a direct relationship with reality. Because a perfect God would not deceive him, Descartes reasoned, his perceptions of a material world must indeed come from and reflect an actual material world.

Seeking to make philosophical truth as firmly grounded as Newtonian physics, empiricist philosophers insisted that any statement that purports to tell us something about the world must originate in sense experience rather than in the mind. If philosophy wished to describe the world, empiricists believed, it must base any description on actual observations of the world itself rather than on our ideas about the world. Because Newton had unlocked the mystery of nature's processes through the formulation of his laws of motion, philosophy ought to begin with observation (as Newton had done) and either describe metaphysical reality or admit that it cannot be done.

Three British philosophers—John Locke in England, George Berkeley in Ireland, and David Hume in Scotland—took up the challenge. Beginning rather modestly with the publication of Locke's *An Essay on Human Understanding* in 1690, the thought processes of these three empiricists evolved over the next century, culminating in Hume's radical skepticism.

THE MAKING OF A PHILOSOPHER

John Locke
(1632–1704)

Locke received a classical education and later trained as a physician, although he seldom practiced that profession. Sympathetic to the Parliamentary Party in England, he later wrote its philosophical defense and remained interested in politics. Best known for his defense of "natural rights," Locke's ideas were influential in the establishment of the American republic as well as the "bloodless revolution" in England in 1688. As a physician, he was well acquainted with the work of his scientific contemporaries and impressed with their attempts to understand nature by "rational experiment and observation." To clear the ground for this work, he was eager to root out the doctrine of innate ideas on which Descartes had built his system.

Creating a Mind-World Connection: John Locke

John Locke began the empiricist tradition in modern Western philosophy by asserting that he saw his task primarily as one of clearing away the metaphysical "rubbish" that was cluttering up the path to knowledge. In his view, before we can speak about the world on the basis of our experiences with it, the "rubbish" left by the rationalists must first be discarded. In particular, Locke rejected the innate ideas that had figured so prominently in Descartes's philosophy.

Two of the most fundamental of the innate ideas claimed by the rationalists are the logical principles of identity—"what is, is"—and of noncontradiction—"it is impossible for the same thing to be and not be at the same time." In his *Essay on Human Understanding,* Locke argued that if there are in fact any innate ideas, they must be assented to by everyone.

Because rationalists believed these ideas to be imprinted on the mind at birth, Locke reasoned that a test might be whether these ideas are present in the minds of every person, no matter how young or unintelligent. If such ideas are truly innate, then they neither require learning nor depend on a high degree of intelligence. Instead, Locke found the principles

> "what is, is," and "it is impossible for the same thing to be, and not to be," not universally assented to.—But, which is worse, this argument of universal consent, which is made use of to prove innate principles, seems to me a demonstration that there are none such; because there

> are none to which all mankind give a universal assent . . . For, first, it is evident, that all children and ideots [sic] have not the least apprehension or thought of them; and the want of that is enough to destroy that universal assent, which must needs be the necessary concomitant of all innate truths . . .[18]

Having criticized the theory of innate ideas, Locke next described the mind as a *tabula rasa*—literally, a "blank tablet"—at the time of birth. Having spent its prenatal life in a warm, dark environment in which all its needs were met, the fetus would have no need of ideas, and no source for them. From the moment of birth, however, the child enters a world of sensation—sights, sounds, textures, tastes, and smells—and experience begins to write upon the blank tablet. This experience, according to Locke, is the only way any of us has of getting to know what the world is like. From these simple sensations, we form simple ideas, and by using our capacity for reflection (by thinking about them), we can combine these simple ideas into complex ones. But all our ideas have their origin in experience. When faced with the basic question of whether our ideas about the world match the world, Locke could not (within the limitations of empiricism) argue, as Descartes did, that the existence of a good God guarantees this connection. Locke does, however, borrow another very useful distinction made by Descartes in the example of the melting wax: Even though every sensation produced by the wax changed during the process of heating, we still understand that it is the same piece of wax.

Descartes had declared that even though the color and scent and solidity of the wax had changed, its essential characteristics—whatever makes it wax—had not. Those primary qualities, the ones that persist through change, must be in the object itself, whereas the secondary qualities, the ones that change, must not. Descartes had used this example, in part, to discredit the senses; Locke picked up the distinction and used it to bridge the gap between ideas of the world and the world itself.

If primary qualities are inherent in objects, then our *ideas* of primary qualities are copies of those qualities as they exist in perceived objects. The ideas are not the objects themselves but they are close enough to provide us a correspondence between mind and external reality. For Locke, primary qualities included solidity (size), extension (occupying space), figure (shape), mobility (in motion or at rest), and number:

> Take a grain of wheat, divide it into two parts, each part has still solidity, extension, figure, and mobility; divide it again, and it retains still the same qualities; and so divide it on till the parts become insensible, they must retain still each of them all those qualities . . . These I call original or primary qualities of body, which I think we may observe to produce simple ideas in us, viz., solidity, extension, figure, motion or rest, and number.[19]

Secondary qualities, according to Locke, are not inherent in the object but are produced in the perceiver by contact with the primary qualities. To put it another way, the primary qualities have the power to produce in us sensations like color, sound, taste, texture, and smell. Because the secondary qualities are not, properly speaking, in the object and because they can be distorted by the medium through which they pass on their way to the perceiver, they do not produce the same kind of reliable knowledge that primary qualities do. If, for example, I am wearing my friend's glasses rather than my own or if I have had drops put in my eyes by an ophthalmologist, I may receive a garbled version of the secondary qualities. Even under these extreme conditions, however, I will recognize whether or not the object is extended, in motion or at rest, and so on.

Locke believed he had created a mind-world connection sufficiently strong to guarantee that our ideas of the world really do resemble the world as it is. Furthermore, he had done it without resorting to Descartes's non-deceiving deity and had used only empirically acceptable methods. As we will see, once the methods of empiricism had been engaged, there was no restraining them. George Berkeley, an Irish bishop and philosopher writing during the first quarter of the eighteenth century, applied all the rigor of the empirical method to Locke's explanation and found it wanting.

THE MAKING OF A PHILOSOPHER

George Berkeley
(1685–1753)

Born in Ireland, Berkeley studied at Trinity College, Dublin, and remained there, after becoming a fellow, until 1713. He traveled extensively in Europe and then spent a decade attempting to found a university in Bermuda. This effort brought him to Rhode Island in 1729 where he was remembered for saying "Westward the course of Empire takes its way." The westward town of Berkeley, California, was subsequently named for him. He spent eighteen years overseeing an Irish diocese as the bishop of Cloyne and died in Oxford, England, in 1753.

Reality as Mind Dependent: George Berkeley

Berkeley reasoned that all the arguments used by Locke to prove that secondary qualities exist only in the mind of the perceiver applied equally to primary qualities (Figure 5.4). In fact, if we know the qualities of extension, figure, and mobility Locke had assigned to solid, senseless matter, those qualities must simply be ideas in our minds. Things, contended Berkeley, can correspond only to things like themselves, so whereas an idea can correspond to another idea, an idea cannot correspond to a piece of unthinking matter. Locke's careful distinction between the reliability of primary qualities and the unreliability of secondary qualities fails on empirical grounds in Berkeley's system. Both are unreliable as proof that a world outside our minds exists:

> Some there are who make a distinction betwixt *primary* and *secondary* qualities: by the former, they mean extension, figure, motion, rest, solidity or impenetrability, and number; by the latter they denote all other sensible qualities as colours, sounds, tastes, and so forth. The ideas we have of these last they acknowledge not to be the resemblances of any things existing without the mind or unperceived but they will have our ideas of the *primary* qualities to be patterns or images of things which exist without the mind, in an unthinking substance which they call Matter. By Matter therefore we are to understand an inert, senseless substance, in which extension, figure, and motion do actually subsist. But it is evident, from what we have already shown, that extension, figure, and motion are only ideas existing in the mind, and that an idea can be like nothing but another idea; and that consequently neither they nor their archetypes can exist in an unperceiving substance. Hence it is plain that the very notion of what is called *Matter,* or *corporeal substance,* involves a contradiction in it.[20]

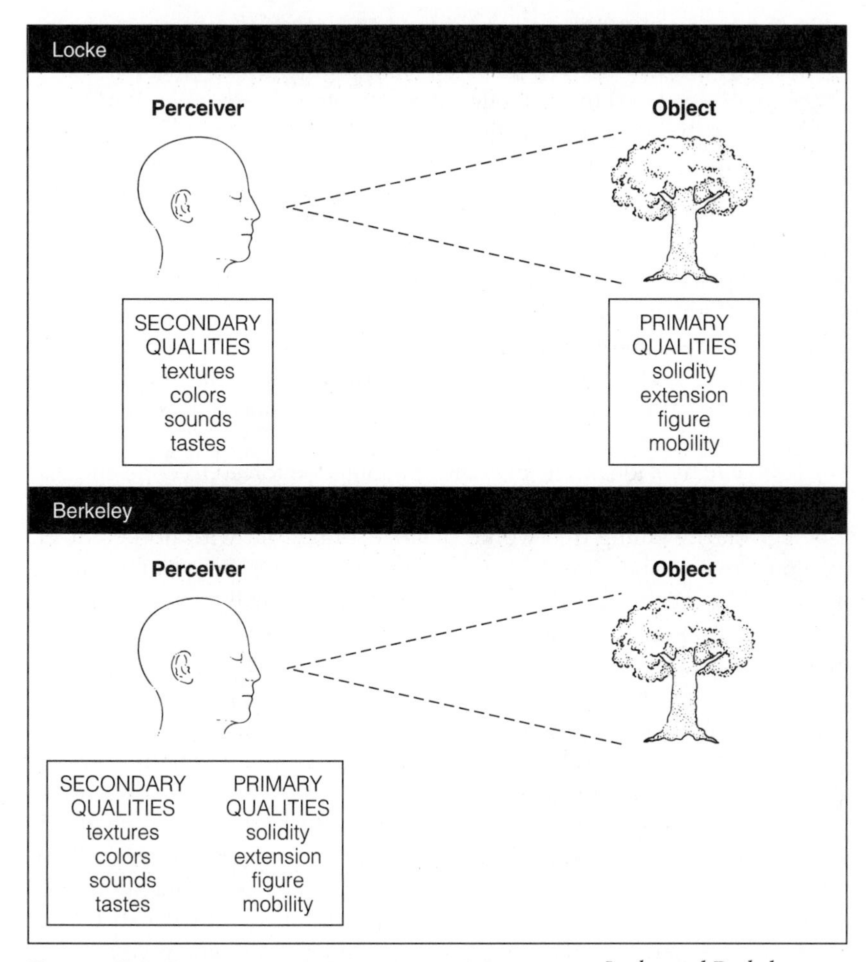

FIGURE 5.4 PRIMARY AND SECONDARY QUALITIES *Locke and Berkeley agreed on the distinction between primary and secondary qualities but disagreed on where each could be found.*

Not only has Berkeley denied the mind-world connection Locke sought to make, he has gone much further and cast doubt on the entire external world. If both primary and secondary qualities exist only in the mind, then, in a very fundamental way, only mental substances (ideas) can be said to exist; physical (material) substances may or may not exist. We have only the contents of our minds to experience, and these contents consist entirely of ideas. The mental gymnastics required to hold primary qualities in one category and secondary qualities in another are too much for Berkeley, who invites you to try your mind on this puzzle:

> But I desire any one to reflect and try whether he can, by any abstraction of thought, conceive the extension and motion of a body without all other sensible qualities. For my own part, I see evidently that it is not in my power to frame an idea of a body extended and moving but I

> must withal give it some colour or other sensible quality which is acknowledged to exist only in the mind. In short, extension, figure, and motion, abstracted from all other qualities, are inconceivable. Where therefore the other sensible qualities are, there must these be also, to wit, in the mind and nowhere else.[21]

If the material world exists only as a mental perception, then, as Berkeley puts it, "to be is to be perceived." If this is true, then it must follow that "not to be perceived is not to be." So in the classic philosophical riddle—if a tree falls in the middle of the forest and there is no one there to hear it—Berkeley's answer must be that it would not make a sound, for sound, like all other perceptions, requires a perceiver. Lacking one, the sound has no real existence even if we admit (as Berkeley might not) that sound waves have been produced.

To Leibniz his nose was a congregation of spiritual beings
To a modern physicist his nose is a wild dance of electrons
To Bishop Berkeley his own nose only existed from time to time when he blew it.
DESMOND MCCARTHY

Following this idea to its extreme, we might be forced to conclude that the world is not the same from one moment to the next. In the presence of a perceiver, the falling tree would make a sound, but with no perceiver, would there even be a tree? Given Berkeley's assertion that "to be is to be perceived," it might be difficult to demonstrate rationally that the car you left in the parking lot is still there. Common sense may tell you it must be there, but if no one is perceiving it, how can you be sure? To be fair to Berkeley, he never took his ideas this far, but if we pursue their implications, some interesting questions arise. How, for instance, can we account for the fact that the world seems to remain intact even when all of us are asleep and not doing our "jobs" as perceivers?

Berkeley distinguishes between ideas of sense and ideas of the imagination. The latter are produced by human free will and tend to be random, whereas the former, ideas of sense, are produced by our perceptions and tend to be more regular and predictable. This distinction implies that there must be some perceiver who is always on the job even when we are not. Perhaps you will not be surprised to learn that Bishop Berkeley next introduces God, the Author of nature and nature's laws, as the source of the regularity in the natural world:

There was a young man who said, "God
must think it exceedingly odd
If he found that this tree
continues to be
When there's no one about in the Quad."

Dear Sir:
Your astonishment's odd
I am always about in the Quad
And that's why this tree
will continue to be
Since observed by
Yours faithfully,
God
RONALD KNOX

> The ideas of Sense are more strong, lively, and distinct than those of the Imagination; they have likewise a steadiness, order and coherence, and are not excited at random, as those which are the effects of human wills often are, but in a regular train or series—the admirable connexion whereof sufficiently testifies the wisdom and benevolence of its Author. Now the set rules or established methods, wherein the Mind we depend on excites in us the ideas of Sense, are called *the laws of nature;* and these we learn by experience, which teaches us that such and such ideas are attended with such and such other ideas, in the ordinary course of things.[22]

The very orderliness and steadiness of our perceptions suggests to Berkeley a constant perceiver. It is this "Author of nature" who is always perceiving everything, who guarantees that objects in your room are where you left them, and that even if a tree falls in the middle of a forest it makes a sound.

But Berkeley, as many philosophers before him and since, had solved one problem only by creating another. Although introducing God, the perpetual perceiver, does restore a sense of order and regularity to nature, Berkeley did not arrive at his conclusion concerning the necessity for such a being on the basis of sense perception. Rather than an empirical demonstration, his "proof" for the existence of the "Author of nature" is a deductive one. Even though Berkeley the empiricist had reasoned his way out of an epistemological dilemma, Berkeley the cleric had in the process violated the assumptions on which empiricism is based. For all the rigor of his attack on Locke, Berkeley had been unable to stay within the first premise of empiricism: Any statement that purports to tell us about the world must originate in sense experience.

You may have noticed that each empiricist philosopher discussed in this section has been more radical than his predecessor. Locke began somewhat modestly with the goal of clearing away the rubbish that lay between him and knowledge of the world. Applying Locke's own methods to his conclusions, Berkeley cast doubt on the independent existence of the material world if there is no mind to perceive it. David Hume, whose philosophy we will consider next, is the most radical of the three. His methods have been ruthless in their destruction of both the content and the methods of traditional philosophy.

Radical Skepticism: David Hume

In Hume we find the rigorous, fully consistent application of empiricist principles. Hume, who died the year the Declaration of Independence was written, does not accept innate ideas, does not believe in God, and limits our knowledge about the character of the world to that which we can know through sense experience. It is, he wrote, "certain we cannot go beyond experience; and any hypothesis, that pretends to discover the ultimate original qualities of human nature, ought at first to be rejected as presumptuous and chimerical."[23]

If we look for the origins of our ideas, Hume argued, we will find them in sense impressions. If I accidentally hit my thumb while hammering a nail, the result is an "impression" that is very strong and vivid. For a moment my entire being seems centered in my thumb where I am experiencing intense pain. When a week later I tell you about hitting my thumb, I draw on my "idea" of the experience—what remains from the initial "impression"—which is much fainter and less powerful:

> All the perceptions of the human mind resolve themselves into two distinct kinds, which I shall call IMPRESSIONS and IDEAS. The difference betwixt these consists in the degrees of force and liveliness, with which they strike upon the mind, and make their way into our thought or

THE MAKING OF A PHILOSOPHER

David Hume
(1711-1776)

Born in Edinburgh, Scotland, and educated at the university there, Hume first studied law but then resolved to become a philosopher. After an argument with a Jesuit over miracles, he began to write his first treatise. Hume spent his twenties working on this project and along the way had what we would today call a nervous breakdown. To make matters worse, the treatise received unfavorable reviews, falling "dead born from the Press" as Hume put it. He tried to restate the ideas more acceptably in *Enquiry Concerning Human Understanding* and was rewarded with critical and philosophical interest. Hume's mother characterized her Davy as a "well meanin' but weak-minded critter," a strange description for a brilliant thinker whose ideas demolished most of traditional metaphysics and epistemology.

> consciousness. Those perceptions, which enter with most force and violence, we may name *impressions;* and under this name I comprehend all our sensations, passions and emotions as they make their first appearance in the soul. By *ideas* I mean the faint images of these in thinking and reasoning . . .[24]

Hume contended that all our ideas are but faint copies of previous sense impressions. Even the idea of something we have not perceived—say, a silver cloud—is a combination of previous impressions of silver and clouds. Hume summed up his general proposition this way: "That all our simple ideas in their first appearance are deriv'd from simple impressions, which are correspondent to them, and which they exactly represent."[25] Complex ideas are combinations of simple ones, and if something does not first exist as an impression, it cannot later exist as an idea.

After advancing this innocent sounding proposition, Hume began to lead his readers through its implications. If all our ideas have their origin in impressions, then surely those who speak of "substance" are dealing in fantasy. What sense impression could we possibly have of either mental or physical "substance"? These may be concepts that philosophers use to entertain themselves, but they can tell us nothing about the nature of reality. Hume admitted to having perceptions of physical objects, but he found no impression in his mind of anything so slippery as physical "substance."

For that matter, he did not even find a "mind." When he went in search of mental "substance," or mind, what he found instead was the contents of what philosophers have called mind. He found a collection of perceptions and nothing else; he found no entity—no mind—that holds these perceptions and has an independent existence. What is called "mind," Hume contended, is really nothing but a "bundle of perceptions."

skepticism *the philosophical doctrine that knowledge is uncertain and (in its strictest sense) that absolute knowledge is unattainable*

In similar fashion, Hume found the supposed "idea" of God to have no basis in sense experience. Because there is no impression, there can be no idea. As Hume's **skepticism** continued to pound at the edifice of traditional philosophy, most of it collapsed under the assault of his radical empiricism. Failing the "impression" test, mental and physical "substance," "mind" or "self," and "God" all become epistemologically meaningless. If people want to talk about them as though something meaningful might be said, they may of course do so, but Hume was clear that such concepts, which do not have their origin in sense experience, can never lead us toward knowledge of the nature and character of reality.

So, to Hume all of metaphysics must be dismissed as a blind alley, of no help whatever in our attempt to understand the world. What then of science, with its empirical methods and its apparent power to explain reality? To examine science's claim to knowledge, Hume looked at the ways in which ideas are connected or associated with each other. He found three patterns of association: resemblance, contiguity, and cause and effect; the first two are described here:

> 'Tis plain, that in the course of our thinking, and in the constant revolution of our ideas, our imagination runs easily from one idea to any

> other that resembles it, and that this quality alone is to the fancy a sufficient bond and association. 'Tis likewise evident, that as the senses, in changing their objects, are necessitated to change them regularly, and take them as they lie *contiguous* to each other, the imagination must by long custom acquire the same method of thinking, and run along the parts of space and time in conceiving its objects.[26]

The mind, of course, is just what the brain does for a living!
SHARON BEGLEY

It seems clear that one of the patterns we follow in associating ideas is resemblance. All the flowers I think of are connected by resemblance. In a similar way, things contiguous (close together) in space-time provide natural associations. The events of my day, as well as all the entities in a given space, are related to one another through the pattern of association.

The "gentle force" responsible for these patterns of association is not reason but the imagination. These connections are not necessary connections like those in mathematics, which lead us to conclude that, based on a proof, two triangles are congruent. The patterns of association, Hume insisted, arise more from feeling than from logic. The third pattern—cause and effect—has a similar origin. Like resemblance and contiguity, cause and effect is a pattern of association and nothing more. Part of our deep, visceral (gut-level) response to the world is that we want it to be an orderly place, so we associate events under the pattern of cause and effect, but the pattern is in us rather than in the events.

Hume analyzed the principle of causation as put forth by scientists and concluded that to have meaning this principle must rest on "some relation" among objects. For causation to exist among objects, three criteria must be met: *contiguity* (the objects would have to be sufficiently close together), *priority of time* (the cause must precede the effect in time), and *necessary connexion* (this effect must follow from this cause). Although Hume granted our experience of the first two, he challenged the empirical basis for the third and crucial requirement: "necessary connexion."

His explanation of what happens is that, as a result of the "constant conjunction" of two events, we apply the pattern of cause and effect. After we have many experiences of two events in which one invariably follows the other, we conclude (with no basis in empirical reality) that the first event has "caused" the second. In fact, we can have no real knowledge of this "causation."

Imagination is more important than knowledge.
ALBERT EINSTEIN

Consider, for instance, a game of billiards or pool. We observe the white cue ball strike one of the striped balls, and then we observe the striped ball rolling into the corner pocket. Our conclusion is that the force of the cue ball "caused" the striped ball to move across the table. But Hume insisted that we have merely observed two events: (1) The white ball striking the striped ball, and (2) the striped ball rolling into the corner pocket. We have not observed any connection between the two events but instead have supplied the connection as a pattern of association:

> We have no other notion of cause and effect but that of certain objects which have been *always conjoined* together, and which in all past instances have been found inseparable. We cannot penetrate into the reason of the conjunction. We only observe the thing itself, and always

> find that, from the constant conjunction, the objects require an union in the imagination.[27]

Notice the use of the word *imagination*. Hume has reduced the foundation of the scientific method—the principle of cause and effect—to a psychological device. Indeed, Hume found the origin of many of our strongest held principles to lie not in reason but in our feelings; they are a consequence of our passionate response to the world. Even though reason is useful in revealing the abstract connections between ideas, it is useless in motivating our behavior. Our moral principles, for instance, derive not from reason, but from how we would prefer the world to be. Acts that preserve our humanity and foster cooperation and honesty bring us pleasure, and it is for this reason that they become enthroned as moral principles.

For similarly emotional reasons, we want to believe in a predictable world, governed by laws of cause and effect. Because Hume has shown that all events are independent (for example, the movement of the billiard balls), science cannot really predict the future based on an analysis of the past. Our psychological pattern of joining two events together to create "cause and effect" is nothing more than a mental exercise; it has no basis in reality. We may feel certain that striking one billiard ball with another in exactly the proper way will drive it into the pocket, and we confidently use this feeling to predict that in the future the same events will lead to the same result; but if the connection exists not in reality but in my interpretation of events, then this confidence is completely unfounded.

Just because the Sun has risen every day of your life so far does not mean that science can guarantee that it will rise again tomorrow. The statement that "The Sun will not rise tomorrow" does not produce a logical contradiction. Like other animals, we rely much more on instinct than on reason. Our instinctual nature allows us to act on our limited empirical knowledge and conclude that there is an external world in which cause and effect rule. Hume simply asks us to admit that we are kidding ourselves. It may be comforting to believe in Santa Claus, but philosophy cannot prove he exists; the same is true for cause and effect.

Hume's radical empiricism created an intellectual dead end for philosophical speculation and scientific reasoning. If Hume was right, there was no point in pretending we could achieve reliable knowledge about the world. It seemed to some that philosophy might have outlived its usefulness.

Implications of Empiricism for Philosophy

During the twentieth century, both logical positivism and language analysis rigorously applied empiricism to ontological questions and concluded that very little of value can be known with certainty about external reality. If we are limited to the data of sense perception and strictly applied rules of logic, the result can be skepticism—a limitation on knowledge that also severely limits philosophy's usefulness in answering basic questions about

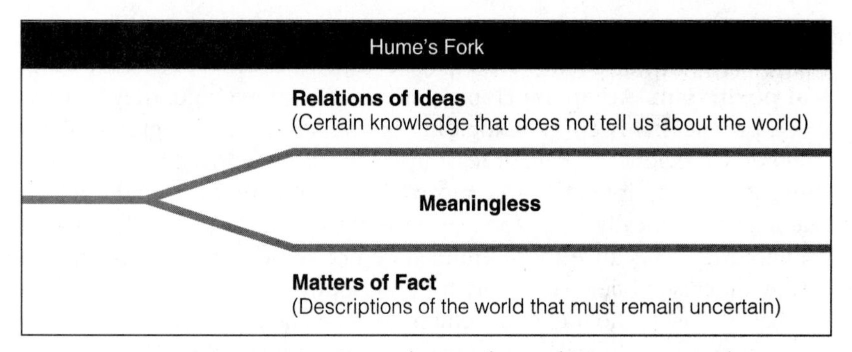

FIGURE 5.5 HUME'S FORK *Hume dismissed everything as meaningless,* except *the two tines of the fork.*

what is real. After having seen where exclusive reliance on either perception or logic can lead, in a later section we step outside Western culture for a moment to consider a traditional African worldview that blends logic with other methods to arrive at reliable knowledge about reality.

Hume's Fork and Logical Positivism

By insisting that we cannot know anything about the character of the world as it exists apart from our sense perceptions, Hume radically restricted the territory in which philosophy can reasonably operate. In what has come to be called **Hume's Fork,** he divided the objects of human inquiry into two types: those that show the relations of ideas and those that describe matters of fact (Figure 5.5).

Hume's Fork *the doctrine that no middle ground exists between necessary truths, based on the relation of ideas, and contingent truths, based on experience; anything other than these two tells us nothing meaningful about reality*

Hume granted that there are truths of reason, which are either intuitively or demonstrably certain. Examples of this kind of knowledge are "the square of the hypotenuse is equal to the sum of the squares of the two sides" and "3 times 5 is equal to half of 30." These statements about the relations of ideas are self-evident or true by definition, but they tell us nothing about the world. They constitute one tine of Hume's Fork, and they provide knowledge about which we can be certain but about which we care very little. The other tine of the fork involves matters of fact that purport to tell us about the world, as in the statement "The Sun will rise tomorrow." As we have seen, however, this knowledge is far from certain, for it is based on our perceptions only and is not demonstrably true. In fact, as we have already noted, there is no logical contradiction in stating that "The Sun will *not* rise tomorrow."

Hume's Fork leaves us a very unappetizing choice between (1) ideas that are certain but do not tell us anything we want to know and (2) ideas that tell us things we want to know but are not certain. Whatever belongs to neither tine meets an even harsher fate: Every supposed "idea" that neither expresses the relationships of ideas nor examines matters of fact is, by definition, outside the scope of knowledge.

logical positivism
a radical empiricist position based on Hume's Fork, asserting that propositions have meaning only if they are either analytic (true by definition) or synthetic (verifiable, at least in principle, in experience)

During the twentieth century, one group of philosophers who took Hume's radical empiricism seriously advocated what came to be called **logical positivism.** Accepting Hume's criteria for knowledge, they insisted that a proposition is epistemologically or cognitively meaningful only if it is either self-evident or can, at least in theory, be empirically verified. Because it is impossible even to conceive of actual conditions under which one might empirically verify the existence of God, the human self, or moral principles and because these entities are not self-evident, the result is a greatly diminished field of activity for philosophy.

Leaving aside the traditional emphasis on metaphysics and ethics, logical positivists have focused on bringing logical clarity to philosophical statements about the world. Real knowledge about the world can be derived only from scientific investigation, and value statements like "Stealing is wrong" are only expressions of emotion (see Chapter 10). Philosophy, however, can perform a useful function by analyzing both everyday language and scientific language.

Language Analysis and the Limits of Philosophy

Much of the original inspiration for logical positivism came from the work of Ludwig Wittgenstein, a Viennese mathematician. Wittgenstein thought philosophical analysis could first reduce complex, descriptive propositions to the simple propositions of which they were composed, and then it could further reduce these to "names" that in combination were the most basic constituents of reality. In Wittgenstein's first work, the *Tractatus Logico-Philosophicus* (1921), he argued that language "pictures" the fact it represents because both the language and the fact share the same *logical form.* A combination of "names" (a proposition) is a picture of a combination of objects (a fact). Language, then, is our key to understanding the world, for if we wish to understand the world, we should begin by analyzing the language we use to "picture" it.

In his second and final work *Philosophical Investigations* (1953), published after his death, Wittgenstein abandoned the idea that language had a universal function—like picturing reality—in favor of a more complex understanding of how language functions. Reasoning that we never have just a picture—we always have a picture of something—Wittgenstein concluded that we also have "language games" that are used to say the same thing in a number of critically different ways.

Wittgenstein believed that we ignore or confuse language games to our peril. Philosophy, in particular, uses perfectly functional words like *mind* and *God* to frame unnecessarily perplexing philosophical problems. Mind can be spoken about quite clearly in psychology, and God can be spoken about quite clearly in theology, but when we remove these words from the language game to which they properly belong, confusion is bound to result.

By Wittgenstein's analysis, philosophy had reasoned itself out of a job. He believed philosophy's task was to decide what could logically be "said" and then let scientists "say" those things. When someone poses a metaphysical question, philosophy's job, according to Wittgenstein, is to point out that the question is meaningless, for most of the propositions in philosophical works are "not false but nonsensical."[28] What a comedown from the time of Descartes, when philosophy seemed to offer a route to certain knowledge about ourselves and about the world!

In the West, logic is assumed to be the foundation of all true knowledge; what cannot survive the rigors of logical analysis has no claim to the status of knowledge or truth. And yet, there is nothing of art or intuition in logic, nothing of human emotion; indeed, these things are specifically and rigorously excluded. In the next two sections we'll look at challenges to these claims. American philosopher Alison M. Jaggar challenges what she calls "the myth of the objective observer" and suggests the value emotions have in identifying deep societal biases. And, in the second section, we learn that some African philosophers are questioning whether Western logic might not profit from a little more intuition.

THE MAKING OF A PHILOSOPHER

Ludwig Wittgenstein
(1889-1951)

Born in Vienna, Wittgenstein was originally attracted to architecture and engineering but later studied pure mathematics and became interested in the philosophy of mathematics, which led him to philosophy. Arguing that philosophy is not a doctrine or set of doctrines but an activity, Wittgenstein insisted that whatever can be said can be said clearly. His emphasis on and investigations into the logical structure of language were major influences on logical positivism. He wrote his first treatise, the *Tractatus,* while serving in the Austrian army during World War I. He also worked as an elementary school teacher and gardener's assistant before taking a doctorate at Cambridge University in England where he used the *Tractatus* as his dissertation. He held a philosophy chair at Cambridge between 1937 and 1947, but during World War II he worked as a hospital orderly and as an assistant in a medical laboratory. His second major work, the *Philosophical Investigations,* was published two years after his death.

Challenging the Myth of the Objective Observer

Within the positivist tradition that we have just been considering, Alison M. Jaggar contends, "the influence of emotion is usually seen only as distorting or impeding observation or knowledge."[29] The very objectivity of Western science allegedly rests on the elimination of emotional and evaluative biases in those doing the investigating. On the level of the individual investigator, Jaggar acknowledges, it might indeed be possible to root out or at least control for biases. But, on the level of society, values and emotions are inevitably woven into our methods and even into the more basic questions about what science is and how it should be practiced. From our vantage point, Jaggar suggests, it is easy to spot the racist biases that underlay nineteenth-century anthropology. But, these biases were not recognized at the time because they were so widely shared. Our own attitudes in the present, favoring some ways of behaving and disapproving others, operate as unchallenged guiding principles because we are too close to them to recognize them for what they are.[30]

There is no dispassionate observer. Those whose emotions and attitudes more closely mirror those of the dominant elements in society may mistakenly believe that these biases are built into the way things are "objectively," but a little distance reveals the falsity of this assumption. Emotions, especially those experienced by less dominant groups, may be our essential clues to the biases of the dominant group. Those who experience what Jaggar calls "outlaw emotions"—socially unacceptable reactions—may be the first to point us toward unacknowledged assumptions that underlie our so-called value-free investigations. "They may provide the first indications that something is wrong with the way alleged facts have been constructed, with accepted understandings of how things are. Conventionally unexpected or inappropriate emotions may precede our conscious recognition that accepted descriptions and justifications often conceal as much as reveal the prevailing state of affairs."[31]

Positivism views values and emotions as "alien invaders that must be repelled by a stricter application of the scientific method."[32] If, however, the scientific method itself is compromised, Jaggar argues that it would be wiser to consider reason and emotion not as opposites but as approaches that mutually constitute each other. This rethinking of the relationship between knowledge and emotion might provide a more reliable path to an accurate understanding of the way things are.

Broadening the Definition of Logic in Traditional Societies

As philosopher S. A. Mwanahewa of Uganda points out, logic can be used (consciously or unconsciously) to mislead society. Through the careful selection of content words, perfectly valid arguments can be framed so that they lead to dangerous conclusions.[33] The "logic" of greed and prejudice can follow this pattern. Is there a way to arrive at useful and important knowledge about the world we live in through a combination of logical analysis and lived experience?

Traditional societies identify what is important and communicate the resulting knowledge to the next generation through the use of proverbs and symbols rather than through logical analysis. In Ghanaian culture, for example, the egg has many symbolic meanings: feminine beauty, for those who find an egg-shaped head beautiful; easy labor in childbirth, since hens seem not to labor in laying eggs; and new and creative life or fertility. One of the more interesting symbolic uses of the egg is to represent love and state power, both of which are considered extremely fragile. Atop the wooden or metal staff of a linguist (who serves as a language medium between a chief and the people at court), one might find a carved hand with an egg in it. The translation of this symbol might be: "Power held in one hand is not safe," and the egg in hand could be seen as a recommendation for shared power, an argument for democracy.[34]

Let's return to the question that has dominated this chapter: What are the sources and foundations of knowledge? We have seen how Descartes and the empiricists answered this question and the implications of their answers for the West. In Ghana, a Yoruba proverb answers the question this way: "Knowledge is like a baobab tree, so no one person can embrace it with both arms." This proverb has several possible meanings, including "He who knows all, knows nothing," "Knowledge is so vast that no one person can grasp all of it," and "Knowledge grows and grows so there is no limit to what any one individual can know."[35]

Common sense is the collection of prejudices acquired by age eighteen.
ALBERT EINSTEIN

Although traditional societies value reason (as Descartes did) and experience (as the empiricists did), their proverb-based epistemology insists that logic is not the only truth test. As we saw in the Chapter 4, the West tends to be skeptical of truth claims based on intuitive knowing. But questions like the existence or nonexistence of God, to use one example, may not be best approached using reason alone. Suppose you lived in a culture that told you about knowledge through the use of simple proverbs rather

HOW PHILOSOPHY WORKS
Proverb as Method

Cultures that rely on the written word use certain methods to test the validity of arguments. In the West, the primary method is logic. What may be sacrificed in submitting everything to the test of logic, however, is the test of experience. Some things that make perfect logical sense fail in practice. Relying only on logic misses an important component in arriving at truth or even accuracy—the validation that only living reality can provide. Traditional cultures communicate the wisdom they have gleaned through the use of proverbs. When you hear a proverb that has the "ring of truth" to it, you are responding from your own lived experience. Proverbs, it is said, have the added merit of including things that logic would certainly omit—like human emotion and an appreciation of beauty. If we are not machines but living organisms, why should we assume that everything worth knowing can and must be expressed logically? Think about the things of which you are most certain. Do you know them logically, or have they become part of you through more intuitive forms of knowing?

than learned treatises? Would you understand knowledge differently? Would your relationship with the world be different?

Mwanahewa argues that, even though the logical approach is mainly scientific and the cultural approach is mainly artistic, both are practical and have cogent objectives. There is a definite logic to proverbs, and there should be an artistic element to logic. Either extreme provides a limited window on the world; balance between them should constitute the ideal.[36]

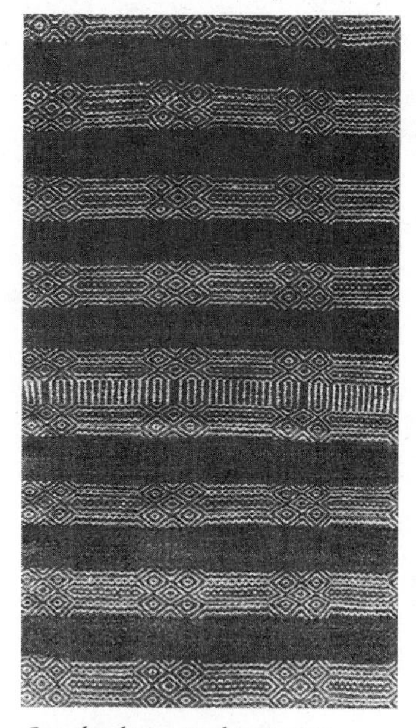

Can the design in this Navajo rug lead us to knowledge about reality?

Navajo rug/Courtesy of Carol Galbraith/Photo by Quentin Kardos.

As we have already seen, Taoism believes that balance is the underlying principle of reality. Too exclusive a reliance on logic might be taking *yang* to the extreme, whereas excessive reliance on emotion might be too *yin*. Having taken our rational, scientific logic to its extreme, maybe we are ready to blend a little of the artistic and the human with deduction. The authenticity of the spoken word is found not only in its internal logic but also in its intuitively obvious application to human life.

We find a similar emphasis on the value of the spoken word in the life of Socrates, who committed nothing to writing. His strong belief was that we are more likely to arrive at truth when we use the testing process of spoken language. Through the dialectic of verbal fencing, weak ideas will be challenged by both logic and experience and then defeated in plain view. When truth is tested in the marketplace or the political forum, only sound reasoning that accurately represents lived experience will survive. What remains unchallenged after the completion of this process of refinement reflects what people agree is true; in many traditional societies these truths are expressed in proverbs.

In the Kinyankore orature (oral literature) of Uganda, the following proverb focuses on hypocrisy: "A woman who has killed her co-wife's child cries louder than the mother of the child." The louder cry, intended by the

DOING PHILOSOPHY
Knowing How to Cure Malaria

When I was six or seven and living in Liberia, I became very ill with malaria. My father, who was a Western-trained physician, treated the disease using quinine and other standard methods, but I did not respond. In fact my fever grew higher and higher. My father respected the healing ability of bonesetters but trusted quinine to cure my illness—he was not going to have any "voodoo medicine" used on his daughter. But, as my condition grew worse, both my grandmothers stepped forward. "Doctor," they said, "we respect you and your methods, but we think you've done all you can do. If we're not careful, this child is going to slip into the spirit world and we're not going to stand idly by and watch this happen." So, they wrapped me in fever leaves and as the leaves dried out from the heat of my skin they wet more and applied them to my burning body. Then they mopped me down with other herbs and finally I broke into a sweat and the fever subsided. With a fever as high as the one I had, I should have hearing loss and other residual effects, but I'm perfectly fine.

SOURCE: Dawn Cooper Barnes, remembering her childhood in Liberia.

The sage embodies the balance and harmony of yin *and* yang *energy.*
Standing sage figure by Hou Rong/Photo by Quentin Kardos.

weeping woman to indicate deep pain and loss, is actually a coverup for guilt.[37] Another Ghanaian proverb stresses the value of freedom over material well-being: "It is only the stupid slave who says that his condition of bondage is good after a heavy meal." And, from the same culture, the following proverb emphasizes the need for adjustment to new situations in life: "If you visit the country of frogs and you find them squatting, you must squat too even though you may find it inconvenient."[38]

In traditional societies, everyone becomes the judge of what is true and therefore what deserves to be passed on to the next generation in the form of a proverb; a proverb that did not "ring true" would simply fade away. Members of a traditional society might laugh at Descartes's philosophical doubts regarding the reality of his body and the external world (at the beginning of his *Discourse on Method*) or at Hume's logical demonstration that God and cause and effect do not exist because they cannot be proved logically.

As we have seen, in the West, one path of reaction to the implications of empiricism (logical positivism, language analysis, and the limitations of logic) seemed in effect to put philosophy out of a job. With the exception of logical analysis of self-evident propositions, there was little if anything for philosophy to do, and nothing that resembled its traditional work of answering important questions about reality. For those who read Hume carefully in the eighteenth century and were stunned by the implications of his ideas, there was another possible response. Immanuel Kant, a Prussian philosopher, took Hume's empiricism seriously but refused to accept the implication that it was impossible to know anything meaningful about the world.

Immanuel Kant

Awakening from what he called his "dogmatic slumber," Kant recognized that any progress in philosophy must take Hume into account. Kant granted what he saw as Hume's most fundamental proposition: All knowledge has its origin in sense experience. This is the basis of all empiricism, and Hume had simply taken the assumption as far as it could logically go. For Kant, however, this proposition about the origin of knowledge in sense experience did not tell the whole story. Even though knowledge must begin with sense experience, it does not end there.

For Kant, the data of sense experience form the *content* of all knowledge, and to these data is added the form of experience, which is supplied by a priori concepts (categories that exist prior to experience in the very structure of the mind). Kant began by asking us to imagine an object, but to imagine that object not existing in space. Although it is easy to imagine space with no objects in it, thinking of an object apart from space seems impossible. Similarly, he invited the reader to think of an event, but to think of it outside a temporal sequence. A little effort here will convince us, Kant believed, that space and time are not themselves perceptions but are patterns of perception through which every datum of sense experience passes.

These two concepts—space and time—may be thought of as analogous to the operating system on a computer. Without an operating system, a computer responds only to on/off electrical impulses, and you will find it difficult to organize electronic bits of information into meaningful sequences. Once you have an operating system, however, data are accepted, stored, retrieved, and manipulated. Space and time may function in this way.

If you think of the sectors on a formatted disk, it may be easier to understand Kant's second level of perception, what he called the categories of quantity, quality, relation, and modality. Like space and time, these categories are "hardwired" into the brain, and they provide a more complete context for incoming data.

Once electronic impulses pass through the operating system and a word processing program and find their way to an identifiable sector on a formatted disk, they are organized meaningfully into words, sentences, and paragraphs and can be retrieved at will. This is Kant's model for the role mind plays in sorting incoming data to make them useful and retrievable. First, everything is placed in space and time. Then, data are perceived under the categories of quantity, quality, relation, and modality. Raw, unprocessed data, Kant thought, would be meaningless and unusable.

Kant took Hume's assertion about the limits of knowledge head on and provided a commonsense solution to it. Granting that Hume is correct in asserting that all knowledge claims must be based in sense experience, Kant nonetheless insisted that all knowledge claims must also take into account the ordering, structuring concepts, or categories supplied by the mind. Even though Hume pointed out that we have no sense experience of "mind," this need not mean there is no mind. For Kant, mind becomes visible when we examine its role in shaping the sense experience we receive.

THE MAKING OF A PHILOSOPHER

Immanuel Kant
(1724–1804)

Kant spent all his life in the city of Königsburg in East Prussia. He studied theology at the university and became a professor of logic and metaphysics there in 1770. He was also interested in natural phenomena and wrote treatises on earthquakes, wind, and the common generation of the Sun and planets, the so-called nebular hypothesis. He led a very patterned life, doing the same things at the same time every day. People in the town used to set their watches by him when he took his daily walk at 3:30. Hume's criticism of causality "awakened him" he said from his "dogmatic slumber."

If this painting seems absurd to you, is it because the idea of causality is hardwired into your brain?

L'Eschelle du Feu, 1939 by Rene Magritte (1898–1967). Ex-Edward James Foundation, Sussex, UK/ Bridgeman Art Library. © 2001 C. Herscovici, Brussels/Artists Rights Society (ARS), New York.

Our knowledge is still restricted to what we can experience through our senses, but we can make meaningful statements about reality (as it appears to us) because of the a priori concepts of the mind. Under the category of relation, for example, Kant included the concept of causality: When we receive our experience of the world, we receive it through the filter of causality. We recognize cause and effect in the world because one of the ways our brains are structured to perceive the objects that present themselves to our consciousness is causality. So we know that the things we experience, as we experience them, are related in a cause-and-effect way.

phenomena *in Kant's epistemology, things as they appear to us under the categories of perception*

noumena *in Kant's epistemology, things as they are in themselves; this is always beyond the limits of human perception and knowing*

synthetic a priori *in Kant's epistemology, a description of statements that tell us something meaningful about reality and are logically prior to (not dependent on) experience*

In a very significant sense, we are still limited in what we can know. We can know things only as they appear to us—what Kant calls **phenomena**—but we can never know things as they are in themselves—what Kant calls ***noumena.*** So, the inner essence of reality remains locked away, but it becomes possible for us to make meaningful statements about the world, at least as it appears to us. Kant calls these **synthetic a priori** judgments, meaning that they say something important about reality (they are synthetic rather than analytic, or merely concerned with definition) and they occur independent of experience (they are a priori, or logically prior, to experience):

> Our critical deduction by no means excludes things of that sort (*noumena*), but rather limits the principles of the Aesthetic (the science

HOW PHILOSOPHY WORKS

Before and After

Philosophers distinguish between knowledge that can be known before or independent of sense experience, and knowledge that can only be known after sense experience since it depends on experience rather than logic for verification. The key question is often phrased this way: Can we have certain knowledge about the world and, if so, which route must we follow?

A priori: logically before, prior to, independent of experience and unable to be challenged by experience. Rationalists like Descartes believed it was possible to have certain knowledge a priori.

A posteriori: after, posterior to, dependent on sense experience for verification. Empiricist philosophers like Locke, Berkeley, and Hume insisted that true knowledge is only possible using sense experience.

Neither: Hume argued that the only a priori or certain knowledge was *analytic* or true by definition, such as "my brother is a boy"; it tells us nothing we don't already know and does not add to our knowledge of the world. What we can know a posteriori, according to Hume, is only probable and not certain.

Both: Kant asserted that the categories of the mind were a priori and therefore certain. Combined with a posteriori sense experience, Kant believed the categories enable us to make synthetic a priori statements about the world. Of course, our knowledge is limited to *phenomena,* or things as they appear to us, and we can never know *noumena,* or things as they are in themselves.

> of the sensibility) to this, that they shall not extend to all things, as everything would then be turned into mere appearance, but that they shall only hold good of objects of possible experience. Hereby then objects of the understanding are granted, but with the inculcation of this rule which admits of no exception: "that we neither know nor can know anything at all definite of these pure objects of the understanding . . ."[39]

Kant is sometimes called the great synthesizer because he took the most significant aspects of both rationalism and empiricism and combined them creatively into a unified system. He accepted the empirical proposition that meaningful knowledge must have its basis in sense experience, but he also validated the rationalist emphasis on the mind as crucial to our understanding of the world. Kant, in a sense, put philosophy back together and allowed it to progress beyond the dead end of radical empiricism, but his ideas have implications as startling as those of Hume.

Reality is not "out there" waiting for me to discover it through passive experience of it. Reality is in my head, shaped by the pure concepts and categories of my mind. Things like cause and effect that seem so obvious to me are part of the map, not part of the territory. Cause and effect does not reside in things but in my understanding of my experience of them. Newton's laws of mechanics exist not in the world but in the forms of consciousness by which we perceive the world. If our way of perceiving the world were to change substantially, our experience of the world would change with it.

Because we cannot know *noumena*—things as they are in their inner essences—we are right back where we started in the egocentric predicament.

I know how reality appears to me, but, according to Kant, I have little idea what it is really like. Indeed, as Kant showed us, the world appears to operate according to the principle of cause and effect, and our shared agreement of this interpretation allows us to reason about the world. However, we are still left to ponder the relationship (if any) between what I think I know and what is actually "out there."

The Knower and the Known

As we try to distinguish between ourselves as knowing subjects and the things of the world as known objects, we raise this question: What is the relationship between the subject and the object or between the knower and the known? As we will see, this is a Western way to put the question. In non-Western cultures, the egocentric predicament seems less significant and perhaps less useful as a way to talk about knowledge. We can begin by reviewing what we have already learned about the Western tradition.

The Western Tradition

Modern Western epistemology began with Descartes's *Cogito*, which assumes a distinction between the knower and the known. After establishing himself as a "knower" (using the *Cogito*), Descartes went on to prove the existence of a nondeceiving God, and as a result, he was able to establish the reliability of his perceptions regarding "known" objects in the material or "clockwork" universe. Since the time of Descartes, Western philosophers have either agreed with Descartes that by thinking (by using rationality) we can know, or they have disagreed with Descartes, arguing that sense experience rather than reason leads to knowing. Both rationalists and empiricists, however, have acknowledged the distinction between the knower and the known. Kant, too, as we have just seen, also honored the separation.

This distinction was not created by Descartes. As you may recall, the pre-Socratic cosmologists assumed this distinction between the knower and the known when they took their first steps in inquiring what everything in the universe is really made of. And, Plato and Aristotle, despite their differences, shared an assumption that the world of Form and matter was one thing, and the human self another. The power of reason, they believed, would allow people to use the methods of inquiry and logic to unlock the apparent mysteries of the cosmos. Subsequent challenges to rationalism from empiricist philosophers insisted on a different way of knowing (through sense experience rather than through rational deduction), but empiricists did not question the basic separation of the knower from the known.

Precisely because every Western philosopher we have studied in this chapter accepts this division, it may be useful to consider non-Western traditions that, on the whole, reject it. The split between knower and known—or to say it another way, between the subject and the object—is

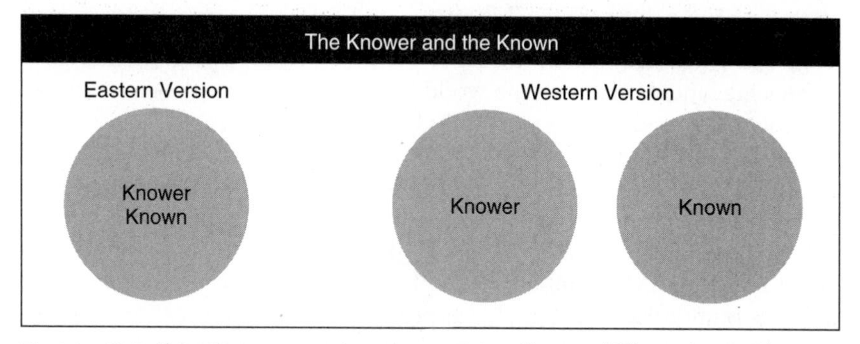

FIGURE 5.6 THE KNOWER AND THE KNOWN *East and West conceive this relationship differently.*

typically Western (Figure 5.6). It characterizes Western epistemology only and does not represent the epistemology of much of the world.

The Non-Western Tradition

In Buddhism, as we saw in Chapter 2, the world of illusion to which we are attached and in which we are ensnared is not what is. In terms of knowledge theory, our everyday experience of the world often presents us with dualistic distinctions—me-you, subject-object—that arise because the artificial boundaries of what we think of as our separate selves (egos) fool us into seeing separation. From the perspective of enlightenment, or true seeing, however, this Western distinction between knower and known is essentially artificial. If I am not a separate self, there is no "me" to serve as knower.

When the mind is most empty, it is most full.
SUSAN FROMBERG SCHAEFFER

Seng-ts'an, a Chinese Zen master who died in the early seventh century, puts it this way in the classic *Hsin-hsin Ming (Affirming Faith in Mind):*

> The object is an object for the subject,
> The subject is a subject for the object;
> Know that the relativity of the two
> Rests ultimately on one emptiness,
>
> In one emptiness the two are not distinguished,
> And each contains in itself all the ten thousand things;
> When no discrimination is made between this and that,
> How can a one-sided and prejudiced view arise?[40]

The knower and the known are one.
MEISTER ECKHART

Subject and object each seem to define the other in a relationship that makes sense from our ego-bound perspective. Seen from what Seng-ts'an calls "the higher realm of true Suchness," however, there is "neither 'self' nor 'other'" and we can only say "not two."[41]

Traditional African epistemology also denies the firm Western distinction between subject and object. This denial is rooted in a deeper unity that insists "man and nature are not two separate independent opposing realities but the one inseparable continuum of a hierarchical order."[42]

Because reality is one, knowledge cannot be based on dualism. Knowledge can occur only when the subject is involved in seeing, thinking, experiencing, and discovering the world as a participant in it, not as detached from it. I can know the world only by being immersed in it, not by attempting to stand apart from it and study it objectively. In truth, the "self of the subject and the objective world outside of the self are really one."[43]

Traditional African epistemology is *always* both theoretical and practical. By contrast in the Western world, theory may address somewhat abstract concepts like numbers or the forces of physics, whereas practice signifies putting ideas into use or applying them in a practical way. We assume that it is possible to have one without the other, and there is even some bias against purely abstract thought—as conveyed in the term *ivory tower.* Ideas conceived and discussed only in the "ivory tower" of a university or a laboratory and never tested in the "real" world are considered suspect in a practical culture like our own. Similarly, philosophy has sometimes been accused of arguing over concepts and ideas that have no bearing on the "real" world. The implication of this criticism is that there is theory and then there is practice.

Postulating a fundamental unity between theory and practice and between knower and known as well eliminates this either/or condition. Knowledge in traditional African culture is always knowledge of something lived—politics, religion, art—not theoretical knowledge separate from the world of lived experience. Consequently, to become knowledgeable—and especially to become wise—one must have many experiences and reflect upon them to understand their meaning. In such a context, it makes no sense to speak of being knowledgeable in an exclusively theoretical sense.

If one learns from others but does not think, one will be bewildered. If, on the other hand, one thinks but does not learn from others, one will be in peril.
CONFUCIUS, *THE ANALECTS*

Being able to deduce the correct lesson from experience is highly valued in traditional societies, as the following proverb illustrates: "It is only a fool who allows his sheep to break loose twice."[44] Sheep can break loose once for any number of reasons, but the person who does not learn from each experience to avoid its repetition is a fool. We have a similar expression in English: "Fool me once, shame on you; fool me twice, shame on me!" Not surprisingly, in traditional societies the elders are looked up to as sources of both knowledge and wisdom; as the Ghanaian proverb reminds us: "You get palm-wine only from mature palm trees."[45]

A similar bias in favor of lived experience as a route to knowledge runs through many ancient Taoist stories. In the tale of "Duke Hwan and the Wheelwright," the message seems to be that knowledge cannot really be transmitted at all. Phien, the wheelwright, asks Duke Hwan what he is reading, and Duke Hwan responds that he is reading "the experts, the authorities." Phien shocks the duke by replying that if these so-called experts are dead, then the duke is only reading "the dirt they left behind." Angered by this contempt for philosophy, Duke Hwan demands an explanation. Phien explains that when he makes a wheel there is a delicate balance between being too gentle and being too rough. "If I am neither too easy nor too violent," he explains, "they come out right. . . . You cannot put this into words: you just have to know how it is. I cannot even tell my own son exactly how it is done, and my own son cannot learn it from me. The men of old took all they really know with them to the grave. And so, Lord," Phien concludes, "what you are reading there is only the dirt they left behind."[46]

Are the words of dead philosophers only "the dirt they left behind"?

Duke Hwan and the Wheelwright, from "For the Love of Wisdom"/Courtesy of Howard Community College.

If you have ever tried to tell someone how to make piecrust or gap a sparkplug, you may understand what Phien is saying. So much of what we call knowledge concerns intangible qualities that are difficult (if not impossible) to put into words. Much of what we know concerns how something "feels" when it is "right." This intuitive knowledge is often the critical part, but it is very hard to speak about it and even more difficult to write about it. Consider the impossibility of proving something like this using logic: When we try, based on our own experience, to save someone pain by advising them not to do something or to do something differently, they are unlikely to take our good advice. What we "know," we know based on our lived experience, which is only theory to the person we are advising.

Apart from lived experience, the only route to knowledge in the Taoist tradition is intuition. Because the *Tao* that can be talked about is not the eternal *Tao,* the deepest reality cannot really be expressed in words. As the *Tao Te Ching* puts it: "Those who know don't talk. Those who talk don't know."[47]

You want knowledge, seek the Oneness within. There you will find the clear mirror, already waiting.
HADEWIJCH II

Summary

We have examined three versions of skepticism. The Taoist version just discussed is a mild form of skepticism; it claims that when we try to know something from the outside we are barking up the wrong tree. If we want to "know" about the world, we must study nature and intuit its wisdom. Nothing lasts forever: Winter turns to spring and then to summer; night becomes day and day night. Paradoxically, it is by yielding that one can conquer. The *Tao,* the oneness that is the source of everything, cannot be spoken of because to speak it puts you immediately into the world of distinctions, the world of what Taoists call the Ten Thousand Things.

Descartes's skepticism was methodic; he used it as a way of getting to the truth. By doubting all knowledge claims, he arrived at what remains—what cannot be doubted—and this he considered to be certain. Descartes never intended to end with skepticism; he always intended to arrive at a place of confidence with respect to knowledge about the world. Once he had proved himself using the *Cogito* and had proved God the nondeceiver, he was restored to certainty that his perceptions of the material world did in fact resemble the world as it existed.

Only in Hume do we find a thoroughgoing skepticism. For Hume, this is no device but an accurate description of what we can and especially what we cannot know. Although we are quite capable of analyzing the relations of ideas, we cannot know anything about the character of the world as it exists apart from our sense perceptions. Our knowledge of the relations of ideas is certain but says nothing meaningful about reality, and our knowledge based on matters of fact informs us about the world but is uncertain because of the limitations of our perceptions. In Hume, we find a philosophical skepticism based on a carefully reasoned analysis of epistemological principles. Faced with such overwhelming limitations on our ability to know, it seems we have no option but to accept that most of our actions are based on feeling rather than on reason.

Even Kant, who struck a balance between the extreme positions of Descartes's rationalism and Hume's empiricism and put human knowing back in place, has left us skeptical about the world. If we can only know the world as perceived by us, and never the world as it really is apart from us, most of our important questions about reality must remain unanswered (at least by human reasoning).

Language analysts like Wittgenstein have reduced the world to "atomic facts" that are composed of simple objects. By naming the objects and combining them into simple propositions, we can depict possible states of affairs in the world. To describe reality we must say which of these possible states of affairs is true and which false. For language analysts, natural science, not philosophy, will define what can be said about reality; philosophy should be thought of as an activity—the clarification of language—rather than as a body of knowledge about the world.

As we have seen, however, this point of view is not without its challengers. If the dream of an objective observer is a myth, we must accept the existence of both individual and societal biases and do our best to get beyond them, using both our reason and our emotions. And, the non-Western world reminds us that intuition can be a very reliable guide to what is, enabling us to find our way to essentials that can be obscured by syllogisms and omitted from narrowly-conducted empirical observations.

In the next two chapters we will further consider how we are to understand the world. Chapter 6 examines truth tests, and we will continue to take seriously the challenge of skepticism by exploring the possibilities and the limitations involved in truth claims. Chapter 7, the final chapter in Part 2, explores the role of art and aesthetic experience in helping us see the world in new ways. Like the proverbs in traditional cultures, visual art can give us fresh eyes and help us see things differently.

For Further Thought

1. Try devising a test to prove to yourself that you are not dreaming right now, that you are actually awake.
2. Compare Descartes' skepticism with Hume's. In what ways are they alike? In what ways different?
3. What changes in thinking would have to occur in the West to eliminate the mind-body problem? What might be some of the implications of these changes? Would the change in thinking create problems greater than the mind-body problem?

4. Try Descartes's experiment in zero-based epistemology. Begin with nothing and see what you are able to establish as certain knowledge.
5. Do you believe any of your current ideas were innate? If so, which ones, and why do you believe them innate? Experiment with a willing young person.
6. Are philosophical proofs for the existence of God possible? Necessary? Explain.
7. Descartes assigned animals to the material side, the "clockwork universe," calling them little robots. Why did he have to do this, based on the system he created? Do you agree or disagree with his classification?
8. Which do you find more persuasive: Descartes's dualism or any of the positions that view everything as one or on a continuum? Why?
9. What does Locke keep from Descartes's epistemology and what does he challenge? Do you find Locke's criticisms of Descartes valid? Why or why not?
10. Does Berkeley's thesis that "to be is to be perceived" solve the mind-body problem? If so, how? If not, why not?
11. Given Hume's denial of the self, would you retain your identity while asleep or unconscious and not perceiving? Explain.
12. Suppose our human way of perceiving the world underwent a radical change (because of a natural or nuclear disaster that altered basic functions). According to Kant, would the world change? Why, or why not?
13. Which aspects of the rationalist and empiricist positions does Kant synthesize? In your opinion, does he keep the best or worst of both worlds? Or some of each? Explain.
14. Gilbert Ryle, a contemporary analytic philosopher has called Descartes's mind-body construction a "ghost in a machine." How is this an appropriate analogy?
15. If space is a category of the mind, what does Euclidian geometry tell us about the world?
16. How, in your opinion, would Socrates judge Descartes's decision not to publish his paper on the Sun-centered universe after noting what happened to Galileo? How do you judge the decision? What might have been some results if Descartes had made the other decision?
17. Does the fact that as a culture we are getting more and more of our knowledge electronically (from TV, Internet, etc.) rather than from books change anything about how or what we know? Explain.
18. Is the knowing that derives from oral cultures in which the treasures of the past are preserved in the memories and spoken words of the wisdom keepers any different from the knowing in cultures in which written language is the storehouse of knowledge and wisdom? How would you test for accuracy and truth in each culture?
19. Have you ever turned on the TV and not been sure whether you were watching an unfolding "live" event, a videotape of something that occurred in the past, or a made-for-TV movie? How did you ultimately "know"? If forced to write a philosophical justification, could you really be sure of what you saw? Explain.
20. Is it possible to deny something others think you know? On what basis might you do this?

For Further Exploration

Fiction and Film

Andrews, Lynn. *Medicine Woman*. New York: Harper & Row, 1987. Like Casteneda (below), Andrews has written a visionary autobiography that is not technically fiction. Also, like Casteneda, Andrews has learned a new way of knowing through her contacts with a shaman known as Agnes Whistling Elk.

Carroll, Lewis. *Alice in Wonderland*. New York: Penguin, 1992. What would happen if everything you thought you knew no longer worked. This is the experience of Alice when she falls down the rabbit hole into Wonderland and has to learn a whole new way of knowing the world.

Casteneda, Carlos. *The Teachings of Don Juan*. New York: Simon & Schuster, 1973. This is actually not fiction, but it reads like fiction. Casteneda, an anthropology student, met a Yaqui Indian named Don Juan and, through him, learned a whole new way of knowing.

Proof. In this Australian film, a skeptical blind man takes photographs of his experiences, asks people to give verbal descriptions of the photographs, translates each description into Braille, and fastens it to the back of the relevant photo. Does he then have "proof" that his experiences were real? Or, is he caught in a Cartesian Circle?

Voltaire. *Candide*. New York: Random House, 1975. In this story, Voltaire satirizes Leibniz's characterization of this world as the "best of all possible worlds." Dr. Pangloss is Leibniz.

Nonfiction

Descartes, René. *Discourse on Method* and *Meditations*. Translated by Laurence J. Lafleur. Indianapolis: Bobbs-Merrill, 1960. Often published together, these two short works reveal the key concepts and methods of Descartes as discussed in this chapter.

Kant, Immanuel. *Prolegomena to Any Future Metaphysics*. Translated by Peter G. Lucas. Manchester, Eng.: University of Manchester Press, 1953. Most of Kant's works are very long and difficult to understand; this slim volume is the exception. As a kind of abstract of the *Critique of Pure Reason,* it traces Kant's chief epistemological argument in a readable format.

Merton, Thomas, trans. *The Way of Chuang-tzu*. New York: New Directions, 1965. Believed to be the disciple of Lao-tzu to whom the *Tao Te Ching* is attributed, Chuang-tzu, in Merton's playful translation, further explains Taoist ways of knowing.

Mitchell, Stephen, trans. *Tao Te Ching*. New York: HarperCollins, 1991. Mitchell gives a very poetic translation of this Taoist classic, using sometimes "he" and sometimes "she" to describe the Master. A good introduction to the *Tao* and the way of knowing associated with it.

Reps, Paul, ed. *Zen Flesh, Zen Bones,* rev. ed. New York: Doubleday, 1989. A wonderful collection of Zen and pre-Zen writings, most of which are stories less than a page long. These stories provide an introduction to an Eastern way of "knowing."

Trueblood, Alan S., trans. *A Sor Juana Anthology*. Cambridge, Mass.: Harvard University Press, 1988. This book contains Sor Juana's poetry and *The Reply to Sor Philothea*.

For Further Research

Try these InfoTrac keywords:

Rationalism

Empiricism

Intuition

Mind/Body Problem

Logical Positivism

African Philosophy

Notes

1. Sor Juana Inés de la Cruz, "The Reply to Sor Philothea," in *A Sor Juana Anthology,* trans. Alan S. Trueblood (Cambridge, Mass.: Harvard University Press, 1988), 211.
2. *A Woman of Genius: The Intellectual Autobiography of Sor Juana Inés de la Cruz,* trans. Margaret Sayers Peden (Salisbury, Conn.: Lime Rock, 1982), 7–11.
3. *A Woman of Genius,* 6.
4. *A Sor Juana Anthology,* 212.
5. *A Sor Juana Anthology,* 5–6.
6. *A Sor Juana Anthology,* 210.
7. René Descartes, *Discourse on Method* and *Meditations,* trans. Laurence J. Lafleur (Indianapolis: Bobbs-Merrill, 1960), 87.
8. Descartes, 82.
9. Descartes, 121.
10. Descartes, 101.
11. Gottfried Wilhelm Leibniz, "The Monadology," in *Philosophers Speak for Themselves: Descartes to Locke,* ed. T. V. Smith and Marjorie Grene (Chicago: University of Chicago Press, 1957), 304.
12. Anne Finch Conway, *The Principles of the Most Ancient and Modern Philosophy* (The Hague: Kluwer, 1982), 211.
13. Conway, 213–216.
14. Kwasi Wiredu, "African Philosophical Tradition: A Case Study," *Philosophical Forum* 24, no. 1–3, Fall-Spring (1992–1993), 48.
15. Wiredu, 51.
16. Wiredu's concept of the human person has been challenged by Kwame Gyekye's *An Essay on African Philosophical Thought* (New York: Cambridge University Press, 1987) in which Gyekye postulates a Cartesian dualism. The balance of contemporary scholarship in this area seems to favor Wiredu's interpretation at this time.
17. Alexander Pope, "Epitaph Intended for Sir Isaac Newton."
18. John Locke, "An Essay Concerning Human Understanding," in *Philosophers Speak for Themselves: Descartes to Locke,* ed. T. V. Smith and Marjorie Grene (Chicago: University of Chicago Press, 1957), 350.

19. Locke, 366–367.

20. George Berkeley, "A Treatise Concerning the Principles of Human Knowledge," in *The Age of Enlightenment,* ed. Isaiah Berlin (New York: New American Library, 1984), 135.

21. Berkeley, 136.

22. Berkeley, 140.

23. David Hume, "Treatise of Human Nature," in *Philosophers Speak for Themselves: Berkeley, Hume and Kant,* ed. T. V. Smith and Marjorie Grene (Chicago: University of Chicago Press, 1969), 105.

24. Hume, 106–107.

25. Hume, 109.

26. Hume, 113.

27. Hume, in *The Age of Enlightenment,* 205.

28. Ludwig Wittgenstein, quoted A. J. Ayer, *Wittgenstein* (Chicago: University of Chicago Press, 1985), 18.

29. Alison M. Jaggar, "Love and Knowledge: Emotion in Feminist Epistemology," in *Gender/Body/Knowledge: Feminist Reconstructions of Being and Knowing,* Alison M. Jaggar and Susan R. Bordo, eds. (New Brunswick, N.J.: Rutgers University Press, 1989), 155.

30. Jaggar, 156.

31. Jaggar, 160, 161.

32. Jaggar, 156.

33. S. A. Mwanahewa, "Logical Heritage: Cogency in Kinyankore Orature," in *The Foundations of Social Life: Ugandan Philosophical Studies,* vol. 1 (Washington, D.C.: Council for Research in Values and Philosophy, 1992), 53.

34. N. K. Dzobo, "African Symbols and Proverbs as Source of Knowledge and Truth," in *Person and Community: Ghanaian Philosophical Studies,* vol. 1, ed. Kwasi Wiredu and Kwame Gyekye (Washington, D.C.: Council for Research in Values and Philosophy, 1992), 88.

35. Dzobo, 95.

36. Mwanahewa, 53.

37. Mwanahewa, 55.

38. Dzobo, 96.

39. Immanuel Kant, "A Prolegomena to Any Future Metaphysics," in *Philosophers Speak for Themselves: Berkeley, Hume and Kant,* ed. T. V. Smith and Marjorie Grene (Chicago: University of Chicago Press, 1960), 314.

40. Seng-ts'an, "Hsin-Hsin Ming," in *Buddhist Scriptures,* ed. Edward Conze (New York: Penguin, 1959), 172.

41. Seng-ts'an, 174.

42. Z. 'b. Nasseem, "African Heritage and Contemporary Life: An Experience of Epistemological Change," in *The Foundations of Social Life: Ugandan Philosophical Studies,* vol. 1, ed. George F. McLean (Washington, D.C.: Council for Research in Values and Philosophy, 1992), 26.

43. 'b Nasseem, 26–27.

44. N. K. Dzobo, "Knowledge and Truth: Ewe and Akan Conceptions," in *Person and Community,* 75.
45. Dzobo, "Knowledge and Truth," 77.
46. Thomas Merton, trans. *The Way of Chuang-tzu* (New York: New Directions, 1969), 83.
47. *Tao Te Ching,* chap. 56, trans. Stephen Mitchell (New York: HarperCollins, 1991), 56.

CHAPTER 6

Truth Tests

Do You Swear to Tell the Truth...?

Before You Read . . .

Ask yourself how confident you are of your own ability to evaluate truth claims in science, history, literary texts, and your personal experience.

Truth—is as old as God.
Emily Dickinson

In courts of law, before a witness is permitted to testify, he or she must be sworn in. In the United States this involves raising the right hand and answering yes to the bailiff's question: "Do you swear the testimony you are about to give will be the truth, the whole truth, and nothing but the truth?" The importance of this ritual seems clear: Jurors must be confident that witnesses are speaking the truth as they know it and not committing perjury—intentional lying on the witness stand. After all, a defendant's life or liberty may hang in the balance.

There is a presumption that we know how to recognize the truth when we see it. Courses you have taken or will take in college purport to tell you what is true. In geometry you may have learned that the square of the hypotenuse of a right triangle is equal to the sum of the squares of the two other legs—the theorem developed by Pythagoras, whom you met in Chapter 1. In biology you were probably told that humans are mammals that bear their young alive rather than laying eggs that hatch later. In history class you read that a civil war was fought in the United States between 1861 and 1865. All of these bits of information were presented to you as true. If you had thought them false, you would not have bothered to remember them.

There may be other truths you believe in. If someone says, "I love you," your life may be significantly changed if you believe it to be true; sadly, those words are not true every time they are spoken. Are there tests we can apply? If so, can we use the same test to identify the truths of geometry, biology, history, and love?

The Issue Defined

Even if you do not know the official names of the following two laws of thought (Figure 6.1), you will probably grant them the status of truth. The first is known as the **law of noncontradiction:** A is not non-A. The second is the **law of the excluded middle:** Something is either A or non-A. Another way of stating the first proposition is to invoke the **law of identity:** A is A (because it cannot be non-A).

law of noncontradiction *states that A cannot be non-A*
law of the excluded middle *states that something is either A or non-A, and no middle ground exists between these two possibilities*
law of identity *states that A equals A*

Every statement we make presupposes these laws of thought. If A is not-A—if a house is *not* a house—we have no way of speaking to one another about houses. Similarly, the second principle states that something is either what we say it is or it is not; this is either a house or not a house, and there can be no middle ground between the two. Logically, there seems to be no way to speak of something that both is and is not a house, so the illogical middle ground is excluded.

Even if you have not formally been taught these principles, they should be obvious to you. They are built into the way we see the world and the way we speak about things. We believe these two principles to be true because if they are not, then all logic and all language simply collapses into meaninglessness. If something is both A and non-A, we are operating under a new set of rules, a set none of us knows anything about. And if there is something that is neither a house nor not a house but something else, then we have no way to speak about this or understand it.

The law of noncontradiction and the law of the excluded middle are part of our heritage from the ancient Greeks, and in particular from Aristotle. These laws have drawn the lines of logic in the Western world for more than 2000 years and have helped us make and clarify our black-and-white distinctions. (To read about an interesting challenge that insists that the world is mostly gray, skip ahead to the "How Philosophy Works" box in Chapter 10 and read about fuzzy logic.) Truth is the arena in which we test those distinctions. Something is either true or false, we insist, and some of the tests you take in college might require you to make such distinctions. We may have faith in a number of things—the love of our family, God, the appropriateness of democracy as a form of government, our own skill as a driver—but it will be another thing altogether to establish that these articles of faith are true.

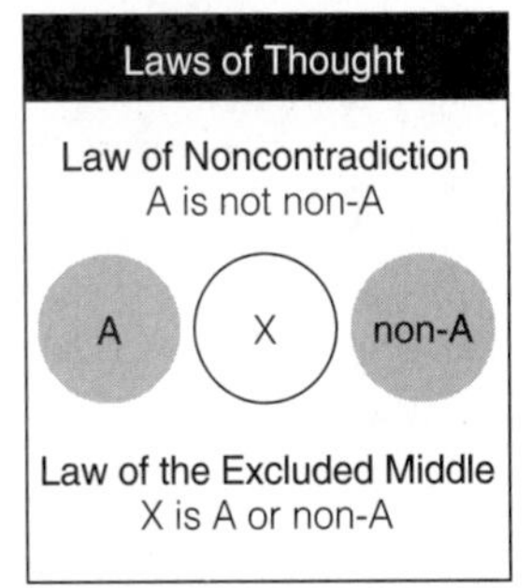

FIGURE 6.1 LAWS OF THOUGHT *According to Western logic, something is either A or non-A; there is no in-between.*

We live in a scientific age and, in part as a legacy of Hume's skepticism (see Chapter 5), we tend to demand proof by which we mean something more than "I believe this to be true." In general, we insist on either logical or empirical proof: Something must either make sense logically, or we must be able to establish it as truth through our senses, by independent testing and verification. As Paul Simon reminds us,

> Faith is an island in the setting sun
> But proof, yes
> Proof is the bottom line for everyone.

We believe many things to be true, but belief alone does not guarantee truth. For many centuries people believed that the Sun moved about Earth, and they had very good reasons for this belief. Every morning the Sun rose above the eastern horizon; all day the Sun moved slowly across the sky; then, in the evening, the Sun sank below the western horizon. Today, we believe something else to be true: The *apparent* motion of the Sun results from the daily rotation of Earth, one of nine planets orbiting around the Sun.

We used to believe that time moved at a fixed and regular pace—until Einstein's relativity formulas convinced us that what is true, instead, is that time is relative and slows down as we approach the speed of light (see Chapter 2). If we are unwilling to grant that truth is somehow relative—true at one time and in one place but not true at other times and places—then we must decide what makes a statement true or false.

Truth is immortal; error is mortal.
MARY BAKER EDDY

In this chapter we explore how we determine which of the many things we believe deserve the label *true*. We look at truth tests and how they work. Once we have established a few ground rules, we turn to the fields of religion, science, history, and literature to see how questions of truth are addressed in each of them.

Truth Tests

Let's consider some of the ways philosophers test for truth. We begin by looking at *warrantability,* the general term for evidence or justification for making a truth claim. Next we turn to three truth tests traditionally employed by Western philosophers—the correspondence, coherence, and pragmatic tests. Finally, we examine an African truth test—the Ewe creativity test.

Warrantability

You may recall that Descartes began his search for truth by doubting the evidence of his senses, whether he was awake rather than asleep, and even the truths of mathematics. After he had established his identity as a thinking self, using the *Cogito,* he moved quickly to find a basis on which to believe in the other commonsense certainties of his life, such as the reliability of mathematics and the evidence from his senses that a material world existed outside himself. If you remember, Descartes could not move outside his own mind until he had established the existence of a nondeceiving God. In Descartes's rationalist system, God was an essential element in the process of establishing truth.

We use the term *warrant* in a legal sense when we say that the police have a warrant for someone's arrest. What we mean is that there is enough evidence or justification to warrant arresting the person. In philosophy we mean much the same thing: A **warrant** provides the evidence or justification that something is so.

warrant *the evidence or justification for a truth claim*

All the philosophers we studied in Chapter 5 were looking for warrantability, and they found it to varying degrees. Descartes found in a nondeceiving God the explanatory principle for everything outside himself.

HOW PHILOSOPHY WORKS

Informal Fallacies—Part One

A *fallacy* makes an argument false in some way. In other chapters we consider formal fallacies in which the rules of inference are not followed and the conclusion is not supported by the premises. In this chapter we want to look at some informal fallacies that attempt to distort an argument and make it appear either to work or not to work falsely. Along with the truth tests discussed in this chapter, another way to test the truth is to inspect an argument for fallacies. These are some of the most common types of informal fallacies:

1. *Appeal to emotion*. If you have ever been at a rousing speech and found yourself agreeing with the speaker but later read a transcript of the speech and found it to be weakly argued or perhaps even lacking in substance, you know how this fallacy works. The personal power and emotional language of the speaker appeal directly to your hopes and fears, bypassing logic and consistency altogether.

2. *Appeal to authority*. Parents try this when all else fails. After arguing unsuccessfully with a child that it is time for bed, a parent who has run out of cogent arguments may resort to "because I said so." Both parent and child probably know that this constitutes a fallacy. The child's version of this fallacy is called *appeal to the crowd* and is most often expressed as "but everyone gets to stay up later than I do."

3. *Begging the question*. This offers as proof the very thing one is trying to prove. Its most common formulation is a more complex version of this: "Janice could not possibly have lied to the house mother. She is not a liar." Critics have accused Descartes of committing this fallacy when he argued: "God must exist because I have a clear and distinct idea of God which must be a true idea since God is its source." These arguments are said to be circular because the premise proves the conclusion that proves the premise.

4. *Appeal to ignorance or incomplete information*. In this fallacy one claims either that something must be true based on the lack of contrary evidence ("There's no proof that picking daisy petals while reciting 'He loves me, he loves me not' does *not* yield accurate information; therefore, we are justified in believing it *does* yield accurate information") or that a conclusion can be drawn from very incomplete information ("John isn't in his room; he must have been taken by extraterrestrials"). In general, arguing from an absence of information or making a case based on very little evidence creates a weak argument.

5. *Ignoring alternatives*. If one claims that the answer is either A or B, when in fact it might also be C–Z, this is the fallacy of ignoring alternatives. "You didn't call me last night as you promised; you either forgot or you purposely didn't call and either way I'm furious with you." It is possible your love or your friend did not call because of illness, being kidnapped, telephone problems, a personal emergency, a confusion about when the call was to be made, etc., etc., etc.

6. *Ad hominem or ad feminam*. This strategy ignores the argument completely and falsely focuses on the person. "No statement by a homosexual can say anything worthwhile about military life" or "If you had a man you would stop making these ridiculous demands for an equality that simply isn't possible or desirable" or "Anyone wearing a tie that bad must be a complete jerk with nothing valuable to say" or "She's a Mormon; I rest my case" or "Anyone from the East (West, South) is so narrow-minded as to have nothing to add to this argument."

7. *Ambiguity*. By using one term in two or more senses or with two or more meanings, you can appear to prove something but in reality prove nothing. "God is love. Love is blind. Stevie Wonder is blind. Therefore, Stevie Wonder is God." Terms must be used consistently.

DISTRICT COURT OF MARYLAND FOR

Case No.:

STATE OF MARYLAND VS

CC#: SID:
Local ID: DL#:
Race: Sex: Ht: Wt: Hair: Eyes:
DOB: Phone(H): (W):

Charge | Statute | Arrest

Charge | Statute | Arrest

ARREST WARRANT ON CHARGING DOCUMENT

STATE OF MARYLAND
TO ANY PEACE OFFICER, Greetings:
YOU ARE ORDERED to arrest and bring before a judicial officer the above-named Defendant as soon as practicable and without unnecessary delay. If a judicial officer is not readily available, this Warrant shall authorize the prisoner's detention until compliance is had with Rule 4-212 and the arresting officer is authorized and required to comply with Rule 4-212.

IF THE DEFENDANT IS NOT IN CUSTODY FOR ANOTHER OFFENSE,
Initial appearance is to be held in county in which Defendant is arrested.
IF THE DEFENDANT IS IN CUSTODY FOR ANOTHER OFFENSE, this Warrant is to be lodged as a detainer for the continued detention of the Defendant for the offense charged in the charging document. When the Defendant is served with a copy of the charging document and Warrant, the Defendant shall be taken before a judical officer of the District Court.

Date: Time: Commissioner:__________ ID:
Given to:

RETURN OF SERVICE

☐ I certify that at ____ M. on ____ at ____
____, I executed this Arrest Warrant by arresting the Defendant and delivered a copy of the Statement of Charges to the Defendant.
☐ I left a copy of the Warrant and Charging Document as a detainer for the continued detention of the Defendant at:
Facility: ____
Location: ____
Signature & Title of Peace Officer: ____
Printed Name of Officer: ____
Agency, Sub-Agency, I.D.: ____
Date: ____

Tracking No.

ARREST WARRANT ON CHARGING DOCUMENT

To obtain a warrant, police need to present evidence or justification for making a search or an arrest.

Police warrant/Photo by Quentin Kardos.

Hume concluded that most of what passes for knowledge is not warranted and is merely belief or feeling. Our certainty about cause and effect, Hume concluded, does not rest on evidence; it is simply a reflection of our psychological need to believe in a predictable world. For Lao-tzu, the Taoist, the whole idea of objective knowledge and logical or empirical warrants seemed to him a distortion of the way things really are.

If we accept the objective character of knowledge and the value of warrants—as the Western world does—then we can divide them into several categories. The laws of identity, noncontradiction, and the excluded middle are examples of *logical warrantability;* these principles are correct, based on the logic of language and thought, and to reject them is to reject all meaning and sense. In contrast, the biological fact that humans are mammals is an example of *semantic warrantability:* a matter of definition or semantics. We have a definition for mammals and humans fit it. Other examples might be "My sister is a girl" or "My bachelor cousin is unmarried." Either these are true or we must amend the definitions of "sister" and "bachelor."

The Pythagorean theorem, sometimes written $a^2 + b^2 = c^2$, represents *systemic warrantability*. This theorem fits into a whole system of axioms and postulates we call Euclidian geometry, all of which are logically interdependent. In theory, if one of these axioms or postulates were erased or cut out from every text, we could derive it again from all the other propositions in the system. This is true of all deductive systems, which operate on principles of logic. The warranty of every proposition within the system ultimately rests on the integrity of the system as a whole. If we were suddenly to find ourselves in a one-dimensional world—a world of points and straight lines and nothing else—the integrity of the deductive system known as Euclidian geometry would unravel.

The historical fact that the United States fought a civil war between 1861 and 1865 has *empirical warrantability;* that is, its warranty is the confirmation of a relationship between an event and the external world. Not so long ago, people who could remember the Civil War were still alive. Today, their descendants have stories, letters, and photographs of relatives in uniforms. The U.S. Government, in its archives, has thousands of records of pay disbursed and rations purchased to feed individual soldiers and entire armies. There are battlefields with monuments erected by those with memories of the events that happened there.

Empiricist philosophers—such as Locke, Berkeley, and Hume—insisted that all knowledge must be derived from empirical experience, by which they seem to have meant direct contact with sense perceptions derived from the external world. Impatient with rationalist philosophers such as Plato and Descartes, they refused to believe that knowledge of the world could be generated by rational processes alone, without reference

TABLE 6.1 WARRANTABILITY *There can be unwarranted true propositions and warranted false propositions, as well as warranted true propositions.*

WARRANTABILITY

	Warranted	Unwarranted
True	Water freezes into ice.	I am the best cook in the class.
False	The Sun revolves around Earth.	The Moon is made of green cheese.

to sense data. Hume, as you recall, demoted all supposed "knowledge" that was not either logically certain or empirically based to the category of meaninglessness.

Another kind of empirical warrantability relates to honestly reported first-person experience. If I tell you that I am thirsty, my experience of being thirsty is what we might call a *testimonial warranty* (assuming, again, that I am representing my experience honestly). If I remark that from an airplane houses and automobiles look like toys, that remark is warranted by my personal experience. It does not make the houses and automobiles toys, but it does warrant both my experience of them and my statement representing that experience. If I say that I love you, my honestly reported experience is my testimonial warranty; your dilemma is deciding whether or not I am honestly representing my experience.

An important aspect of warrants to keep in mind is that they operate independently from truth. Sometimes warrants and truth occur together, but sometimes they do not, and one does not logically imply the other. What this means is that not only can warranted beliefs be true and unwarranted beliefs false, but also warranted beliefs can be false and unwarranted beliefs true. Let's take a look at how this might be so.

At present, we believe the claim that Earth revolves around the Sun to be a *warranted true belief*. A systemic warrant in the form of the Copernican system of astronomy explains the movement of the planets, and on the basis of this warrant we believe a heliocentric, or Sun-centered, system to represent reality. A few centuries ago, people accepted a strong empirical warrant for the belief that Earth is stationary and the Sun moves. Even today, our senses provide us with this apparent warranty, but we now assert that the medieval confidence in the Earth-centered–hypothesis constituted a *warranted false belief* (Table 6.1). A warranty existed—the evidence of common sense and sense experience—but it did not make the theory true.

Family heirlooms like these can help us verify the reality and accuracy of historical facts.

The mess cup and kerchief belonging to Louis Russell LeClear during the U.S. Civil War/Courtesy of the Howard County Historical Society/Photo by Joseph Mitchell.

It is fairly easy to imagine what an unwarranted false belief might look like. "The Moon is made of green cheese" would be one example. We have all had the experience of saying to someone, "You have no proof for that, so it's false." Without a warranty of some kind, you will have a difficult time convincing anyone, even yourself, that something is true. Unwarranted true beliefs are also possible. You may in fact be the tallest, or the most athletic or musical, or the smartest person in your college or university, but you probably have no warranty to that effect.

We can look to warrants as a first step in determining whether or not to believe a truth claim, but as we have seen, statements without warrants can be true and warranted statements can be false. We must make further distinctions to determine whether or not any given statement is true. In fact, Western philosophers have traditionally used three tests to determine truth: the correspondence test, the coherence test, and the pragmatic test. In the next few sections, we will consider each of these in turn.

THE MAKING OF A PHILOSOPHER

Bertrand Arthur William Russell
(1872–1970)

Born in Wales, Russell was the grandson of Lord John Russell who had twice served as prime minister under Queen Victoria. Both his parents died while Bertrand was young, and he was raised by grandparents with John Stuart Mill (see Chapter 9) as an informal godfather. He had a lonely, troubled adolescence and was often on the verge of suicide. He always claimed he was "restrained by the desire to know more mathematics." He was a fellow in the Royal Society and opened an experimental school called the Beacon Hill School. He may be best known popularly for his antiwar views. He was jailed twice—once in 1918 (during World War I) because of a supposedly libelous article he wrote for a pacifist journal, and again in 1961 at the age of eighty-nine because of his campaign for nuclear disarmament.

The Correspondence Test

Put simply, the **correspondence test** demands that, to be true, a proposition must correspond with an object or event. Derived from the correspondence theory of the nature of truth, it asserts that if things are as we say they are, then we have a true state of affairs. If someone tells you snow is falling, you can verify this truth claim by looking out a window. To determine whether it is true that the soup is too salty, you can taste it. This is the commonsense view of truth; it has a strong empirical flavor and probably makes a good deal of sense to you.

correspondence test
a true proposition must correspond with a fact or state of affairs

One of its developers and leading exponents was twentieth-century philosopher Bertrand Russell, who maintained that a world of facts existed independent of our minds. When we speak about reality, Russell says, we order the terms that refer to it. We might say "The Orioles beat the Phillies in the World Series," for example. This would be true if and only if the Orioles won. If we kept the same terms but reversed the order, the resulting statement—"The Phillies beat the Orioles"—would be false (assuming the Orioles won). The difference between the two statements, according to Russell, is that the first corresponds with a fact, whereas the second does not.

There are two possible relationships between a proposition and a fact. Either the proposition is true, meaning the fact to which it refers exists in the world, or it is false, meaning the fact to which it refers does not exist in the world. If I say that Dublin is the capital of France, you will tell me that my statement is false—that Dublin is the capital of the Republic of Ireland and that Paris, not Dublin, is the capital of France. The true version of the proposition must match the fact to which it refers.

What does it actually mean to say that there is (or is not) a correspondence between a proposition and a fact? Suppose I made a statement that unicorns are white and dragons are green. In what sense could we speak about my statement (proposition) as corresponding or not corresponding with a fact, since unicorns and dragons are mythical creatures and thus cannot be said to "exist" in any commonsense definition of the term? What about events from the mythical/historical past? If I say that Arthur was king of Camelot and Guinevere his queen, how would we go about testing the correspondence, or lack of it, between this statement and fact?

Some conditions limit the usefulness of the correspondence test, the most serious of which concerns the assumption upon which the correspondence theory of truth rests—namely, that there is a mind-independent reality. The correspondence test posits an external world that exists "out there" and is available for comparison with statements made about it, but this realist view is not universally accepted. Kant, for instance, argued that reality, having been filtered through the intuitions of space and time and through the shaping categories of the mind as well, was not available for mind-independent reference. We can, he observed, never know things in themselves, or *noumena,* but only things as they appear to us (i.e., phenomena).

If Kant is correct, then there is no world "out there" that we can know about; the only knowable reality is the one in our heads. Since Kant assumes all of us share the same world in our heads, because we share the same mental categories, he asserts that we can make statements about the world that correspond to the world *as we experience it.*

Philosopher W. V. O. Quine goes further. He suggests that physical objects may be no more than **theoretical posits**—that in response to sense data we hypothesize the existence of physical objects to make sense of our experiences. Neurophysiologists provide some evidence for this view. Each of us has a blind spot in each eye, through which the optic nerve passes as it takes visual stimuli from the retina to the brain. Most of the time we are completely unaware of this, because our brains fill in the image with what seems to make sense—more blue sky, more human skin, a continuation of pattern and shape.

theoretical posits *our mental construction of physical objects in an attempt to make sense of our experience, according to Quine*

For Quine, only sense data are real; the rest we create out of our need to make sense of the world. This is also reminiscent of Hume, who insisted that we imagine we see cause and effect because of a similar psychological need. Hume's theory was that we cannot live without predictability and order; Quine's theory is that we cannot live without sense. In both cases our brains provide what we need on a feeling level, but this is a far cry from philosophical realism.

According to the **realist/representationalist view** upon which the correspondence test rests, actual states of affairs exist in reality and true beliefs accurately represent them. Proponents of the **antirepresentationalist view** counter that, because of the egocentric predicament, no one can climb outside his or her own perspective long enough to speak about the world "as it really is." Because each of us is limited to our own private perspective, it makes no sense, according to twentieth-century philosophers such as Richard Rorty, to speak about the mind or even language as representing reality.

realist/representationalist view *there is an external world outside our minds to which we may appeal for verification*

antirepresentationalist view *we are limited by our own perspective and cannot rationally speak about a world that exists outside it*

When we say a belief is true, Rorty asserts, what we really mean is that we are applauding the belief for having been proved in terms of our own standards of rationality. The entire process of comparing a belief against a truth standard is going on within us because there is no possibility of comparison with something outside us. Antirepresentationalists think we should start being honest about what we can and cannot do and stop pretending that "the world as it really is" is available for comparison.

If the reality of an external world is in doubt, it seems we must seek alternative methods of truth verification. Under conditions in which the correspondence test seems inadequate or inappropriate, Western philosophers have used a second truth test that appears to bypass the need for an external world of reality.

The Coherence Test

coherence test *measures coherence and consistency among statements within a system*

The **coherence test** of truth measures coherence and consistency among statements within a system. According to the coherence theory of truth, a belief or statement is true if and only if it *coheres* (literally, "sticks together") with other beliefs that together form a comprehensive account of reality.

If you have ever served on a jury, you have been called upon to use the truth test that derives from this theory, whether or not you accept the coherence theory of truth. Each of the two attorneys, representing the prosecution and the defense, tries to construct as coherent a system as possible by ordering existing facts in a particular way. The task of the jury is to decide which has done a more effective job. In which case do the facts seem to cohere, or hang together, more effectively? Often the evidence itself is not at issue, but rather the relationship among the facts that each attorney assembles and constructs.

Much of mathematics operates from this kind of test. In our example of the Pythagorean theorem, the statement that the square of the hypotenuse of a right triangle is equal to the sum of the squares of the two other sides is judged to be true because it fits so well with other geometric statements. If we did not know that was an accepted theorem, we might subject it to the coherence test to determine how well it fits with other things we know about lines and angles and particularly about the properties of triangles. Because we know that the sum of the interior angles in a triangle always equals 180 degrees, or two right angles, we know that the right angle in a right triangle equals 90 degrees and the other two angles must total the other 90. Given this, it seems both coherent and consistent to assert a similar relationship between the line opposite the right angle (the hypotenuse) and the other two lines.

Science, too, offers many examples of apparently coherent systems. Indeed, we will see later that it is in the nature of science to construct *paradigms,* or tightly coherent explanations of reality. One example of a paradigm is the theory of quantum mechanics we discussed in Chapter 2. Although at first quantum theory clashed with existing scientific explanations, it has been verified as a coherent explanation of reality in the world of the very small. To describe atoms and their smaller constituent parts today, one must speak from within the paradigm of quantum mechanics.

Often there are competing, even conflicting paradigms that purport to explain the same reality. Two hundred years ago, for example, we believed the body was controlled by so-called humors; their balance meant health and their imbalance meant illness. If choler, the element representing anger or heat, were out of balance, the physician might try bloodletting. The prescription made perfect sense within the coherent theory of diseases and their cures then popular. Today, we subscribe to the *germ theory* of disease, and our repertoire of defenses includes antibiotics designed to kill germs.

Today most of us would not dream of submitting to bloodletting, even though some people get better after such a practice. Blowfly maggots do a better job of eating dead tissue and the gangrene-producing bacteria in it than any modern scientific procedures, including aggressive drug therapy.[1]

Even though patients improve, the treatment does not fit our current model of medical theory. These graphic, perhaps repulsive, examples point us to one of the weaknesses of the coherence test. Where there are competing and apparently equally coherent models, how do we choose among them? Indeed, taking a very broad view, it is difficult to imagine any statement that does not fit into one coherent system or another. So, what does it really mean to speak of this as the coherence test of truth?

A related problem is that even if all the statements in a system cohere beautifully, what guarantees the truth of the whole system? Each belief may be verified for coherence with the other beliefs within the system, but such verification does not prevent the entire system from being wrong. Until about 500 years ago, a very coherent system insisted that Earth was flat. When people looked in any direction, their eyes fell on the horizon, the place where land (or water) and sky meet, and the line they saw was always flat.

For many people who never traveled more than a few miles from the place of their birth, the 20 or so square miles visible in all four directions constituted the known world—and it certainly looked flat. If the Sun dropped below a flat line and disappeared, what else could that mean except that Earth ended at that point? By every reasonable measure and piece of evidence then, Earth was flat. No wonder people warned Columbus that his ships would sail off the edge of the world before reaching the wonders of Cathay. Without the careful distinctions that arise from critically examining competing systems, consistent error may seem just as coherent as consistent truth.

Are we not at some point required to find out whether any part of the system (or the system as a whole) connects with reality (assuming that reality exists)? If we insist on correspondence, we find ourselves back where we started. If we do not, we may be forced to join the Flat Earth Society. There is a third possibility: the pragmatic test.

The Pragmatic Test

The **pragmatic test** of truth derives from the distinctly American contribution to philosophy known as *pragmatism,* perhaps best embodied in popular culture by former President Harry Truman, who was famous for saying "I'm from Missouri, show me!" What is real, according to the pragmatic theory of truth, is what works. Thus, pragmatists care more about results than theories; something is true, they say, if it makes a difference, if its power to explain clarifies our understanding and changes our lives.

Here's a little bottom-line nineteenth-century American pragmatism for you from William James, the philosopher who insisted we choose between theism and atheism because the decision would make a difference in the way we lived our lives (see Chapter 4): "Grant an idea or belief to be true, what concrete difference will its being true make in any one's actual life . . . What, in short, is the truth's cash-value in experiential terms?"[2] Whether Earth is flat or spherical may not make much difference to me, but whether or not you love me certainly does; the latter truth has a real "cash-value" in terms of my lived experience.

THE MAKING OF A PHILOSOPHER

William James
(1842–1910)

Born into a family with wide-ranging cultural and intellectual interests, William James and his brother, the novelist Henry James, enjoyed frequent trips to Europe and a feeling of comfort in the entire Atlantic community. Henry James, Sr., was a theologian and philosophical writer. As a young man, William pursued a career as a painter, and—although he later turned to medicine, the natural sciences, and eventually philosophy—he retained the ability to capture in words the immediateness of a situation (as an artist might) and the discipline of using language exactly (as a scientist must). His book *Pragmatism* and his other writings have come to represent not only pragmatism but also American thought in general. They are characterized by an emphasis on immediate, concrete experience, and they recognize that no philosopher can set his or her own temperament aside—even though many try to cite "impersonal reasons only" for the conclusions they draw. Pragmatism, James believed, is like a corridor opening into many rooms. Since it is neutral, it can lead to many results.

pragmatic test *what is true is what works*

THE MAKING OF A PHILOSOPHER

Charles Sanders Peirce
(1839–1914)

The son of a Harvard professor—Benjamin Peirce, who was probably the premier American mathematician of his day—young Charles developed an early interest in mathematics and logic. Before turning to philosophy, he worked for ten years in a chemistry lab. It was his interest in exact sciences like chemistry and in logic that led him finally to philosophy. After graduating from Harvard in 1859, Peirce did some college lecturing—at Harvard (1864–1865 and 1869–1870) and at Johns Hopkins University in Baltimore (1879–1884)—but his independent and even rebellious nature made universities reluctant to hire him as a professor. Instead, he worked for thirty years as a physicist with the U.S. Coast Guard and Geodetic Survey. Peirce receives the credit for developing and bringing to clarity the ideas that became the core of pragmatism. Most of this work was done in informal gatherings of the "metaphysical club" in Cambridge, Massachusetts, where he conversed with Justice Oliver Wendell Holmes, philosopher William James, and others.

From the beginning of their history, Americans have seen themselves as more practical and down to earth than the worn-out (in their opinion) European societies they had left behind. While Europe was fighting its dynastic wars and debating between rationalism and empiricism, Americans saw themselves as carving a society out of the wilderness. Lacking easy access to ready-made materials, they learned to "make do," and the "Yankee ingenuity" in which they took so much pride was a reflection of their ability to use whatever was at hand to solve a problem. Moving ever westward, Americans saw themselves as living on the "frontier" of civilization, both literally and figuratively.

Philosophical pragmatism was developed primarily by three nineteenth-century American philosophers who were weary of the debate between idealism and materialism (see Chapter 2), which seemed to them only slightly more valuable or interesting than a discussion of how many angels can dance on the head of a pin. The outcome of such a debate, they felt, would make no difference in most people's lives. Charles Sanders Peirce, William James, and John Dewey offered the philosophical system of pragmatism as an alternative.

For Peirce, truth is revealed in practical experience with concrete things, and beliefs are really "rules for action." Thinking is but one step on the road to action. When we speak about truth, Peirce believed, what we really mean is that belief in a particular proposition would, "with sufficient experience and reflection," lead us to action that will in turn satisfy our desires. If you tell someone that philosophy is difficult or interesting, that assessment may be "true" for you, but it can never be true for the person you tell unless he or she takes a philosophy course or begins reading philosophy books. Truth is revealed through lived experience rather than through logical proofs or laboratory experiments.

William James developed this idea into a truth test for the proposition "God exists." James advised us that being an agnostic was not a viable option, for deciding to believe or not to believe in God is, in his view, a "live, forced, momentous option." In other words, whether you do or do not believe in God makes a tremendous difference in your lived experience. James applied Peirce's original principle to a specific philosophical problem.

To understand the truth test aspect of this theory, we must first understand James's definition of truth. Like all pragmatists, James rejected the traditional idea of truth as absolute and unchanging; instead, he saw truth as relative and dynamic. In other words, truth is not a fixed or static quality but a part of the unfolding meaning that lived experience gives to something. "Truth *happens* to an idea," James wrote; "it *becomes* true, is *made* true by events."[3] Thus, the truth of our assertion that democracy is the best form of government will be found, or not found, in our lived experience.

Pragmatism arose as a conscious rejection of what seemed to be stagnant methods then in use in philosophy. Pragmatism was a turning away from abstraction and a turning "towards concreteness and adequacy, towards facts, towards action, towards power."[4] For a pragmatist like James, the definition of a true idea is a very straightforward one: "True ideas are those that we can assimilate, validate, corroborate and verify. False ideas are those that we can not."[5]

Our third pragmatist, John Dewey, applied his ideas to education and is known as an advocate of *learning by doing*. One of Dewey's chief objections concerns the Cartesian separation of mind and body and its consequent negative results in the field of education:

> More than anything else it explains the separation of theory and practice, of thought and action. The result is a so-called cultural education which tends to be academic and pedantic, and in any case aloof from the concerns of life, and an industrial and manual education which at best gives command of tools and means without intelligent grasp of purposes and ends.[6]

Both extremes (one addresses the mind; the other, the body) are distortions because they fail to further the pragmatic goal of integrating intellectual learning with lived experience. The false separation of thinking and action that is our legacy from Descartes results, Dewey argued, in an inadequate education for both academics and technicians.

Properly understood, education "is a constant reorganizing or reconstructing of experience."[7] In its ideal form, there is a *progressive* quality to it. At the beginning, the study of any subject will focus on materials available in ordinary life experience. Gradually, the learner's experiences will modulate from a "social and human center toward a more objective intellectual scheme of organization . . ."[8]

All of this assumes the integration of theory and practice. "When education is based on theory and practice upon experience, it goes without saying that the organized subject-matter of the adult and the specialist cannot provide the starting point."[9] Learners must always begin with their own experiences. If theory and practice travel different paths, there may be no place where the beginner and the expert can meet—no place of connection possible between teacher and student. Thus, educational pragmatism insists that theory must always be based in practice.

As the most fundamental discipline, philosophy, in Dewey's judgment, had a critical role to play in shaping our collective intellectual life. He was even willing to define philosophy as "the general theory of education."[10] To be effective, however, a philosophy "and its program of values must take effect in conduct."[11] In other words, it must pass the pragmatic test:

> A first-rate test of the value of any philosophy which is offered us is this: Does it end in conclusions which, when they are referred back to ordinary life-experiences and their predicaments, render them more significant, more luminous to us, and make our dealings with them more fruitful?[12]

The pragmatic test is perhaps most easily applicable in response to statements involving values and emotions. Correspondence and coherence tests are not likely to do us much good in testing the truth of statements

THE MAKING OF A PHILOSOPHER

John Dewey
(1859-1952)

Born in Burlington, Vermont, Dewey soon left the East to venture west, spending nearly twenty years teaching at the universities of Minnesota, Michigan, and Chicago, before returning east to join and later lead the philosophy department at Columbia University. He had seen a good deal of the continent, and his philosophy—when he came to write it—reflected all of it. He apparently never lost a kind of rustic simplicity, which he learned in Vermont, and he retained a respect for the naturalism that characterized much of America at the turn of the century. He put his philosophy to work on educational reform, insisting that book learning should never take place in isolation from practice. Schools should teach what students need to know to be productive and happy in an industrial democracy; education, far from being a once-and-for-all enterprise, should be a process of continual, lifelong growth and illumination. At the celebration of his ninetieth birthday, Dewey remained optimistic. To lose faith in each other would be, he thought, to lose faith in ourselves, and that he labeled "the unforgivable sin."

such as "I love you," but it may be very easy to see the practical difference this declaration can make in a person's life. If you are willing to consider my welfare in addition to your own, to give me your time and attention and to listen when I need to talk, I may very well conclude that you do love me. If instead you make your declaration of love but continue to focus entirely on your own needs and to ignore mine, I may conclude that your declaration is nothing more than words; it will have failed the pragmatic test of truth.

The truth will set you free. But first it will make you miserable.
SEVENTIES POSTER

The biggest difficulty with pragmatism is that it is frequently unclear about the actual meaning of such terms as *reality* and *truth,* and so critics fault pragmatists for fuzzy thinking. An interesting variation on the pragmatic test among the Ewe people of Ghana takes a step in overcoming this objection.

The Ewe Creativity Test

In the creativity, or *nyanono,* theory of truth from West Africa, it is not only "the workability of an idea that makes it true, but its power to bring about a better human situation."[13] In the Ewe word *nyano, nya* is the root word for "truth," and *no* represents "woman, mother, the female principle associated with life, creativity, growth." Used as a term for truth, *nyano* means that a statement is alive with creative power. One way to command a person to speak the truth in Ewe is to say *do nyanono,* meaning "plant the truth" (Figure 6.2). The understanding is that if the statement is the truth, it will "germinate, grow and bear fruit."[14] Falsehood, being dead, does not have the power to germinate and grow.

creativity test *what is true is what promotes life and growth, according to the Ewe*

In the *nyano* or **creativity test** of truth, it is not enough that truth work in a pragmatic way; truth must also bear fruit. Using only the pragmatic test, a student might be tempted to conclude that "cheating is good" because he or she might have gotten a better grade on a test or paper by cheating. The richer rendering of the *nyano* truth theory, however, helps us realize that although cheating might work in the short term, it certainly will not generate better life situations over time.[15]

Knowing the truth is finally a matter of doing the truth . . . that is, knowledge is alive . . . and doing the truth takes courage and demands risks.
DR. ELIZABETH TIDBALL

Like English, the Ewe language also has a correspondence test and a coherence test of truth claims. But, because in Ewe culture truth is seen as the highest spiritual value, the creativity test offers an added dimension to the pragmatic test. If truth is life promoting and falsehood leads to death, it is said that the person who loves truth will live a long life—a very pragmatic reward.

It is probably clear to you by now that each of these theories makes sense under certain conditions but that none is universally applicable to all times, places, and situations. When we are considering empirical questions, the correspondence test may be of greatest value; logical, semantic, and systemic truth can be evaluated most easily using the coherence test; and value judgments must pass the pragmatic test of truth, and perhaps the creativity test as well.

FIGURE 6.2 *DO NYANONO* ("PLANT THE TRUTH") *If you plant the truth, it will grow—falsehood will not.*

Truth and the Really Real

What we clearly want to know is the truth about reality. Both our own true nature and the true nature of external reality matter to us. Let's look now at two very different attempts to ascertain what is really real—Zen Buddhism and Christianity—to see how truth is tested in each of them.

Truth in Zen

Like the Buddhism from which it is derived, Zen Buddhism does not assert the existence of a divine being. In fact, Zen has only one "goal": the direct experience of what is. Truth cannot be discovered in any objective way, and both warranties and truth tests badly miss the point. What we need to do is still our mental chatter and experience what is right in front of us *directly*—without the intervention of words and concepts. If we can get beyond words and concepts to direct experience, then and only then is truth possible.

As the fletcher whittles
and makes straight his
arrows,
so the master directs his
straying thoughts
THE BUDDHA

Truth is the present—past and future do not exist—and truth is the everyday, the mundane, the earthy: doing our work, eating our food. As the Zen masters put it: Draw water, chop wood. Live your ordinary life, but be there for the experience. If you are present—instead of letting your idea of something predetermine what you experience—you may be able to see truly. The only warranty is your own experience.

No one can explain Zen to you, not even the most fully enlightened person (or perhaps especially such a person), because to explain something is to know it and speak about it from the outside. Truth lives instead on the inside, at the heart of life, and it must be experienced directly rather than talked about. There is no substitute for experience—your only entry point for a true encounter with the way things are.

Unarmed truth is the most
powerful thing in the
universe.
MARTIN LUTHER KING, JR.

Koans *are intended to stop logical thought.*

Zen Comics by Joanna Salajan. Used with permission.

In contrast with religions that rely on sacred texts, Zen insists that the way to truth is not through reading or instruction. In fact, there is a real danger that teachers and concepts can get in the way, for it is easy to confuse the message with the messenger. If the master points at the Moon, do not confuse the master's finger with the Moon. Put in its most extreme form: "If you meet the Buddha on the road, kill him." All concepts—even the concept of the Buddha, the Enlightened One—that interfere with your direct experience can only get in your way; therefore, you must "kill" them. Seek instead the direct uncovering of truth.

This excerpt from Antoine de Saint-Exupery's *The Little Prince* may help us understand the Zen approach to truth. Although the story of "taming the fox" is primarily a story of intimacy, it provides a metaphor for the process of apprehending truth about what is. We might think of the fox as the way things are and taming as the process of quieting our minds to become one with it:

> [The fox said] "To you, I am nothing more than a fox like a hundred thousand other foxes. But if you tame me, then we shall need each other. To me, you will be unique in all the world. To you, I shall be unique in all the world . . . One only understands the things that one tames," said the fox.[16]

Truth is the vital breath of beauty; beauty is the outward form of truth.
GRACE AGUILAR

In the process of taming (learning the truth), you must first sit very far away from your fox (the way things are). The next day you may be able to move a little closer, but you must still sit quietly and wait. Day after day you move closer; if you are patient, focused, and attentive enough, one day you will recognize that your fox has been tamed (and that you have been tamed by your fox). Practice in Zen means sitting meditation, or *zazen*. Every day Zen monks, nuns, and others spend hours sitting, often facing a wall. The first goal is to quiet the mind and gain control over it.

In Zen, studying and trying hard to "get it" are the things most likely to keep you from ever getting it. The truth cannot be commanded to appear; it cannot be conquered by reading, studying, and talking. You must patiently sit, like the Little Prince, until you have tamed your mind. Like the fox, truth will only open itself to you through patient, persistent, direct experience.

So, the Zen method of seeking truth is not the traditional Western method of study: reading and thinking, listening to and learning from experts. Indeed, Zen masters are known for saying very little or nothing. They might sit in stony silence or dismiss you, or even hit you if you give a wrongheaded answer. The chief teaching method of the Rinzai branch of Zen is the ***koan***—a kind of riddle. One of the best known is this: "You know the sound made by two hands clapping. What is the sound of one hand clapping?" *Koans* are not meant to be answered in the ordinary way; they are instead designed to *stop* logical, analytical, discursive thought and force you into a direct encounter with what is.

koan *[KO ahn] a Zen riddle designed to stop rational, discursive thought in order to permit or force the direct experience of what is*

A Zen master who knows you well may assign you a *koan*. The best way to "attack" a *koan* is not to think about it and try to figure out what it means. The best way to begin may be to meditate, to empty your mind of all thought. If you persist, you may catch a glimpse of what is. Truth may reveal itself to you. Zen practitioners use **sitting** in silent meditation every day to quiet the mind and become receptive to experiencing the truth about the way things are.

sitting *the Zen practice of silent meditation, designed to quiet the mind*

This is a much more difficult task than you might imagine. If you have never done so, try sitting quietly for five minutes and thinking about nothing. It is perfectly all right to notice the bird singing or even the refrigerator motor humming, but "replaying" the jingle from the TV commercial or reviewing your "to do" list or your plans for the rest of the day or evening is off limits; all thoughts must go. If you are like most people, you will find it extraordinarily difficult to control your own mind. Zen advocates do not find anything wrong with thinking; it is very useful for solving all kinds of complex problems, especially scientific and technical ones, and it has a clear and important role to play in the world. They just reject its value in finding the truth about existence.

The Buddha was known for delivering sermons with no words. The emptiness of his silence created a meditative space in which his listeners sometimes "heard" important truths. His own enlightenment—coming to grips with the truth about what is and what is not—occurred when he sat silently all night, beneath the bodhi tree, vowing not to get up until he became enlightened. In the same way, Kasyapa became enlightened when the Buddha simply held up a flower.

Man will occasionally stumble over the truth, but usually manages to pick himself up, walk over or around it, and carry on.
WINSTON S. CHURCHILL

Truth is right there, at the heart of the universe, waiting to be experienced. Warranties and truth tests will be useless. You will never find truth by walking around it, observing it from the outside and trying to analyze it. You must come face to face with it, so to speak. The best way to do this is to have what is called **beginner's mind.** Consider this description of how to do calligraphy:

beginner's mind *according to Zen, the state of openness in which one can directly access the truth about what is*

> The Zen way of calligraphy is to write in the most straightforward, simple way as if you were a beginner, not trying to make something skillful or beautiful, but simply writing with full attention as if you were writing for the first time; then your full nature will be in it.[17]

When we think we already know the truth about what is, we become expert at life and believe we have nothing much to learn from it. Think about the first time you drove a car. Every action was important, and you approached the task with full concentration. Once things have moved to the automatic level, you really do not need to "be there." That may be fine for driving, but it is not so good for living. If our experience of existence moves to the automatic level, we may miss it and the truth it has to tell us.

Zen is unique in urging people to look for truth in direct experience rather than in sacred texts. By contrast, three religions that originated in the Middle East locate truth within a sacred book, and each urges the study of texts as one method of learning the truth about reality.

PHILOSOPHERS SPEAK FOR THEMSELVES
Hadewijch of Antwerp (a mystical vision)

One Christmas night, when I was lying in bed in a very depressed frame of mind, I was suddenly taken up in the spirit. There I saw a very deep whirlpool, wide and extremely dark. And in this vast abyss all things were included, packed together and compressed. The darkness illuminated and penetrated everything. The unfathomable abyss was so deep and so high that nobody could reach it. I shall not describe it now, for it is not the moment to speak of it, and I cannot put into words what is indescribable. Moreover, I would not have time to do so, for I saw many other things: all the omnipotence of our Beloved. I saw the Lamb take possession of our Loved One. In the vast spaces I looked upon festivities, such as David moving his fingers over the harp strings. Then I saw a Child being born in the secret part of loving souls, souls hidden from their own eyes in the deep abyss of which I speak, and lacking nothing, except to be lost forever in this abyss. I perceived the forms of many souls, according to what the life of each had been. Those I saw and had already known [in life] remained familiar to me and those I had not known before became familiar to me; I received interior knowledge about some and also exterior knowledge about a great many. And some I knew inwardly, although I had never seen them outwardly . . .

Eleventh Vision, from *Women Mystics in Medieval Europe,* Emilie Zum Brunn & Georgette Epiney-Burgard, eds., translated from the French by Sheila Hughes (New York: Paragon House, 1989).

For Jews and Christians, these Scriptures provide access to God's truth.

Silver-covered Torah/Courtesy of Sara Baum/Photo by Quentin Kardos.

Truth in Religions of the Book

In Judaism, Christianity, and Islam, the so-called religions of the Book, the Book (Torah, Bible, or Qur'an) is regarded as the source of truth. God or Allah is believed to have communicated the words of truth that are recorded in the Book. When debates in philosophy classes reach a point at which a theist says, "It's true because God says so" or "It's true because it's in the Bible," an atheist, or an agnostic, or a theistic philosophy student replies, "In philosophy, that is not enough."

As we have observed, this is one of the major points of departure between theology and philosophy. For theists, however, God or the Bible can provide the ultimate warranty. For believers, a sacred text or the words and deeds of a religious leader can offer lessons in truth. Revelation, the direct revealing of truth by a divine figure, has a powerful warranty for those who accept it.

Mystics, such as Mechtilde of Magdeburg and Hildegard of Bingen (whom we met in Chapter 4), asserted a truth claim based on their direct, personal, intuitive experience of the divine. Notice that this is quite different from the Zen path of direct, personal, intuitive experience of everyday existence. In both cases truth is possible, but mystics claim access to a reality that lies beyond the ordinary, everyday one. Zen insists there is only the everyday one—truly seen.

Nearly every day, between 1376 and 1380, Catherine of Siena, after receiving Holy Communion, went into a trancelike state and spoke with God in a voice quite different from her ordinary one. She believed these mystical experiences to be revelations of truth. In a letter to another nun, Catherine explains that truth lies:

> . . . where the soul tastes the ineffable love that God has for his creature, shown to us through that Word who ran, like someone in love, to the shameful death of the cross, for the honor of the father and our salvation. When the soul has known this truth with perfect light, it rises above itself . . .[18]

Catherine used what she believed to be her access to divine truth to mediate when the Vatican declared war on Florence. Although this effort ultimately failed, she became advisor to Pope Gregory XI, once persuading him to walk barefoot to the Vatican as an act of penitence.[19] Convincing a powerful person like the pope that he needed to acknowledge and share her sense of sin was clearly very risky business, but Catherine stayed alive and kept her freedom because she claimed God as her warranty in a way that was credible to the powerful Church hierarchy.

As we saw in Chapter 4, a person who claims to speak with the authority of God behind him or her can be seen (by those who share these assumptions) to have a powerful truth claim. Catherine's right to speak derived not from her own insights but from the revelations of God she claimed to have received during her mystical trances. Her case seemed strengthened when marks resembling the nail wounds of Christ (called the stigmata) mysteriously appeared on her body. Only an extremely holy person, it was believed, would be marked by God in such a way. Catherine of Siena was named a Doctor of the Church in 1970 (one of only three women ever to receive this honor; the other two were Teresa of Avila and Thérèse of Lisieux, both mystics who also claimed direct revelation of truth from God).[20]

Women like Catherine of Siena made truth claims based on belief in an extraordinary reality to which they had access through mystical experience. Let's turn now to a more ordinary kind of reality—the subject matter of science, history, and linguistics—to examine how truth claims are made and tested in each of these fields of study.

THE MAKING OF A PHILOSOPHER

Catherine of Siena
(1347?–1380)

Catarina Benincasa was born in the city of Siena and died in Rome. She had her first vision while still a young girl. When she joined a religious order, she chose not to live in a convent. Instead, she lived as a recluse in her parents' home. Since she had received no formal education, she was illiterate at the time she took her vows. Often, she dictated what she had learned from her mystical visions to a group of secretaries. In 1370 she received what she interpreted as a divine command to go out into the world and save souls. Five years later she received the stigmata, the marks of the wounds of Christ, and this greatly increased her credibility. Because she believed she conveyed the will of God, Catherine became bold enough to intervene in the dispute between Pope Gregory XI and the city of Florence. She did persuade the pope to return to Rome from Avignon in France. This done, she composed the *Dialogue,* her major visionary work, and died at the age of thirty-three.

Truth in Science

The search for truth in science would seem to be a straightforward enterprise. After all, science is the realm of empirical data and logical theory in which ideas are tested and compared with the real world, so truth must be easy to spot and even easier to define. And aren't scientists, more than the rest of us, committed to remaining objective, even dispassionate? Not exactly, according to Thomas Kuhn, whose 1970 book *The Structure of Scientific Revolutions* revealed a much more complex picture of how scientific statements are confirmed or accepted as true within the scientific community. According to Kuhn, science operates within a prevailing paradigm—a shared assumption or view of what the world is like—and this paradigm determines how questions of truth will be asked and answered.

The Nature of Paradigms

During the period of what Kuhn calls *normal science,* students learn the prevailing paradigm in college, textbooks are written to reflect that paradigm, and anything that does not fit into it is more or less ignored. "Normal science . . . often suppresses fundamental novelties because they are necessarily subversive of its basic commitments."[21] As an explanation of the world, a **paradigm** is highly coherent, and it becomes the truth test in the field in which it operates. Let's look at what this means.

paradigm *according to Kuhn, a model that produces a coherent tradition of scientific research*

Before the development of a paradigm, various competing explanations of reality, each based on the facts at hand, exist in the scientific community; in the absence of an accepted paradigm, "all of the facts that could possibly pertain to the development of a given science are likely to seem equally relevant."[22] People looking at the same range of phenomena (although not necessarily the same phenomena) tend to interpret their meaning differently, but once a spectacular advancement gives one theory about the phenomena widespread acceptance, a paradigm has been created.

"To be accepted as a paradigm, a theory must seem better than its competitors, but it need not, and in fact never does, explain all the facts with which it can be confronted." The new paradigm does, however, more rigidly define the field in which it operates. "Those unwilling or unable to accommodate their work to it must proceed in isolation or attach themselves to some other group."[23] Once agreement has been reached, writers of textbooks then explain the field in terms of the new paradigm, and researchers—operating from within the paradigm—take it as their starting point.

Because the paradigm has already been justified in the academic community and by textbooks and teaching methods, individual scientists are free to explore specialized implications of the new theory (without having to justify the theory itself). Publications are addressed to colleagues "whose knowledge of a shared paradigm can be assumed and who prove to be the only ones able to read the papers addressed to them."[24] What this means for the general public, and even for other members of the scientific community, is that the paradigm is accepted as a given within a particular field and assumed without being explained. Reading about and analyzing scientific explanations of reality becomes possible only within the highly specialized knowledge and methods of the prevailing paradigm.

Only when a problem that ought to be solvable within the rules of the paradigm is not or a piece of equipment, designed for "normal research," fails to perform as expected does a scientific revolution occur. (For a simple exercise that illustrates this point, see Figures 6.3 and 6.4.) *Scientific revolutions* are the "tradition-shattering complements to the tradition-bound activity of normal science."[25] After a revolution, an existing paradigm is replaced "in whole or in part by an incompatible new one."[26] From the point of view of philosophy, what is most interesting is that the truth test applied is both a coherence test and a correspondence test. Scientists never reject one paradigm without accepting another at the same time, and the decision to do so rests on "the comparison of both paradigms with nature and with each other."[27]

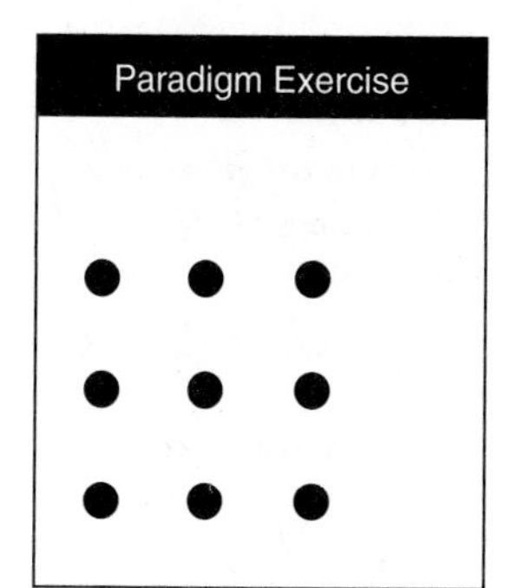

FIGURE 6.3 NINE-DOT PROBLEM *Using four lines, hit all nine dots without lifting your pencil from the page. The answer appears in Figure 6.4.*

Before Copernicus described the Sun-centered view of our solar system we accept today, the prevailing paradigm—Ptolemy's commonsense Earth-centered system, developed between 200 B.C.E. and 200 C.E.—predicted the changing positions of stars and planets well enough, but the predictions never quite matched the best data gathered by observation. Ptolemy's successors continued to make minor adjustments to his system of "compounded circles" to make the theory more closely match observed reality. By the time of Copernicus, however, the calculations were very cumbersome and unwieldy. Nothing that complex, it seemed, could really describe how things actually are.

The crisis that was produced when Ptolemy's theory became increasingly difficult to apply to reality led to what we know as the *Copernican revolution*. Once the Sun was accepted as the center of the solar system, many of the difficulties of the Ptolemaic Earth-centered system simply disappeared. Copernicus's explanation was finally accepted because his mathematical calculations and formulas were so much simpler. The revolution led to a new period of what Kuhn calls normal science, in which relatively detailed puzzles within the theory continue to be explored, but the paradigm remains intact.

From the point of view of philosophy, the implications of a paradigm shift can be enormous. If Earth is no longer the center of the universe, but merely one of a group of planets circling the Sun, our worldview—including Earth as the unique site of human creation and salvation—must change to accommodate this new understanding. This helps explain why the Roman Catholic Church invested so much energy into suppressing this new paradigm and waited until late in the twentieth century to officially grant that Galileo's Copernican views were correct after all. What was at stake was not merely a scientific debate over theory but the very way we see ourselves in relation to the rest of the cosmos.

The impact of paradigms on our ability to test for truth in science can be significant. Because the paradigm structures how we see the world, truth tests must operate from within it; this makes the objectivity for which science is known much more difficult to achieve.

Truth Tests

Once accepted, a paradigm, as we have observed, becomes *the* explanation for a range of phenomena. Conflicting data and theories are ignored or discredited until it is no longer possible to do so. "Normal science," Kuhn says, "does not aim at novelties of fact or theory and, when successful, finds none."[28] Even when one paradigm replaces another, the newer one does not disprove the coherence of the former one. Ptolemy's theory remains coherent. Here we see one of the shortcomings of the coherence

Who built the Seven Gates of Thebes?
The books are filled with the names of kings
Was it kings who hauled the craggy blocks of stone?
BERTOLT BRECHT

test of truth in science. Two theories can be consistent and apparently coherent, and one is judged to more accurately *correspond* with reality—but only from within the rules of the new paradigm.

Reality is always filtered for us through the lens of the version of it we currently accept. This is a very Kantian notion of perception. The paradigm provides a kind of mental category through which we interpret our perceptions of the world. We may be convinced that cause and effect exist or that the Sun (and not Earth) is the center of our solar system, and these beliefs may be thoroughly justified, according to the paradigm that provides the internal system of verification in our heads. But if we have already "agreed to agree" on a paradigm, then we have no way to independently prove the correspondence of those beliefs with the real world. Kuhn has provided support for Kant's claim that "mind is the lawgiver to nature," rather than the other way around.

Let's look at how scientists decide to accept one paradigm over another and to reject other apparently coherent systems as "unscientific." Both astrology and creationism appear to some people to provide coherent explanations of reality. What scientists find lacking in these two systems is the deep connections among underlying subsystems and the capacity to explain wide ranges of phenomena that they insist on in a fully coherent scientific paradigm. A completely coherent system, scientists say, is superior to a superficially coherent one. For people outside a field, however, such comparisons are nearly impossible to make.

Another difficulty is that both theories accepted by the scientific community (like quantum mechanics) and those rejected by the scientific community (like astrology and creationism) fail the correspondence test of truth. Only from within quantum mechanics, astrology, and creationism do the truth claims of the system make sense. If we cannot apply the coherence test and the correspondence test is not appropriate, we are left with the pragmatic test. Although this test apparently works for particle physicists, as we observed in discussing quantum mechanics (see Chapter 2), most of us are unable to see the "cash value" of quantum mechanics in our own lives. The nonexpert seems doomed to accept on "faith" the judgments of the scientific community as expressed in its prevailing paradigms.

Paradigms exist in all academic fields. In history, the tension that exists among paradigms is reflected in the reciprocal relationship between the present and the past. Although they strive for objectivity, as scientists do, historians know that they inevitably see the past through the lens formed by the concerns of the present.

Truth in History

When we begin to talk about truth in history, it is a little easier to see from the start that we are on a slippery slope. Unlike science, history cannot claim to speak in a purely logical and empirical way. Historians are aware that their field is very largely governed by interpretation and that interpretations change over time. Even so apparently simple a matter as what constitutes history has undergone a significant revision during the past few decades.

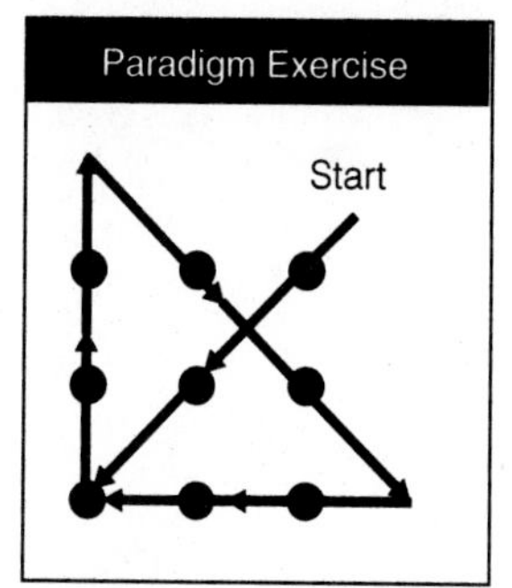

FIGURE 6.4 ANSWER TO THE NINE-DOT PROBLEM *If the paradigm requires your pencil not to extend beyond the dots, the puzzle cannot be solved—to solve it you must break the paradigm.*

The Changing Definition of History

Fewer than fifty years ago, historians were more or less in agreement about what constituted history: The story of the past could best be told in terms of kings, presidents, battles, and political events. The "great man" theory of history asserted that history was molded by great men rather than the reverse. Whereas a powerful and influential man could alter future events by his actions, the poor, the weak, women, children, and minorities—all those without political power—were at best marginal to the great events of history that swirled around them. The important documents of history were those that created governments or defined rights, such as the Magna Carta or the Declaration of Independence and, to a lesser but significant degree, the private papers of influential men. The diaries, letters, and other private glimpses into the personal motivations of these leaders were believed to round out our picture of history in any given period. History, then, was a narrative that weaves together pivotal events and great men into a compelling story, explaining who we are now by telling us who we once were.

Today, things are quite different. Some historians are writing history "from the bottom up" rather than from the top down, beginning with the lives of ordinary people and describing what it was like to be a peasant, slave, maid, or factory worker. To tell the truth in history, they argue, we must include the poor and the powerless as well as the rich and influential. Social differences are being taken seriously. Is it really possible to speak about what it was like to be an eighteenth-century American without specifying this American's race, sex, and social class?

Race, Class, and Gender in Historical Interpretation

Racism is used both *to create false differences among us* and *to mask very significant ones.*
MIRTHA QUINTANALES

Nobody ever helps me into carriages, or over mud-puddles, or gives me any best place! And ain't I a woman?
SOJOURNER TRUTH

It was one kind of experience to be Abigail Adams, writing to her husband as he attended the Continental Congress while she ran the farm in Braintree, Massachusetts, and quite another to be a slave on a tobacco plantation in Virginia. Even if we accept that we must include the experience of women as well as men in evaluating the past, we still must specify which woman we are looking at and when and where she lived. Put another way, we might ask what is true with respect to what it was like to be a woman at a particular moment in history?

Was it, for example, more significant for a woman that she was white rather than black, middle class rather than poor, living in the South rather than the North? Under certain conditions, race can be the most important factor. African Americans in post–Civil War America were discriminated against on the basis of their race—regardless of their gender or social class, slave or free status before the war. Women living under Reconstruction may have felt more solidarity with those of their own race than they felt with women of other races.

At other times, gender may have been the key concept. Vastly different as their lives were on many levels, the middle-class white woman whose children were apprenticed out by the father to pay his gambling debts may have had more in common with the slave woman whose children were sold to a neighboring planter than the white woman had with white men of her class or the black woman with black men of her class and condition.

And there were times when social class was more significant than either race or gender. Even today, the very rich will always receive the best table in the restaurant, regardless of the feelings of the maître d' about their race or gender. Once a person has achieved economic success, he or she may find more in common with other successful people and be criticized for forgetting "where you came from." Similarly, to be poor is to be poor, and it may not be materially different to be poor and Latina or poor and Caucasian.

It is important for historians to find out which of these three factors—race, class, or gender—was the most significant one in shaping the life of a particular historical subject. Also, if we want to learn the complete truth about the historical past, the research methods of the "old history" will not suffice because the marginal and the powerless do not leave many written documents. A revolution within the field of history has produced a new subfield—social history—with its own focuses and methods.

Racial oppression of Black people in America has done what neither class oppression or sexual oppression . . . has ever done: destroyed an entire people and their culture.
ELEANOR HOLMES NORTON

Research Methods of Social History

Historians in this first decade of the twenty-first century are looking at court documents, geological data, and what they call *material culture* (material objects left behind by individuals, in bequests, or by societies, in trash piles and graveyards) in an attempt to understand the past. If we want to know what it was like to be a peasant in the fourteenth century, it may be very significant to find out how many eating utensils the family owned, how large the family was, and how much rain fell in any given year. Although our subject may not have left a diary or written letters, this kind of information can tell us a lot about what life was like for him or her. Did the family have barely enough to survive? Was the crop good? Was there plenty of food to go around and, perhaps, some to sell?

Comparing marriage dates with baptismal records reveals the amount of time a couple was married before the first child was born. Fewer than nine months may indicate a premarital pregnancy and can tell us something about how acceptable it may have been to engage in premarital sex. In a similar way, what items a person left in an estate at death can reveal much about the kind of life that person lived. Having a plow or not having a plow made all the difference between mere survival and some modest comfort. Bones of the dead can reveal nutritional levels and tell us how hard the person may have worked while alive.

After all this has been done, however, we still have some fundamental questions to ask about truth in history. In the first place, facts never come to us as "pure" facts. They are always subject to interpretation. If you have ever been involved in an automobile accident, you already understand how one fact or set of facts can easily have more than one interpretation. Second, facts always occur in a particular historical situation; to speak about them at all, we must speak about them in the context in which they occurred. And the historian is almost never an eyewitness, so our understanding of the past is filtered through the assumptions of those who reported the facts. In addition, our present concerns, as well as our current understanding of the world, provide the context in which we consider the facts of history. As historian Edward Hallett Carr points out, "The world of the historian, like the world of the scientist, is not a photographic copy of the real world, but rather a working model which enables him more or less effectively to understand it and to master it."[29] Accepting this, historians must strive for objectivity. They must not be limited by the vision of the present or of the particular circumstances in which they write.

Truth Tests

The correspondence test of truth is really not a possibility because of the ambiguous nature of historical facts. A fact, it seems, is never entirely separate from the values that surround it. An historical fact lies somewhere between a valueless fact, such as "Most American slaves lived on plantations housing nine or fewer slaves," and a value judgment, such as "Slavery is a great moral evil."[30] To illustrate this point, let's look at the fact of American slavery. It is a fact that several million people, mainly Africans, were brought forcibly to the Americas, denied all legal rights and even personhood while being forced to do the work assigned them by their "masters." One question we might ask is, What effect did this have on slaves themselves?

Historians have given various interpretations. Until the 1950s, U.S. history textbooks typically described slavery as a paternalistic institution in which slave owners brought both civilization and Christianity to savage and heathen Africans. Although they were bought and sold, history students were told, slaves were provided with food, clothing, and medical care into their old age and remained passive, happy-go-lucky children.

Looking at slavery from the slaves' point of view, some revisionist historians found the slaves rebellious—overtly when it was possible, covertly when it was not. Others compared slavery with conditions in a Nazi concentration camp. Slaves living under such dysfunctional conditions, they argued, adopted the values of the master's "superego" and adapted, rarely running away or attempting to rebel. This view considers accommodation to be a successful survival strategy.

Do not cheat me of the truth. Not to know the truth—that indeed would be my hurt.
SOPHOCLES

Current debates focus on how much of African culture survived the brutal attempt to smash it and how much autonomy slaves experienced within their own community. Were they able to forge a stable family life and a separate spiritual life through worship, especially in free, black churches and in secret gatherings? Did acceptance of Christianity enable slaves to control their own religious activities and, in the process, resist some of the most dehumanizing aspects of the slave system?[31]

To come back to our original question: What is the truth about slavery in the United States, and how can we discover it? If we grant that any truth must contain some value judgment (otherwise, it is a statement like "Slavery existed," which is not really true or false in an historically meaningful way), we eliminate the correspondence test of truth from consideration. Although we might be able to test correspondence with a "pure" fact, testing correspondence with a value is impossible. All the theories described earlier were coherent to some degree, in that they provided an explanation, based on data, that hung together well enough to convince some people. But because these theories differ so radically, it seems clear they cannot all be true; how can we determine which is coherent truth and which equally coherent falsity?

Each of these theories made sense to at least some people living in the historical time period in which they were written. Although we might be able to agree on a core of independently derived facts, the interpretations based on those facts are likely to continue to vary. Unless we believe that our own era has somehow reached the ultimate in historical interpretation, it seems we must leave open the question of final truth based on the possibility of further developments and deeper understandings.

History, like science, appears to be the product of a pragmatic test of truth: What is true in any given time period is what fits best within current understandings of life and human nature. G. W. F. Hegel, whose ideas we will consider in Chapter 8, saw history as a great mind coming to greater and greater self-consciousness, through the workings of the Absolute. According to Hegel's model of the *dialectic,* history is spiraling upward. A *thesis* gives rise to its opposite, which he calls the *antithesis,* and from the tension between thesis and antithesis something new is created: a *synthesis* that combines valuable parts from both the thesis and the antithesis. When a historian departs from the views of a predecessor, it is rarely to say that the previous view was just plain wrong. Usually, as we have seen with the *historiography* of slavery, each successive historian accepts some of what the previous generation of historians has said and adds a new twist in a dialectic method of truth evolution. Full truth lies somewhere in the future, and what the historian conceives of as truth today is what works with the materials and theoretical constructs available.

If truth can be somewhat arbitrary, as in the paradigms of science, and constantly evolving, as in the methods of history, we must also carefully examine how language can subtly be employed to support existing power relationships. As words and concepts pass through a language system, they can take on hidden meanings. If we are to test for truth, we must at least acknowledge these underlying assumptions. Let's turn now to the question of language and meaning.

"Tomorrow I'll deconstruct 'Little Red Riding Hood' for you again. But now it's time for bed."

What is the meaning behind the meaning in any text?

Reprinted from *The Chronicle of Higher Education*. By permission of Mischa Richter and Harald Bakken.

Truth in Texts: The Deconstruction Test of Truth

Beginning in the twentieth century, and especially since the early 1970s, much attention has been paid to the "deep structures" that lie within language systems and determine meaning. The question has been whether fixed or stable meanings are possible within a text. The word text provides the key to understanding what all of this has to do with truth. The book you are currently reading is obviously a text; however, so is the conversation you just had with a fellow student and the advertising slogan you heard on the radio this morning. In short, because everything intelligible to us becomes intelligible by passing through a language system, everything that uses language of any kind becomes a text.

Our strong tendency is to assign stable meanings to terms and to assume that we understand what a given text means. In fact, according to *deconstructionists,* meaning occurs only through experience, and texts are being reinterpreted continuously. As we saw in the previous section, the meaning of slavery has continued to change and will continue to change as people encounter the text in which its meaning occurs; slavery will mean different things to different people, and it may mean different things to the same person at different times. We must, according to French philosopher and literary critic Jacques Derrida, the originator of the term **deconstruction,** continue to "question" the text to discern the multiple meanings it contains.

deconstruction
a method used to "question" texts and take apart their artificial constructions in order to reveal their hidden meanings

DOING PHILOSOPHY
Deconstruction: Where Do We Stop?

African philosopher Kwasi Wiredu claims that throwing the colonizing power out of your country is much easier than throwing the colonizer out of your mind. The real damage to indigenous people who are colonized by a foreign power or indeed to any group that internalizes negative assumptions about itself is the colonization of the mind. Women, gays, lesbians and bisexuals, and members of racial and ethnic minorities are especially vulnerable to mental colonization. We form our identity in large part from images of ourselves we find in visual media and in language systems. If we accept the premise that all texts are constructed, one task might be to uncover assumptions of superiority-inferiority built into the language system. In this chapter we've looked at some of the more obvious tasks of deconstructing racist, sexist, and classist assumptions about reality. Many of us would agree that deconstructing these often harmful assumptions is a good thing and will help us reach a more neutral way of describing reality. But our second challenge is, Where do we stop? If everything is a text—your conversations and even your thoughts—and if all texts are constructed, must we keep deconstructing until there is nothing left? At its extreme, the process of deconstruction seems to take us precisely to this point. In a certain sense, there are no "neutral" statements. Every statement contains assumptions about reality, about the characteristics of what is being described, about what is "right," "wrong," "valuable," "worthless." When we start peeling away the constructed layers of meaning, we might agree that prejudice should go as should certain narrow ways of viewing the world that are based on economic system and lifestyle, but where do we stop? And, if there is no place to stop, what remains?

If texts have no fixed meanings, then the question becomes, How is it that some terms have become *privileged,* whereas others—often those paired with the privileged term—have become almost invisible? Our language structure contains many *dyads,* or pairs of words, that tend to be used together as opposites; the first term in the pair is the privileged term. Some common dyads are male-female, white-black, and mind-matter. What Derrida wants us to understand is that male has no meaning without female in this dyad, white has no meaning without black, and mind has no meaning apart from matter.

Think about Descartes's careful distinction between mind and matter discussed in Chapter 5. Mind was thinking, unextended substance, whereas matter was unthinking, extended substance. The meaning of mind could not be clear unless it were contrasted with matter. Mind was thinking, whereas matter was unthinking; mind was unextended, whereas matter was extended. We clearly consider mind to be the superior term in the mind-matter dyad. To speak about one in this dyad is to simultaneously speak about the other. The meaning of each is implied in the other in much the same way that we can hardly imagine the front of a coin apart from the back of that same coin.

Some interesting theories about the white-black dyad suggest that just such a pairing of implied opposites was absolutely necessary in order for one group to enslave the other. If *white* meant "civilized and Christian" and *black* meant "savage and heathen," then a pairing of white and black in the institution of slavery could be justified. Master-slave is also a dyad; it is impossible to be a master if there are no slaves, and vice versa. Historians have struggled to understand what it meant to be a master and what it meant to be a slave. By questioning the text created by the social institution of slavery, the terms *master* and *slave* are revealed not as fixed entities but as terms in a dynamic relationship.

By bringing the less privileged term to the foreground, Derrida thinks we can learn a lot about the assumptions built into our language system. When we use the male-female dyad, for example, male is the *normative* term, and *female* exists in relation to the standard set by the term male. This helps explain why it became acceptable to use the term men and maintain that it included men and women. If *white* sets the standard for what is normal, then *black* may appear aberrant or deviant.

If language is not correct
then what is said is not
what is meant;
if what is said is not what
is meant,
then what must be done
remains undone;
if this remains undone,
morals and art will
deteriorate;
if justice goes astray, the
people will stand about
in helpless confusion.
Hence there must be no
arbitrariness in what is
said.
This matters above every-
thing
CONFUCIUS

As long as all models of beauty were white, black children would be very tempted to look at their own skin and hair and find them abnormal, to even be tempted to lighten their skin and straighten their hair. When women entered the business world in large numbers during the 1970s, they often wore business suits and little ties, trying very hard to mirror the male stereotype as much as possible to fit in. Only recently have we discovered that "Black is beautiful" and that women may have an extremely effective style of leadership even if it does not fit the male model.

When we pursue the truth, we must refuse to take these dyads at face value. Instead, we must *deconstruct* them, or take them apart, to learn about the ideas and processes embodied in them. If we do this, we will discover that these oppositions are not "natural" oppositions, as they may appear to be (and are often claimed to be), but oppositions that are *constructed* for specific purposes. Let's take a look at how this might operate in the current "equality-versus-difference" debates concerning women's rights and civil rights.

"Equality-versus-difference" appears to offer a choice. A group seeking justice can either claim equality (and deny all difference) or assert difference (and give up all hope of attaining equality). According to the terms of this dyad, women can either claim equality with men (in which case they'd better not ask for maternity leave), or they can argue from difference, demanding maternity leave as a necessity that also serves the good of society (and give up all hope of equal pay for equal work because they are clearly conceding that they are different from men). Deconstruction reveals this to be a false dichotomy.

"In fact, the antithesis itself hides the interdependence of the two terms, for equality is not the elimination of difference and difference does not preclude equality."[32] To accept this false choice is to guarantee failure. Deconstruction reveals that it is not the case that equality and difference are opposites of which people may claim one but not the other. Instead of remaining within the *discourse* created by the term *equality-versus-difference,* we must critically examine the terms themselves. When we do, we will discover that the dyad is not an accurate one.

In the context of justice claims made by excluded groups, equality contains within it an acknowledgement of difference. When the Fourteenth

Amendment to the U.S. Constitution was ratified in the years immediately following the Civil War, African-American men gained the right to vote, whereas women of all races continued to be excluded. The equality implied in opening the franchise did not presume that no differences existed between former slaves and former slave owners or between free blacks and white industrial workers. In fact, the amendment was a tacit agreement to ignore the differences between these groups of men, while insisting on the difference remaining between men as one group and women as another group. Indeed, "If individuals or groups were identical or the same there would be no need to ask for equality. Equality might well be defined as deliberate indifference to specified differences."[33]

An early example of this kind of deconstruction can be found—believe it or not—in Plato's *Republic,* when Socrates discusses whether both women and men should be eligible for the guardian class from which the philosopher-kings would ultimately be selected. Socrates and Glaucon agree that women and men are different; men beget and women bear children. The question, they agree, is whether this difference is a relevant one with respect to the question at hand. After all, some men are bald and others hairy, and this too is a clear difference. But does it make sense to forbid bald men to be shoemakers? They agree that it does not because hair on one's head (or lack of it) has nothing to do with shoemaking ability.

Being absolutely consistent, they then also decide that bearing or begetting children is not a relevant factor in governing. What they will carefully consider are the qualities necessary to be a guardian. Using those qualities as a standard, they will select those individuals best suited by nature to rule and then educate and train them accordingly. (You may want to look ahead to the "How Philosophy Works" box in Chapter 8 to see how the argument progresses.)

The Elusive Nature of Truth

Plato lived in a very stable world, one in which a philosopher might be very confident of his ability to arrive at the truth about those best qualified to rule. In the postmodern world, we must consider the possibility that absolute truth—a truth for all times and places—or even a definitive truth for right now might not be possible. Yet, in the absence of clarity, we will still be called upon to make important decisions about how to live our lives. Can we bypass the formal systems of logic and empiricism and step outside the conventions of academic fields if we wish to ascertain what is true? If so, how?

Truth and Time

Let's consider something basic: the nature of time. One hundred years ago, the Western world was in virtual agreement that time was absolute—ticking along at a fixed rate, regardless of whatever else might be going on.

Given the widespread acceptance of relativity theory, as we have seen, time is currently acknowledged not only to seem faster or slower but actually to be faster or slower, depending on the speed of moving systems. If this is so, what is the truth about time?

To complicate matters further, outside the Western world, other truths are known about time. Visitors to West Africa report that in that part of the world "time just is." As we think of water as an inexhaustible resource, so Africans see time as an ever-present medium in which things happen. It can't be managed—who would want to try? And it doesn't limit what you do. Activities take whatever time they take, but there is no time pressure, no anxiety about time being out of control.[34] This can be very disconcerting for Westerners who expect the ten o'clock meeting to start at ten and are surprised to find it beginning at two or even the next day.

What does this timeless design tell us about the relationship between past, present, and future?

Acoma pot/Courtesy of Carol Galbraith/Photo by Quentin Kardos.

Time, it seems, is an abstraction that helps us account for apparent change around us—more useful to some people than to others. According to Pulitzer Prize–winning fiction writer N. Scott Momaday, we think of ourselves as remaining in place and observing the passage of time. Past and future tenses in English indicate the distance of events from us—either backward or forward from our place in the present. We imagine time moving and ourselves standing still.[35] But, is this a true representation?

"Much has been written," Momaday says, "concerning the Indian's conception of time." Stories about his long-dead grandfather, Momaday recalls, might begin in the past tense but slide imperceptibly into the present tense:

> For the Indian there is something like an extended present. Time as motion is an illusion; indeed, time itself is an illusion. In the deepest sense, according to the native perception, there is only the dimension of timelessness, and in that dimension all things happen.[36]

This description resembles the conviction of the aboriginal people of Australia that everything arises from and returns to "dreamtime."

For time-obsessed Westerners, this nonlinear sense of time as a kind of eternal present may seem like a fantasy. People with daily planners, fax, phone, and e-mail messages to read and meetings to attend may be completely unable to imagine a time that "just is" and seems to go on forever in what we call the present moment. Does anyone know the truth about time?

Believe nothing merely
because you have been told it.
Do not believe what your teacher tells you
merely out of respect for the teacher.
But whatsoever, after due examination and analysis,
you find to be kind, conducive to the good,
the benefit, the welfare of all beings —
that doctrine believe and cling to,
and take it as your guide.

THE BUDDHA

Truth and "Gut Feelings"

For much of what we call ordinary life, truth tests and issues of warrantability will have little to offer. Yet, despite our inability to "prove" something true, we often have a conviction about what to do. Have you ever decided something was either true or not true, good or bad, based on a "gut feeling" you had?

The results of an experiment conducted by neuroscientist Anthony Damascio indicate that we have a covert system in our brains, based on emotional memories, that tells us when our decisions are good and when they are bad. In a "rigged" card game, people rapidly reached a "hunch" stage at which, on some level, they could distinguish "good" from "bad" decks. Damascio speculated that what has happened to us in previous situations is drawn into the brain through a circuit in the decision-making prefrontal lobes.

Although the memories we draw on remain covert, they provide us with valuable information on which to base decisions. In the game we call life, many of our decisions about relationships, career moves, and major purchases will not necessarily lend themselves to standard truth tests. Is it possible that we have a truth-testing mechanism "hardwired" into our neurobiology?[37]

Summary

We may agree with Paul Simon that "proof is the bottom line for everyone," but that does not mean we agree, or even have a clear idea about, what constitutes truth and what does not. The further we investigate this concept, the more complex it seems to become. Warranties are fairly clear and easy to apply; the difficulty is that they provide no assurance of truth. Truth can exist without them, and their presence does not and cannot guarantee truth.

Truth tests have built-in limitations and require so much qualification that we may be unsure of what we are left with even if a statement does indeed "pass" one or more truth tests. Even if we can decide what it means to say that a fact must correspond with a state of affairs, we are still left with the more basic question of whether or not there is a world out there with which facts can be said to correspond. Coherence can be very compelling, but it seems equally capable of leading us to coherent falsity as to coherent truth. When this occurs, we find ourselves back with the correspondence test and the problems it presents.

Most of us probably live our lives relying more on the pragmatic test. We clearly understand what it means to say that something is true if it works, makes a difference, or changes things. The difficulty here is that we seem cut off from all standards of meaning and value. Is the simple fact that something works enough to make it true? Perhaps the Ewe creativity test provides the needed corrective: Only those things promotive of growth and life pass the test of truth.

The status of truth seems much more complicated than we may have suspected. Science, despite its reliance on logic and empirical warrants, is caught in paradigms and cannot see the world except through the lenses paradigms provide. History seems to move dialectically, as Hegel explained, continually opposing antithesis to thesis and arriving at a new synthesis. Even if our understanding is increasing, it seems clear that we have not arrived at any absolutes.

Indeed, the very search for absolutes seems misguided when we consider the deconstruction test of truth. If texts are always changing and everything of meaning is a text, then how can we hope to pin anything down? By deconstructing we can reveal hidden meanings and consider things that were always present in the text but had remained hidden. This examination is useful, even educational, but it will not bring us to certainty.

Have we then exhausted all hope of learning the truth about our world? Are there times when we should abandon all formal processes and trust our "guts"? Or, should we simply give up and settle for uncertainty and relativism? Is every statement potentially just as true as every other? When we become frustrated with truth tests, we are left with a more fundamental question: What does it mean to say something is true?

Is truth something we discover—something that already exists in the world—or is truth something we create through active involvement with it? If we think it is the former, then things can, according to Friedrich Nietzsche, only end in confusion:

> What then is truth? a movable host of metaphors, metonymies, and anthropomorphisms: in short, a sum of human relations which have been poetically and rhetorically intensified, transferred, and embellished, and which, after long usage, seem to a people to be fixed, canonical, and binding. Truths are illusions which we have forgotten are illusions; they are metaphors that have become worn out and have been drained of sensuous force, coins which have lost their embossing and are now considered as metal and no longer as coins.[38]

If truth is a kind of collective illusion, a useful fiction on which we have agreed to agree, then it will have little capacity to tell us anything we really want to know about the world or about ourselves. If, on the other hand, truth is the product of our creative involvement with the world, then its power to reveal is greatly enhanced.

In Chapter 7 we will consider the lively relationship that can exist between beauty and truth by examining the aesthetic experience and what it might have to teach us about the nature of truth. As we observed in Chapter 4, the rationalist way is not the only route to knowledge of God. The same might be said about knowledge of the world. Just as the mystics claimed certain knowledge based on intuition, there are ways to learn about the world that do not depend on logic and truth tests. As we turn to an investigation of the nature of truth, we will look at art and its power to help us see the world differently—and possibly more truly.

For Further Thought

1. Think of something you are confident is true. On what basis do you believe it to be true? How would you prove or demonstrate its truth if called upon to do so?
2. The next time you say "That's not true!" to someone (or to the TV set), stop for a minute and analyze why you are so sure the statement or claim is false. What is the basis for your objection?
3. We seem to hear conflicting empirical claims on a regular basis: Coffee is bad for you/coffee, taken moderately, is good for you; alcohol is dangerous/

alcohol (in certain forms) prevents heart disease; butter is a killer, use margarine/ margarine is worse, go back to butter. From what you know about the methods of science, why do you think this happens?

4. If every age must reinterpret history for itself, will we ever reach the final revision? Is something or someone directing the process toward its own ends, as Hegel suggested, or does the process operate autonomously? If the latter, are we moving closer or farther from the truth? How can we know?
5. Is "proof" the bottom line for everyone? Can you think of instances in which something other than proof functions as the bottom line in determining truth? Or are we dealing with varying definitions of the word proof and still insisting on proof of some kind?
6. Try to prove one very simple statement to be true. It might be best to choose something you don't have a strong emotional stake in. Notice how you construct your proof, what you choose as your warranty, and whether you rely on one or more of the truth tests discussed in this chapter.
7. What does it mean to be "true to yourself"? What is the standard against which your actions will be compared? Is this kind of truth different from the truth of propositions? How?
8. If deconstructionists are right and all language systems are texts, how can we "escape" the thought system of language to pursue the truth? Listen to a conversation and observe any dyads or other assumptions built into what is being said that the speakers may not be aware of. Find whatever hidden meanings you can find and write the subtext for the conversation whose text you heard.
9. What happens to our notion of truth if Zen masters are right and most of what we think we see and know is really illusion—a product of our conception of the way things are rather than the way things are? Is it possible to restructure our truth tests to match this understanding of reality? How?
10. In traditional societies, everything must meet the test of lived experience. What has enabled our technological society to produce ideas that are "true in theory but not in practice"? Does the division between mind and matter expressed by Plato and Descartes define traditional societies as it does our own?
11. Do you believe there is a world "out there," independent of your mind? If so, on what basis? If not, on what basis? (Thinking about your own truth tests may help here.)
12. How much of what you believe to be true have you taken on "faith"—that is, how much rests on the authority of a textbook, a teacher, parents, or friends telling you something is true? Augustine thought most of what we believe to be true fell into this category, and he didn't mean only religious truths. If he is right, is your confidence (in what you "know" to be true) shaken or fortified?
13. It has been said that pragmatism is a distinctly American contribution to philosophy. From what you know of American history and culture, explain why this might be so. How has America's experience as a nation led to a pragmatic approach to life?
14. Imagine you are a slave owner writing what is "true" about slavery. Now imagine you are a slave engaging in the same exercise. Assuming your account is substantially different from the account given by the slave owner, how can we assess which of you has rendered a "truer" account? Is there some truth in what each of you write, or is one of you correct and the other incorrect?

15. Imagine you are a neutrino with virtually no mass, no electrical charge, and no magnetic field. You can travel at the speed of light through "solid" objects, including the earth itself and human beings, as if they were not there. What is "true" about the world from your point of view? Since you see the world so differently from the rest of us, are you right and we wrong, or vice versa? Who can decide which version is closer to the "truth"?
16. Suppose we discover a race of aliens (or they discover us) for whom space and time do not exist. They can be wherever or whenever they want to be just by thinking about it. Is it still "true" that space and time exist since they exist for us?
17. Can truth ever be absolute? Is there anything that will always be true at all times and under all circumstances? If you answer yes, what is your proof? How might someone question your proof?
18. If all truth is relative, we can make no definite decisions about reality or how to live our lives. Since we do make decisions of this type, on what basis do we decide among competing truth claims?
19. If we decide that information is exploding at such a rapid rate that we can never assess enough of it to make a truth claim, what implications would this decision have for our society? What would be your response to someone who announced that decision?
20. Here is a philosophical riddle: If I say "All statements are false," is this a true statement? Why or why not?

For Further Exploration

Akutagawa, Ryunosuke. "Rashomon." In *Rashomon and Other Stories.* New York: Prentice-Hall, 1952. A man has been murdered, and we read seven versions of what might have happened, including that of the murdered man as told to a medium. What really happened, and how would we go about deciding this? There is also an excellent film of the same name by Japanese director Akira Kurasawa.

Pirsig, Robert. *Zen and the Art of Motorcycle Maintenance.* New York: Bantam, 1974. A man and his son travel across the country on a motorcycle in search of truth and meaning. The protagonist, who calls himself Phaedrus (a character in one of Plato's dialogues), has had a nervous breakdown after discovering that the number of scientific hypotheses expands much faster than our ability to test them. Science, he realizes, is leading us away from "single absolute truths to multiple, indeterminate, relative ones."

Shakespeare, William. "As You Like It." In *The Complete Works of William Shakespeare: The Cambridge Edition.* New York: Doubleday, 1936. Rosalind disguises herself as a man and as Ganymede meets her lover Orlando in the forest, promising to cure him of love sickness if he will woo her as if she were Rosalind (which of course she is). This play, like several of Shakespeare's comedies, plays on the notion of what is true.

Spinrad, Norman. *Deus X.* New York: Spectra, 1993. Before dying, people encode their entities onto the big electronic board that essentially represents reality. Do they have souls (as they claim), or have the souls left and gone before God for judgment? Which position is true? A dying priest promises the female pope that he will conduct an experiment to prove them wrong, but he ends up arguing that they are right (from the board).

The Usual Suspects. This film is reminiscent of "Rashomon." Be aware of the language and violence in this fascinating exploration of the changing nature of truth in a police investigation.

Woolf, Virginia. *Orlando.* New York: Penguin, 1946. In the sixteenth century, a young man named Orlando is granted a house by an aging queen on condition that he never grow old. He lives until the present, changing sexes along the way and remarking as he sees his female body in the mirror, "Same person. No difference at all. Just a different sex." What is the truth about Orlando? About time? About the world? There is an excellent film by the same name.

For Further Research

Try these InfoTrac keywords:

Truth
Deconstruction
Paradigms
Zen Buddhism
Social History

Notes

1. Carl Zimmer, "The Healing Power of Maggots," *Discover,* August 1993, 17.
2. William James, "Pragmatism," quoted in William James: *Pragmatism and Four Essays from The Meaning of Truth* (New York: World, 1970), 133.
3. James.
4. James, 45.
5. James, 133.
6. John Dewey, "Body and Mind," quoted in *Intelligence in the Modern World: John Dewey's Philosophy,* ed. Joseph Ratner (New York: Modern Library, 1939), 606.
7. Dewey, 627.
8. Dewey, 677.
9. Dewey, 677–678.
10. Dewey, 259.
11. Dewey.
12. Dewey, 1046.
13. N. K. Dzobo, "Ewe and Akan Conceptions of Knowledge and Truth," in *Person and Community: Ghanaian Philosophical Studies,* vol. 1, ed. Kwasi Wiredu and Kwame Gyekye (Washington, D.C.: Council for Research in Values and Philosophy, 1992), 81.
14. Dzobo, 80.

15. Dzobo, 83.
16. Antoine de Saint-Exupery, *The Little Prince,* trans. Katherine Woods (New York: Harcourt, Brace & World, 1943), 66–67.
17. Richard Baker, introduction to *Zen Mind, Beginner's Mind,* ed. Shunryu Suzuki and Trudy Dixon (New York: Weatherhill, 1991), 21.
18. Catherine of Siena to Sister Daniella of Orvieto in *Medieval Women's Visionary Literature,* ed. Elizabeth Alvilda Petroff (New York: Oxford University Press, 1986), 271.
19. Catherine of Siena, 55.
20. Catherine of Siena, 226–227, 225, 228.
21. Thomas Kuhn, *The Structure of Scientific Revolutions,* 2nd ed. (Chicago: University of Chicago Press, 1970), 5.
22. Kuhn, 15.
23. Kuhn, 17–18, 19.
24. Kuhn, 20.
25. Kuhn, 5–6.
26. Kuhn, 92.
27. Kuhn, 77.
28. Kuhn, 52.
29. Edward Hallett Carr, *What Is History?* (New York: Vintage, 1961), 136.
30. Carr, 175. The distinction, not the example, is Carr's.
31. *Taking Sides: Clashing Views on Controversial Issues in American History,* vol. 1, 2nd ed., ed. Eugene Kuzirian and Larry Madaras (Guilford, Conn.: Dushkin, 1987), 248–249; and 5th ed., ed. Larry Madaras and James M. SoRelle (Guilford, Conn.: Dushkin, 1993), 238–239.
32. Joan W. Scott, "Deconstructing Equality-Versus-Difference: Or, the Uses of Poststructuralist Theory for Feminism," *Feminist Studies* vol. 14, no. 1 (1988): 38.
33. Scott, 44.
34. Reported by Willie Cardwell, May 1997.
35. N. Scott Momaday, *The Man Made of Words* (New York: St. Martin's, 1997), 52.
36. Momaday, 53.
37. "In Work on Intuition, Gut Feelings Are Tracked to Source: The Brain," *New York Times,* 4 March 1997, C1.
38. Friedrich Nietzsche, "On Truth and Lies in a Nonmoral Sense," in *Philosophy and Truth: Selections from Nietzsche's Notebooks of the Early 1870's,* ed. and trans. Daniel Breazeale (Atlantic Highlands, N.J.: Humanities Press, 1992), xxxi–xxxii.

Aesthetic Experience

Is Truth Beauty and Beauty Truth?

BEFORE YOU READ . . .

Ask yourself what you might have learned from the arts that you could not have learned elsewhere.

All things are artificial, for nature is the art of God.
THOMAS BROWNE

Have you ever looked at something really beautiful and found yourself with no words to describe what you were feeling? An incredible sunset, the smile of a baby, the first flower of spring—all these and many more experiences of beauty have the ability to "take our breath away" and with it the power of speech. Like these experiences of what we might call "natural art," or the art of nature, the art humans create has the same potential to render us speechless. When we look at something beautiful, sometimes it seems that in the process of seeing we "know" something very certainly; and yet, if someone asked us what it is we "know," we would probably be at a loss for words.

The Issue Defined

noetic *having the quality of knowledge, seeming to be knowledge*

Art is like other intuitive experiences: It provides a way of knowing that runs parallel to the rational, linear, logical kind of knowing with which we are very familiar and comfortable in the Western world. Like the intuitive knowing of the mystics we discussed in Chapter 4, this experience carries with it a conviction of certainty that seems to defy verbal description. This **noetic** quality—the sense of "knowing" associated with nonrational knowledge about reality—seems present in the experience of genuine art. It can bring instant and "irrational" tears to our eyes, and yet the experience seems **ineffable,** unable to be spoken in words.

ineffable *unable to be spoken in words*

If you have ever had a brush with death, you know what it feels like to see the world as precious and new, to judge everything to be beautiful because you are truly seeing and knowing it, maybe for the first time. Walking away from an auto accident or breathing the relief that comes from a negative lab test, you may find even the ordinary and boring things of life charged with intensity and overflowing with meaning. Most of the time the incredible stamina of a dandelion or the simple elegance of a cat curled up in the Sun are invisible to us because we are preoccupied by very important tasks; we have places to be, things to do, schedules to keep. Let the ordinariness of life be threatened, however, and we may, perhaps for the first time, really begin to look at life and to see it.

In his classic play *Our Town,* Thornton Wilder has the stage manager allow Emily, who has died as a young woman, to select one day of her life to live over again. She chooses her twelfth birthday. From her present state, death, there is nothing about her house, her family, or the ordinary life she has left behind that she can treat casually, as if it did not matter or would always be there tomorrow. Things she had never really noticed while alive are suddenly filled with a poignant and unspeakable beauty. "I didn't know Mamma was ever that young," Emily gulps through her tears. In the end she is unable to finish the day; her emotions are too intense and she cannot bear the beauty and the loss associated with everything she has loved and no longer has. She chooses to go back to the graveyard, and in her final speech she cries, "Oh earth, you're much too wonderful for anybody to realize you."

Here should be a picture of my favorite apple. It is also a nude and bottle. It is also a landscape. There are no such things as still lifes.

ERICA JONG

Faced with the loss of life, we would take a new look and probably find incredible satisfaction in the most humdrum of things. The thought that tonight's sunset would be the last we would ever see would certainly charge it with intensity and focus our attention on it. Art, and the experience we have in viewing it, has the same kind of power; it can clarify and crystallize our perceptions by clearing away all of today's superficial concerns and by cutting through our belief that we have unlimited tomorrows. If there are a thousand rainbows waiting to be seen, it may not be worth my time to turn off the TV or wake up from my nap to go out and see one, but if today is my last, I may find that the rainbow reveals the world to me in a wholly new and meaningful way.

I got the idea from Ernest Hemingway . . . instead of eating lunch, he would go to a museum and look at paintings on an empty stomach. When he looked at art with that edge of hunger, he saw more . . . that's the point of all the great spiritual teachings and paths: to become awake.

DAN WAKEFIELD

Art can stop us in our tracks, wake us up, and bring us face to face with what is real. In the presence of genuine art, we come to know things about the world, and about ourselves, that seem certain to us even if we cannot put them into words. A number of philosophers have suggested that the search for truth leads us inevitably to the realm of the aesthetic—that through art we can learn the truth about reality. In this chapter we consider the medium of *aesthetic experience,* look at some philosophical reflections on the beautiful, and examine the role art can play in bringing us to aesthetic forms of knowing. Our focus will be less on **aesthetics** than on an aesthetic approach to examining truth.

aesthetics *a philosophical reflection on art and the beautiful*

Our first task will be to survey the role of art in Western, Asian, and African societies and the special position held by the artist. As we will see,

HOW PHILOSOPHY WORKS
Informal Fallacies—Part Two

Several philosophers, discussed in this chapter, favor approaches to truth that rely on the aesthetic experience rather than on logic. One of the advantages they see to the aesthetic experience is that it bypasses words altogether. Although language is a wonderful tool that allows us to discuss certain aspects of reality with great precision, it can mislead us or fail us completely in certain other areas. Philosophers try to avoid confusion in language. To assist us in this effort, let's examine several potential traps in the hope of avoiding them ourselves and spotting them in the writings of others.

Fallacies of Ambiguity

Amphiboly. This is a grammatical construction that can be understood in more than one way and thus is ambiguous. For example, in the sentence "This blood test will evaluate you for hepatitis, anemia, and AIDS, which you will receive absolutely free" it is not clear whether the test or the diseases are yours at no charge. We should try to say exactly what we mean so that our meaning will be clear to others.

Composition. This fallacy attributes what applies to the parts of something to the whole thing. For example, "Since every word in this essay is a good word, the whole essay must be a good essay."

Division. Division reverses the process and attributes the characteristics of the whole thing to one or more of its parts. For example, "Since this is a good essay, every word in it must be good."

Equivocation. This fallacy involves changing the meaning of a word or expression in the course of an argument. For example, "That suit doesn't suit you very well, and if you don't change it immediately, I will bring legal suit against you." We can also observe equivocation in this syllogism:

All men are mortal.
No woman is a man.
Therefore, no woman is mortal.

In the first premise, men clearly includes all human beings, whereas in the second it clearly includes only those of the male gender—hence, the confusion.

Hypostatization. In this fallacy, abstract words are treated as if they were concrete. In literature, this is known as PERSONIFICATION and is perfectly acceptable as a method of comparison. In philosophy, however, we need to avoid this confusion. When we say "Life owes me a better deal" or "You know the truth will set you free," we aren't speaking precisely enough to construct a valid argument.

Misplaced accent. This fallacy misleads by de-emphasizing or omitting relevant information. For example, "Double coupons at this store" may be followed in smaller print by "coupons for 50¢ or more redeemed at face value."

the artist can serve as a mediator between reality as it is and our perception of it, interpreting significant knowledge that cannot be adequately expressed in words. Although we begin with Plato's and Aristotle's views on art, love, and the beautiful, our main focus will be on the relationship between beauty and truth, as we explore the writings of four philosophers from the last two centuries: Friedrich Schelling, Arthur Schopenhauer, Friedrich Nietzsche, and Martin Heidegger. In the final section of this chapter, we look at art as a vehicle for helping us to see the world differently.

Functions of Art in Society

Let's begin by looking at the sharply contrasting views of art expressed by Plato and Aristotle. If art represents reality, Plato fears it will lead to confusion, but Aristotle is confident it can convey truth. As we consider three representative artists—Michelangelo in the West, Khing in Asia, and Edogo in Africa—the artist's role as a kind of priest emerges. Artists, it seems, can understand important truths and illuminate them for the rest of us, capturing reality in terms we can understand. Plato, however, remained skeptical.

What an artist is for is to tell us what we see but do not know that we see.
EDITH SITWELL

Art as Representation of Reality

Plato and Aristotle both believed that art tries to represent the universal and is one source of information about reality. The term ***mimesis*** refers to this quality of representation, and the classical theories of art developed by Plato and Aristotle assume that the purpose of art is to represent reality. Because of his metaphysics, Plato was wary of art and artists because he saw art as being an image of an image and thus twice removed from the Form itself.

mimesis *[mih MEE sis] the aesthetic theory of art as representation*

If you recall from Chapter 1, Plato believed that true reality can be found only in the Kingdom of Ideas, or the World of Forms, in which the perfect prototype of everything in this world exists. Artisans represent ideas in their work. A carpenter, for example, must have the idea of a Table in mind as he sets out to construct a table—the carpenter's image, or idea, of "tableness" made concrete in a particular object. What the carpenter makes is once removed from the Form of a Table that is its source and inspiration. Artists, Plato concluded, work one step farther removed from reality. Because they begin with the images found in this world, artists make what amount to copies of copies.

Not only are these imitations of imitations twice removed from the real thing; they are also *illusions* of reality. If our goal is to know the Forms ever more truly and accurately, then—rather than helping—art is more likely to get in the way. Operating through the medium of the senses, art can entertain and provide pleasure, Plato believed, but it is unlikely to lead us to true knowledge of the Forms—the only kind of knowledge worth having. Even worse, we may be manipulated by art in the form of propaganda. A skillful artist can make us accept a false view of the world and perhaps even arouse us to immoral action. This is the view of current critics of TV violence who make similar claims.

Art is a lie that makes us realize the truth.
PABLO PICASSO

Aristotle was much kinder to artists than Plato was. Far from being mere imitators or reporters of experience (a job he reserved for historians), Aristotle contended that artists showed nature not as it is but as it could be. Believing that they began with the ideal or universal aspects of human nature, Aristotle applauded the brilliant Athenian playwrights for their depictions of deep (as well as universal) human feelings. A well-constructed tragedy could, he thought, arouse in the audience feelings of pity and fear (for the characters in the play) and free people of the need to act out in their own lives the mistakes depicted in the tragedy. By experiencing rage, resentment, and jealousy secondhand, spectators could also experience a **catharsis,** or purging of those emotions.

catharsis *the emotional cleansing achieved by viewing tragic drama, according to Aristotle*

Leaving an amphitheater after watching a tragedy, Aristotle believed, viewers would be purified of any desire to repeat the mistakes made by

The sense of the absurd, the ability to defamiliarize, the absurd humor, these are the possible routes by which the contemporary man achieves catharsis; they are possibly the only ways of "cleansing" him adequate to the world in which he lives.
VACLAV HAVEL

the protagonist. Unlike Plato, who worried about the potential of art as propaganda, Aristotle was confident that a tragedy would teach a lesson to the audience even as it entertained them. Rather than being stirred to imitate the tragic actions they have just seen enacted on stage, people may avoid tragedy because they have already *experienced* the emotions those actions generate and been cleansed of them, just as if they had taken the actions themselves.

Because Plato believed the Forms to be outside the sense world, he understandably assumed that each representation took the viewer farther and farther from what is real. Aristotle—who insisted that the Forms can only be found in this world, joined with the concrete objects that embody them—found Greek tragedy to be a transparent medium for universal ideas. Thus, although Plato and Aristotle agree that the universal Forms are the basis of knowledge and that the function of art is mimesis, or representation of the Forms, they reach very different conclusions about the effect this mimesis might have on observers. Plato fears art's potential for manipulating observers, whereas Aristotle applauds its potential for eliciting catharsis.

Both the sculptors Plato may have had in mind and the Athenian playwrights praised by Aristotle were well known in Greek society. Artistic competitions were routinely held and widely attended. Prizes raised the individual artist's status in society. Many centuries later, when art in Western society had become almost exclusively associated with and in service to the Christian Church, the identity of an individual artist was regarded as unimportant, perhaps irrelevant.

The Role of the Artist in Western Society

What image of human nature is Michelangelo able to convey through this statue that appeared to him in marble?

The *David* by Michelangelo/ © Robert Frerck/Odyssey Productions/Chicago.

During the Middle Ages, it would have been unthinkable for artists to sign their work. Almost all art had a religious theme, and artists saw themselves as a kind of medium for religious messages, as if the goal were to be as invisible as possible so that the glory or majesty of God could shine through. With the Renaissance came a new enthusiasm for the powers of human reason and creativity, with an accompanying shift in theme: Subjects of art were as likely to be idealized human beings as divine personages, and artists dared to claim credit for their work.

Upon hearing a debate about the identity of the sculptor of a particular work (neither name mentioned was his), the creator of that work got his chisel and carved "Michelangelo Buonarotti, the Florentine, made this!" on its base. Although he is well known for his masterful Sistine Chapel ceiling, which is filled with religious imagery from Hebrew and Christian Scriptures (the Old and New Testaments), Michelangelo also took pride in accurately sculpting the human form. By stealing and dissecting corpses, he learned the relationship of muscles and ligaments to bones and his statues have an amazingly lifelike quality.

One of his best-known sculptures is a fourteen-foot-high marble figure of the young David, with his slingshot in hand, soon to hurl the stone that will fell the giant Goliath (as described in the Bible). What one sees is the

PHILOSOPHERS SPEAK FOR THEMSELVES
Plato and Aristotle

Let's consider why dramatic poetry must be banished from our republic. We must begin with the notion of imitation or representation. A carpenter who wishes to make a bed or a table relies on the idea or type of a bed or a table, which contains its essence. But, we understand that the carpenter does not make the idea or type itself. Now, let's broaden the focus and consider all the particular things, both natural and manufactured, that exist in the cosmos. Can you imagine one craftsperson capable of making all these things? What if you yourself were that person?

Suppose you carried a mirror around with you everywhere you went. You could capture images of everything that exists, but they would be appearances only and not the things themselves. That's basically what a painter does. The painter creates a bed on canvas—an apparent bed rather than a real one. Even the carpenter is making only a particular bed and is incapable of making the type on which every particular bed is based. So, although the bed made by the carpenter seems more real than the bed made by the painter, it still lacks the complete reality—what we might call bedness—that exists only in the original type.

Plato, from *Republic,* Book X

A tragedy is an imitation of an action; it is serious, self-contained, described in poetic language, told dramatically rather than narratively, and it uses plot twists to first arouse pity and fear and then resolve them through the purging of catharsis . . .

Of the six ingredients that together make a tragedy—plot, character, diction, thought, spectacle, and song—plot is the most vital. Since tragedy imitates life rather than persons, it must follow the pattern of our own lives in revealing its truth through action. Character gives us certain qualities, but it is our actions that lead us either to happiness or unhappiness. Dramatic action rather than character development is what drives the tragic drama to its climax . . .

The function of a poet or playwright is to describe not what has happened—that is the job of the historian—but what might happen, according to the laws of probability and necessity. And, contrary to popular opinion, it is more than the choice of prose or verse that separates historians from poets. Put the work of Herodotus into verse and it would still be history. Poetry is closer to philosophy than to history and, like philosophy, it has the high calling of dealing with universals rather than particulars . . .

Aristotle, from *Poetics,* [6, 9]

zestful energy of a youth on the verge of manhood—an image as well of the emerging power of the city of Florence. Michelangelo's work is only part mimesis; the rest is the vision of the artist. In this combination, Renaissance artists believed, true art is born. The goal is not the most accurate possible representation of a subject but a kind of blending of what we might call photographic accuracy and interpretation. Indeed, being capable only of flawless representation came to be seen as not nearly enough.

In one of his most famous poetic monologues, the nineteenth-century British poet Robert Browning criticizes Andrea Del Sarto, the "faultless" painter. "That arm is wrongly put," he has Del Sarto remark about a work by Raphael, "its soul is right . . . still, what an arm! and I could alter it." The arm is technically flawed, but Raphael's work as a whole is an artistic success, while the work of Del Sarto is technically perfect, but lacks "soul." An artist must have both vision and technique; to lack either is to be less than whole, but vision is the indispensable ingredient.

Art is why I get up in the morning,
but my definition ends there.
You know it doesn't seem fair,
that I'm living for something
I can't even define.
And there you are
right there in the mean time.

ANI DIFRANCO

To be a "faultless" painter like Andrea Del Sarto is to be a technician, but art must do more than imitate; it must be more than what Plato would call a copy of a copy. What we value most in art is what the artist brings to the work. We might say that technique is a necessary but not a sufficient gift to bring. Although an artist, even one with a superb vision of reality, who is unable to render proportion correctly may be unable to share that vision with others through the medium of painting, a technician, who is only that, has nothing of what matters most to offer. Thus, Raphael's work endures, despite a badly drawn arm, because of the vision he saw and was able to create using materials in the visible world. Real art, like real philosophy, has something to offer us each time we look at it. It is larger than itself and points beyond itself.

Visual arts may be the clearest medium for communicating a vision, but they are not the only one capable of doing so. Another kind of artist uses words and music to connect listeners with a more inclusive reality. In the ancient Celtic world, the poet, who was often a harper as well, was second only to the king in status and power because he, like the king, had the power to call the people to action and show them their true identity. Working in a culture in which the line between history and myth was not so rigidly drawn as it is today, the poet told the story of the past in its *truest* way. This task was *not* understood to mean telling the story with historical accuracy. As we discussed in Chapter 6, facts and experiences rarely exist in an objective state—that is, out there somewhere pristinely waiting to be analyzed and studied. Instead, meaning seems intimately connected with subjective overlays.

What a poet does is evoke a larger vision within which ordinary events of the present can be interpreted. We retain a sense of this poetic function even in our very rationalist, Western culture of the late twentieth century when we celebrate national holidays like the Fourth of July. Reverential readings from the Declaration of Independence, with their emphasis on the Enlightenment idea that "all men are created equal," tell us something true about ourselves as a people even as we realize that we have in practice treated people unequally. What is honored is not the scientific or historical accuracy of the concept of equality, but rather the truth that equality is what we stand for.

Reformers know this, and by calling us to our ideals, they can successfully negotiate change. If standing for equality were not a part of what we truly are as a people, modern reformers such as Martin Luther King, Jr., and Betty Friedan who called people to action and a larger vision, as the ancient Celtic poet-harpers did, would have been ignored. In his "I Have a Dream" speech, King called America to the dream of racial equality, and in *The Feminine Mystique,* Friedan described "The Problem That Has No Name" and launched twentieth-century feminism. Reformers are not poets, but they express a larger vision as poets do. The poet-harper of the Celtic world, as he sang his stories, called the people to their greatness by reminding them of their noble past and challenging them to create a noble future. Whether the call was to war or to peace, it was the poet as much as the king who understood what was real and what was true. In the presence of this kind of art, the audience might be moved to tears or to battle, but they would recognize what they know because the poet sings so truly of what is real.

The Role of the Artist in Asian Society

Because the Western distinction between the knower and the known (see Chapter 5) is absent or at least significantly blurred in Asian cultures, the idea that artists succeed by becoming one with their creations seems much more natural in Asian art. When artists forget their own small concerns, they can become mediums of expression for a deeper reality as truth and beauty express themselves through the work of the artist. In the third century B.C.E., Chuang-tzu told a wonderful story of Khing, a master wood-carver, who made a bell stand of such beauty that all who saw it were amazed. Some thought that an artistic creation of such perfection must be the work of spirits. When questioned by the Prince of Lu, Khing gave this explanation: "I am only a workman," he said. "I have no secret. There is only this."

Khing began by focusing his spirit on the task at hand and by fasting "in order to set my heart at rest." After a week of fasting, he had left behind thoughts of success, of possible criticism, even of the prince and his court. Everything that might distract him—including the awareness of his own body—had been banished. "I was collected in a single thought: of the bell stand." In this state Khing went to the forest to see the trees in their natural environment, and "when the right tree appeared before my eyes, the bell stand appeared in it." Khing's explanation to the Prince of Lu is that his focused and collected thought met "the hidden potential in the wood," and the rest was only technical work.[1]

Today, like every other day, I wake up empty and frightened. Don't go to the door of the study and read a book. Instead take down the dulcimer, let the beauty of what you love be what you do. There are a thousand ways to kneel and kiss the ground, there are a thousand ways to go home again.
RUMI

The idea of a union between raw material and artist's vision is not a uniquely Asian one. Aristotle also spoke of the statue existing potentially in the marble and being made actual by the sculptor, and Michelangelo told a similar story when asked about the creation of his incredible David. According to Michelangelo, when he set off in a focused state to look for a piece of marble, it was just a question of finding the right one—the one with the David already in it. Once he had found that piece of marble, all that remained to be done was to chip away the pieces of marble that did not belong. When looking at a group of unfinished Michelangelo statues today, you get a strong sense of figures straining to emerge from the marble.

Mathematics, rightly viewed, possesses not only truth, but supreme beauty—a beauty cold and austere, like that of sculpture.
BERTRAND RUSSELL

There is, then, something that happens when the focused idea of the artist meets the exactly right medium, the right tree or the perfect piece of marble; the result is unmistakably a work of art, a work of vision. The bell stand appears in the tree, the David appears in the marble. Once the vision of the artist has fused with the medium, there is nothing left to do but remove what does not belong. In the presence of works like these, viewers can learn something about themselves.

The aesthetic experience of the viewer comes close to the creative experience of the artist. In this sense, art is a window on truth not only for its creator but also for those who enjoy it. Just as the audience at a Greek

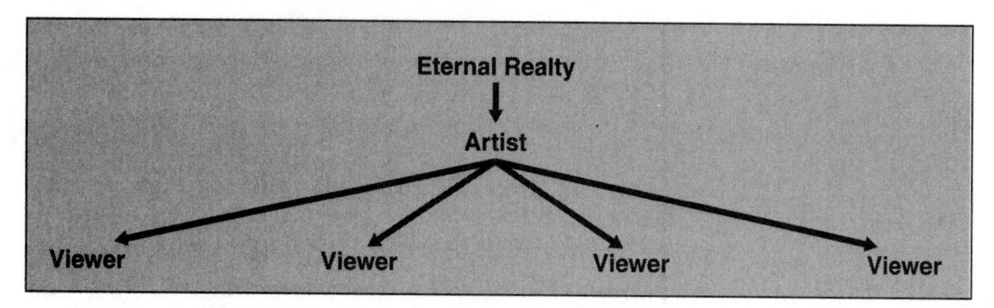

FIGURE 7.1 ARTIST AS MEDIATOR *The artist mediates between eternal reality and temporal reality.*

tragedy could experience secondhand the emotions of the characters on stage—without having to repeat their tragic mistakes—the viewer of the bell stand or the David has at least partial access to the vision of the artist. What we learn can often not be put in words, but it is knowledge all the same.

As a mediator of ultimate or eternal realities and values, the artist serves as a connection between the spiritual and the temporal (Figure 7.1). This kind of art elevates by pointing to what is finally real. We might see the connection between reality, artist, and viewer more easily by looking at two of the arts associated with Zen—calligraphy and sand gardens. Both of them should be created (and appreciated) in a meditative state.

beginner's mind
according to Zen, the state of openness in which one can directly access the truth about what is

As we saw in Chapter 6, the ideal state of mind or of being, in Zen, is described as **beginner's mind.** In this state, one resembles Khing the master carver or Michelangelo the sculptor. No longer the expert, one sees the world as if for the first time, focused entirely on the task at hand. Like Emily in *Our Town,* every simple, ordinary thing is charged with meaning and beauty because we are really seeing it with fresh appreciation and a sense of wonder. From the state of Beginner's Mind, one is able to put one's whole self into a task as only a beginner can do. Once we have done something repetitively, it loses its freshness, and the experience can all but disappear for us. Even the pleasures of eating and sexual intimacy can become dulled if we perform them mechanically without really being present to ourselves and to our experience.

When I am working on a problem, I never think about beauty. I only think of how to solve the problem. But when I am finished, if the solution is not beautiful, I know it is wrong.
BUCKMINSTER FULLER

The intention in Zen is to do whatever you are doing mindfully, fully present in the task, instead of thinking ahead to the next thing on your busy schedule or back to the events of the past. To do calligraphy in this state is to do it naturally, from the heart, rather than in a practiced way. To draw a Chinese character with your whole being is to be both artist and priest in the sense of being mediator between the temporal and the spiritual. In the same manner, a Zen rock garden can be an exercise in meditation for the person who creates it and the visitor who experiences it.

Zen gardens have none of the elements usually associated with gardens: flowers, trees, living plants, and insects; instead, they are large rectangles of flat, raked gravel, standing stones (alone or in groupings), and empty space. To view a Zen garden is to be soothed and startled at the same time. Perhaps it is the emptiness, the space going on to what seems

Raking a sand garden can be an experience in active meditation.
Zen sand garden/Photo by Quentin Kardos.

infinity, that is the most unexpected and that calls us to empty ourselves of our usual mental clutter, our preconceived notions of what reality is all about. If we do, we may see anew, with the immediacy and spontaneity of a child, into the depths of what is. A similar experience is possible with a miniature Zen garden made of sand and stones and raked with a wooden rake into swirls of pattern. To create a Zen garden yourself, mindfully and fully present, is to be (at least in a limited way) an artist and a priest.[2]

Unlike the West, the East blurs the distinction between professional artist and layperson. The tea ceremony, flower arranging, archery, and martial arts are all available to people who may not call themselves artists. Once the artist has showed us what is and allowed us to glimpse a vision of something larger and more complete, we are empowered to do some exploring on our own.

Life, religion and art all converge in Bali. They have no word in their language for "artist" or "art." Everyone is an artist.
ANAÏS NIN

The Role of the Artist in African Society

The role of the artist as intermediary between the divine and the human is clearly evident in traditional African societies. Even in the case of court art, which proclaimed the power and glory of kings on palace walls and entrance arches, the individual artist was not considered to be acting alone. Instead, according to W. Emmanuel Abraham, the work of art was often described as "the self expression of the Supreme Being himself relying on human instruments."[3]

The artist who produced ritual objects was regarded as a kind of priest. "He was steeped in the metaphysics of his people and possessed the skill to concretize it in his creations." Like Khing the master carver or Michelangelo

Even in making a decorative mask such as this one, the artist must work in a focused state.

West African decorative mask/ Courtesy of Dawn Cooper Barnes.

the sculptor, the African artist at the peak of his work "enters into a trance-like condition and becomes oblivious of the public and its doings."[4] Here is Edogo, the carver of ritual masks, in Chinua Achebe's novel *Arrow of God:*

> The hut was dark inside although the eye got used to it after a short while. Edogo put down the white *okwe* wood on which he was going to work and then unslung his goatskin bag in which he carried his tools. Apart from the need for secrecy, Edogo had always found the atmosphere of this hut right for carving masks . . . Edogo sat down on the floor near the entrance where there was the most light and began to work. Now and again he heard the voices of people passing through the market place from one village of Umuaro to another. But when his carving finally got hold of him he heard no more voices. The mask was beginning to come out of the wood when Edogo suddenly stopped and turned his ear in the direction of the voices which had broken into his work.[5]

Within his ritual space, insulated from everything that might distract him, the artist is free to become tuned to the ideas he wishes to make concrete. Once the right material has been selected and the proper incantations recited, the artist invokes the forces that will animate his creation. In the process he becomes "a channel of communication with them, the means of mediation between them and his society, he constitutes a priest-like figure."[6] As contemporary philosopher Roger Scruton points out, art may serve in the modern world, as prayer has traditionally done, to awaken the "memory of enchantment," for art "properly understood, is a kind of prayer; it is an attempt to call the timeless and the transcendental to the scene of some human incident."[7]

Art objects, produced in this way, are clearly sacred; they are frequently used in connection with public festivals and religious ceremonies. The purpose of such ceremonies is often to "restore and strengthen the orderliness of nature and of society and to evade the tragedy which a disconnection from that orderliness would entail."[8] The sacred art object cannot merely represent order, but must embody order: It must itself *be* the order it illustrates. The power of the artist lies not in the degree of individuality he brings but in the degree of universality he is able to evoke. Like the Greek tragedies we have already examined, village ceremonials involve everyone. After days of drumming, dancing, chanting, and sacrifice, throughout which negative and destructive feelings that have been suppressed build, the peak of the ritual creates a release of passions and a joyous celebration of a return to stability. Once this emotional purging has occurred, the ritual objects are again put away out of public view.

Real art has the capacity to make us nervous.
SUSAN SONTAG

We see in a traditional African society exactly the same function of art and the same role of the artist as we saw in ancient Greece as described by Aristotle. Whether by drumming and dancing or by intensely watching a play, people are drawn into the destructive possibilities of anger, envy, and resentment that are ever present in the human person and in human society. Then, at the moment of climax, these negative emotions are released and the comfort of order is restored. Having seen an alternative vision—a negative and frightening one—people may be more open to seeing and appreciating the value of order with fresh eyes.

Like the rituals of priests, the rituals presided over by artists bring us in touch with bigger things and take us out of the every day—if only for a moment. The Celtic poet-harper, the Zen master in the teahouse, the African mask dancer—all mediate at public ceremonies as priests sometimes do. The artist becomes a luminous figure, almost transparent, a medium through which important knowing can be transmitted. Just as in a religious ritual we often cannot speak what we feel, in the presence of genuine art we may find no words to express our experience.

While our own culture has compartmentalized art and restricted it to museums, many societies have given art a more central and less formal role. As we have just seen, the arts of Zen are available to all, and the African carver makes his mask for a public ceremony to be enjoyed by everyone in the community. Such was also the case in ancient Athens where subjects like the role of art and the always-interesting topics of love and beauty were regularly discussed. Love was recognized as intimately connected with the Idea of Beauty and Art—not separate from it. Indeed, for Plato, love appeared to be one route to the contemplation of pure Beauty.

The artist, like the God of Creation, remains within or behind or beyond or above his handiwork, invisible, refined out of existence, indifferent, paring his fingernails.
JAMES JOYCE

Art and Beauty

Art is, at least in part, concerned with beauty, and the branch of philosophy called aesthetics describes what we mean by the beautiful and how we apply standards of value in judging art. We turn now to Socrates' education in how Platonic love can lead to beauty itself, and then we explore the question of taste and how we separate "good" art from "bad" art. Once we have made this connection, we move on, in the next section, to examine the relationship between truth and beauty.

Socrates and Diotima

Much of what we have to say about art begins with the idea of beauty. In the playful Platonic dialogue called the *Symposium,* we find Socrates at the age of fifty-three enjoying with a group of much younger men an evening of light conversation that ultimately turns to the relation between love and beauty. According to the protocol of a ***symposion*** (symposium), each man in turn would drink and speak on a given subject (frequently, love or sex).

The fourth speaker is Aristophanes, the comic playwright, who offers a fascinating myth to explain the erotic attraction we have for each other. In the beginning, he says, we were two-headed, four-armed, and four-legged creatures. Because we threatened the gods with our ***hubris,*** or arrogance, Zeus retaliated by splitting all the creatures in half. Each of these creatures—now possessing only one head, two arms and two legs—wanders the world,

symposion *[sim PO zee ahn] a male drinking group held in an andron, or men's room*

hubris *[HEW bris] human arrogance or pride*

looking for its "other half." Earthly love is only the yearning to regain our original wholeness.

When his turn arrives, Socrates declares that all the previous speeches have been lies, and his conversational contribution is a retelling of instructions in love he received from Diotima, a holy priestess. According to Diotima, ***eros*** (earthly love) offers us a way to go from the human to the divine. In other words, love functions as art sometimes does—as a link between the temporal and the spiritual.

eros *[AIR ros] earthly love, the love of bodies*

To be fully initiated into the mysteries of love, one must pursue beauty throughout his life. First, he will fall into Platonic love with one particular, beautiful person. This will ultimately lead him beyond the love of one beautiful body to the love of all physical beauty. Next he will learn to find the beauty of the soul more valuable than that of the body and be able to love a "beautiful" soul, even if it is housed in a less than beautiful body. From this, he will be led to contemplate beauty as it exists in abstract thought and the moral law. This, at last, will bring him to the true object of the whole enterprise—the love of beauty itself:

> This is the right way of approaching or being initiated into the mysteries of love, to begin with examples of beauty in this world, and using them as steps to ascend continually with that absolute beauty as one's aim, from one instance of physical beauty to two and from two to all, then from physical beauty to moral beauty, and from moral beauty to the beauty of knowledge, until from knowledge of various kinds one arrives at the supreme knowledge whose sole object is that absolute beauty, and knows at last what absolute beauty is.[9]

Is Beauty in the Eye of the Beholder?

This brings us to the question of beauty itself. Is there an objective or perfect standard of beauty (as Plato would assert), or does the definition of beauty vary from person to person? Can we agree on what is beautiful, or is beauty really in the eye of the beholder—so that what seems beautiful to me may not seem so to you, and vice versa?

There are actually two ways in which we speak about beauty: a subjective way and an objective way. When we speak subjectively about beauty, we are actually saying something about ourselves and our preferences rather than passing judgment on an object. Often when we exclaim, "How beautiful!" what we really mean is something like "This pleases me!" To speak about beauty in the objective sense is to suppose that there are qualities inherent in the object that make it objectively beautiful and, perhaps, subjectively beautiful as well. The twentieth-century philosopher Mortimer Adler addresses this distinction by using the terms **enjoyable beauty** and **admirable beauty.** If we can speak only of enjoyable beauty, then we must conclude that beauty is indeed in the eye of the beholder.

enjoyable beauty *personal preference in art, according to Adler*

admirable beauty *intrinsic excellence or perfection in art, according to Adler*

Admirable beauty, like enjoyable beauty, is partly based on taste, Adler admits. But, it also "may be mediated by thought and dependent upon knowledge."[10] The concept of admirable beauty rests on the assumption that there are qualities in objects of art that produce *intrinsic excellence or perfection*. These qualities are internal ones, part of the object itself and independent of whether or not they produce enjoyment in anyone who contemplates them. The question then arises of who is competent to judge whether an object possesses intrinsic excellence or perfection and, if it does, to what degree it possesses these qualities. The answer, Adler asserts, is that the expert and only the expert is qualified to make that judgment.

George Dickie, another philosopher, suggests that judgments are to be made by the *art-world public*. Members of the art-world public understand that their role requires "knowledge and understanding similar in many respects to that required of an artist."[11] Those who have the abilities and sensitivities to understand and appreciate a particular kind of art, Dickie says, make up the art-world public, and they are qualified to judge what is art from what is not, as well as to distinguish good art from bad.

What appeals to people in one culture and is believed to have intrinsic excellence or perfection may be quite different from what passes the test of objective beauty in another culture. The art-world public associated with Western art, for instance, may be totally unmoved by Japanese Zen gardens, people in Eastern cultures may not be able to discern the objective beauty in African sculpture, and Africans may be left cold by Western painting. This does not mean there are no objective standards of beauty; what it does mean is that members of the art-world public exist in a relationship with the artist and must share certain knowledge and experiences with him or her.[12]

Critic Clive Bell, a member of the influential Bloomsbury group—which included Virginia Woolf—believes that all genuine art transcends cultural limitations. Art, he says (in an echo of Diotima) can be fully appreciated only by one who approaches as a lover:

> To him who woos, but woos impurely, she returns enriched what is brought . . . But only to a perfect lover does she give a new strange gift—a gift beyond all price. Imperfect lovers bring to art and take away the ideas and emotions of their own age and civilisation . . . But the perfect lover, he who can feel the profound significance of form, is raised above the accidents of time and place . . . Great art remains stable and unobscure because the feelings that it awakens are independent of time and place, because its kingdom is not of this world.[13]

If art has this potential—to take us beyond time and place—then beauty will have at least the possibility of leading us to truth.

If truth is beauty, how come nobody has their hair done in a library?
LILY TOMLIN

Truth and Beauty

To speak about truth and beauty, we will use art forms themselves. In considering the West, our subject will be a poem by John Keats that equates truth with beauty and beauty with truth. To explore aesthetic experience in Asia, we will focus on Chinese and Japanese landscape painting and calligraphy.

Truth and Beauty in the West

What is the relationship between beauty and truth? What did the English Romantic poet John Keats mean when he wrote in his ode "On a Grecian Urn" that "beauty is truth, truth beauty"? Is there in beauty something beyond enjoyment and admiration that might lead us to truth?

In art there is no such thing as universal truth. A truth in art is that whose contradictory is also true . . . the truths of metaphysics are the truths of masks.
OSCAR WILDE

Looking at a Grecian urn (like the one in the photo), Keats is struck by two things: the permanence of the life depicted in the painted scenes, which will endure long after he has passed away, and the cold, static quality of the frozen moments they depict. The youth whose lips are poised above those of his love will never kiss the maiden; the people of the town will never return home from the sacrifice; the trees will never bear fruit. In short, there is no life on the Grecian urn. Keats is keenly aware of the irony. An artistic rendering of life in an ordinary, little Greek town has made it immortal (as long as the urn endures, at least), but it is an unappealing sort of immortality—the villagers on the urn no longer have access to life.

There is, however, something in that cold beauty that can lead us (its viewers) to truth. Great art, Keats seems to say, has the power to fix beauty in such a way that those who contemplate it can continue to be stirred in the imagination just as the artist was in the original creation of the work of art. The villagers are long dead, but an artist's rendering of them retains the power to inspire us. As a glimpse of unchanging perfection, great art is superior to nature. Unlike nature, it has a direct link with knowledge of the truth.

"Beauty is truth, truth beauty," wrote Keats, and he concluded "that is all ye know on earth and all ye need to know." Somehow, understanding this mystery would be a sufficient task for a human life. The powerful message here is that beauty and truth are two aspects of one ultimate reality. We will experience and express each of them in different ways—beauty through the medium of the senses and the exercise of the imagination, and truth through thought, knowledge, and wisdom—but the two are no less identical. What we experience as beautiful would, if it were adequately expressed intellectually, be a truly conceived reality. Similarly, truth, if it were adequately transformed into sensation or imagination, could only be beautiful.

Images and sometimes whole stories were told in paint on Grecian urns, one of which inspired John Keats to write "truth is beauty, beauty truth."
Grecian urn/Photo by Quentin Kardos.

One of the difficulties, as we have already noted, is expressing beauty in words; very often words simply fail us. Language works quite well in describing many aspects of life, but it seems to fall short in the expression of deep feeling of any kind. As contemporary American philosopher Susanne Langer observes, there is "an important part of reality that is quite inaccessible to the formative influence of language; that is the realm of so-called 'inner experience,' the life of feeling and emotion."[14] People sometimes conclude that feelings and emotions are irrational because they cannot be spoken through language, but Langer disagrees.

Art serves as the translator of this "inward experience"; it "objectifies the sentience and desire, self-consciousness and world-consciousness, emotions and moods, that are generally regarded as irrational because words cannot give us clear ideas of them."[15] When an artist apprehends a truth about reality, the resulting work of art becomes an expression of that truth. Those of us who are not creative artists can still share the experience of the artist when we contemplate the work because the artist has translated his or her experience into the medium of the work and left it there for us to "read."

Most of us seem to be constantly in motion, always "on the go." To have the aesthetic experience we have been discussing, the first thing we will have to do is stop long enough to really look at the natural and artificial beauty all around us. Adler suggests that we might begin with the notion of enjoyable beauty and the rest it can introduce into our lives. One ingredient in the happiness of a well-lived life is the rest that the contemplation of art can provide. When we pause in our very busy lives to look with pleasure on the art of nature or the art of human artists, we give ourselves a breather and open the possibility for deeper thoughts to arise.

And beauty is, or can be, a window on reality; it has its own kind of truth. A gifted artist can show us or tell us truths about the world that may not be available to us in any other way. Alfred North Whitehead, who was Susanne Langer's teacher, believes that the art we produce has a unique role to play in inspiring us to pursue perfection: "A million sunsets will not spur on men towards civilization. It requires art to evoke into consciousness the finite perfections which lie ready for human achievement."[16]

Art, like science, seeks to uncover the harmony of the universe. Both are, Whitehead insists, "the consciously determined pursuit of Truth and of Beauty. In them, the finite consciousness of mankind is appropriating as its own the infinite fecundity of nature."[17] Both science and art capture a manageable slice of the infinite richness of nature for us and let us glimpse a moment of perfection.

Just as exemplary individuals held out as role models can inspire us to greater civic achievement, so a civilization "interfused with art" can reveal infinite or immortal possibilities to very finite humans. Great art, Whitehead seems to be saying, always points beyond itself to the source of its vision. As we contemplate great art, we get a glimpse of something larger and more perfect than what we see around us. Where "precision of consciousness fails" we have the possibility of "a message from the Unseen."

In the West, truth and beauty can be seen as two aspects of one reality. Let's examine whether this is also true in Asia.

Truth and Beauty in Asia

Like the Zen gardens we previously considered, Chinese and Japanese landscape paintings speak to the inner life of the person who looks at them. The first thing you might notice is the amount of empty space. In contrast with Western art, which often fills the canvas, Asian art uses emptiness as an ingredient in the composition. The message seems to be that emptiness is a significant part of existence itself and must be an essential quality in the person who seeks to understand existence.

The next thing likely to reveal itself is the smallness of any human figures present and the vastness of nature; if emptiness or the white silk or paper background is the main component, nature is second, and the

THE MAKING OF A PHILOSOPHER

Susanne K. Langer
(1895–1985)

Born into Manhattan's German-American community, Susanne Knauth acquired a love of music and the ability to play the cello from her father and, under her mother's influence, learned to read, recite, write, and love poetry. From these early experiences, she began to develop what would become a deep understanding of a work of art as a "non-discursive symbol that articulates what is verbally ineffable, the logic of consciousness itself." She studied philosophy at Radcliffe College in Cambridge, Massachusetts, where she also met and married historian William Leonard Langer. In a distinguished career of teaching at Radcliffe, Wellesley, and Smith Colleges, Langer worked out her conviction that humans are symbol-making creatures—in art, myth, and science. For Langer, the arts are no less significant as forms of knowledge than are mathematics and physics. Books in symbolic logic and aesthetics followed, explaining the function and value of symbols in conveying meaning. Art presents emotional experience or the nature of emotion to us through a symbol system, Langer believed, and the role of the artist is to portray not his or her own particular feelings but the nature of feeling itself.

Art is the objectification of feeling, and the subjectification of nature.
SUSANNE K. LANGER

Art is not a luxury, but a necessity. Art is, at least in part, a way of collecting information about the universe.
REBECCA WEST

human presence is a distant third. This tells us something about the proportion of things, that we are specks in the natural world and that even nature exists amidst the emptiness that characterizes the way things are. Human figures are not seen as dominating or imposing order on nature, but rather as being dwarfed and rendered insignificant by nature and by the even greater emptiness.

As you may recall from Chapter 3, in much of Asian thought, distinctions are not made among the human, the natural, and the emptiness; everything is connected. Only our human eyes see division and multiplicity where there is essential unity. As the "Heart Sutra" put it, form is emptiness and emptiness is full of form.

Often the human figure is entirely absent from works of art. An entire painting may consist of a few simple strokes of brush and ink, producing a single stem and perhaps a bird. If only we could empty ourselves of all our judgments and assumptions, the painting seems to say, perhaps we could get close to our original nature and regain the ability to react freshly to life or to conceive an original idea of our own. According to Zen, words put up a screen between us and what is; we have an inner wisdom that is sometimes thwarted or confused by the words we tell ourselves or hear. Turn them off and the inner life can flourish.

When we look at Chinese and Japanese landscape painting, we can reach beyond words to the inner knowledge or wisdom that lies too deep for words but is clearly recognizable when we reach it and allow it to speak. A scroll painting might be the source of meditation, one of those moments of rest Adler spoke about that give us a window on larger concerns. To sit quietly and observe such a painting is to be drawn both into oneself and out into the larger reality.

If you could read the calligraphy, would it enhance your understanding of or appreciation for this painting?

Boy with Tree Apple by Yifei Gan/Photo by Quentin Kardos.

Some Asian art combines both painting and words. On the scroll or canvas is a traditional painting of a human subject or of nature, and of course the emptiness in which nature moves, but across the top or down the side there may be a series of Chinese characters in the beautiful calligraphy that is itself an art form. To the Western mind, this might seem a complete painting, one that speaks to both the heart and the head, because those who understand the language can read the words as well as contemplate the brush strokes that constitute the painting and the calligraphy. But the point, of course, is not to read the words, as you might read the words in this text or even in a novel, but to see them with Beginner's Mind—as separate from and yet a part of the more clearly visual art of the remainder of the painting.

These ink drawings and paintings are sometimes called "landscapes of the soul." For the artist-priest who painted them, they were a product of intense contemplation, of an active meditation by their creator that may inspire a similar response in those who view them. The "technique" of such paintings is rather unconventional. The painter strives to empty himself or herself as much as possible of ego, of preconceived ideas and judgments, so that in the contemplation of what is the essential will be revealed. In a state of deep meditation, the artist then executes the brush strokes without

With an artist's skill, a few simple lines can convey an entire world of reality.
Early Spring by Yifei Gan/Photo by Quentin Kardos.

consciously controlling the brush. From this state of emptiness, the painting can almost be said to paint itself, just as a poem sometimes seems to write itself or the runner becomes the race. What we see in contemplating such a work, then, is not so much the work of a particular artist, as the glimpse of reality that artist's egoless work has brought into being.

The possibility exists that the viewer and the painter can become one across cultures, oceans, and centuries in a mutual act of creativity. As an empathetic observer, you may be open to the nonanalytic truth a particular painting reveals. If you grasp it, you share in that moment the experience of the artist who "discovered" the truth and passed it on. For an instant, something of his vision is yours and can remain a part of you forever. For that moment, you too have an artist's or a philosopher's vision because you see directly into what is—in Western terms, you have moved from beauty to truth. In Zen art, beauty (as well as worth and social correctness) really is in the eye of the beholder. These judgments are part of our evaluation of things and have nothing to do with the way things are. Everything, it is said, exists in its own nature; it simply is. The rest are labels we attach and should not be confused with reality.

There is something very calming about contemplating Asian art. At the heart of all nature in the Chinese system is the mysterious *Tao,* which appears to do nothing but accomplishes everything, seemingly without effort. There is a restfulness in this and in our connection with the earth itself and with our own distant ancestors:

> How can we fret and stew . . . under the calm gaze of ancient *Tao*? The salt of the sea is in our blood; the calcium of the rocks is in our bones; the genes of ten thousand generations of stalwart progenitors are in our cells. The sun shines and we smile. The winds rage and we bend before them. The blossoms open and we rejoice. Earth is our long home.[18]

The very words *truth* and *beauty* seem out of place here. But, we can see that a work of art has the power to reveal what is. Keeping in mind the connection art can help us make between beauty and truth, we turn now to four Western philosophers who wrote about aesthetics: Schelling, Schopenhauer, Nietzsche, and Heidegger. Each of them sees a way in which art can overcome divisions that appear to exist and lead us to a true understanding of reality.

Truth and Beauty in Western Philosophy

The first two philosophers, Schelling and Schopenhauer, began with the dilemma created by the philosophy of their contemporary Immanuel Kant (see Chapter 5). If we can know only phenomena, or things as they appear to us, then *noumena,* or things as they are in themselves, will remain hidden from us. In other words, truth about reality becomes impossible because we have no independent way of knowing that reality.

THE MAKING OF A PHILOSOPHER

Friedrich Wilhelm Joseph von Schelling
(1775–1854)

Schelling was known as Proteus because he shared a character trait with the mythological shape-shifter known as the master of changes. As a young man, Schelling fascinated those he met with his flexible and agile mind; he was full of new ideas and an astute judge of people and situations. The great German poet Goethe considered him the most "congenial" of philosophers. Some believe Schelling inspired Hegel. As an old man Schelling became intellectually rigid and repudiated many of his earlier views. Although he became a defender of religious orthodoxy and an extreme conservative in politics, many continued to quote the writings of his youth on transcendental idealism.

Overcoming the Subject-Object Split: Friedrich Wilhelm Joseph von Schelling

In his philosophy of transcendental idealism, Schelling posed this question: Is there a way to re-create the original unity between subject and object and then understand it? If this were possible, we might be able to speak about truth. If our ambition is to know things in themselves and not merely things as they appear to us, then, Schelling was convinced, we cannot use cognitive processes that employ logical analysis in arriving at concepts. The "in-itself" cannot be known from the outside the way we can know appearances, but only from the inside, through the process of intuition. You might be reminded here of the mystics (see Chapter 4) who rejected the possibility of knowing God rationally in favor of knowing God intuitively.

Schelling's solution to the Kantian dilemma relies on the kind of knowing that only art can make possible for us. To begin, he made very clear the distinction between true art, which can only be produced in aesthetic freedom, and ordinary art, which may be in the service of sensuous enjoyment or even utility or usefulness. Genuine art, Schelling insisted, can be recognized because it alone depicts the unconscious in action as well as its "original identification with the conscious":

> Art is paramount to the philosopher, precisely because it opens to him, as it were, the holy of holies, where burns in eternal and original unity,

> as if in a single flame, that which in nature and history is rent asunder, and in life and action, no less than in thought must forever fly apart. The view of nature which the philosopher frames artificially, is for art the original and natural one . . . Each splendid painting owes, as it were, its genesis to a removal of the invisible barrier dividing the real from the ideal world . . . Nature . . . is . . . simply the ideal world appearing under permanent restrictions, or merely the imperfect reflection of a world existing, not outside him, but within.[19]

Like Hegel (see Chapter 8), Schelling adopted an organic rather than a mechanistic view of reality. Earlier, Hegel had insisted that nothing could be understood apart from the whole to which it belonged, including its historical circumstances. For both Schelling and Hegel, the world more closely resembles a living organism than it does a machine. A gear may be understandable, have meaning, and even function separately from the machine of which it is a part, but my hand cannot function, and indeed has very little meaning, apart from my body. Cut off from the living organism of which it is essentially a part, the hand will quickly wither and die. In fact, for Schelling, the self and the world are two aspects of one organic unity.

Differences between mind and matter, which were so critical to a rationalist philosopher like Descartes, are, in Schelling's philosophy, only apparent and not real differences. From the point of view of the Absolute, these distinctions are irrelevant, and the Absolute is indifferent to them, much as a magnet is indifferent to our observation that it has negative and positive poles.

Schelling contended that the Absolute, or creative spirit in the universe, creates nature and operates at an unconscious level in its processes (chemical reactions, the force of gravity, the instincts of animals, etc.). When the creative spirit reaches the level of human development, it becomes free and rational; it attains self-consciousness. The highest human function, therefore, is imitation of and participation in this same creative process. As self-conscious subjects, we are able to imitate the creative activity of the Absolute through creative art, which is the highest possible activity for a person. In aesthetics Schelling saw a joining of the world of phenomena, or appearances (the sense world), and the world of the mind.

An artistic creation represents a fusion of object and subject, according to Schelling. The artist experiences the original harmony, or identity, between subject and object through the creative process and then represents it in an object we can contemplate:

> It is as if, in the exceptional man (which artists above all are, in the highest sense of the word), that unalterable identity, on which all existence is founded, had laid aside the veil wherewith it shrouds itself in others, and, just as it is directly affected by things, so also works directly back upon everything. Thus it can only be the contradiction between conscious and unconscious in the free act which sets the artistic urge in motion; just as, conversely, it can be given to art alone to pacify our endless striving, and likewise to resolve the final and uttermost contradiction within us.[20]

Art accomplishes what philosophy alone cannot do: It provides a finite rendering of an infinite reality. Like the mystics, we cannot approach this artistic creation logically or rationally; it is not knowable through these means. We can, however, use a particular kind of intuition. We are not talking here about intellectual intuition, which is the province of philosophy and may lead us to some level of understanding. Schelling called the kind of intuition we need **aesthetic intuition** and defined it as intellectual intuition become "objective and universally valid."

aesthetic intuition
knowing available through aesthetic experience, according to Schelling

Through the creative process, the artistic genius can apprehend the truth about reality in a way that simply is not available to the philosopher who uses only intellectual intuition. Once an artistic genius has created the fusion between subject and object, however, then through aesthetic intuition or contemplation the philosopher can share in the knowledge that is revealed.

Schelling was clear that even though philosophy, acting according to its own scope and methods, can approach an understanding of reality, only art can arrive at certainty:

> The one field to which objectivity is granted is art. Take away objectivity from art, one might say, and it ceases to be what it is, and becomes philosophy; grant objectivity to philosophy, and it ceases to be philosophy and becomes art. Philosophy attains, indeed, to the highest, but it brings to this summit only, so to say, the fraction of a man. Art brings *the whole man,* as he is, to that point, namely to a knowledge of the highest and this is what underlies the eternal difference and the marvel of art.[21]

Here we have a powerful affirmation of Keats's observation that truth is beauty and beauty truth. When the whole human person contemplates the whole of reality and is able to fuse its apparent divisions, between matter and mind, between the unconscious and the conscious, what we have is art. It renders objectively what philosophy, acting alone, can only render subjectively:

Make your life a work of art.
JILL KER CONWAY

> The ideal world of art and the real world of objects are themselves products of one and the same activity; the concurrence of the two (the conscious and the nonconscious) *without* consciousness yields the real, and *with* consciousness the aesthetic world. The objective world is simply the original, as yet unconscious, poetry of the spirit; the universal organon of philosophy—and the keystone of its entire arch—*is the philosophy of art.*[22]

Art, according to Schelling, can give us access to the world as it is in-itself. This was also the view of Schelling's contemporary Arthur Schopenhauer, although Schopenhauer used a somewhat different process to arrive at a similar conclusion.

Escaping the Force of Will: Arthur Schopenhauer

Schopenhauer began where Schelling did—with the dilemma posed by Kant's metaphysics: our inability to know *noumena,* or things as they are in themselves (and independent of our perceptions of them). If we are confined to knowledge of the world of phenomena, or appearances, then real knowledge and the possibility of truth remain hidden. Unlike Kant, however, Schopenhauer did not locate reality in idea; instead, he asserted that the thing-in-itself is what he called the Will. The Will—which he understood as the ultimate, primeval principle of being—is the source of the world of appearances and in fact the source of all life. The Will is the will to live, a blind, uncaused, unmotivated impulse to achieve and cling to life. The Will is neither the perceiving subject nor perceived matter; in fact, both proceed from the Will.

Existing outside time, space, and causality—the filters that Kant insisted shape all our perceptions of reality—the Will greedily and ruthlessly demanded life and thus its own objectification. In its blind urge toward life, the Will objectified its original unity into the multiplicity of the phenomenal world. The Will also created mind to be a light for it in its higher stages of evolution. Notice here the inversion of more traditional philosophical thought, which declares the intellect primary and the will secondary. Plato, for instance, declared that to know the good was to do the good; will, in other words, would follow intellect. Schopenhauer reversed this order. For him, intellect, like everything else in the phenomenal world, is in the service of the Will and owes its very existence to it.

In his master work *The World as Will and Idea,* Schopenhauer, like Schelling, saw the route to knowledge as lying in **aesthetic contemplation.** Schopenhauer began by considering various kinds of knowing, including natural science and mathematics, and ended with this question:

aesthetic contemplation *a route to knowledge, according to Schopenhauer*

> But what kind of knowledge is concerned with that which is outside and independent of all relations, that which alone is really essential to the world, the true content of its phenomena, that which is subject to no change, and therefore is known with equal truth for all time, in a word, the *Ideas,* which are the direct and adequate objectivity of the thing-in-itself, the will? We answer, *Art,* the work of genius.[23]

Ideas, understood in the sense in which Plato used the term as the eternal, primeval, original forms of all things, are the Will made objective. We may try to frame or explain the world through concepts, but our efforts are doomed to fail, in Schopenhauer's view. It is a case of using the wrong medium, the wrong kind of language. The proper (indeed the only) medium that is adequate for this task is art.

The Idea can be expressed in a variety of forms that Schopenhauer viewed hierarchically. On the most primitive level, the Idea may be expressed in architecture, and it may ascend through sculpture, painting, and literature (especially tragedy in which events happen of necessity because of the reality of the situation and the being of the characters) to music. Music, in Schopenhauer's view, has the capacity to leave the world behind and express the very heart of reality. All the other arts are copies of the Ideas; music, alone, is the copy of the Will itself.

All of us have the capacity to know the Idea in things—to transcend, if only for a moment, our own individual personality. A genius excels by "possessing this kind of knowledge in a far higher degree and more continuously."[24] Even though both nature and works of art have the power to reveal the Idea to us, works of art are more effective because of the genius of their creators. The artistic genius grasps the pure Idea and is able to express it in a work of art.

Here, we are reminded of Khing, Michelangelo, and Edogo who in focused states became oblivious to the world of actual things and understood something of the thing-in-itself (to use Kant's term). According to Schopenhauer's theory of knowledge,

> The artist, who knew only the Idea, no longer the actual, has reproduced in his work the pure Idea, has abstracted it from the actual, omitting all disturbing accidents. The artist lets us see the world through his eyes. That he has these eyes, that he knows the inner nature of things apart from all their relations, is the gift of genius, is inborn; but that he is able to lend us this gift, to let us see with his eyes, is acquired, and is the technical side of art.[25]

With the help of the artistic genius, we have the ability to become what Schopenhauer called a "pure will-less subject of knowledge." As long as our consciousness is occupied with the "endless stream of willing," we can never really be happy or have peace of mind. Our natural state, the natural state of everything in the world, is slavery to the Will. Only by going beyond personal interest and losing ourselves in the pure contemplation the aesthetic experience offers can we escape time and place and achieve peace of mind.

Of all the arts, Schopenhauer found music the most sublime. Because it does not rely on visual images, music has the capacity to bring us more directly to the state of pure contemplation that leads to true knowledge. Schopenhauer regarded music as a direct expression of the Will itself:

> Music is as *direct* an objectification and copy of the whole *will* as the world itself, nay, even as the Ideas, whose multiplied manifestation constitutes the world of individual things. Music is thus by no means like the other arts, the copy of the Ideas, but the *copy of the will itself,* whose objectivity the Ideas are. This is why the effect of music is so much more powerful and penetrating than that of the other arts, for they speak only of shadows, but it speaks of the thing itself.[26]

The kind of music Schopenhauer seemed to have in mind is Baroque music in which form predominates over content. A Bach fugue, for example, in which a particular musical form repeats many times with many variations, fulfills Schopenhauer's requirements. Popular music, with its sensuous, emotional content leaves us firmly in the grasp of the Will. Even more formal classical music like Handel's Pastoral Symphony might conjure up visual and sensual images of a pastoral scene. The goal of art, in Schopenhauer's system, is to take us out of the world of the devouring Will and into the contemplation of the Ideas.

Clearly, Schopenhauer was not an optimist. Seeing the world as a manifestation of blind, voracious Will did not make him hopeful about what

THE MAKING OF A PHILOSOPHER

Arthur Schopenhauer
(1788–1860)

Born in the free city of Danzig, Schopenhauer spent time living in France and England before taking an extensive European tour. His father, a wealthy merchant, apparently committed suicide, releasing young Arthur from the obligation to work in his father's business. His mother, a novelist, established a literary salon whose circle included the poet Goethe. Schopenhauer quarreled with his mother over her love affairs and her "romantic" friends, and they parted company, hating each other until their deaths. At the University of Göttingen, he studied Plato and Kant before moving to Berlin where he explored the natural sciences. At Jena, he submitted the work that would become known as *The World as Will and Idea* as his doctoral dissertation. Disregarded during his lifetime, the book became famous after his death. He lectured briefly at the University of Berlin but lived most of his life in solitude, accompanied by his poodle Atma whose name means "world soul."

Music, my joy, my full-scale God.

GWEN HARWOOD

humans would do if left to their own devices. As slaves to the Will we act in its service, seeking first of all to procreate and continue life, and then to fulfill our own desires for more, more, more! Freud's concept of the id—the pleasure principle that is such a strong ingredient in the human personality—owes much to Schopenhauer. Much of Schopenhauer's pessimism, as well as his vision of the liberation offered by the aesthetic, was shared by Friedrich Nietzsche.

The Merging of Dionysus and the Separation of Apollo: Friedrich Nietzsche

In his remarkable first book, *The Birth of Tragedy,* written in the 1870s, Nietzsche draws our attention from the modern world back to the world of Aristotle and the classic Greek dramatists of the fifth and fourth centuries B.C.E. Like Aristotle, who saw the ability of the Greek tragedy to transform human understanding, and like Schopenhauer, who saw the tragedy as second only to music in its power to help us escape the Will, Nietzsche evoked the power of tragic drama. In the culture of ancient Athens, he believed, the tragic poets fused the insights of two Greek gods, Apollo and Dionysus. The gift of Apollo is the state of contemplation in the presence of a world of beautiful appearances, whereas the gift of Dionysus is the wild intoxication of creation and destruction.

Greek tragedies combine both Apollonian and Dionysian elements. As Aristotle pointed out, the audience could achieve a catharsis by seeing the wildness and violence of human nature expressed and resolved on stage. To watch a Greek tragedy is to lose one's everyday sense of optimism and confidence in an ordered world. When Medea, in order to avenge herself on her husband Jason, kills their children by her own hand, we see a side of human nature we would prefer to ignore. Although few of us will ever act as Medea did, many of us can identify with the rage and irrationality that can consume us when we feel we have been wronged. Aristotle felt that we had to periodically come face to face with the darker side of human nature—through the relative safety of drama—so that we can avoid its consequences in our lives.

Nietzsche shared this pessimism about what psychologist Carl Jung calls the **shadow self,** those parts of ourselves we prefer not to own but that travel with us, like our shadows, whether we will them to or not. He found it unfortunate, and a little frightening, that we are apparently no longer able to confront the vitality of our dark human nature as the Greeks were able to do. Our arts have, in his judgment, become far too tame, and as a result they have lost their power to warn us of our potential for violence and evil. Nietzsche's answer to the question "What killed Greek tragedy?" is Greek philosophy.

shadow self *unaccepted parts of the self, according to Jungian psychology*

Nietzsche claimed that **theoretical man**—of which Socrates was perhaps the best example—arrived to calm our fears and represent nature as perfectly rational, understandable, and intelligible. With the advent of

theoretical man *the philosopher who imposes reason on reality, according to Nietzsche* philosophy in Athens, art was replaced by philosophy. The method of understanding reality became not the drama but the dialectic. We could, theoretical man assured us, reason our way to an understanding of both the world and human nature; what is more, the will is in service to the intellect. What we understand with our minds, we will be able to will in our lives.

This exclusive reliance on reason was, in Nietzsche's view, a very grave mistake:

> Socrates might be designated as the specific *non-mystic,* in whom the logical nature is developed . . . to the same excess as instinctive wisdom is developed in the mystic . . . But then it seemed to Socrates that tragic art did not even "tell the truth" . . . Optimistic dialectics drives music out of tragedy with the scourge of its syllogisms: that is it destroys the essence of tragedy, which can be explained only as a manifestation and illustration of Dionysian states . . .[27]

In this view, tragedy appears illogical to the philosopher who believes that reason explains the world and its human occupants, for tragedy is full of causes that seem to be without effects and effects that seem to lack causes. There is nothing logical about Medea's slaughter of her children. The adoration of reason, which theoretical man brought, also cuts us off from much of what makes us feel alive and makes life worth living:

> Dionysian art, too, seeks to convince us of the eternal joy of existence . . . We are to perceive how all that comes into being must be ready for a sorrowful end; we are compelled to look into the terrors of individual existence—yet . . . we are really for brief moments Primordial Being itself, and feel its indomitable desire for being and joy in existence . . .[28]

The appeal of the Dionysian, for Nietzsche, is that it opens for us the universal and takes us out of the particular. In this, he agrees with Schopenhauer about the role of art and the function of the artist.

Whereas Schopenhauer's vision is of quiet contemplation in the presence of a work of art, Nietzsche's vision is alive with passion:

> Let no one attempt to weaken our faith in an impending re-birth of Hellenic antiquity; for in it alone we find our hope of a renovation and purification of the German spirit through the fire-magic of music . . . how suddenly this gloomily depicted wilderness of our exhausted culture changes when the Dionysian magic touches it! A hurricane seizes everything decrepit, decaying, collapsed, and stunted; wraps it whirlingly into a red cloud of dust; and carries it like a vulture into the air.[29]

What Nietzsche believed (or at least hoped) is that "the time of the Socratic man is past." With the rebirth of tragedy will come the rebirth of the **aesthetic hearer**—the person able to respond with feeling and involvement to art.

Nietzsche was also distressed with the attitude of the critic—the person who watches a play dispassionately and is therefore incapable of enjoyment. It is easy to be a critic. The spirit of his age he saw as a

THE MAKING OF A PHILOSOPHER

Friedrich Wilhelm Nietzsche
(1844–1900)

Nietzsche was born on October 15, just as the church bells were ringing to celebrate the birthday of Friedrich Wilhelm IV, then king of Prussia and patron to the new baby's father who was a Lutheran minister. Young Friedrich was named for the royal benefactor. After his father's death from an accidental fall, Nietzsche returned with his mother to her family home where he was raised by five women: his mother, grandmother, aunts, and sister. At Bonn University, he studied philology (the structure of languages) and theology. He also exhibited musical talent and did a lot of drinking. Following his teacher to the University of Leipzig in 1865, he met both Schopenhauer (whose book *The World as Will and Idea* impressed him) and the composer Richard Wagner (whose force of character Nietzsche admired). Nietzsche's brilliant beginnings as a professor and writer as well as a composer of symphonies was cut short when he contracted syphilis, a then incurable disease, and experienced bouts of apparent madness. Although he was considered a genius, many found him difficult if not impossible to live with. As an adult he was often in poor health, suffering migraine headaches and nausea.

criticohistorical spirit that kills myth and approaches all of life with detachment and distance:

> He who wishes to test himself rigorously as to how he is related to the true aesthetic hearer, or whether he belongs rather to the community of the Socrato-critical man, has only to enquire sincerely concerning the sentiment with which he accepts the wonder represented on stage: whether he feels his historical sense, which insists on strict psychological causality, insulted by it, whether with benevolent concession he as it were admits the wonder as a phenomenon intelligible to childhood, but relinquished by him, or whether he experiences anything else thereby.[30]

aesthetic hearer *a person who can respond to art with feeling and involvement, according to Nietzsche*

According to Nietzsche, art, science, and philosophy are all forms of illusion. They are all methods for ordering the meaningless swirl of experience into a meaningful whole. In his view, we need the spirits of both Apollo and Dionysus—both the impulse of Apollo toward individuation and the delights of the world of appearance and the impulse of Dionysus toward the merging of self into oneness symbolized by intoxication. If either predominates excessively, a culture will suffer. Both are needed to present a unified vision of reality.

The people who passionately love bad music are much closer to good taste than the wise men who love with good sense and moderation the most perfect music ever made.
STENDHAL

Nietzsche felt that the defeat of the Dionysian elements in Western culture began with the advent of philosophy in the Western world. Just before the rise of Socrates—the ultimate theoretical man—both elements were fused in Greek tragedy. Then, when it became too painful for us to look unflinchingly at the tragic elements in human life, we learned to tame them, to intellectualize them, by denying their reality and insisting that everything is explainable and controllable by reason. We may have gained a certain amount of security (false though it is), but in Nietzsche's view what we have sacrificed is the truth about reality.

Our culture has no rival in the realm of technology; we understand how to use logic and the methods of science to solve problems and to impose order. What we lack, however, is access to the irrationality Nietzsche saw in Dionysus. When we shut off the irrational impulses that Dionysus represents, we become critics of life rather than participants in it. We have, he believed, closed our eyes to a vital portion of the truth.

Opening our eyes, however, solves only part of the problem. Martin Heidegger argued that being must also open itself to us. If both processes occur, we have the possibility of truth.

Truth as Unconcealment: Martin Heidegger

The question of truth cannot be separated from the question of being, according to Heidegger, the twentieth-century intellectual heir to Schelling, Schopenhauer, and Nietzsche. Although he originally wanted to go directly to phenomena, or "the things themselves," he soon focused more directly on being, rejecting in the process the Cartesian view of the human person as a thinking substance and the world as extended substance. This image of the world as a container with people inside is a false one, he argued, because people and the world share a much more dynamic and intimate relationship: The natural state of the human person is as a **Being-in-the-world.**

Being-in-the-world *the natural state of the human person, according to Heidegger*

Heidegger wanted to ground truth in something deeper than phenomena—in Being itself. If the natural state of human beings is one of dwelling in the world, then the Western scientific view of ourselves as masters of nature is not only arrogant but also false. Being exists prior to thought and makes thought possible; if we want to discover the truth, we must look to Being. Verifying the truth about something is not a process of representation (or mimesis); it is more accurately a process of **unconcealment,** or **revealment.** If something lays itself open to us—if it unconceals itself—we may learn the truth about it.

unconcealment/ revealment *the disclosure of Being as truth, according to Heidegger*

Our stance toward the world, Heidegger contended, is crucial. Systematic philosophy, with its mind-matter split and other dichotomies, must give way to a more poetic kind of thinking. In fact, Heidegger described poetry, which he defines quite broadly to mean any authentic writing or speaking that has not lost its magic and power by being overused or abused, as "the saying of the unconcealedness of what is."[31] Thought must be expressed poetically because poetry is the saying of truth. We might say that truth, in Heidegger's way of thinking, can only be expressed poetically because it concerns being.

Furthermore, only as Being-in-the-world does the human person have the possibility of discovering the truth. This idea is similar to knowing the world from within it and is very different from the standpoint of the natural sciences, which try to understand the world from the outside. The truth is first and foremost the action of letting something become accessible—that is, uncovered or disclosed—and only secondarily the thing that becomes uncovered.

The quiet, simple way of thinking that Heidegger advocated led him to readings in Eastern philosophy and to the composition of original poetry. His new way of thinking has much in common with both Taoism and Zen in seeking the wisdom found in nature and in believing that most of what passes for knowledge is really ignorance. To Heidegger, the poetic element opens for us the possibility of authentic human existence; without it, we are, in his view, either brutes or robots (their twentieth-century counterparts) living by the dictates of self-will. The artist, and indeed anyone who lives poetically, escapes this fate by being willing to stop, listen, and respond to the call that comes from Being.

Good art speaks truth, indeed is *truth, perhaps the only truth.*
IRIS MURDOCH

We have made what Heidegger thought were unhelpful distinctions between, for example, the fine arts (which produce the beautiful) and the applied arts (which produce the useful). Truth has been said to belong to logic and beauty to aesthetics. Heidegger found an integration of truth and beauty in a work of art:

> In the work of art the truth of an entity has set itself to work . . . Some particular entity, a pair of peasant shoes, comes in the work to stand in the light of its being . . . The art work opens up in its own way the Being of beings. This opening up, i.e., this deconcealing, i.e., the truth

of beings, happens in the work. In the art work, the truth of what is has set itself to work. Art is truth setting itself to work.[32]

One of our mistakes is the assumption that truth exists ". . . in itself beforehand, somewhere among the stars, only later to descend elsewhere among beings."[33] Only the openness of beings provides a "somewhere" for truth to happen. Through the creative process, the unconcealedness of what-is is brought forth into "movement and happening."

What a work of art does is preserve truth in the work. "The nature of art," Heidegger wrote, "on which both the art work and the artist depend, is the setting-itself-into-work of truth."[34] In a way, it is art that lets truth originate or come into being. Art, Heidegger believed, is a distinctive way in which "truth comes into being, that is, becomes historical."[35]

If art can perform a function nothing else can perform, it is uniquely responsible for making truth historically available to us. If Heidegger is right, this restores to art the vitality that Nietzsche feared had been killed by Greek philosophy. Let's look now at how art functions in our own time.

Art as a Vehicle for Seeing the World Differently

At the very least, visual art and the artists who create it have the potential to give viewers a new experience of reality. When it is well done, art can re-order and re-form the world for us in a way that words alone cannot do. A gifted artist, like a skilled philosopher, can lead us to question our commonsense version of reality and call us to see the world differently. In this section we consider Impressionism, Cubism, and an inventive art installation to see how they are able to accomplish this visionary task. Finally, we will look at art's ability to widen our world.

Moving away from mimesis, modern artists have sometimes intentionally created works that do not imitate reality the way a snapshot does but, rather, reconstitute it in new forms. As we will see, theories of art have arisen that credit the artist with creating new forms every bit as real as the old ones. Although someone outside the art world might fault an artist for failing to successfully imitate reality, it is equally possible to see that artist as having captured reality more accurately (or at least equally so) by not employing mimesis.[36]

Leonard Shlain, whose book about the impact of alphabet literacy on image and the feminine we looked at briefly in Historical Interlude A, contends that artists are the harbingers of major shifts in our worldview. In *Art and Physics: Parallel Visions in Space, Time, and Light,* Shlain examines concepts of space, time, and light as they have been understood by artists and scientists over the past few millennia. His discovery is a recurring pattern: again and again, "the artist introduces symbols and icons that in retrospect prove to have been an avant-garde for the thought patterns of a scientific age not yet born.[37] For Shlain, art and physics are complementary partners; like the two manifestations of light as wave and particle that we examined in Chapter 2, art and physics should be seen as an "integrated

THE MAKING OF A PHILOSOPHER

Martin Heidegger
(1889–1976)

Heidegger had a sense of being called to do philosophy. He believed it is in the nature and vocation of all of us to ask what it means to be. When we fail to do this, it is the task of philosophy to call us back to ourselves and warn us of our failure. The question of what it means to be dominates *Being and Time,* which Heidegger published in 1927. Most people, he said, do not confront the question of being. They prefer to accept society's values rather than struggle to formulate their own. As a result, they live inauthentically, having forfeited the defining human characteristics of freedom and creativity. These ideas form the core of existentialism, which we will explore in the next chapter. Heidegger saw his own country of Germany as existing between two barbarian superpowers—the United States and the Soviet Union—and he believed philosophizing was possible only in the German language (or possibly German and Greek). This extreme nationalism also led him to join the National Socialist Party in 1933, and he publicly praised both Hitler and the Nazi regime. His sympathy for Nazi ideals has caused some to dismiss his ideas.

duality: They are simply two different but complementary facets of a single description of the world."[38]

From idealized Greek sculptures and Euclid's crisp geometric theorems, to the Renaissance discovery of perspective and Newtonian physics, through modern art and the breakthroughs of quantum mechanics and relativity theory, Shlain shows the artist anticipating in image what the scientist will later explain in words. To use only one example, Claude Monet announced the impressionist discovery that "the real subject of every painting is light." Einstein would later agree: "For the rest of my life I want to reflect on what light is." And, Shlain concludes this comparison by reminding us that God's act of creation did not involve space or time. Instead, we have creation out of nothing in God's fiat: "Let there be light!"[39]

Perhaps the most interesting comparison Shlain makes is between the startling and impossible to picture claims of quantum mechanics and relativity theory on the one hand and the parade of ever more obscure forms of art, such as Fauvism, Cubism, Expressionism, Dadaism, and Surrealism, on the other. In a bizarre but perfectly predictable coincidence, "the branch of science primarily responsible for explaining the nature of physical reality became unimaginable at the very moment that art became unintelligible."[40] Although they apparently did not read about or understand the emerging theories in physics, surrealists like Rene Magritte (whose painting "L'Eschelle du Feu" we looked at in Chapter 5) did image in their work concepts such as the flattening of space that occurs as we approach light speed (in "The Glasshouse") and the stopping of time at the speed of light, as described in Einstein's Special Theory of Relativity (in "Time Transfixed"). The difficulty we experience trying to picture the four dimensional space-time continuum is partially alleviated by Salvador Dali's "Crucifixion." The suffering Christ is pressed against a three-dimensional rendering of a four-dimensional hypercube, which according to mathematical calculations would consist of eight cubes, seven of them sharing one contiguous side, and one cube (the central one) that shared all of its sides.[41]

Keeping all of these possibilities in mind, let's look at the ways in which art has what might be a unique power to help us see the world differently. Impressionism, Cubism, and art installations all invite us to reconsider the common sense version of reality that presents itself to us minute-by-minute.

Impressionism

One of the clearest examples of the power of art to raise metaphysical and epistemological questions is the Impressionist revolution of the nineteenth century. Impressionist painters have showed us that once we move beyond the conventions of studio painting, the material concreteness of reality breaks down into *impressions* of light and color. Their great discovery was that light accounts for the changes in how we see things. Given the seemingly infinite variety of light effects, the universe seems to be in per-

DOING PHILOSOPHY
Artist as Philosopher

Art can offer us a window into the heart of reality, but only if it also serves as a mirror in which we can see ourselves. Mexican artist Frida Kahlo painted a number of self-portraits, including this one for Leon Trotsky, the Russian revolutionary with whom she had a romantic liaison. It was presented to him on his birthday November 7, 1937, which was also the twentieth anniversary of the Bolshevik Revolution. Perhaps the portrait is meant to reflect the couple's shared political beliefs. What aspects of the exterior persona Kahlo shows us might indicate that intention? What insights about the inner Frida is Kahlo communicating to Trotsky? We know that in adolescence her body was crippled by a trolley accident, which severely injured her spinal cord. Are there any hints of pain and struggle in this portrait? We can speak about our identity, our human nature, using words, with all their built-in limitations, and we can also use images, the symbolic language of art. In what sense might Frida Kahlo be said to be doing philosophy in this self-portrait?

petual movement, ever changing and never fixed into a finished product. (See Virgil's experience in Chapter 2.)

Seen through the eye of an Impressionist painter, reality appears to be composed of the many and varied discrete bits of sensation described by empiricist philosophers. The apparently stable and quite rational knowledge of the world that realistic art seems to offer is dethroned by Impressionism. What is revealed instead is a volatile succession of colored snapshots. The same object can appear endlessly varied as light modulates over its surfaces.

If you stand directly in front of an Impressionist painting, it may be difficult to determine what the painting represents; all your eye can take in are the many dots of color. It is necessary to step back and view the painting from a distance before you can really see the people and objects it contains. Once you have gained this needed perspective, the artist seems to be telling you, your eye can form images of objects out of the multiplicity of sensations. If you focus too closely on some of the splotches to the exclusion of others, you will see nothing at all.[42]

A self-portrait of Frida Kahlo (1907–1954).

Frida Kahlo (Mexican, 1907–1954). *Self-Portrait Dedicated to Leon Trotsky,* 1937. Oil on masonite. 30 × 24 in./The National Museum of Women in the Arts, Washington, D.C./Gift of the Honorable Clare Booth Luce.

Cubism

If Impressionism tends to resolve images into bits of light and color, Cubism makes an even more radical statement about reality by breaking up objects to such an extent that they must be reconstituted by the observer. Believing that the senses deform objects, Cubist painters sought to reduce or eliminate the distorting effects of light and color. Cubist art dissects a form—takes it apart—and then reconstructs it, using the entire surface area of the painting. The artist represents the subject of the painting from every conceivable point of view—from above, below, the front, the back, and

Are we able to "see" reality more clearly when Picasso dissects it into geometrical planes and draws masklike faces?

PICASSO, Pablo. *Les Demoiselles d'Avignon*. Paris (June–July 1907). Oil on canvas, 8' × 7'8" (243.9 × 233.7 cm). The Museum of Modern Art, New York. Acquired through the Lillie P. Bliss Bequest.

each side—to in effect let the viewer move around the subject the way one moves around a piece of sculpture, without moving at all.

When looking at a Cubist painting, you see not what the ordinary casual gaze might reveal but focused glimpses of reality. The artist can draw our attention to small bits of form by disconnecting them from any natural surrounding. Bits of form are in effect highlighted the way a strobe light can bring something into momentary illumination before dropping it back into darkness. Cubism is an assault on—a radical dissection of—the wholeness that ordinary vision presents us.

In Picasso's *Les Demoiselles d'Avignon,* we see the bodies of the young women from the "red light district" as smooth, geometric fragments. Body parts seem almost disconnected, some are distorted, and there is an overall sense of violent energy. Picasso had recently discovered the art of African masks, and we can see that influence as well, especially in the stylized and staring quality of the eyes.

Apparently far removed from reality, Cubism offers access to another kind or level of reality. As Picasso explained it, "I paint things as I think them, not as I see them."[43] Do we see more or less truly when we focus first on one plane and then on another? Is reality unified and continuous or broken and distorted? How much of what we think we know about reality is a fiction created by our minds?

Mining the Museum

There is another way in which art can pose questions about reality and make us question what we really know. A permanent exhibit at the Maryland Historical Society uses juxtaposition of objects to consider the experiences of African Americans and Native Americans in Maryland. The issue being explored is the extent to which the experience of these two groups of people is reflected (or not reflected) in the Society's collection.

By placing slave's shackles in the same case with a beautiful silver service and by placing velvet Victorian chairs in front of a whipping post, New York installation artist Fred Wilson encouraged visitors to reexamine their attitudes and their understanding of history. An empty pedestal bearing the name of Frederick Douglass placed next to a bust of Andrew Jackson dramatizes omissions from both history and art.

Called "Mining the Museum," the exhibit speaks to the descendants of both slaves and slave owners. Both experience a jolt and feel compelled to rethink their assumptions about history, race, and art itself. Record crowds have visited the exhibit, and Wilson has found the experience very satisfying: "It made my faith and trust in others bloom—and my faith that art can make a difference in people's lives, museums can make a difference in society and I can make a difference as an artist."[44]

Opening a Wider World

It was precisely this challenge to the content of museums that led artist Judy Chicago to create an installation she calls *The Dinner Party*. On a huge equilateral triangle (48 feet on each side) are thirty-nine place settings honoring women from history and legend, including many who appear in this text. Each woman has her own unique porcelain plate with a raised design; a fabric placemat-runner, with needlework techniques appropriate to her period; and a drinking chalice. On the marble floor beneath the dinner table are the names of an additional 999 women. More than 100 women joined Chicago in bringing this design to completion.

"Mining the Museum" and *The Dinner Party* aim to bring the previously excluded within the walls of the museum. This is also the intention of the Mexican Fine Arts Center Museum in Chicago. According to the Museum's

What do we learn by placing slave shackles next to a silver tea service?
Metalwork/Fred Wilson, The Maryland Historical Society.

driving force Helen Valdez, "This museum is about people and about freedom . . . This is about breaking stereotypes that limit not only our community but the whole country. It's about possibilities."[45] Committed to connecting popular and high culture, the Museum features so-called fine art as well as the arts of the people:

> We are not creating something that isn't already there. We are formalizing it, enhancing it, highlighting it, celebrating it. You know all those little *quinceaneras,* the celebrations of a girl's fifteenth birthday, that go on in church, the music, the beliefs, all those are parts of the culture in its most popular form and in its most sophisticated form as well.[46]

Art, like philosophy, has the possibility of opening us up to ourselves and to our world. It can be our window on a wider world—but only if it is also a mirror, reflecting back something we already recognize.

Summary

Art appearing on the walls of caves is dated to 30,000 years ago—masterpieces of sophisticated realism, impressive even by today's standards.[47] And, 50,000 years ago, Neanderthals fashioned musical instruments—flutes and tubas, triangles and xylophones—from bone. There is even evidence of a bagpipelike instrument made from the bladder of some large animal.[48] Art appears to be co-extensive with human existence. What essential function does it perform?

American artist Audrey Flack has this to say:

> Art is a powerful force in the world. It is the visual representation of what we think . . . what we feel . . . how we think . . . how we feel. Art makes life more livable, more beautiful, more comprehensible. It helps us deal with . . . all that is perishable in the world, and attempt to reach a higher reality—to fill the soul, to excite the mind, to go beyond. Its message cuts through time and space and lasts for centuries. Art is a protest against death.[49]

We have considered in this chapter the role that beauty, especially the beauty created by visual art, can play in helping us arrive at truth. From the classic understanding of art as mimesis (representation of reality), we have moved through history, exploring Western, Asian, and African art and artists. Like philosophers, artists seem to bridge the distance between the commonsense world of appearances and whatever underlies it. As priestlike figures, artists speak the transcendent to us in a language without words.

Art is an affirmation of life, a rebuttal of death . . . To serve a work of art, great or small, is to die, to die to self.

MADELEINE L'ENGLE

Though we may not be able to speak the insights we receive in the presence of genuine art, there is a kind of certainty we feel. Art has a language of its own that codifies inner experience, just as language codifies outward experience. Traditional philosophy, relying as it does on language, has its own built-in limitations; knowing what is true may be more a question of seeing truly than of speaking accurately, and art can be the vehicle for a critical kind of knowing.

Every culture produces art, and art has a way of signaling new ways of seeing and being. When a society's artistic forms change, we may be fairly confident that society has found a new way of seeing itself and reality. Art takes us out of ourselves and out of our ordinary concerns, and it gives us access to a wider world. Although words may fail us, we should not be misled into thinking that we have learned nothing; real art speaks to us just as truly as words do, and perhaps more deeply.

This helps explain why we often keep coming back to the same painting or sculpture, the same symphony or concerto, the same ritual mask or sand garden. As a work of art continues to reveal itself to us, we get ever-new meanings, each one full of richness. When it works, art seems to be a window on a fuller reality. Beauty is truth and truth beauty. If we can understand this, we will have learned something really worth knowing.

Once we know what is true and what is real, we are in a position to consider what we value. Part 3, the next and final section, deals with questions of **axiology** and asks this question: By what values shall I live in the world? We will look at the relationship between the individual and the state, consider the extent to which we are or should be connected with one another, and explore what moral standards are appropriate in the living of an individual life. Before we begin this section, however, let's explore the transition from the modern to the postmodern world and its effect on values.

axiology *the branch of philosophy dealing with the study of values*

For Further Thought

1. Are there things you know with certainty that you cannot put into words? If so, what kinds of things are they, and why is it so difficult to verbalize them? Does the fact that they cannot be spoken make them any less certain?
2. What kind of window on a culture does art provide? In other words, what kinds of things can we learn about a culture by studying its art?
3. If we study only the written documents of a culture or only the visual arts, are we getting an incomplete and perhaps inaccurate picture of the culture? Explain.
4. Why do people turn to artistic expression in times of emotional pain or confusion? What does the experience of being a performing artist (even if you are the only audience) provide that seems unavailable outside it? How is it that one can lose oneself in playing the piano or guitar, painting, woodworking, sculpting, or writing?
5. What kind of culture would we have if artists played the role traditionally played by priests? What might our "religious rituals" look like if they were based in art rather than religion?
6. Why do people return time after time to a favorite piece of music or a favorite painting? What is being communicated?
7. Give some thought to what you feel you can be certain about. If you conclude there is something, decide the basis for your certainty. Does aesthetic experience play any role in giving you certainty?
8. Can you think of some examples of art being used for propaganda purposes? (HINT: Remember the "good guy/bad guy" stereotypes. What function is being served by portraying a group of people as "bad guys"? This is clearly a perversion of art, but is it functional? Does it work?)
9. Talk to an artist or read a biography of an artist whose work you know something about. If you are an artist yourself, think about this question: What is it like to create a work of art? What does it cost the artist? What does the artist receive? How does it feel?
10. Have you ever seen a movie or play about an event that you witnessed or even lived through yourself and found your emotional reaction to the staged event stronger than your emotional reaction to the actual event? What, if anything, does this tell us about the relationship between art and truth?
11. What is the sense in which art is a mirror of the culture that produced it? Does this have any connection with questions of truth? Explain.
12. What role does perspective provide in art and in the assessment of reality? What is our feedback mechanism for determining whether our own perspective is accurate or not? Who ultimately decides what an accurate or appropriate perspective is? Who should decide?
13. Why do people differ so profoundly in their opinions of art objects?
14. Who decides when something moves from the category of "mindless garbage" to that of "sheer genius"? How does a person become an "expert" in matters of aesthetic judgment? What kind of knowledge does that person have to have?
15. Are there conditions under which art could be used for purely instrumental purposes (as something to be used rather than admired)? Do we want our art to be useful as well as beautiful? As we move toward the useful and away

from the beautiful, is there a point at which an object stops being art and starts being something else?

16. How does "folk art" differ from "fine art"? What do the two art forms have in common? Where do the differences exist? Is folk art, like quilting, a legitimate art form? Why, or why not?
17. Some serious questions about censorship in art are being raised today. Under what circumstances would a work of art, in your judgment, be deserving of censorship?
18. Should we allow the "expert" to determine when a work of art becomes "pornographic"? Current Supreme Court guidelines rely on "community standards," which seems to imply that something can be pornographic in one community and not pornographic in another. Who should make these judgments, and how should they be made?
19. If artists were the arbiters of truth and were looked to for decisions about what is true and what isn't, do you think our understanding of truth would undergo a radical change? Explain. It might help to consider who we now acknowledge to be arbiters of truth.
20. Think of something that offers you a genuine "aesthetic experience" when you are in its presence (a painting, a piece of sculpture, a piece of music). When you contemplate this art form, do you learn anything you might classify as knowledge or truth? If so, think about the nature of that knowledge. (NOTE: It may be difficult for you to put what you think you know into words.)

For Further Exploration

Achebe, Chinua. *Arrow of God*. New York: Anchor, 1974. Achebe describes what it is like being an artist in a traditional African society.

Asimov, Isaac. *The Foundation Trilogy*. New York: Ballantine, 1983. Asimov offers the saga of a thousand years of a galactic empire (the Foundation) dedicated to art, science, and technology.

Herrigel, Eugen. *Zen in the Art of Archery*. Translated by R. F. C. Hull. New York: Vintage, 1953. Herrigel shows why it takes years to learn the art of archery, why it has nothing to do with hitting the target, and why if you learn it you will hit the target every time—even blindfolded.

James, Henry. "The Real Thing." In *The American Novels and Stories of Henry James*. New York: Knopf, 1947. Issues addressed in this story are why real people can't portray themselves as effectively as actors can and why a movie can affect us more powerfully than the event on which it was based.

Kafka, Franz. "Hunger Artist." In *The Complete Stories and Parables*. New York: Schocken, 1983. This short story centers around an artist whose "art" consists of fasting for many days.

Langer, Susanne. *Philosophical Sketches*. Baltimore: Johns Hopkins University Press, 1962. Langer offers philosophical musings on reality and the value of art in helping us manage our dealings with it.

Merton, Thomas, trans. *The Way of Chuang Tzu*. New York: New Directions, 1965. This book provides insight into the experience of being an artist in a traditional

Eastern society. See especially "Cutting Up an Ox," "The Fasting of the Heart," "Duke Hwan and the Wheelwright," and "The Need to Win."

Plato. *The Symposium*. Translated by Walter Hamilton. New York: Penguin, 1951. This work contains meditations (some humorous) on beauty.

Stone, Irving. *The Agony and the Ecstasy*. New York: Anchor, 1989. This historical novel depicts the experience of being an artist (Michelangelo) in a traditional Western society.

Yalom, Irven. *When Nietzsche Wept*. New York: Basic, 1992. This is an imaginary encounter between Joseph Breuer, Friedrich Nietzsche, and Sigmund Freud (Breuer's student in the emerging field of psychoanalysis); Breuer tries to analyze Nietzsche and ends up being analyzed; a good introduction to Nietzsche's ideas.

For Further Research

Try these InfoTrac keywords:

Aesthetic Experience
Cubism
Installation Art
Impressionism
Nietzsche
Heidegger

Notes

1. "The Woodcarver," in *The Way of Chuang Tzu,* trans. Thomas Merton (New York: New Directions, 1969), 110–111.
2. Abd al-Hayy Moore, *Zen Rock Gardening* (Philadelphia: Running Press, 1992), 16–34.
3. W. Emmanuel Abraham, "Sources of African Identity," in *Person and Community: Ghanaian Philosophical Studies,* vol. 1, eds. Kwasi Wiredu and Kwame Gyekye (Washington, D.C.: Council for Research in Values and Philosophy, 1992), 50.
4. Abraham, 51.
5. Chinua Achebe, *Arrow of God* (New York: John Day, 1967), 62–63.
6. Achebe.
7. Roger Scruton, "The Philosopher on Dover Beach," in *The Philosopher on Dover Beach* (New York: St. Martin's, 1990), 10.
8. Scruton, 49.
9. Plato, *The Symposium,* trans. Walter Hamilton (New York: Penguin, 1951), 94.
10. Mortimer J. Adler, *Six Great Ideas* (New York: Macmillan, 1981), 112.
11. George Dickie, "The New Institutional Theory of Art," in *Aesthetics: A Critical Anthology,* eds. George Dickie, Richard Sclafani, and Ronald Roblin (New York: St. Martin's, 1989), 202.

12. Dickie.
13. Clive Bell, "Art as Significant Form," in *Aesthetics,* 83.
14. Susanne Langer, "The Cultural Importance of Art," in *Philosophical Sketches* (Baltimore: Johns Hopkins University Press, 1962), 88.
15. Langer, 90.
16. Alfred North Whitehead, *Adventures of Ideas* (New York: Free Press, 1967), 271.
17. Whitehead, 272.
18. Stewart W. Holmes and Chimyo Horioka, *Zen Art for Meditation* (Tokyo: Tuttle, 1990), 37.
19. Friedrich Wilhelm Joseph von Schelling, *System of Transcendental Idealism* (1800), trans. Peter Heath (Charlottesville: University of Virginia Press, 1978), 231–232.
20. Schelling, 222.
21. Schelling, 233.
22. Schelling, 12.
23. Arthur Schopenhauer, *The World as Will and Idea,* ed. Will Durant (New York: Ungar, 1955), 105.
24. Schopenhauer, 117.
25. Schopenhauer, 117.
26. Schopenhauer, 150.
27. Friedrich Nietzsche, *The Birth of Tragedy: Or Hellenism and Pessimism,* trans. Wm. A. Haussmann (New York: Russell & Russell, 1964), 105, 107, 111.
28. Nietzsche, 128.
29. Nietzsche, 156.
30. Nietzsche, 173–174.
31. Martin Heidegger, "The Origin of the Work of Art," in *Poetry, Language, Thought: Martin Heidegger,* trans. Albert Hofstadter (New York: Harper & Row, 1971), 74.
32. Heidegger, 36, 39.
33. Heidegger, 61.
34. Heidegger, 71, 72.
35. Heidegger, 78.
36. Arthur Danto, "The Artistic Enfranchisement of Real Objects: The Artworld," in *Aesthetics,* 173.
37. Leonard Shlain, *Art and Physics: Parallel Visions in Space, Time, and Light* (New York: Quill, William Morrow, 1991), 19.
38. Shlain, 24.
39. Shlain, 179.
40. Shlain, 222.
41. Shlain, 236, 233, 230.
42. Gina Pischel, *A World History of Art: Painting, Sculpture, Architecture, Decorative Arts,* rev. ed. (New York: Simon & Schuster, 1975), 611–612.
43. Pischel, 649–650.

44. Fred Wilson, in the *Baltimore Sun,* 1 March 1993.
45. Helen Valdez, in *Barrios and Borderlands: Cultures of Latinos and Latinas in the United States,* ed. Denis Lynn Daly Heyck (New York: Routledge, 1994), 297.
46. Valdez, 297.
47. "The Birth of Cro-Magnon Art," *Baltimore Sun,* 23 August 1996, 19A.
48. "Human Origins," *Discover Magazine* (April 1997): 19.
49. Audrey Flack, "Some Notes on Art and Life," in *Audrey Flack on Painting* (New York: Abrams, 1981), 28.

PART THREE

By What Values Shall I Live in the World?

Questions of Axiology

HISTORICAL INTERLUDE D

From the Modern to the Postmodern World

There was a time, not so very long ago, when life began at birth and ended with death—events that were clear and obvious to everyone. Babies were born to two people who had sexual intercourse; for the most part, people knew who their parents were. When someone died, a death certificate was signed. Most people were born at home and died at home. Today, most of us are born in hospitals, and many of us will die in hospitals.

Wars have been common throughout history, but there used to be rules governing what was acceptable and what was not. In Descartes's day, wars stopped during the winter. If you fought a particularly bloody war, you might have killed large numbers of men and even boys, but the tribe or the village or the culture would remain. Not so long ago wars were fought in person; to kill the enemy you had to smash his skull with an axe or shove your sword through his body, you had to look your enemy in the eye as you killed him. Later, the crossbow and the gun were invented, enabling killing from a distance. Use of the crossbow was almost forbidden because it was perceived as such a powerful weapon of destruction.

In the not-so-distant past, people lived and died according to a natural cycle. When the rains came, there was a good harvest; when they did not, there was

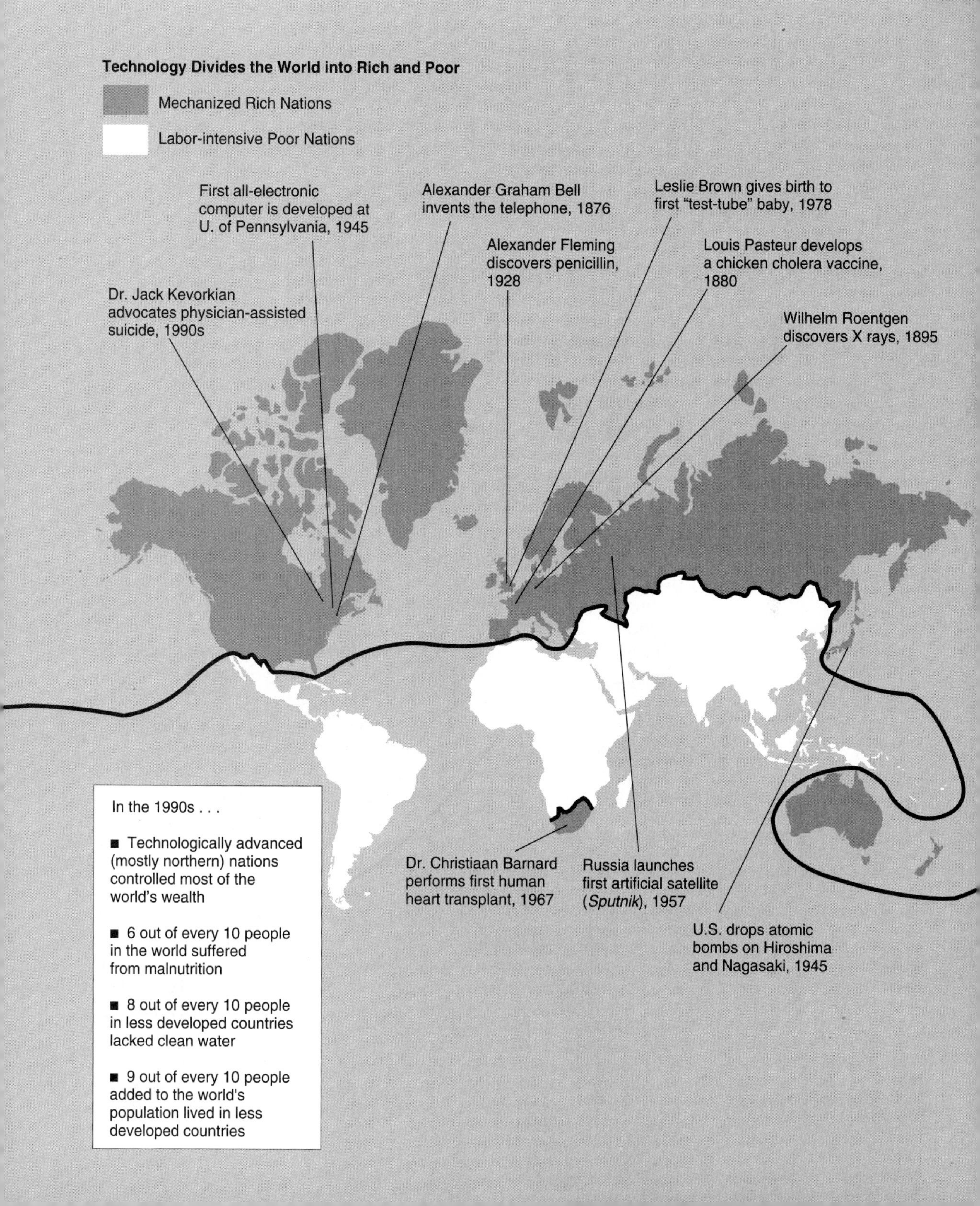

Technology Divides the World into Rich and Poor

Mechanized Rich Nations

Labor-intensive Poor Nations

First all-electronic computer is developed at U. of Pennsylvania, 1945

Alexander Graham Bell invents the telephone, 1876

Leslie Brown gives birth to first "test-tube" baby, 1978

Alexander Fleming discovers penicillin, 1928

Louis Pasteur develops a chicken cholera vaccine, 1880

Dr. Jack Kevorkian advocates physician-assisted suicide, 1990s

Wilhelm Roentgen discovers X rays, 1895

Dr. Christiaan Barnard performs first human heart transplant, 1967

Russia launches first artificial satellite (*Sputnik*), 1957

U.S. drops atomic bombs on Hiroshima and Nagasaki, 1945

In the 1990s . . .

- Technologically advanced (mostly northern) nations controlled most of the world's wealth
- 6 out of every 10 people in the world suffered from malnutrition
- 8 out of every 10 people in less developed countries lacked clean water
- 9 out of every 10 people added to the world's population lived in less developed countries

famine. Now we make the deserts bloom by irrigation, but famine is still with us. Microbes used to take the lives of thousands, wiping out almost entire villages, before we discovered antibiotics; now we have miracle drugs that routinely defeat microorganisms with stunning efficiency—except for increasingly common drug-resistant strains. And viruses continue to resist our attempts to kill them. There have always been plagues that killed massively and without warning or explanation about why one person lived and another died; AIDS seems to fit this model.

Once upon a time, when your heart—or liver or lungs or kidneys—wore out or became diseased, you died. Now we have developed the ability to transplant organs from person to person. After your death, your eyes can help another person see; your organs can give life to someone who may not even know you are the one to be thanked. As Paul Simon reminds us in "The Boy in the Bubble," "These are the days of miracle and wonder. So, don't cry baby, don't cry."

The Advent of the Technological Age

It takes very little reflection to realize what incredible progress has been made over the past few centuries. Imagine a person who died 100 or even 50 years ago reanimated and transported to the present time (as people who have undergone cryogenic suspension hope to do some time in the future). How easily you might impress that person, even with the most mundane routines of your daily life. Satellites and cable television bring the world into your living room. Someone in your family can spend the day in a distant city and jet home in time for dinner. Information flies by phone and fax machine around the world, and money goes into your bank account and out to your creditors without ever passing through your hands. Very likely, your home maintains a comfortable temperature year-round, heated in winter and cooled in summer. Machines do most of the backbreaking, spirit-breaking work that only a century ago was done by humans, and before that by animals—at least in Western Europe and the Americas.

Technology is the miracle of Western science, and it has been harnessed to make our lives easier, safer, and more comfortable in countless ways. One hundred years ago, people looked at the progress that had already been made and optimistically envisioned a future in which all human problems would be solved and life would be close to perfect. What we have learned since is that technology seems to have a life of its own. Even though splitting the atom provides a power supply, it also produces bombs powerful enough to wipe out life as we know it and radioactive wastes we don't yet know what to do with. And, once discovered or unleashed, technology is difficult to ignore. Because we *can* do such a staggering number of things that once seemed impossible, we often *do* them. There has been too little time for our philosophy to keep pace with our technology. The question philosophy must ask is, *Should* we do something simply because it is possible to do it?

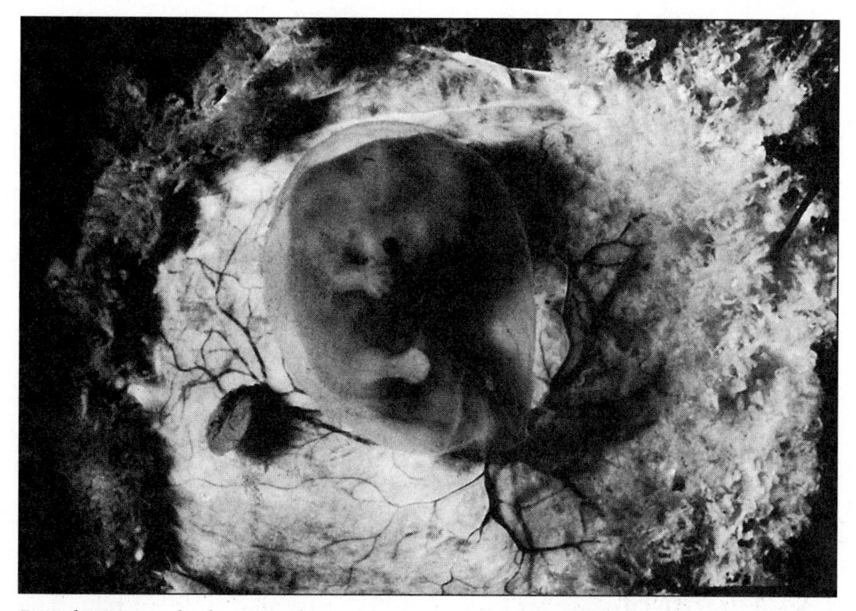

Does this stage or birth or something in-between represent the beginning of new life?

The Philosophical Implications of Technology

In Part 3 of this text, we will be considering the issues of axiology, or values, under the topics of political philosophy, social philosophy, and ethics. Some of the questions we will be asking are these: How large (or small) a role should government play in people's lives? Who should enjoy the benefits, and who should bear the burdens in a society? How shall I as an individual make moral choices? At the beginning of the millennium, we cannot ask these questions without considering the role of technology and its implications for our lives as individuals and members of a larger society. As it blurs the lines surrounding birth and death, makes possible technological warfare, and intervenes to alleviate famine and prevent disease, technology raises philosophical questions.

The Blurred Definitions of Birth and Death

Exactly when life begins and ends is no longer as clear-cut as we once thought it to be. Does life begin when an egg and sperm unite, before the newly formed zygote has attached to the wall of the uterus with its rich blood supply that will make life possible? Does it begin, as Thomas Aquinas believed in the thirteenth century, with "quickening," when the mother feels the baby move, or at the time after which the fetus is able to survive unassisted outside the mother's body, or at birth? Today, we can separate these processes, and that separation makes the questions possible.

Egg and sperm can now be united in a petri dish. Is this the moment when life begins? A divorced couple in Tennessee fought in the courts for years over "custody" of seven frozen fertilized embryos the couple "produced" by donating eggs and sperm while they were still married. The man wanted the embryos destroyed because he no longer wished to become a parent, whereas the woman wanted the embryos to be used, possibly to be donated to another couple. And supposing the embryos were donated—who would be the parents of the resulting child?

Since adoption has become more commonplace, we have begun to distinguish between birth parents and legal parents. A parent, we have said, is the person who sits beside your bed all night while you burn with fever, who wipes your tears when you are frightened or emotionally bruised by life, who opens his or her life to you. These are compelling arguments, and they feel "right" to us. Still, some adopted children cannot suppress the desire to meet their birth parents, even if only to explore their biological "roots" and see whether they resemble anyone physically or psychologically.

Trickier still is the issue of donor artificial insemination. Beginning with the desire to breed better cows, the technology of sperm collection and storage provided an answer for couples who desired children but could not conceive because of the man's infertility. Many formerly infertile married women (as well as unmarried heterosexual and lesbian women) have been able to conceive and bear children using donated sperm. Unlike adoption, this process could be kept secret even from the child. Aside from a feeling of doing something to help someone else, many sperm donors may have given little or no thought to the matter. Today, however, some children of artificial insemination are asking to meet their biological "fathers." Anonymity was promised to the sperm donors, and that may decide the legal question. But what of the matter of the child's identity? Does the child, now grown, have the moral right to know his or her biological parents, if they are different from the people called Mom and Dad?

When a woman is infertile, technology now makes it possible for her eggs and her husband's sperm to be extracted and brought together in a petri dish. Called *in vitro fertilization,* this process can also employ donor eggs. Along with *surrogate motherhood*—in which a woman donates her body as incubator for a developing fetus—these technological miracles (discussed in greater detail in Chapter 10) further cloud the question of who the parents of any given child actually are.

Amniocentesis and other related procedures allow physicians, with minimal risk, to extract a few cells from the amniotic fluid during the fourth or fifth month of pregnancy and "read" the genetic code of the developing fetus. The purpose is to screen for genetic defects such as Tay Sachs disease or Down syndrome. A good report sets the parents' minds at ease, and discovery of some chromosomal abnormality gives the parents the option of terminating the pregnancy. Among the information in the genetic code is, of course, the sex of the child. What if the parents really were holding out for a girl (or a boy) and decided to terminate this pregnancy simply to gamble that in a future pregnancy they can conceive a child of the desired sex?

With all our medical technology, we are now able to "save" tiny babies who weigh less than a pound and can fit in the palm of a hand. Born prematurely, they lack many systems they need to survive, and before the advent of technology they would certainly have died. Some of these babies grow into fully functioning "normal" children, whereas others are so damaged or incomplete at birth that they never leave the hospital. Medical personnel are obliged to fight for the life of every one of these babies, and because of our technology we save more each year. We make no decisions about which babies to save and which to "allow to die." Technology often makes the decision for us.

The same sorts of dilemmas occur at the end of life. People who only a few years ago would have died of "natural causes" are automatically hooked up to life-support systems today. If the patient fully recovers, the family is grateful, but if the patient is physically alive but mentally dead, the family is faced with wrenching decisions about "pulling the plug." The concept of brain death is a relatively new one. When no detectable pulse or breathing meant the death of the person, there were fewer decisions to make. If we could keep the body alive, we did; if we could not, the person died. Today, when technology can keep either a body or a brain alive when the other can no longer function on its own, the definition of death is so very much more complicated.

Suicide was once a very private matter, and the methods available were often a deterrent. With physician-assisted suicide, however, death can be almost painless. Sworn to preserve life, physicians are now faced with gut-wrenching decisions. If life has become intolerable for a terminally ill patient and that patient desires a "death with dignity," is it the physician's duty either to refuse that request or to assist in a dignified death? Less often reported in the headlines are the hundreds, probably thousands of families and friends of terminally ill people who cross the border into Mexico, buy drugs that are illegal in the United States or Canada, and deliver them to those they love for the purpose of suicide. To be sure, legal questions are involved here, but of more interest are the moral ones. If a person asks your help in committing suicide, should you help? And how might you make that decision?

Waging War and Making Other Political Decisions

These are the days of technological war. We have only to push a button, and we are capable of raining unimaginable destruction on another country, perhaps even of destroying the entire Earth. Apart from the moral questions related to war, we must consider how decisions about war should be made. Is the decision easier or more difficult to make when you meet the enemy face to face? And who, after all, is the enemy?

If your government orders you to fight as a soldier (or face serious, equally life-threatening consequences as a "draft dodger"), in what sense are you the enemy of a soldier from the opposing camp whose government has imposed a similar burden on him or her? You have no personal quarrel with the enemy soldier. You have in fact never met. There are no blood feuds between your families, no vengeance you feel compelled to visit on the other. You are simply fighting because your government has ordered you to fight. Perhaps you agree with the political posture of your government, perhaps you simply agree a citizen must do what the government asks, perhaps you disagree entirely but cannot refuse to serve without risking jail or worse.

Wars used to be a lot more spontaneous. If a neighboring village raided your cattle, you went to war to get them back. The threat or the wrong was obvious and clearly present. You fought, if you did, because you wanted to right a wrong. Wars today are declared and "fought" by large impersonal governments over sometimes difficult-to-understand theoretical and geopolitical issues. If you are asked or ordered to fight, you automatically become the enemy of thousands of other people against whom you have no grievance. Like the young protagonist in Ernest Hemingway's *A Farewell to Arms,* you may find yourself wondering why you are killing someone so much like yourself.

In Chapter 8, "Political Philosophy," we will examine who makes decisions such as the commitment to go to war, and how these decisions are made. Should government shape or reflect the will of the people? Who really knows best? Less dramatic but equally important powers, like the power to tax and spend, are also the province of government. How much say should elected representatives have over how to spend money collected from the citizens? Should power rest in the hands of ordinary people, or would it be wiser to provide some backup systems to prevent the public from choosing unwisely?

Preventing Famine and Controlling Disease

We are no longer bound by the limits of Earth's natural cycles—or are we? Evidence is everywhere of successful attempts to exert human control over nature. We stay comfortable in our homes, our cars, our offices, and our schools, no matter how brutal the weather—unless of course the electricity goes out. Water is piped into arid regions, and deserts bloom with produce and even flowers—unless of course a drought ensues and water is rationed. Levees hold back mighty rivers—except when they break. Vaccines administered in childhood protect against diseases that used to be epidemic—except that measles is making a comeback on college campuses.

There seem to be some natural limitations to the application of human technology. Perhaps the world's systems are more complicated than we realize; when we fix something in one place, we create a problem in another, like trying to smooth out the bumps in a carpet. Another set of questions, though, addresses the extent of our responsibility to take care of our fellow human beings—at home and abroad. In Chapter 9, "Social Philosophy," we will look at where we believe our obligations lie. If we have machines to do our work while people in third-world countries use the brawn of animals or their own bodies, should we feel any obligation to share the fruits of our technology with them? Can we share technology without altering other factors (like population density), or might we be doing more harm than good?

Social philosophy looks at who should enjoy the benefits in a society—like health care and education and the rights to vote, to drink, and to drive—and who should bear the burdens—such as paying taxes, serving on juries, and fighting in wars. More important, who should decide, and how should the decisions be made? Traditionally, those with wealth, power, and status make those decisions. What of the poor, the powerless, and those without status? Are they on their own to do whatever they can do, or do we have obligations arising out of the benefits we enjoy?

Should North Americans turn inward, focusing on our own problems and trying our best to solve them? Or are we so much a part of the "global village" that it is an illusion to speak of our problems in isolation from those that affect the world as a whole? Would it have been possible to keep AIDS out of the United States during the early days of the epidemic, and if so, would this have been an acceptable posture for us to take?

Axiology in a Postmodern World

In the 200 years since Kant wrote his philosophy, we have moved from a modern to a postmodern world. As we saw in Chapters 2 and 3, defining what we think is real and what it means to be a human person seems more difficult than ever before. Along with uncertainty over basic issues such as these has come the suspicion, or the fear, that there may be no underlying order to the cosmos, no fundamental meaning to human life. The Greek assumption that the world is an intelligible place whose secrets rational human beings can unlock has come into question. Ironically, as we have learned to penetrate and control what used to be called life's mysteries, meaning seems to fade away like a receding tide.

Women and racial/ethnic minorities in Western societies may agree that this is not all bad news. Among the certainties 200 years ago was an unchallenged assumption that a white patriarchy was destined by God and nature to rule the world. Philosophers like Kant assumed that there was one and only one framework for interpreting reality, and textbooks even 100 years ago reflected a world very different from the world we see today.

As travel and communication shrink the world into a global village, diversity and pluralism are natural consequences. For those whose existence is valued and whose ideas are included, multiculturalism makes perfect sense and feels "right"; for those used to a more unitive view of the world, the result may seem more confusing and perhaps even a little threatening. If others whom I have assumed should learn from me begin trying to teach me, the world may appear to me to be falling apart.

One aspect of postmodernism is the loss of certainty. In a world modeled on the Great Chain of Being, everyone and everything (at least in theory) has a place. When even the notion of hierarchy is questioned, we may feel the ground crumbling under our feet. In a postmodern world, many more things are possible and many fewer things are certain. What has changed most appear to be the values we hold as individuals and as a society. The relationship between the individual and the state, the definition of justice, the presumption that there are objective standards for moral decision making—all these have shifted dramatically over the past 200 years.

Once we have grappled with what constitutes reality—in the world and in the human being—and struggled to understand how we know what we think we know, we come to the final set of questions: How do we act based on what we know? Our moral decisions will be based on our beliefs about what reality is like and on how we define the human person. How we think we know will influence and be influenced by what we think we know. And what we believe to be true will guide us in our actions as individuals and as a society. The issues of this final section involve the application of philosophy to the dilemmas we face individually and collectively and assess how our incredible success with technology has made these issues infinitely more complicated.

CHAPTER 8

Political Philosophy

Is Big Brother Watching?

BEFORE YOU READ . . .

Ask yourself how you think human beings would behave in a theoretical "state of nature," with no political authority to restrain their natural impulses.

Part 3 of this text considers values, a branch of philosophy sometimes referred to as *axiology*. The overall question we will be asking is, By what values shall I live in the world? As we end one millennium and begin another, we are able to do incredible things, many of which were impossible even fifty years ago. The issue we will consider in these final three chapters is whether we *should* use all the capabilities we have and, if we should, by what rationale or set of values we should decide in any given situation which things to do and which not to do. Technology has exploded on the scene with such force and speed that philosophy has found itself running somewhat breathlessly behind it, asking whether we really want to incorporate all these technological miracles into our daily lives. The "shoulds" and the "oughts" are being decided in the courts, and there seems to be little time for deep, thoughtful consideration. As we try to make the instant moral judgments needed in a rapidly changing world, philosophy can help us ask the right questions.

The Issue Defined

In this chapter, we focus on political philosophy, particularly the relationship between the individual and the **state,** a formal word for what we mean when we say "the government." The information explosion has put enormous power into the hands of those who control data,

state *the ruling political power within defined borders*

The stakes are too high for government to be a spectator sport.
BARBARA JORDAN

and it seems that even our friends may know less about us than the data banks do. Computer technology has made it simple to store your school records; organizations you belong to; your financial transactions; records of your political contributions; the kinds of clothes you buy, whom you talk to on the telephone, and where you stay when you are out of town; your medical and driving records; and much, much more. Although we do not have a national data bank like the one George Orwell described in his novel *1984,* these many smaller databases can easily be linked together. Incorrect or inaccurately entered information can be used to deny you credit or a job; sometimes we do not even know that damaging information is contained in our files until we are turned down for a car loan or are unable to rent an apartment.[1]

Our nine-digit Social Security number is used so frequently, and the information associated with it is tied together so effectively, that there seems to be no place to hide from the data banks, which today constitute a billion-dollar-a-year industry. In the fictional *1984,* the government controlled all information in Oceania and reminded its citizens of this control by constant repetition of the phrase "Big Brother Is Watching You." As the controller of information, the party also continually rewrote history. If Oceania were at war with Eastasia, history showed that its ally Eurasia was a noble country. When alliances shifted, however, and Oceania was fighting Eurasia, all history books were changed to show that Eurasia was and had always been a bitter enemy and a despicable and evil place. As we noted in Chapter 6, the "truth" of history depends to a great extent on who is reporting it.

He who makes the gunpowder wins the battles.
DAHOMEAN PROVERB

The law is the traditional dividing line between the individual and society (as represented by the state), and there are laws to protect protesters. But what if a protester found that his or her income tax return was audited every year? Would this constitute an abuse of the state's authority? What if the government decided it knew what was best for its citizens and began systematically persecuting dissenters in the name of the public good? The question philosophy asks is this: Where do the individual's rights end and the rights of the state begin, and which should receive the benefit of the doubt in cases of conflict?

Some philosophers have argued that the state exists to serve and to protect the rights of the individual; others have insisted that (in part for the individual's own good) the individual exists to serve the state. There is a range of opinion from **totalitarianism,** the belief that the power of the state should be absolute, to **anarchism,** the belief that ideally there should be no state at all. To a great extent your view of human nature will determine where on this continuum your own views fall. If you have confidence in the basic goodness and decency of people, you may be more willing to trust them to behave correctly with little or no interference from the state; if, on the other hand, you view humans as more than a little selfish, you may want to control their tendencies toward aggression with the power of a strong state.

totalitarianism *the political belief that power to rule must be given exclusively to the state*

anarchism *the political belief that all forms of government should be abolished since they interfere with the rights of individuals*

The question to ask yourself is where your sympathies lie: with the rights of the individual or with the duty of the state to regulate society? Consider this situation. Operation Rescue is a large, nationally organized group of individuals who believe that the U.S. Supreme Court made a tragic error in the *Roe v. Wade* decision that liberalized abortion laws. To the members of Operation Rescue—who protest and pray at abortion clinics and sometimes harass women arriving for abortions and the physicians who perform them—the state is morally wrong to permit abortions. They believe that the state is failing to protect the lives of the unborn, and their protests are attempts to block an existing legal right that violates their moral principles.

When the interests of individuals clash—as they clearly do when women seeking abortions are confronted by people opposing abortion—should the state have the power to resolve the existing conflict, or should we leave such matters in the hands of the individuals? Would the state be justified in arresting the protestors, or should their individual rights of protest be upheld? Both the protestors and the women seeking abortions believe that their individual rights are protected under federal law. Do you find yourself more in sympathy with the rights of the individual, or more supportive of appropriate power from the state?

In conflicts between the individual and the state, both sides are likely to claim they have moral right on their side. Another issue we must consider is whether there is some kind of **natural law** ("the way things ought to be") or whether all law is artificial and the product of a particular society at a particular time. If you believe in natural law, then the implication is that laws must exist in the form they take because they are rooted in the nature of things. If you deny this assumption, then you consider all laws as temporary and subject to change as circumstances change.

natural law *a rational principle of order, often the logos, by which the universe was created or is organized*

A related question asks whether or not people have **natural rights** that are theirs at birth and that a government cannot and should not take away. If people do have natural rights, then these rights must be honored (even protected) by any state that attempts to govern. If, on the other hand, people have no natural rights, then the state may be better positioned to determine what is best for its citizens.

natural rights *rights, such as those to life, liberty, and property, with which an individual is born*

The labels **liberal** and **conservative** have referred, at least in part and especially in the United States, to the amount of authority government should have to legislate what is in the public interest. Should the power of government be restricted, or is government our best hedge against anarchy and chaos?

liberal *one who believes in the primary importance of individual freedoms*

conservative *one who values the preservation of established traditions*

Where does the right to rule originate? Must a ruler receive authority from a higher power, or does the right to govern derive from the consent of the governed? And if the latter is true, can the people be trusted to choose their leader wisely?

Theories of the Right to Rule

sovereignty *a term used to describe where political authority does or should reside*

When we consider the relationship between the individual and the state, a useful concept to keep in mind is **sovereignty.** In general this term describes where political authority does or should reside. In a totalitiarian dictatorship, the state is supreme and sovereignty resides in a single tyrant. Under the opposite condition, known as anarchism—a position advocated by Robert Nozick in the next chapter—we find the near absence of sovereignty. With a very minimal state, whose authority extends only to the safeguarding of individual rights, there may be no sovereign in the traditional sense. Between these two extremes lies the position sometimes known as popular sovereignty, which makes the assumption that a certain degree of political authority is necessary and it should reside with the people. Using this understanding as a guideline, sovereignty is sometimes vested in an entity smaller than the nation state. During the sectional crisis that led up to the Civil War in the United States, for instance, those supporting "popular sovereignty" argued that the decision to either support or reject slavery should be left to the states and, ultimately, to citizens residing within those states.

As you read through the positions outlined in this chapter, ask yourself where each of these thinkers and thought systems believes sovereignty should reside. Although Plato and Aristotle differ at some points, both agree that an elite class, and not the common people, should rule. Closer to our own historical period, questions of natural law—a built-in "way things ought to be"—and natural rights—inborn rights of citizens—inform the issue of sovereignty. If there is (or should be) a kind of contract that citizens make with their state, where does sovereignty reside under these conditions? Let's look first at Plato's reasons for thinking democracy a singularly bad form of government.

The Philosopher-King: Plato

Plato's image of what the ideal society might be like begins with recognition of a harsh political reality, and his analysis anticipates contemporary urban problems. The city, he argued, was really two cities—one rich, the other poor—at war with each other. To solve the problems of the city, he believed, it is essential to have a wise and competent ruler who understands what is wrong and has the knowledge and power to make it right. We have no trouble recognizing the need for an expert in many other areas of our life, Plato said, but when it comes to politics or statecraft, we seem to believe that anyone who can collect the necessary votes is able to rule. This, he believed, is a serious, perhaps tragic error.

If your dog is sick, would you ask advice from your neighbor (who is, say, a lawyer), or would you take your dog to the veterinarian, in such matters the acknowledged expert? Faced with a legal problem, would you turn to the vet, or would you make an appointment to tap your neighbor's legal expertise? The wise, Plato believed, clearly understand the role of the expert and make important choices only after consulting with someone knowledgeable and experienced in the field. In everything from shoemaking to psychology, we seem to have no trouble recognizing the need for a trained and practiced expert, but when we think of politics our minds seem to cloud over and we apply a different set of standards.

It was Plato's firmly held opinion that we do so at our own peril. The qualities necessary to get elected to political office have little or no relationship to the qualities needed to govern. A person who is articulate, quick witted, and a charming conversationalist may be very electable, but are these the traits you believe to be most valuable in a ruler? Would you not agree that the ability to think clearly, to analyze shrewdly, to command an army (if necessary), and to negotiate compromise are the abilities really necessary in a political leader? If you do, then Plato's writings challenge you to explain why the process used to select a leader in a democracy tests none of these qualities and instead tests a completely unrelated set of traits.

They are wrong who think that politics is like an ocean voyage or a military campaign, something to be done with some particular end in view, something which leaves off as soon as that end is reached. It is not a public chore to be got over with. It is a way of life.
PLUTARCH

In our own era, the advent of instantaneous media coverage has further confused the situation. Being able to answer complex questions with answers that fit the fifteen- or thirty-second soundbites that make up the evening news seems to be the most important skill in winning a presidential election. Many political analysts believe that one key reason Richard Nixon lost the very close 1960 presidential election was that during the televised debates his "five o'clock shadow" made him look sinister, while John F. Kennedy's suntanned good looks accented his youthful, energetic image.

This kind of situation is a classic example of why Plato hated democracy and mistrusted the people's ability to choose a good leader. The question of who might be the better candidate aside, it is superficial qualities, rather than those of substance, that determine public opinion. Plato saw that people could learn to manipulate images so that vital decisions such as who should be chosen to rule would be made on superficial grounds. As a result, instead of democracy he advocated the careful education and training of a leader from youth. The people would have no say in the selection of this leader because the people are easily fooled and manipulated; they rarely know what is good for them and do not have the objectivity to select a leader with the qualities required to govern wisely.

Few men are placed in such fortunate circumstances as to be able to gain office, or to keep it for any length of time, without misleading or bamboozling the people.
F. S. OLIVER

Before you reject Plato's idea out of hand, think for a minute about your friends and family. How many vote? Of those who do, how many give serious consideration to the issues when casting their ballots? Do you know anyone who votes for the person who is better dressed or better looking? How many try to select the candidate who will benefit the country as a whole, not just their own private interests? If Plato were here, he would urge us to take a good honest look at the political process in place today, to ask ourselves whether it is designed to find the person who is best suited for the job.

In the utopia described in Plato's *Republic,* the most promising toddlers would be taken from their parents and raised by the state. For the first ten years, their education would be mainly physical, concentrating on gymnastics. (Recall that the Greek ideal was a sound mind in a sound body, and that the two elements were considered to be closely related.) During the second ten years, music and mathematics would be added to the curriculum. At the end of twenty years, a process called The Great Elimination would use academic exams as well as toils, pains, and conflicts to weed out those unqualified to continue. Those who remained would receive ten more years of training in body, mind, and character. The survivors of a second test, more severe than the first, would then be ready to study philosophy.

HOW PHILOSOPHY WORKS

The Hypothetical Chain Argument

In a hypothetical chain argument, a series of propositions is linked in such a way that the first antecedent is connected with the last consequent:

If A, then B
If B, then C
If C, then D
If D, then E
If A, then E

Plato's argument in book 5 of the *Republic*—that women, as well as men, should be eligible for the role of guardian (and therefore potentially philosopher-king)—operates this way.

If A, then B: If a woman wishes to be guardian, she must have the right nature.
If B, then C: The right nature means the necessary abilities and attitudes.
If C, then D: Those with these qualities will be trained and educated.
If D, then E: Those who survive the training are eligible to be guardians.

Plato's conclusion is that a woman who wishes to be a guardian (A) is eligible to be a guardian (E), assuming she has the right nature (B), meaning the necessary abilities and attitudes (C), is trained and educated (D), and survives the rigors of the process, becoming eligible to be a guardian (E).

The key component is B. The right nature in this argument is logically restricted to the qualities necessary to make a good guardian. Whether a person bears or begets children, Plato asserts, has no bearing on these qualities. It is not, to use modern language, a bona fide occupational qualification. Therefore, it would be illogical as well as unjust to exclude women from the guardian class on the basis of an irrelevant quality. It would be just as illogical and unjust to say that bald men cannot be shoemakers, since baldness has nothing to do with shoemaking ability. Bearing or begetting children has, in Plato's view here, nothing to do with guardian potential.

Plato was wary of putting the tools of philosophy into the hands of the unworthy, for he feared they might do what, in his opinion, the Sophists had done: Use it to exploit and confuse the unwary, making money and trivializing it in the process. After five years of training in philosophy, the candidates would be sent back to the "cave" for further seasoning. If you recall the "Allegory of the Cave" from Chapter 1, you know that for Plato the sense world was a world of illusion; any future ruler must learn to survive in that world as well as in the world of the academy. In today's terms, we might be tempted to say that any well-rounded education must include "street smarts," the ability to survive and even prosper in the rough-and-tumble world of everyday life. A future ruler was not to be an ivory tower intellectual who had no idea how theories were implemented and lacked the common sense needed to survive.

At this stage of preparation, the remaining candidate or candidates would be over fifty years old. Having passed all these tests, such an individual would be qualified to serve as *philosopher-king,* Plato's ideal ruler. Once chosen, the philosopher-king would rule with absolute authority as a benevolent dictator. After all, who among the general population would imagine himself or herself better able to guide the state than this clear expert in statecraft?

It is interesting to note that in a society that allowed only restricted roles for women, the *Republic* makes the job of philosopher-king open to women and men alike. The key attribute is not gender but the right "nature" for the job. Those who have the right nature are subjected to training and discipline to shape them for the role and, Plato argues, it would make no more sense to eliminate women on the basis of gender than to forbid bald men to be shoemakers. Granting that men beget children whereas women bear them and that men are generally physically stronger than women, Plato insists that we must look at individuals and find those individuals with the right nature to be philosopher-king:

> So if either the male or the female gender turns out to be better than the other gender at some profession or occupation, then we'll claim that this is an occupation which ought to be assigned to that gender. But if the only difference turns out to be that females bear offspring, while males mount females, then . . . we'll continue to think that . . . there's no administrative job in a community which belongs to a woman *qua* woman, or to a man *qua* man . . . Innate qualities have been distributed equally between the two sexes, and women can join in every occupation just as much as men, although they are the weaker sex in all respects.[2]

Aristotle shared Plato's mistrust of rule by the common people, agreeing with Plato that ordinary citizens might be unable or unwilling to look at society's needs as a whole and might instead act to further their own selfish ends. Although Aristotle criticized some key concepts outlined in the *Republic*—including the radical ideas of women as rulers, state-controlled mating, and communal child rearing—he supported Plato's basic assumption that the people could not be trusted with so important a process as choosing a ruler. Rule by an elite was clearly the best alternative, and Aristotle defended this assumption in terms of natural law.

Natural Law: The Stoics, Aristotle, and Thomas Aquinas

More than 2000 years ago, the Stoics (see Historical Interlude B) introduced the idea that reason was the identifying principle for both the natural world and for human beings. Heavenly bodies move through the cosmos in an orderly progression, while here on Earth season follows season with a comforting regularity. In the human person, logic enables us to control our passions and behave rationally. Thus, both the natural and human domains are governed by reason, by what the Stoics and other early Greek philosophers called the logos. Human reason was seen as a "spark" of the logos that created and directs the natural system. You may recognize this concept that humans share a spark of the divine, for it has found its way into Judaism, Christianity, and Islam as a way of explaining the unique position human beings occupy—between the nonhuman and the divine.

In this ordering of society, the Stoics have given us the concept of a natural law that flows from the logos and expresses the rationality of the universe. Just as there are appropriate places for the Sun and the Moon and appropriate relationships between them (the Sun has precedence during the day and the Moon at night), so in human society there is a given order and hierarchy. Some are emperors and others slaves, but all can understand the grand scheme of the universe and their own place within it.

Applying a similar concept, Aristotle declared the state to be a "creation of nature," one of the logical "givens" in the cosmos. How we organize ourselves politically is not, for Aristotle, entirely our choice. Using our reason we can discover the natural order of things and put it into place in human society. Whereas Plato argued for a strong state on the basis of weak human nature, Aristotle considered a strong state to be a part of the natural order of things. Like Plato, Aristotle believed that individuals will be better off if they are directed by a wise state that is logically prior to the individual and is necessary for the cultivation of virtue:

> Further, the state is by nature clearly prior to the family and to the individual, since the whole is of necessity prior to the part; for example, if the whole body be destroyed, there will be no foot or hand, except in an equivocal sense as we might speak of a stone hand . . . The proof that the state is a creation of nature and prior to the individual is that the individual, when isolated, is not self-sufficing; and therefore he is like a part in relation to the whole. But he who is unable to live in society, or who has no need because he is sufficient for himself, must either be a beast or a god . . .[3]

Aristotle described the human person as a "political animal," meaning that by nature we will organize ourselves into political structures. The important thing for Aristotle and others who follow in the natural law tradition is to discover the preexisting proper order and put this order into practice. Plato had reasoned his way to the ideal society in the *Republic;* Aristotle approached the same problem by studying 158 actual constitutions and ascertaining which of them created well-ordered states.

During the Middle Ages (see Historical Interlude C), Christian theologians picked up the idea of natural law and applied it to their own society. As we saw in Chapter 4, Thomas Aquinas used Aristotle's proofs for an unmoved mover, a first efficient cause, and a necessary being to rationally establish the existence of the Judaic and Christian God. He also examined the natural law (which he identified with the law of God) in relationship to the secular laws of society.

eternal law *the law or reason of God, according to Aquinas*

divine law *that portion of eternal law applicable to human beings, according to Aquinas*

If the natural law, which the Stoics had seen as flowing from the logos, or rational principle of the universe, were derived from God, then divine law must be the basis for human society. This was exactly the way Aquinas understood the situation (Figure 8.1). He began by saying that "all laws derive from the Eternal Law in so far as they are right and reasonable."[4] That portion of the **eternal law** that applies to humans is called **divine law.** Aquinas called the rather self-evident principles deduced from the eternal law (that we should tell the truth, not commit murder, etc.) the natural law. Finally, there is *human law,* which is created by civil society.

There is a clear hierarchy among these laws. At the top is the eternal law, established by God and unchangeable; included in it is the divine law, the portion directly applicable to us as creatures made by God. Occupying the middle position is the natural law, a set of principles that are a reflection of the way things are, the way God has made things; human reason can discern these principles. In the lowest position is human law, and Aquinas clearly stated his belief that human law has its limitations: "Human law cannot repeal any part of divine law or Natural Law."[5]

Thomas Aquinas's Hierarchy of Laws
Eternal Law
Natural Law
Human-Made Laws

FIGURE 8.1 NATURAL LAW *Thomas Aquinas conceived a hierarchy of laws.*

All these laws are binding on us—meaning we are obliged to obey them—but some are clearly more binding than others. In the normal course of events, a citizen is expected to obey the civil law. Aquinas did not wish to exempt us from things like stopping at red lights or serving on a jury. However, if a civil law conflicts with the natural law or with the eternal law, not only may we violate it—we *must* violate it.

In the *Crito* Socrates decided that he must drink the hemlock precisely because the laws of Athens (under which he had lived happily all his life, with no complaint) required him to do so. Aquinas took a significantly different position here. For him, civil law, no matter how well crafted, can never be the final authority; there is always a "higher law" that must be considered and must be obeyed.

Claiming the obligation to obey a "higher law" has led many people to break civil laws by taking actions called **civil disobedience.** Mohandas K. Gandhi used this practice very effectively in India when he led thousands to nonviolently oppose the laws of British colonial rule, which he believed to be unjust. In nineteenth-century America, Henry David Thoreau was jailed for refusing to pay taxes he felt were being used for immoral purposes. In our own century, Martin Luther King, Jr., found himself in a Birmingham jail for a similar refusal to obey the civil law. And even though people who perform acts of civil disobedience typically cite obedience to a higher moral law, whether it be divine or eternal law, they may also cite higher humanistic principles. During the Vietnam War, a number of young men, some of them atheists, refused induction into the armed services because they believed killing to be morally wrong. Whenever individuals commit acts of civil disobedience, civil authority is threatened. During the Middle Ages, however, an even more troubling thesis stated that the Church, not the state, must be the final authority. Both Augustine and Aquinas insisted that although the state has rights and duties proper to its sphere, it must be subordinate to the Church, just as the state's laws must always be subordinate to divine law.

civil disobedience *breaking of a civil law in protest by citing obedience to a higher law*

My life is my message.
MOHANDAS K. GANDHI

Although both Augustine and Aquinas saw the natural law as deriving from a divine, eternal law, not all natural law theorists do so. Aristotle, of course, did not, and neither did Thomas Hobbes, a seventeenth-century political philosopher who was a thoroughgoing materialist. In Hobbes's system, there is no higher power beyond nature, but it is in our own rational self-interest to obey natural laws. One should, for instance, seek peace as long as there is any hope of achieving it, but once there is no such hope one should use all available means of self-defense. This is a law of survival that presumes a hostile environment.

There is an echo of Hobbes in Malcolm X's admonition to seek justice "by any means necessary." He challenges the government to do its job and warns that citizens will take the law into their own hands if it does not:

> Concerning nonviolence: it is criminal to teach a man not to defend himself when he is the constant victim of brutal attacks. It is legal and lawful to own a shotgun or a rifle. We believe in obeying the law . . . When our people are being bitten by dogs, they are within their rights to kill those dogs. We should be peaceful, law-abiding, but the time has come for the American Negro to fight back in self-defense whenever and wherever he is being unjustly and unlawfully attacked. If the government thinks I'm wrong for saying this, then let the government start doing its job.[6]

What Malcolm X concluded is that the government and the people have an implied contract; if the government does not uphold its end of the contract (by protecting the people), the people are free to disregard their obligations (to remain law-abiding citizens) as well.

THE MAKING OF A PHILOSOPHER

Thomas Hobbes
(1588–1679)

Born prematurely as a result of his English mother's anxiety over the approach of the Spanish armada, Hobbes spent much of his life in fear, since his philosophy of materialism appeared ungodly and made him seem threatening to both the Puritan Party and the Church of England. There were times when his life was in danger because of his ideas. At Oxford University he studied Greek and Roman authors and later made his living as a tutor in both England and Europe. He lived for a while among the philosophers of Paris and was influenced by the thought of Descartes, Montaigne, and Galileo. *Leviathan* angered even royalists (who might have been expected to support the idea of a strong, authoritarian state) because it lacked religion. When he died, some judged him to be a sage, but others cursed him as an enemy of virtue.

Social Contract Theory

We next consider some political theorists who share Malcolm X's understanding that citizens and the state enter into an implied contract. Thomas Hobbes argued that our aggressive, destructive human nature forces us to set up a powerful, restraining state, whereas John Locke saw the need for a state arising out of a citizen's benign human nature. Both Hobbes and Locke base their arguments on what human beings would be like in a hypothetical "state of nature." This concept also intrigued Jean-Jacques Rousseau, Aphra Behn, and Clarisse Coignet.

The Leviathan: Thomas Hobbes

The need for a strong state to protect us from the worst of our selfish and aggressive human impulses appears in Thomas Hobbes's best-known book, *The Leviathan*. Having lived through the Thirty Years War (1618–1648)—an ugly European free-for-all in which soldiers raped women, pillaged villages, and left thousands as homeless refugees—as well as civil war in England, Hobbes developed a somewhat jaundiced view of human nature. Having seen the brutality and mindless cruelty humans were capable of inflicting on each other, Hobbes was unwilling to trust people to govern themselves.

The state of nature, he feared, would be the "war of all against all," and life for Hobbes seemed "solitary, poor, nasty, brutish and short." Under these conditions a strong state was needed to protect people from other people. During the seventeenth century, as Europeans developed national states, they came to view the government power to which citizens owed political obligations as a *secular state*. Being a secular entity, the state did not derive its power from God or the Church, and within its own borders the state regulated all institutions, including (at least by implication) the Church. Augustine

DOING PHILOSOPHY

The Fuzzy Social Contract

Bart Kosko, in his book *Fuzzy Thinking,* includes this fuzzy social contract written by computer engineer Robert Alexander and distributed via the Internet. You and I did not sign this contract, but its terms are binding. The state says that by residing in the United States we have consented to its terms. Much of its duties, benefits, and costs are fuzzy—not clearly defined—and capable of delivering surprises.

Social Contract
between an individual and the
United States Government

WHEREAS I wish to reside on the North American continent, and

WHEREAS the United States Government controls the area of the continent on which I wish to reside, and

WHEREAS tacit or implied contracts are vague and therefore unenforceable,

I agree to the following terms:

SECTION 1: I will surrender a percentage of my property to the Government. The actual percentage will be determined by the Government and will be subject to change at any time. The amount to be surrendered may be based on my income, the value of my property, the value of my purchases, or any other criteria the Government chooses. To aid the Government in determining the percentage, I will apply for a government identification number that I will use in all my major financial transactions.

SECTION 2: Should the Government demand it, I will surrender my liberty for a period of time determined by the Government and typically no shorter than two years. During that time, I will serve the Government in any way it chooses, including military service in which I may be called upon to sacrifice my life.

SECTION 3: I will limit my behavior as demanded by the Government. I will consume only those drugs permitted by the Government. I will limit my sexual activities to those permitted by the Government. I will forsake religious beliefs that conflict with the Government's determination of propriety. More limits may be imposed at any time.

SECTION 4: In consideration for the above, the Government will permit me to find employment, subject to limits that will be determined by the Government. These limits may restrict my choice of career or the wages I may accept.

SECTION 5: The Government will permit me to reside in the area of North America that it controls. Also, the Government will permit me to speak freely, subject to limits determined by the Government's Congress and Supreme Court.

SECTION 6: The Government will attempt to protect my life and my claim to the property it has allowed me to keep. I agree not to hold the Government liable if it fails to protect me or my property.

SECTION 7: The Government will offer various services to me. The nature and extent of these services will be determined by the Government and are subject to change at any time.

SECTION 8: The Government will determine whether I may vote for certain Government officials. The influence of my vote will vary inversely with the number of voters, and I understand that it typically will be minuscule. I agree not to hold any elected Government officials liable for acting against my best interests or for breaking promises, even if those promises motivated me to vote for them.

SECTION 9: I agree that the government may hold me fully liable if I fail to abide by the above terms. In that event, the Government may confiscate any property that I have not previously surrendered to it, and may imprison me for a period of time to be determined by the Government. I also agree that the government may alter the terms of this contract at any time.

____

SIGNATURE

____

DATE

Are you ready to sign?

and Aquinas had argued that the state must submit to the Church, but several hundred years later that equation was being reversed.

Hobbes considered himself a realist. Looking at the same kind of world that Malcolm X would later describe, Hobbes concluded that only a strong state could guarantee personal survival and make possible a certain degree of peace and prosperity. In a "dog-eat-dog" world in which people would do anything to get the upper hand, government must regulate human behavior; if left to their own devices, people will lie, cheat, steal, and even kill, and the result will be chaos. The solution, for Hobbes, was to create a strong central state, which he called the Leviathan. People would have to recognize that it was in their own best interest to enter into a *contract* among themselves, exchanging their personal rights and power for civil order and safety:

> This is more than consent or concord; it is a real unity of them all . . . as if every man should say to every man, I authorize and give up my right of governing myself to this man or to this assembly of men, on this condition that thou give up thy right to him, and authorize all his actions in like manner. This done, the multitude so united in one person, is called a COMMONWEALTH, in Latin *Civitas*. This is the generation of that great LEVIATHAN, or rather (to speak more reverently) of that mortal God to which we owe under the immortal God our peace and defense. For by this authority, given him by every particular man in the commonwealth, he has the use of so much power and strength conferred on him, that by terror thereof, he is enabled to form the wills of them all, to peace at home, and mutual aid against their enemies abroad.[7]

social contract *an agreement among citizens or between the ruler and the ruled that defines the rights and duties of each party*

This kind of **social contract** among citizens to create the state, once made, would be irrevocable. No individual could, at a later date, take back his individual rights, and the state once created would be like a Leviathan, a giant sea monster, more powerful than any fish in the sea. Only by this power could the state ensure the development of commerce and trade, the arts, and intellectual progress for all. Notice the similarity with Plato's philosopher-king, who would rule absolutely to ensure a well-administered state. But whereas Plato's argument is rooted in a mistrust of people's ability to wisely choose a ruler, Hobbes goes much further and insists that without a dictator we would destroy each other and civilization, too.

William Golding's novel *Lord of the Flies* also takes on this issue. A group of English choirboys, stranded on an unpopulated island, begin by establishing rational rule (as symbolized by the conch shell, the possessor of which had the right to speak). Eventually, though, many of them revert to a primitive state, and, led by a renegade boy named Jack, a band of hunters is driven by bloodlust to kill not only wild pigs but other boys, their former friends and companions. This is precisely Hobbes's point: Without a strong, authoritarian ruler, we risk chaos. It may seem harsh to give up your rights and power unconditionally, but the alternative is so much worse; the social contract among the ruled saves them from a far more serious danger.

The price, however, is high. Once created, the Leviathan cannot be restrained in any way; the sovereign may put in place any laws he can enforce. Subjects may reject him and choose another sovereign, but they cannot take back their consent to be ruled by someone other than themselves. Under the thin skin of apparent civilization, Hobbes believed, we are all just like Jack and his band of killers.

A useful way of thinking about this might be to consider the relationship between the police, as agents of the state, and the citizens of the state. The videotape of Los Angeles police officers repeatedly beating motorist Rodney King struck fear into the hearts of some Americans, whereas others defended the officers' use of force as necessary and expedient. Are the inner cities "war zones" in which the police must presume they are dealing with Jack and his band of killers? Is it a kill or be killed situation, or has the power to carry a night stick and a gun made some officers preemptively aggressive?

The Natural Rights of Citizens: John Locke

Locke, whose knowledge theory we discussed in Chapter 5, had a more benign view of human nature than Hobbes did, and it is reflected in his version of contract theory. Whereas Hobbes had believed that a social contract was necessary to protect us against the worst in ourselves and others, Locke valued a social contract to preserve what is best in us—namely, our natural rights. Rooted in the natural law tradition, Locke's concept of natural rights assumes that anyone consulting the law of reason will recognize the God-given rights of others to life, health, liberty, and property:

> The state of nature has a law of nature to govern it, which obliges every one: and reason, which is that law, teaches all mankind, who will but consult it, that being all equal and independent, no one ought to harm another in his life, health, liberty, or possessions . . .[8]

Born during a more tranquil time than Hobbes, Locke had seen the peaceful transformation of England, from a monarchy to a constitutional government that assigned a more powerful role to Parliament, in the so-called Glorious Revolution of 1688. Looking at a theoretical "state of nature," Hobbes saw chaos and anarchy, but Locke saw the natural rights of citizens. Having been created by God, human beings are, in Locke's phrase, "God's property"; as such, we are made for God's use, not one another's, and we are made to last according to God's pleasure. We are about God's business, Locke says, so we each must have the right to our lives, our liberty, and whatever property we are able to amass through our ingenuity and hard work:

> To understand political power aright, and derive it from its original, we must consider what estate all men are naturally in, and this is, a state of perfect freedom to order their actions, and dispose of their possessions and persons as they think fit, within the bounds of the law of Nature, without asking leave or depending upon the will of any other man.[9]

Endowed with natural rights, Locke asserted, citizens may voluntarily create a state to assist them in safeguarding those rights (Figure 8.2). The

FIGURE 8.2 LOCKE'S VERSION OF THE SOCIAL CONTRACT *Locke believed the contract between the individual and the state to be conditional; individuals retained the option to withdraw their natural rights.*

resulting social contract among citizens, however, is *conditional* rather than absolute. Living in a state may entail consent to a social contract, but if the state abuses the power entrusted to it by its citizens, they retain the right to rebel. Unlike Hobbes's Leviathan, the state for Locke exists only at the pleasure of the citizens who have created it. The bargain is that we give up certain rights in exchange for others. Accordingly, stopping at traffic signals and even paying taxes are legitimate prices to pay for an orderly society with public schools and police protection:

> If man in the state of nature be so free as has been said . . . why will he part with his freedom, this empire, and subject himself to the dominion and control of any other power? To which is it obvious to answer, that though in the state of Nature he hath such a right, yet the enjoyment of it is very uncertain and constantly exposed to the invasion of others . . . it is not without reason that he seeks out and is willing to join in society with others who are already united, or have a mind to unite for the mutual preservation of their lives, liberties and estates, which I call by the general name—property.[10]

The point for Locke was that the contract is temporary and contingent upon the good performance of the state, which is the servant of the people. At such time as the state becomes tyrannical, it has broken the terms of the contract and no longer deserves the support of the people. If we believe those we have elected to govern us are abusing power, we are justified in overthrowing the government and establishing a new one. In effect,

PHILOSOPHERS SPEAK FOR THEMSELVES
John Locke

The State of Nature has a law of nature to govern it, which obliges every one: and reason, which is that law, teaches all mankind, who will but consult it, that being all equal and independent, no one ought to harm another in his life, health, liberty, or possessions: for men being all the workmanship of one omnipotent and infinitely wise Maker; all the servants of one sovereign master, sent into the world by his order, and about his business; they are his property, whose workmanship they are, made to last during his, not another's pleasure: and being furnished with like faculties, sharing all in one community of nature, there cannot be supposed any such subordination among us, that may authorize us to destroy another, as if we were made for one another's uses, as the inferior ranks of creatures are for ours. Every one, as he is bound to preserve himself, and not to quit his station willfully, so by the like reason, when his own preservation comes not in competition, ought he, as much as he can, to preserve the rest of mankind, and may not, unless it be to do justice to an offender, take away or impair the life, or what tends to the preservation of life, the liberty, health, limb, or goods of another . . .

From *Treatise of Civil Government*

we also renegotiate our social contract whenever we vote elected officials out of office or remove them midterm through impeachment.

So ingrained are Locke's ideas in our own notions of government that they probably seem perfectly natural to you. Indeed, Locke's ideas provided the intellectual inspiration for both the American and French Revolutions. The U.S. Declaration of Independence asserts that governments "derive their just powers from the consent of the governed." This phrase is at the heart of Locke's political theory. Without the consent of the governed, continually given, the state has no justification for its existence. Locke was willing to trust people to know when their government had exceeded its authority and to take back their assent to the social contract.

The Value of the State of Nature: Jean-Jacques Rousseau, Aphra Behn, and Clarisse Coignet

We have seen that both Hobbes and Locke felt that people were better off living under a well-formed state than in a state of nature, but Jean-Jacques Rousseau disagreed. At least in his early eighteenth-century political writings, Rousseau put forth the idea that perfect freedom exists only in the state of nature. Before civilization, before the advent of the state, before the creation of private property, individuals enjoyed a kind of pure liberty. In this state of nature, people were naturally innocent and therefore good.

Under a state of civilization, Rousseau favored what we might call a pure democracy over a representative one. For the social contract to work, he was convinced that all citizens must retain an active, ongoing interest in the laws being passed. Delegating that responsibility to elected representatives simply would not work because the laws would lack legitimacy. To give others the responsibility of legislating for us is to give

THE MAKING OF A PHILOSOPHER

Jean-Jacques Rousseau
(1712–1778)

Born in Geneva, Switzerland, Rousseau spent much of his life as a wanderer. His mother died giving birth to him, and his father abandoned him when he was twelve years old. In his thirties he moved to Paris; was befriended by writers, musicians, and scientists; and took a lover with whom he is said to have had five children—all of whom went to a foundling home. He married the woman twenty years later. The theme of his writings—that civilization tends to corrupt people's natural goodness—helped launch the Romantic movement, which glorified impulse and emotion over discipline and reason. His deistic ideas angered Church authorities, and he was forced to leave Geneva after his house was stoned. David Hume, another freethinker, invited him to England, but Rousseau later suspected Hume of conspiring against him and returned to Paris in 1770.

Individuals retain the right to withdraw their consent to the social contract.

up our freedom, Rousseau insisted. For him pure freedom and civilization are incompatible concepts; only in the state of nature can we hope to be truly free.

Some who read Rousseau's early works drew the logical conclusion that society was the cause of much of humankind's woes and that the solution was to return to a simpler, more natural state. The concept of the "noble savage," living in close communion with nature and far from the corrupting influence of civilization is often attributed to Rousseau but was in fact developed earlier by an English writer, Aphra Behn.

In her novel *Oroonoko: Or The Royal Slave,* published in 1688, nearly a century before Rousseau's death, Behn gives us a fictional vision of the state of nature. Oroonoko, a handsome, black, warrior prince is taken into slavery trying to rescue his beloved in Surinam. Raised in the state of nature, Oroonoko believes in "virtuous action voluntarily practiced by individuals"; the colonial rulers who brutalize him use the law to enforce their supremacy, but there is no moral foundation for their actions. In the end, it is Oroonoko's personal moral code of "honesty, honor, loyalty, and fortitude" that makes him vulnerable. He expects others to behave similarly and they do not.[11]

It is only to the state of nature that nineteenth-century French author Clarisse Coignet believed human beings could look to discover their freedom—the basis of the *independent morality* she and others advocated. In her major work, *The Independent Morality,* Coignet imagined an uneducated tribal chief who beats his wife and is stopped in the act when she realizes her own worth and freedom and regards him with reproach, awakening his conscience. This internal morality, which derives from human freedom, is superior to an external morality, derived from philosophy or natural science.[12]

Mohandas K. Gandhi, known for his effective use of nonviolent protest, told a story of his own conversion to the principles of independent morality that seems to bear out Coignet's thesis of how it arises from within the human individual:

> I learnt the lesson of nonviolence from my wife when I tried to bend her to my will. Her determined resistance to my will on the one hand and her quiet submission to the suffering my stupidity involved on the other ultimately made me ashamed of myself and cured me of my stupidity. Thinking that I was born to rule over her, in the end she became my teacher in nonviolence.[13]

Natural Rights and Feminism

Women in Europe and the United States read with interest arguments over the legitimacy of the social contract and assertions of natural rights and began to apply these principles to their own social situation. American women such as Elizabeth Cady Stanton and Susan B. Anthony skillfully used documents like the Declaration of Independence to make a case for extending equal political rights to women. English writer Mary Wollstonecraft believed that Rousseau and others had excluded women from the social contract.

> *Many who have at last made the discovery that the negroes have some rights as well as other members of the human family, have yet to be convinced that women are entitled to any . . . "Right is of no sex."*
>
> **FREDERICK DOUGLASS, PUBLISHER OF THE *NORTH STAR***

Gender Equality: Mary Wollstonecraft

One of Rousseau's writings, *Emile or a Treatise on Education,* aroused the ire of the eighteenth-century philosopher Mary Wollstonecraft, an early advocate of women's equality. Rousseau, in laying out the ideal education for his male title character, Emile, had declared that the whole purpose of a woman's education should be to render her "pleasing to men"—her father, her husband, her sons. Wollstonecraft dedicated *A Vindication of the Rights of Woman* to the French statesman Tallyrand, whose proposed French Constitution would have educated girls in school only to the age of eight, at which time they would be permanently returned to the home where they would spend the rest of their lives. Clearly, she hoped her dedication would compel Tallyrand to read her analysis. Wollstonecraft's arguments follow the same lines as those of Locke and Rousseau, but they urge that one consistent set of standards be applied to women and men alike.

Like Plato, Wollstonecraft believed that the only differences between the genders are that men beget and women bear children and that men are, generally, physically stronger than women. Individuals, she said, must be treated as individuals rather than as members of groups about whom assumptions have been made. Just as Plato concluded that no rational argument could be made for excluding women from the guardian class (and therefore eligible for the position of philosopher-king), so Wollstonecraft contended that no rational case could be made for educating girls differently from boys. Innocence is fine for children, she agreed, but adults of both sexes must be treated as rational creatures:

> Men, indeed, appear to me to act in a very unphilosophical manner when they try to secure the good conduct of women by attempting to keep them always in a state of childhood. Rousseau was more consistent when he wished to stop the progress of reason in both sexes, for if men eat of the tree of knowledge, women will come in for a taste; but, from the imperfect cultivation which their understandings now receive, they only attain a knowledge of evil . . . In fact it is a farce to call any being virtuous whose virtues do not result from the exercise of its own reason. This was Rousseau's opinion respecting men; I extend it to women . . .[14]

She agreed with Rousseau on one significant point: If we wish to see what human beings are like by nature, the best way to do this is to observe those who have been the least corrupted by civilization. Men's greater physical strength is a law of nature, she granted, but all other differences come from education and socialization. Wollstonecraft found Rousseau's assertion that women are natural coquettes (flirts) before society trains them to be that way particularly unphilosophical, and she asserted that he could never have drawn this conclusion from reason but instead reached it because it was his already-held opinion:

> I have probably had an opportunity of observing more girls in their infancy than J. J. Rousseau—I can recollect my own feelings, and I have looked steadily around me; yet, so far from coinciding with him in opinion respecting the first dawn of the female character, I will venture to affirm, that a girl, whose spirits have not been damped by inactivity, or innocence tainted by false shame, will always be a romp, and the doll will never excite attention unless confinement allows her no alternative. Girls and boys, in short, would play harmlessly together if the distinction of sex was not inculcated long before nature makes any difference.[15]

Published simultaneously in London and New York in 1792, Mary Wollstonecraft's *Vindication* was but one early example of many treatises by women and men advocating equality between the sexes. Among the many people Wollstonecraft influenced was Elizabeth Cady Stanton.

THE MAKING OF A PHILOSOPHER

Mary Wollstonecraft
(1759–1797)

Born into what we would today call a dysfunctional family (her father drank and was abusive), Mary Wollstonecraft played the role of "helper and protector" for her mother as well as for her siblings. In 1786 she began her formal career as a writer and reviewer with Joseph Johnson's publishing house. Johnson offered thoughtful and caring criticism of her writing, and under his influence, she matured as a writer. She had a long liaison with the socialist William Godwin, and the two eventually married, but they maintained separate residences. Godwin wrote every morning in his own apartment and sometimes returned to the house he shared with Mary for dinner. She maintained her own study where she did her writing. Like many women of her day, Mary Wollstonecraft died from complications surrounding the birth of her second child, Mary Wollstonecraft Shelley, the author of *Frankenstein*.

Liberty is the mother of virtue, and if women be, by their very constitution, slaves, and not allowed to breathe the sharp invigorating air of freedom, they must ever languish like exotics, and be reckoned beautiful flaws in nature.
MARY WOLLSTONECRAFT

"Declaration of Sentiments": Elizabeth Cady Stanton

The principal nineteenth-century theoretician of feminism in the United States was Elizabeth Cady Stanton. Like Wollstonecraft, she based her arguments on Enlightenment principles of rationality and equality. Stanton had the advantage of living in a country that proclaimed equality in many public documents, and she used this advantage to point out the many ways in which women were denied their "natural rights."

One of her most thought-provoking treatises was the "Declaration of Sentiments," written for the Seneca Falls Convention, the first women's rights convention ever held in America. It was 1848, and all over Europe revolutions were breaking out as people took to the streets to demand the rights promised in the great documents of the American and French Revolutions. Karl Marx and Friedrich Engels that year published the *Communist Manifesto,* which urged: "Workers of the world unite. You have nothing to lose but your chains!" In the United States a debate was forming over the legitimacy of holding human beings in chattel slavery and declaring them to be less than full persons.

Elizabeth Cady Stanton based her "Declaration" on a more famous one, the Declaration of Independence, following the latter line by line with carefully placed modifications:

> We hold these truths to be self-evident: that all men and women are created equal; that they are endowed by their Creator with certain inalienable rights; that among these are life, liberty, and the pursuit of happiness; that to secure these rights governments are instituted, deriving their just powers from the consent of the governed. Whenever any form of government becomes destructive of these ends, it is the right of those who suffer from it to refuse allegiance to it and to insist upon the institution of a new government . . . Such has been the patient sufferance of the women under this government, and such is now the necessity which constrains them to demand the equal station to which they are entitled.[16]

In place of the grievances against King George III that the colonists had listed in the Declaration of Independence, Stanton listed grievances of women against men:

> The history of mankind is a history of repeated injuries and usurpations on the part of men toward women . . . Having deprived her of this first right of a citizen, the elective franchise, thereby leaving her without representation in the halls of legislation, he has oppressed her on all sides.[17]

Notice that the call for equal rights for women is couched in the already familiar language of natural rights and social contract theory. Arguing, as Locke and Rousseau did, that citizens themselves provide the authority to government, Stanton and her colleague Susan B. Anthony were able to raise awareness of the injustice of excluding women from the social contract.

Addressing the New York State Legislature in 1860 on behalf of a bill to grant property rights to American women, Stanton compared the legal situation of women to that of slaves:

> The negro has no name. He is Cuffy Douglas or Cuffy Brooks, just whose Cuffy he may chance to be. The woman has no name. She is

THE MAKING OF A PHILOSOPHER

Elizabeth Cady Stanton
(1815–1902)

As a child in Johnstown, New York, Elizabeth Cady studied Greek and later Latin and mathematics, joining her male schoolmates at the Johnstown Academy in horseback riding and chess. When she married Henry Stanton, an abolitionist, the word *obey* was omitted from the wedding service at her insistence. She became interested in women's rights on her honeymoon in London where women delegates to the World's Anti-Slavery Convention were denied their seats. Back in America, she and Lucretia Mott designed the first Women's Rights Convention in 1848. In 1851 she met Susan B. Anthony with whom she would spend the next half-century working to secure the vote for American women. As the mother of seven children and a charming extrovert, Stanton was a popular speaker. With Anthony she coauthored the multivolume *History of Woman Suffrage;* toward the end of her life, she alienated many by writing *The Woman's Bible,* which reinterpreted derogatory references to women in the light of context and common sense.

Were women in the United States in 1848 denied the basic rights of citizenship as Stanton claimed?

Elizabeth Cady Stanton addresses the Seneca Falls Convention, from "For the Love of Wisdom"/ Courtesy of Howard Community College.

> Mrs. Richard Roe or Mrs. John Doe, just whose Mrs. she may chance to be. Cuffy has no rights to his earnings; he can not buy or sell, or lay up anything that he can call his own. Mrs. Roe has no right to her earnings; she can neither buy nor sell, make contracts, nor lay up anything that she can call her own. Cuffy has no right to his children; they can be sold from him at any time. Mrs. Roe has no right to her children; they may be bound out to cancel a father's debts of honor . . .[18]

The effectiveness of this appeal (which was ultimately successful in establishing some property rights for the married women of New York State) rested on its ability first to evoke the principle of natural rights and then to illustrate how women, living in a supposedly free republic, had been denied those rights. Theoreticians for the nineteenth-century American women's movement skillfully used comparisons not only with slaves but also with the American colonists before independence from Great Britain.

THE MAKING OF A PHILOSOPHER

Susan Brownell Anthony
(1820–1906)

Born near Adams, Massachusetts, Anthony was a Quaker who never married and devoted her energies to the struggle for woman suffrage. Male reformers were frequent guests in her childhood home, and Susan began early to identify with the struggles of laborers. Her exceptional organizational ability was the perfect complement to Elizabeth Cady Stanton's graceful writing and speaking style. From 1868 to 1870 she published a radical newspaper, *The Revolution*. In February 1906, a month before her death, she defied a doctor's orders and spoke to the suffrage convention meeting in Baltimore. With women such as these, she declared, "Failure is impossible!"

The Struggle for Suffrage: Susan B. Anthony

Tried in federal court in June 1873 on the charge of attempting to vote in a federal election, Susan B. Anthony, the more activist member of the Stanton–Anthony team, was not allowed to speak on her own behalf during the trial. Her defense had been that she considered herself a citizen under the Fourteenth Amendment, and she was therefore eligible to vote. At the conclusion of arguments presented by her male attorney, the judge pulled a prewritten opinion from his pocket and declared that the Fourteenth Amendment did not apply. Then he made the tactical error of asking the prisoner if she had anything to say before sentence was pronounced. Here is part of what she replied, taken from the transcript of *The United States of America v. Susan B. Anthony:*

> Yes, your honor, I have many things to say; . . . Robbed of the fundamental privilege of citizenship, I am degraded from the status of a citizen to that of a subject . . . Your denial of my citizen's right to vote, is the denial of my right of consent as one of the governed, the denial of my right of representation as one of the taxed, the denial of my right to a trial by a jury of my peers as an offender against the law; therefore, the denial of my sacred right to life, liberty, property and . . .[19]

At this point the judge interrupted and ordered the prisoner to sit down, but Anthony was far from finished and simply resumed speaking. Her final point made an explicit comparison of her own status as a disenfranchised person with that of the colonists under British rule before the revolution:

> Of all my prosecutors, from the corner grocery politician who entered the complaint, to the United States marshal, commissioner, district-attorney,

> district-judge, your honor on the bench—not one is my peer, but each and all are my political sovereigns . . . Under such circumstances a commoner of England, tried before a jury of lords, would have far less cause to complain than have I, a woman, tried before a jury of men . . .[20]

Is a woman, facing a jury of men in 1873, being tried by a jury of her peers as guaranteed by the U.S. Constitution?

Susan B. Anthony on trial for voting, from "For Love of Wisdom"/Courtesy of Howard Community College.

Women in the United States did not receive the right to vote until 1920 when the Nineteenth Amendment declared, "The right of citizens of the United States to vote shall not be denied or abridged by the United States or by any state on account of sex." Anthony had drafted the amendment, which was first introduced into Congress in 1847 by a friend of hers. Neither Anthony nor Stanton lived long enough to enjoy the privilege of voting.

The criticisms of these eighteenth- and nineteenth-century feminists raised questions about the right of the government to rule. Their focus was on the deprivation suffered by women when the state denied their natural rights, but the debate their ideas engendered also spoke to a larger issue—the legitimacy of the state.

The Right to Govern

Resolved, that the women of this country ought to be enlightened in regard to the laws under which they live that they may no longer publish their degradation by declaring themselves satisfied with their present position, not their ignorance, by asserting that they have all the rights they want.

SENECA FALLS WOMEN'S RIGHTS CONVENTION, 1848

When we turn our attention from the rights of the individual to the authority of the state, we find Western, Asian, and African political theories

Many times suffrage seemed just around the corner, but the struggle to gain it took almost a century and women like Susan B. Anthony did not live to vote.

Suffrage banner/Courtesy of the National Woman's Party.

justifying a strong central government. In all three cases, a kind of divine sanction is invoked to legitimize the power of the state.

The Absolute: Georg Wilhelm Friedrich Hegel

In some significant ways, G. W. F. Hegel's philosophy is the very antithesis (opposite) of the natural rights positions of Locke, Rousseau, Wollstonecraft, Stanton, and Anthony. The focus for Hegel was not on the individual but on the sweep of history. According to Hegel, the Idea, or the *Absolute*—which at times seems very like God—has its fullest expression in history. We might liken this to Spinoza's idea (Chapter 5) that God was expressed or embodied in nature.

The whole system of the world was for Hegel a kind of theology. The divine thinker conceives the world as an idea and then embodies this thought in history, which is the progressive self-expression of the Absolute. History is moving in the direction of greater freedom through a dialectical process of thesis-antithesis-synthesis.

In this process, a *thesis,* or idea, gives rise to its opposite, or *antithesis.* From the tension between the two a new reality emerges, a synthesis, which contains the best elements of both the thesis and the antithesis (Figure 8.3). It may be useful to recall the historical development of ideas about knowledge we explored in Chapter 5. Understood in terms of **Hegel's dialectic,** Descartes's rationalism would be the thesis; Hume's empiricism, the antithesis; and Kant's epistemology, the synthesis. The extreme of Descartes's emphasis on mind (which led him to separate mind from matter, thus yielding the mind-body problem) gave rise to an opposite system. Empiricism rejected mind as the route to certain knowledge and insisted instead that knowledge be based on sense perception. Taken to the extreme in Hume, we were left with a radical skepticism and no certainty about anything worth knowing. Kant wove together the empiricist insistence on perception and the rationalist confidence in mind to form a new epistemology in which perception is filtered through the *categories* of the mind.

Hegel's dialectic *the progress of ideas through opposition and resolution in the form of thesis-antithesis-synthesis, according to Hegel*

For Hegel, however, the synthesis Kant achieved could not be the end of the process. In Hegel's system, the synthesis becomes a new thesis, and the whole process continues spiraling toward ever-greater clarity. In fact, although Hegel was Kant's intellectual heir, his philosophy is in some ways a reaction against Kant. For Hegel, the important questions are those of metaphysics (reality), rather than those of epistemology (knowledge theory). In the process of the dialectic, Hegel saw the Absolute, or Reason, working itself out, thinking itself more fully real.

Recall that Kant said that we could not know noumena (things as they are in themselves) but only phenomena (things as they appear to us). Hegel disputed this. Even God, or perhaps especially God, is expressed in history and is therefore knowable:

> I have touched on a prominent question of the day, the question, namely, whether it is possible to recognize God—or, since it has ceased

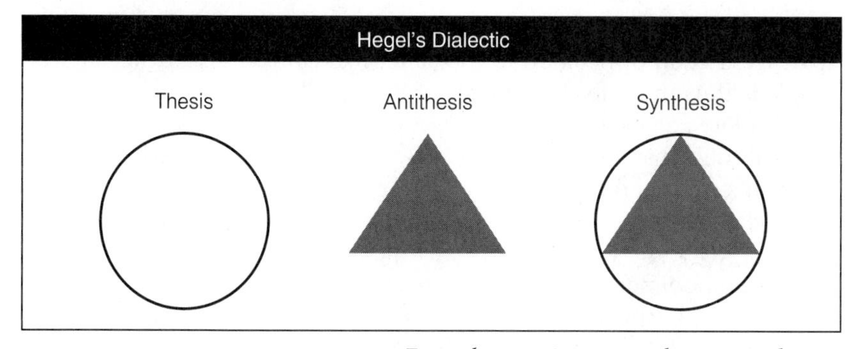

FIGURE 8.3 HEGEL'S DIALECTIC *From the creative tension between a thesis and an antithesis, a new synthesis emerges.*

> to be a question, the doctrine, which has now become a prejudice, that it is impossible to know God . . . I wanted to discuss the connection of our thesis—that Reason governs and has governed the world—with the question of the possible knowledge of God . . . In the Christian religion God has revealed Himself, which means He has given man to understand what He is, and thus is no longer concealed and secret.[21]

Hegel believed that we can understand the highest reality—and indeed, all of reality—by studying its expression in history. In particular, Hegel focused on nations or, to be more accurate, cultures, which are ways of organizing the principle of freedom. It is only through a particular culture that the Absolute becomes concrete; and in the same manner the spiritual nature of an individual may find its completion only through a nation or culture and not in isolation.

Here is the most controversial aspect of Hegel, and the way in which he differs so dramatically from Locke. A culture, for Hegel, is the actualization of the Absolute. To understand your culture's law and religion, its literature and philosophy, is to understand yourself as a cultural individual and thus to have the possibility of developing your capacities, what Hegel would call your full freedom. Recall that Aristotle said that we are all "political animals" and that anyone who could live outside the *polis,* or the cultural life of the city, would have to be either a beast or a god. Hegel put the same idea this way:

> In summary, the vitality of the State in individuals is what we call Morality. The State has its laws, its institutions are the rights of its citizens; its nature, its soil, its mountains, air and waters are their land, their country, their external property . . . Their minds are full of it and their wills are their willing of these laws and of their country. It is this temporal totality which is One Being, the spirit of One People. To it the individual belongs . . . This spiritual being is his—he is one of its representatives—it is that from which he arises and wherein he stands. For the Athenians Athens had a double meaning, the totality of their institutions as well as the goddess which represented the spirit and the unity of the people.[22]

THE MAKING OF A PHILOSOPHER

Georg Wilhelm Friedrich Hegel
(1770-1831)

Hegel was an intelligent and tireless student, but also something of a rebel, taking the unpopular position of defending the French Revolution and writing a life of Jesus that described him as the son of Mary and Joseph with no divine connections. According to his graduation certificate from Tübingen University, Hegel was proficient in theology and philology (language) but had no ability in philosophy. He was a contemporary of the great poet Goethe and the Romantic composer Beethoven. Hegel's philosophy of history centered on the *Zeitgeist* (spirit of the age) and the dialectical process through which history unfolds. Most of his writings, like those of Aristotle, consist of his own lecture notes or those of his students. He held several professorships, ending at the University of Berlin where his ideas had a profound impact on Karl Marx. Hegel died in the cholera epidemic of 1831, after only one day's illness.

When modes of music change, the fundamental laws of the state change with them. Let me write the songs of a nation and I care not who makes its laws.

DANIEL O'CONNELL, IRISH LIBERATOR

According to this explanation, to speak of the rights of the individual, apart from or in opposition to the state, makes no sense. The state, for Hegel, is thus the true "individual" of history, the vehicle through which the Absolute comes to greater and greater self-realization. As the Absolute moves through history, first one culture and then another takes center stage as the fullest (until then) expression of the Absolute. Perhaps it was Athens in the classical period; France and England certainly had their moments. But, for Hegel, the Prussian state in which he lived was the then-current highest embodiment of the Absolute. "Only the Germanic peoples," he said, "came, through Christianity, to realize that man as man is free and that freedom of Spirit is the very essence of man's nature."[23]

It may be interesting to think in these terms about the history of the United States. For much of its history, the young nation seemed to grow in power, and it finally came to occupy the center of the world stage. It may, in Hegel's terminology, be the embodiment of the Absolute for the second half of the twentieth century. But like Athens, Rome, Paris, and Berlin before it, the United States will—according to Hegel's dialectic—eventually decline, and some other culture will become the dwelling place of the Absolute—perhaps a culture from the Middle East.

cunning of reason *the method by which the Absolute, in Hegel's philosophy, uses the talents and ambitions of world historical individuals to advance its own ends*

Hegel said that the Absolute moved through history, expressing itself in various cultures and using what he called the **cunning of reason** to manipulate even "world-historical individuals" in the service of its self-expression. Dominant personalities such as Alexander the Great, Julius Caesar, and Napoleon had their own selfish aims, but they also acted "instinctively" to bring about what the times required. In such actions Hegel saw the hand of the Absolute at work:

> Such individuals have no consciousness of the Idea as such. They are practical and political men. But at the same time they are thinkers with insight into what is needed and timely. They see the very truth of their age and their world, the next genus, so to speak, which is already formed in the womb of time. It is theirs to know this new universal, the necessary next stage of their world, to make it their own aim, and put all their energy into it . . . Their whole life was labor and trouble, their whole being was in their passion. Once their objective is attained, they fall off like empty hulls from the kernel. They die early like Alexander, they are murdered like Caesar, transported to Saint Helena like Napoleon . . .[24]

For Hegel—as for Plato, but for different reasons—the state knows better than the individual what is best for him or her. The practical result is the same and contrasts sharply with the conclusions of natural rights advocates. The individual can do no better than to seek direction from the state. Plato put his faith in the competence (from nature and training) of the philosopher-king, whereas Hegel relied on the Absolute to direct the culture through its presence within it.

Government! Government! What do I get for all I give, I'd like to know! Pot holes and bombs!

CECIL DAWKINS

We must also contrast Hegel's idea of the state with Hobbes's. For Hobbes, the state functions pragmatically to protect the people from the worst they are capable of doing to one another. The state is a convenience, a necessity, but something contrived by people for their own purposes. It is absolute because it must be, but this necessity is rooted in brutal human nature and does not serve a larger purpose. Hegel's state, by contrast, is the current fullest expression of the Absolute. Unlike Hobbes's mechanical state, Hegel's state is organic; every aspect of it is related to every other aspect, and everything is as it must be. Because the state is for Hegel a reflection of the divine, it is a living entity that grows and develops as the Absolute becomes ever more conscious of itself.

This conception of the state leads Hegel to an interesting view of freedom. The traditional protections offered, for example, by the Bill of Rights in the U.S. Constitution—freedom from search and seizure; freedom from the interference of the state in the free practice of speech, the press, and religion—are merely *formal freedoms*. To seek *freedom* from oppression is to think abstractly and negatively. As the individual moves through three dialectically related stages—from the family where love creates a unit, to civil society where individuals relate to one another through their work, to the moral perspective of the state that reconciles and unites all conflicts in society—he or she reaches what Hegel calls *substantial freedom*.

At this stage of moral development, the individual seeks the freedom to define himself or herself in terms of wider cultural values. Having achieved moral maturity by moving progressively from family to civil society to the state, Hegel believes, one will no longer see the laws of the state as oppressive. That person will then be able to move beyond a narrow search for freedom from oppression to a much broader freedom to align his or her own will with the will of the state. Since the Absolute directs the state, an individual could have no higher aim. The substantial freedom Hegel advocates is the freedom to further the work of the Absolute. This is perhaps the most controversial of Hegel's ideas.

The Mandate of Heaven: Rule in China

There is something very Hegelian (or perhaps it is the other way around) about the ancient Chinese understanding of the right to rule. The emperor, it was said, ruled because he had the Mandate of Heaven; he stood at a midpoint between heaven and Earth and mediated between the two. In terms of metaphysics, all human beings were seen as reflecting that balance. Recalling the principles of *yin* and *yang* from Chapter 2, you may think of *Chi'en,* the Father in Chinese cosmology, as *yang,* bursting with energy, full of light and activity; and you may think of *K'un,* the Mother, as *yin,* deeply meditative, full of nurturing and receptivity. It is inconceivable to think of either *Chi'en* or *K'un* as existing without the other, for they have reality only in the dance of energy between them.

In Hegel's system, even the Absolute (like *Chi'en*) is not real until expressed in the world (like *K'un*). Hegel's way of saying it was that the universal fulfills itself in the particular and the particular in the universal. The

In chains for teaching the truth, this figure may indicate his government's loss of the Mandate of Heaven.

Si Ma Qian by Hou Rong/Photo by Quentin Kardos.

Chinese way of expressing the same thing is that as *Chi'en* sends out its energy to be embodied in *K'un;* Earth receives and makes real the heavenly *ch'i,* or energy. You might think of *ch'i* as a kind of life force. Nothing is fixed, nothing is static; energy is continuously moving between heaven and Earth, giving life to the world of particular things and expression to the oneness of the *Tao*.

So it is that the emperor stands between heaven and Earth and receives the Mandate of Heaven. It is not the emperor as an individual human person who rules, but rather heaven (in its dance with Earth) that rules *through* him. As semidivine beings, the emperors mediated between heaven and the world, called "Under Heaven," only as long as their rule remained pure; when it became corrupt, the Mandate of Heaven passed to another dynasty. Here is the story of the collapse of the Shang dynasty around 1000 B.C.E. and the transfer of the Mandate of Heaven to the Chou dynasty, as represented by Wen Wang:

> Wen Wang is placed above—
> How radiant in Heaven!
> Although Chou is an old domain,
> its Mandate is a new one.
> The holders of Chou—
> were they not brilliant?
> The Mandate of god—
> is it not timely?
> Wen Wang ascends, descends,
> to the left and right of god.[25]

What a powerful support for the ruling family it is to be regarded as comfortable in heavenly realms. Such a belief made government a sacred and awe-inspiring function. Still, popular belief insisted that the government observe the Confucian virtues of propriety (or order) and human heartedness; failure to do so would bring heavenly indications of displeasure such as the birth of a two-headed baby or the appearance of a meteor. If these early signs were ignored, more severe disasters might follow, including drought, floods, and even wars. Ultimately the ruling house would fall, final proof that it had indeed lost the Mandate of Heaven.

The absolute authority available to Chinese emperors rested to a certain extent on popular belief in the Mandate. The ethical demands the Mandate placed on the ruling house, if it wished to retain its power, served as a moral restraint on potential tyranny. Only by acting benevolently could the ruling dynasty demonstrate that it continued to enjoy the Mandate of Heaven; any attempt to rule without the welfare of the people in mind would result in a loss of the Mandate.[26]

According to Chinese political philosophy and metaphysics, other restraints on the power of the ruler exist in the natural order. In classical Taoist philosophy, the only way to rule is to dance the dance of *ch'i,* to observe how things are going in their own *Tao*-inspired way and let them fulfill their nature. The *Tao Te Ching* puts it this way:

Governing a large country is like frying a small fish.
You spoil it with too much poking.
Center your country in Tao and evil will have no power.
Not that it isn't there, but you'll be able to step out of its way.
Give evil nothing to oppose and it will disappear by itself.[27]

This is the principle the Chinese call ***wei-wu-wei*** (or sometimes ***wu-wei***), which literally means "doing without doing." To understand *wei-wu-wei,* it is only necessary to look at how nature moves the natural system. Day turns to night and night to day; winter turns to spring and autumn follows summer. There is no effort involved, no striving. These processes show us the power of the *Tao,* which never seems to do anything; yet, somehow, through it everything gets done. There is a built-in order to nature and a built-in order to human affairs that will become perfectly obvious to us if we will only open our eyes.

wei-wu-wei (wu-wei) *[WAY WOO WAY] literally, "doing by not doing"; in Taoism, the method of blending your individual effort with the great power of the* Tao *in the world of created things*

In another translation of the *Tao Te Ching,* written to reflect the concerns of the twentieth century, John Heider describes how *The Tao of Leadership* functions:

It puzzles people at first, to see how little the able leader actually does, and yet how much gets done. But the leader knows that is how things work. After all, Tao does nothing at all, yet everything gets done. When the leader gets too busy, the time has come to return to selfless silence.

Silence gives one center.
Center creates order.
When there is order, there is little to do.[28]

It is tempting to think we have the "mandate" to tell people what to do, or even to force them to do certain things. This approach, however, can only end in frustration. It is much wiser, and incredibly more efficient, to step back and create openings for things to happen:

The greatest martial arts are the gentlest. They allow an attacker the opportunity to fall down. The greatest generals do not rush into every battle. They offer the enemy many opportunities to make self-defeating errors. The greatest administrators do not achieve production through constraints and limitations. They provide opportunities. Good leadership consists of motivating people to their highest levels by offering them opportunities, not obligations. This is how things happen naturally. Life is an opportunity and not an obligation.[29]

The Divine Right to Rule

Royal Families in Europe

In Europe, hereditary rulers claimed the right to rule as a mandate from God. Known as the *divine right of kings,* this claim was especially influential in France and England from the fourteenth to the seventeenth century. In an absolute monarchy, the glory of the king and the power or sovereignty of the state were complementary; each supported and enhanced the other. To rule as God's anointed was to have divine authority for very earthly decisions, but unlike the Chinese emperors, European monarchs claimed the right to act as individuals with an implied stamp of preexisting heavenly approval.

The great Bourbon kings of France—Louis XIII and Louis XIV (known as the Sun King)—and the first two Stuart kings of England—James I and Charles I—are perhaps the best-known European advocates of the divine right of kings. They saw no need to have the consent of their subjects because their authority to rule came, in their opinion, from God. If the people objected, they could always be suppressed or killed. Louis XIV once remarked, "*L'etat, c'est moi!*"—"I am the state." If a king rules as an individual by divine right, then there is no recourse for dissatisfied subjects; there is no higher authority to which they can appeal.

Nearly all men can stand adversity; but if you want to test a man's character, give him power.
ABRAHAM LINCOLN

Royal Families in Africa

During the same time period in Buganda (modern Uganda, East Africa), the hereditary king was a limited monarch rather than an absolute monarch on the model of Louis XIV. His authority, according to E. Wamala, was shared with a council of the heads of clans, which acted as parliament, and, further down the line, with a system of chiefs and subchiefs who assisted in social and political decision making. Myths, however, claimed that kings had a quasi-divine origin, and the right to rule was automatically transferred to the son of a king who had been born with the "signs."[30] The king, for his part, was obliged to behave benevolently toward the people God had given him. Whereas the European kings used the theory of divine right to rule autocratically, the kings of Buganda, by contrast, ruled by consensus, or group agreement.

As a limited rather than an absolute monarch, the king ruled through the council of heads of clans and the whole structure of subheads and chiefs down to the level of the village. The role of all these councilors was to debate an issue fully until consensus was reached. Once consensus was established, it was taboo for the king to reject the conclusion. In fact, the king rarely took part in the discussion, preferring to send his own ideas to the debate through a trusted councilor rather than risk prejudicing the debate by his presence. Although the heads of clans were chosen by the king rather than by the people, this consensus form of government was an early, weak form of *representative democracy*.[31] The interests of the people were represented through subchiefs, chiefs, and councilors at the highest levels of decision making.

One head does not go into council.
GHANAIAN PROVERB

Among the Akan people of Ghana in West Africa, the consensus model of government was also traditional. The chief, chosen from the royal line to govern, could issue only those commands that had been agreed upon by the council, whose members had sought public opinion before any debate took place. It was well understood that each council member (usually the head of a clan) was obliged to seek the advice and consent of his people in the same way that the chief was expected to seek the concurrence of his councilors. Any formal commands would be issued in the name of "the chief and his elders," and a chief who acted without this concurrence could expect to be deposed.[32]

At the time of his formal installation, the chief had to take a public oath to observe the formal and informal laws of the town or village. On this occasion, according to Kwame Gyekye, a series of expectations submitted by the people would be recited before the chief as a definition of the scope and limitations of his political authority. These expectations constituted a kind of social contract between the people and the chief who was "bound by law to rule with the consent of the people." The following are some typical examples of the people's expectations:

> We do not wish that he should treat us unfairly. We do not wish that he should act on his own initiative (. . . without reference to the views or wishes of the people). We do not wish that it should ever be that he should say "I have no time," "I have no time."[33]

By listening to a formal reading of this mandate, the ruler bound himself to rule by popular consent. To visually underscore this concept, the staff held by the chief's linguist (spokesperson) might be topped by a gold- or silver-embossed hand holding an egg. The message was a reminder of the need for appropriate and judicious use of political power. Squeeze the egg too hard and it breaks; hold it too loosely and it can fall, with the same result.[34]

Claiming divine support can provide powerful authority to a ruler in a variety of cultural settings; the wise ones, however, have understood that divine support alone is not enough. If they acted without reference to (or worse, in opposition to) the wishes of the people, rulers often learned too late how fragile the Mandate of Heaven could be. There may not have been two-headed babies or meteors to give warning, but the dynastic kings of Europe who lost touch with the people and acted in isolation from them ended up deposed or beheaded. It seems that at least an implied social contract is necessary for the successful exercise of political power.

Carved out of a single block of wood, this statue recognizes the interdependence of family members on which a consensus model of decision making might be based.

African house post by Lamidi Fakeye/Courtesy of the African Art Museum of Maryland/Photo by Quentin Kardos.

Political Theory

Political theory addresses the balance of power between the people and the state. At the extremes are anarchism, belief that no government would be best, and totalitarianism, belief that government must have absolute power. The labels *liberal* and *conservative,* which reflect moderate positions between anarchism and totalitarianism, meant one thing in the nineteenth century and quite another in the twentieth century. After examining the changes in meaning these terms have undergone, we will turn to American constitutional theory and the issue of civil rights.

Philosophers . . . conceive men not as they are, but as they would wish them to be. The result is that they write satires instead of ethics, and that they have never produced a political theory which is of any use.

SPINOZA

Liberalism and Conservatism

A built-in tension exists between the liberties claimed by individual citizens and the power inherent in political institutions. Each society must decide what is an appropriate balance between the two. When we speak about political theory, the terms *liberal* and *conservative* are often used. In general, liberals favor individual freedom, whereas conservatives advocate respect for tradition and established institutions. These terms can be confusing because what they meant during the nineteenth century, when they became popular, and what they mean today are significantly different in some respects. Let's take a look at the origins of these terms and their development over time.

Liberalism had its beginnings in the political philosophy of John Locke, who assumed the right of people to be free. Although the Western world now assumes basic rights for individuals—known as the theory of *individualism*—the idea that people were born free was a relatively new one when Locke published his treatises. Among the natural rights Locke believed we all possessed was the right to property, and the philosophy of liberalism had its first powerful expression in a book on economic theory, Adam Smith's *The Wealth of Nations*. Published in 1776, this book was enormously influential during the nineteenth century. Beginning with an assumption of individualism, Smith advocated what has come to be called ***laissez-faire* economics.**

***laissez-faire* economics** *the economic theory that if government stays out of the economy, market forces will regulate it in a harmonious and productive manner that will benefit all*

Smith's theory was that individuals should be left alone (the basic meaning of *laissez-faire*) to pursue free-enterprise capitalism. Without government regulation, Smith believed, the market forces of *supply and demand* would regulate the economy, and competition would keep prices reasonable. If too great a supply of a product existed, prices would drop, and there would be less incentive to produce more of it. When the product became scarce, however, demand would force prices up, and entrepreneurs would respond by increasing the supply. Smith's theory was that by acting in their own self-interest, producers would serve the common good.

Locke's political philosophy and Smith's economic theory combined to define nineteenth-century liberalism. If individuals were born free with natural rights, then the implication was that the power of government to restrict an individual's rights should be severely restrained. Everyone would be better off (individual freedom would be best served) with as little government interference as possible. The liberal ideal of individual freedom was rooted in limited state power.

There is no such thing as good government.
EMMA GOLDMAN, ANARCHIST

Today our economic system is quite different. Rather than many individual entrepreneurs or even family-owned businesses, a relatively few huge multinational conglomerates control much of the economy and seem to rival the government in power. Modern liberals still value individual freedom, but they now find themselves in the somewhat strange position of asking government to guarantee that freedom. It was private enterprise, twentieth-century liberals point out, that made African Americans ride in the backs of buses and declared them ineligible to eat lunch in certain restaurants or sleep in certain hotels. Private enterprise had the audacity to give female job applicants pregnancy tests and to ask them during job interviews what methods of birth control they were using. Only government, say twentieth-century liberals, has enough power to ensure individual freedom.

Nineteenth-century conservatism found its classic expression in the backlash against the wars of revolution in Europe and America. Edmund

Burke, a contemporary of Adam Smith, was an English political philosopher who mistrusted the judgment of the "common man," somewhat in the style of Plato. Left to their own devices, Burke pointed out, individuals became a mob—witness the atrocities of the French Revolution. The state, for Burke, was not an artificial structure, but an embodiment of tradition and all that is best in human nature. Although he may not have gone quite as far as Hegel, Burke had the same sense of the state as a living, organic focus of a culture's values.

Nineteenth-century conservatives, like Burke, looked to the state to provide continuity with the great traditions of the past and to guide individuals toward the kind of freedom Hegel talked about: the freedom to fulfill one's culture's ideals. As in Hegel's philosophy, to speak of the rights of the individual apart from this cultural matrix is to speak nonsense. In Burke's ideal state, as in Plato's *Republic,* the best of those people who by breeding and education were ideally suited to rule would decide what was in the best interest of individuals who are too frivolous to decide wisely for themselves.

In the new code of laws which I suppose it will be necessary for you to make, I desire you would remember the ladies and be more generous to them than your ancestors. Do not put such unlimited power into the hands of the husbands. Remember, all men would be tyrants if they could.

ABIGAIL ADAMS, TO HER HUSBAND JOHN AT PHILADELPHIA FOR THE CONTINENTAL CONGRESS

After all, conservatives would argue, is it really in the individual's best interest to choose without having the "big picture" that centuries of connection with tradition provide? Ask children to decide for themselves, and they will watch TV all day, eating sweets until their teeth rot, and doing nothing to improve themselves. Leaders of the state must act in the same way that parents act within the family, depriving individuals of freedoms that are not in their own best interests.

One clear vestige of this political philosophy is embedded within the U.S. Constitution: the electoral college. Many people believe that individuals, by their votes, elect the president. However, the president is actually

What do you notice about the race, gender, and social class of this group of people?
Signing of the Declaration of Independence/North Wind Photo Archive.

elected by the electoral college, composed of individuals chosen by political parties. These 538 individuals, some of whom are not bound to vote the way their state's popular vote decrees, elect the president. We have the electoral college because the framers of the Constitution, for all their Lockean rhetoric, didn't fully trust the wisdom of the ordinary citizen in so important a choice. The electoral college, composed of hand-picked people with knowledge of the great traditions and values of the past, could override any mistakes the people, acting as individuals, might make.

Twentieth-century conservatives oppose government interference in economic matters every bit as vehemently as Adam Smith and nineteenth-century liberals did. The *supply-side economics* advocated by President Ronald Reagan was based on Smith's theory that individuals, acting in their own self-interest, would create profits that would "trickle down" to benefit all levels of society through the creation of wealth and jobs.

Current conservatives also tend to believe that today's big government is not serving people's needs. If individual communities, for instance, were to be allowed to decide that they wanted creationism or prayer to be part of their public schools, today's conservatives believe that everyone would be better off. Only when a sufficiently significant (to them) value seems threatened (such as the natural right to life they see threatened by abortion or the right to public prayer in school) do conservatives look to government to restore what they view as traditional moral order. Respect for traditional moral values remains at the heart of conservative thinking.

Depending on the circumstances, twentieth-century liberals and conservatives may find themselves advocating more or less government involvement in the lives of private citizens. The clear distinctions between the two positions that were possible during the nineteenth century have broken down; what remains is a liberal bias in favor of individual rights and a conservative bias in favor of the value of tradition.

American Constitutional Theory and Civil Rights

In our discussion of Locke's view of the social contract, we saw that his emphasis on the need to limit state power is embodied in the Declaration of Independence. Some of Locke's ideas are also reflected in the U.S. Constitution. James Madison, its chief architect, insisted on a system of **checks and balances** to prevent the federal government from becoming tyrannical or falling completely under the influence of a particular interest group, rather than representing the interests of all the people. Three branches of government were established: *executive,* the president and the cabinet agencies; *legislative,* the two houses of Congress; and *judicial,* the system of courts, culminating with the Supreme Court.

checks and balances *the system by which each of the three branches of the U.S. government restrains the power of the other two, keeping any one from becoming too powerful*

In theory, each branch can check the power of the other two to ensure a balance among them for the public good. Presidential treaties and nominees for cabinet posts must be confirmed by the Senate; the president has the power to veto laws passed by Congress, but Congress can override a veto with a two-thirds majority; the laws created by Congress are subject to interpretation by the courts.

As we have seen, American political theory as expressed in the Constitution represents a blend of liberal and conservative values. The chief executive officer, the president, is chosen by the people (a liberal respect for individual rights), with the electoral college acting as the final selector (a conservative mistrust of individual judgment). In the legislative branch, the same sort of balance existed. Originally, the House of Representatives was directly elected by the people, whereas the Senate was chosen by the state legislatures. Direct election of senators, the current method, required a constitutional amendment.

We must have government, but we must watch them like a hawk.
MILLICENT FENWICK

The judicial branch is charged with interpreting the laws passed by Congress, which the president agrees to enforce. This power to interpret the law has become especially significant in the twentieth century. As precedent-setting cases make their way to the Supreme Court, decisions affecting individual rights are increasingly made by the judicial branch. Because appointments to the Supreme Court are for life, the individual political philosophy of a Supreme Court justice can have very far-reaching implications.

From the beginning, American citizens have been guaranteed *civil rights*. Ratification of the Constitution would not have been possible without the promise of prompt action to include a Bill of Rights. These first ten amendments guarantee, among other freedoms, the right to free speech, freedom of the press, and the right to practice freely the religion of your choice (or no religion at all). Individuals are also promised the right to peaceably assemble to demand change, to bear arms, to have a speedy and public trial, to protection from search and seizure and from cruel and unusual punishments. The Fifth Amendment guarantees that no individual shall be deprived of "life, liberty or property" (in John Locke's words) without "due process of law."

What this means is that the state, through its judicial branch, must move slowly and carefully in restricting individual rights, even those of suspected criminals. As a result of the *Miranda v. Arizona* case, a captured suspect has the right to remain silent and to have an attorney present during questioning. Police officers are reminded, when arresting suspects, to "read them their rights." Failure to do so can result in a case being thrown out of court. The rights referred to are civil rights, the rights of a citizen to protection against the power of the state. In many countries, people have no such protection and are subject to arrest—and perhaps indefinite imprisonment and torture—without being informed of the charges against them and with no means whereby they can assert their individual rights.

Freedom of speech . . . Just watch what you say!
ICE-T

The U.S. Government and Human Rights

What happens if people who fear torture, unjust imprisonment, and even death in foreign countries seek political asylum in the United States? If those fleeing political persecution have entered the United States illegally, does the

U.S. government have the duty to send them back or the obligation to shelter them? This conflict was highlighted in the 1980s when churches began offering "sanctuary" to those fleeing persecution in their country of origin.

Under the Refugee Act of 1980, immigrants who have a "well-founded fear of persecution" because of their nationality, race, religion, or political opinion have the right to asylum in the United States. One of the problems has been that refugees from Guatemala and El Salvador were granted asylum between 1983 and 1989 at a much lower rate (2 to 2.5 percent) than were those from the former Soviet Union (73 percent) and Iran (62 percent) because the United States was unwilling to admit its support for military dictatorships in those Central American countries, according to a suit brought by religious and refugee assistance groups.[35]

The Immigration and Naturalization Service agreed to settle the suit by allowing many to reapply, and 280,000 did by the 1991 deadline. Under a 1997 law, most of these Centro-Americans risked being deported. With death squads continuing to roam the streets, the homicide rate remained high in El Salvador: 114 per 100,000 people compared with 11 per 100,000 in the United States. Should these asylum seekers be sent home?

Rigoberta Menchú recalls an experience when she was twelve years old and working on a cotton plantation in Guatemala:

> When the owner began to speak, he spoke in Spanish. My mother understood a little Spanish and afterwards she told us he was talking about the elections. But we didn't even understand what our parents told us—that the *ladinos* [children of Spaniards and Indians who speak Spanish] had a government. . . . They told us we all had to go and make a mark on a piece of paper . . . He warned us that anyone who didn't mark the paper would be thrown out of work . . . They came to the *finca* and told us that our President had won, the one we had voted for. We didn't even know that they were votes they'd taken away. My parents laughed when they heard them say, 'Our President,' because for us he was the President of the *ladinos,* not ours at all.[36]

With no protection for individual rights, citizens of Guatemala were extremely vulnerable. The first to be tortured and killed was Rigoberta's younger brother; then her father died in the occupation of the Spanish embassy,[37] and later her mother was kidnapped, raped, tortured, and eventually killed.[38]

To die for the revolution is a one-shot deal; to live for the revolution means taking on the more difficult commitment of changing our day-to-day life patterns.
FRANCES M. BEAL

The sanctuary or asylum movement insists that those who flee conditions such as these deserve the political protection of stable democracies such as the United States. This is especially the case if that government has played a covert or overt role in supporting military dictatorships. If there is no guarantee of individual rights in the country of my birth, do I have the right to expect the government of another country to offer me protection?

Summary

The framers of the U.S. Constitution felt very strongly that the liberal regard for individual rights must be built into the structure of government, alongside a conservative respect for traditions that have served humankind well over many centuries. The Constitution reflects the Enlightenment respect for the individual—advocated by Locke, Rousseau, Wollstonecraft, Stanton, and Anthony—and balances it with protection for politically sacred traditions in the same way that Plato, Aristotle, Hegel, and Burke wished to do. A sense of natural law, or the way things are meant to be, is blended with respect for natural rights that belong to citizens from birth.

There is an ongoing tension between belief in divine authority to rule, which the absolute monarchs of Europe and the Chinese emperors claimed, on the one hand, and belief in the *consent of the governed* as the basis for any legitimate state authority on the other. If there is no formal or implied social contract between the citizens and their rulers, changes in government can be violent, for those who claim that God wishes them to rule can be convinced this is not the case only by forcibly depriving them of power. One of the great advantages to government by social contract is the peaceful transition of power.

It is something we take for granted in the Western world, but when Republican administration gives way to Democratic, or vice versa; when Liberal, Labor, Social Democrat, and Conservative can take turns as prime minister without bloodshed or violence in the streets, this is cause for gratitude. Elections for prime minister or president are often bitter, with mudslinging on both sides, but after the votes are counted, the loser congratulates the winner and the processes of government move on.

This kind of stable government was one of the ideals of classical political theorists such as Plato and Aristotle, who had watched Athenian democracy deteriorate into mob rule. All the political philosophers we have met in this chapter shared the desire to create a government that helps individuals live full and happy lives and permits society to develop economically, culturally, and intellectually. Even Hobbes, the most pessimistic of the group, valued public order as one of the most essential conditions within a state.

Whether sovereignty should reside with a political elite, shaped by birth and tradition for the exercise of political authority, or with the people, however informed or ignorant, interested or bored they might be, is a matter of dispute among the thinkers and thought systems surveyed in this chapter. All agree, however, that the way we define sovereignty will have a profound and far-reaching effect on the lives of all citizens and even on the fortunes of non-citizen residents within a state.

The *Republic* begins with the question "What is justice?" and looks for the answer to this societal question by examining the nature of the individuals that make up the society. A society, the *Republic* concludes, is what it is because the individuals who make it up are what they are. In the next chapter, on social philosophy, we will begin as we did in this chapter—by looking at the *Republic*. The question we will be examining involves the relationship between the individual and the community, rather than between the individual and the state. Once a state has been constituted, how will justice be done? What is the proper balance between the needs and wants of the individual and those of the society in which he or she lives?

And what can the nature of individuals tell us about how we should think about community?

For Further Thought

1. Are you more willing to trust the good judgment of the individual or the benevolence of a strong state to produce a well-ordered society? Explain.
2. Is there a natural law at work behind the structures of society, or are there many possible ways a society might be organized? Explain.
3. If there are natural rights, is it the duty of the state to protect them? Why, or why not?
4. What do you see as the proper balance between liberal support for individual rights and conservative respect for tradition?
5. Is civil disobedience ever justified? If not, why not? If so, under what conditions and on what grounds?
6. Are you inclined to agree more with Hobbes or with Locke on the need for a strong state? Why?
7. Under what conditions would people be justified in thinking their rulers had broken the social contract and should be replaced?
8. Is an independent morality (originating inside the person rather than imposed from the outside) possible? Desirable?
9. Does history move through the dialectic process outlined by Hegel, or does it—as others have suggested—move in repeating cycles?
10. How convinced are you that some higher power uses world historical individuals for its own purposes through the cunning of reason?
11. Is a social contract possible when the ruler believes he/she rules by divine right or with the Mandate of Heaven? Why, or why not?
12. How is it possible for a leader to do without doing? What must the leader give up to practice rule by *wei-wu-wei*?
13. In your judgment, what qualities make an effective ruler? An ideal ruler? A dangerous ruler? How might society cultivate or protect against these types of rulers?
14. What are the potential dangers inherent in a democracy? What can go wrong, and how might it do so?
15. For a democracy to be successful, what obligations do citizens have?
16. What happens when there is too much government? Too little? Which groups are more likely to prosper and suffer under each of these conditions?
17. If we create artificial intelligences, will they have natural rights? If so, on what basis? If not, why not?
18. In today's global economy, is it possible for market forces like supply and demand alone to regulate the economy?
19. Why do citizens need civil rights?
20. In a country with more than 200 million citizens, is it possible for consensus to be reached? If so, how? If not, why not?

For Further Exploration

Hegel, G. W. F. *Reason in History*. Translated by Robert S. Hartman. Indianapolis: Bobbs-Merrill, 1953. This slim volume gives the essentials of Hegel's philosophy of history and is both readable and manageable intellectually.

Heider, John, trans. *The Tao of Leadership: Lao Tzu's Tao Te Ching Adapted for a New Age*. New York: Bantam, 1986. Heider offers a translation of Lao-tzu's classic *Tao Te Ching,* using the word *leader* instead of *master* or *sage* and offering an alternative style of leadership based on *wei-wu-wei* (doing without doing). Many successful businesses are using this approach.

Machiavelli, Niccolo. *The Prince*. New York: Scholar Press, 1969. *The Prince* is a masterpiece of practical politics, written in the form of advice for a Renaissance prince. One piece of advice is that it is better to be feared than loved.

Orwell, George. *1984*. New York: Harcourt Brace Jovanovich, 1984. Orwell's novel predicted a future in which government would control every aspect of a citizen's life through the control of information. Even though 1984 is now history, the issues remain live ones.

Schneir, Miriam, ed. *Feminism: The Essential Historical Writings*. New York: Vintage, 1972. This is an anthology of short excerpts from the speeches and writings of the eighteenth- and nineteenth-century women's movement. The Seneca Falls Convention and *The United States of America v. Susan B. Anthony* are both included.

For Further Research

Try these InfoTrac keywords:

Sovereignty

Anarchism

Totalitarianism

Liberalism

Conservatism

Social Contract Theory

Notes

1. Patrick G. McKeown, "Is 'Little Brother' Watching You?" *National Forum* (Winter 1993): 46.
2. Plato, *Republic,* trans. Robin Waterfield (New York: Oxford University Press, 1994), 166–167.
3. Aristotle, "Politics," in *The Pocket Aristotle,* ed. Justin D. Kaplan, trans. W. D. Ross (New York: Washington Square, 1958), 281.
4. Thomas Aquinas, "Summa Theologica" (1a–2ae, xciii, 3), in *St. Thomas Aquinas: Theological Texts,* ed. and trans. Thomas Gilby (New York: Oxford University Press, 1955), 146.
5. Aquinas, lxvi. 7.

6. *The Speeches of Malcolm X at Harvard,* ed. Archie Epps (New York: Morrow, 1968), 34.
7. Thomas Hobbes, *The Leviathan* (New York: Prometheus, 1988), 89–90.
8. John Locke, "Two Treatises on Government," bk 2, chap. 2, in *Philosophers Speak for Themselves: From Descartes to Locke,* eds. T. V. Smith and Marjorie Grene (Chicago: University of Chicago Press, 1960), 457.
9. John Locke, "An Essay Concerning the True Original Extent and End of Civil Government" in *Great Books of the Western World,* ed. Robert Maynard Hutchins (Chicago: Encyclopaedia Britannica, 1952), 25.
10. Locke, 53.
11. Lore Metzger, introduction to *Oroonoko: Or the Royal Slave,* by Aphra Behn (New York: Norton, 1973), xiv.
12. Clarisse Coignet, *La Morale Independante dans son Principe et dans son Objet* (Paris: Germer Bailliere, 1869, facsimile from UMI), pp. 107–109.
13. Mohandas K. Gandhi, in "Family Satyagraha" by Eknath Easwaren, from "Gandhi, the Man" found in *Alternatives to Violence,* ed. Colman McCarthy (Washington, D.C.: The Center for Teaching Peace, 1987).
14. Mary Wollstonecraft, *A Vindication of the Rights of Woman* (New York: Norton, 1967), 50, 52.
15. Wollstonecraft, 81.
16. Elizabeth Cady Stanton, "Declaration of Sentiments and Resolutions, Seneca Falls," in *Feminism: The Essential Historical Writings,* ed. Miriam Schneir, (New York: Vintage, 1972), 77–78.
17. Schneir, 79.
18. Schneir, 118.
19. Schneir, 134.
20. Schneir, 135.
21. G. W. F. Hegel, *Reason in History,* trans. Robert S. Hartman (Indianapolis: Bobbs-Merrill, 1953), 16.
22. Hegel, 66.
23. Hegel, 24.
24. Hegel, 40, 41.
25. Quoted in Edward H. Schafer et al., eds., *Ancient China, Great Ages of Man: A History of the World's Cultures* (New York: Time-Life Books, 1967), 82.
26. John Meskill, ed., *An Introduction to Chinese Civilization* (New York: Columbia University Press, 1973), 652.
27. Stephen Mitchell, trans. *Tao Te Ching,* chap. 60 (New York: HarperCollins, 1991).
28. John Heider, *The Tao of Leadership: Lao Tzu's Tao Te Ching* Adapted for a New Age (New York: Bantam, 1986), 73.
29. Heider, 135.
30. E. Wamala, "The Socio-Political Philosophy of Traditional Buganda Society," in *The Foundations of Social Life: Ugandan Philosophical Studies,* vol. 1, ed. George F. McLean (Washington, D.C.: Council for Research in Values and Philosophy, 1992), 37–39.

31. Wamala, 40–41.
32. Kwame Gyekye, "Traditional Political Ideas and Contemporary Development," in *Person and Community: Ghanaian Philosophical Studies,* vol. 1, ed. Kwasi Wiredu and Kwame Gyekye (Washington, D.C.: Council for Research in Values and Philosophy, 1992), 242–244.
33. Gyekye, 243.
34. Gyekye, 251.
35. Demetria Martinez, "Time to Take a Stand Against Deportation," *National Catholic Reporter,* 18 April 1997, p. 15.
36. *I Rigoberta Menchú: An Indian Woman in Guatemala,* ed. Elisabeth Burgos-Debray, trans. Ann Wright (New York: Verso, 1984), 25–27.
37. *I Rigoberta Menchú,* 183.
38. *I Rigoberta Menchú,* 195.

CHAPTER 9

Social Philosophy

Am I My Brother's or My Sister's Keeper?

BEFORE YOU READ . . .

Ask yourself how you would decide what constitutes justice.

Those who tell stories hold the power in society. Today, television tells most of the stories to most of the people, most of the time.
GEORGE GERBNER

Political philosophy focuses on the relationship between the individual and the state and considers where the rights of one end and the rights of the other begin. In social philosophy we look at a related set of questions that arise out of the tension (or lack of it) between the individual and the community. Living in cultures as devoted to individualism as those in the West, it may be difficult for us to understand that in Japan, for example, it is the group, not the individual, that matters. To be singled out for individual accomplishment is cause for embarrassment rather than pride.

The Issue Defined

Perhaps you have heard some of the following views expressed: If the individual is the significant unit in society, then my attention should be devoted to myself—to getting enough education to ensure a good job and the financial and social rewards that go with it. If things go wrong, I must look to myself for explanations and solutions. Maybe I am not smart enough, or did not work hard enough, or I am the wrong race/gender/age. If other people are homeless, hungry, or out of work, they obviously have some problem, but the responsibility for finding solutions is theirs. Each of us needs to pull ourselves up by our own bootstraps. Look at the individuals who have "made it" against all odds;

they are our inspiration; they show us it can be done. Anyone who does not make it is just not trying hard enough.

A society that focuses instead on the community may look at these same issues rather differently. We have heard a lot lately about the Japanese auto industry, with its high quality standards, pride in product, and company songs that everyone sings each morning with a kind of patriotic fervor. In Japanese culture, it is the group that matters, and the success of the team that makes the well-built car is shared. Not to work hard is to let down the team as well as yourself; your efforts have little meaning apart from those of the group to which you belong. You cannot build a car by yourself, but you can do your job as well as you possibly can, and you can cooperate with the other members of your team rather than compete with them.

A similarly communal lifestyle was prevalent not so long ago in eighteenth-century Europe and England. People lived in individual homes, but there was common land on which all the cattle in the village grazed. Family members who worked for wages pooled their earnings in a common fund known as the "family wage economy," and it would have been unthinkable to say, "These earnings are mine, and I will do with them what I like." It was the family and the village that mattered; their survival was the goal, and each individual had a part to play.

The native cultures of the Americas have also emphasized communal values, assuming that some resources belong to the entire group and insisting that some resources—such as the land and water—belong to no one. In cultures of this type, a hungry person is fed, an ill person is cared for, a dying person is comforted. People and material goods alike are seen as part of the culture's wealth.

We cannot think of ourselves save as to some extent social beings. Hence, we cannot separate the idea of ourselves and our own good from our idea of others and their own good.

JOHN DEWEY

To emphasize individualism, as we now do in the West, is to de-emphasize communalism—the one-for-all, all-for-one village or work group, tribe, or team. In a communal society, the poor and the mentally and physically ill are the community's responsibility. When people are born at home and die at home, or at least are born and die in the same village, there is a sense of belonging that is second nature and personal. When people become ill or drought ruins the crop, the family and the village step in to help. Even criminals are part of the community and are seen as a community problem to be "rehabilitated" within the embrace of society.

Because most of us are born in a hospital and die in a hospital and because most of us have been taught individualism all our lives, these communal ideas may seem quaint. Most of us neither live in the city of our birth nor live near the extended family of parents, siblings, grandparents, aunts, and uncles who supported our ancestors through good times and bad. Economic mobility has severed many of such ties; when we live in apartment or condominium complexes surrounded by people whose names we do not even know, the notion that we might be responsible for them or for others outside our immediate family may seem extraordinary.

Questions of justice—the primary philosophical issue of social philosophy—are rooted in whether we see our own welfare and the welfare of others as connected or separate. How should people be treated, for

I have a dream that one day this nation will rise up and live out the meaning of its creed, "We hold these truths to be self-evident, that all men are created equal."

MARTIN LUTHER KING, JR.

instance? On the basis of their merit? Should the beautiful/handsome, talented, and high born be treated according to one standard and the ordinary by another? Should those who may be expected to advance the social good be given special advantages and rewards? Is it fair to treat everyone equally when some will abuse that good treatment and waste the advantages and rewards, whereas others will use them to benefit all of us? What kind of message are we sending as a society when we pay athletes $2 million a year, the president of the United States $200,000, and a beginning teacher/police officer/nurse $20,000?

Even though we are intellectually committed to the idea of equality, we do not treat everyone equally. Some people are rewarded extraordinarily with wealth, prestige, and power, while others struggle to eat and to have a safe place to sleep. It seems that our notion of equality is closely linked to our equally powerful idea of individualism. We say that people have equality of opportunity and that what they make of that opportunity is up to them, but does everyone really have an equal chance? Supported by local property taxes, public schools in the United States vary greatly in quality from state to state, and even from county to county. Even though every child in the country has access to a free public education, the resources of one school district may put a computer in each child's hands, while the resources of another may be so scant as to be unable to provide each child a textbook. Do children in these two districts start life equally?

What is looked upon as an American dream for white people has long been an American nightmare for black people . . . We didn't land on Plymouth Rock. Plymouth Rock landed on us.

MALCOLM X

To what extent is a society obliged to make up for past abuses? Because their ancestors brought Africans to the Americas in chains and denied them basic personhood and civil rights for centuries, do present-day Latin Americans and Anglo Americans have ongoing societal obligations to the descendants of these former slaves? How long does the legacy of broken families and exclusion from economic opportunity last? When does society's obligation to make amends end, and the obligation of individuals to make something of themselves begin?

With a fraction of the world's population, North Americans use a large portion of the world's resources, many of which we convert into technological marvels. We have a very high standard of living, plenty of agricultural and material goods for those who can afford to buy them. But what of so called third-world countries that use resources at a much lower rate and have fewer ways to intervene when nature brings a drought? When people are starving halfway around the world, are we noble to help them, or are we only paying our debts for using such a disproportionate share of the world's natural bounty of oil, coal, and natural gas?

These are not easy questions. They lie at the heart of this chapter's question, which asks "Am I my brother's or my sister's keeper?" In other words, is someone else's misfortune also my problem as a fellow human being, or is it that person's problem, which I am free to ignore? If my country goes to war, should I be obliged to fight the "enemy" my country has identified? Should everyone—male or female, rich or poor, employed or unemployed, in or out of school, black/white/brown—be subject to an involuntary military draft, or should the future mother, the wealthy person who can pay for a substitute, or the person with special talents be exempt?

DOING PHILOSOPHY
Freedom Versus Tradition

In the Sudan, an eight-year-old girl is given by her family to a priest in a neighboring village. She is told to serve him and obey all his wishes. Someone in the girl's family has offended someone in his family, and she is part of the reparation. When she reaches puberty, she will become his sex slave as well. She understands none of this. In this cultural context, individual freedom must take a back seat to respect for tradition. Neither the young girl nor her family share the Western assumption that individuals have "inalienable rights" that must be protected. In honoring an ancient tradition, the wishes of the young girl play no role at all. Excesses of individualism in our own society have caused some to fear that we are losing touch with valuable traditiuons. Where does the balance lie? At what point must the rights of the individual be protected against the power of the state, and when must they bow to the enduring value of respected tradition?

Put another way, what is justice, and how can we decide what constitutes a just society? Who should receive the benefits, and who should bear the burdens? Equally important and difficult to decide, how shall we determine what standard of justice to use? As Peter, Paul, and Mary told us in the 1960s, justice can be a hammer and freedom a bell, but the real answer may be love. Let's begin as we did in Chapter 8 by looking at Plato's *Republic,* which asks the question "What is the just society?" and answers it by arguing that a society is what it is because the individuals who make it up are what they are.

Classical Theories of Justice

The classical tradition of Greek philosophy explores how justice might be cultivated and expressed. Plato's theory of a just society focuses on the Greek cultural idea of the *polis* in relating the good of the individual to the good of society. Aristotle's contribution highlights the role of the state in educating virtuous citizens.

Justice in the *Polis:* Plato

Who thinks of justice unless he knows injustice?
DIANE GLANCY

To understand how a just society might be constituted, Plato argued, we must begin by looking at how individuals are constituted. If we can decide what makes an effective individual, we will be well on the way to knowing what makes an effective society. (The reverse is also true.) In book 2 of the *Republic,* Socrates, the central character in the dialogue, suggests that justice may be easier to grasp when observed on a larger scale, in the life of the city. Justice in the *polis* will also be justice for the individual.

We usually translate the Greek word *polis* as "city-state," but for Plato, Aristotle, and their contemporaries, the *polis* was much more than a political entity, much more than what we mean today by the word *state*. The *polis* was the source of culture as well as government, and it was where citizens received training in virtue. Recall Aristotle's claim that to live apart from the *polis*, one would have to be either a beast or a god. When Pericles said with pride, "We make our *polis* common to all," he meant much more than outsiders might live in the city; he offered the gift of the common cultural life to Athenians and non-Athenians alike, and he invited all to share in the development of mind and character a well-formed society provides.

To understand the difference between the Greek *polis* and our modern state that is based on individualism and natural rights, it may be helpful to consider the contrast between the Greek theater and the movie theater. Comedy and drama were at the heart of the cultural life of the Greek *polis*; by watching the tragic fate of proud Oedipus or the bitter fury of scorned Medea while sitting in an outdoor amphitheater in the company of people from all ranks in society, one could learn that killing begets more killing and that too much pride always comes to a bad end. We go alone to our movie theaters and sit in the dark, ignoring those around us and hoping to be entertained.

The idea of the common life as expressed in the Greek theater was crucial to the question of justice for Plato. Justice, he had Socrates argue, is not the right of the stronger but the effective harmony of the whole. Justice, in other words, is having and doing what is one's own. The cobbler must make shoes, the shepherd must guard sheep, the warrior must guard the city, and the ruler must rule—each person must do what he or she is fitted to do so that both the individual and society will prosper.

Each person, Socrates pointed out, is composed of three elements: a rational part, a spirited part, and a desiring part:

> One part we say was that by which a man learns, one by which he is angry and spirited; the third has many forms, and we could not give it a proper name of its own, but we named it the desiring part because of its powerful desires for food and drink and love-making and all that attends these, yes and money-loving too, because these desires are fulfilled mostly through money.[1]

Socrates further explained that the three elements of a person correspond to three classes in society, each governed by one of the three qualities.

Most people in any society, Socrates conceded, prefer to be producers who desire to enjoy the fruits of their labors. The farmers and artisans in the *Republic* provide for the bodily needs of all, and their function corresponds to the desiring element in a person. Soldiers perform the function that corresponds to the spirited element in the person; they live a spartan life and guard the safety and security of the city. A few in any culture are motivated primarily by the quest for knowledge and wisdom; they are governed by the rational element, and it is they who must govern the *polis*.

Justice waits upon the great,
Interest holds the scale, and
Riches turns the balance.
MARY DELARIVIÈRE MANLEY

A society is just, according to the argument in the *Republic,* only when each person does what it is proper for him or her to do, what he or she is suited by nature to do. Ideally, this harmony of purpose is also reflected in the life of the individual:

> Then it is proper for the reasoning part to rule, because it is wise and has to use forethought for the whole soul; and proper for the high-spirited part to be its ally and subject . . . These two, then, thus trained and educated, will . . . preside over the desiring part, which is the largest part of the soul in each man . . . they will watch it lest it be filled full of what are called the bodily pleasures, and so growing great and strong may no longer do its own business but may try to enslave and rule the classes which it should not, and so overturn the whole life of all.[2]

Molding Citizens for Society: Aristotle

You may recall from Chapter 1 that Aristotle also found harmony to be the key to happiness. The idea of the "golden mean" between two extremes that forms the core of the *Nicomachean Ethics* finds its counterpart in Aristotle's *Politics*. Aristotle writes, "For if what was said in the *Ethics* is true, that the happy life is the life according to virtue lived without impediment, and that virtue is a mean, then the life which is in a mean, and in a mean attainable by every one, must be the best."[3]

Aristotle was very critical of Plato's *Republic* because of its radical proposals and because it set out to describe the ideal state. For Aristotle, what really matters is not what state is best in theory, but what kind of state is possible in practice. In his judgment, a mixed government combining a monarch and a parliament would be the most stable and therefore the most lasting.

He did agree with Plato that the key to good government was the type of education the state afforded its citizens. Plato's elaborate system for discovering and shaping the philosopher-king is echoed in Aristotle's assertion that "the citizen should be moulded to suit the form of government under which he lives."[4] The diversity of the state, the fact that it is made up of different sorts of people, makes a state system of education not only desirable but also necessary; only by such a system can a plurality be made into a community.[5]

Aristotle contended that it is not the desires of the individual but the needs of the state that should dictate the content and methods of public education. Training in things that are of common interest for the good of the city should be available to all, but the intention is to create good and useful citizens: "Neither must we suppose that any one of the citizens belongs to himself, for they all belong to the state."[6]

Both Plato and Aristotle focus on the good of the community. Because each assumes that like people will be treated similarly, we might say that they conceive of justice in terms of **merit;** but neither assumes a completely egalitarian society in which natural rights might determine how a citizen interacts with government. In fact, both assume a hierarchical society in which some will rule and others will be ruled. Plato and Aristotle agree that a kind of benevolent dictatorship would be the most ideal form of government because the ordinary mass of people is simply not to be trusted with important decisions; they cannot be relied upon to act rationally.

merit *a fixed condition—such as wealth, talent, intelligence, race, or gender—on the basis of which justice may be dispensed*

In a system of justice based on merit, people get what they deserve commensurate with their innate abilities and their status in society. In Plato's *Republic,* for instance, the guardians are allowed/expected to rule but prohibited from owning private property and from marrying and raising their own children individually. Members of the producer class, by contrast, are permitted to marry and raise their own children, but prohibited from ruling. What we "merit" seems to be fixed, and there is no social mobility such as people anticipate in a democracy; that is, people are unable to "earn" or "achieve" their way to a higher social status. Although people are treated unequally, Plato seems to believe they are, nonetheless, treated fairly because each person gets what they merit.

The consensus of these classical theorists seems to be that justice will be achieved when people do what their nature and status in life call them to do. Their merit determines what benefits they receive and what burdens they bear. Because what matters most is a well-ordered society, individuals must do what society determines is best for them to do. If they play their parts well, the result is a harmonious social order that benefits everyone. The luxury of individual choice may be sacrificed, but all will flourish in a just society. To retain individual rights but live in an unjust society would be a much less desirable state of affairs—for the individual and for society alike.

Nearly 2000 years later, a group of British political theorists—Jeremy Bentham, John Stuart Mill, and Harriet Taylor Mill—took as their starting point these basic assumptions articulated by philosophers of the classical period. Their concept of justice, however, focuses on the distribution of pleasure and pain.

Utilitarianism as a Measure of Justice

Like the classical theorists, utilitarians argue that the social good, or the good of society, is what really matters. Unlike Plato and Aristotle, however, they define what is good in terms of pleasure. The question they pose is a simple one: What is most useful, or utilitarian? Their answer is also simple: more pleasure and less pain for the greatest number of people. If we really want to have a just society, then according to **utilitarianism,** right or just actions are those that ordinarily produce the greatest amount of happiness and the least amount of unhappiness in the world at large.

utilitarianism *the theory that an action is right if it seeks to promote the greatest amount of happiness in the world at large*

We must also consider matters of degree, for there may in fact be cases in which the mild unhappiness of many might be offset by the extreme happiness of a few. Living as we do in a society rooted in basic freedoms, the idea of being *forced* to donate blood is a repugnant one. Still, if my demanded pint of blood saves a life, might it not be possible to argue that the greater good more than balances the lesser evil?

When we use words like *good* and *evil,* what we really mean, utilitarians insist, is pleasurable and painful. We often pretend that these words have some independent reference, that they represent the will of God, for instance, but in truth we do not know what the will of God is. What we do know is what gives us pleasure, and we simply assume that those same things must be pleasing to God. As Feuerbach pointed out (see Chapter 4), humans have a strong tendency to project their own human characteristics, including their needs and wants, onto God. Utilitarians believe that we should be honest about seeking pleasure and trying to avoid pain, rather than dressing up those desires in abstract language and pretending they are divinely decreed.

Utilitarianism is, then, a sort of social **hedonism;** the individual hedonist seeks pleasure for himself, whereas the social hedonist seeks pleasure for the society. Social good is advanced and justice is done, according to utilitarians, if more people experience a balance of pleasure over pain than vice versa. It is all a kind of math problem on a social scale. Produce more pleasure than pain, and the result will be justice; produce more pain than pleasure, and the result will be injustice.

hedonism *the theory that pleasure is the highest good*

Jeremy Bentham

Jeremy Bentham, the first modern utilitarian, had in mind exactly this kind of mathematical conception of pleasure over pain. As a British critic of crown policy toward the American colonies and a supporter of their subsequent revolt in 1776, Bentham declared the U.S. government the only existing one that upheld utilitarian principles. When we speak of a community, Bentham wrote, we speak of a fictitious concept, for a community is nothing more than the individuals of which it is made; make them happy as individuals and you make a happy community. Those who fashion the law ought to have this goal in mind, and they must recognize that their only hope of enforcing the law lies in the promise of pleasure or the threat of pain:

> The happiness of the individuals, of whom a community is composed, that is their pleasures and their security, is the end and sole end which the legislator ought to have in view; the sole standard, in conformity to which each individual ought, as far as depends upon the legislator, to be made to fashion his behaviour. But whether it be this or any thing else that is to be *done,* there is nothing by which a man can ultimately be *made* to do it, but either pain or pleasure.[7]

Because a community is nothing but the sum total of its individuals, it is in the life of the individual that the principle of utility can be most clearly stated and understood. According to Bentham's theory, moral dilemmas can become a sort of arithmetic exercise in which we add up the units of pleasure and pain and subtract one from the other. For Bentham, the quantity of pleasure mattered most; the greater the quantity of pleasure, the more desirable and useful the result.

Suppose you are considering two job opportunities. In one you will make a large salary and have many "perks," but you will have to relocate

THE MAKING OF A PHILOSOPHER

Jeremy Bentham
(1748–1832)

Nicknamed "philosopher" at the age of five, Bentham had already begun studying Latin at the age of four and went on to finish college and law school while still a teenager. He grew up to write commentaries on English law and society and became a supporter of both the American and French Revolutions. As the good friend of James Mill, Bentham became godfather to Mill's son John, and together they crafted an ambitious program of study for the young boy. Unfortunately, it focused exclusively on reason and ignored the other aspects of a growing boy.

TABLE 9.1 BENTHAM'S QUANTITATIVE CALCULUS *In this calculus, each plus and minus would be weighted before the final calculation is performed. What matters is the quantity of pleasure—more is definitely better.*

BENTHAM'S QUANTITATIVE CALCULUS

+ Keep apartment I like	+ Exciting new opportunity
+ Keep friends and kin nearby	+ Significant raise
+ Same, predictable work	+ Challenging
+ Comfort of the familiar	– Must find new apartment
+ Have job down to a routine	– Must make new friends, travel to see kin
+ Know I can be successful	– Risks of the unknown
– Existing salary	– Must work hard learning new job
– Boring	– Fear I might fail

to another city and leave your family, friends, and significant other behind. In the second job, located in your current city of residence, the salary and "perks" are fewer, but you will retain a very satisfying social and emotional life. Bentham would suggest that you simply assign values to each of these units of pleasure and pain and then make the calculation. The result will tell you clearly what you should do (Table 9.1).

Societies, Bentham contended, must do something similar to this on a communal scale. Whereas the individual has only his or her individual pleasure and pain to consider, society must consider the happiness of all, and thus the utilitarian solution calls for social rather than egoistic hedonism. The task is to calculate the sums of all pleasures and pains before selecting the right or just action to take.

Sometimes called the *hedonic calculus,* Bentham's method of calculation offers a guide to what is good and what is bad both for the individual and for society:

> Sum up all the values of all the *pleasures* on the one side, and those of all the pains on the other. The balance, if it be on the side of pleasure, will give the *good* tendency of the act upon the whole, with respect to the interests of that *individual* person; if on the side of pain, the *bad* tendency of it upon the whole . . . Take an account of the *number* of persons whose interests appear to be concerned; and repeat the above process with respect to each . . .[8]

One danger here is the temptation to be very aware of your own pleasure while minimizing another's pain. In the antebellum American South, for instance, slave owners had clearly persuaded themselves that the pleasure a slave society brought them exceeded the pain slavery caused the slaves. Had slaves been making the calculation, they might have reached a different conclusion.

TABLE 9.2 MILL'S QUALITATIVE CALCULUS *What matters is the quality of the pleasures—more is not necessarily better.*

MILL'S QUALITATIVE CALCULUS

+ Days in the Sun and mud	+ Pleasures of the intellect
+ Food provided, no work	+ Pride of accomplishment in work
+ Don't know life is limited	+ Existential courage in face of death
+ Sleep whenever I like	+ Variety in my life—work, play, culture
+ Goal is to become fat	+ Goal is to achieve my own objectives
+ Other pigs don't take up much room	+ Pleasure in companions

John Stuart Mill

Bentham's intellectual heir and the better-known nineteenth-century utilitarian philosopher was John Stuart Mill. Although he accepted much of what Bentham wrote, Mill contended that the *quality* of pleasure was more important than the mere *quantity* of pleasure. Here we have echoes of Plato and Aristotle, who believed pleasures of the mind to be superior to those of the body. Mill insisted that none of us would trade the pleasures of being human for the pleasures of being a pig, no matter how juicy the mud or how many days of lying contentedly in the Sun awaited us (Table 9.2).

When we compare higher pleasures with lower ones, Mill pointed out, only those who have experienced both are competent to judge which is better:

> From this verdict of the only competent judges, I apprehend there can be no appeal. On a question which is the best worth having of two pleasures, or which of two modes of existence is the most grateful to the feelings, apart from its moral attributes and from its consequences, the judgment of those who are qualified by knowledge of both, or, if they differ, that of the majority among them, must be admitted as final.[9]

Mill applied the principle of quality over quantity to one of the great debates of his day, the question of intellectual and social equality for women, arguing that the legal subordination of one sex to the other, besides being wrong, was "one of the chief hindrances to human improvement." In his famous essay "The Subjection of Women," Mill argued for gender equality on utilitarian grounds: If women were liberated, all of society would benefit.

Nobody's free until everybody's free.
FANNIE LOU HAMER

Mill saw the family as the prototype for society. If relationships in the family were based on the right of the strong father over the weak mother and children, it would be difficult to imagine relationships in the wider society based on anything other than might. In the primary social unit, the family, children learn what it is appropriate and inappropriate for members of each sex to do. If both girls and boys have the experience that men make decisions while women make bread, they will likely repeat these expectations in their own lives. If, on the other hand, social roles assigned to men and women are to be altered for the ultimate good of society, then these alterations must begin—if not first, at least simultaneously—in the family:

> What marriage may be in the case of two persons of cultivated faculties, identical in opinions and purposes, between whom there exists that best kind of equality, similarity of powers and capacities with reciprocal superiority in them—so that each can enjoy the luxury of looking up to the other, and can have alternately the pleasure of leading and of being led in the path of development—I will not attempt to describe. To those who can conceive of it, there is no need; to those who cannot, it would appear the dream of an enthusiast.[10]

A house is not a home unless it contains food and fire for the mind as well as for the body.
MARGARET FULLER (1845)

The condition of married English and American women during this time was in fact one of civil bondage. A husband had the power to control his wife's inherited property, her wages, and even the lives of their children. As Mill put it in his essay "The Subjection of Women," "Marriage is the only actual bondage known to our law. There remain no legal slaves, except the mistress of every home."[11] To those who demanded to know whether humanity would be better off if women were free, Mill responded that "all the selfish propensities, the self-worship, the unjust self-preference, which exist among mankind, have their source and root in, and derive their principal nourishment from the present constitution of the relation between men and women."[12]

How can this experience of inequality not have a profound effect on a young boy, who quickly comes to see himself as superior to his mother? Like a hereditary ruler, Mill argued, the boy grows up with "unearned distinctions, and he may well turn a deaf ear to the notion that only good conduct entitles one to respect." The law of justice—the principle that the weak have equal rights with the strong—can never "get possession of men's inmost sentiments" as long as a strong contrary lesson is imbibed along with mother's milk.[13] It is not surprising that Elizabeth Cady Stanton, after reading this essay in 1869, wrote Mill to say:

> I lay the book down with a peace and joy I never felt before, for it is the first response from any man to show he is capable of seeing and feeling all the nice shades and degrees of woman's wrong'd state and the central point of her weakness and degradation.[14]

Harriet Taylor Mill

Like her husband, John, Harriet Taylor Mill constructed her essay "Enfranchisement of Women" on utilitarian principles, asking whether the condition of women in her day really furthered society's overall good. If a man wishes to cultivate his character and improve his intellect, she asserted, he must associate with those who, if not his superiors, are at least his equals. Under the prevailing conditions, Harriet Mill argued, women, although intelligent, were often so limited in their concerns by societal restrictions that they could not help but drag their husbands down morally and intellectually:

> If one of the two has no knowledge and no care about the great ideas and purposes which dignify life, or about any of its practical concerns save personal interests and personal vanities, her conscious, and still more her unconscious influence, will, except in rare cases, reduce to a secondary place in his mind, if not entirely extinguish, those interests which she cannot or does not share.[15]

Yet the answer is not to give women a smattering of general knowledge, of art, poetry, even science and politics, because the question of power remains the central one. "The most eminent men cease to improve," according to Harriet Mill, "if they associate only with disciples,"[16] and a woman will be forced to gain her own ends by manipulation, by contriving to make her husband think something is really his own idea. Thus, both partners are corrupted: "In the one it produces the vices of power, in the other those of artifice."[17] If it were in fact deemed either necessary or just to keep one portion of humankind "mentally and spiritually only half developed," then the wisest course would be to keep the remaining group "independent of their influence."[18] Because in marriage exactly the opposite occurs, the half-developed women exert their influence on men, it is not in society's best interest to perpetuate the incomplete development of women. Elsewhere in the essay, Harriet Mill argues that it is also unjust to do so, but here her argument, like John's, rests on the implied benefit to the community: Justice for women will be accompanied by an elevation in the condition of all society.

Although the object is the same—equality of rights for women—the arguments made by the Mills differ from those made by advocates for women's rights in Chapter 8. There, women such as Mary Wollstonecraft and Elizabeth Cady Stanton argued from a belief in natural rights and from an Enlightenment presupposition of the inherent natural equality of all human persons. For them, the issue is simply one of right: It is unjust and not rationally defensible to deprive women of their rights as citizens. For the Mills, equality of rights for women is urged primarily on the basis of utilitarian principles: Not only will women benefit, but men as well—and more important, society as a whole will be better off.

Like Bentham, the Mills advocated pleasure over pain; unlike Bentham, however, they looked more for a qualitative experience of pleasure than a merely quantitative measurement. For the Mills, more might not necessarily be better; indeed, many people of their day argued that women had more pleasures than men, being able as they were to stay within the family circle, protected from the demands of earning a living and free to read magazines and eat sweets. The Mills and others like them could not be convinced that any amount of the pleasures of interacting with children and servants might compensate for lacking the benefits of full citizenship and personal autonomy, especially when the things they were missing included independence and political decision making.

THE MAKING OF A PHILOSOPHER

John Stuart Mill
(1806–1873)
Harriet Taylor Mill
(1807?–1858)

These two philosophers had a twenty-eight-year relationship. John was a precocious child, raised by his father James Mill and the utilitarian philosopher Jeremy Bentham to become their intellectual heir. He was reading Greek at age three, and the rigorously rationalist education he received did not include any of what we would call "social skills." At age eighteen he was emotionally impoverished and described himself as a "dry, hard logical machine." After a crisis in his twenties, he resolved to cultivate his feelings. In late 1830 Mill met Harriet Taylor at a dinner party, and over the next two years the two wrote essays for each other on the subject of women and the marriage relationship. Harriet took the more radical position, arguing for the elimination of all laws on marriage and giving women full responsibility for their children even in the event of divorce. John's more moderate position called for postponement of childbearing until a couple tested their compatibility and for communal living so that in the event of divorce children could be provided for by a kind of extended family.

John Stuart Mill's contribution to the intellectual defense of women's rights has been enormous. As the first man in the modern Western world to apply the best arguments of his day in support of the movement for women's equality, Mill forced many who might not have done so to take the issue seriously. He always insisted that his works represented a collaboration between himself and Harriet; in his *Autobiography of John Stuart Mill,* he wrote explicitly about his powerful essay "The Subjection of Women":

> As ultimately published it was enriched with some important ideas of my daughter's, and passages of her writing. But in what was of my own composition, all that is most striking and profound belongs to my wife; coming from the fund of thought which had been made common to us both, by our innumerable conversations and discussions on a topic which filled so large a place in our minds.[19]

Although the utilitarian argument can be a powerful one, not all social philosophers find it adequate. Let's consider another alternative.

THE MAKING OF A PHILOSOPHER

Karl Marx
(1818–1883)

Marx was born into a comfortable middle-class family that included generations of venerable Jewish rabbis. At age seventeen he went to the University of Bonn to study law, but after a year spent mostly in writing poetry, drinking, and dueling, his father urged him to transfer to the University of Berlin. There he came under the influence of Hegel. In 1843 he married his childhood sweetheart, the beautiful and refined Jenny von Westphalen, and the two moved to Paris. After co-editing a radical magazine and becoming converted to communism, Marx was expelled from Paris in 1845 and later from Brussels; after the 1848 revolution failed, the Marxes were again deported from Germany. Karl and Jenny pawned her grandmother's silver and moved to London where they lived in poverty for the remainder of their lives. Three of their children died because they could not afford medical care, and Karl wrote his manuscripts in the British Museum because it had heat. At his death Marx was practically unknown.

Justice Expressed as Fairness

Karl Marx in the nineteenth century and John Rawls and Robert Nozick in the twentieth century have insisted that the only credible standard of justice was fairness. In the modern world, therefore, the question of what constitutes a just society has focused not on what is useful for society but on what is fair to the individuals that make it up. After considering these three modern philosophers, we conclude our discussion with a review of a consensus model of justice from the ancient African kingdom of Buganda, in present-day Uganda.

Utilitarians contend that a society is really nothing more than the individuals who constitute it; make individuals happy and you produce a just society. For Karl Marx, however, economic forces that are larger than the individual determine whether a society is just. In his view, individuals cannot be made happy and society cannot be made just without changing these fundamental and extremely powerful economic forces.

The Alienation of Workers: Karl Marx

Marx's vision of a perfectly communistic (and therefore just) society was his answer to the question of human alienation. For Marx, a just society would be one in which people were not alienated from their work and their lives because of the destructive relations flowing from capitalism. As long as a few wealthy people own private property and grow rich from its use while millions of others lead a life of drudgery in exchange for mere survival, justice can never be achieved. Let's look at how he conceived the problem and the solution he proposed.

Living in industrializing Germany in the middle of the nineteenth century, Marx saw the worst of the exploitation and human misery that made possible what we celebrate as the Industrial Revolution. As machines took over production, workers became not artisans with skills but robots with repetitive tasks to perform. In these early years, fourteen-hour days were not uncommon, and workers (who might be women or children, as well as adult men) in effect had no life outside the job. It was not only the long hours, however, but the nature of the work that caused the workers' **alienation:**

alienation *in Marxist thought, the estrangement of workers from their work, their fellow citizens, and ultimately themselves as the direct result of capitalism's exploitative nature*

> What, then, constitutes the alienation of labour? First, the fact that labour is *external* to the worker, i.e., it does not belong to his essential being; that in his work, therefore, he does not affirm himself but denies himself . . . the worker therefore only feels himself outside his work, and in his work feels outside himself. He is at home when he is not working, and when he is working he is not at home . . . Lastly, the external character of labour for the worker appears in the fact that it is not his own but somebody else's, that it does not belong to him, that in it he belongs, not to himself but to another.[20]

Instead of creating a product with the skill and pride learned in the artisan system of apprenticeship and then selling that product to a fellow villager, industrial workers had only their labor to sell; and the harder they worked, the richer the factory owner became. Rather than being fulfilling and a source of gratification, work became a drudgery. No one saw a completed product; workers saw only their little segment of the production

Workers can be dehumanized and alienated as a result of the work they are forced to do in an industrializing society.

Technique Metal Work by Henrich Kley ca. 1900/AKG, London.

process. When the product was finished, middlemen took it away to another city, where it was bought by people who neither knew nor cared about who had made it. With industrialization, products were cheaper, so if something broke or wore out, you could always buy another. Some critical links—between artisan and product and between producer and consumer—had been broken, and Marx saw these disconnections as the explanation for why society was so unjust and workers so miserable.

By selling your labor, Marx believed, you became a kind of wage slave. Capital, or money, became the only means of exchange and a kind of god. People, it seemed, were willing to do just about anything for money, and if by exploiting workers they could make even more money, they seemed perfectly willing to do so. To change this unjust arrangement, Marx believed, the economic foundations of society would have to be radically restructured. Capitalism was inherently exploitative and could not be repaired; it would have to be overthrown in a workers' revolution. Only if the workers owned what Marx called the "means of production" would they be able to share in the profit produced by their labor.

Justice was dependent on forces too large and complex to be controlled by a single individual. To create fairness, Marx's precondition for justice, society's unfair economic structure would have to be understood for what it is and then transformed:

> The mode of production in material life determines the general character of the social, political, and spiritual processes of life. It is not the consciousness of men that determines their existence, but, on the contrary, their social existence determines their consciousness. At a certain stage of their development the material forces of production in society come into conflict with the existing relations of production . . . then comes the period of social revolution. With the change of the economic foundation the entire immense superstructure is more or less rapidly transformed.[21]

Like classical theorists, Marx looked to the structure of society as the basis for justice; unlike them, he found harmony among groups desirable only if the individuals who make up those groups feel they are being treated fairly. He might have accepted a utilitarian understanding of justice as more pleasure and less pain, but he rejected the idea that individuals can be made happy without transforming the structures of the society in which they live. His concept of the alienation of workers also links him with existentialism, which we will discuss in Chapter 10.

THE MAKING OF A PHILOSOPHER

John Rawls
(1921-)

A living philosopher, Rawls until 1991 taught a course entitled "Justice" at Harvard. As many as 1000 students would attend his lectures each semester. Rawls earned a doctorate in philosophy from Princeton in 1950. His teaching career has spanned the Ivy League colleges, beginning in 1953 when he accepted a position at Cornell, continuing at the Massachusetts Institute of Technology (MIT) in 1959, and concluding at Harvard from 1962 to 1991. Rawls's first book, *A Theory of Justice,* is an elaborate defense of the liberal tradition in America, and it has been called "the most ambitious and influential work in social philosophy of the later twentieth century." His second book, *Political Liberalism,* was published in 1993.

The Equal Liberty and Difference Principles: John Rawls

The twentieth-century social philosopher John Rawls shares Marx's belief that fairness or *equality* is the true test of justice. In his best-known work, *A Theory of Justice,* retired Harvard professor Rawls explicitly rejects the utilitarian conception of justice as inherently indifferent to the fate of individuals. Even though in theory the utilitarian concern for the overall good of society benefits everyone, in practice an individual may have to suffer or be deprived of certain rights for the greater good of the whole social order, as we saw in considering slaves and slave owners. Rawls rejects this as inherently unjust.

Instead, Rawls begins where some of the philosophers we studied in Chapter 8 began: with natural rights and the theory of the social contract. For Rawls, every individual has a "natural right, which even the welfare of every one else cannot override. Justice denies that the loss of freedom for some is made right by a greater good shared by others."[22] If justice is defined in terms of the individual, then its first principle must be that each individual be treated equally or fairly by society.

In fact, Rawls's theory of justice has two principles: the equality principle and the difference principle; the first, the equal liberty principle, is fundamental and logically prior to the second. Consider Rawls's description of the relationship between the two:

> First: each person is to have an equal right to the most extensive basic liberty compatible with a similar liberty for others. Second: social and economic inequalities are to be arranged so that they are both (a) reasonably expected to be to everyone's advantage, and (b) attached to positions and offices open to all.[23]

The first principle, the **equal liberty principle,** defines justice as encompassing all the things we have come to take for granted in a democratic society, including the right to vote and hold office; the freedom to speak, worship, assemble, and hold property; and the freedom from arbitrary arrest and seizure. The second principle, the **difference principle,** insists that whereas the distribution of income and wealth "need not be equal, it must be to everyone's advantage, and at the same time, positions of authority and offices of command must be accessible to all."[24] The equal liberty principle is the primary one; it cannot be compromised, even if greater social and economic advantages were offered, and still result in a just society.

equal liberty principle *Rawls's primary condition of justice that insists people must be treated equally and be guaranteed minimum natural rights*

difference principle *in Rawls's system of justice, permission to treat people differently as long as the least well-off benefit from the different treatment*

Because it seems that in a large and complex society there is no alternative to treating people differently, how can such treatment exist within the theory of justice that Rawls outlines? The answer lies in his difference principle: Those who are "better situated" will naturally have higher expectations for themselves. For Rawls, these higher expectations "are just if and only if they work as part of a scheme which improves the expectations of the least advantaged members of society."[25]

What might this mean in practice? Rawls uses as an illustration the relationship between an entrepreneurial, property-owning class and an unskilled-worker class. (Notice that this is the same relationship Marx thought to be inherently responsible for injustice and doomed to destruction by a workers' revolution.) Rawls argues that even if current social injustices such as discrimination were removed, these two groups would still face very different and unequal life prospects. According to his theory of justice, "the inequality in expectation is permissible only if lowering it would make the working class even worse off."[26]

In theory, the advantages enjoyed by entrepreneurs encourage them to improve the efficiency of the economic process and increase the rate of innovation so that over the long term the benefits spread throughout the economic system and the prospects of the working class are also improved. Rawls is clear that this is a theoretical model, and he does not speculate about how well it works in practice. He does insist, however, that this kind of model is the only justification for treating individuals differently; the difference principle is secondary to the equality principle. The first and most binding requirement of justice is that individuals have equal rights and open opportunities.

Perhaps the most interesting aspect of Rawls's theory of justice is his model for constructing a just society. He defines justice as a system of principles to be used in "assigning rights and duties and in defining the appropriate division of social advantages."[27] How might we decide who should enjoy the benefits and who should bear the burdens in a society? Rawls's answer is that a kind of social contract must be developed, but it will not resemble the contract to live in a particular society. Instead, it will be a general contract, defining fundamental principles of justice and ensuring that every party to the contract will be treated fairly.

original position
Rawls's hypothetical position from which a general social contract may be constructed; since the parties do not know which position they will occupy in society, they are likely to create a truly just society

Rawls suggests that this kind of contract could only be constructed from what he calls the **original position,** a hypothetical situation in which "no one knows his place in society, his class position or social status, nor does any one know his fortune in the distribution of natural assets and abilities, his intelligence, strength and the like."[28] Imagine how careful the parties to a contract would have to be if they did not know which race or gender they would be, whether able bodied or physically challenged, gay or straight, Mensa material or developmentally delayed (Figure 9.1).

Behind this *veil of ignorance,* people would be forced to consider what actually constitutes a just society. Rawls believes that the original position would lead rational people to embrace the equal liberty and difference principles as necessary for establishing justice. This mental exercise is his way of pressing us to step outside our own situation in society and dispassionately consider what justice means and how it might be implemented.

Human nature being what it is, we all seem to be tuned in to the world as it appears to us. If you break your leg in a skiing accident, you may suddenly acquire empathy for what a person in a wheelchair faces every day; from your previous position of privilege or fortune, you may not have even seen the obstacles faced by someone differently positioned in society. Something of this empathy was captured in the television series *Quantum Leap* in which Dr. Sam Beckett "leaps" from life to life, finding himself perhaps a middle-aged African American in the American South of the 1950s, then a pregnant unwed teenaged girl, then a Native American accused of murder. The world looks very different from the perspectives of people with different bodies and alternate complexes of skills and attitudes.

We must be the change we wish to see in the world.
MOHANDAS K. GANDHI

Rawls's idea of making a contract from behind a veil of ignorance calls us to a kind of rational disinterest, to a kind of radical fairness, in which we cannot, however innocently, structure a world that is comfortable for ourselves but insensitive to the needs of others. Slave owners in the American South believed their system operated in the best interests of everyone

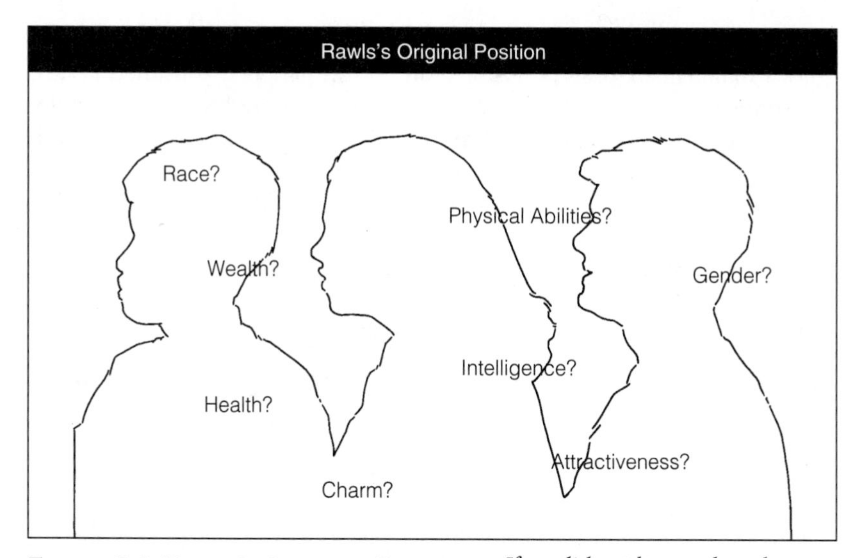

FIGURE 9.1 RAWLS'S ORIGINAL POSITION *If we did not know what place we would occupy in society, we would be more likely to create a society that would be fair to everyone.*

involved; when they had an opportunity to speak, slaves of course told a different story that surprised and confused their former "owners." Even if we make a special effort to be sensitive to the needs of those who pass through life differently equipped, however, we may still miss the little crucial things that make all the difference to someone else.

The principles of justice in Rawls's system, then, are "those which rational persons concerned to advance their interests would consent to as equals when none are known to be advantaged or disadvantaged by social and natural contingencies."[29] Under these conditions and acting from behind the veil of ignorance, individuals might be able to create a truly just society—one in which Rawls's first principle of fairness or equality would be met.

The Theory of Entitlement: Robert Nozick

Rawls's Harvard colleague Robert Nozick agrees that justice must be done but strongly questions the role of the state in promoting justice. If you recall the terminology from Chapter 8, Nozick comes close to anarchism in arguing that only a very minimal state can be justified. "Individuals have rights," he says in the preface to *Anarchy, State, and Utopia,* "and there are things no person or group may do to them (without violating their rights). So strong and far-reaching are these rights that they raise the question of what, if anything, the state and its officials may do."[30]

Nozick believes the state may legitimately use its power to protect citizens against force, theft, and fraud, but, he insists, "the state may not use its coercive apparatus for the purpose of getting some citizens to aid others, or

THE MAKING OF A PHILOSOPHER

Robert Nozick
(1938-)

Another living philosopher, Nozick has taught philosophy at Harvard since 1965. Born in New York City, he became a socialist while at Columbia University. While in graduate school at Princeton, however, he underwent a conversion experience after discovering and confronting libertarianism. His transformation from socialism to a radical espousal of individual rights is reflected in his best-known book, *Anarchy, the State, and Utopia,* which won the National Book Award in 1975. His most recent book, *The Nature of Rationality* (1993), continues Nozick's practice of making complex and highly theoretical philosophical debates accessible to the general, educated reading public.

in order to prohibit activities to people for their *own good or protection*."[31] If only a minimal state can be justified and if the state is not justified in forcing some citizens to aid others, how can justice be done? Nozick's definition is known as the **entitlement theory.** Fairness for Nozick does not lie in wealth redistribution, as Rawls seems to suggest, but rather in safeguarding what people have legitimately acquired and are entitled to keep. What Nozick is concerned with is how things come to be held by some and not by others and how holdings come to be transferred from one party to another. In a completely just world, he asserts, everyone would be entitled to what they presently hold. Here are his rules of entitlement:

entitlement theory
Nozick's theory that justice should be conceived in terms of entitlements (what individuals are entitled to), rather than in terms of fairness or equality

1. A person who acquires a holding in accordance with the principle of justice in acquisition is entitled to that holding.
2. A person who acquires a holding in accordance with the principle of justice in transfer, from someone else entitled to the holding, is entitled to the holding.
3. No one is entitled to a holding except by (repeated) applications of 1 and 2.[32]

The situation is further complicated by the fact that some people deprive other people of their rights, by stealing from them or even enslaving them and thus preventing them from competing in exchanges. Since there have been violations of the first two principles—justice in holding and justice in transfer—we must also address the rectification of injustice in holdings. However, Nozick wants to be clear that these three principles refer to an ongoing process but they do not prescribe any specific result.

The very idea of a utopia is problematic for Nozick. The best of all possible worlds for me will not necessarily be your ideal, and vice versa. As Nozick puts it, "There is no reason to think that there is *one* community which will serve as ideal for all people and much reason to think that there is not . . . Utopia will consist of utopias, of many different and divergent communities in which people lead different kinds of lives under different institutions."[33] People will be free to choose among different communities and to move among them freely.

Although a particular community might opt to redistribute holdings or give to another community, there would be no nation to compel redistribution among communities. Since Nozick values liberty over equality, he is concerned to protect the rights of individuals. Rawls's emphasis on benefiting the least well-off seems to Nozick to imply a role for the state in redistribution. To this he is vehemently opposed. Individuals might choose to belong to a community that practiced Rawlsian justice, but Nozick believes only a minimal state provides the framework for the many possible utopias that will satisfy all of us.

Justice in Buganda

Let's look at how justice was conceived in the African kingdom of Buganda. There, the small size of villages, the stability of a society in which people lived in extended families, and the many people who knew one another permitted justice to operate according to *societal norms,* rather than according to an elaborate code of laws. This model has something in common with the smaller, individual utopias Nozick sees as ideal. Keep in mind, however, that there is also a major contrast between justice in Buganda and Nozick's entitlement theory; in Buganda, fairness was defined within the context of societal norms rather than individual rights.

In any society, one of the fundamental questions concerns reconciling the interests of the individual with those of society. According to philosopher E. Wamala, in a traditional society the individual and the community are more closely intertwined than in a large industrial and technological nation. Whereas North Americans put great emphasis on the independent identity and rights of the individual, a traditional Bugandan might have thought more like this: "I am because we are and because we are I am."[34]

consensus *a meeting of the minds after rational discussion and the give and take of dialogue*

As a result, justice was seen to rest on **consensus,** or group agreement. Suppose a young married couple quarreled, and the young woman ran back home to her father's house. Contrary to what you might expect if you have grown up in a traditional Western culture, the couple would not be expected to work things out between themselves; the traditional concept of justice would require that elders representing the two families meet and settle the case.

The first condition would be that both "sides" of the story be heard, both the young woman's version and the young man's version of why they quarreled and she ran away. Then a judgment would be rendered that represented a consensus reached by the elders from both sides. If the decision was that the husband had wronged the wife, he might be required to pay a fine before being allowed back into the mainstream of society. If, however, the wife were judged to have overreacted, her prompt return to her husband's house might be seen as justice. It would be understood by both young people that the elders, acting by consensus, knew best.[35] This system, which may sound strange to many of us, guarantees both the offender's right to be heard and a prompt rendering of justice. In a small, closely knit society, everyone would likely agree that justice had been done. The emphasis was on the creation of *social harmony,* and, to this extent at least, Buganda shared a conception of justice with Plato and Aristotle.

In a small and stable community, the chief's royal gong can summon everyone to celebration or to dispense justice.

Royal gong/Courtesy of the African Art Museaum of Maryland/Photo by Quentin Kardos.

Because justice was defined in terms of *societal norms,* there is also a utilitarian element to the traditional Bugandan understanding of justice. Justice was that which would enable the values of the community to continue, and a stable society was both more important than and inseparable from the needs of individuals. In fact, one or the other members of the couple or perhaps both might still feel aggrieved; and yet a good had been accomplished on the community level. A couple would stay together. Presumably they would bear and raise children and form a stable family to support the needs of the village. This *good* was seen as far more important than the right of either individual to a particular version of justice.

A person old enough and wise enough to sit in this chair would wear the symbolic badge of authority.

Dan chair, Liberia/Courtesy of the African Art Museum of Maryland/Photo by Quentin Kardos.

The right of the individual to a fair hearing was built into the Bugandan concept of justice, for consensus could not be reached until both young people had told their "side" of the story. Marx and Rawls both insist on the primacy of right over good, and yet if an overall social good is achieved at the expense of fundamental individual rights, justice has not been served. Like the Bugandans, both Marx and Rawls understood that fairness begins with human rights and that only after human rights are secured can we move on to a discussion of the social good. We are still grappling with these issues, for today they remain at the forefront of racial relations in the United States.

African-American Political Philosophy

Focusing on the question of social justice, African-American social philosophers have explored the question of assimilation versus separatism. Would justice be more achievable in racial isolation or from within the dominant culture? In this section we examine a nineteenth-century debate on this subject between Martin Delany and Frederick Douglass and its twentieth-century echoes as expressed by Martin Luther King, Jr., and Malcolm X. Such twentieth-century figures as W. E. B. Du Bois, the Negritude poets, and Cornel West will also speak to the question of racial justice.

Assimilation or Separatism?

Justice is not cheap. Justice is not quick. It is not ever finally achieved.

MARIAN WRIGHT EDELMAN

For African Americans, the question of what constitutes a just society has not been and is not today an academic matter. Struggling first against slavery and then against oppressive and discriminatory segregation laws, African Americans have wondered what road might finally lead to justice. In the face of ongoing racism, the question has sometimes been: Are we more likely to attain justice by being assimilated as much as possible into the dominant white society or by retaining our separate identity as a race?

assimilationist *one who believes that blending as much as possible with the dominant culture will produce justice*

separatist *one who believes that blending with the dominant culture is not possible, desirable, or both*

According to the assimilationist view, a color-blind society in America is both possible and desirable. **Assimilationists** define or conceptualize justice as a state of affairs in which one's race would have no political, social, or economic implications. Racial differences would exist but would be irrelevant, much as the color of one's eyes is irrelevant to the question of justice. To be a **separatist** is to believe that this kind of assimilation is either impossible or undesirable or both. Some African-American separatists think that race has been a defining characteristic for far too long—with advantages going to those with white skin and disadvantages to those with black skin—to make it possible for race to cease being relevant; others

HOW PHILOSOPHY WORKS

The Disjunctive Syllogism

A *disjunctive syllogism* proposes alternatives, at least one of which is true; it is possible that both are true. In a disjunctive syllogism, the first premise is a disjunctive statement (either P or Q). The second premise either affirms (P, Q) or denies (not-P, not-Q) one of the disjuncts. The conclusion affirms or denies the other disjunct (P, Q, not-P, not-Q)

These are the valid forms of the disjunctive syllogism:

Either P (You've eaten my chocolate candy) or Q (We've been robbed).

Not-P (You haven't eaten my chocolate candy).

Therefore, Q (Oh my goodness, we've been robbed!).

Either P (You've eaten my chocolate candy) or Q (We've been robbed).

Not-Q (We haven't been robbed).

Therefore, P (You must have eaten my chocolate candy!).

The valid forms of the disjunctive syllogism deny one of the disjuncts, thus making the other one true. Since it is possible that both disjuncts may be true, the other two forms are invalid:

Either P (You've eaten my chocolate candy) or Q (We've been robbed).

P (You have eaten my chocolate candy).

Therefore, not-Q (At least we haven't been robbed).

It's possible someone has eaten the chocolate and a robbery has occurred.

Either P (You've eaten my chocolate candy) or Q (We've been robbed).

Q (We have been robbed).

Therefore, not-P (At least you didn't eat my chocolate candy).

Not necessarily; both might have occurred.

This kind of argument can be illustrated using the assimilationist-separatist debate in the African-American community:

Either P (We should assimilate) or Q (We must remain separate).

Not-P (Assimilation is neither possible nor desirable).

Therefore, Q (We must remain separate).

or

Either P (We should assimilate) or Q (We must remain separate).

Not-Q (There is nothing compelling us to remain separate).

Therefore, P (We should assimilate).

Notice that it is possible for both disjuncts to be true. It's possible that we should assimilate (for our own good) and yet we must remain separate (since we are not welcomed by the majority culture). It is also possible that we must remain separate (despite our desire to assimilate) and yet we should assimilate (if the opportunity presents itself).

The validity test is: Look for one premise to deny one disjunct and the conclusion to affirm the other. Any other form is invalid.

think that it is possible for African Americans to assimilate but that it may not be in their best interest to do so.

As the issue has been debated by African-American social philosophers during the nineteenth and twentieth centuries, two clear poles have emerged. At one extreme have been those who fought to integrate into and blend with the white majority as much as possible; at the other have been those who felt that the best course was to maintain, and even emphasize, differences from the majority, to remain distinct rather than integrate. At the heart of the issue is the question of race identity: What does it mean to be an African American?

What have these people gained and lost by assimilating so fully into the majority culture in American society?

Underwood Photo Archives, SF.

The Dilemma of Being Both an African and an American: W. E. B. Du Bois

The problem of the twentieth century is the problem of the color line . . . Am I an American or am I a Negro? Can I be both: Or is it my duty to cease to be a Negro as soon as possible and be an American?
W. E. B. DU BOIS

Speaking on the subject a hundred years ago, professor and social philosopher W. E. B. Du Bois insisted that maintaining race identity was an important duty for African Americans and an important ingredient in the quest for social equality, or what he called *race uplift*. We need to keep in mind here that although an African American is obviously in some sense both an African and an American, the question is, Which of the two will be emphasized? Of course, all of us have an ethnic identity; we are Irish American, Italian American, Chinese American, Jewish American, or one of many other possible variations. The difference, according to African-American social philosophers, is the negative associations attached to being of African descent. Historically, making this a matter of pride has been difficult because of the negative stereotypes constructed by the dominant white society.

In a racist society, good reasons may exist for minimizing or playing down one's color or African heritage. What Du Bois sought was a way for African Americans to affirm their distinctness while contributing culturally to American society. In his view this would lead to social equality, whereas a "servile imitation of Anglo-Saxon culture" would do nothing for African Americans as a race. Du Bois seems to have believed that by making economic, literary, legal, and spiritual contributions to the wider society, African Americans would win acceptance of themselves and their African heritage and make a unique contribution to American culture. They could be Africans *and* Americans.[36]

The pre–World War II philosophy of *Negritude,* developed in Senegal and Martinique by Leopold Sedar Senghor and Aimé Césaire, was an extreme statement of this position. It contrasted the communal society of Africa, which functioned organically and in close connection to nature, with the soulless materialism of technological European culture. According to the Negritude poets, Africans and those of African descent had a lot to teach driven, alienated Europeans who had lost the ability to enjoy life. We might think here of Marx's critique of rapidly industrializing Germany and the alienation of the worker. To assimilate too quickly or too thoroughly might be to lose this essential and uniquely African cultural contribution that European and American societies desperately needed.[37]

The lure of assimilation is a very strong one. For people whose racial or ethnic group has experienced prejudice or discrimination, it might seem very appealing to join the majority culture to the extent possible and deny differentness. In fact, some African Americans have a derogatory expression for a person who tries to do this: An "oreo," like the cookie, is black on the outside but white on the inside. Du Bois seems to have feared that if the restrictive segregation laws then in effect were repealed, African Americans would begin assimilating as fast as they could, and the value of the black experience would disappear.

Du Bois was a very influential thinker, and his ideas help us understand the tension between the two positions of separatism and assimilationism. What Du Bois appears to advocate is a separatism that makes possible an assimilation that retains a certain amount of separateness. It may be easier to unravel this position by looking at assimilation for twentieth-century Americans who are not of African descent. Although every arriving immigrant group has faced prejudice and discrimination, there is today relatively little or no injustice for, say, Irish Americans or Italian Americans, based on their ethnic heritage. In fact, it is somewhat "in" to be "ethnic" in America today.

What these groups have achieved may be what Du Bois had in mind. It is quite possible to consider yourself and be considered by others to be fully American and at the same time to celebrate your Irishness or your Italianness by listening to ethnic music and eating certain foods. Cultural and religious traditions associated with these ethnic groups have become integrated into the mainstream of American culture, creating a certain amount of ethnic pride for those claiming genealogical connections. What

THE MAKING OF A PHILOSOPHER

W. E. B. Du Bois
(1868–1963)

Born only a few years after slavery was declared unconstitutional, William Edward Burghardt Du Bois died the day before the historic march on Washington, D.C., at which Martin Luther King, Jr., delivered his "I have a dream" speech. His ancestry included African, French, and Dutch roots. He graduated *cum laude* from Harvard in 1890, becoming in 1895 the first African American to receive its Ph.D. degree. In 1905 he helped found the Niagara Movement, a forerunner of the NAACP. He spent many years as a college professor and was accused of being an "unregistered agent" of Russia because of his work for peace. Indicted by a New York City grand jury in 1951 but acquitted, he became increasingly pessimistic about the liberation of people of color in the United States and looked to the Soviet Union and China for leadership in world peace and justice. Invited by President Kwame Nkrumah of Ghana to live in the capital city of Accra, Du Bois accepted and in 1963 became a citizen of Ghana. When he died, he was honored with a state funeral.

Was justice a possibility for African Americans in the nineteenth-century United States?

Martin Delany and Frederick Douglass debate assimilation versus separatism, from "For the Love of Wisdom"/Courtesy of Howard Community College.

Du Bois was hoping for was not only an end to the injustice suffered by African Americans but also a retention of the cultural values and traditions that bound them together as a race and that would, in his judgment, enrich the dominant culture.

The separatist-assimilationist debate took shape during the nineteenth century. Let's look now at how two key thinkers arrived at their views of the best way to achieve justice for African Americans.

The Nineteenth-Century Debate: Martin Delany and Frederick Douglass

Martin Delany, author of *The Condition, Elevation, Emigration and Destiny of the Colored People of the United States,* argued that "enlightened freemen" and "colored adventurers" should emigrate from America to the east coast of Africa, where they would found a powerful black nation.[38] He reasoned that Africans had been enslaved by European capitalists in America because neither Native Americans (unaccustomed to forced labor) nor the white European underclass (not sufficiently "foreign" to be exploited harshly) was suitable. An enslaved class had to be both able to withstand the hardship of the work and appear "foreign" enough to the sympathies of their masters to make this exploitation acceptable.

Once this mental shift had been made and Europeans grew comfortable enslaving Africans, Delany believed, all hope of eliciting their sympathy and receiving justice from them was lost; only a new country could provide a new beginning for African Americans. Although he originally urged emigration to Mexico or South America, believing the American continent to be "home" in a vital sense, he eventually abandoned this idea in favor of a new state in Africa in order to put as much distance as possible between his "colored adventurers" and capitalist Europeans. Eventually, he thought, a powerful black capitalist state would win the respect of Anglo-Americans.[39]

black power *a movement to achieve legal, economic, and social power for African Americans and for all black people*

Delany was an early advocate of **black power,** and separatism was for him a necessary step on the road to achieving this goal. Africa was chosen, not for its sentimental role as fatherland or motherland, but because of its "agricultural, mining, and commercial possibilities" and for its distance from slaveholding America. Because slaves could not go with Delany and many freemen showed great reluctance to do so, Africa's other great advantage was that it was filled with black people. Black power would only be possible in an already black nation, in Delany's view, and a few emigrants with a strong vision might be able to mobilize others to accept that vision.

Martin Delany's friend, the abolitionist newspaper owner-editor Frederick Douglass, disagreed that emigration was the only answer to the obvious lack of justice being afforded African Americans. Having taken

Martin Delany hoped to merge capitalism with the community power, represented by this stool, that was already present in black Africa.

Stool of authority of the type used by the Asante Hene of Ghana/Courtesy of the African Art Museum of Maryland/Photo by Quentin Kardos.

seriously John Locke's theory of natural rights (see Chapter 8), Douglass argued that justice was morally demanded, and he believed rational people (white as well as black) would be persuaded by such a logical case. Once human rights had been established—as they had been, in Douglass's opinion, in the Declaration of Independence—there was no need to make a separate case for black human rights. If blacks self-evidently possessed human rights, then, Douglass believed, appealing to the world to stop violations against those rights might very well be effective.[40]

As a former slave, Douglass understood that the only way to prevent the enslaved and oppressed from rebelling against the obvious injustice of their condition is to inflict pain or death at any sign of revolt; therefore, slavery as an institution *must* be cruel. This *necessary cruelty* formed the core of Douglass's case against slavery, which he used to "engage the sympathies of an otherwise disinterested world, and to impel it thereby to see that slavery violated self-evident human rights, and therefore should be abolished."[41]

When moral argument failed, Douglass advocated rebellion, an action that clearly disproved the slaveholder's claim that his "property" did not desire liberty. Douglass understood only too well from personal experience the risks slaves took if they let their desire for liberty be known, but slaveholders cited the very lack of rebellion as proof that slaves were happy

THE MAKING OF A PHILOSOPHER

Malcolm X
(1925–1965)

Born Malcolm Little, Malcolm X was the son of a Baptist minister, who was also an organizer for Marcus Garvey's "Back to Africa" movement, and a light-skinned mother from Grenada. Called "Red" because of his light skin, young Malcolm tried to assimilate into white society. Sent to prison in 1946, he converted to the Nation of Islam and began thinking of the white man as responsible for rewriting history and exploiting all people of color. Out of prison, Malcolm took the name "X" to symbolize the "true African family name" he never could know. As a minister of Islam, he advocated voluntary separation of the races until a pilgrimage to Mecca revealed the "color blindness" of Muslim society. He returned to America aware that some white people were working against racism to create a just society. He was assassinated while speaking in the Audubon Ballroom in New York City in 1965.

Men would rather be starving and free than fed in bonds.
PEARL S. BUCK

and their slavery was justified. In fighting back, Douglass believed, slaves would gain a sense of moral equality.

Douglass's argument is an assimilationist argument. Believing that all Americans had the natural rights promised in the Declaration of Independence, Douglass was not willing to give up these rights by emigrating to another country. Instead, he took the moral high ground and insisted on what was called moral suasion, calling everyone to a rational analysis of human nature and the rights that pertain to it. In this respect his method is similar to that of Rawls.

Delany agreed that slavery was morally wrong but doubted the capacity of slaveholders to be persuaded to end it. To achieve his goal of black power, he could see only one possibility: Put as much distance as possible between African Americans and their oppressors and find a place with an indigenous black population and the natural resources required as a base for black capitalism. The separatist solution was not his preference, but it was a practical solution to what he saw as an untenable situation.[42] His method is closer to that advocated by Nozick.

In the next century, this still unresolved dilemma once again received expression at the hands of two eloquent writers and speakers—Martin Luther King, Jr., and Malcolm X. The strains of assimilationism and separatism continued to appear in social philosophy at the turn of the century.

THE MAKING OF A PHILOSOPHER

Martin Luther King, Jr.
(1929–1968)

Born into a middle-class family in Atlanta, Georgia, King followed his father into the Baptist ministry. Raised in a loving family "where love was central," young Martin learned an optimistic view of life and the possibility of change. The civil rights tradition he came to lead stressed nonviolent protest as a way of obtaining equal rights and liberties for African Americans. Armed with a doctorate from Boston University, King was serving his first church in Montgomery, Alabama, when Rosa Parks refused to give up her seat to a white person; he became the leader of the Montgomery bus boycott (1955–1956). Sit-ins followed, and they led to freedom rides, protest marches, and finally to the march on Washington in June 1963. There he delivered his "I have a dream" speech appealing for justice for Americans of African descent. Named *Time*'s "Man of the Year" (the first African American) in 1963, he was awarded the Nobel Peace Prize (the youngest recipient) a year later. He was assassinated in April 1968 while standing on a motel balcony.

A Twentieth-Century Approach: Cornel West, Malcolm X, and Martin Luther King, Jr.

In the final chapter of his 1993 book *Race Matters* (published on the first anniversary of the acquittal of the four white police officers accused of beating motorist Rodney King), the American philosopher Cornel West discusses "Malcolm X and Black Rage." In the twentieth century the assimilationist strain in African-American social philosophy is represented by Martin Luther King, Jr., and the NAACP, whereas the separatist tradition is reflected in the life and writings of Malcolm X. What Malcolm X advocated was a **psychic conversion** in which black people would "affirm themselves as human beings, no longer viewing their bodies, minds, and souls through white lenses, and believing themselves capable of taking control of their own destinies."[43]

The devaluation of black people by white America might easily be seen, West suggests, by looking at Michael Jackson's facial revisions. Although Jackson may be striving to reach a state that is neither black nor white, West believes Jackson's new face reveals a "self-measurement based on a white yardstick."[44] This is the modern version of what Du Bois had called **double consciousness,** looking at oneself through the eyes of another—in this case, white society—and it is especially a problem for black professionals, like Jackson, who live between the black and white worlds and have complete acceptance in neither.

psychic conversion
Malcolm X's prescription for African Americans, involving a shifting away from white standards of beauty, success, and the like to black-defined standards

The ideas espoused by Malcolm X and King mirror the differences between Delany and Douglass during the nineteenth century. Like Delany, Malcolm X was deeply pessimistic about the possibility of white Americans shedding their racism, and his solution was a kind of cultural separatism within the United States. Black spaces—networks and groups "in which black community, humanity, love, care, concern, and support flourish"—would provide an antidote to white supremacist ideology and promote the psychic conversion of black people.[45]

King was more optimistic; he shared with Douglass an unshakable belief in the moral rightness of the black struggle and in the ultimate triumph of justice. King saw blacks and whites sharing "one garment of destiny"; whatever happened to one group would profoundly affect the other. "His project of nonviolent resistance to white racism was an attempt to channel black rage in political directions that preserved black dignity and changed American society," West says. Both Martin Luther King, Jr., and Malcolm X were assassinated.[46]

Although he takes seriously the reality of black rage, West broadens its target to include, in addition to racism, sexism, homophobia, economic injustice, and anything else that prevents ordinary people from living lives of "dignity and decency." In a metaphor he admits would be foreign to Malcolm X, West closes his book with a picture of what justice might look like for African Americans (and, by implication, for everyone). Rejecting both the either/or nature of separatism and the blurring of all distinctions that assimilationism seems to imply, West prefers the image of a jazz ensemble:

> The interplay of individuality and unity is not one of uniformity and unanimity imposed from above but rather of conflict among diverse groupings that reach a dynamic consensus subject to questioning and criticism. As with a soloist in a jazz quartet, quintet or band, individuality is promoted in order to sustain and increase the creative tension with the group—a tension that yields higher levels of performance to achieve the aim of the collective project.[47]

For most women, separatism is not an option. By cultural practice and custom, women are typically assimilated with men in families. Living in a **patriarchal** society, in which power is exercised chiefly by men, some women have objected to the lack of justice afforded women. We now consider the philosophical analyses of a French woman, Simone de Beauvoir, and an American woman, Charlotte Perkins Gilman, as they address the question of social justice for women.

double consciousness *Du Bois's analysis of the psychic division in many African Americans in terms of which they see themselves through the lens of their own culture and through the lens of the dominant culture—as Africans and as Americans*

THE MAKING OF A PHILOSOPHER

Cornel West
(1953-)

Another living philosopher, West is professor of philosophy and African-American studies at Harvard University. His wife, Elleni, is from Addis Ababa, Ethiopia, and they have a son Clifton. West has been called "the preeminent African American intellectual of our generation" and "one of the most prophetic and healing voices in America today." The grandson of a Baptist minister, West combines the ethic of love at the heart of Christianity with Marxist economics and the political savvy of the Black Panthers.

patriarchal *characterized by male dominance*

Feminist Social Philosophy

Women are all the same tribe.

East African Delegate to United Nations Conference

Feminist social philosophy begins with the same type of assessment made by Delany and Douglass, King and Malcolm X. In the present-day United States, feminist thinkers point out, comparing the average of salaries earned by all men with the salaries earned by all women reveals that women earn about 75 cents for every dollar men earn. This is true even when women have equal or superior education; a woman with a college degree has the earning power of a man with a high school diploma. Of course, any discussion of this type is complicated by racial factors too, but on average, women earn significantly less than men.

The personal is the political.
WOMEN'S MOVEMENT SLOGAN

Another area of perceived injustice concerns women's sexuality. Why does blame fall on the pregnant teenager (but not the baby's father), the prostitute (but not her client), the rape victim (as well as on the rapist)? What is there about women's bodies that makes the state feel it can legislate their activity? Like African Americans, women cannot be disinterested about questions of justice for their gender because the issues affect their daily lives. As we saw in the previous section, social philosophy touches matters of life and death and involves deeply felt emotions. It is difficult to be objective when you *experience* injustice.

People who have confronted injustice on behalf of women and argued for justice have been called **feminists.** (Neither of the women we discuss in this section used that term to describe herself, but we may group them under that label for our purposes here.) We have already seen how Harriet Taylor Mill and John Stuart Mill confronted the injustice experienced by women from a utilitarian perspective; let's look now at how some other nineteenth- and twentieth-century women have constructed feminist arguments on behalf of justice for women.

feminists *those who promote political, legal, economic, and social equality for women, in opposition to the structures of a patriarchal society*

Woman as the Other: Simone de Beauvoir

We begin with a description of injustice from a feminist standpoint taken from a powerful modern book, *The Second Sex.* Until she published this book in France in 1949, Simone de Beauvoir was best known as the longtime companion of Jean-Paul Sartre, whose philosophy of atheistic existentialism we touched on in Chapter 3 and will discuss further in Chapter 10. As a philosophy professor in the 1930s, de Beauvoir felt no frustration over the fact that women could not vote (French women did not gain this right until 1947), and she was puzzled that some women did. Her wealthy, powerful family had trained her to expect a career, and she enjoyed an egalitarian relationship with Sartre, whose friends treated her just as they treated him. Only when she began to write an essay defending Sartre's controversial philosophical positions and their own unmarried liaison did de Beauvoir make the troubling discovery that women did not enjoy equality in society.

What she found was that she was different from Sartre because he was a man and she was something else. A year in America and extensive interviews with African Americans and both American and French women, convinced de Beauvoir that in Western societies white men had defined for themselves a central role, leaving black men and all women the position of **alterity,** or *otherness. The Second Sex* is largely about what it means to be the other. De Beauvoir begins book 2 as follows:

alterity *De Beauvoir's term for the "otherness" experienced by women and nonwhite men in relation to the power positions staked out by white men in Western society*

> One is not born, but rather becomes a woman. No biological, psychological, or economic fate determines the figure that the human female presents in society; it is civilization as a whole that produces this creature, intermediate between male and eunuch, which is described as feminine. Only the intervention of someone else can establish an individual as an Other.[48]

From boyhood, according to de Beauvoir, men learn that they create their existence by doing; women, on the other hand, are trained in passivity. Taught that to please others she must make herself an object, a woman learns to renounce her autonomy:

> She is treated like a live doll and is refused liberty. Thus a vicious circle is formed; for the less she exercises her freedom to understand, to grasp and discover the world about her, the less resources will she find within herself, the less will she dare to affirm herself as subject.[49]

Indeed, women are told that passivity is in their own best interest, a phenomenon that echoes the slave owners' view of their slaves.

De Beauvoir argued that the devaluation of femininity was a necessary step in human evolution and that, as a consequence of it, the economic system defines women's place in society. Here de Beauvoir closely follows Marx's economic analysis. Women, like the alienated workers Marx described, have been excluded from the economy, but unlike the male workers, they have been told they have the "better part":

> We have seen what poetic veils are thrown over her monotonous burdens of housekeeping and maternity; in exchange for her liberty she has received the false treasures of her "femininity" . . . Like the carefree wretches gaily scratching at their vermin, like the merry Negroes laughing under the lash and those joyous Tunisian Arabs burying their starved children with a smile, woman enjoys that incomparable privilege: irresponsibility.[50]

It is pointless to assign blame singlehandedly since "justice can never be done in the midst of injustice." Here de Beauvoir joins Marx in asserting that it is the system that must be changed: "A colonial administrator has no possibility of acting rightly toward the natives, nor a general toward his soldiers; the only solution is to be neither colonist nor military chief."[51] This option is at first glance clearly not available since, as de Beauvoir points out, men cannot stop being men and women cannot stop being women. Caught in an unequal situation, not of their own making, what are men and women to do?

Even though oppressors can rarely be counted on to grant privileges to the oppressed, men have at times considered giving partial emancipation to women to be in their own interest. Coupled with occasional revolts of their own, women can use these new openings to achieve full economic and social equality, which in turn will produce an inner transformation: "Let the Negroes vote and they become worthy of having the vote: let woman be given responsibilities and she is able to assume them."[52]

THE MAKING OF A PHILOSOPHER

Simone de Beauvoir
(1908–1986)

Born in Paris to an intellectual and affluent family, de Beauvoir was educated at the Sorbonne and enjoyed a career as a philosophy professor and novelist. Until 1949, when *The Second Sex* was published, she was primarily known for her fiction and her association with the existentialist philosopher-playwright Jean-Paul Sartre. After the publication of *The Second Sex* in France and in America in 1953, she became known primarily as a feminist theoretician. When the book appeared in France, one of her friends commended her for her courage and added, "You're going to lose a lot of friends." Twenty-two thousand copies were sold the first week, and de Beauvoir was quickly accused of being "unsatisfied, frigid . . . nymphomaniac, lesbian, a hundred times aborted" and even "an unmarried mother." The book has now been translated into nineteen languages. In 1972 de Beauvoir published a book on aging, entitled *The Coming of Age*.

PHILOSOPHERS SPEAK FOR THEMSELVES
Mary Wollstonecraft

As the rearing of children—that is, the laying a foundation of sound health both of body and mind in the rising generation—has justly been insisted on as the peculiar destination of women, the ignorance that incapacitates them must be contrary to the order of things. And I contend that their minds can take in much more, and ought to do so, or they will never become sensible mothers. Many men attend to the breeding of horses, and overlook the management of the stable, who would—strange want of sense and feeling!—think themselves degraded by paying any attention to the nursery; yet, how many children are absolutely murdered by the ignorance of women! But when they escape, and are destroyed neither by unnatural negligence nor blind fondness, how few are managed properly with respect to the infant mind! So that to break the spirit allowed to become vicious at home, a child is sent to school; and the methods taken there, which must be taken to keep a number of children in order, scatter the seeds of almost every vice in the soil thus forcibly torn up ...

But, we shall not see women affectionate till more equality be established in society, till ranks are confounded and women freed, neither shall we see that dignified domestic happiness, the simple grandeur of which cannot be relished by ignorant or vitiated minds; nor will the important task of education ever be properly begun till the person of a woman is no longer preferred to her mind. For it would be as wise to expect corn from tares, or figs from thistles, as that a foolish ignorant woman should be a good mother ...

From *A Vindication of the Rights of Women* (New York: Norton, 1967), Sect. V.

Justice is not always freely given.

BIZARRO © Dan Piraro. Reprinted with permission of Universal Press Syndicate.

Although de Beauvoir was clear that economic emancipation alone would not be enough to render woman man's equal, she maintained that it was an essential first step. This was also the view of one of the women whose writing inspired *The Second Sex.*

An Approach to Economic Independence: Charlotte Perkins Gilman

In her 1898 analysis of economic injustice for women, Charlotte Perkins Gilman observed: "We are the only animal species in which the female depends on the male for food, the only animal species in which the sex-relation is also an economic relation."[53] Rejecting the view that by performing household and maternal duties a woman contributes economically to a marriage as an equal partner, Gilman granted that women's labor in the home enables men to produce more wealth than they could if they also had to do all the work done by women. Considered in this light, women are economic factors in society, Gilman agreed. "But so are horses."[54]

Her modern-sounding solution is for household tasks to follow the pattern of other work in society and become specialized. All the work usually done by every individual woman would be done by specialists in the various fields. Instead of every woman being an amateur cook, for example, skilled food preparation would be available communally for women and their families. This approach would permit women to work outside the home without jeopardizing the needs of the family. A century ago, Gilman wrote:

> If there should be built and opened in any of our large cities today a commodious and well-served apartment house for professional women with families, it would be filled at once. The apartments would be without kitchens; but there would be a kitchen belonging to the house from which meals could be served to the families in their rooms or in a common dining-room as preferred. It would be a home where the cleaning was done by efficient workers, not hired separately by the families, but engaged by the manager of the establishment; and a roof garden, day nursery, and kindergarten, under well-trained professional nurses and teachers, would insure proper care of the children.[55]

In the suburbs, Gilman envisioned adjacent homes, each with a yard but no kitchen and connected with the central kitchen by covered walkways. People would soon come to appreciate, she believed, the cleanness of a home in which the grease and ashes connected with food preparation are missing. Once the tasks of cooking, cleaning, and household management were professionalized, they would become honored work that some women would choose to do for pay. There would be great savings in labor under this system because a few trained people would do everything quickly and efficiently. What an improvement, in Gilman's opinion, over twenty women working all the time in twenty homes and accomplishing their duties less efficiently.[56]

Like de Beauvoir, Gilman realized that women would remain both dependent on men and (to use de Beauvoir's term) other as long as they remained passive consumers rather than active producers. Economics was somehow intimately tied up with the question of justice for women, according to feminist social philosophy. Women who must depend on men for the very food they eat cannot be autonomous beings.

THE MAKING OF A PHILOSOPHER

Charlotte Perkins Gilman
(1860–1935)

Gilman, who referred to herself as a sociologist, believed the chief obstacle in the way of progress for women was their economic dependence on men. Soft-spoken and genteel, she was known as the "militant madonna." Self-sufficient at a very young age, she could not adjust to the restrictive role of a nineteenth-century wife and mother. Her depression lifted when she traveled alone to California for rest and recuperation but returned when she tried to resume her life. Seeing no alternative, she gave the custody of her daughter to her husband. After the successful publication of *Women and Economics,* a second marriage brought her peace. Told that she had inoperable breast cancer in 1932, she bought enough chloroform to end her own life. After her husband's death in 1934, she went to California to live with her daughter Katherine, and in August 1935 she took the chloroform.

Women Redefining Difference: Audre Lorde

Charlotte Perkins Gilman was part of the so-called first wave of feminism that emphasized the ways in which all women were alike in being oppressed by a patriarchal society. The twentieth-century second wave of feminism, which included Simone de Beauvoir, made some similar assumptions about sameness and difference which third-wave feminists such as Audre Lorde were quick to observe. As she points out, being "a forty-nine-year-old Black lesbian feminist socialist mother of two, including one boy, and a member of an inter-racial couple, I usually find myself a part of some group defined as other, deviant, inferior, or just plain wrong."[57]

A recognition of difference is crucial for feminists like Lorde. Although she might agree with de Beauvoir and Gilman that economic independence is a necessary condition for women's independence, Lorde would be unlikely to accept it as a sufficient condition. White women face the patriarchy, whereas, women of color must also deal with racism, lesbians must deal with heterosexism and homophobia, and everyone struggles with issues of discrimination based on age and class. De Beauvoir and Gilman believed they were speaking for all women, but Lorde questions this assumption.

Responding as a woman of color without acknowledging sexism or as a woman without acknowledging racism would equally distort Lorde's integrity as a person; ignoring her lesbianism, her age, her social class, or her political views would further fragment the self she would ideally bring whole to the struggle for human liberation.[58] Rather than dividing women, Lorde believes the naming and understanding of difference offers the key to a larger unity for all women. "It is not our differences which separate women, but our reluctance to recognize those differences and to deal effectively with the distortions which have resulted from the ignoring and misnaming of those differences."[59] Justice will require all of us to uncover "that piece of the oppressor which is planted deep within each of us, and which knows only the oppressors' tactics, the oppressors' relationships."[60]

Communitarianism

communitarianism *the theory that both individuals and society will be best served by balancing their needs*

In this chapter we have been looking at one aspect of the tension that can exist between the individual and the society. Where shall the balance lie: on the side of the individual in the best tradition of natural rights or on the side of the community? **Communitarianism,** a growing philosophical movement, suggests that the liberal theories that have shaped government in the English-speaking world may place too much emphasis on individual rights and not enough on community needs and civic obligations. If we see ourselves exclusively as isolated, atomic individuals, rather than as linked by shared values and goals with others in a community we share, the result may be an unhealthy society that is inhospitable to the individual. Notice that the modern communitarian vision takes us back to some of the values held by Plato and Aristotle about the primacy of communal needs (although clearly not to other assumptions they made) as well as to justice as practiced in ancient Buganda. In a contemporary context, Ignacio Ellacuría, a Spanish Jesuit priest, and Charles Taylor, a Canadian professor, both engage this issue.

Human Rights in a Communitarian Perspective: Ignacio Ellacuría, S.J.

If we were to shrink the world's population to a village of 100 people, keeping all existing proportions, there would be 57 Asians, 21 Europeans,

14 from the Americas, and 8 from Africa. Seventy would be unable to read, half would suffer from malnutrition, only one would have a college education; half the village's wealth would be owned by six people, all of them citizens of the United States.[61]

According to Ellacuría, this is an inherently unjust distribution. If we accept the analyses of Aristotle, Rousseau, and Hegel (among others), we will have to grant that the common good is above the particular good and insist that everyone put the common good first. Ellacuría goes further: "No one is good except in relation to the common good; furthermore, one who prefers his or her private good to the common good is not an ethical person."[62]

This is the essence of a communitarian philosophy. Because we live in what has been termed a "global village," there is clearly a single human race and a single common good:

> In itself humanity has a single universal common good, however much this is divided into distinct national common goods, which are always subordinate as parts of the whole which is humanity . . . Humanity today is a single humanity and its common good is obligatory, because it is necessary both for the existence of humanity itself and for the sake of justice . . . If human rights are derived from the common good, then they will appear as obligatory for all who make up humanity, since all would have a fundamental right to share in the common good as well as to contribute to its realization.[63]

If seventy of the villagers are illiterate and half are malnourished, Ellacuría is arguing that it is the duty of all to put the common good before any individual or particular good. Apply this to the village we call the world, and you see the demands a communitarian philosophy makes on all of us.

Both the traditional liberal defense of individual rights and the assumptions behind "trickle-down" economic theories are denied by communitarianism. We cannot assume that individuals seeking their own good will automatically create a common good. Furthermore, only if everyone enjoys minimal benefits and no one exploits the system can the common good be said to be promoted:

> No structuring of society and no government is legitimate, if they do not foster an effective promotion of the common good. The real proof of such promotion occurs when no one feels deprived of the basic conditions for personal development and when no one profits from the common good at the expense of the right of others to avail themselves of this common good.[64]

Adherence to communitarian values makes the whole world one community. Seeking the common good might entail a radical redistribution of the world's wealth as well as restrictions on the use of natural resources. In its purest formulation, communitarianism requires that pursuit of the common good precede the pursuit by individuals of their own particular or private goods.

THE MAKING OF A PHILOSOPHER

Ignacio Ellacuría Beas Coechea, S.J.
(1930–1989)

Born in the Basque region of Spain, Father Ellacuría lived and worked in Central America for over twenty-five years. Having trained as a philosopher, he began teaching philosophy at the Universidad Centroamericana in Managua, Nicaragua. After living and working in El Salvador, he became a naturalized Salvadoran. As a professor of philosophy and theology at José Simeon Canas University in El Salvador, Ellacuría was also known as a strong advocate of human rights and especially the social justice teachings of the Roman Catholic Church that stemmed from the second Vatican Council. He was serving as rector of the university in November 1989 when thirty uniformed soldiers entered the university grounds and killed Ellacuría, as well as five other Jesuit priests, their cook, and her daughter. His best-known book is *Freedom Made Flesh: The Mission of Christ and His Church* (Orbis, 1976). On questions of justice, his concern is that the common good be respected and sought in preference to a narrow individualism.

The Ethics of Authenticity: Charles Taylor

Canadian philosopher Charles Taylor is one of the leading Western communitarian thinkers. According to his formulation, we must respect the rights of individuals to define themselves and their goals, but we must insist that they do so through dialogue with others. Somewhat on the lines of justice as practiced in Buganda, we must give a fair hearing to the needs of individuals without sacrificing the overall health of the community. Active in Canadian politics, Taylor has energetically participated in the debate over Quebec separatism and has applied communitarian principles to it.[65]

I remember, we must remember until justice be done among us.
ROSARIO CASTELLANOS

As a French-speaking province, Quebec has sought separate status, apart from the dominant English-speaking culture and its strong ties with Great Britain. The problem is how to honor Quebec's need for a separate cultural identity while maintaining the unity of Canada as a political entity. Taylor maintains that people who live together in society must reach agreement on their common aims and not simply settle for morally empty procedures that prescribe rules of fairness.

What is needed is a pragmatic solution, and Taylor has spent a lot of time and energy supporting a proposal that would maintain the existing Canadian federation of provinces but grant limited autonomy to Quebec province. He distinguishes between *fundamental rights*—like those of life, liberty, free speech, and due process of law—which must be guaranteed to everyone, and *lesser privileges,* which may be denied under certain circumstances.

Whereas fundamental rights cannot be compromised, lesser privileges may have to be sacrificed to promote justice. Quebec's right to require that certain commercial transactions be conducted in French in order to maintain its own distinct culture might require English speakers to adapt, as French speakers already do in the dominant society.[66] It is not a matter of right to have commercial transactions conducted in one's native language, as speakers of French observe in the other provinces.

Taylor argues that an *ethics of authenticity* must involve both an affirmation of our individuality and a recognition of what we have in common:

> If authenticity is being true to ourselves . . . then perhaps we can only achieve it integrally if we recognize that this sentiment connects us to a wider whole. It was perhaps not an accident that in the Romantic period the self feeling and the feeling of belonging to nature were linked.[67]

The fragmentation so often described and lamented in society today arises, in Taylor's view, when people come to see themselves more and more atomistically, existing as separate atoms, and "less and less bound to their fellow citizens in common projects and allegiances."[68]

Taylor's ideal seems to be somewhat along the lines of Du Bois's solution, individualism within a communal context. Lesser privileges must be compromised so that fundamental rights may be upheld. For Quebec, there must be some accommodation to the wider culture, and for the English-speaking majority there must be some accommodation of Quebec. Authenticity will sacrifice neither the rights of the individual nor the integrity of the community.

A Covenanted Society

This ideal was articulated in the establishment of the Massachusetts Bay Colony as a **covenanted society.** The original Puritan vision rested on a covenant between God and society; stripped of its religious content, the idea of a secular covenant between citizens and their government is making a return. During the 1992 U.S. presidential election campaign, both Bill Clinton and Al Gore made repeated references to a **new covenant** among Americans that would overcome divisions and re-create a sense of common purpose. As president, Clinton promoted volunteerism and spoke of "a new spirit of community, a sense that we are all in this together."[69]

covenanted society *a society that functions as one and as a party to a covenant, or sacred relationship*

new covenant *a Clinton–Gore campaign slogan in the 1992 U.S. presidential election, used to evoke the Puritan ideal of a covenanted society and to revive communitarian principles*

In his first inaugural address, President Clinton called on "a new generation of young Americans" to "recognize a simple but powerful truth: We need each other and we must care for one another." He urged a rededication to what he called the "very idea of America":

> An idea born in revolution and renewed through two centuries of challenge; an idea tempered by the knowledge that but for fate we, the fortunate and the unfortunate, might have been each other; an idea ennobled by the faith that our nation can summon from its myriad diversity the deepest measure of unity . . .[70]

A covenant that includes everyone would redress some of the inequities entailed by the original compromises that made the Constitution possible, such as excluding the one-fifth of the nation consisting of enslaved African Americans and all women. The Clinton covenant would include African Americans as Americans, not Africans. The emphasis in any communitarian vision is on what binds us together, rather than what separates us; the aim is to include everyone in available rights and to expect of everyone commensurate responsibilities. Each faction in society can expect benefits, and each must be prepared to accept the entailed duties that accompany those benefits.

But it is not really difference the oppressor fears so much as similarity.
CHERRIE MORAGA

Communitarianism in Africa

If communitarianism is the newest old idea in America, it has never gone out of style in traditional societies. Speaking of tribal life in Kenya, former President Jomo Kenyatta observed, "According to Gikuyu ways of thinking, nobody is an isolated individual. Or rather, his uniqueness is a secondary fact about him; first and foremost he is several people's relative and several people's contemporary."[71] This does not mean that the person is not an individual with rights and privileges, but it does mean that the person is not merely an individual. The person is conceived dualistically, "as an autonomous, self-determining entity capable of evaluation and choice and as a communal being."[72]

African philosopher Kwame Gyekye believes that Rawls's *Theory of Justice,* conceived in individualistic terms, resonates very well with "communitarian expressions, meanings and content."[73] Speaking of the difference

A person is not a palm tree that he should be self-complete or self-sufficient.
AKAN PROVERB

principle, which permits unequal treatment of individuals if and only if the least well-off benefit, Rawls uses phrases like "sharing one another's fate," "collective assets," "common benefit," and "participating in one another's nature," all very *communitarian* ideas. Indeed, Gyekye believes that Rawls's ideas have a much better chance of being realized in a communal society than in one strongly based on individualism.

The balance between rights and duties in a communitarian framework is achieved by accommodating both individual and communal values in one system:

> Communitarian ethical and political theory, which considers the community as a fundamental human good, advocates a life lived in harmony and cooperation with others, a life of mutual consideration and aid and of interdependence, a life in which one shares in the fate of the other . . . such a life, according to the theory, is most rewarding and fulfilling.[74]

Summary

In examining the crucial question of justice, we must ask ourselves whether it is possible to focus exclusively on our rights as individuals without taking into account the common social order all of us share. The issue does not turn entirely on altruism; rather, the question may be whether it is in my own best interest as an individual to invest in the common good, to think of myself as my brother's or my sister's keeper as a way of achieving my individual goals. In societies founded on the principle of natural rights, we are very unlikely to give these rights up, and indeed it would be unwise to do so. What we must consider is whether an exclusive emphasis on personal rights is possible or desirable apart from a concern for the common good.

Consider for a moment what restrictions, if any, were placed on your freedom to take the philosophy course you are now taking. There may have been a financial restriction, but let's assume that you were either able to pay for the course or you received financial assistance in doing so. Was there a prerequisite for the course? Did you have to demonstrate basic proficiency in reading or writing? Did you have to take a test to show your competence to do the work required in the course? Typically, philosophy students must read long, complex chapters in a textbook and write at a pretty sophisticated level on essay examinations and in papers. Let's suppose for a moment that there were no restrictions whatsoever on admission to philosophy courses.

Freedom is not free.
MARTIN LUTHER KING, JR.

Your basic freedom would certainly have been respected; your right to take the course of your choice would have been honored. However, you may have been granted only the freedom to fail. If you lack the required reading and writing skills, the lectures and reading material will go over your head. You will be lost almost from the start, and you will have taken the seat of someone who might have been successful. Does this serve your interests? Is it a good use of the professor's time and energy? Is it fair to other students and to the college or university as a whole?

The placement office or counseling center may be doing you a favor to test and advise you or to provide prerequisites for entry into the course. Your pure freedom will be restricted, but your GPA will be protected and your ego will have been spared the bruise that a failing grade would inflict. In addition, the college or university will be able to use its limited resources more efficiently, and all students will benefit, including you. Perhaps your fate and your own long-term interest are more bound up with those of others than first appearance might have suggested.

Aldous Huxley's classic novel *Brave New World,* written more than fifty years ago, describes a totalitarian state in which babies are "decanted" in laboratories rather than born; the process yields five levels of intelligence. Alphas are the very brightest, whereas Epsilons, at the bottom, are decanted with just enough skill to do the most menial work in society and to find satisfaction in it. All children are conditioned from birth to be happy with their state in life by listening to tape recordings whenever they are asleep. "I'm so glad I'm a Beta. Alphas work so frightfully hard and Deltas wear those ugly khaki uniforms." There is almost no individual freedom.

There is also no crime, no unemployment, no war, no poverty or homelessness, no job dissatisfaction—in fact, no dissatisfaction of any kind. At the slightest twinge of any unpleasant sensation, people could go to a government store and pick up the legal drug Soma. Clearly, things have gone too far. Huxley was writing to warn future readers (like us) of the inherent dangers of a technological society. While you are using technology to solve society's problems, he seems to be saying, be careful that you do not forget about individual freedom.

The question remains: Have we gone too far in pursuit of individual freedom and lost our investment in what used to be called the commonweal, or the good of all? Just as an excess of government control over individual lives has a terrible cost (read *Brave New World* or George Orwell's *1984*), perhaps an excess of individualism has a cost as well. It seems that we cannot even achieve our individual goals unless we have a strong, healthy society in which to enjoy them. We might decide that Plato and Aristotle were correct to emphasize the harmony among all elements. The balance between a utilitarian concern for the social good (perhaps at the expense of individuals) and an aggressive insistence on individual rights (perhaps at the expense of the social good) may lie in a communitarian concern with both needs.

We will not easily give up our strong sense of individual rights, nor should we, but we may want to consider the question of justice in terms of what is most fair for ourselves and for everybody else. It is tempting to see the choice as an either/or one, either me or the other person. In a world as complex as our own, it may be a matter of both/and, both my rights and the good of all. The two may be more difficult to separate than we have supposed.

Wealth is strength. Wealth is power, wealth is influence, wealth is justice, is liberty, is real human rights.
MARCUS GARVEY

As Buckminster Fuller reminds us, we are living on "spaceship earth." It is an illusion—and a dangerous one—to think we can act in isolation and not affect the welfare of all. Obvious things like war and disease—but also not-so-obvious things like overpopulation, species elimination, and pollution—will affect us all and can threaten the very existence of life on Earth. As both Ellacuría and Taylor remind us, the common good is in everyone's best interest.

In the next and final chapter, we will look at ethics. As the final response to the overall section question—by what values shall I live in the world?—ethics considers individual moral decision making. What is the morally right thing to do, and on what basis will I decide how to act? We have been looking at political and social philosophy, but a society is only as moral as the individuals in it. In the final analysis, justice can be secured and a healthy state established only if individual citizens act in an ethically sound manner.

For Further Thought

1. You have been asked to design a just society. Where will you begin, and what considerations will you use to ensure that justice is achieved?
2. Are the classical theorists right that people are happiest doing what they do best, rather than what they might choose to do if given the opportunity? Why, or why not?
3. Would it be possible for you to make an important decision using Bentham's hedonistic calculus of pains subtracted from pleasures? Try it and see how happy you are with the result and the method.
4. Do you agree with John Stuart Mill that the quality of a pleasure is much more significant than the mere quantity of pleasures? Would you rather have a large number of superficial pleasures or several really meaningful ones? Explain.
5. Is Marx right that capitalism alienates workers from their work and from themselves? Ask three people you know how they feel about their work and what they would change to make it more meaningful and pleasant.
6. Choose a condition currently liable to receive discriminatory treatment in our society (a disability, low intelligence, homosexuality, racial minority status), imagine that you occupy that position, and write an essay about your experiences. This will give you a taste of Rawls's original position.
7. How did traditional Bugandan society balance the rights of the individual with the social good? Were they successful in your judgment? Explain.
8. Is it fairer to group students homogeneously (with others of the same ability) or heterogeneously (by locker number, for example, with people of varying abilities in one class)? Which is fairer to the individual student and which to the group? Explain.
9. Under what circumstances might it be wise to adopt an assimilationist strategy? Under what circumstances might separatism be a better choice? How would you decide which strategy to pursue if you were (or are) a member of a minority group? This could be the minority of students not using drugs or the minority practicing sexual abstinence, for instance.
10. If you have ever played on a team, acted in a play, or sung in a chorus, describe the experience of being both an individual and a member of something

larger than yourself. Were you able to achieve a satisfactory balance between your own individual needs and the needs of the group? If so, how? If not, why not?

11. Is justice promoted by urging everyone to "get out and vote," whether or not they have followed the issues and understand what the candidates stand for? Should the right to vote have more restrictions on it? Why, or why not? At the present time, if 50 percent of the eligible people vote this is considered an excellent turnout.
12. Make a list of expressions using the words black and white (black magic and lily white, for example). Are there any differences between the associations the two lists bring to mind? Explain. Some people contend that discrimination is built right into our language and to speak it is to take on subtle judgments about race.
13. Utopian communities have been formed throughout the history of the United States. Often they have been situated on a farm, and every member contributed to the work of raising food for the community. In most cases, gender roles blurred so that both men and women worked in the fields and both cooked, cleaned, and engaged in child care. In the "hippie" communes of the 1960s and in an Israeli kibbutz, the children are raised primarily in a group rather than in a nuclear family. What effect do you think this kind of arrangement might have on the children, especially as they grow up to establish families of their own?
14. In a monastery, the individual is very much a part of a group, usually working, eating, and praying with others on a scheduled basis. At the same time, the person is very much alone, living in a small cell with only minimal furnishings. The idea is to be alone with yourself (and God or the cosmos) while engaging in a group effort. Does this model seem to you to fulfill or contradict the communitarian model? How?
15. A short film called *Second Coming* shows a black Jesus confronting discrimination in modern American society. The premise is that his ideas could never be heard and he would most likely end up in jail (which is where he is when the movie opens). Discuss the implications of this. Would people be open to the message of a female Prophet or Savior, or would her "otherness" get in the way too much? Explain.
16. To promote equality, affirmative action programs offer compensatory help to groups who have suffered from past discrimination. There have been objections that these programs are actually discriminatory since, in helping a whole group, some people receive help who need it far less than others. Historian Garry Wills argues that government disaster help after a hurricane or flood does exactly the same thing, that it is a kind of "affirmative action" program to help the disadvantaged catch up and so is the GI Bill (affirmative action for veterans) and the FHA mortgage program (affirmative action for young people getting their first mortgage). Do you agree or disagree with his analysis? Why?
17. Speaking about our current family model in which the mother is expected to cook for her family, Charlotte Perkins Gilman writes: "Our general notion is that we have lifted and ennobled our eating and drinking by combining them with love. On the contrary, we have lowered and degraded our love by combining it with eating and drinking." Do you agree or disagree with her? Why?
18. Can a woman be said to be free if she cannot determine whether or when to bear children in a society that insists children are the mother's responsibility (if

the father or other family members are not around to help)? If it is in the best interest of society for a woman to bear a child she has not chosen to conceive, should society share responsibility for the rearing of that child? If not, does society have the right to demand the woman bear the child? Explain.

19. What do you think about a program of national service that would require a one- or two-year commitment from everyone at the age of eighteen? The person could choose from a wide range of service—environmental work, teaching in a city school, military service—and would earn a small salary as well as financial credit toward a college education.
20. During the crisis time of separation from Great Britain, the leaders of the American Revolution agreed on this: "We must all hang together [one-for-all-and-all-for-one] or surely we shall all hang separately [by the neck until dead]" Do you agree that unless we cooperate on a social level we are doomed as individuals? Why, or why not?

For Further Exploration

The Autobiography of Malcolm X, as told to Alex Haley. New York: Ballantine: 1986. This is Malcolm's life story as told to writer Alex Haley over a two-year period. Spike Lee used it, with some variations, as the script for his popular film *Malcolm X.*

Du Bois, W. E. B. *The Souls of Black Folk.* New York: Fawcett, 1961. This book is a readable classic in African-American philosophy. It is a collection of essays, short fiction, poetry, elegy, allegory, and a treatise on ethnomusicology, which includes data-laden studies of rural poverty in the Black Belt of the South, a short history of Reconstruction, and impassioned objections to racial violence, as well as philosophical reflections on racial identity.

Gilman, Charlotte Perkins. *Herland.* New York: Pantheon, 1979. Gilman offers a feminist fantasy in which women rule and society prospers.

Huxley, Aldous. *Brave New World.* New York: Harper & Row, 1969. In this novel, Huxley has created a dystopia (the opposite of utopia, like a dysfunctional family on a large scale) featuring the worst tendencies of the technological era run amok.

The Insider. In this film a courageous whistle-blower and a determined investigative reporter expose corporate malfeasance within the tobacco industry and reveal the connection between cigarette smoking and nicotine addiction.

Orwell, George. *Animal Farm.* New York: New American Library, 1946. This influential novel is a Marxist parody set on a farm. After the revolution, the animals declare that "all animals are equal," but later, under the influence of Napoleon the pig, another phrase is added: "Some animals are more equal than others."

Rossi, Alice, ed. *The Feminist Papers: From Adams to de Beauvoir.* New York: Bantam, 1974. This comprehensive anthology contains primary source readings that deal with feminism and political/social philosophy, written by both women and men.

Soderberg, William. *Game of Philosophy.* Lanham, Md.: University Press of America, 2000. Of particular interest is "The Rawls Game" in which players try to implement a just and workable society, using the principles laid out by John Rawls.

West, Cornel. *Race Matters*. Boston: Beacon, 1993. West provides a short, readable analysis of the problems facing American society from an African-American perspective and offers a communitarian solution.

For Further Research

Try these InfoTrac keywords:

Distributive Justice
Assimilation
Communitarianism
Utilitarianism
Feminism
Marxism

Notes

1. Plato, *Republic,* bk. 9, in *Great Dialogues of Plato,* trans. W. H. D. Rouse, ed. Eric H. Warmington and Philip G. Rouse (New York: New American Library, 1956), 380.
2. Plato, bk. 4, 242.
3. Aristotle, "Politics," in *The Pocket Aristotle,* ed. Justin D. Kaplan, trans. W. D. Ross (New York: Washington Square, 1958), 330.
4. Aristotle, bk. 8, 335.
5. Aristotle, bk. 2, 290.
6. Aristotle, bk. 8, 335.
7. Jeremy Bentham, "An Introduction to the Principles of Morals and Legislation," in *Treasury of Philosophy,* ed. Dagobert D. Runes (New York: Philosophical Library, 1955), 132.
8. Jeremy Bentham, "An Introduction to the Principles of Morals and Legislation," chap. 4, in *John Stuart Mill: Utilitarianism, On Liberty, Essay on Bentham, Together with Selected Writings of Jeremy Bentham and John Austin,* ed. Mary Warnock (New York: New American Library, 1974), 66.
9. John Stuart Mill, "Utilitarianism," chap. 2, in *John Stuart Mill,* 261.
10. John Stuart Mill, "The Subjection of Women," quoted in John Stuart Mill and Harriet Taylor Mill, *Essays on Sex Equality,* ed. Alice S. Rossi (Chicago: University of Chicago Press, 1970), 235.
11. Mill, "The Subjection of Women," 217.
12. Mill, "The Subjection of Women," 218.
13. Mill, "The Subjection of Women," 220.
14. Alma Lutz, *Created Equal: A Biography of Elizabeth Cady Stanton* (New York: Day, 1940), 171–172.
15. Harriet Taylor Mill, "Enfranchisement of Women," in *Essays on Sex Equality,* 111.
16. Harriet Taylor Mill, 112.

17. Harriet Taylor Mill, 114.
18. Harriet Taylor Mill, 117.
19. "Autobiography of John Stuart Mill," in *Essays on Sex Equality,* 57.
20. Karl Marx, "Economic and Philosophic Manuscripts of 1844," in *The Marx-Engels Reader,* ed. Robert C. Tucker (New York: Norton, 1972), 60.
21. Karl Marx, "A Contribution to the Critique of Political Economy," in *Marx & Engels: Basic Writings on Politics and Philosophy,* ed. Lewis S. Feuer (New York: Anchor, 1959), 43–44.
22. John Rawls, *A Theory of Justice* (Cambridge, Mass.: Harvard University Press, 1972), 28.
23. Rawls, 60.
24. Rawls, 61.
25. Rawls, 75.
26. Rawls, 78.
27. Rawls, 10.
28. Rawls, 12.
29. Rawls, 19.
30. Robert Nozick, *Anarchy, State, and Utopia* (New York: Basic, 1974), ix.
31. Nozick.
32. Nozick, 151.
33. Nozick, 310, 312.
34. J. S. Mbiti, quoted in E. Wamala, "The Socio-Political Philosophy of Traditional Buganda Society," in *The Foundations of Social Life: Ugandan Philosophical Studies,* vol. 1, ed. A. T. Dalfovo et al. (Washington, D. C.: Council for Research in Values and Philosophy, 1992), 38.
35. Wamala, 44.
36. Bernard R. Boxill, *Blacks and Social Justice* (Totowa, N.J.: Rowman & Allanheld, 1984), 173–185.
37. Boxill.
38. Martin Delany, quoted in Bernard Boxill, "Two Traditions in African American Political Philosophy," *Philosophical Forum* 24, no. 1–3 (1992–1993): 123.
39. Delany, 124.
40. Delany, 125–126.
41. Delany, 127.
42. Delany, 131–132.
43. Cornel West, *Race Matters* (Boston: Beacon, 1993), 96.
44. West, 96.
45. West, 99.
46. West, 102.
47. West, 105.
48. Simone de Beauvoir, *The Second Sex,* trans. H. M. Parshley (New York: Vintage, 1952), 267.
49. De Beauvoir, 280.

50. De Beauvoir, 720.
51. De Beauvoir, 723.
52. De Beauvoir, 728–729.
53. Charlotte Perkins Gilman, *Women and Economics: A Study of the Economic Relation Between Men and Women as a Factor in Social Evolution,* ed. Carl N. Degler (New York: Harper & Row, 1966), 5.
54. Gilman, 13.
55. Gilman, 242.
56. Gilman, 244–245.
57. Audre Lorde, "Age, Race, Class, and Sex: Women Redefining Difference," in *Sister Outsider* (Watsonville, Calif.: Crossing Press, 1984), 114.
58. Lorde, 120–121.
59. Lorde, 122.
60. Lorde, 123.
61. "Summary of the World," *Baltimore Sun,* 2 June 1997, 3D.
62. Ignacio Ellacuría, S.J., "Human Rights in a Divided Society," in *Human Rights in the Americas: The Struggle for Consensus,* ed. Alfred Hennelly, S.J., and John Langan, S.J. (Washington, D.C.: Georgetown University Press, 1982), 53.
63. Ellacuría, 55.
64. Ellacuría, 56.
65. "A Scholar Seeks the Multicultural Middle Ground," *Chronicle of Higher Education,* 9 December 1992, A8.
66. "A Scholar Seeks."
67. Charles Taylor, *The Ethics of Authenticity* (Cambridge, Mass.: Harvard University Press, 1991), 91.
68. Taylor, 112–123.
69. Orlando Patterson, "Our History vs. Clinton's Covenant," *New York Times,* 13 November 1992, A29.
70. William Jefferson Clinton, quoted in the *New York Times,* 21 January 1993, A15.
71. Jomo Kenyatta, quoted in Kwame Gyekye, "Person and Community in African Thought," in *Person and Community: Ghanaian Philosophical Studies,* vol. 1, ed. Kwasi Wiredu and Kwame Gyekye (Washington, D.C.: Council for Research in Values and Philosophy, 1992), 102.
72. Gyekye, 115.
73. Gyekye, 117.
74. Gyekye, 120.

CHAPTER 10

Ethics

What Will It Be: Truth or Consequences?

Before You Read . . .

Ask yourself what standard you currently use for your own, personal moral decision making.

Love in action is a harsh and deadly thing compared with love in dreams.
Fyodor Dostoyevsky

A baby has just been born, but no one is behaving the way people typically do at a birth because this baby has been born without a complete brain. In medical terms, this baby is anencephalic; she has only the most primitive part of her brain, the part just above the spinal cord that controls heartbeat, breathing, and the other autonomic (more or less automatic) functions that keep a body alive. This baby, whose parents name her Theresa, will never recognize them or anything else in her world. She will never think or speak or interact with anything or anyone. The medical staff agree that within a few days or weeks at most she will be dead.

Seeking to find some meaning in this tragedy, her parents make the painful decision to donate her organs so that other children might live. In their minds, this means her short life and death will have meaning. If they wait for her natural death, the organs will have deteriorated to such an extent that they will be unsuitable for donation. Should they be permitted to authorize the donation of Baby Theresa's organs while she is still alive (according to some medical definitions but not necessarily all of them, and according to the laws of some states but not others)?

The parents' wishes are based on outcomes. Much as they would wish it otherwise, their baby will never go home from the hospital with them. She will never have "life" in the sense in which they understand the word. Their interest is in investing Theresa's brief existence and untimely death with meaning. If another child (or several other children) might live after receiving Theresa's donated organs, they would feel consoled. Their grief would be tempered by the knowledge that their child was, in a sense, living on in other children. For some of the recipients, a heart or a liver could mean the difference between life and death; for others, a donated organ might significantly improve the quality of life.

The outcome they would most wish for—a healthy baby to take home and love—has been denied them, but from among the remaining possible outcomes, the parents select organ donation as the best possibility for themselves, the other children, and their daughter. There is, in their view, absolutely nothing to be gained by watching her organs deteriorate until, at the moment of her inevitable death, they are worthless.

Having heard the parents' wishes, the hospital ethics board is assembled in emergency session to decide the question. Although all members are committed to doing the morally right thing, they are also aware of the honest differences of opinion that exist on the subject. Everyone is sensitive to the pain of the parents but also to the publicity sure to surround this case with its many legal ramifications. What they decide may have far-reaching implications.

One member, a physician, begins by reminding the medical staff that they have sworn an oath to preserve life. As physicians, they cannot take the life of one patient to save the lives of others, even if Theresa's life is sure to be very brief. While she lives she is entitled to their care and protection, and it is not their place to "play God" and "harvest" her organs while her body sustains them. Her life (and her organs) are in their hands. When she dies, her parents may make any decision they wish about the disposition of her organs, but while she is a living patient, they must use all medical means to ensure that Theresa's life is preserved.

Another member of the board, a lawyer, draws attention to parallels with mature people whose bodies "live" but who lack brain activity. There are legal and medical precedents for removing those patients from life-support systems and allowing them to die. Baby Theresa is in a similar situation. Because she has no brain activity—an electroencephalogram (EEG) would show a flat line—Theresa is essentially a body without a brain. She cannot be confused with other patients who—though ill or injured, even severely—retain their rational powers and have a mental existence. We might even, this member observes, be doing Theresa a favor by ending her brief, pointless, and possibly painful life. The difference in Theresa's case is that organs would have to be removed while a "beating heart" was present.

A third member, a clergyperson, disagrees, observing that whether or not Baby Theresa fits our definition of a person, she is surely a person according to the laws of the state and the laws of God who created her. Only by respecting life in all its forms—those similar to our own and those radically different—can we follow a truly moral course of action. If we lose a vital respect for individual life, we open the door to abuses such as those in the Nazi death camps and in prison torture cells around the world today. We can never do what is merely expedient when we are dealing with human life; we must always ask ourselves what we owe this person as an individual. Logically, we owe Theresa life for as long as she can live it; other arguments do not apply.

The next speaker, a nurse, wonders about the other lives—some of them in this very hospital—that might be saved if we shorten this child's life by a week at the most. After citing the cases of several babies and young children, all of whose prognoses are very poor, the nurse observes that without donated organs most of them will be dead within a month because none of them is high enough on a waiting list to be certain that an organ will become available in time. We're playing roulette; we're risking a certain good against an uncertain evil. Theresa has no "quality of life" at all, for she is unaware of everything going on around her. Being a person means being aware of your world and capable of interacting with it. We should certainly not cause her undue pain, but we gain nothing by honoring a personhood she clearly lacks.

A community representative observes that debates about what constitutes a person and other theoretical, ethical discussions are not going to solve our problem. We can—and will—disagree on these abstract issues for the rest of the night, and that will not help us decide what to do here. Ethics, for this person, involves care, and that makes this issue a very simple one: We must care for Theresa. If she lives two days, a week, two weeks, a month, or fifty years, our job remains making her life as pain free and as comfortable as possible. We are healers, and failing that, we are caregivers. No one should be allowed to die without being lovingly cared for. This argument applies equally to an old and terminally ill patient and to Baby Theresa. If we lose sight of this important consideration, we might as well think of ourselves as a corporation and start basing all our decisions on the "bottom line."

That might not be such a bad idea, a hospital administrator says. It's all well and good to talk about care and the quality of Baby Theresa's life, but the bottom line is this: While she is using the expensive resources of this hospital to live one or two additional days, we are spending precious health-care dollars that could buy prenatal care for inner-city mothers or provide immunizations against childhood diseases. Why should we use our limited resources to help a patient who, everyone agrees, will not live past the fifteenth of this month? We can't help her, and we'll tie up our already overburdened staff. There isn't any rational basis for committing ourselves to keeping this baby alive after her parents have made the sensible choice to donate her organs.

The Issue Defined

ethics *the branch of philosophy concerned with judgments about moral behavior and the meaning of ethical statements and terms*

Deciding what we should do in the case of Baby Theresa—and all the other moral dilemmas of the modern world—is the province of the branch of philosophy called **ethics.** Some basic ethical questions are these: Should we consider the long-term consequences for ourselves and society in deciding what is the right thing to do? Are there rules governing moral choices? If so, where can they be found? Are we bound to respect the integrity of a person under all circumstances, and (most difficult to agree on) what constitutes a person? Are there principles such as "care" or "help" that should be our guiding lights in making moral choices?

In this chapter we look at the major theories of **normative ethics**—what constitutes moral behavior and intention—and how those theories may be applied to the living of our own lives. Philosophers are also concerned with **metaethics,** which studies the meaning of ethical terms and the justification of ethical theories. Some issues raised in metaethics include: (1) the question of whether absolute moral values exist (Are there actions that are always right/always wrong, or is morality determined by the customs of a particular society?); (2) the meaning of ethical statements (When I assert that a particular action is right or good, do I mean anything other than that I or a majority of people approve that action?); (3) the meaning of ethical terms (When I say, "Cheating is *wrong,*" there seems to be no way to verify the statement without using other ethical terms: "Cheating is *bad,*" or "people *shouldn't cheat*"). Metaethics also poses the ultimate ethical question: Why be moral?

normative ethics *the branch of ethics that makes judgments about what constitutes moral behavior and intention*

metaethics *the branch of ethics that studies the meaning of ethical statements and terms*

These considerations underlie the debates of normative ethics, and how we answer them will affect our ability to talk about and reason our way through ethical theories. In this chapter we focus on *applied normative ethics,* which applies general ethical principles to specific moral problems—such as the life and death of Baby Theresa. In all normative ethics, the emphasis is on what we *ought* to do. When we face moral choices, normative ethics supplies guidelines to help us with those choices—to suggest how we might decide what we ought to do in any given situation.

Though the dialogue among the members of the ethics board presented here is fictitious, the case of Baby Theresa is real. Her brief life and death in 1992 set off a controversy covered by many newspapers and discussed in a number of magazines around the world. In the actual case, for legal and ethical reasons, the hospital made the decision not to hasten Theresa's death and "harvest" her organs. As a result, she was allowed to die naturally, which she did ten days after birth. Deprived of oxygen, none of her organs was suitable for transplantation purposes.

One of the complicating factors was that Florida, where Theresa was born, uses a *whole-brain* concept of death: A person is legally dead only if the whole brain, including the brain stem, has ceased to function. Baby Theresa's parents sued the hospital in which their child was born to have her declared legally dead so that her organs could be donated. She died of natural causes while the legal and ethical debate raged around her.

Twenty-five years ago the question of when life began and ended was a much simpler one: A person with breathing lungs and a beating heart was alive; a person with neither was dead. Now that machines can do the job of heart and lungs, most hospitals and most states use the much more abstract whole-brain definition of life and death: A person with a functioning whole brain is alive (even if sustained by a heart-lung machine); a person whose *entire* brain has ceased to function is dead (even if a heartbeat and respiration are present). Baby Theresa was legally alive (because part of her brain was functioning), and the Florida hospital could not legally treat her as dead.

Using this case as a starting point, we can look at the major ethical theories and how they apply to the complex moral decisions of the modern world. We begin with some traditional Western theories and then consider Asian and African approaches to ethics.

Western Ethical Theories

Most of our own choices are neither as dramatic nor as ambiguous as the sad case of Theresa and her parents, but we may use the stark choices presented by this case to frame our discussion. Following the sequence of deliberations from the fictitious hospital ethics board, we begin with consequentialist and nonconsequentialist ethical theories—those that look to outcomes and those that do not—then revisit natural law theory, discuss the sacredness of human life, consider the interest view, and conclude with virtue ethics.

Consequentialist, or Teleological, Ethical Theories

teleological ethical theory *an ethical theory that evaluates behavior in terms of consequences*

Baby Theresa's parents adopted a **teleological** (*telos* means "purpose") approach to their moral dilemma. They looked to the consequences of possible actions and tried to choose the most desirable option among those available. If they could not take home a healthy child (clearly the most desirable consequence), the next best alternative seemed to them investing her brief life with meaning by donating her organs to other children who desperately needed them. From their point of view, the morality of the situation depended on the consequences of their decision. If you recall our discussion of social philosophy in Chapter 9, this is a *utilitarian* solution.

As with all utilitarian approaches, the goal is to maximize pleasure and minimize pain. It is possible to make a utilitarian choice using your own long-term interests as the measuring stick; it is also possible to use the greater good of society as a way of determining whether a proposed choice is a moral one (along the lines of the *communitarian* position we explored at the end of Chapter 9). If in either case you choose to focus on consequences, you will be acting so as to increase pleasure and decrease pain. It may seem odd to use the word *pleasure* in this case; the issue clearly has more to do with avoiding pain or choosing the less painful alternative. Yet for Theresa's parents, there would have been a kind of pleasure in knowing that their daughter's death was not entirely without meaning. To think of other children living because of the gift of Theresa's organs would have brought them pleasure and would, over the long term, have diminished the pain they felt in losing their child.

They may have had a wider view in mind as well. If Theresa's death was a certainty (as everyone agreed it was), then how could the overall good of society be best served? Several children could live or have a better quality of life with Theresa's donated organs, but if she died of natural causes, no one would receive any benefit. In this case, the utilitarian principle must be seen in communitarian as well as in personal terms.

Nonconsequentialist, or Deontological, Ethical Theories

In sharp contrast with consequentialist ethical theories, **deontological ethical theories** (from *deon-*, meaning "obligation") do not take consequences into account; instead we must follow our duty, regardless of the consequences. According to deontology, how things turn out is really not the point. If you, as an unmarried person, have sexual intercourse with another unmarried person, some deontological theories would judge you as having committed an immoral act, no matter what the consequences for yourself or the other person; other deontological theories might find you to have acted morally. What matters is doing one's duty; if you want to know what that means, look to ethical laws and principles rather than to consequences.

deontological *[DAY AHN tah lah juh kuhl]* **ethical theory** *an ethical theory that evaluates behavior in terms of adherence to duty or obligation, regardless of consequences*

Baby Theresa's case brought medical personnel, especially physicians, into conflict with a clear and well-established duty. By tradition, a physician must swear an oath, which dates back to the time of the early Greeks, to protect life and relieve suffering. Known as the *Hippocratic Oath* after the Greek physician Hippocrates who formulated it, the oath requires the physician first and foremost to *do no harm*. In the murky case of Theresa, taking organs from a body with a beating heart certainly seems to do harm to Theresa. Living in a time when life and death were determined by the presence or absence of a beating heart, Hippocrates clearly could not have imagined a case of brain death or absent brain within a living body. Before the advent of today's sophisticated technology, what it meant to do no harm was considerably clearer.

Deontological ethical theory may invoke the will of God. If one of the Ten Commandments (accepted by several major religious traditions) says "Thou shalt not kill," what could be clearer? We may want to hide behind medical terminology such as euthanasia (literally, "good death"), but the truth is that in order to relieve suffering, the physician may have to assist the patient in killing himself or herself, a violation of God's law. Similarly, to take Theresa's organs, we would have to kill her or at least hasten her death. If killing is strictly forbidden, there is no arguing against it; consequences do not matter: Killing is killing and God does not allow it.

Making a distinction between killing (which can sometimes be justified) and murder (which can never be justified) allows some people to condemn abortion while supporting capital punishment (execution by the state of a convicted felon) or subscribing to the theory that there are just wars in which killing of the declared enemy is justified. It is difficult for humans to speak with absolute certainty about what the *will of God* might be in a particular situation, and disagreements (among and within religions) as well as apparent exceptions only complicate the picture. Still, one possible interpretation

DOING PHILOSOPHY

Cultural Relativism: Has It Gone Too Far?

In the 1930s and 1940s, anthropologist Ruth Benedict told the world that "normal" was relative to the culture in which a person lived. What is accepted and even valued in one culture can be condemned and even punished in another. What we call "cultural relativism" replaced the absolute moral standards and accompanying value judgments of the nineteenth century. The question for us today is, Has cultural relativism gone too far? A growing number of students, according to John Leo (*U.S. News & World Report,* 21 July 1997), seem unwilling to condemn human sacrifice, ethnic cleansing, and slavery because they believe no one has the right to criticize the morality of another culture. "Of course I dislike the Nazis," one student said, "but who is to say they are morally wrong?" What do you think? Is everything culturally relative? Or are there some actions that should be prohibited and punished no matter where they occur? If there are some moral universals, who should decide what they are? Are they intuitively obvious? Can we all, for instance, agree that large-scale genocide is wrong? Or are we prepared to consider mitigating circumstances even for the Holocaust? Are you willing to live in a world in which there are no moral standards and everything is culturally relative? At the other extreme, how do I prevent someone else's moral code from making illegal what I choose to do with my own life (assuming that I injure no one else in the process)?

clearly is that the preservation of life is always one's duty and the intentional taking of life is always a moral wrong.

Immanuel Kant, whom we met in Chapter 5, believed ethical principles to be self-evident. All a person needed to do, Kant thought, was to consider whether a proposed action could serve as a universal law without self-contradiction. Kant called this principle the **categorical imperative** because it was an imperative (demanded action) and it was categorical (was necessary in itself). Kant suggested that when you are faced with a moral choice, you should imagine a world in which everyone was required to do precisely what you are proposing to do right now. If you favor such a world, you should act as you are proposing; if you do not favor it, you should not do what you propose.

categorical imperative *a deontological ethical principle, developed by Kant, that states unconditionally that one must act in such a way as to desire his or her actions to become universal laws binding on everyone*

Sometimes called the *universalizability principle,* Kant's ethical guideline asks you to mentally universalize your proposed action and imagine it as a moral law, binding on everyone. If you can will that what you are about to do should become the law of the land, and can do so without self-contradiction, Kant urges you to go ahead and do it; if you find the prospect of your private action becoming universalized frightening, you should not do it. Kant thought that if you are tempted to kill someone when your anger is aroused, you will easily see that a society governed by this principle would be uninhabitable and, in a short time, uninhabited. If you are considering telling a lie to protect yourself, Kant believed that you would reject living under conditions that would make truth telling a rare or nonexistent act.

Let's consider Baby Theresa's case from the Kantian perspective. The key question is where to draw the line? Would we be willing to universalize the principle that organs must be taken if the patient fails to meet certain

Philosophers Speak for Themselves

Immanuel Kant

An action done from duty derives its moral worth not from the purpose or outcome which is to be achieved through it but from the maxim on which it is based. Therefore, the action does not depend on the achievement of its objective but only on the principle of volition [willing] on which the action is based, independent of desired outcomes . . . Being truthful from duty is quite a different matter from being truthful out of fear of consequences. In the first case the concept of acting out of duty already contains its own law; in the second, I must look elsewhere to see what effects for myself might be connected with an action. It is undoubtedly evil for me to deviate from the principle of duty, but if I betray my maxim of prudence, this can sometimes be advantageous to me, even though, overall, it is better to obey it.

The most direct and objective way to resolve the problem of whether a false promise is ever consistent with duty is to ask myself: would I be content to have my maxim (to get myself out of difficult situations with false promises) become a universal law? Would I dare say to myself that anyone facing an embarrassing situation and seeing no other way out may make a false promise? This immediately makes clear that, while I can defend the lie, I cannot support lying as a universal law. If this law were in effect, there would, in reality, be no promises at all, since it would be pointless for me to make promises to others who would not believe me or, even if they did believe me, might repay me with a false promise of their own. In other words, as soon as my maxim was made into a universal law, it would self-destruct.

From *Foundations for the Metaphysics of Morals.* Translation:

criteria and the organs are needed? In Theresa's case, this principle might seem reasonable. However, if it is permissible to remove the organs from the body of Theresa while her heart beats, would we consider *requiring* the same action with respect to the 5000 to 10,000 U.S. citizens currently in a "persistent vegetative state" and permanently unconscious? Suppose a person we loved was in the twilight world between life and death and we wanted to preserve his or her life, but that option was not available to us because of a precedent set in an earlier case?

Another way of expressing Kant's categorical imperative states that we must always treat people as ends in themselves, never merely as means to an end. You may be pursuing a college degree as a perfectly legitimate means to a good job, a satisfying and productive career. There is absolutely nothing wrong with this. One might even argue that the purpose or the nature of a degree is to serve as the means to an end. Even if your only goal were to increase your knowledge and wisdom, the degree would not be an end in itself but a means to help you achieve your goal.

Kant asserted that even though things like degrees can appropriately serve only as means, people most certainly cannot. To use a person only as a way of making a sale, getting invited to join a club, or being promoted is to behave immorally, according to Kant. It is never permissible to treat people as if they were valued merely as a way of achieving something else. People are people, not things, and as such they have a fundamental human dignity that can never be compromised.

In the moral twilight zone of the intensive care unit, medical personnel are called on daily to make choices with less-than-clear guidelines. When a patient has suffered a stroke or been in an accident involving head trauma and has no measurable brain activity, it may be possible to unplug a respirator and *allow* the patient to die without facing an ethical dilemma. Removing what are sometimes called "extraordinary means"—the technological marvels that sustain life artificially—is a different thing from removing organs from a body with a beating heart. Still, the advent of heart-lung machines has made much more uncertain what it means to *cause* someone's death.

Come, come, whoever you are
Wanderer, Worshiper, Lover of Leaving
It doesn't matter
Ours is not a caravan of despair
Come, even if you have broken your vow a thousand times.
Come, yet again, come come.
RUMI

What happens if you "pull the plug" and the patient's body continues to live? The parents of Karen Ann Quinlan, Nancy Kruzan, and others, having made the agonizing choice to remove technological support from their child's comatose body, faced such a situation; their children remained permanently unconscious and had no possibility of returning to what their parents would call life, and yet their brain stems continued to drive the heart and work the lungs. And what about parents who have sued to stop intravenous nourishment and allow their permanently unconscious child to die but have been prevented from doing so? No one wants to make value judgments of this kind.

Using Theresa's organs to benefit other ill children might seem like a commendable thing to do in terms of teleological (consequentialist) ethical theory, but according to Kant it would be using Theresa merely as a means to an end (that of saving the lives of other ill children) and not treating her as an end in herself (a person with human dignity that can under no circumstances be compromised). If we use Kant's categorical imperative as our yardstick *and* if Theresa qualifies as a person, we must conclude that no moral justification exists for taking Theresa's organs; in fact, to do so would be immoral.

Natural Law Theory

natural law theory
in deontological ethical theory, the belief that the rational principle of order that underlies the cosmos also contains a basis for moral action that is discoverable by reason; in Christian versions of this theory, we find the belief that humans, created in the image and likeness of God, deserve special moral status on that account

So much turns on our definition of a person, and Kant, who seemed to use reason as the criterion for personhood, might have found the case of Baby Theresa especially problematic. Are a beating heart and breathing lungs enough to qualify one as a human person? Using Kant's definition of personhood, the answer is no. There are, however, traditions asserting that a person—even one with no brain activity—is still a person. Every person, according to **natural law theory,** has worth, and this intrinsic worth cannot be compromised.

The question of personhood is at the heart of the abortion controversy as well as the debate over cloning human beings. For instance, at what point does a fertilized egg qualify as a person? At conception? When the mother begins to feel movement inside her body? At the time of viability, when the fetus can survive on its own outside the womb? If persons have intrinsic worth, defining what constitutes personhood becomes a critical task. In the world after Dolly—a sheep cloned by scientists in Scotland—some are

HOW PHILOSOPHY WORKS
Fuzzy Logic

This new way of thinking already is used in air conditioners, enabling them to constantly adjust the room temperatures with varying amounts of cooling air instead of operating as either "off" or "on." Its major contention is that only mathematics is really *bivalent*—either/or, right/wrong, 1/0—and that everything else is *multivalent*—a matter of degree. Most of reality is neither black nor white but gray, as Descartes discovered when he melted the ball of wax. At some point it changed from wax ball to non-wax ball, but where exactly was that point? You can try the experiment yourself, suggests Bart Kosko in his antiscience science book, *Fuzzy Thinking* (see "For Further Exploration").

Place an apple in your hand and ask yourself, "Is this an apple?" Your answer will clearly be yes. Now eat the apple and ask yourself the same question. Just as clearly, your answer will now be no. The issue is, At what point did the apple cease to be an apple? Kosko explains, "When you hold half an apple in your hand, the apple is as much there as not. The half apple foils all-or-none descriptions. The half apple is a *fuzzy* apple, the gray between black and white."

Fuzzy logic is commonplace in "smart" computers that recognize and translate handwritten characters; camcorders; auto engines, transmissions, brakes, cruise controls; elevators; microwave ovens; televisions and many other electronic devices. It works because it takes into account the reality that nothing is absolute, that everything is a matter of degree.

Aristotle taught us *bivalence*—something is either A or not-A—and this logic prevailed for 2000 years. Eastern systems, like Taoism and Buddhism, have always recognized the contradictions at the heart of what-is and asserted that things are both A and not-A. We can see glimmers of this *multivalent* view in the ancient paradoxes of Western thought. If a liar from Crete says that all Cretans are liars, does he lie? It seems the only way out of the paradox is that the Cretan both lies and doesn't lie at the same time (A is not-A).

Applied to ethics, fuzzy logic helps us see that a person may not be clearly either alive or not alive, a person or not a person, but somewhere on the line between those two alternatives. Instead of arguing violently about whether life begins at conception, quickening, viability, or birth, fuzzy logic suggests we begin by granting that life begins at all those times—to a certain degree.

urging a ban on human cloning. If we could clone an adult human being, would the resulting organism be a person? Suppose we made many copies for the sole purpose of having organs available for later transplantation? Would this be a moral course of action? Natural law theory insists that Theresa was a person, even though she lacked many of the defining characteristics of a human person. Others are not so sure, but everyone is nervous about declaring a body with a beating heart a nonperson.

Science cannot stop while ethics catches up—and nobody should expect scientists to do all the thinking for the country.
ELVIN STOCKMAN

At the other end of life, we are on an equally slippery slope. Does a patient with Alzheimer's disease who does not recognize loved ones and cannot perform basic feeding or cleaning functions still qualify as a person? Again, natural law theory is clear; there is no point at which a human organism is not yet or is no longer a person.

Leaving aside the legal questions, should a physician be allowed to assist a person in committing suicide, as Dr. Jack Kevorkian and others are alleged to have done on several occasions? Is the decision about when human life is over the physician's, the patient's, the bioethics board's,

God's? In other words, can someone decide he or she no longer feels like a person and wishes to stop the charade? Should someone else (a relative or a dear friend) be permitted to decide on that person's behalf?

The natural law tradition insists that there is an "objective moral order" and that "there are certain moral absolutes that ought never be violated if one hopes to attain personal wholeness or societal health."[1] Things are wrong because they are wrong, not because they are forbidden. One of these principles is that human life has intrinsic worth. According to the natural law tradition, killing must harm not only the individual who is killed but the entire social fabric.

If we grant personhood, we may still encounter situations in which two persons appear to have conflicting rights. In late 1993 a pregnant Chicago woman learned, at a routine prenatal examination during her third trimester, that her developing baby was not receiving adequate oxygen or nutrition through the placenta. The physician recommended inducing labor or performing a cesarean section; if she did neither, he advised, the baby would either die or suffer severe brain damage. The woman, who described herself as a Pentecostal Christian, believed that God wanted her to have a natural delivery and rejected her physician's advice, preferring to trust in the Lord and hope for a miracle.

A publicly appointed guardian for the fetus argued in court that the woman be forced to undergo a cesarean birth. The American Civil Liberties Union (ACLU), defending the woman's rights to privacy and to her own religious beliefs, insisted that she have control over her own body. It was a peculiar case. The woman, whose beliefs would ordinarily have led her to argue for the **sacredness of human life** and oppose abortion, found herself insisting on her right to a natural delivery—a right that many insisted would lead to the death of her child. The ACLU, a champion of individual rights (including a woman's right to decide whether or not to have an abortion), found itself supporting a very traditional, even fundamentalist religious position.

sacredness of human life *the religious or philosophical belief that human life is sacred and must be respected in all instances*

Two courts in Illinois, including the state Supreme Court, found in the woman's favor, and she was permitted to let the pregnancy, labor, and delivery take their own natural course (which resulted in the birth of a healthy child). The case was further complicated by the maturity of the fetus. Probably capable of surviving outside the womb, this fetus met nearly everyone's definition of a baby. Outside the womb, the right of a baby to medical attention is protected, even if the parents' religious beliefs oppose providing it and favor trusting in the Lord to provide. Almost no one on either side of the abortion debate opposes this position. Similarly, almost no one favors tying a woman down and forcing her to have a cesarean section against her will. Arguing on the basis of *rights*—those of the woman versus those of the fetus—seems incapable of resolving cases like this one.

Nevertheless, people on both sides of the abortion issue insist that their position cannot be compromised. In March 1993, Dr. David Gunn was shot and killed in front of a Florida abortion clinic. His killer insisted that taking one life (Dr. Gunn's) to save hundreds, maybe thousands, of the unborn was legitimate. This utilitarian argument was picked up by a Roman Catholic priest who tried (unsuccessfully) to run a newspaper ad calling the death of an abortionist "justifiable homicide." "If 100 doctors need to die to save over 1 million babies a year, I see it as a fair trade," he said.

Many people have been alarmed by the escalating level of violence, and compromise is beginning to seem more out of reach than ever. Law professor Ronald Dworkin argues that most Americans misunderstand what abortion and euthanasia arguments are really about. In a 1993 book, *Life's Dominion,* he suggests that a shared belief in the sacredness of human life, rather than a debate over personhood and interests, is what is at issue:

> We disagree about abortion not because some of us think, and others deny, that an immature fetus is already a person with interests of its own but, paradoxically, because of an ideal we share. We almost all accept, as the inarticulate assumption behind much of our experience and conviction, that human life in all its forms is *sacred*—that it has intrinsic and objective value quite apart from any value it might have to the person whose life it is.[2]

For some, Dworkin writes, this belief in the sacredness of human life is a matter of religious faith; for others, it is a deeply held philosophical principle.

We can see how deeply this value is embedded in our culture if we look at the debate about euthanasia or, as it is sometimes called, mercy killing. Doctors who knowingly prescribe enough pills for a patient to kill himself or herself or inject a suffering person with lethal drugs, as well as family members who respond to the desperate plea for relief from suffering by a loved one in agony with a bullet through the head are condemned as murderers. Even if people are willing to concede that such a death is in a person's best interest, they may object to taking that life because of the independent and sacred value of all human life.

We routinely use this line of argument in other matters, Dworkin points out. Great works of art, for instance, are preserved not because we believe they have rights or interests, but because of their intrinsic value. The same can be said for an endangered species: What matters is not their rights, but the value they have as living beings that matters. Those on both sides of the debate over abortion and euthanasia share a belief in the sacredness of human life, Dworkin insists; where they differ is in how best to preserve it.[3]

This more abstract argument about the meaning and value of human life both unites us and divides us. As the final act in the drama of life, a death with dignity upholds for many people the sacredness of life. To have our own death managed technologically seems to some a violation of life's sacred character:

> People who dread being kept alive, permanently unconscious or sedated beyond sense, intubated and groomed and tended as vegetables, think this condition degrades rather than respects what has been intrinsically valuable in their own living. Others disagree: They believe, about euthanasia as about abortion, that mere biological life is so inherently precious that nothing can justify deliberately ending it.[4]

If Dworkin is right, the shared belief in the sacredness of human life has at least the potential for shifting the debate over abortion and euthanasia from violent confrontation to dialogue. Many abortion opponents recognize an exception in cases of rape or incest; few advocates of freedom of choice believe an abortion should be undertaken frivolously. Perhaps there is some common ground somewhere in the middle. Would it, for example, be possible to consider as justification for abortion conditions that would seriously damage human life in another form—a child who would be born seriously deformed or the economic burden of another child for a family already living in poverty? Could a belief in the sacredness of human life help us resolve the issue of the woman in Chicago who clearly valued human life even as she put her fetus at risk?

The Interest View

interest view *an ethical principle stating that moral status is based on interests; this is derived from Feinberg's interest principle—to have moral status is to have rights; Steinbock's application is that the capacity for conscious awareness is both a necessary and a sufficient condition for possessing interests*

moral status *existing in such a way as to have claims on others that must be considered from a moral point of view*

In considering the question of moral status, another group of philosophers favors what has come to be called the **interest view,** which maintains that to have **moral status** someone or something must have interests, must be capable of being benefited or harmed or both. This view is derived from philosopher Joel Feinberg's *interest principle* and holds that to have moral status is to have rights—claims against others that they act (or refrain from acting) in certain ways. One clear illustration of the question of rights deriving from moral status is the current debate concerning the rights of both smokers and nonsmokers. According to all moral theories, both smokers and nonsmokers (as human beings) have moral status, which means that their claims must be considered from a moral point of view.[5] The question in this case is, Whose interests should prevail—those of smokers or those of nonsmokers?

The larger ethical question is, Do the dead and the unborn, those in persistent vegetative states, those born without a brain, and other animals and plants have moral status and therefore interests? Applying the interest principle, ethicist Bonnie Steinbock argues that the capacity for *conscious awareness* is both a necessary and a sufficient condition for the possession of interests. By a *necessary condition* we mean one without which the possession of interests cannot apply; a being without conscious awareness does not meet the necessary condition and therefore lacks both interests and moral status. Conscious awareness is also a *sufficient condition,* meaning it alone fulfills the requirement; the possession of some other characteristic—say, language ability—is not also required. So, "nonlinguistic beings, like animals and babies, can have interests, and so, moral status."[6]

According to Steinbock's interpretation of the interest principle, all beings that possess (or once possessed) conscious awareness possess both interests and moral status, which means that they can make claims on us. Conscious awareness implies the ability to be happy or miserable, to feel pleasure or pain, to care what is or is not done to you. Human beings ordinarily meet the requirement of conscious awareness with ease; so do higher animals because they clearly have the capacity to experience pleasure and pain and care what is or is not done to them.

People in a persistent vegetative state, by contrast, lack conscious awareness; they are in the same physiological state as those rendered unconscious through anesthesia, who are incapable of experiencing pain (we know this because they tell us so after they return to consciousness). "The biographical life of the PVS [persistent vegetative state] patient is over, even though he is not biologically dead," Steinbock contends. Whatever reasons we may have for continuing or ceasing treatment, they are not based on the interests of the person.[7]

Oh the tiny cry
Of a pitiful
Cricket
Caught in a hawk's beak
RANSETSU

A similar standard may be applied to anencephalic infants like Theresa. If we determine that they lack conscious awareness, we may conclude they do not have interests because they are incapable of caring what is or is not done to them. Unlike conscious human beings or even dogs and cats, anencephalics may be beyond caring what happens to them and therefore incapable of being harmed. If so, they lack moral status. Does this mean we have the right to harvest their organs? Not without being very clear about when this would and would not be morally acceptable. The same might be said for PVS patients, and we may need to think even longer about harvesting their organs because the issue of *consent* applies to PVS patients (as it does to dead people). Organs cannot and should not be removed without consent. People once alive but now dead, or once alive but now in a persistent vegetative state, have interests based on the conscious awareness they once possessed. Thus, some interests may be understood to survive people's biological lives.

Anencephalic infants, by contrast, have never had conscious awareness and therefore lack interests. Because they have parents (and perhaps siblings), their place in a "network of human relationships" may very well qualify them as persons. Certainly, they deserve to be treated with dignity and respect; certainly, they are the children of their parents, who will love them and grieve for them. In terms of the interest view, however, they may be described as "people who, due to their devastating neurological deficit, cannot be benefitted or harmed." Their parents may well decide, as Theresa's did, that they could best honor her dignity and show her respect by donating her tissues and organs so that others might live.

In contrast with Dworkin's view, which considers the sacredness of human life to be central to the issue, the interest view would not favor protecting persons or things because of intrinsic value. Great works of art, however beautiful and representative of enduring cultural values, do not and cannot have interests. As a result, they can have no claim on us. We must view persons who lack conscious awareness in just this way. Like great works of art, they lack moral status. They are essentially indifferent to what happens to them, and as a result, they have no claims on us for protection.

Virtue Ethics

Whether we look to consequences or the course of duty, natural law, the sacredness of human life, or interests, the question of what to do has become very complex. An alternative ethical tradition shifts the focus from "What should I do?" to "What kind of person should I be?" Ethical questions, according to this tradition, must be based in the larger context of a virtuous character. Sometimes we have the luxury of engaging in debate with others (or within our own minds) about possible alternatives, but in other instances we have no time to think; then our "habits of character" (to use Aristotle's phrase) will prevail. Under these circumstances we will act virtuously (or we will not) because of the kind of people we are.

Action is indeed the sole medium of expression for ethics.
JANE ADDAMS

Consider this illustration: In August 1987, Northwest Airlines Flight 255 crashed within one minute of takeoff. The single survivor was spared because her mother, realizing the plane was going down, unhooked her seat belt, left her own seat, and went to her daughter's seat where she draped her body over the child. The woman's six-year-old son, who perished in the crash along with 155 others, may have seemed to her more able to seek help on his own. For whatever reasons, Paula Ciamaichela Chichan did the one thing that had any chance of helping and succeeded in saving her daughter's life. There was no opportunity for deliberation. From the point of view of **virtue ethics,** we would have to say that she acted from a virtuous character formed long before the tragedy.[8]

virtue ethics *an ethical theory that uses as a moral standard what a virtuous person would do, as opposed to consequences or obligations; the primary question is, What kind of person should I be?*

For Aristotle, *virtue* involves acting according to our highest (and, he believed, uniquely human) ability: the ability to reason. It must be our rational self that informs our ethical choices, even if we lack the time to engage in rational thought. As we observed in Chapter 1, the *Nicomachean Ethics* described the moral virtues as *means,* or midpoints, between two extremes. To behave virtuously or morally, Aristotle believes, one must cultivate the habits of character that lead to moderation. If courage is the mean between rashness and cowardice, then one must reason this to be so and practice acting courageously.

In recent years there has been a resurgence of interest in virtue ethics. Its proponents continue to emphasize that virtue consists in habits of character—that is, in ways of being, rather than in adherence to rules or concern with consequences. The question remains: "How shall I be?," not "What shall I do?" A significant difference, however, is that some modern advocates of virtue ethics disagree with Aristotle that reason is the highest or defining human characteristic. Some philosophers have suggested that reason has gotten us into some strange situations. We have, for instance, reasoned our way into killing each other and exploiting the limited resources of our planet. If reason can lead to such (in their view) unethical outcomes, then perhaps we should look elsewhere for our guiding principle. One place some philosophers are looking these days is to the emotions.

I can reflect light into the dark places of this world—into the black places in the hearts of men—and change some things in some people. Perhaps others may see and do likewise. This is what I am about. This is the meaning of my life.
ALEXANDER PAPADEROS

If we follow the classic Western model for understanding human nature that was laid out for us by Plato and Aristotle and reinforced strongly by Descartes, we will conclude that reason is what sets us apart from other animals and makes us uniquely human. Following this line of reasoning then, it makes perfect sense that living in accordance with our reason will produce a virtuous character. This traditional model of the human person rests on the presumption of the *autonomous self* as the norm and the goal of adult human persons. An autonomous self would and should seek to act in accordance with rational principles.

What if we instead focus on the ideal adult human person as one who is connected with other human persons and is not strictly speaking

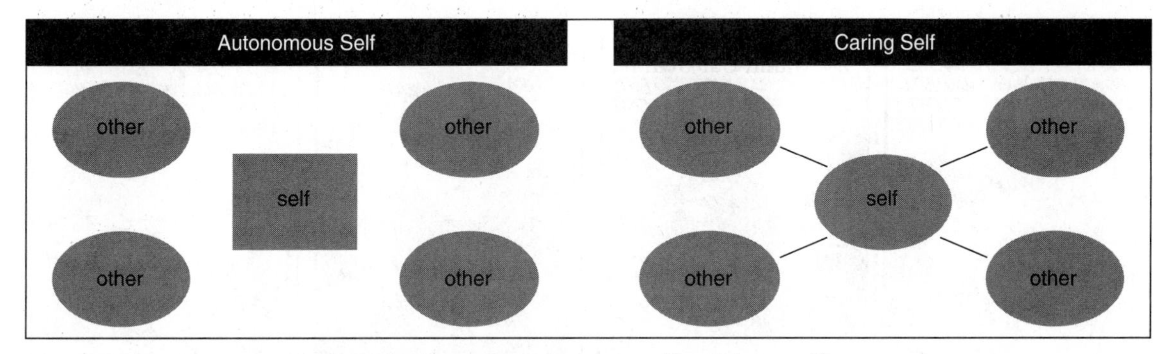

FIGURE 10.1 AUTONOMOUS SELF VERSUS CARING SELF *The virtuous self can be conceived of as separate from or connected with other selves.*

autonomous? Suppose we conclude that reason ought to be practical as well as theoretical and that there should be no sharp divisions between reason and emotion? If we made these assumptions, we might conclude that the norm would be the *caring self* rather than the autonomous self (Figure 10.1). A caring self would cultivate a habit of caring, of being concerned with relationships, of considering the needs of others; the ideal would be interconnectedness rather than autonomy or separateness. Moral behavior would be that which takes an **ethic of care** as its guide.

ethic of care *an ethical theory, which is a variation on virtue ethics, that holds as an ideal the caring self*

Carol Gilligan, in her 1982 book *In a Different Voice,* explains that an autonomous self sees morality in terms of justice, fairness, rules, and rights, whereas a caring self focuses more on people's needs, wants, and aspirations. In our culture, Gilligan argues, men's concern for autonomy tends to lead them to the first viewpoint, whereas women's concern for relationships often leads them to the second. Frequently, Gilligan found, only the male model was regarded as reflecting moral maturity. By this standard, women were sometimes seen as morally immature because of their attention to care rather than abstract standards of justice and right.

Her pathbreaking, although controversial, book has led to a renewed interest in virtue ethics with a focus on emotional rather than rational ways of knowing. As Rita Manning explains, the cultivation of habits of virtue still applies, but the ideal is of a caring self rather than a rational self. The question then becomes, not "What would a rational person do in this situation?" but "What would my ideal caring self do?"

According to virtue ethics, I, as a moral agent, am called upon to adopt a certain perspective and to internalize that perspective so that it becomes a part of me. When this occurs, I will behave according to that perspective as it arises from the depths of my being, rather than applying rules to a given situation. A high level of internalization is what creates a virtuous character. In an ethic of care, the emphasis shifts from knowing to caring. Adopting and internalizing a perspective of caring rather than knowing gives me a caring context from which to act.[9]

As moral agents, our concern would be "to advance the good of the other(s) in the context of a network of care."[10] If we recognize that autonomy

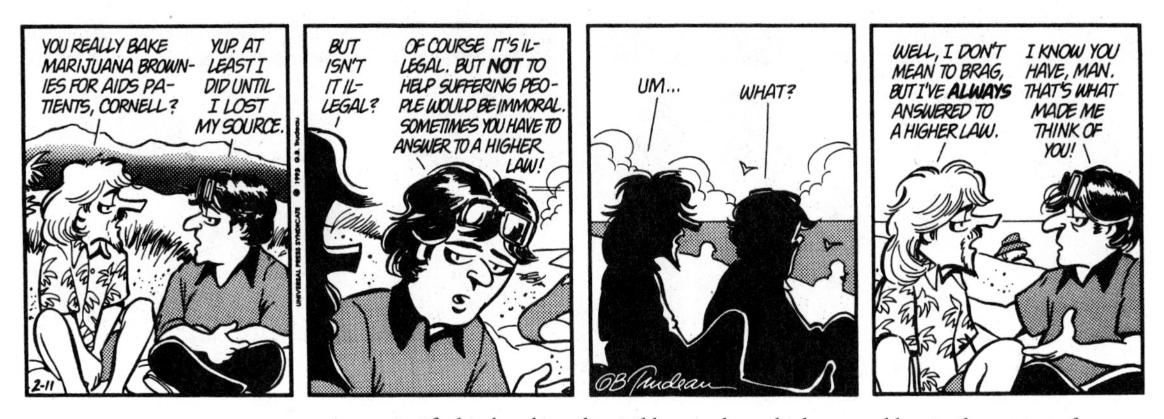

Are we justified in breaking the civil law to obey a higher moral law in the context of an ethic of care?

The dehumanizing of subordinates then appears to have begun with the dehumanizing of oneself. To undo one is to undo both.

R. G. H. SIU

is not the only, or maybe even the most important, value, we may see all our actions in the context of a network of care. This image is significant because a network of care sustains all its members, including the most autonomous and the relatively helpless. There is an element of reciprocity, of alternative giving and receiving, that recognizes that all relationships are mutual. Instead of debating about people's rights, we would focus on caring for them.

Theresa would become a child to be cared for, as would the other children whose failing organs make them vulnerable. Indeed, children and the parenting relationship might become a major focus of ethical theorizing (traditionally, they have not been). Other animals would be seen as part of the network of care, as indeed the whole natural world would be. The net might be cast very wide. If one sees oneself primarily as an autonomous self, there is the temptation to distance oneself from other creatures and from the earth itself, but to see oneself as a caring self is to recognize the deep interconnectedness that exists between all living beings and to recognize mutual obligations among them.

Virtue is not left to stand alone.
He who practices it will have neighbors.

CONFUCIUS

An ethic of care represents something of a departure from a Western tradition that has emphasized individuality and freedom, as well as the separation between knower and known. As Western ethicists consider the caring self as a model, they draw closer to the Asian and African worldviews we have been considering. And there are also resonances with communitarianism.

Asian and African Ethical Theories

The image of a network of care is quite compatible with some Asian and African ethical systems. Arising as it does out of metaphysics, ethics reflects how we see the world and our place within it. The Buddhist and African ethical traditions we examine next have a communitarian focus—that is, the context of moral decision making is larger than the rights or interests of individuals.

Buddhist Ethics

Before we examine Buddhist ethics in some detail, it may be useful to recall that Buddhism offers both a diagnosis of the human condition (as characterized by suffering resulting from attachment) and a prescription for that condition (in the form of nonattachment). The Buddha claimed neither to be a theistic being like Jesus in Christianity, nor a prophet like Muhammad in Islam; the Buddha was instead someone who "got it," who saw the world as it was and is. This is the definition of *enlightenment:* the ability (and the willingness) to see life as it is and to accept it (because there is really no other choice; life is what it is, whether we like it or not).

The Buddha's *sutras* (sermons) were attempts to aid others in seeing things as they really are. In one of the most famous of these sutras, the Buddha simply held up a flower. One person in the crowd smiled, and the Buddha understood that person had become enlightened. When the Buddha spoke, it was to offer suggestions for living life in a less painful way. Unlike the religions of the Book (Judaism, Christianity, and Islam) in which rules for living are laid down by a superior being who demands obedience and judges disobedience, in Buddhism there is only the imperative to wake up and see things as they are.

We are free to remain in ignorance, but our ignorance will cause us suffering. By attachment to things and people, by giving them the power to make us happy or miserable, we make ourselves vulnerable to the inevitable suffering that results when these things or people change, die, or no longer bring us pleasure. If we wish to suffer less, there is only one way to do it: Align ourselves and our actions with the way things actually are. No one is keeping an account book of our good and bad deeds; the suffering we feel is not divine punishment but simply the consequence of our ignorance of the way things are.

The Buddha's suggestions for living are the suggestions of an enlightened person, guideposts along the way from someone who has traveled farther and can help show the path. You are under no obligation to follow them, unless you wish to suffer less. Consider an analogy with the laws of the natural world: Even though in very cold temperatures human flesh will freeze, you may, if you wish, ignore this natural law and remain outside in the cold until you die or at least get frostbite. You may rant and rave about how unfair it is that you cannot go outside in a bathing suit without paying a penalty, but it will not change the way things are. The Buddha advises you to wear a jacket, light a fire, or stay inside.

According to religions of the Book, the human condition is a *fallen* one. Having lost our original innocence in the Garden of Eden, humans are predisposed to brokenness, inauthenticity, and sin. Certain ideal ways of being, often symbolized in the West as a loving attitude toward God and one's fellow beings, represent the goal of human life. We are working toward being loving and are sometimes more and sometimes less successful in our attempts. We might diagram the condition this way:

is . . . ideal

What *is* now exists at some distance from the *ideal.*

In Buddhism, a person who does not understand the true nature of the world is variously described as asleep or drunk; the goal is to wake up or sober up. In this image, the sleeping or drunk person is already conscious of the way things are, even if that consciousness exists at another deeper level; such a person already has the full consciousness that is the goal. We might diagram the condition this way:

is (at a superficial level)
.:
ideal (at a deeper level)

Right now you already possess Buddha-nature; you need only to wake up to that realization.[11] As contemporary Zen Roshi Philip Kapleau puts it, "Buddha-nature is our common birthright. Confirmation of this comes from the highest source, the Buddha himself. On the occasion of his supreme enlightenment he exclaimed, 'Wonder of wonders! All living beings are inherently buddhas . . .'"[12]

Having spoken ill
My lips now
Feel the cold of
Autumn's fatal wind
BASHO

As you may recall from Chapter 2, Buddhism conceives the world as a web of interconnectedness; the Net of Indra, with its grid of crystals reflecting other crystals, captures this image. Nothing stands alone; nothing is or can be separate from anything else. Harm to one part is harm to another; benefit to one part benefits others as well.

This is the foundation for Buddhist ethics. Everything done to any part of the Net affects other parts of the Net. In a very meaningful sense, then, what one person does to another, that person does to himself or herself. This is the meaning of the law of ***karma,*** sometimes called the law of sowing and reaping: Whatever good I do, I do to myself; whatever evil I do, I also do to myself. In my ignorance it may seem to me that I can inflict harm on my foot without harming the rest of me, but if I think this I am simply deluded. As the *Dhammapada* puts it, "For whatever you do, you do to yourself."[13]

karma *in Hinduism and Buddhism, the principle that all actions operate according to causal laws and what I do to another I do to myself; sometimes this law is referred to as the law of sowing and reaping*

Because the Net is a net of interconnectedness, all actions bind us to the chain of cause and effect that keeps us on the wheel of *samsara,* repeating the cycle of birth-death-rebirth. Escape from the wheel can be gained only by recognizing our true nature. Once we wake up and treat others as ourselves, we will have become enlightened, like the compassionate Buddha, and be free from rebirth. The good news is that everyone will make it—eventually; the bad news is that some of us will have to live many lives and suffer many painful experiences until we finally realize the way things really are.

Perhaps the Buddha's counsel "Refrain from harming living things" sounds like "Thou shalt not kill," but by now the difference should be clear. Whereas "Thou shalt not kill" is a divine edict to be disobeyed only at the cost of divine anger, "Refrain from harming living things" is a tip—from someone who sees truly—that may help us wake up sooner and suffer less in the living of our lives. We are of course free to ignore the Buddha's advice—to go on treating others as if they were separate from us.

Things may seem fine until one day they no longer are. Sometimes the law of *karma* is slow in working, but it always works.

All the time I pray to Buddha
I keep on
killing mosquitoes
ISSA

African Ethical Theories

Some of this emphasis on interconnectedness that defines Buddhist ethics also exists in traditional African thought. Like Buddhism, African ethics is not derived from God (even though, unlike Buddhism, traditional African cultures typically assume a supreme being). African ethics springs from a deeply held concept of human nature. We may think of African ethics as a kind of humanism.

A traditional Akan proverb from West Africa states, "When a human being descends from on high, he or she alights in a town." Instead of emphasizing the autonomous individual, African ethics tends to focus on the communal nature of human society and consequently on the reciprocal character of human moral obligations; in this sense, there are some similarities with an ethic of care. "It is a human being that has value," another proverb asserts, emphasizing both the preeminent value of the human person and the importance of human fellowship.[14]

If you do not allow your neighbor to reach nine, you will never reach ten.
AKAN PROVERB

What is therefore good will be that which promotes human interests and is conducive to harmonizing the conflicts that inevitably arise among them. The image of a crocodile with a single stomach but two branching heads locked in conflict depicts the ethical principle that conflicts must be resolved if the organism is to survive. Put another way, moral questions must take the community into account. Although a person is an individual, he or she is not an autonomous individual:

> A human person is essentially the center of a thick set of concentric circles of obligations and responsibilities matched by rights and privileges revolving round levels of relationships irradiating from the consanguinity of household kith and kin, through the "blood" ties of lineage and clan, to the wider circumference of human familihood based on the common possession of the divine spark.[15]

In Akan thought, a person is composed of three elements (*mogya, sunsum, okra*), the last of which comes directly from God and is "a spark of the divine substance" conceived as the **life principle.** As you may recall from Chapter 5, in the Akan language it is called *okra;* in the Ewe language, it is expressed as *Se.* As a direct result of this concept, there is an irreducible human dignity that every person possesses; even a person who does wrong or fails to live up to full personhood cannot forfeit his or her essential value.

life principle *the spark of the divine in each human person that is responsible for an irreducible human dignity, according to traditional African ethical systems*

Because all people possess the divine spark—the life principle—all people deserve the same kind of treatment you expect for yourself. In any interpersonal situation, the test is to put yourself in the other person's position and consider the consequences of your proposed action. This is a modification of the ethical principle that is sometimes called the **golden rule:** "Do unto others as you would have them do unto you." This variation, which we might call the **silver rule,** advises: "Do not do unto others what you would not have them do unto you."[16]

golden rule *"Do unto others as you would have others do unto you."*

silver rule *"Do not do unto others what you would not have them do unto you."*

syntropy *[SIN troh pee] the tendency toward building up, as opposed to entropy, which is a tendency toward falling apart or the breakdown of synthesis*

The divine life force is always working dynamically toward wholeness and healing, "towards building up and not pulling down, towards creating and not destroying and towards synthesis and not conflict."[17] A Western word for this concept is **syntropy**—the tendency toward creative synthesis; this is the opposite of *entropy*—the tendency toward disarray and the breakdown of synthesis. In West African ethical theory, morality is defined in terms of syntropy. Human behavior is right or good not because it conforms to a set of rules, but because it builds up instead of tearing down.[18] In this sense, the Akan ethical system has something in common with Western consequentialist, or teleological, ethical theories.

To behave morally is to behave in conformity with your human nature. Your spark of the divine life principle is both your gift and your obligation. Your behavior can never be evaluated in a vacuum because inevitably you live in a social network with other human beings who, like yourself, possess a spark of the divine. One inescapable fact is the mutual dependence of all people on each other: "A human being is not a palm tree so as to be self-sufficient."[19]

Some African philosophers believe that Western culture has lost sight of this essential truth. The Greek division, begun with the pre-Socratic cosmologists, has led Europeans and North Americans to the mistaken notion that they exist apart from nature and from human society. Living an artificial life divorced from nature, the modern Western person has, in the opinion of African philosopher P. Kaboha, reached a crisis point:

> The person who has broken away from his parents, his society and his roots and is living a new life supported by artificial systems in a cultural and metaphysical vacuum . . . cannot hold the Gods or God as sacred since he does not see his parents, society and ancestors as so sacred. In ancient Greek terms he has committed "hubris," which always led to tragedy.[20]

In both Greek and African traditions, people who fall into *hubris* (arrogance resulting from excessive pride or passion) are always given enough rope to hang themselves. In Kaboha's view, this is just what is happening now that technology has become a god in Western culture. "'Western' or 'Westernized' man . . . inevitably is being taught a lesson. He has created toys that can destroy him and, like a forest fire started by a child, are out of control."[21] It is time for a humbler approach to nature, and Kaboha suggests that it may be Africa's turn to play the role of missionary to Europe, the Americas, and Asia.[22]

One person's path will intersect with another's before long.
AKAN PROVERB

When one lives closer to nature rather than in artificial, constructed surroundings, one realizes that scientific logic does not explain every phenomenon. The integration of all life and the influence of the life principle are immediate and obvious.[23] An ideal life would be defined by such events as getting married and having children, good health, and a natural death in old age, rather than by the achievement of power, prestige, and financial success.[24] Creativity in all its forms would be esteemed as expressive of the life principle and as conducive to the good of the person and the culture.

If the ideal life revolves around a good marriage and well-raised children, then it would be irrational to place restrictions on sexual relations between unmarried people. Whereas married people, who would be expected to form and maintain a stable union, might be prohibited from engaging in sexual activity outside the marriage bond, an unmarried couple would be encouraged to seek "full knowledge of each other, moral, psychological, sexual and so on."[25] Abstract laws, such as those in the Judaic and Christian traditions, would make no sense in a society that honors the creative principle of the world as the highest good. Clearly, there would be no sexual free-for-all, but sexual curiosity would seem as natural and as healthy as scientific curiosity currently seems in more technological cultures.

We have been looking at different ways in which three cultures—Western, Asian, and African—have conceived ethical theories. One of the basic ethical questions is indeed how one ought to behave, but there is another fundamental question to address: How free are we to choose what we do and do not do?

Everybody is important. There is strength in unity. If we take any part away, we no longer have a complete work of art. It's good to stick together, good to work together. It takes a whole village to raise a child.

Makonde community sculpture/Courtesy of the African Art Museum of Maryland/Photo by Quentin Kardos.

The Question of Human Freedom: How Much Do We Have?

To explore this question, we begin with theories of determinism that assert constraints on human freedom—ways in which we are unfree. Next we examine existentialism, an ethical position that insists we have a total, radical freedom. Finally, we consider conditions under which a person might be found not morally accountable for committing immoral acts, and we conclude by looking at the appropriate response to massive evil on the scale of the Holocaust.

Determinism

Among the central issues raised by ethical theory is, How much freedom do we have? If we lack freedom, then we cannot be held responsible for our moral choices. If our actions are determined, then human nature, society, God, or other forces beyond our control must be held accountable for what occurs. Only if our actions are free can we be held accountable. As the rock group Rush points out, "Free Will" is the real issue in ethical theory.

Some philosophers have held that human actions are not free. Known as *determinism,* this position holds that causal laws rule all occurrences in the universe. Let's distinguish between two major forms of determinism—**hard determinism** and soft determinism (Figure 10.2). Although we may believe we are acting freely, hard determinism would insist that this belief

hard determinism
the view that the will of an individual is not free and is instead determined by factors beyond his or her control and/or responsibility

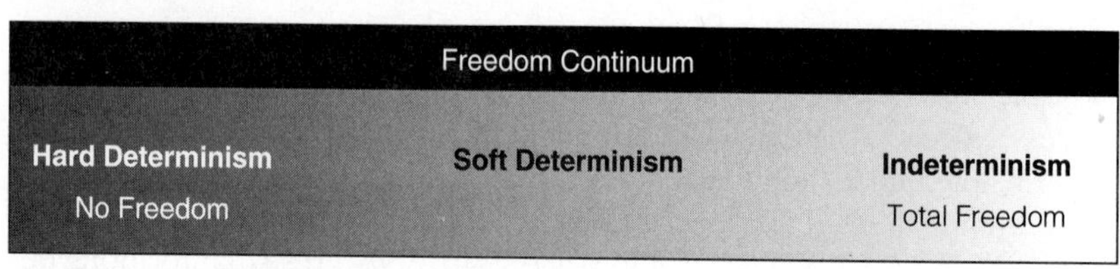

FIGURE 10.2 THE FREEDOM CONTINUUM

is an illusion; the truth is that each of our actions is determined by factors beyond our control. From the point of view of hard determinism, there can be no real moral responsibility; a life of crime that may appear to be freely chosen is actually the result of heredity and environment, and we cannot legitimately indict an individual for genetic and societal influences that are beyond his or her control.

soft determinism/compatibilism *the view that the will of an individual remains free even if some of that individual's choices are determined by previous experiences*

Soft determinism, or **compatibilism,** asserts that determinism and free will (its opposite) are compatible. It shares with hard determinism the belief that all human actions are determined and accepts the role of our early experiences, including choices made for us in childhood, in shaping us into the people we are today. To the extent that my action is caused by some outside force, I cannot be held responsible for it—that is, if I am forced to do something or constrained from doing something. In most cases, however, I must indeed accept responsibility. If the "causes" of my actions are internal ones—part of my reasoning process—then my will remains free and I am responsible for my choices.

Recent work in the field of psychology has added an interesting twist to the question of human freedom. Beginning with John Gray's assertion that men are from Mars and women are from Venus, there has been a tendency among some psychologists to claim innate or nearly innate gender tendencies. If we are born a certain way, how can we be held responsible for being that way? Some theorists working in a field called evolutionary psychology have made even bolder suggestions that have been turned into sound bites: Men are polygamous, women monogamous. Women select mates on the basis of wealth and status; men select mates based on reproductive potential. Early in 2000, Dr. Randy Thornhill and Dr. Craig Palmer claimed that rape could be best understood as a sexual act with its roots in evolution. Their book *A Natural History of Rape: Biological Bases of Sexual Coercion* (MIT Press, 2000) seemed to suggest that much of what humans do today is a result of behavior that evolved during the Pleistocene Era, millions of years ago.[26] One question to ask ourselves here is the following: Even if this is the case (which many people question), would there be any basis in the modern world on which to excuse rape—a crime with no social approval?

existentialism *emphasizes the uniqueness and freedom of the human person as an individual (what makes each life a unique, personal experience) as opposed to the essence of a human being (what makes all of us alike)*

Existentialism: A Radical Concept of Freedom

In dramatic contrast with determinism, **existentialism** affirms the absolute freedom of the individual—what we might call indeterminism. We studied some religious existentialists (Kierkegaard, Buber, and Tillich) in Chapter 4, but here we will concentrate on **atheistic existentialism,** which developed in Europe during the chaotic time between the two world wars. Shocked at the reality of "man's inhumanity to man," some philosophers rejected the old certainties that, in their judgment, might have produced the postmodern world or were at least inadequate to deal with it. Rejecting claims to universal truth and belief in God as incompatible with the uncertainty and brutality of reality, they affirmed the uniqueness of the existing individual.

atheistic existentialism *the view that, since there is no God and no resulting moral laws, individuals are free to determine their own human nature through choices for which they stand accountable*

There are no *fixed essences,* insisted French philosopher Jean-Paul Sartre. A person is neither fixed by heredity nor trapped by environment, but instead is free at every moment to actualize any possibility. The Greek rationalist tradition and the Judaic and Christian religious traditions had erred, in Sartre's judgment, by claiming that each person had some essence as a thinking thing or a divine creation. These essences had the effect of limiting a person's possibilities and determining what that person's life and choices might be.

As an alternate vision, Sartre proposed the theory that *existence precedes essence.* In other words, first a person exists as a unique individual with no preconceived definition determining what he or she will become; all possibilities are open to him or her:

> What do we mean by saying that existence precedes essence? We mean that man first of all exists, encounters himself, surges up in the world—and defines himself afterwards. If man as the existentialist sees him is not definable, it is because to begin with he is nothing. He will not be anything until later, and then he will be what he makes of himself. Thus, there is no human nature, because there is no God to have a conception of it . . . Man is nothing else but what he makes of himself.[27]

Programming Language #17, named SARTRE after the existentialist philosopher, is extremely unstructured. Statements in SARTRE have no purpose; they just are. The SARTRE programs are left to define their own functions.
AUTHOR UNKNOWN

In the choices of a life lived *authentically,* each individual has the potential to become a self that is of his or her own making. The crucial difference between existentialism and previous views is that the emphasis is on the radical freedom of the person to do and be anything at all. There are no limitations; everything is possible, and all choices are free choices.

Indeed, Sartre used a startling phrase. We are, he said, *condemned to be free.* At first glance this may seem more than a little strange, especially to Westerners nurtured on freedom and raised to value highly the rights of the individual. What Sartre meant is that we have no option but to be free, and we cannot claim unfreedom:

> Everything is indeed permitted if God does not exist, and man is in consequence forlorn, for he cannot find anything to depend upon either within or outside himself. He discovers forthwith, that he is without excuse . . . there is no determinism—man is free, man is freedom. Nor, on the other hand, if God does not exist, are we provided with any values or commands that could legitimize our behavior . . . That is what I mean when I say that man is condemned to be free. Condemned, because he did not create himself, yet is nevertheless at liberty, and from the moment that he is thrown into the world he is responsible for everything he does.[28]

Where there is no freedom, there can be no morality.
ALISON NEILANS

All of us, at times, want to say that we could not help doing what we did, that we are not really responsible. Sartre asserted that this attempt to

bad faith *in the existentialist philosophy of Sartre, acting as if one is not free (being-in-itself), denying the freedom and responsibility of the human person (being-for-itself), behaving inauthentically*

THE MAKING OF A PHILOSOPHER

Jean-Paul Sartre
(1905–1980)

This leading French existentialist was a precocious child who read voraciously and chose a literary career while still very young. At the Sorbonne he excelled in philosophy and met Simone de Beauvoir with whom he would share a lifelong relationship. During a period of study in Berlin, he became acquainted with the writings of Kierkegaard and Heidegger while witnessing Hitler's rise to power. Back in France, he was drafted into the French army as a private and, in 1940, was taken prisoner by the Germans. This experience helped form his radical concept of existential freedom—even under outward conditions of unfreedom. Nine months later he was back in France, writing for a lively underground paper published by the Resistance and edited by Albert Camus. After the war, Sartre toured the United States and lectured in American colleges and universities. His literary works include plays, novels, and short stories and have contributed as much as his formal philosophical writing to interest in existentialism.

avoid freedom constitutes **bad faith** for it denies the freedom that makes humanity possible and tries to place responsibility on someone or something other than ourselves. This is an inauthentic way to live, and it denies us the possibility of becoming a self.

Sartre referred to trees and rocks as being-in-itself because they are passive and cannot shape what they will be; unlike humans, they are acted upon and do not act independently. Humans, by contrast, are being-for-itself, and our lives are literally in our own hands. For whatever we become, we have only ourselves to thank or blame; there is no one else, nothing else to praise or curse. Even if we are physically imprisoned, as Sartre was during the Nazi occupation of his native France, options are open to us.

If we are left with only the choice between giving in to despair or retaining an attitude of resistance, we still have options; this is what distinguishes us from trees and stones. As we act and accept responsibility for our actions, we are going about the task of creating a human nature for ourselves. Traditional thought had given that privilege and responsibility to God, but Sartre insisted that it is the human person—the *being-for-itself*—who has the power of creation. We might think of ourselves as potters, shaping the artistic creation that is ourselves.

To deny this uniquely human freedom is to act in bad faith. In Sartre's ethical system, this is the only immoral thing that it is possible to do. If I pretend I am being-in-itself and blame forces outside myself for what is happening to me, I am denying reality and acting immorally. It is sometimes tempting to do this, Sartre admitted, but to do so is to pass up the power and beauty of the human condition.

As an illustration, Sartre told the story of a young woman who consents to go out with a young man who, she knows, is intent on seducing her. In the course of the evening, the young man takes her hand and says, "I find you so attractive," and she allows her hand to be held without making a decision either to consent to or to reject the seduction.[29] It is tempting, Sartre admitted, for her to postpone such a decision, to pretend that her hand somehow does not belong to her. If she does this, she avoids the decision of whether to take the first step in the dance of seduction or to announce her intention not to dance; either decision is completely morally acceptable to Sartre. Either one affirms her status as being-for-itself. She can in good faith accept his advance and let nature take its course, or she can, also in good faith, reject it—for any number of reasons. She can say, "I don't engage in premarital sex" or "I'm afraid of getting AIDS" or "You don't turn me on." All these responses are also morally acceptable; what is not morally acceptable is pretending that there is no decision to be made. A human being is not a table or a stone, and to pretend to be one is to break the moral code of existentialism.

Atheistic existentialists assert that existence is absurd. There is no God and therefore no moral law. Life is filled with uncertainty and despair, and at the end death awaits. All the comforts of the old certainties no longer apply, if they ever did. The good are not rewarded and the evil go unpunished; we are born, we live briefly, and we die. Between birth and death there is the opportunity, unique to human beings, to fashion an authentic self. It is all we have—and for existentialists like Sartre, it is quite a lot.

What must be avoided at all costs is the *groupthink* that exists in large, dogmatic organizations. If you belong to a church, for example, there are some tenets you must believe in and others in which you may not believe; your individual choices are precluded. The same is true for informal membership in a group or a gang: Certain attitudes and judgments will be expected of you; you will be strongly discouraged from adopting any opinion that differs from the group's position. To submit to this kind of pressure, Sartre felt, is to act in bad faith.

I am the master of my fate
I am the captain of my soul.
Oh S---!

SEEN ON A BUTTON

When he joined the Communist Party, Sartre's friends accused him of this very error, insisting he was acting in bad faith. How, they demanded, can you join a political party, any political party, and expect to live authentically? Although he was persuaded of the rightness of the goals of the Communist Party, Sartre eventually felt compelled to resign. He was unable to reconcile membership with his own views about the necessary independence of the individual.

Ziggy cannot be held responsible—but can we?

Similarly, Sartre argued that love automatically puts a person in bad faith. Even though in an absurd world it might seem that love would provide needed comfort and ease the despair engendered by absurd existence, for Sartre the price seemed much too high. Once we love and are loved, we become slaves to love, modifying our opinions and our actions to retain the favor of the beloved. For fear of losing the love we have become dependent upon, we do certain things and do not do other things. For Sartre, living an authentic existence is impossible if we must check each action against the imagined judgment of the person who fulfills our need for love. We might observe, however, that just as Sartre spent some years as a member of the Communist Party, he also spent twenty years in a long-term love relationship with Simone de Beauvoir, whose ideas we discussed in Chapter 9. For Sartre, as for most of us, some ideas about which he had intellectual certainty were very difficult to live. He remained persuaded that organizations and love relationships put a person in bad faith, but he followed the natural human tendency to ally himself with both.

Excusability

Existentialists like Sartre seem unwilling to excuse anyone from responsibility for their moral choices; for them, the making of a self depends on being accountable, a condition that is directly responsible for personhood. If we grant this premise as a moral ideal, then we must still consider whether there are any conditions under which we might hold a person *not morally accountable* for an objectively immoral act.

Today we live in a society suffering from ethical rickets.

RITA MAE BROWN

Late in 1993 we learned that researchers had deliberately subjected 800 people, without their informed consent, to radiation exposure in an experimentation program during the Cold War. In one study, terminally ill patients were given plutonium; in another, the testicles of male prisoners were irradiated to determine how much exposure to X rays made a man sterile; a third project fed "mentally retarded" children trace amounts of radioactive elements in their breakfast cereal to measure their effects on human metabolism. Defenders of the program argue that much of value has been learned, and they point out that much less was known then about the effects—especially the long-term effects—of radiation. Critics attack the arrogance of the experimenters and cite the similarity of these experiments to those conducted in Nazi death camps, where informed consent was also totally lacking.

With the hindsight of today, are we justified in pointing the finger at these scientists, or should their actions be excused because they were acting according to then-accepted research norms and available knowledge? So little was known then about X rays that devices emitting them were used to measure foot size in shoe stores and their power was offered as an advanced method for removing tonsils. We reject these methods today because of what we now know, but how much of what happened in the past are we willing to attribute to *excusable ignorance of consequences*?[30]

In a classic ethical dilemma, another problem is posed this way: Mr. X's wife is dying. There is a drug that can save her life, but it is very costly and he cannot afford to buy it. The pharmacist understands the problem but is unwilling to establish a precedent by giving away the drug. Should the man steal it? If he does, would we be willing to excuse him from an objectively immoral act (stealing) because of a lack of alternatives? Think about some of the ethical positions we have discussed in this chapter; should we focus mainly on the sacredness of human life, or consider the interests of all the parties, or adopt an ethic of care? Is stealing really the only alternative open to Mr. X?

Suppose we learn that a mass murderer was subjected to extreme and sadistic brutality as a child; was this person warped irreparably by those early experiences of cruelty? Even though this person has murdered several children with no remorse and has even expressed an inclination to do the same thing given similar circumstances, would we grant that the murderer's actions should be excused because he was acting under constraints? Or are there crimes so unacceptable there is no appeal to **excusability?**

excusability *the state of being excused from moral responsibility for an act that is objectively immoral*

Radical Evil and the Question of Punishment

What about crimes so brutal and so large-scale that we barely have moral language in which to speak about them? The Nazi Holocaust in which millions of people were systematically exterminated is such a case. So are the atrocities committed by the military dictatorship of Argentina between 1976 and 1983. The contemporary philosopher Carlos Santiago Nino believes we must confront massive human rights violations and exact some kind of retroactive justice:

> How shall we live with evil? . . . Massive human rights violations involve what Kant called "radical evil"—offenses against human dignity so widespread, persistent, and organized that normal moral assessment seems inappropriate. If someone had confronted Adolf Hitler and told him that his acts were wrong, it would have sounded almost laughable. Wrong is

> too weak an adjective . . . Other words of moral condemnation, like "atrocious" or "abhorrent," express our emotional revulsion more strongly, but do not clarify the descriptive content. Thus our moral discourse appears to reach its limit when dealing with deeds of this type.[31]

The first problem we must face is that those who perpetrate radical evil seem to be operating outside the moral system most of us accept. Their actions seem as alien to us as would those of a people who did not share our concepts of space and time. How, Nino wonders, can we legitimately judge such actions in terms of our own morality? Furthermore, dictators such as Hitler clearly have a strong and sincere conviction that what they are doing is right. If we accept the lawbreaking of civil disobedience, even when we may dispute the convictions behind it, does this muddy our moral condemnation of radical evil? Most ambiguous of all is the realization that massive human rights violations can only be carried out if many people participate to a greater or lesser extent, or at least acquiesce, or perhaps ignore what is going on. If almost everyone is guilty, whom do we try?[32]

In a larger sense, how can any punishment be appropriate, given the magnitude of the crime? If capital punishment is the sentence for murder, what more can or should we do to the person who plans or orders the murder of millions? Another modern philosopher, Hannah Ahrendt, studied the character of Adolf Eichmann, one of the last Nazi war criminals to be apprehended. He had no special hatred toward his victims and was extremely respectful of "law and order." His personal objective was furthering his own career; causing harm to others was a necessary consequence of pursuing this objective. Shocked by this indifference, Ahrendt called it the "banality of evil." For Eichmann, the deaths of millions had no more significance than our destruction of an anthill might have.[33]

If there is no really proportionate punishment, what can a society do to achieve justice retroactively? Nino favors trials on the model of the Nuremburg Trials that followed World War II. The first benefit is a public acknowledgment of the scope and nature of the atrocities, something that repressive regimes take great pains to conceal. The very nature of a trial, especially one in which the legal rights of the defendant(s) are meticulously protected, highlights (by contrast) the unlawful actions of the accused. Perhaps the most significant benefit, Nino believes, is that:

> Trials enable the victims of human rights abuses to recover their self-respect as holders of legal rights . . . their suffering is listened to in the trials with respect and sympathy. The atrocities are publicly and openly discussed and their perpetrators' acts are officially condemned. The true story receives official sanction. This process not only assuages the desire for revenge but reconstitutes the self-respect of the victim.[34]

Trials promote a public discussion that is emotionally cathartic (in somewhat the same way Aristotle saw Athenian tragedies to be) and builds public solidarity. Their value is not compromised even if pardons are issued at the end of the trial, as was the case in Argentina.

THE MAKING OF A PHILOSOPHER

Carlos Santiago Nino
(1943–1993)

Born in Buenos Aires, Argentina, Nino trained in the law and held a doctorate in jurisprudence (J.D.). He became involved in politics during the early 1980s in an effort to restore democracy in Argentina. The atrocities committed by the military dictatorship prompted him to think deeply about human rights and especially about their violation in instances of radical evil. How a society can best recover from massive human rights violations is the topic of his final book, *Radical Evil on Trial.* As a professor in the philosophy of law and as advisor to Argentine President Raul Alfonsin on human rights and constitutional reform, Nino helped the modern world cope with the results of radical evil. Besides his work in Latin America, Nino was a visiting professor at Harvard Law School, Yale Law School, New York University School of Law, Miami Law School, and the University of California at Los Angeles. In 1993 Nino died suddenly while working on reform of the Bolivian constitution.

The hottest places in hell are reserved for those who, in a time of great moral crisis, maintain their neutrality.

DANTE

The Question of Human Freedom: How Much Should We Have?

In one sense, the technology of war makes modern holocausts possible. Technology is of course neutral, but as it grows, so do our options. Because we can know and do so many new things, most of which lack an ethical framework, the question of how much freedom we should have is a crucial one. How much, for instance, do we want to know (and want others to know) about who is genetically ensured of getting certain diseases during their lifetimes? Once we have knowledge, it becomes difficult to ignore because "bad genes" create ethical dilemmas. What we know about the effects of a pregnant woman's lifestyle on a developing fetus creates another set of problems. How extensive are our obligations to one another? We'll explore some dramatic and some everyday issues that touch on the ethical dilemmas created by this world of seemingly unlimited possibilties. How much freedom should we have?

The Human Genome Project, Cloning, and In Vitro Fertilization

There is no monster more destructive than the inventive mind that has outstripped philosophy.
ELLEN GLASGOW

In the late 1980s the U.S. government undertook an ambitious project to map in detail the human genome and to determine not only what separates us from chimpanzees but also to locate the gene for each trait that makes up a human. Within each human cell, there are somewhere between 50,000 and 100,000 genes, "spread through twenty-four chromosomes, ordinarily X and Y, and the twenty-two others." The genes are strands of deoxyribonucleic acid (DNA) arranged in a double-helix pattern, and the sequence in which the rungs that join the two strands of the helix are arranged determines the genetic code—the hereditary information that makes us what we are.[35]

In June 2000, scientists announced that they had nearly finished sequencing the entire human genome, the first phase in compiling a "complete operating manual of the human machine." Although each of us, with the exception of identical twins, is one of a kind, the sequencing of the human genome also reveals our overwhelming similarities. Announcing the breakthrough, President Clinton said, "In genetic terms all human beings, regardless of race, are more than 99.9 percent the same. Modern science has confirmed what we first learned from ancient faiths. The most important fact of life on this earth is our common humanity."[36]

The next step involves annotation, finding all the genes and figuring out what they do. Dr. Victor A. McKusick of Johns Hopkins University likens this task to discovering a vast encyclopedia of information (in this case life's encyclopedia) that lacks any kind of organization. "There is no index, no table of contents, no headings, no nothing," according to one of Dr. McKusick's colleagues Dr. David Vale, thus, no efficient way to extract the sea of information the genome contains. Annotation will clear the way for other breakthroughs—pinpointing diagnoses of illnesses, creating drugs that target metabolic processes like smart bombs, identifying the families of genes that predispose people to cancer, mental illness, Alzheimer's, asthma, and so forth. "Almost any disease you can think of has at least some genetic predispositon," McKusick said.[37]

And, therein lies the problem. Emerging information from what has been called "The Book of Life" is already creating ethical dilemmas. As we learn to read the genetic code prenatally, we will inevitably sort what we find into "good" and "bad" genes. Is there a danger of creating a genetic underclass? People can already be genetically screened for certain inherited diseases such as cystic fibrosis and Tay-Sachs disease and then advised, if they are carriers, about whether or not to conceive a child.

Because Tay-Sachs appears 100 times more frequently among French Canadians and Ashkenazi Jews from Central and Eastern Europe, the Committee to Prevent Jewish Genetic Diseases is currently offering a blood-screening test to young Orthodox Jews in the United States, Canada, and Israel and making dating recommendations. Once the blood test is done, each person receives a six-digit identification number; when couples start dating, they can exchange numbers. Of the 50,000 people tested by 1994, eighty couples were told they were "genetically incompatible"; a few decided to marry anyway and take the 25 percent risk a child born to them would develop the disease.

The Foundation on Economic Trends is calling for a public debate on the issue.[38] Although the Committee for Prevention of Jewish Genetic Diseases refuses to label individuals "carriers" and advises only on the "genetic incompatibility" of the couple, the implications of labeling are far reaching. Once people are labeled as "carriers" of certain diseases, should businesses be allowed to genetically screen applicants with an eye to keeping down future health-care costs? Many insurance companies are already refusing coverage to people who are genetically predisposed to developing certain conditions (like colon or breast cancer).

When we acquire information, the ethical question is, What should we be allowed to do with it as a society? If health care is supported in part by your tax dollars, should I be allowed to conceive a child genetically likely to have a severe abnormality? Many ancient societies, including the highly sophisticated cultures of Greece and Mandarin China, permitted (even urged) infanticide in the case of deformed or otherwise unthriving babies. Facing a population explosion, modern-day China has been limiting family size by government decree. Should there be unlimited freedom to bear children if some will be killed through infanticide, others will have lifelong illnesses requiring public support, and all children place a strain on an already overburdened ecosystem? Who should make these decisions?

Perhaps even more problematic is the issue of cloning. After we learned about Dolly, the sheep clone, and a Texas millionaire offered $5 million to clone a dog named Missy, it was only a matter of time before someone tried to clone a human being. Dr. Richard Seed got a lot of publicity when he claimed to be in the process of working out the details of how to clone himself, using his wife as the "surrogate mother." This, he claimed would defuse criticism that he was taking advantage of women desperate to be mothers by using an unproven procedure. Meanwhile, at the Roslin Institute in Scotland, where Dolly was cloned, they are working on trying to create a genetically altered cloned pig that can produce harvestable pig organs that the human body won't reject. The goal, according to a Roslin spokesperson, is "a production line," serving up organs on demand.[39]

And, it's only a matter of time, according to some theorists, before we have computer chips powerful enough to store your knowledge and even your "consciousness" so that, after the death of your body, they could be uploaded into the brain of a clone. Rosalind Picard, an M.I.T. computer expert predicts that people will not be able to resist calling it a "soul chip," although she personally believes the only way to impart a soul is through procreation.[40] This highlights the key issue of concern for most people. Would cloning generate a soul—something only God is supposed to be able to do—or would the resulting clone be souless? These alternatives may be equally frightening if you believe in the existence of something called a soul. If you don't, cloning does not present those problems. Whether or not cloning will be banned will ultimately be a political decision, but one with ethical implications.

Technology evolves so much faster than wisdom.
JENNIFER STONE

An interesting twist on the issue of reproductive technology and human freedom has surfaced in the context of *in vitro fertilization*. Several women who were long past the age of natural childbearing have opted for implanted donor eggs that were fertilized by their husbands' sperm. A wealthy London businesswoman, aged fifty-nine, and her husband, aged forty-five, became the parents of twins, igniting a significant ethical debate. "Women do not have the right to have a child," the British secretary of health told the BBC, "the child has a right to a suitable home." Charging sexism, the woman's physician said there was no reason a woman in her fifties should not have a child. "A man can have a child at that age and everyone says, 'Isn't he clever,'" Dr. Severino Antinori insisted, "but those same people say that a woman of fifty-five is a dishrag."[41]

Another of Antinori's patients was even older. Rosanna Dalla Corte, believed at age sixty-one to be the oldest woman ever to become pregnant, made the decision, along with her husband Mauro, to have a baby when their only son was killed in an automobile accident.[42] According to Mark Siegler, director of the Center for Medical Clinical Ethics at the University of Chicago, "The history of medicine has been devoted to overcoming the natural lottery, the hand fate has dealt each one of us. We are already pushing the bounds of attractiveness, sexuality, human well-being. Why draw the line at reproduction?"[43] One critical issue may be who will rear the children if older parents die while their offspring are still young.

Because donor eggs are in very short supply and the wait is often three years or more, some physicians have begun using eggs from aborted female fetuses for in vitro fertilization. At a relatively early period in prenatal development, female fetuses already possess their full lifetime complement of millions of eggs. This practice has provoked an even more intense ethical controversy. It is one thing to have a biological mother you have never met (the egg donor); it is quite another to have as a biological mother someone who has never lived at all. How would a ten-year-old child react to learning that his or her mother was an aborted fetus? Of course, the alternative is that the child asking the question would not exist at all.

Slightly less disturbing is the practice of producing offspring from the gametes of dead people. Those who are facing life-threatening illnesses might have their eggs or sperm frozen before undergoing chemotherapy and being rendered infertile. With the help of a surrogate mother, grandparents are getting to know the grandchildren from their long dead children (using eggs fertilized and frozen before their deaths). And, in a procedure some have likened to rape, sperm can be removed from comatose and even dead men to be saved for future paternity. According to a 1997 survey, 14 clinics in 11 states were engaged in sperm retrieval. There is even a term for the no-longer-living father—sperminator![44] In some cases, the surviving spouse uses the harvested egg or sperm to complete the parenthood the couple had dreamed about or at least discussed. But, in other cases, it is the grandparents or other relatives who are choosing to bring a child into the world with one dead parent and one unknown parent (the donor of the missing gamete—egg or sperm). What are the moral implications of this kind of technology-driven wizardry?

Couples who conceive a child in the usual way are already able to know many characteristics of their unborn child through *amniocentesis,* a procedure in which fetal cells are removed from the amniotic fluid and analyzed. Suppose a couple decided to abort all female fetuses and wait for a male child, or the reverse? When the human genome project is completed, should people be permitted to abort a child with undesirable or less desirable characteristics? What about *gene splicing*—substituting one trait for another?

Maternal Obligations to Fetuses

A pregnant woman, injured in an accident on the German autobahn, entered a persistent vegetative state. Even though no one expected her ever to recover or even regain consciousness, the hospital decided to keep her body alive to allow her unborn child to develop to term. While the controversy over this decision raged, she miscarried and was then allowed to die. In Washington, D.C., a young woman who was dying of cancer was ordered by the court to undergo a cesarean delivery in an attempt to save her twenty-six-week-old fetus; both died.[45]

Cases like these raise the question of maternal obligations to fetuses. Suppose I smoke, drink alcohol, or use drugs, all of which are known to be harmful to developing fetuses. Should I have the freedom to continue doing these things while I am pregnant? Should the health-care system or the government be permitted to intervene and enforce behavior changes in me on behalf of the fetus I am nurturing?

What if I refuse to abandon these practices; should my child, after birth, be allowed to sue me? A Florida woman was convicted of delivering cocaine to her newborn through the umbilical cord, and a Massachusetts woman was charged with vehicular homicide after she crashed her car while intoxicated, killing her 8½-month-old fetus.[46]

No woman wants an abortion as she wants an ice cream cone or a Porsche. She wants an abortion as an animal caught in a trap wants to gnaw off its own leg.
FREDERICA MATTHEWES-GREEN

Opponents of abortion claim that pregnant women owe developing fetuses the right to life. Whatever sacrifices may be necessary, they say, we must respect the fetus's right to life. In response to this argument, philosopher Judith Jarvis Thomson has developed an interesting thought experiment. Imagine that you wake up and find yourself connected by tubes with an unconscious person you are told is a famous violinist. He has, it turns out, a fatal kidney disease, and because you alone have the correct blood type to filter his blood (as well as your own), the Society of Music Lovers has kidnapped you and is forcing you to provide this service for nine months, after which time the famous violinist will have recovered.

If we grant that the famous violinist is certainly a person with a right to life, do we also grant that you would be violating his right to life by unplugging yourself? Thomson believes that it is possible to terminate the life of an innocent person (the violinist) without violating his right to life. Her thesis is that the right to life "does not necessarily include getting whatever you need to live."[47] To understand this thesis, let's consider another example.

Our Obligations to One Another

A friend of mine has a brother who also has a serious kidney disease. It turned out that my friend was a good tissue match for his brother, and the family put strong pressure on him to donate a kidney to his brother. The situation seemed clear to them: He could save his brother's life by donating one of his two healthy, functioning kidneys. Although my friend loved his brother, he was not immediately prepared to undergo painful and serious major surgery, especially since his brother's disease would destroy the donated kidney after five years or so and require the whole process to begin again. In the end, he gave in and donated the kidney.

What do you think his ethical obligations were? Would he have been justified in refusing? Did his brother's right to life require him to donate a kidney? A couple whose teenaged daughter developed leukemia made the decision to conceive another child so that (if their tissues matched) cells from the baby's umbilical cord could be used to save the older girl's life. Many criticized their actions on Kantian grounds, claiming they were using the unborn baby merely as a means to an end. Although the story had a happy ending—the easily donated cells from the baby saved the older sister's life—the case raises interesting ethical issues. What if a couple chose to have a baby in order to harvest its heart or liver to save an existing child? How could the right to life be applied in situations like this?

These are troublesome questions, and there appear to be no easy solutions to them. As we observed in Chapter 9, where one person's rights end and another's begin is sometimes difficult to decide. In a culture strongly committed to freedom and individuality, asking a person to consider the greater social good may provoke an angry response. The technological advances of the past few decades have made it increasingly more likely that at some point in our lives each of us will face the wrenching life-and-death decisions or the troubling moral dilemmas described earlier. It's important to remember, though, that ethics concerns all moral choices, even those made in the course of living an everyday, unextraordinary life.

Everyday Ethics

Would you lie to protect a friend? Work for a company that engaged in what you considered unsavory practices? Tell someone you loved him or her in order to have sex with them? Ask your family to cover for you as you engage in forbidden activities? Sell secret knowledge about a now-famous person to the tabloids? Ethical challenges that will never make the headlines arrive unannounced into every person's life. Now that you have some knowledge about theories of ethical decision making, let's take a look at some everyday challenges you might have already faced.

True friendship is never tranquil.
MARIE DE RABUTIN-CHANTAL, MARQUISE DE SÉVIGNÉ

Friendship lightens our burdens and magnifies our joys. A friend can be a sounding board, a shoulder to cry on, a kick in the pants. Bound by neither blood nor law, most of us would willingly do a lot for our friends. Friendship seems sacred. That's why so many people were outraged to learn that Linda Tripp had drawn out her friend Monica Lewinsky in taped phone conversations and then made those emotional and intimate exchanges public. Tripp herself has claimed she was doing her patriotic duty by exposing the President's immoral behavior. Does a duty such as this justify betraying a friendship? Can you imagine a situation in which obedience to a higher moral principle might lead you to betray a friendship? What if the person in a high-profile F.B.I. case was your best friend or, even more problematically, your brother?

Friendship is a difficult, dangerous job. It is also (though we rarely admit it) extremely exhausting.
ELIZABETH BIBESCO

As the Unibomber case unfolded and people worried about where the next set of victims might show up, Ted Kaczynski's brother David was doing some private investigating of his own. Hoping against hope that he would be wrong, David Kaczynski finally reached the awful conclusion that his own brother was the person the F.B.I had been trailing for 18 years and turned him in. It was a wrenching decision and one that has cost David a lot, but he said he could not permit more maiming and killing from his brother's bombs. What would you do? Are there circumstances under which you might feel compelled to turn a friend or relative in to the police? The novelist E. M. Forster is supposed to have said, "If I had to choose between betraying my country and betraying my friend, I hope I should have the guts to betray my country." Do you think the decision is that simple—that loyalty must supersede everything else? When we asked, "Am I My Brother's or my Sister's Keeper?" in the last chapter, we probably were not thinking about David and Ted Kaczynski.

Always be smarter than the people who hire you.
LENA HORNE

Work is seen as the key to status, material prosperity, and often self-concept. Having a well-paying job that offers us tangible and intangible rewards has been seen as the pinnacle of the American Dream. Ideally, the work you love to do will be possible under conditions that don't challenge your personal moral framework. But, what if you are the human relations director in a prestigious law firm and learn that the firm is engaging in practices you consider unethical? You are not contributing directly to any of these shady practices. Will your conscience permit you to go on working there? What if the company merely mistreats some of its employees, paying them unequally, say, or denying them promotion on prejudicial grounds? The employees themselves might not know, but you do. Will you feel morally obligated to quit? What if you're the billing clerk or the maintenance supervisor or the groundskeeper? Does this diminished responsibility make your decision any easier?

A bit more complex is the question of whistle-blowing. If you learn that something criminal (as opposed to merely illegal in a non-criminal sense) is going on, is it your obligation to turn the company in? Or is it enough to make a silent protest by quitting? Even quitting would mean economic disruption for yourself and your family. And, after all, someone else will simply be hired to take your place. Yet, the only way to stop the reprehensible activity might be to notify the government. Being a whistle-blower can be risky. People have been killed for knowing and telling too much. Would your moral code require you to take these drastic steps the way the protagonist in the movie *The Insider* did by taking on the tobacco industry?

On a more personal level, does any amount of coercion seem ethical to you in the pursuit of sexual conquest? Even if the thought of date rape drugs appalls you, would you consider telling someone you love them or otherwise implying a deeper commitment that did not in fact exist, to increase your chances of having sex? Does "no" ever mean "yes"? Is it ethical to date someone you really don't care for because it raises your social status? How do you feel about lying to break up a couple so that you have a chance at a relationship with one of the partners? Does the situation change if the information you supply is true but your goal is still to break up the couple? Would you misrepresent yourself as richer, smarter, more moral than you actually are? Suppose you are cruising the "net." Is it unethical to describe yourself in ways that obscure who you really are or create a false "persona" that is not the real you? "The Talented Mr. Ripley" stole someone's identity and eventually stepped inside that person's life.

Do you consider it a family or friendship obligation that people lie for you? Suppose you go somewhere you have promised not to go? Is it your buddy's responsibility to deny you went there, even if he went there with you? Do you expect your colleagues to lie when you've been caught padding your expense account at work or to back you up in false claims of innocence at an I.R.S. audit? Should your best friend be expected to tell the professor that your car was indeed stolen (with the paper and disk in it) when you don't have time to complete an assignment? Is it unethical for you to ask or expect others to lie for you?

What if someone you knew in grade school becomes famous or infamous and the tabloid press is looking for information you know this person would not like revealed? Would you be willing to violate a kind of trust by telling what you know? Would the fact that the press was offering large sums of money make your decision easier or more difficult? Suppose you know that a person running for political office did drugs in college? Do you feel, like Linda Tripp, that it is your patriotic duty to share this information? Or, are the bonds of acquaintanceship strong enough to keep you silent? Would you tell your best friend her husband (or his wife) made a pass at you? Is this something she (or he) needs to know? What if you know, but others don't, that a high-profile person is a closeted gay or lesbian? Do you consider this relevant information that should be shared? Suppose you saw someone cheat and get a much better grade than you did. Should you tell? What would be your motivation in each case?

The Global Community

Just how far should our personal freedom and responsibility extend? When Peter Singer arrived at Princeton University in the fall of 1999 to take up his new post as Ira W. DeCamp Professor of Bioethics at Princeton's Center for the Study of Human Values, he was greeted by protesters representing disability advocacy groups who had read or heard that Singer supports the euthanasia of severely disabled babies. It is true that Singer takes a strictly utilitarian position and also believes there is no moral distinction between a fetus and a newborn—he considers neither a person. As a result of this assumption, in cases where "you can judge that a child's life would be a miserable one with a lot of pain and suffering and without the things that might redeem a life despite the pain and suffering," he favors the euthanasia option.[48]

Equally controversial, however, are Singer's less-often-discussed views on what he calls "companion animals" and on our obligations to charitable giving. In one of his famous illustrative examples, Singer asks us to imagine that a child is in the path of a runaway train. Would we throw the switch diverting the train to another track where it will smash the Lexus we have just acquired? For Singer, this is the same moral question as whether we should go without luxuries to save the lives of starving children. Once necessities for ourselves and our families have been secured, Singer believes we are obligated to give until it hurts. In his view, it is our moral responsibility to do all we can to relieve world hunger. All humans, not just those we love or those we see every day, have a claim on us.

And, Singer does not stop with humans. Using animals for food and in experiments is morally repugnant to him, and he thinks it should be to all of us. The suffering involved in raising animals for food and in physically and emotionally cruel experiments should inspire us, he thinks, to examine our own ethical positions. If we care only for our own species and disregard others, he believes we are in the same moral position as those who act from prejudice regarding a person's race or sex. Calling our narrow preference for humans "speciesism," Singer issued a call to action in his 1975 book *Animal Liberation*.[49]

We call them dumb animals, and so they are, for they cannot tell us how they feel, but they do not suffer less because they have no words.

ANNA SEWELL

Only by hardening our own emotional responses are such practices possible, according to Singer. Recognizing a similar kind of callousness, Gloria Anzaldúa, in *Borderlands/La Frontera,* asks the Anglo culture in the United States to come to terms with its own "shadow"—the psychological term for disowned and dishonored parts of ourselves. "Where there is persecution of minorities, there is shadow projection," Anzaldúa writes. "Where there is violence and war, there is repression of shadow." Calling on white society to acknowledge that "you looked upon us as less than human, that you stole our lands, our personhood, our self-respect," Anzaldúa urges the Anglo culture to heal "the intracultural split" by recognizing Mexico as a shadow double, tied to the United States and reflecting its rejected and dishonored parts.[50] This is in essence the same argument Peter Singer is making in asking us to think of the child or animal we never see as intimately linked with us and worthy of our ethical response.

As a Mexican from the Anglo point of view and an Indian within Mexican culture, Anzaldúa has come to terms with the "mestiza consciousness" she thinks will break down the divisions that enable us to treat someone else or some different culture as the "other."[51] Shouting across a divide will do nothing but highlight our differences. Only by being able to stand on both shores at once is it possible to see the deeper unity that binds us all into one global community. To miss this opportunity would be to disregard something essential we need to learn about ourselves.

Benjamin Hoff makes a similar claim with a much broader scope in *The Te of Piglet*. Reconnecting with other humans and then, perhaps, with companion animals is only part of the journey. To reclaim our original state of wholeness, Hoff argues that we need to go back to the time when humans lived in harmony with the rest of the world and communicated easily with plants, animals, and all other forms of life. Before what Hoff calls the "Great Separation" of humans from the rest of nature, humans saw themselves as the equals rather than the superiors of other life forms and found it natural to learn from them.[52] What he is describing is a kind of Taoist Eden in which people are at home in the natural world.

In China, the Great Separation of humans from the rest of nature is reflected in the Confucian tradition of ritual conformity and authoritarianism that Hoff compares unfavorably with the serentiy and gentleness of Taoism. According to Hoff, Taoism's key principles are "Natural Simplicity, Effortless Action, Spontaneity, and Compassion," whereas, the key principles of Confucianism are "Righteousness, Propriety, Benevolence, Loyalty, Good Faith, Duty, and Justice."[53] Because Taoism is "a way of living in harmony with *Tao,* the Way of the Universe, the character of which is revealed in the workings of the natural world," its worldview is very compatible with the worldview of those who are now applying traditional ethical concerns to a consideration of the relationship between humans and the environment—the field we call Environmental Ethics.

Environmental Ethics: Healing the Greek Division

We began our study of Western philosophy by looking in some detail at the ideas of the early Greeks. Beginning with the pre-Socratic cosmologists and continuing through Plato and Aristotle to Descartes, Western philosophy has separated mind from matter. As both Plato and Descartes told us, mind is superior to matter and appropriately dominates it.

The first chapter of Genesis, the first book in the Bible, describes the spirit of God moving over the darkness, separating dry land from water, making the Sun and Moon, and then creating all living things—first plants, then animals, and finally human beings. The assumption of species superiority that can flow from this worldview has been more or less taken for granted for centuries in the Western world. Cultures in Africa and Asia, by contrast, have a more integrated view of living things, tending to see everything as part of an organic whole, with no part being inherently superior to any other part. Native American cultures, similarly, often have a reverence for Earth and all its creatures that is as instinctive as the Greek sense of division and opposition.

Does your moral web include the environment?

Francis of Assisi, from "For the Love of Wisdom"/Courtesy of Howard Community College.

There have, of course, been exceptions in the Western world. One of them is the view of Francis of Assisi, the thirteenth-century founder of the Franciscan Order who is well known for his sense of intimacy with other animals and birds and his gentle attitude toward all living things. We can see how far this intimacy extends by looking at the first few verses of the following well-known hymn of praise. Notice all that Francis considers members of his family:

> ***Canticle of Created Things***
>
> Most high, all powerful, good Lord
> Praise, glory, honor and every blessing are yours.
> To you alone, most high, are these rightly given
> And none of us is worthy to name you.
>
> Be praised, my Lord, with all your creatures
> Especially the master, our brother sun.
> Each day is illuminated by him
> And he is beautiful, radiant with splendor
> From you, most high, his significance comes.
>
> Be praised, my Lord, for our sister moon and for the stars,
> In the sky you have formed them—clear, precious, beautiful.
> Be praised, my Lord, for brother wind,
> For air, cloudy days and sunny ones,
> For all weather that sustains your creatures.
>
> Be praised, my Lord, for sister water
> Who is so useful, yet humble, precious and pure.
> Be praised, my Lord, for brother fire
> Whose power lights the night.
> He is beautiful and playful, sturdy and strong . . .[54]

This sense—that we share a family relationship with all of nature—is the basis for the modern environmental movement. Environmental ethics assumes that we may have moral obligations not only to each other and to other animals but also to the environment itself. If, as Francis says, the wind, water, fire, and the Sun and the Moon are our siblings, perhaps life itself has moral standing. Biocentric ethics makes this claim and rejects the hierarchy of more traditional theories that confer moral status on human animals only.

Ecocentrism and Ecofeminism

ecocentrism *puts the ecosystem first and assumes, as a philosophical position, that the natural world has intrinsic value*

Ecocentrism puts the ecosystem first and assumes, as a basic philosophical position, that the natural world has intrinsic value. Quite apart from its value to us in ensuring the future survival of the human species, nature is seen as valuable in and of itself. According to "the land ethic" branch of ecocentrism, humans have a responsibility toward the land. A shift to this point of view requires giving up the human claim to superior status, also known as anthropocentrism. Instead, this approach sees humans as ordinary members (along with many other participants) in the land community. Deep ecology, another expression of ecocentrism, looks beyond short-term or shallow responses to environmental problems such as pollution and toward a deep understanding of how humans should relate with the environment. A deep response to this challenge may inspire lifestyle choices that involve living simply and honoring the right of all life-forms to live and flourish, creating a rich diversity of human and non-human life. There are many resonances with the Taoist worldview in the goals of ecocentrism.

ecofeminism *links the dominance of women by men and the dominance of the environment by humans and challenges both systems of domination*

Ecofeminism makes connections with the overall goals of feminism and the honoring of "feminine" values that we have explored in earlier chapters. The term ecofeminism highlights both the intimate connection between the dominance of women and the dominance of the environment and the special potential women have to create an ecological revolution. By challenging such harmful dualisms as "superior man versus inferior woman" and "superior human versus inferior natural environment," ecofeminists hope to counter two structures of dominance and subordination at the same time. In fact, coming to terms with one form of subordination brings us automatically to consideration of the other—because they are linked. Both patterns of oppression must be challenged simultaneously. As the "subordinate" members in one pattern of dualistic thinking, women stand in the same relationship to men as the environment stands in relationship to humans. It is in women's best interest, ecofeminists believe, to challenge both of these value-laden dualisms.

We may be on the verge of rethinking the Greek division between mind and matter—between ourselves as rational, human creatures and the rest of the world as lacking in rationality or even inanimate—between rational men and emotional women. The decisions we make in ethical theory will have implications for metaphysics as well. If we choose to move closer to Asian and African worldviews, our understanding of our place in the cosmos will have to shift accordingly.

Summary

A traditional Chinese blessing-curse is "May you live in interesting times." Certainly, the times we live in seem to qualify. The natural boundaries of birth and death have become blurred. For those whose own lives (or the lives of those they love) are saved or extended, this is undiluted good news. Many who would have died in infancy live to a healthy old age, and all of us can expect to live longer, healthier lives than our parents. As we have seen, however, these gifts are not without their complications.

When death becomes a mechanical event—such as turning off a respirator—we face new ethical challenges that did not exist when death occurred "naturally" or as the result of an "accident." In the light of astounding scientific breakthroughs, making babies can now be thought of as a technological rather than a biological process. Again, under these conditions, we must assume responsibility for what we do. If a woman's fertility is no longer simply "in God's hands," we might well ask whose hands are in control.

In the absence of an ethical framework, many decisions are currently made on the basis of feasibility: If we can do it, we do it. In the long run, this is ethically insupportable. Thus, philosophy finds itself poised to speak to crucial questions about when life begins and ends, as well as what exactly constitutes life itself. We are facing an identity crisis as a species when we ask ourselves, What constitutes a human person? How we answer questions like these may change the way we think about ourselves, the way we govern our societies, and the ways in which we decide what we are sure we know is true.

We seem to have a great deal of freedom. If we can extend the very boundaries of birth and death, can there be any limits at all on what we are capable of doing? Ethics may press us to ask the more fundamental question we posed in this chapter—How much freedom should we have?—and its corollary question—Who should decide? What is justice in a world in which the rich and powerful can choose to prolong their lives artificially while the poor and powerless cannot? Can my government enforce obligations it might decide I bear to the fetus in my womb? Are we all on our own to wrestle with this immense and frightening freedom? Do we want to be?

As we chew on these questions with our families, friends, and coworkers, we must also take a fresh look at what the modern world loves to call the "big picture." If life is confined to the material realm, then these questions must be determined by us and us alone. If there is a transcendent realm, a divine plan, then we must at least take it into account. Who, as we asked in Chapter 4, is in charge?

Of equal importance, where will we get the answers? Is our knowing entirely a rational (or perhaps intuitive) process, or must we base all theories on empirical information and use that to shape our hypotheses? Will we turn to art for a new understanding of what seems in many ways to be an entirely new world, or will we continue to rely on traditional methods of knowing?

Other species as well as the entire environment may need to be included in the new ethics we are about to create. It seems appropriate to end our first look at philosophy with the basic issues that are being raised in ethics. One danger is that the whole field of ethics will seem so overwhelming that we will become frozen between choices and be unable to commit to any of them. Although we may have more freedom than we are sure we want, confronting the ethical challenges this freedom brings will help us take major steps in the other branches of philosophy as well.

In the final Historical Interlude, we look at new research into the neurophysiology of the brain and its implications for values, human identity, and knowing. How would we feel about ourselves if scientists convinced us that our brains operate modularly, with different modules doing different tasks and no one module having executive authority? Would we have moral responsibility for what we do? Are we willing to consider the possibility that there may not be an "I" in the sense we have always assumed? If these hypotheses are sustained, will we find ourselves closer to Asian and African worldviews or lost in a Western identity crisis?

For Further Thought

1. According to a recent survey, 61 percent of high school students admit to cheating, 33 percent admit to shoplifting, and 31 percent admit to lying. Do they regard these actions as immoral and do them anyway, or do they not regard cheating, shoplifting, and lying as immoral? What implications do these two interpretations have for society? Ask some high school students their opinion.
2. In the new catechism of the Roman Catholic Church, which is the first update in more than 425 years, the definition of stealing has been broadened to include both paying low wages and performing low-quality work. Does this broader definition seem appropriate or inappropriate to you? Explain.
3. Do human beings have an innate, or inborn, moral sense? If you answer yes, what is its source? If you answer no, why is there such general agreement about what is truly immoral?
4. Under what conditions would you be willing to excuse a person from moral responsibility on a large scale? Consider for instance, a baby addicted to crack cocaine in the womb who grows up addicted and, as a result, steals and even kills to feed a habit acquired before birth. At what point do you grant determinism, and at what point do you require responsibility—no matter what that person's past influences have been?
5. In the United States, April 30 is National Honesty Day. The person who proposed it, M. Hirsh Goldberg, chose the last day of April since the first day of the month (April Fool's Day) celebrates lying. Do we need a National Honesty Day? Why, or why not?
6. To what extent do you personally feel morally free? To what extent do you feel constrained by forces in your past and present life? Is total freedom a desirable thing, in your view? Why, or why not?
7. Many have claimed they were not responsible for acts they committed under orders from a superior. This defense, sometimes called the Nuremberg defense (after the city in which Nazis were tried for war crimes after World War

II), was rejected even though lower-ranking officers insisted they had been taught to obey orders without questioning them. Under what circumstances would you disobey a commanding officer, a boss, an older relative who, in your opinion, was asking you to do something immoral?

8. Look at the Doonesbury cartoon in which Zonker is asked to bake marijuana brownies to relieve the suffering of AIDS patients (page 438). Could you feel morally justified in doing something like this even though you were breaking the law? Is it possible to act legally but still behave immorally? Under what conditions?
9. Do obligations of friendship include helping a friend to commit suicide? If so, what ethical theory would support your decision? If not, how would you explain to your friend that you could not help?
10. Suppose a dear friend or relative had decided to commit suicide and had secured enough drugs to do it but asked you to be present. If the clear wish of the person was to die and the drugs did not kill him or her, would you be willing or able to "finish the job" by suffocation? How would you decide?
11. Are racism, sexism, ageism, speciesism immoral? How would you decide the morality of prejudice?
12. On a flight from Chicago to Spokane, Washington, the pilot learned shortly after takeoff that two pets—a golden retriever and a cat—had mistakenly been loaded into an unheated cargo compartment. Knowing that when the plane reached 30,000 feet temperatures in the unheated portion of the cargo bay would drop to 55 degrees below zero and the pets would die, the pilot dumped 16,000 pounds of jet fuel worth about $2300 and made an emergency landing at a nearby airport. The pets arrived safely, but the human passengers were delayed by about two hours. Did the pilot do the right thing? Why, or why not?
13. Are there any circumstances under which you would grant moral status to an artificial life-form like Data, the sophisticated android on *Star Trek: The Next Generation*? If so, what are they? If not, why not?
14. Should intention and not action be the real basis for morality? During the 1970s, U.S. President Jimmy Carter became the butt of many jokes when he admitted in a *Playboy* interview that he had "lusted in his heart" after women other than his wife. If you determine to do an immoral thing but are stopped by someone or something before you get a chance to do it, are you absolved of any responsibility for your immoral intention? Why, or why not?
15. If we buy products produced under brutal and exploitative working conditions, do we bear any moral responsibility? Do our dollars support the brutality and make us accomplices in it, or are the workers better off, relatively speaking, with an exploitative job than with no job at all? In other words, should we withhold our financial support of what is often called "sweated labor"? Explain.
16. In 1993 a London man was denied bypass surgery by Britain's National Health Service after his first heart attack because he smoked twenty-five cigarettes a day. He finally quit smoking but, before surgeons could operate, had a second (fatal) heart attack. Physicians insist that patients who continue to smoke after bypass surgery don't live any longer and waste resources that can be used to help those with a more healthy lifestyle. What is the moral thing to do in cases such as this one? What is your ethical framework?

17. Cold War experiments using radioactive materials, which came to light in the 1990s, raise issues about what is called informed consent. Do you consider it immoral to use someone in an experiment in which they have not consented to participate? How much difference does it make whether the person is exposed to any pain or danger or is simply an unwitting subject? Explain.
18. In the Milgram studies, experimental subjects administered what they thought were painful and potentially very harmful doses of electric shocks to other people (who were actually part of the experiment) when instructed to do so by people wearing white lab coats. The other variable is that the experimental subjects were being paid to participate. Are we more likely to bend our ethical principles when we are being paid and/or instructed by someone in authority to behave in a certain way? What implications do these factors have for our moral lives?
19. How far would you be willing to bend your own moral code to save someone you love from pain/suffering? Would you be justified in doing so? What if you were instead securing a greater good for the loved person? Would you feel more or less justified in modifying your own principles? Explain.
20. Spend some time thinking about the origin and ethical basis of your own, deepest-held moral principles. It is useful to do this when there is no pressing moral issue so that you know what really matters to you, as well as when and under what conditions you might be willing to bend your principles and why.

For Further Exploration

Fiction and Film

Atwood, Margaret. *The Handmaid's Tale.* New York: Ballantine, 1987. In a future society, women are kidnapped, brainwashed, and forced to have sex and bear children as surrogates for infertile wives. The movie is also pretty good.

Bova, Ben. *Multiple Man.* Indianapolis: Bobbs-Merrill, 1976. When several clones of the U.S. president are found dead, no one is sure whether the original or a copy is occupying the Oval Office.

Camus, Albert. *The Stranger.* Lanham, Md.: University Press of America. A French Algerian shoots an Arab on the beach for no real reason but accepts responsibility for his action in this dark, existentialist novel of absurdity and alienation.

Cook, Robin. *Coma.* New York: Little, Brown, 1977. Vital organs are removed from patients who have deliberately been rendered comatose. Also a movie.

Cook, Robin. *Mortal Fear.* New York: Putman, 1988. This novel asks, Is it morally justifiable to let the older members of an HMO die, or even hasten their deaths, in the interest of saving money to be used for younger members?

Flatliners. In this movie some bright medical students simulate death to find out "what's on the other side" but learn that they have brought bad *karma* from their own pasts into the present and must set things right before being able to move on.

Keneally, Thomas. *Schindler's List.* New York: Simon & Schuster, 1982. This is actually a nonfiction novel about a not very admirable character (the hard-drinking, womanizing, war-profiteering Oskar Schindler of the title) who does an admirable act (risks everything as a member of the Nazi Party by saving the lives of Jews). The movie was a critical and box-office success.

Levin, Ira. *The Boys from Brazil.* New York: Random House, 1976. Inept neo-Nazis clone several Hitlers but cannot replicate the evil of the original because they fail to replicate the real Hitler's early life experiences. Also a movie.

Sartre, Jean-Paul. *No Exit.* New York: Knopf, 1947. In this play, three people realize they are dead and discover that torturers will be unnecessary since they will torture each other eternally. Hell, it seems, is other people.

Sartre, Jean-Paul. "The Victors." In *Three Plays.* New York: Knopf, 1949. "The Victors" is a play about the moral dilemma of six French resistance fighters who strangle the youngest in their group after he reveals that he will "tell all" rather than be tortured. One of the rebels is the boy's sister.

Styron, William. *Sophie's Choice.* New York: Random House, 1979. A woman lives with the memory of a choice she was forced to make in Nazi Germany between the life of her son and the life of her daughter. A great movie.

Weldon, Fay. *The Cloning of Joanna May.* New York: Penguin, 1991. A man dumps his unfaithful wife but not before cloning her so that he can produce a better version of her later on. Also a British TV miniseries.

Westlake, Donald E. *The Ax.* New York: Mysterious Press, 1997. Downsized and unemployed, Burke Devore systematically kills other middle managers (his competition for remaining jobs) using a utilitarian justification: The end I seek is a good end (taking care of my family, contributing to society, putting my skills to work); therefore, the means to that end (killing the competition) can be justified.

Nonfiction

Bok, Sissela. *Lying: Moral Choice in Public and Private Life.* New York: Pantheon, 1978. Is it ever acceptable to lie in politics, medicine, research, and so on?

Bok, Sissela. *Secrets.* New York: Pantheon, 1983. Bok discusses the ethics of revealing and concealing secrets in such areas as journalism, government, and police work.

Camus, Albert. *The Rebel.* New York: Knopf, 1961. This book expresses the view that by creating value through rebellion, the rebel becomes part of humanity and creates values for everyone.

Kant, Immanuel. *Foundations of the Metaphysics of Morals.* Indianapolis: Bobbs-Merrill, 1969. Kant outlines the ethical foundations of the categorical imperative.

Kosko, Bart. *Fuzzy Thinking: The New Science of Fuzzy Logic.* New York: Hyperion, 1993. This book includes the application of fuzzy logic to such ethical puzzles as when life begins (at many different stages—to a certain degree).

Sartre, Jean-Paul. *Being and Nothingness.* New York: Washington Square, 1966. This is primarily a work of existential metaphysics that contains the philosophical origins of the ethical condition known as bad faith.

Swimm, Brian and Thomas Berry. *The Universe Story.* New York: HarperSanFrancisco, 1992. Brian Swimm, a mathematical cosmologist, and Thomas Berry, a historian of culture, offer what they call "a celebration of the unfolding of the cosmos" that stretches from "the primordial flaring forth" to what they term "the ecozoic era," a new era that conceptualizes the universe as a "communion of subjects rather than a collection of objects." Good insight into the underpinnings of the ecological movement.

For Further Research

Try these InfoTrac keywords:

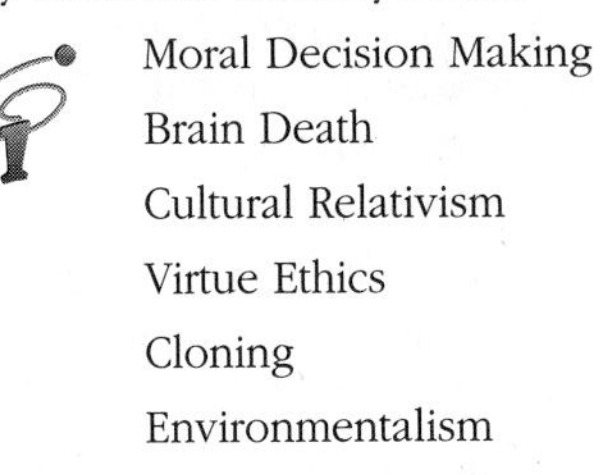

Moral Decision Making
Brain Death
Cultural Relativism
Virtue Ethics
Cloning
Environmentalism

Notes

1. John Haas, "Thinking Ethically About Technology," *Intercollegiate Review* (1992): 9.
2. Ronald Dworkin, "Life Is Sacred. That's the Easy Part," *New York Times Magazine,* 16 May 1993, 36.
3. Dworkin, 60.
4. Dworkin.
5. Bonnie Steinbock, *Life Before Birth: The Moral and Legal Status of Embryos and Fetuses* (New York: Oxford University Press, 1992), 10.
6. Steinbock, 13.
7. Steinbock, 29.
8. Margie Burns, "A Mother's Astonishing Act," *Baltimore Evening Sun,* 18 August 1993.
9. Rita C. Manning, *Speaking from the Heart: A Feminist Perspective on Ethics* (Lanham, Md.: Rowman & Littlefield, 1992), 82–83.
10. Manning, 89.
11. For this illustration, I am indebted to John Greenfelder Sullivan who develops it in his book *To Come to Life More Fully: An East-West Journey* (Columbia, Md.: Traditional Acupuncture Institute, 1990), 18–21.
12. Philip Kapleau, Zen: *Merging of East and West* (New York: Anchor, 1989), 131.
13. *The Dhammapada, The Sayings of the Buddha,* trans. Thomas Byrom (New York: Vintage, 1976), 118.
14. Kwasi Wiredu, "The Moral Foundations of an African Culture," in *Person and Community: Ghanaian Philosophical Studies,* vol. 1, ed. Kwasi Wiredu and Kwame Gyekye (Washington, D.C.: Council for Research in Values and Philosophy, 1992), 196–197.
15. Wiredu, 199.
16. Wiredu, 196–198.
17. N. K. Dzobo, "Values in a Changing Society: Man, Ancestors and God," in *Person and Community,* 227.
18. Dzobo, 228.
19. Wiredu, 201.

20. P. Kaboha, "African Metaphysical Heritage and Contemporary Life," in *The Foundations of Social Life: Ugandan Philosophical Studies,* vol. 1, ed. A. T. Dalforo et al. (Washington, D.C.: Council for Research in Values and Philosophy, 1992), 74.
21. Kaboha.
22. Kaboha, 76.
23. Kaboha, 71.
24. Dzobo, 233–234.
25. Wiredu, 205.
26. Erica Goode, "Human Nature: Born or Made? Evolutionary Theorists Provoke an Uproar," *New York Times,* 14 March, 2000, D1, D9.
27. Jean-Paul Sartre, "Being and Nothingness," in *Existentialism: From Dostoevski to Sartre,* ed. and trans. Walter Kaufmann (New York: New American Library, 1975), 349.
28. Sartre, 353.
29. Sartre, 309–310.
30. *New York Times,* 1 January 1994.
31. Carlos Santiago Nino, *Radical Evil on Trial* (New Haven, Conn.: Yale University Press, 1996), vii–viii.
32. Nino, ix–x.
33. Nino, 142.
34. Nino, 146–147.
35. Daniel J. Kevles, "Social and Ethical Issues in the Human Genome Project," *National Forum* (spring 1993): 18.
36. Nicholas Wade, "Now the Hard Part: Putting the Genome to Work," *New York Times,* 27 June 2000, D1.
37. Douglas Birch, "Code Warrior," *Baltimore Sun,* 1 July 2000, 1E, 5E.
38. Debate between Kalman Weiss of the Committee to Prevent Jewish Genetic Diseases and Jeremy Rifkin of the Foundation on Economic Trends, *CNN News,* 7 December 1993.
39. "Better Make Mine a Double," *The New York Times Magazine,* 19 April 1998, 19.
40. "Better Make Mine a Double," 19.
41. William E. Schmidt, "Birth to 59-Year-Old Generates an Ethical Controversy in Britain," *New York Times,* 29 December 1993, A6.
42. Schmidt.
43. Susan Chiva, "Of a Certain Age, and in a Family Way," *New York Times,* 2 January 1994.
44. "The Sperminator," *The New York Times Magazine,* 28 March 1999, 62.
45. Steinbock, 3, 4.
46. Steinbock, 4.
47. Steinbock, 77.
48. Arthur Hirsch, "Generating a storm over ethics," *Baltimore Sun,* 20 November 1999, 2A.

49. Hirsch, 2A.
50. Gloria Anzaldúa, *Borderlands/La Frontera* (San Francisco, Aunt Lute Books, 1987), 85–6.
51. Anzaldúa, 79.
52. Benjamin Hoff, *The Te of Piglet* (New York: Dutton/Penguin, 1992), 13–14.
53. Hoff, 19.
54. "Il Cantico delle Creature," attributed to St. Francis of Assisi, in *Poems from Italy,* ed. William J. Smith (New York: Crowell, 1972), 10. My translation.

HISTORICAL INTERLUDE E

A Revolution in Philosophy?

So much of what matters most in philosophy arises out of our view of human nature. In the West, beginning with the pre-Socratics and Plato and reinforced by Descartes, a strong tradition of the individual, rational "I" has predominated. The East, by contrast, has either denied (in the case of Buddhism) or blurred (in the case of Taoism) the distinction between the separate, knowing "I" and the world. African philosophy represents in some ways a blend between East and West—an integrated ontology that emphasizes knowing from the inside as well as the outside. Almost all the philosophical speculation you have been reading has taken place without reference to what actually happens in the brain; assertions have followed the rules of philosophy but ignored the facts of physiology. This Interlude summarizes recent encounters between philosophy and physiology.

Over the last forty-five years or so, a quiet revolution has been going on in our understanding of the neurobiology of the brain: the scientific study of how single neurons communicate with one another and how, in doing so, they produce complex brain activity. This research attracted general notice with the popularization of studies on the asymmetry of the human brain—the so-called left-brain/right-brain phenomena. Most of us were surprised to learn that the two halves of our brains are far from identical. In 99 percent of right-handed people and in 67 percent of left-handed people, the left hemisphere

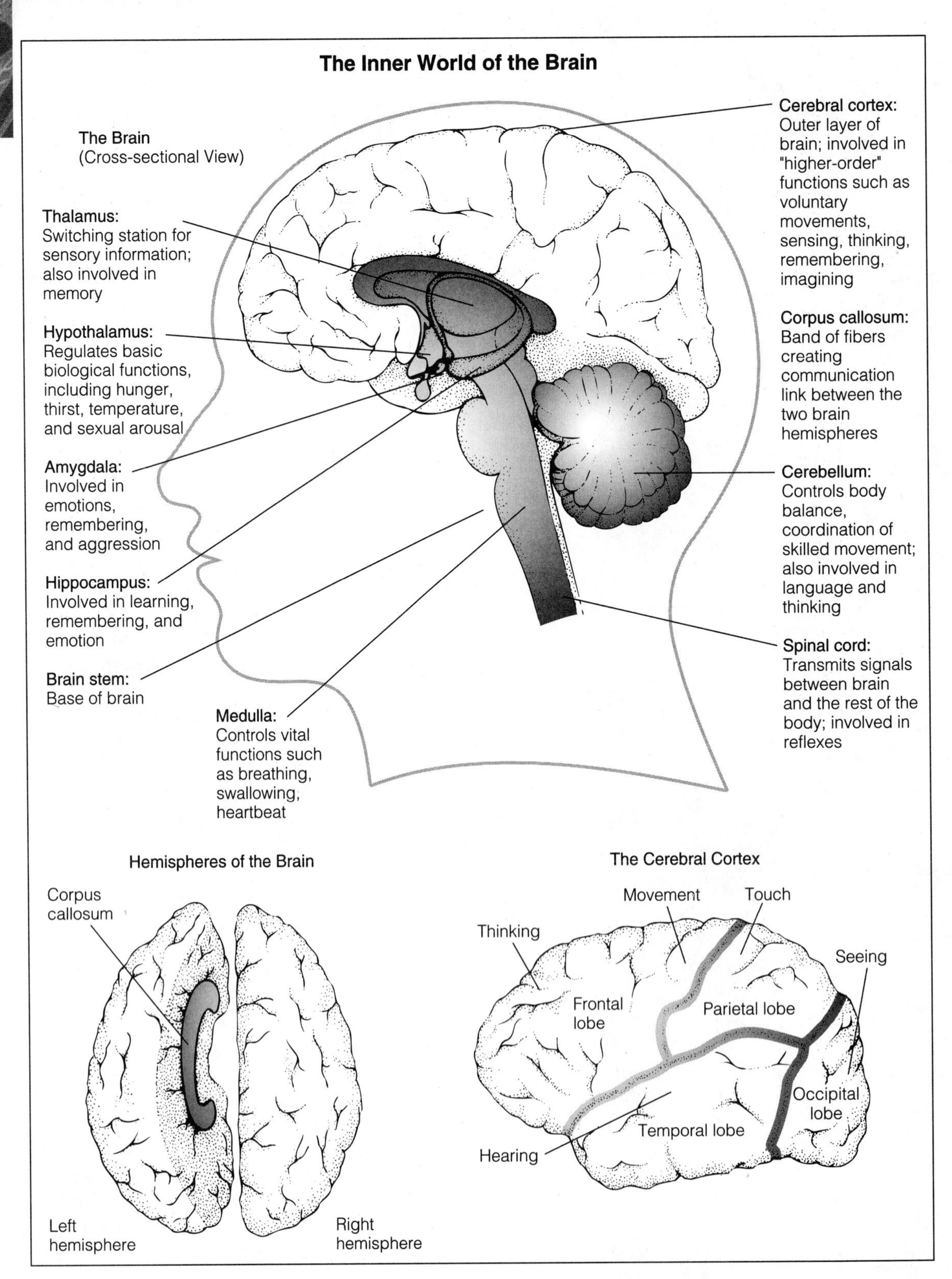
The Inner World of the Brain
The Brain
(Cross-sectional View)
Thalamus:
Switching station for sensory information; also involved in memory
Hypothalamus:
Regulates basic biological functions, including hunger, thirst, temperature, and sexual arousal
Amygdala:
Involved in emotions, remembering, and aggression
Hippocampus:
Involved in learning, remembering, and emotion
Brain stem:
Base of brain
Medulla:
Controls vital functions such as breathing, swallowing, heartbeat
Cerebral cortex:
Outer layer of brain; involved in "higher-order" functions such as voluntary movements, sensing, thinking, remembering, imagining
Corpus callosum:
Band of fibers creating communication link between the two brain hemispheres
Cerebellum:
Controls body balance, coordination of skilled movement; also involved in language and thinking
Spinal cord:
Transmits signals between brain and the rest of the body; involved in reflexes
Hemispheres of the Brain
Corpus callosum
Left hemisphere
Right hemisphere
The Cerebral Cortex
Movement
Touch
Thinking
Seeing
Frontal lobe
Parietal lobe
Occipital lobe
Temporal lobe
Hearing

primarily controls reading, writing, language acquisition, arithmetic calculation, and complex voluntary movement. The right hemisphere performs the complementary functions of complex-pattern recognition in vision, hearing, and touch, as well as a spatial sense, musical/artistic ability, and intuition.

Neurobiologists have located what appear to be highly specialized areas in the brain, particular places where certain, very specific functions are carried out. By studying people who, through injury or surgery, have lost the use of precisely known areas of their brains, neurobiologists have found that a person may, for instance, retain recognition of nouns while losing the ability to recognize or process verbs. Even individual letters such as vowels and consonants are apparently processed in highly specific and precisely located but separate parts of the brain, so it is possible to lose the ability to deal with one while retaining the ability to deal with the other. The abilities to match like colors and to say the names of those colors also appear to be two separate functions. Some people can correctly match like colors and can even match a yellow square with a banana but no longer have the word yellow to associate with either the color or the banana. Others have the words but cannot match them with appropriate colors.

In an uninjured brain, the two hemispheres communicate back and forth through a bundle of billions of nerve cells called the corpus callosum. When this connection is severed (as it sometimes is as a surgical last resort in the control of epileptic seizures), we are able to study what happens when brain activity that occurs on one side cannot be communicated to the other. People who have undergone this surgical procedure appear to function normally when they perform the ordinary activities of life; under controlled, experimental conditions, however, processing abnormalities become apparent.

If you were to fix your gaze on a point on the wall, everything to the left of that point would be projected to and processed by the right hemisphere of your brain, and everything to the right would be projected to the left hemisphere. Assuming that your brain is functioning normally, it would make no difference which side of your brain receives the information because your corpus callosum is sending information from side to side. For those who have had the surgery severing the corpus callosum, however, each half of the brain functions more or less autonomously and independent of the other half.

When asked to fix visually on a point, some split-brain subjects cannot name objects from the left side of the visual field that are fed into the right half of the brain. Because the right half cannot communicate with the language center in the left half, the patient denies seeing anything from the left visual field. Another blindfolded split-brain subject could correctly name objects held in the right hand (because the information went to the left, language center of the brain) but could not name objects held in the left hand (because the right half of the brain does not have language ability).[1]

In cats in which not only the corpus callosum but also the anterior commissure and optic chiasm were divided, what was learned through one eye was unavailable when the other was used. A cat can learn very quickly that pushing a panel with a triangle yields delicious liver pâté, but if the

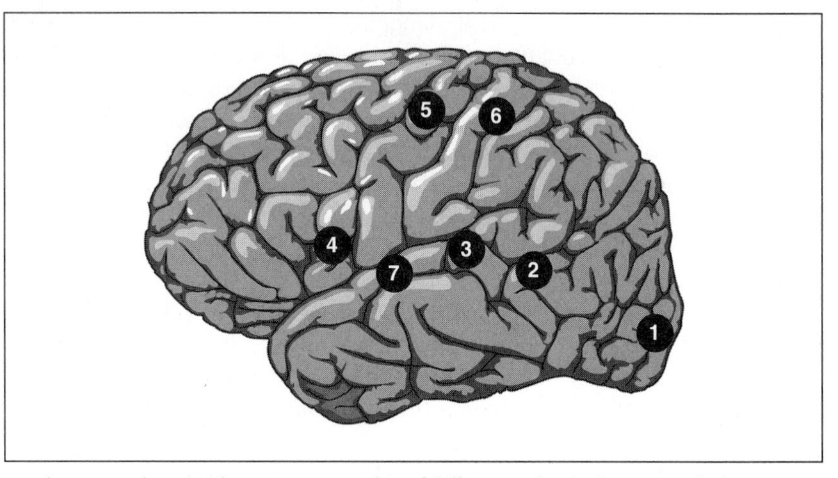

Reading a word out loud activates a number of different individual areas in the brain to work as a "team," including (1) the visual cortex, for seeing the word; (2) an area adjacent to Wernicke's area, for matching the word's visual form with its spoken sound; (3) Wernicke's area, for understanding the word; (4) Broca's area, for producing the word; (5) the motor area, for moving the muscles of the lips, tongue, and mouth in order to actually speak the word; (6) the somatosensory cortex, for feeling the movement of the lips, tongue, and mouth; and (7) the auditory cortex, for hearing the word as it is being spoken.

cat learned this skill with the right eye open and the left eye closed, it lost the skill when the left eye was open and the right eye was closed. It was because the cat behaved as if it had two separate brains that the term split-brain was coined.[2]

Brain Modularity: Independent Parts Working as a Team

Thousands of experiments and observations over the last forty years have led to a now widely accepted theory of brain modularity. It appears that far from being one unified system, the brain is a group of separate and semi-independent modules that communicate with one another; it also appears that these modules usually operate in parallel rather than in serial fashion. That is, instead of information being passed on from system to system in a single line (much as you would pass buckets of water from hand to hand to put out a fire), the modules seem to work beside each other at different tasks while they communicate the results of this work back and forth (much like one group passing water buckets and another smothering sparks, but all working together to put out the fire).

Certain kinds of unusual abilities support conjecture that our brains can be extremely efficient in one area while being very inefficient or even nonfunctioning in others. At the age of four, Mozart's extraordinary musical ability was already obvious; yet in most other ways, he behaved like a "normal" child, becoming distracted by the arrival of a pet cat and "galloping" around the room with a stick horse between his legs. In the movie *Rain Man,* the autistic savant had amazing abilities both to count (as the Las Vegas card-counting experiment proved) and remember numerical information, while remaining dysfunctional in other major areas of his life. If the brain were a unified system, the argument goes, this kind of lopsided development would be impossible.

To understand this modularity model, it may be helpful to liken it to the U.S. government. In the early years of its independence from Great Britain, the United States had no central government. It functioned as a confederation of loosely joined states; each state was independent, formed and enforced its own laws, issued its own currency, and so on. Since the ratification of the Constitution, the United States has had a federal government; many functions that were once assigned to the separate states have now been centralized. Although states can and do have their own laws, federal law is superior to state law in the event of a conflict. The U.S. Supreme Court issues interpretations of federal, state, and even local laws in a way that is binding on all citizens. Recent brain research indicates that our brains are more of a confederation than a federation; each module functions pretty much independently, and much communication travels back and forth between it and other modules.

Another way to understand modularity is to think about a football or soccer team. The modules are the individual players, each in a position with a specific assignment, while being a member of something larger called a team. If one of the players is injured, for example, and replaced with a less skilled one, that position suffers as does the entire team. Similarly, when a particular module of the brain is not functioning well, the particular activity it governs falters or fails, and the individual as a whole functions less well.

The goal of the team is to win games and, perhaps eventually, a championship. Some neurobiologists argue that winning a championship is like consciousness, an *epiphenomenon* (secondary phenomenon), a sort of side effect of winning many games that has no possible existence apart from the games, the team, and ultimately the players. This is the point at which neurobiology challenges some of the most basic assumptions of traditional Western philosophy. If consciousness depends on neurons, just as a championship depends on functioning ballplayers, perhaps consciousness has no real existence of its own. Descartes's certainty about his mental existence or consciousness (in the *Cogito*) while he is still uncertain about material reality is directly challenged by this explanation. If consciousness is an epiphenomenon, it cannot have an independent existence apart from the brain; it is only a by-product of the brain's activity—just as a championship is a by-product of the players winning games.

Implications of Brain Modularity for Philosophy

The neurophysiology of the brain has quite a lot to do with the issues of philosophy. Philosophers speak about the "mind" as something separate from the brain. Aristotle believed that the mind was centered in the heart, but since Descartes many philosophers have agreed that the mind is allied with although separate from the brain. Descartes himself, you may recall, located a transfer junction between mind and body in the pineal gland. From the marriage between biology and philosophy comes the revolutionary idea that the mind is nothing more and nothing less than what the brain does. The brain, some say, is an extremely complex and incompletely understood organ that produces thoughts and ideas through the interaction of its billions of neurons.

Consciousness, according to this view, is thought to be one aspect of mind. Daniel Dennett of Tufts University talks about a "multiple drafts" model of consciousness. Different parts of our brains are working on various drafts or versions of what is going on in the world (much as a group of students might work on individual drafts of an essay), and the drafts weave together to make apparent sense of things (just as if the students pooled their drafts to produce one essay). There does not seem to be a central point at which everything is experienced as a whole by our conscious selves.

Even more disturbing to philosophers is research that indicates that actions may arise within us before we consciously will them to occur. We are not speaking here of a reflex action, like removing the hand from a hot stove or even driving a car, which have long been understood to occur without conscious intervention. What is apparently occurring here is an act that seems to have chosen itself before we consciously "choose" to do it.

In carefully controlled experiments, in which subjects were asked to wriggle a particular finger whenever they felt like it, electrical activity in certain specific areas of the brain seemed to indicate a decision to move the finger two-fifths of a second before the conscious command to actual movement. Further, the brain activity that precedes movement is specific to the type of movement; foot movements are different from finger movements, and preparatory brain activity takes longer before a complex task (such as playing a melody) than it does before a simple task (such as playing a single note).

"A 'spontaneous' act therefore begins before we are aware we have 'decided' to act. The decision, then, is often not up to 'us,' our conscious selves. Rather we watch a part of the mind begin action on its own and we can sometimes veto the order before it travels out to the muscles."[3] Thus, the modules of our brains are quite capable of acting on their own; do they then merely give us the illusion of being in control? As we discussed in Chapter 2, is the "world" actually real or virtually real? Is it "happening now," or did it happen a short time ago?

We have known for a long time that electrical stimulation of specific parts of the brain makes us feel sensations as if they were occurring in other parts of our bodies (a hand or a foot, for example). One experiment compared electrical stimulation of the wrist with direct electrical stimulation of the corresponding area of the brain. It found, surprisingly, that although the wrist stimulation was consciously felt almost immediately, a half-second of stimulation was necessary before the sensation registered when the corresponding area of the brain was directly stimulated. Put another way, if the stimulus is strong enough or lasts long enough to keep the neurons active for a half-second, then the conscious mind becomes aware of it. The strange part is that the conscious mind "believes" that the stimulation began only when it became aware of it—after the half-second delay.

"It is as if the brain, below our awareness, spends a half second deciding whether we should be allowed to know about what just happened. If it decides that it is best that we know, then it also informs us of when the event happened."[4] We are constantly operating on a half-second delay, much as the seven-second delay in radio talkshow broadcasts enables program directors to edit out offensive language before it airs.

Like the sprinter who is out of the starting block within a tenth of a second after the gun fires (long before the required half-second it takes to be conscious of the sound), we appear to behave largely as the result of nonconscious processes. The runner claims to have heard the gun before sprinting because the brain makes sense of the situation by referring the sound of the gunshot back before the beginning of the sprint. The runner did not consciously hear the gun first, but the brain insists that the gunshot came before the sprint.[5] Thus, "reality" appears to be "reconstructed" by the brain out of input from modular activity.

This phenomenon illustrates one of the activities most characteristic of the human species: our need to make sense out of what happens. If we have no sensible explanation, our brain will make one up because it seems to be our nature to make sense of things. This is one of the most important things brains do. Dreams, for instance, may be the result of brain neurons firing at random and the brain's creation of a story to make sense out of the jumble. This might explain the very random, jumpy character of some dreams in which scenes shift and people from one part of your life appear with others from different parts. The drive to make sense of neural activity seems to be a very basic and powerful one.

Recall that we learned from split-brain patients that it is possible for the right hemisphere of the brain to "know" something, and even to act on that knowing, without being able to communicate it to the language center of the left hemisphere. In one experiment, the left hemisphere is shown and sees a picture of a chicken claw while simultaneously the right hemisphere is shown and sees a picture of a snow scene. The person's task is to choose from a series of pictures of objects (lawnmower, rake, shovel, pick, apple, hammer, toaster, chicken) the appropriate answer to the question "What goes with what?" The correct answer is that the chicken goes with the claw and the shovel goes with the snow scene.

One split-brain patient correctly chose the claw and the shovel, but when asked why he responded, "The chicken claw goes with the chicken and you need a shovel to clean out the chicken shed."[6] The right brain "knew" the shovel correctly matched the snow scene, but the snow scene could not be communicated to the language-making left brain. Without knowing about the snow scene in his left, language-producing brain, the subject nevertheless had to make sense of his verbalized choice, and so he supplied the "logical" explanation that the shovel was needed to clean out the chicken shed.

Like the split-brain patient in this experiment, the sprinter needs to believe he heard the gun before moving, and so the brain creates the story arranged in an acceptable time sequence. If you suddenly find yourself behaving in a way that is not consistent with your beliefs, you are very likely to invent a new story to explain the change. If the brain were a monolithic system, the argument goes, our beliefs would never change. Because the brain appears to be a series of connected but semi-independent modules, however, one module can "try out" a behavior different from the beliefs maintained by the cognitive systems of the left brain.[7]

One big advantage of semi-independent modularity is the phenomenon that occurs when you are one with your body and your conscious mind is out of the way, as when the dancer is the dance, the poem writes itself, or the race runs you rather than you running the race. There is wonderful efficiency in these times of peak performance; as you become one with the act, there is nothing to get in the way of perfect responsiveness. In terms of brain neurophysiology, one of the many brain modules is simply doing its own thing, as it always does, but competition from other modules has been reduced or eliminated. You have given up the "illusion" of a conscious self and allowed the appropriate module to operate purely and directly.

Can you hear Descartes turning over in his grave? If all this is true, then there is no "I" to think and therefore exist. Critics have always argued that his *Cogito,* which we discussed in Chapter 5, really only establishes that "thinking exists," not that "I" exist. If the illusion of conscious control is something the modules of our brain allow us to maintain, what does this do to the Western concept of the responsible individual acting ethically to shape a life and a future? Does the story creator in our brain simply feed us a fiction of consciousness while other modules carry on the real work of the brain, including choosing how to act? What if we have, at best, only a partial or delayed veto power over the nonconscious activity of our brains? Who or what are we then?

A Quantum Mechanical Theory of Consciousness

One of the most interesting new theories about consciousness is based on quantum mechanics. If you recall our discussion from Chapter 2, one theory is that the cat in the box may exist as both alive and dead; only when we open the box is one or the other "reality" activated. Roger Penrose, an Oxford mathematician and physicist, uses this quantum mechanical model to explain consciousness. Out of a mix of billions of possible patterns in the brain, one pattern fulfills the task at hand, and it "clicks" and becomes a conscious thought.[8]

Unlike some of the neurobiologists whose ideas we have been discussing, Penrose believes that consciousness exists and is noncomputable; that is, it can never be broken down into a series of steps or a recipe that can then be taught to computers. Penrose goes so far as to assert that consciousness has a physical root in the brain—in microtubules, the "long, thin hollow tubes of protein . . . [that] form alongside one another to create long bundles, a bit like loosely wrapped fistfuls of drinking straws." All living cells contain microtubles, and they behave in interesting ways.[9]

For instance, they appear to play a key role in cell division. Under ordinary conditions, microtubules serve as a kind of "skeleton" for the cell, providing structure as well as pathways for the transport of chemicals. When a cell is just about to divide, however, the microtubules dissolve and "reform in new configurations that pull the cell apart in exactly the right place." Anesthetics such as ether appear to disable consciousness while allowing most brain function to continue by temporarily crippling neuron microtubules.[10]

Thus, microtubules seem to provide a kind of information-processing network at the level of the individual neuron, or brain cell. The question then becomes, If the brain is already functioning as a computer via its network of neurons, why would it need each individual neuron to function as a kind of computer within a computer? One clue can be found in a task we all take for granted: the ability to instantly recognize every object in a room we enter for the first time. If you recall Virgil's experience (see Chapter 2), the enormity of this task may become clearer to you. This is such a huge feat of information processing that even a dozen of the largest supercomputers cannot come close to replicating it.

For tasks like this (tasks we continually face), it seems we need the boost provided by the microtubules working within each neuron. According to Penrose's theory, microtubules, because of their structure, permit the energy in the brain to exist in "a quantum mechanical mixture of states." Normally, the dense matter and "noisy" activity in the brain could be expected to function like the opening of the box (in the cat thought experiment) and force the choosing of a single state. The tubular structure, however, seems to insulate a pulse of energy, allowing that pulse of energy to explore simultaneously a wide range of possible patterns, within its own microtubule and in communication with others.[11]

Microtubules enable the brain to generate the mind, "that intangible, unbounded entity that provides us with an inner voice, imagination, emotions, thought, and our very sense of self." Working quantum mechanically, they generate and keep as options many possible states, until the "right one" emerges to fulfill a particular task. For Penrose, this explanation also means that computers will never be able to "intuitively assess the truth in a subtle argument or see the humour in a joke, to . . . philosophize about the meaning of life, or come up with counterintuitive solutions to unfamiliar problems."[12]

Consciousness, Penrose believes, is a uniquely human ability. Although Descartes's pineal gland theory was woefully inadequate to explain the connection between mind and body, he may have been correct to hypothesize a physical location for consciousness. Like the other theories in this Historical Interlude, Penrose's is conjecture. Much work remains to be done concerning the neurophysiology of the brain and its possible connection with quantum mechanics, but Penrose thinks nature's great practical joke on us may have been to weave a big clue to the ultimate explanation for reality itself into the very process of thought.

Whether consciousness is real or an epiphenomenon, the view of the person constructed from our knowledge of brain neurophysiology seems closer to the Eastern worldview than to the traditional Western one. The distinction between the knower and the known may not be so clear as Plato and Descartes believed; we may be more a shifting, changing composite than a pure, unchanging Cartesian "I."

The Brain and Moral Accountability

In the West we have insisted on the freedom of the conscious self to choose and stand accountable for its choices. Jewish, Christian, and Islamic religious systems are all founded on belief in the power and obligation of the individual self to choose good over evil and on the moral accountability that follows from this assertion. Our legal system insists that we have the ability to distinguish right from wrong and the freedom to choose one over the other.

Yet, what of a person with a brain injury or disorder who suddenly begins to behave differently? Shall we acknowledge a neurologically caused loss of freedom based on physical changes and thereby relieve that person of moral and even criminal responsibility? Suppose for a moment that most wrongdoers could be found to have physiological abnormalities (as some brain researchers are tentatively beginning to suggest) and, like the person with a brain injury, are unable to behave otherwise. Would we be forced to revise our definitions of legal and moral accountability? How far would we be willing to go?

In 1848 an explosion drove a metal tamping rod through the skull of Phineas P. Gage, a twenty-five-year-old foreman for a New England railroad. Although he lost his left eye, Mr. Gage could walk and speak normally. His memory and high intelligence were unimpaired, yet he had lost the ability to make ethical decisions. According to neurobiologists Hanna and Antonio Damasio, "Before the accident, Mr. Gage had been an intelligent, socially responsible, hard-working fellow who was well-liked by all who knew him . . . But in the weeks after the tamping rod pierced his brain, he began using profane language, lied to his friends and could not be trusted to honor his commitments."[13]

The Damasios have theorized the existence of a special region for making personal and social decisions, located in the frontal lobes of the human brain (which are situated behind the forehead and the eyes). In twelve modern-day counterparts to Phineas Gage, people whose frontal lobes have also been damaged through accident or stroke, the results are consistent: Once upright citizens, they can no longer be trusted. Even though they continue to perform well on intelligence tests, speak normally, use logic flawlessly, form new memories, and make new associations, their processing of emotional input is impaired. They have difficulty making rational decisions about personal and social matters, and they cannot keep a job.

The neurophysiological paradigm of brain function is in its infancy; where the next generation of research will take us is anybody's guess. It is a pretty good bet, however, that whatever we learn about how our brains work will have important, perhaps revolutionary, implications for how we see ourselves and how we write our philosophy. Just as you would have little confidence in a TV repairperson who claimed not to know how your set was wired, philosophers may be forced to study how the brain is wired before constructing theories about how it works. As you think about the questions of philosophy raised in this book, keep reading about new research and keep rethinking your own conclusions. That, after all, is the very nature of philosophy: to question the obvious and to keep a sense of wonder about everything that is apparently decided once and for all.

For Further Exploration

Calvin, William H. *The Cerebral Symphony: Seashore Reflections of the Structure of Consciousness.* New York: Bantam, 1990. A highly readable discussion about thought consciousness by a world-class neurologist.

Dowling, John E. *Neurons and Networks: An Introduction to Neuroscience.* Cambridge, Mass.: Harvard University Press, 1992. An introduction to the basic principles of the field written for beginning college students and other interested people. Terms are explained, and each chapter is clearly and fully summarized.

Gazzaniga, Michael S. *The Social Brain: Discovering the Networks of the Mind.* New York: Basic, 1985. A readable introduction to the modular view of brain function. The thesis is that, since the modules work beside each other rather than in unison, we are more a sociological entity than a single, unified, psychological entity. The modules of the brain, Gazzaniga argues, frequently operate apart from our conscious, verbal selves.

Hobson, J. Allan. *The Dreaming Brain.* New York: Basic, 1988. An entirely new, non-Freudian view of the causes of dreams based upon contemporary findings in neurophysiology. The book also provides an excellent history of past theories of dreaming as well as a brief overview of brain physiology and some current concepts of consciousness.

Ornstein, Robert. *The Evolution of Consciousness: Of Darwin, Freud, and Cranial Fire—The Origins of the Way We Think.* New York: Prentice Hall, 1991. Ornstein's thesis is that we are adaptive rather than rational creatures and that Darwin, rather than Freud, is the central scientist of the modern mind. We have many minds that shift into place as needed, and "we" are not the same person from moment to moment. The world we adapted to is gone, and we need to adapt again. A tribal mind, he says, has no place in a global world.

Penrose, Roger. *The Emperor's New Mind: Concerning Computers, Minds, and the Laws of Physics.* New York: Oxford University Press, 1989. A basic introduction to physics, information science, and neurobiology that closes with the theory of quantum mechanical choosing among brain states as the model for a uniquely human consciousness.

Scientific American, September 1992. This is a special issue devoted entirely to "Mind and Brain." Articles cover the range of current research, including: The world we see is literally an invention of the brain, constructed from a constantly changing flood of information; language ability depends on concepts being produced in one area, words and sentences constructed in another, and mediation between the two; brain computations are largely unconscious, and what we become aware of is the result of these computations.

Notes

1. Michael S. Gazzaniga, *The Social Brain* (New York: Basic, 1985), 40–45.
2. Gazzaniga, 29.
3. Robert Ornstein, *The Evolution of Consciousness: Of Darwin, Freud and Cranial Fire—The Origins of the Way We Think* (New York: Prentice Hall, 1991), 147.
4. Ornstein, 149.
5. Ornstein.
6. Gazzaniga, 72.
7. Gazzaniga, 139.
8. David H. Freedman, "Quantum Consciousness," *Discover* (June 1994): 94.
9. Freedman, 95.
10. Freedman, 97.
11. Freedman.
12. Freedman, 94.
13. Sandra Blakeslee, "Old Accident Points to Brain's Moral Center," *New York Times,* 24 May 1994, C1.

APPENDIX

A Few Final Words About Philosophy

How to Read It
How to Write It

As a philosophy student, your first challenge is learning to navigate through an academic subject that was probably not part of your high school experience. This includes mastering a specialized vocabulary, as you must do when you study a foreign language, and understanding a particular approach to knowledge. The goal of this appendix is to help you do that so effectively that you will be able to turn the process around and do philosophy yourself—that is, write the philosophical essays and answer the essay questions your professor is likely to assign. We'll be using the contents and especially the design and format of this book as our curriculum, examining how it does philosophy, so it can serve as a guide to a new field and a model for your own philosophical writing.

The first sentence in the Preface reads: "As we learn in our first course in philosophy, the concerns of this ancient discipline are those of people everywhere—who we are, how we know, how we should live." There you have the thesis of this book—the philosophical premise that this book will spend several hundred pages trying to validate. *Roots of Wisdom* asserts that philosophy is a worldwide enterprise, not just the province of ancient Greeks and their intellectual heirs in Europe and North America. This is not a universally accepted proposition and that means that I face special challenges when I introduce thinkers and thought systems not traditionally included in philosophy texts. In every case, my task is to demonstrate how these ideas qualify as part of the human love affair with wisdom we call philosophy. You will ultimately be the judge of how successful this effort has been. Let's consider some key ingredients in this process.

A well-written book (and a successful student essay) states a premise and then defends it. The entire work (this book or your essay) is a matrix in which ideas are meant to cohere, to literally "stick together" in a convincing way. In a very important sense, you must know where the entire project is going before you construct any portion of the matrix. This book has three sections—one for each of the major divisions within philosophy (metaphysics, epistemology, and axiology) and ten chapters, each devoted to a specific topic. Each chapter must function as an integrated whole and must fit successfully into its appropriate section. And the three sections must work together to advance the thesis of the book and accomplish all its other goals, which include introducing you to a number of thinkers and thought systems as well as to the major questions about reality, knowing, and valuing posed by philosophy. Your essay faces the same challenges, on a smaller scale. After you state your thesis, you will want to divide your essay into sections. Each paragraph must work within its appropriate section and all the sections must combine to support your thesis.

The opening chapter of *Roots of Wisdom* functions the way the opening paragraph of your essay should. It asks the question: Why Philosophy? In other words, what does philosophy have to offer humankind and each of us as individuals? Why should we bother to study it? This chapter begins with the ancient Greeks and their early attempts to ask and answer philosophical questions, moves to the classical period in which the three Western masters—Socrates, Plato, and Aristotle—taught, and then considers how the same questions that puzzled the Greeks have been pondered and addressed in Asia, Africa, and the Americas (especially by indigenous peoples). I conclude this chapter with a few examples of how philosophy makes a practical difference in the lives of contemporary people and then offer a preview of what lies ahead in the next nine chapters. Your challenge as a writer is the same. You need to convince the reader that what you have to say has merit and offer some guidance about where your essay is headed. This chapter finishes with a summary, and so should your essay. Begin by telling us what you hope to prove, spend the bulk of your essay doing just that, and then tell us what you have demonstrated.

If you think of your essay as providing a map for the reader, your matrix will be easier to construct. Transitions are particularly important, so the reader can follow as you take a turn or introduce a new point of discussion. In a larger work, such as this text, headings are a key part of the mapmaking skills and will be useful to you in your own mapreading. As the mapmaker, try to think of your essay as following a route from beginning thesis to summary and then help the interested reader to join you on your journey. If you look at the short paragraph that follows each new heading in this book, you will find a brief preview of what is to follow and how it fits into the existing matrix of the chapter. Transitions are links between what has already been stated and what is to come. Smooth and effective transitions make for convincing essays.

One key distinction here is between descriptive and analytic writing. Many students are skilled at describing what a philosopher has said, and this is a useful skill. In a philosophical essay, however, your task is to persuade rather than to describe. You are not reporting on someone's views; instead, you are using the views of that thinker or thought system to support a thesis of your own making. In *Roots of Wisdom,* I have taken as one of my challenges the legitimizing of some of the thinkers and thought systems that have been omitted in the past. My task as author, therefore, is to demonstrate how these new players in the game belong on the team, so to speak. Merely describing their ideas is not enough. The ideas must be analyzed and presented in such a way that they are seen to fit into the existing body of philosophical thought. To use a few examples from the first chapter of this text, both Perictyone and Rigoberta Menchú are included alongside more traditional philosophers. It happens that Perictyone writes about a tripartite or three-part soul in ways that are very similar to Plato's writings. This places Perictyone within the same Pythagorean tradition that shaped Plato. Rigoberta Menchú's description of the welcoming of a baby into the community of the Quiché Maya reveals a cosmology in which the sun and moon are evoked as "pillars of the universe." Did I convince you that these women are philosophizing? Ultimately, you will be the judge. And, the person who reads your essay will, similarly, determine whether you have analyzed your sources in such a way as to convincingly support your thesis.

As you draw your map, think about convincing the reader to come with you one more step, to follow you in one more turning. Each of these advances requires analysis. How does the new idea fit with what has gone before? Are you using it to pave the way for something yet to be stated? If you would like some practice with using the philosophical method of analysis, visit the publisher's Web site at: www.wadsworth.com, select "the Wadsworth Philosophy Shoppe" and then the Web page for this text. The longer selections from philosophers, included in each chapter as Philosophers Speak for Themselves, and the selection of philosophical writings, both fiction and nonfiction, found in the reader *Readings from the Roots of Wisdom* that supports this text will also give you practice in following the maps drawn by philosophers and determining how successful you think they have been.

One of the requirements of philosophical writing is that it must be logical; that is, your philosophical argument cannot violate the rules of logic. If it does your argument is rendered invalid and your conclusion is not supported. A good way to make sure you don't fall into this trap is to become familiar with the standard forms of argument and their valid and invalid forms. Beginning with Aristotle, Western philosophers have placed a very high premium on logic and there are many patterns that, if followed correctly, will enable you to reach a valid conclusion. There is a very significant difference, however, between a valid argument and a true or accurate conclusion. Logic will help you establish a valid claim, but, if you begin with a false premise, you cannot reach a true conclusion. The logic boxes in each chapter of *Roots of Wisdom* will help you learn to follow the rules of inference that underlie successful analytic writing. These rules are mathematical in nature. Just as there are algebraic rules to follow, there are also logical rules to follow. Certain patterns lead to valid conclusions, whereas others do not. The first and most important step in crafting a philosophical argument is to make sure you follow the correct deductive forms and avoid the traps of informal fallacies. These less formal but equally devastating errors, examples of which may be found in Chapters 6 and 7, can also render what you have to say invalid. Once you are sure you have argued in a valid manner, your next imperative is to be very certain that you have used true premises.

Chapter 3 of *Roots of Wisdom* includes a discussion of Elizabeth V. Spelman's essay on Aristotle. Her assertion is that Aristotle's claim that rational men must rule over irrational women is an invalid one. Professor Spelman faults Aristotle, the master of logic, for arguing circularly. That is, each of his premises—that men appropriately rule women in the political realm and that the rational part of the "soul" (weaker in women) appropriately rules the irrational part—supports the other, but there is no independent validation for either outside this self-validating system. This claim has been implicitly accepted for centuries and used as the basis for men ruling women in society, so a charge of invalidity requires our careful scrutiny. Does Spelman skewer Aristotle successfully? Her entire essay appears in Chapter 3 of *Readings from the Roots of Wisdom*. Although logic can seem "dry," it is not without its moments of drama.

Ideas can easily become ideologies and, when they do, they seem to be immune to challenges. If men must rule women because women have a weaker rational element, then women's demands for fuller participation in the political arena must be rejected. Clearly, ideology has no place in philosophical writing. Large belief systems—such as socialism, communism, democracy, and feminism—run the risk of turning into ideologies. The test for whether you are reading (or writing) ideologically is whether or not evidence is provided. Ideologies assert themselves as self-evident and, therefore, not requiring any defense. Effective analytic writing makes no such assumptions. Even something that seems quite self-evident to you will need to be supported in some way if you hope to convince your professor that you have written a philosophical essay. It is not enough to assume that democracy is the best form of government, particularly if emerging nations don't agree. Their refusal to accept our "self-evident" assumption might be the first clue that we are operating in the realm of ideology.

Philosophical arguments may be defended logically or through appeal to empirical evidence found in the world. Arguing inductively, from many particular examples to a general conclusion, is often the method preferred in science. Within the Western world, these have been seen as the only two valid knowledge claims. Other cultures, however, have accepted intuitive ways of knowing and the testimony of lived experience to a far greater degree than we in Western society have done. Many people also rely on faith—in religion or the paradigms of science, for instance—to make the practical and more far-reaching decisions of their lives. In writing a philosophical essay, though, it is safest to rely on logic and empirical evidence.

As you read through *Roots of Wisdom,* pay particular attention to the way its argument—that philosophy is a worldwide enterprise—is built. If the argument is successful, all the thinkers and thought systems that appear in each chapter will seem to be peers; each will appear to have a legitimate claim to space within the chapter. Use your analytic skills to evaluate each section, each chapter, and the entire book as an extended philosophical essay. The Special Content Features, Visual Features, and In-Text Learning Aids described in the Preface will guide you in getting the most out of your first experience with philosophy. If you use these features wisely, they can also assist you in crafting the kinds of philosophical writings your professor is expecting. Good Luck!

Glossary

admirable beauty intrinsic excellence or perfection in art, according to Adler
adwene [ahd WAY nay] the mind, meaning the capacity to think and feel in the Akan system
aesthetic contemplation a route to knowledge, according to Schopenhauer
aesthetic hearer a person who can respond to art with feeling and involvement, according to Nietzsche
aesthetic intuition knowing available through aesthetic experience, according to Schelling
aesthetics a philosophical reflection on art and the beautiful
agnosticism the philosophical position that whether God exists or not cannot be known
alienation in Marxist thought, the estrangement of workers from their work, their fellow citizens, and ultimately themselves as the direct result of capitalism's exploitative nature
alterity De Beauvoir's term for the "otherness" experienced by women and nonwhite men in relation to the power positions staked out by white men in Western society
anarchism the political belief that all forms of government should be abolished since they interfere with the rights of individuals
anatman [ahn AHT muhn] the Buddhist doctrine that there is no permanent, separate, individual, ego-self
androgyny [an DRAH jin ee] the state of having all or some of the characteristics of both sexes/genders
anima Latin word meaning "spirit"
animism the philosophical theory that all being is animate, living, contains spirits
anthropomorphism representing something nonhuman (such as animals or God) in human likeness
antirepresentationalist view we are limited by our own perspective and cannot rationally speak about a world that exists outside it
apology a philosophical defense of an action, position, or viewpoint
archē [AHR KAY] the first principle or basic stuff from which everything derives
asceticism the view that the body requires the discipline of mind or spirit, resulting in self-denial and even self-torture as a way of renouncing worldly longings in preparation for a happier existence after death
assimilationist one who believes that blending as much as possible with the dominant culture will produce justice
atheism the denial of theism, usually on the basis that everything can be explained without God
atheistic existentialism the view that, since there is no God and no resulting moral laws, individuals are free to determine their own human nature through choices for which they stand accountable
atman [AHT muhn] in Hinduism, the Self or soul, which endures through successive reincarnations as an expession of the divine and as a carrier of *karma*
axiology the branch of philosophy dealing with the study of values
bad faith in the existentialist philosophy of Sartre, acting as if one is not free (being-in-itself), denying the freedom and responsibility of the human person (being-for-itself), behaving inauthentically
beginner's mind according to Zen, the state of openness in which one can directly access the truth about what is
behaviorism a psychological theory that focuses on objective or observed behavior, as opposed to introspection or reflections about inner states
Being-in-the-world the natural state of the human person, according to Heidegger
black power a movement to achieve legal, economic, and social power for African Americans and for all black people
bodhisattva [bohd hee SAHT vuh] in Buddhism, a wise and enlightened person who postpones *nirvana* to help others gain enlightenment

Brahman [BRAH muhn] in Hinduism, the ultimate, absolute reality of the cosmos, the world-soul with which *atman* is identified and seeks union
Cartesian circle the argument by which Descartes uses his clear and distinct idea of God to prove God's existence and uses God's existence as the justification for the accuracy of his clear and distinct ideas; each proves the other, but there is no outside justification for either
categorical imperative a deontological ethical principle, developed by Kant, that states unconditionally that one must act in such a way as to desire his or her actions to become universal laws binding on everyone
catharsis the emotional cleansing achieved by viewing tragic drama, according to Aristotle
checks and balances the system by which each of the three branches of the U.S. government restrains the power of the other two, keeping any one from becoming too powerful
ch'i [CHEE] in Taoism, the energy of the life force that flows between heaven and Earth and within nature
civil disobedience breaking of a civil law in protest by citing obedience to a higher law
Cogito [KO ghi toe] the proof by which Descartes established his mental existence
coherence test measures coherence and consistency among statements within a system
communitarianism the theory that both individuals and society will be best served by balancing their needs
consensus a meeting of the minds after rational discussion and the give and take of dialogue
conservative one who values the preservation of established traditions
correspondence test a true proposition must correspond with a fact or state of affairs
cosmogony [kos MAH go nee] theory about the origins of the cosmos
cosmological argument an argument for the existence of God, based on the contingent nature of the physical world, developed by Aristotle and popularized in the Middle Ages by Aquinas
cosmology the branch of metaphysics dealing with the study of the principles underlying the cosmos
cosmos the world as an ordered whole
covenanted society a society that functions as one and as a party to a covenant, or sacred relationship
creativity test what is true is what promotes life and growth, according to the Ewe
cunning of reason the method by which the Absolute, in Hegel's philosophy, uses the talents and ambitions of world historical individuals to advance its own ends
darshan [DHAR shan] in Hinduism, uplift in the presence of greatness and, in *puja,* a moment of fusion with the divine
deconstruction a method used to "question" texts and take apart their artificial constructions in order to reveal their hidden meanings
deism the belief that an impersonal, mechanical genius began the world and has since left it alone
deontological [DAY AHN tah lah juh kuhl] **ethical theory** an ethical theory that evaluates behavior in terms of adherence to duty or obligation, regardless of consequences
dialectic a method of questioning used by Socrates in pursuit of the truth
difference principle in Rawls's system of justice, permission to treat people differently as long as the least well-off benefit from the different treatment
divine law that portion of eternal law applicable to human beings, according to Aquinas
double consciousness Du Bois's analysis of the psychic division in many African Americans in terms of which they see themselves through the lens of their own culture and through the lens of the dominant culture—as Africans and as Americans
ecocentrism puts the ecosystem first and assumes, as a philosophical position, that the natural world has intrinsic value
ecofeminism links the dominance of women by men and the dominance of the environment by humans and challenges both systems of domination
egocentric predicament the human condition of being unable to leave the boundaries of our individual selves to determine what anything is really like, as opposed to how it seems to us
empiricism the belief that meaningful knowledge can be acquired only through sense experience
enjoyable beauty personal preference in art, according to Adler
enlightenment the Buddhist term for the realization that comes from seeing the world as it actually is
entelechy [EN tuh leck ee] in Aristotle's ontology, the inner purpose, or end, in something that brings it to actuality
entitlement theory Nozick's theory that justice should be conceived in terms of entitlements (what individuals are entitled to), rather than in terms of fairness or equality
epistemology the branch of philosophy dealing with the study of knowledge, what it is, and how we acquire it
equal liberty principle Rawls's primary condition of justice that insists people must be treated equally and be guaranteed minimum natural rights
eros [AIR ros] earthly love, the love of bodies
eternal law the law or reason of God, according to Aquinas
ethic of care an ethical theory, which is a variation on virtue ethics, that holds as an ideal the caring self
ethics the branch of philosophy concerned with judgments about moral behavior and the meaning of ethical statements and terms
excusability the state of being excused from moral responsibility for an act that is objectively immoral

existentialism emphasizes the uniqueness and freedom of the human person as an individual (what makes each life a unique, personal experience) as opposed to the essence of a human being (what makes all of us alike)
feminism the theory that women should have political, legal, economic, and social rights equal to those of men and should define their own roles
feminists those who promote political, legal, economic, and social equality for women, in opposition to the structures of a patriarchal society
Forms in Plato's ontology, intelligible Ideas, the ultimate realities from which the world of objects has been patterned
golden mean the moderate action between undesirable extremes; used by Aristotle to describe an ethical ideal
golden rule "Do unto others as you would have others do unto you."
hard determinism the view that the will of an individual is not free and is instead determined by factors beyond his or her control and/or responsibility
harmonia [har moh NEE uh] the Pythagorean principle of desired harmony among elements
hedonism the theory that pleasure is the highest good
Hegel's dialectic the progress of ideas through opposition and resolution in the form of thesis-antithesis-synthesis, according to Hegel
henotheism [HEN oh THEE ism] attributing supreme power to a number of deities, one-at-a-time, so that each becomes a window on the One or the All
hubris [HEW bris] human arrogance or pride
Hume's Fork the doctrine that no middle ground exists between necessary truths, based on the relation of ideas, and contingent truths, based on experience; anything other than these two tells us nothing meaningful about reality
idealism in metaphysics, the belief that the most real entities are ideas and other immaterial entities
imago dei [ih MAH go DAY ee] literally, "image of God"; how humans picture an infinite deity, using finite terms
immanent indwelling within a process, as God is described as indwelling in creation
ineffable unable to be spoken in words
innate literally, "inborn," present from the moment of birth, not learned or acquired
interest view an ethical principle stating that moral status is based on interests; this is derived from Feinberg's interest principle—to have moral status is to have rights; Steinbock's application is that the capacity for conscious awareness is both a necessary and a sufficient condition for possessing interests
karma [KHAR muh] in Hinduism and Buddhism, the principle that all actions operate according to causal laws and what I do to another I do to myself; sometimes this law is referred to as the law of sowing and reaping
koan [KO ahn] a Zen riddle designed to stop rational, discursive thought in order to permit or force the direct experience of what is
***laissez-faire* economics** the economic theory that if government stays out of the economy, market forces will regulate it in a harmonious and productive manner that will benefit all
law of identity states that A equals A
law of noncontradiction states that A cannot be non-A
law of the excluded middle states that something is either A or non-A, and no middle ground exists between these two possibilities
liberal one who believes in the primary importance of individual freedoms
life principle the spark of the divine in each human person that is responsible for an irreducible human dignity, according to traditional African ethical systems
Lisa [LEE sah] the male principle in West African thought
logical positivism a radical empiricist position based on Hume's Fork, asserting that propositions have meaning only if they are either analytic (true by definition) or synthetic (verifiable, at least in principle, in experience)
logos the rational, ordering principle of the cosmos, for the Greeks
materialism in ontology, the belief that reality is essentially matter
Mawu [MAH woo] the female principle in West African thought
merit a fixed condition—such as wealth, talent, intelligence, race, or gender—on the basis of which justice may be dispensed
metaethics the branch of ethics that studies the meaning of ethical statements and terms
metaphysics the branch of philosophy investigating what is real
mimesis [mih MEE sis] the aesthetic theory of art as representation
mind-body problem a problem of metaphysics created when Descartes divided reality into mind and matter, making each a separate substance; how can two completely distinct substances interact in one person?
modernism the quest for certainty and unitive truth, a single and coherent explanation of reality that gives it meaning
mogya [MAHG yah] bloodline and clan identity in the Akan system
monad Leibniz's word for the simple, unextended, teleological substances that make up the universe
monist a pre-Socratic philosopher who believed the *archē* was a unified whole or any philosopher who believes reality is one

monotheism belief in one God
moral status existing in such a way as to have claims on others that must be considered from a moral point of view
mystical experience intuitive knowledge of a larger reality, based on personal experience that convinces the recipient of its accuracy
natural law a rational principle of order, often the logos, by which the universe was created or is organized
natural law theory in deontological ethical theory, the belief that the rational principle of order that underlies the cosmos also contains a basis for moral action that is discoverable by reason; in Christian versions of this theory, we find the belief that humans, created in the image and likeness of God, deserve special moral status on that account
natural rights rights, such as those to life, liberty and property, with which an individual is born
natural theology the pursuit of knowledge of God, using natural intelligence rather than supernatural revelation
Net of Indra in Buddhism, an image of the world as interrelatedness and interconnectedness—pictured as a net of jewels, each of which reflects all others and itself
new covenant a Clinton-Gore campaign slogan in the 1992 U.S. presidential election, used to evoke the Puritan ideal of a covenanted society and to revive communitarian principles
Nirguna Brahman [NIR goon uh BRAH muhn] in Hinduism, the absolute conceived without attributes
nirvana a state in which individuality is extinguished or the state of enlightenment in which all pain, suffering, mental anguish, and the need for successive rebirths disappear
noetic having the quality of knowledge, seeming to be knowledge
normative ethics the branch of ethics that makes judgments about what constitutes moral behavior and intention
noumena in Kant's epistemology, things as they are in themselves; this is always beyond the limits of human perception and knowing
nous [NOOS] Greek for "mind," expressing the rationality of the cosmos
okra [OAK rah] the life force in the Akan system
omnipotence the state of unlimited power, usually attributed to God
omniscience the state of unlimited knowledge, usually attributed to God
ontological argument a logical argument for the existence of God, based on the nature of thought, developed by Anselm and used by Descartes
ontology the branch of metaphysics dealing with the study of being
original position Rawls's hypothetical position from which a general social contract may be constructed; since the parties do not know which position they will occupy in society, they are likely to create a truly just society
panentheism the belief that God is expressed in the world and that the world and all that is exists in God
pantheism the belief that God is fully expressed in nature or the material world
paradigm according to Kuhn, a model that produces a coherent tradition of scientific research
Pascal's wager the advice to wager and live your life as if God exists, in case God does
pathe [PAH thay] the plural of *pathos,* a Greek word that, when used in connection with the soul, means "emotion" and "passion"
patriarchal characterized by male dominance
patriarchy a form of social organization in which the father is recognized as head of the family or tribe and men control most of the formal and informal power, as well as define the role of women
phenomena in Kant's epistemology, things as they appear to us under the categories of perception
philosophy literally, the "love of wisdom"
plastic capable of continuous changes in shape or form
pluralist a pre-Socratic philosopher who believed the *archē* was multiple or any philosopher who believes reality is plural
polytheism the belief in many gods
postmodernism the recognition that certainty and unitive truth are not possible because existence and reality are partial, inconsistent, plural, and multiple
pragmatic test what is true is what works
pragmatism in ontology, the belief that what is real is what works and predicts what is likely to happen next
preestablished harmony the harmony between body and soul or between the world of efficient causes and the world of final causes established by God, according to Leibniz
psychic conversion Malcolm X's prescription for African Americans, involving a shifting away from white standards of beauty, success, and the like to black-defined standards
puja [POOH jah] in Hinduism, personal ritual worship, either at home or in a temple
realist/representationalist view there is an external world outside our minds to which we may appeal for verification
relativism the view that truth has no objective standard and may vary from individual to individual, from group to group, and from time to time
sacredness of human life the religious or philosophical belief that human life is sacred and must be respected in all instances
Saguna Brahman [SA goon uh BRAH muhn] in Hinduism, the absolute conceived with attributes

samsara [sahm SAHR uh] the continuous cycle of births, deaths, and rebirths resulting from karma
separatist one who believes that blending with the dominant culture is not possible, desirable, or both
shadow self unaccepted parts of the self, according to Jungian psychology
silver rule "Do not do unto others what you would not have them do unto you."
sitting the Zen practice of silent meditation, designed to quiet the mind
skandhas [SKAHN duhs] in Buddhism, the five elements (feeling, perception, impulse, consciousness, and form) that make the world and the person of appearances
skepticism the philosophical doctrine that knowledge is uncertain and (in its strictest sense) that absolute knowledge is unattainable
social contract an agreement among citizens or between the ruler and the ruled that defines the rights and duties of each party
Socratic method the method of the dialectic, reported in Plato's dialogues
soft determinism/compatibilism the view that the will of an individual remains free even if some of that individual's choices are determined by previous experiences
solipsism belief that only my mind exists and everything else is a perception of that mind
Sophist a teacher of practical applications for philosophy in early Greece
sovereignty a term used to describe where political authority does or should reside
state the ruling political power within defined borders
Stoicism [STOW us sism] the belief that virtue and happiness are achievable by mastering oneself and one's passions and emotions
substance the underlying reality of something, containing its primary qualities; the essence of something that remains constant despite changes in its perceptible qualities
sunsum [SUHN suhm] the distinctive aspects of personality in the Akan system
symposion [sim PO zee ahn] a male drinking group held in an andron, or men's room
synthetic a priori in Kant's epistemology, a description of statements that tell us something meaningful about reality and are logically prior to (not dependent on) experience
syntropy [SIN troh pee] the tendency toward building up, as opposed to entropy, which is a tendency toward falling apart or the breakdown of synthesis
Tao the Way, the fundamental principle of the world, the cosmic order, nature in Taoism
teleological argument an argument for the existence of God, based on the design, order and apparent purpose of the universe, developed by Aquinas and attacked by Hume
teleological ethical theory an ethical theory that evaluates behavior in terms of consequences
teleology the theory that there is order and purpose in reality
theism the conception of God as a unitary being
theocracy literally, "rule by God"; the fusion of church and state
theodicy [thee AH dih see] the justification of the goodness of God in the face of the fact of evil
theology the rational organization of religious beliefs into a logical system
theoretical man the philosopher who imposes reason on reality, according to Nietzsche
theoretical posits our mental construction of physical objects in an attempt to make sense of our experience, according to Quine
totalitarianism the political belief that power to rule must be given exclusively to the state
transcendent existing beyond and thus independent of the space-time world
Trinity the Christian doctrine asserting that God is three persons in one nature
tripartite soul Plato's theory of a three-part human nature ideally ruled by reason
unconcealment/revealment the disclosure of Being as truth, according to Heidegger
utilitarianism the theory that an action is right if it seeks to promote the greatest amount of happiness in the world at large
virtual reality a computer-generated reality that is fully interactive for the participant
virtue for Aristotle, a life lived in accordance with the highest human capacity, reason
virtue ethics an ethical theory that uses as a moral standard what a virtuous person would do, as opposed to consequences or obligations; the primary question is, What kind of person should I be?
warrant the evidence or justification for a truth claim
wei-wu-wei (wu-wei) [WAY WOO WAY] literally, "doing by not doing"; in Taoism, the method of blending your individual effort with the great power of the *Tao* in the world of created things
yang the active, male principle associated with action and doing
yin the receptive, female principle associated with quiet and being
yin and yang the complementary principles through which the *Tao* is expressed; *yin* reflects receptivity and being, whereas *yang* reflects activity and doing

Index

Note: Page numbers in **boldface** indicate location of term definition. Page numbers in ***italics*** indicate location of biographical sketch in sidebars.

B

E

Modern and Post-Modern Eras

1500 C. E. | **1600 C. E.** | **1700 C. E.**

CONTINENTAL

Continental Rationalists

1596 René Descartes

1632 Baruch Benedict de Spinoza

1646 Gottfried Wilhelm Leibniz

European Enlightenment

1712 Jean-Jacques Rousseau

1724 Immanuel Kant

BRITISH

1588 Thomas Hobbes

1631 Anne Finch, Viscountess Conway

1759 Mary Wollstonecra

British Empiricists

1632 John Locke

1685 George Berkeley

1711 David Hume

AMERICAN

ca. 1650 Sor Juana Inés de la Cruz

REFORMATION

1517 Martin Luther begins Protestant Reformation

1543 Copernican theory of solar system published

SCIENTIFIC REVOLUTION

1609 Galileo constructs astronomical telescope

1665 Isaac Newton formulates law of gravity

AGE OF ENLIGHTENMENT

1751–1772 Publication of French *Encylopédie*, grand attempt to summarize all rational knowledge

1492 Columbus discovers "New World": beginnings of European expansion and colonialism

1619 First African slaves in North America (Virginia)